GEOGRAPHY AND POLITICS IN AMERICA

Harper & Row Series in Geography
Donald W. Meinig, Advisor

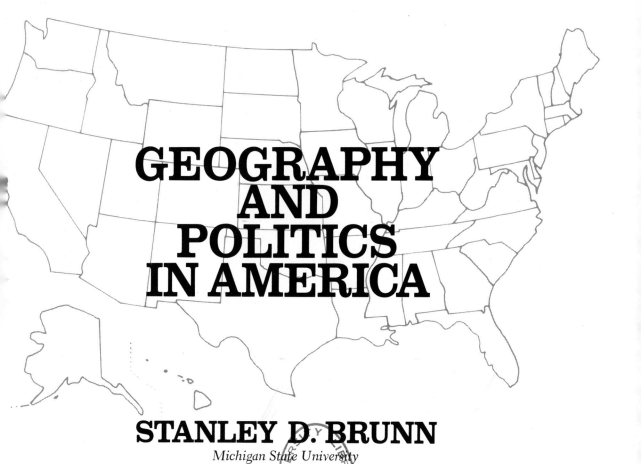

GEOGRAPHY AND POLITICS IN AMERICA

STANLEY D. BRUNN

Michigan State University

HARPER & ROW, PUBLISHERS
New York   Evanston   San Francisco   London

Sponsoring Editor: Ronald Taylor
Project Editor: Holly Detgen
Designer: T. R. Funderburk
Production Supervisor: Stefania J. Taflinska

Geography and Politics in America

Library of Congress Cataloging in Publication Data

Brunn, Stanley D.
   Geography and politics in America.

   (Harper & Row series in geography)
   Includes bibliographical references.
   1.   Geography, Political.   2.   Political sociology.
3.   Regionalism—United States.   4.   United States—
Politics and government.   I.   Title.
JC319.B78   320.1'2   73–17670
ISBN 0–06–041018–3

for the Joy that is Beverly

CONTENTS

Part II Patterns and Organization

Part III The Future

PREFACE

Political geography is perhaps the most human phase of
geography, since it deals so largely with the strengths,
weaknesses, and ambitions of men.

John K. Wright

A variety of expressions of political activity and political phenomena are found within the space filled by the confines of the United States. Some states exhibit a more progressive political philosophy than others and are the first to adopt political reforms. There are cities that receive and are willing to accept larger amounts of federal support for defense contracts, Model Cities, or environmental cleanup. Federal installations are not located in equal numbers in all states. Laws are more stringent for certain crimes in some locales. All these and many other examples of politically related phenomena and systems can be discerned by examining the political geography of the United States.

This book represents a breakthrough in the field of political geography. Whereas most books have emphasized the world scale and international themes, this is an attempt to focus on the variety and diversity of forms of political behavior, organization, and structure of one particular nation. Most regional texts on the United States give scant attention to the nation's political geography or the significance of regional diversity in political behavior. Prescott has commented in this regard by stating that "the excellent regional geographies which are published normally neglect the political aspects of the state and make only brief reference, for

xi

example, to international boundaries, the arrangement of civil divisions, electoral patterns, and regional alliances." It is hoped that in this first attempt at a regional political geography of the United States the student will gain a greater awareness of the exciting and fascinating political spaces in his backyard.

Political geographers have been most widely known for their treatment of select themes, such as boundaries, capitals, growth of nation states, and national voting. There has been little attempt to examine the behavior and patterns of contemporary politics. Soja remarked that "many political geography textbooks appear to be little more than catalogues of states and their characteristics (political or otherwise), with incidental notes about current events." These traditional themes are discussed as well as new inputs that have developed in the past decade. The behavioral school in geography has yielded some valuable insights into the notions about political space, especially as they relate to perception, attitude-formation, location of public facilities, delivery of public services, power and conflict, territorality, and organization. Facets of the behavioral school comprise a major segment of this book. Likewise, a number of themes treated by political scientists and political sociologists are placed in a geographic framework, for example, political recruitment, legal variations, and political cultures. The importance of the environment (physical and human) in recent years has political and social ties that are important in policy formulation. This theme is also treated as is the role and activities of minority groups, blacks, Chicanos, and Indians. In essence the author agrees with Cox, who, in commenting on the geographic nature of many current problems, stated that "many of these political issues [urban housing, welfare, and pollution] have a very strong locational component."

ORGANIZATION

The book is organized into three major parts and thirteen chapters. Part I is devoted to behavioral facets of the political geography of the nation; Part II deals with specific political patterns and organization. The marriage of both schools provides a sound basis for understanding and analyzing the geographic components of American politics. Each chapter in this book treats a particular aspect of the political geography of the United States. The first seven chapters examine the role of man and groups in political space. Much of this discussion is placed within the current thinking of the behavioralists. Part II contains five chapters that consider the organization, structure, and patterns of selected themes. Some themes and topics, such as boundaries and elections, are familiar to the political geography field. Others, such as the relations of political geography to laws, government programs, environment, and political cultures as well as the behavioral materials in Part I, are new to the field. The book concludes with Part III, a discussion of some likely behaviors and patterns of political geography for the future and a suggested political reorganization of the United States.

Throughout the thirteen chapters a number of major threads are woven.

The first is to present the materials in a fashion so that the student will be cognizant of the varieties of political geography existing in the United States. Examples of regions, states, and cities in all parts of the nation are provided throughout. The United States is a single nation but within are many sharply contrasting views and uses of space. Because over half the population lives in ten states and within their largest cities, these areas and points in space are emphasized with maps, tables, and examples. However, there are a variety of political expressions existing in both small-sized and populated regions and states. Thus the process of filling in threads to form a national fabric is a major aim. All areas, local to national, can be viewed in terms of political geography.

That the United States is an urbanized unit, population-wise if not politically, is the second thread. If most Americans are not already living in or near large urban complexes, they will be soon. Urban and suburban units are emphasized. Cities may be similar in population size but often their location dictates differing views on government assistance, political extremism, environmental quality, political party allegiance, and legal interpretation. Urban political geographies are illustrated throughout.

The third major thread is how man as an individual or as a member of groups fits into political spaces. In Part I, the concern is how man perceives, identifies, interacts, and organizes himself with reference to political spaces. Not all men view local, state, or national space alike. Man can do many things with the political spaces around him. He can perceive them as being alien to his particular philosophy, he can manipulate them to serve his own gains, or he can become involved in a national organization by interacting with a local affiliate. In the second part of the book the focus is on political organization and structure. The enactment of laws, the patterns of voting, and the characterization of political cultures are some of the subjects handled. In Part III, the aim is to establish the impress of man and politics on the geography of the future in the United States.

RATIONALE

An additional objective of this book is to present some notions of how the political geographer looks at space. His spatial perspective on the political activities, phenomena, and processes lends him a different slant than the political scientist or political sociologist. The focus on the variations, organizations, and behaviors of the political world (local to international) offers him more than an ample supply of materials for scrutiny.

A word is in order about the illustrative materials in the book. The maps are an important part of the treatment of materials in all chapters. They not only illustrate various concepts or patterns, but also stimulate the reader to view political geography materials in other ways than he is presently familiar with. Although a number of the maps are derived from the works of other political and social geographers, many are newly constructed and specifically designed for this book.

Related social science materials form the basis for some of the maps and tabular data. These graphic materials are used to convey behavioral and structural notions—one major way geographers differ from those in sister disciplines who study political processes and patterns. Many of the political scientists whose materials are discussed throughout the book are, in essence, regional political geographers.

In this initial attempt at a political geography of the United States, there is much material that is new. Some geographers and even those in related disciplines may question whether certain topics are genuinely part of political geography. All too frequently political geographers have remained shackled by traditional approaches and select themes. However, if one accepts the catholic view that political geography is concerned with the structure, character, organization, and behavior of phenomena in political spaces, the world of possible topics and themes is wide open. This book does not purport to define what is or what is not political geography. Nor will a defense be offered stating what is political geography and how it differs from political science or political sociology. Rather, the aim is to integrate where possible a select number of themes and approaches into a spatial consideration of politics within the United States. There can be no doubt that there is much material available in the social sciences for the writing of a political geography of the nation. Where such ideas and themes are deemed worthy of analysis, they are included.

A geographer desiring to write about the political geography of the United States can adopt various approaches. At his disposal are historical or contemporary treatments as well as those relating political processes and phenomena to a variety of theories and models. Most of the latter have been borrowed from fellow social scientists. The text focuses primarily on contemporary America, that is, post-1960. It is an attempt to concentrate on the salient facets of American life and society that are part of the everyday world of the American citizen. There is much that a political geographer can write about and analyze on the local, state, regional, or national scene that is reflected in the daily life of politicians, students, and citizens. Contemporary political allegiances, fiscal programs, forms of international assistance, location of facilities, organizational schemes, and environmental crises are topics that, when examined in present light, are useful in understanding the place of man in the United States.

UTILITY

As designed, this book could be adopted in courses dealing specifically with political geography as well as courses dealing with social geography, urban geography, and the geography of the United States or North America. The political, social, and urban themes that are emphasized would suggest use in introductory and advanced courses in political systems, political cultures, or American politics. Colleges and universities that offer programs in American studies may find a geographic perspective on the political process a most valuable insight. Because sections of the book consider economic, environmental, and social themes, as well as minority groups, parts may be useful in specific courses.

Finally, a word is in order about the task of writing such a book. Discussing politics and the effects of politics on individuals, groups, regions, and the nation calls for an objective appraisal. Frequently it would seem that political analysts favor a particular region or population segment. It is considered essential that a proper balance be struck that aims for truth in analyzing the political processes, events, and structures. While some biases are almost certain to creep in when specific topics are handled, the attempt is to strive for a contemporary critical analysis of the political geography of the United States. It is realized that there may be differences in the interpretation of some political and social events that are treated. Such diversity is expected and accepted as a part of the search for truth in and behind politics. The realization of such differences and writing about them is one of the hallmarks of political geography writings in the past few years. Rather than restricting their research to some of the time-honored themes, political geographers are writing about such controversial topics as the uses and misuses of power, justice, and areal administration. The final section on the future may well trigger the most discussion, as thinking about and planning the political geography or any geography of the future often takes on an emotional air.

It is hoped that this book will serve to stimulate the reader to explore the exciting field of a nation's political geography. If the reader in only a minor way gains some of the enthusiasm that inspired the writing of this book, the effort will not have been in vain. There is much we do not know about the political geography of the United States. Continued study and discussion on this fascinating subject by student, teacher, politician, and citizen will lead to a greater appreciation of the fascinating world of politics in the United States.

S. D. B.

ACKNOWLEDGMENTS

The stimulus to write a book on geography and politics in the United States stems from my personal and professional interests in American society and politics, plus the realization that there is much inherently spatial in the behavior and structure of both that merits the serious attention of political and social geographers. While political geographers traditionally have been associated with studies of the international world and selected themes, it seems the time has arrived for geographers to focus on political and social facets of the United States. To be sure, there are ample spatial expressions of political processes and patterns existing in metropolitan areas, in states, and in the nation itself.

This book probably would not have been written at this point in time had not the Department of Geography at Michigan State University and especially Professor Lawrence Sommers given me the opportunity to develop a political geography course that included many of the approaches and topics covered. The actual release from teaching during the 1972–1973 year was made possible by Professor Sommers and by Professor Charles Wrigley of the Computer Institute for Social Science Research. This research position enabled me to complete the manuscript during the academic year. For this support I am most grateful.

In writing this book there are several individuals whose contributions deserve mention. Especially, I am appreciative of the numerous discussions on various topics with graduate students: Gerald Ingalls in particular, Jack Ford, Robert

Pierce, John Catau, Terry McIntosh, and Walter Farrell. They were instrumental in bringing various politically related notions to my attention as well as completing assignments on certain topics. Assistance in obtaining valuable maps and data came from fellow geographers Richard Morrill, Robert Mings, Ron Sheck, Mel Albaum, and Joe Darden. The librarians in the Michigan State University documents section, Eleanor Boyles, Diane Marin, and Carol Manning, were most helpful in tracking down often inaccessible data and maps.

Special recognition is merited for my typist and cartographer. The typing of all manuscript materials was accomplished by Joyce Ingalls, who performed competently, admirably, and cheerfully in the midst of the author's deadlines and reading from sometimes illegible manuscript copy. Maps for the book were done by Sherman Hollander, staff cartographer in the Department of Geography, Michigan State University. His excellent drafting abilities plus his creativeness as evidenced in preparing some fascinating cartographic representations are responsible for making the maps a most important part of the book. To both Joyce and Sherm go special thanks.

PART I
MAN, BEHAVIOR, AND SPACE

Chapter 1

IDENTIFICATION AND ATTITUDES

I am a member of no organized political
party, I am a California Democrat.

Will Rogers, Jr.

IDENTIFICATION AND INTERACTION

Americans identify themselves and possess different views about their local community, state, region, and nation. Even though 200-plus million Americans reside in the same national territorial space, their identities and attitudes are far from uniform. Some may label themselves conservatives or Democrats; they may have beliefs and impressions about federal government limitations that place them in agreement with the majority of other citizens. On the other hand, they may identify themselves primarily with their local town politics should they be lifetime residents in rural Maine or they may be basically adherents of preserving states' rights. The attitudes they have are reflected in their reaction to political leaders as well as to economic or social programs affecting them and those residing in the other political spaces.

Political Identification. Man identifies himself in various ways with the political world and political space. His attachment is dependent on his own awareness of political spaces and the identification and attachment he has as a member of political groups at various levels, from local to national.[1]

One important way an individual identifies himself with political space is by political participation. A suburban Democrat may identify with those candidates and issues that support his basic ideology. He may not only be a registered Democrat but may maintain that he is a liberal Democrat on most issues. This label separates him, in his view and the view of his friends and neighbors, from conservative Democrats and from the Republicans. His loyalty is demonstrated by his consistent support for the national party. Although he consistently supports Democratic party candidates and issues at local and state levels, frequently his identification weakens at national levels. He has been known to support moderate and even liberal candidates in national elections because he does not believe the Democratic party candidate always speaks for him and his political spaces, be they city or state. Thus he has maintained a strong party and ideological loyalty, but a loyalty that could be altered at national levels.

In addition to voting, ideology, and party loyalty, political man in a spatial context identifies in other ways with the political world. One such way is as a contributor to organizations and candidates. If he believes that civil rights or environmental protection or women's liberation are crucial issues he may decide to contribute financially to local, state, regional, or national candidates espousing these views. These he may support irregardless of the party. His main concern is that the solutions to many world problems demand support—financial and voluntary—hence his decision to embrace those potential leaders aiming to make the political world more to his liking. The support he lends to particular candidates for public office may be made in spite of the stances adopted by his labor union, veterans group, or business organization. The choices an individual makes to support with token or major contribution a local school board candidate, a moderate nonpartisan mayoral candidate, and a conservative Republican presidential candidate are all examples of ways man participates in and identifies with the varying problems and issues existing at different scales of political space.

Other than contributing financially to a particular political party or a particular issue, there are additional ways political man may identify with his known political space. He may assume door-to-door campaigning for a candidate, circulate petitions for effective political action at the county fair, or assume a leadership role in the local fight to halt industrial pollution. The decision to place bumper stickers on his car advocating "Don't Californicate Colorado" or "Save Lake Erie" or "Another Family for Peace" or "Get the U.S. out of the UN or "Don't Blame Me—I'm from Massachusetts" are outward ways in which some of his political philosophy and ideology are displayed. Also the wearing of other politically related attire such as army fatigues may suggest a protest against United States policy in Vietnam. Flying the American flag daily may represent a true exhibition of his patriotism. Wearing a lapel with a clenched black fist or a black beret may show sympathy for militant black organizations. Marching in a demonstration advocating abortion reform or in a parade for victory in Vietnam are additional ways man chooses to identify with political space. Thus we find that man's political behavior and especially his identification take on particular forms that reveal his sentiments and attitudes about his political worlds.

Political Interaction. Being a social animal, man interacts with other men at various scales for a variety of reasons. In the political arena, there are various kinds of interaction that serve to heighten man's cognizance of the political and social world. Interaction serves as a basis for presenting his own conception of problems and solutions to others whose worlds are different.

Interaction in the political world occurs on all scales from individual citizen exchanges to discussions by state, national, and world leaders. The interaction on political issues occurring at the family level is but one example of the many others that take place, such as local Republican party caucuses, Senate subcommittee hearings, or discussions in the United Nations General Assembly. The issues may vary and the ramifications of the pending discussions may be greater but the reasons for such interactions are basically the same.

Outside the family atmosphere, at the local level, interaction on political issues may take place between friends, relatives, or neighbors. The discussions may be between like-minded persons or between those having different views. The place and the form of interaction may vary from over the back fence, informal coffee breaks, business luncheons, or church discussion groups to regular organization meetings devoted to informing the membership and exchanging views with candidates for public office or representatives for certain politically related issues.

A more formal organizational structure for interaction is provided by political or quasipolitically related state, regional, and national organizations. State and national conventions of the AFL–CIO, the General Assembly of the Presbyterian Church, the American Legion, the American Civil Liberties Union, the American Association for the Advancement of Science, and the National Association for the Advancement of Colored People are concerned with exchanging and disseminating information among the membership about crucial issues. Although not all issues discussed in panels or small discussions at such meetings are of a political nature, frequently there are resolutions adopted that attempt to encourage political and social interactions on issues facing cities, states, the nation, and the world.

Traveling through spaces and particularly spaces that are dissimilar from one's own presents an opportunity for interaction with local citizens or relatives and thereby enlarges one's political horizons. Knowledge about these "foreign" political spaces, gained through reading magazines or local newspapers and by watching television news coverage, are other ways an individual acquires knowledge about the political world.

Spatial contacts are particularly important in the development of a political self. These may come from personal travels or experiences, or from interaction with people in "foreign" spaces. The individual identified as a liberal, whether in New

York or in South Carolina, is one who frequently has a greater amount of spatial contact with other peoples and other places. Whites who have traveled outside their home state and outside the South are more likely to have progressive views about blacks than those not having such experiences. Experience in the military or childhood experiences in northern states often are reflected in views that are not a part of the accepted views of southern rural areas, small towns, and cities. While these whites may not be as liberal on certain social issues as liberal whites in the northern cities, they are more in support of granting voting privileges, equal employment, improved housing, and better education to blacks.

Similar background experiences in the adjustments to immigration and American life may lead to the feelings of hostility some eastern and southern European ethnic groups have toward Chicanos, Puerto Ricans, blacks, or Indians. The absence of much open and intense racial hatred toward minority groups in cities in the American West may be attributed to the fact that most of the region's residents are themselves recently transplanted. Once an individual moves to a new location or political region, he finds his identification and interaction may also change. That is, the lack of a sizable portion of the population with deep roots in the Southwest may be reflected in the open nature of the society. Much of the growth of this area is due to Midwest, South, and Northeast migrants. These heterogeneous groups cluster into cities and suburbs where occupation, income, and social status are more important than tradition, race, and ethnic status. This is not to say that racial sentiments are absent, but suggests that the transferring of large numbers of citizens to a new and distant space results in the openness of society. The realization that blacks can win statewide offices in California or the Los Angeles mayoral race illustrates the more receptive nature of such candidacies in a region and city that many consider almost as conservative as parts of the South.

MAN'S POLITICAL SPACE: LOCAL PERSPECTIVES

Citizens identify themselves politically in different ways both ideologically and with respect to their party preference. Much of their classification of themselves and their neighbors and their community is based on their own social and economic background and position, their levels of interaction with others, and their sources of information. Furthermore, the importance of place is not to be overlooked as a salient ingredient in identifying political behavior. Where a person resides is likely to influence his position of himself, his neighbors, and his friends. Also how much and what kinds of interaction he engages in are reflected in his location.

In an effort to discern some of the spatial components of political activity and identity, a survey of residents of East Lansing, Michigan, was taken in June 1971. The homeowners interviewed were asked about their general background as well as their levels of political activity, their perceptions of themselves and their neighborhood, and their sources of politically related information. A random sample was conducted in three easily identifiable sections of the city: (1) Towar Gardens, which is a low-income white area; (2) Whitehills, immediately adjacent, which is a very high-income white section; and (3) an area referred to as Saginaw-Burcham, which is medium to medium-high income and white. These three areas are north of Michigan State University and beyond the concentrations of the student residential units. Occupationally the three areas are somewhat different. The Towar Gardens area is mainly manual blue-collar workers, some are Mexican-Americans and a few are retired workers. Whitehills is comprised of a professional, business, and state government elite. Few professors live here; they live primarily in the third area along with local businessmen and some retired citizens. On a map these three are contiguous, but important transport lines serve to easily demarcate the three neighborhoods. A major four-lane state highway separates the Whitehills from the Saginaw-Burcham areas. A two-lane road plus a concrete fence encircling Whitehills Estates separates it from Towar Gardens. In essence these three neighborhoods are self-contained in that the transport routes may be considered barriers to social as well as possible political interaction.

Party-wise, conservative Democrats dominate Towar Gardens and conservative Republicans Whitehills. A mixed group comprised of moderate liberals and Independents as well as conservative Republicans and liberal Democrats live in the Saginaw-Burcham area. It is only in the third area that political party loyalties were sharply divided. In general the area can be categorized as moderate to liberal Independent. The party label that the individuals attached to themselves was maintained by most citizens at local, state, and national levels. The Democrats were somewhat more likely to abandon their party label at the local level. Independents were just that at all levels; if they shunned the label and identified with a party, it was more likely to be the Republicans.

When the residents of all three areas were asked to indicate the levels and amounts of political discussion, some definite variations emerged (Table 1-1). About half of all the 107 respondents do not discuss politics with their neighbors. Moderates are the most reluctant. However, they are more willing to discuss political matters with their friends. This is especially true of the conservative Republi-

TABLE 1-1   East Lansing Survey: Political Identification and Interaction
(C = conservative; M = moderate; L = liberal)

		Republicans			Democrats			Independents		
		C	M	L	C	M	L	C	M	L
Discuss Politics	Yes	9	7	4	2	7	8	3	7	6
With Neighbors	No	7	7	2	2	9	8	3	13	3
Discuss Politics	Yes	13	13	5	3	8	14	4	17	9
With Friends	No	3	1	1	1	8	2	2	3	0

Source: Seminar in Political Geography, Michigan State University, June 1971.

cans in Whitehills and the very liberal Democrats and moderate Independents and Republicans in the Saginaw-Burcham area. The moderate Democrats are least likely to discuss politics with their friends.

There are a number of ways citizens involve themselves in the political processes. Voting is the most accepted form and most stated they were voters. The most regular voters in the East Lansing survey were the Republicans regardless of their ideological orientation. The conservative and the liberal Republicans had slightly better records than the moderates. Democrats as a party had the worst record. The very liberal Democrats were the best voters and those of moderate persuasion were like their Republican counterparts, the worst.

Besides voting for local, state, and national candidates and issues, the residents participated in other forms of political activities. A total of ninety-three said they signed petitions for one or another purpose; again, the moderate Democrats comprised half of those who did not sign. About half the respondents stated they would fly the American flag, write letters, or contribute monies to campaigns. Flag flying was most popular with moderate and conservative Republicans and least so with Democrats, especially of a liberal persuasion. Writing letters and contributing to campaigns proved most frequent among the conservative and moderate Republicans and the liberal Democrats, both groups whose socioeconomic position could afford donations. Bumper stickers, an increasingly popular and free political advertisement so popular in the 1960s, were displayed on automobiles of a third of those interviewed. They were equally popular among the Republicans, Democrats, and the Independents. Those who identified themselves as moderate and liberal Democrats, as moderate and conservative Republicans, and as Independents were the most frequent adopters. The wearing of pins advertising a party or an issue was associated primarily with conservative and moderate Republicans and liberal and very liberal Democrats and Independents. Door-to-door campaigning was popular with the Republicans interviewed and marching in demonstrations with Independents.

As mentioned earlier, a person's perception of politicians and political issues of local, state, national, and international concerns is formed by his interaction with his friends and neighbors, his engagement in varying forms of political activities, and finally his sources of information. Specifically television and radio news programs, newspapers, and magazines are important in helping form the individual's attitudes and opinions about the political world around him.

East Lansing receives clear reception from all three major national television networks. The vast majority of those interviewed, over 90 percent, watched the television news daily. CBS was the most popular network. Only about one-third stated they relied on the radio for news. CBS was the most popular network watched by Democrats and Independents, those who classed themselves as conservatives or liberals. NBC and ABC were watched mainly by Republicans.

In terms of newspaper coverage, the *Lansing State Journal*, the only daily newspaper published in the metropolitan area, had the widest appeal; over 90 percent subscribed to it. It was the only paper read by the conservative Democrats.

The second most popular paper was the *Detroit Free Press*, a paper read by all shades of political and philosophical opinion. It was the least popular among liberals and Democrats. The *New York Times* was read by about 10 percent of those interviewed and those primarily who were liberal and/or Democrats. The *Wall Street Journal* was read by about the same percentage but by conservative and moderate Republicans and Independents. The greatest variety of newspapers was found in the homes of moderate Independents and liberal Democrats.

Certain weekly and monthly magazines were also important in helping East Lansing residents keep abreast of the political world and help form their opinions. The most widely read weeklies were *Time* and *Life* followed by *Newsweek* and *U.S. News and World Report*. *Time* had the greatest appeal, as it reached all groups on the political spectrum. It was especially popular among conservatives and moderate Republicans, moderate and liberal Democrats, and moderate Independents. *Life* was looked at primarily by the moderates of all three political groups; the liberals read it the least. *Newsweek* was more popular with liberal Democrats than with Republicans or Independents. *U.S. News and World Report* was read mainly by conservative and moderate Republicans. Other magazines were read much less but had a distinct clientele. *Look* was evenly distributed among all parties and all philosophical persuasions. *Saturday Review* was read by liberals. *National Geographic* and *Reader's Digest* were especially popular with conservative and moderate Republicans and Independents and very unpopular with Democrats and liberals. Just as in the case of newspapers, the moderate Independent had the greatest variety of reading materials. If members of the two major parties are considered, the Republicans were more avid readers than the Democrats.

Thus, it may be seen that citizens in this mid-Michigan city can be grouped into several classes when their information fields and interaction levels are considered. There are some striking parallels when party and ideology are juxtaposed, and it becomes possible to typify, for example, the conservative Democrat in East Lansing as relying mainly on CBS news, the *Lansing State Journal*, and *Life* for his news sources.

REGIONAL VARIATIONS IN ATTITUDES

Politically Related Organizations. Probably no politically related organization has been more opposed to the civil rights gains made since 1960 than the Ku Klux Klan. Their position as antiblack, anti-Jewish, anti-Catholic, and anti-Communist has varied from loud rhetoric at rallies, parades, and marches to their association with cross-burnings, church- and school-burnings, bombings, kidnappings, and shootings. These have been concentrated mainly in southern states, but not exclusively. Historically these men in white sheets and peaked hoods ruled the rural South by frightening blacks and engaging in varying acts of violence against property and person (black and sometimes white). They are dedicated to a United

States that is white supremacist and free of communism, socialism, and the mixture of races.

Klan membership increased during the 1960s, from what it had been several decades earlier, with the progress being made nationally and especially in the South in the civil rights arena. These gains for blacks accounted for more whites joining the Klan in the South; riots and disturbances augmented the numbers in the North. The violence that was associated with the Ku Klux Klan led the House Committee on Un-American Activities to issue a report on the present-day strength of the movement. This study focused especially on the numerical and geographic strength and influence of the KKK in the 1964–1966 period. The highly secretive nature of the Klan precluded earlier accurate assessments of its strength. However, by calling in a number of witnesses and carrying out extensive field investigations and analyzing bank records, a fairly accurate and current report was filed. The Committee identified 714 klaverns (local units of the KKK) that were in operation from 1964–1966; these had a combined membership of 16,810 in early 1967.[2] Although membership fluctuates according to the issues of the day and during the year (high membership in summer when cow pastures are amenable for rallies and other stunts), the Committee reported that probably not all klaverns were found. Their error was estimated to be less than 10 percent.

The report includes the names and geographical location of each of the 714 klaverns. This figure includes fifty-six ladies' klaverns; they are located particularly in North Carolina. At the time of the writing there were fifteen major Klan organizations in the United States. The United Klans of America headed by Imperial Wizard Robert Shelton and headquartered in Tuscaloosa, Alabama, is the largest. Its membership is over 15,000. Most of the UKA members live in North Carolina (7500), Georgia (1400), Virginia (1250), and Alabama (1200). Numerous small-sized splinter groups comprise the remainder of the KKK total membership; some have less than fifty members.

The membership of the KKK, as measured by the location of klaverns, is concentrated in six major locations: eastern North Carolina (definitely Klan country), northern South Carolina, central Florida, southern Mississippi, and northern Louisiana (Fig. 1-1). Less dense concentrations are found in southern Virginia, Alabama, southern Arkansas, and east Texas. It might be expected that the klaverns would be most numerous in those parts of the South where the black population is highest. Yet this only holds true in part, especially in eastern North Carolina, South Carolina, and southwest Mississippi. In southwest Georgia, central Alabama, the Mississippi Delta, and Florida panhandle, where the black population is above 40 percent, the Klan membership is low. These are also some of the poorest parts of the South. It may be that the paying of dues precludes joining a klavern or that if violence or vigilante action is deemed in order against the blacks, no formal structure is needed. Possibly the membership is low because the whites who might engage in these violent activities feel the blacks in these rural and isolated parts of the South simply "know their place." That is, the KKK may

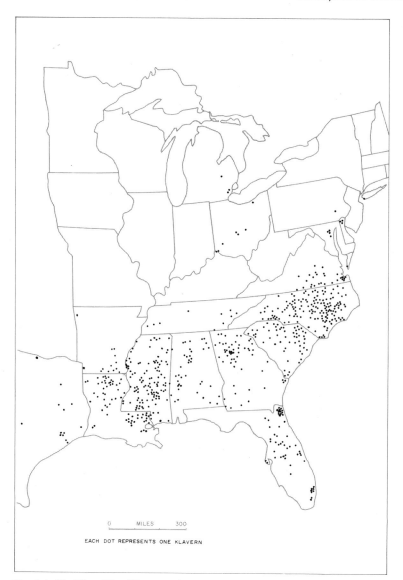

Fig. 1-1 Ku Klux Klan Klaverns. (U.S. House of Representatives, Committee on Un-American Activities, *The Present-Day Ku Klux Klan Movement*, Report, Ninetieth Congress, Second Session, Washington, D.C., 1967.)

become an active organization in locations where there are black gains in civil rights. These would probably be in the not-so-poor rural areas and in the cities. The number of klaverns in large cities in the Deep South and in cities at the periphery suggests that the membership may be strongest where blacks are a large part of the population, especially due to recent migration. Witness for example the number of klaverns in Atlanta, Birmingham, and Jacksonville. The klaverns in Ft. Lauderdale, West Palm Beach, and Miami (all with a relatively low percentage of black population) may be formed by recent white southern migrants who organized a klavern to maintain sociopolitical ties and to combat any future black gains. Outside the South, the klaverns are few. They tend to be in large eastern cities where the black population is large, such as New York City, Detroit, and Cleveland. White suburbs with first or second generation southern migrants would seem likely foci for a klavern.

Americans for Democratic Action. One of the more liberal politically related groups is the Americans for Democratic Action. In its advocacy for government programs in the areas of civil rights, social welfare, and foreign policy the ADA is one of the most influential liberal organizations. Often the policies and programs it supports are legislated by Congress five or eight years after they were proposed in the national conventions. The present membership of some 40,000 is not distributed equally in all parts of the United States.[3] Rather, the chapters are located primarily in large cities in the Northeast and California as well as in major university communities (Fig. 1-2). The largest number of chapters are in Ohio, Pennsylvania, New York, New Jersey, Michigan, and Texas. In membership alone the chapters in and around Chicago, Los Angeles, New York, Philadelphia, and Washington, D.C., are the largest. Individuals belonging to the Americans for Democratic Action are identified as political liberals, and their concentration in states and environments (university) that support progressive or liberal causes and concerns sharply contrast with the klavern locations of the Ku Klux Klan.

FIG. 1-2 Chapters of the Americans for Democratic Action.

Gallup Public Opinion Polls. Politicians at all levels and of all parties are interested in the views and opinions of citizens. These may often help a decision maker to support a particular piece of legislation or may lead to his clarifying his constituents about his stances on critical national and international issues. The importance of attitudes in national politics has been reflected in the polling agencies and organizations that have made it a business to take an accurate pulse of the public on issues, programs, and personalities. Polling has probably become most popular in presidential years when trial heats and preferential polls are taken to measure the support for a party, candidate, and issue.

The Gallup Poll has become one of the most widely recognized scientific barometers developed in the past twenty-five years. By taking a representative sample of 1200 to 1500 residents of varying backgrounds in widely scattered parts of the United States, the agency is able, with only a small margin of statistical error, to predict the pulse of the nation on critical issues and key personalities. The import of these polls to a political geographer is that they reveal spatial variations in the responses themselves. While a national average citing support for the Vietnam War or for busing is an important figure in its own right, the concern here is how much and where the geographic variation exists. Varying opinions about issues would be expected to be revealed in the stances taken by senators, congressmen, governors, as well as by those elected to lower offices. The attitudes taken by citizens or politicians may be related to the social development of the area, its economic orientation, the role of the individual in the federal bureaucracy and the prevailing political tenor of the times. Regional variation in opinions as revealed in polls indicates that seldom is there equal support nationwide for a particular issue or candidate. Almost always there are variations (Table 1-2).

In Table 1-2 the political cultures of regions are revealed in some of the questions asked in Gallup Polls during 1971.[4] The South is often considered as a region at variance with the East and this appears in its greater support for the Vietnam War and defense spending and greater opposition to the admission of China to the United Nations and the use of busing to achieve racial balance in schools. However, the respondents in the South reflected similar attitudes to those in the other three regions in favoring the death penalty for murder. This same region expressed the strongest support for lowering the voting age to eighteen; the major opposition came from the Midwest and West. Of the items presented in the table, while the South has less support for many issues that would probably lead it being labeled conservative, the West is more conservative in some (death penalty) and the Midwest in others (voting age). In general the East has the most progressive or liberal views of those issues presented, but in some cases the region is not distinctly different from the other three. It is worth noting that the metric system has as much appeal as it does. In the East and the Midwest, the two regions with probably the most contact with industrial countries using the metric system, it has its greatest support.

Regional variations in political philosophy are revealed in the respondents' request to position themselves in one of the six categories. When this poll was taken in May 1971, the slightly conservative nature of the populace was considered an accurate barometer of citizen's feelings. Even regionally this conservative sentiment was apparent in national and international politics at that time. This can be measured by presidential and congressional statements and legislation. This conservative view was more apparent in the South and West than in the East. It is interesting that in the two liberal categories the percents for those in the Midwest and South are almost identical. Of the four regions and the five categories, the Midwest most closely approximates the national average followed by those in the West. Those interviewed in the East deviated most from the national averages.

Bellwether Counties in Presidential Elections. Political parties have expressed a great interest in public opinion polls in recent decades in an effort to test the support of candidates and issues nationally as well as regionally. In key presidential races as well as key Senate, House, and gubernatorial races, opinion polls have been taken to project election results quickly and accurately. The search for counties or states or urban precincts that have been consistently not only in the winning camp but within a small percent of the total victory by the winner is a task that concerns both parties, television networks, and polling agencies. At the national level the slogan of "As Maine goes, so goes the Nation" indicated to party leaders that this state was considered a meaningful barometer in presidential races. However, in recent years the state has not been in concert with the remainder of the nation very frequently. In the fourteen presidential elections since 1920, Maine has elected the winner on only seven occasions. Illinois and New Mexico are states that consistently have voted for the winners.

At the county level, the search for counties that have consistently voted within a few percentage points of the winning party is expected to reveal something of the nature of the citizenry that makes them bellwether counties. Counties that fall into this category are those not affected drastically by the political schisms that have occurred in both parties nationally since 1960. Once these counties are identified, pollsters from all parties and networks could conduct surveys in them to identify support for candidates as well as reactions to crucial national and international issues. The behaviors of the residents would prove useful in projecting winners once election day statistics become available. The sampling of pertinent areal units—whether they be precincts, wards, or counties—can be conducted to measure the varying responses of citizens regionally as well as nationally.

In the past four presidential elections (1960, 1964, 1968, and 1972), there have been six counties that have always voted within 2 percent of the winning party's vote (Table 1-3). These bellwether counties are not restricted to only one section of the nation.[5] The fact that no southern counties appear in the table is not surprising since 1964 and 1968 were years when the region deviated strongly from the national election averages. Both years and 1972 may be considered as deviating elections. That is, the attitudes of the citizenry and allegiances to and platforms of the political parties had little in common with previous election results. Thus the past four presidential elections cannot be considered, according to some political analysts, as true political party elections. Therefore any areal unit, county, precinct,

TABLE 1-2   Regional Variations in Public Opinion: Gallup Poll Results

	National	East	Midwest	South	West
U.S. Made Mistake to Send Troops to Fight in Vietnam (percent Yes)[a]	50	62	61	54	60
Lower Voting Age to 18 (percent Yes)[b]	60	62	54	65	57
Admit Communist China as Member of United Nations (percent Yes)[c]	45	49	47	33	51
Favor Busing to Achieve Racial Balance (percent Yes)[d]	19	22	17	15	22
Would Like to See U.S. Adopt Metric System (percent Yes)[e]	42	44	45	36	39
Favor Death Penalty for Those Convicted of Murder (percent Yes)[f]	49	49	48	47	54
Defense Spending: (percent)					
Too Little	11	9	6	17	13
Too Much	49	55	52	37	54
About Right	31	26	34	36	26
No Opinion[g]	9	10	8	10	7
Political Philosophy: May 1971 (percent)					
Very Conservative	11	11	13	12	8
Fairly Conservative	28	24	26	31	30
Middle Road	29	30	31	25	30
Fairly Liberal	19	22	18	17	20
Very Liberal	7	7	7	7	9
No Opinion[h]	6	6	5	8	3

Source: American Institute of Public Opinion. [a] *Gallup Opinion Index*, March 1971, Report 69; [b] Ibid., March 1971, Report 71; [c] Ibid., June 1971, Report 72; [d] Ibid., September 1971, Report 75; [e] Ibid., October 1971, Report 76; [f] Ibid., December 1971, Report 78; [g] Ibid., May 1971, Report 71; and [h] Ibid., June 1971, Report 72.

or city that exhibited a profile similar to the winning party's vote must be considered. The consistency of even six counties in the Kennedy, Johnson, and Nixon elections is remarkable considering the political and social dynamics associated with each election.

As stated above it can be argued that the past three elections are distinctly different from 1960 in that realignment in presidential voting began to occur in the South in particular. The support of Republican Goldwater in 1964 was garnered by the AIP (American Independent party) candidate Wallace in 1968 and Republican Nixon in 1972. For this reason consistency in county voting in the southeastern states for one political party has not been a marked trait of recent presidential voting. In considering only the 1964, 1968, and 1972 elections, there were sixteen counties that voted within 2 percent of the winning party's final vote. As in

TABLE 1-3 Bellwether Counties in Presidential Elections

Elections	Elections
1960, 1964, 1968, 1972	1964, 1968, 1972
New Castle, Delaware	Napa, California
St. Joseph, Indiana	Fulton, Illinois
Vigo, Indiana	Harrison, Indiana
Glacier, Montana	Pike, Indiana
Lake, Ohio	Greenup, Kentucky
Okanogan, Washington	Powell, Kentucky
	Clark, Nevada
	Harris, Texas
	Tarrant, Texas
	Putnam, West Virginia

Source: Governmental Affairs Institute, *America Votes*, vol. 4 (1960), vol. 6 (1964), vol. 8 (1968); and the 1973 *World Almanac*, New York, Newspaper Enterprise Association, 1973, pp. 42–69.

the four most recent elections, these appeared in all parts of the United States. No Deep South counties appeared, yet several did in Kentucky and Texas. Some of the fifteen were urban, some suburban, and some distinctly rural. They were marked by varying occupation, education, and income levels.

Newspaper Endorsement for President. Another way of discerning the variation in political attitudes of an area is to examine the content and editorial support of its newspapers. The syndicated columnists as well as the editorial slant often reflect the prevailing views of management as well as the subscribers. Inasmuch as newspapers depend on advertising for much of their income, it behooves the publishers and editors to take stands on issues and candidates that will engender such support and be acceptable to readers at the same time. On the other hand, the newspaper is an important organ for molding public opinion as perceived by the management. They may attempt to sway public opinion in directions they think are beneficial and desirable. This is accomplished by endorsing stands on particular issues or supporting certain candidates.

When viewing newspaper endorsements for political candidates, they may be expected to reflect elements of a region's political philosophy and culture. Simply plotting on a map the newspapers who supported President Nixon in 1968 or those that favored the 1970 invasion of Cambodia should reveal spatial patterns reflective in part of the area's prevailing attitudes and philosophy.

The majority of newspapers since 1896 have preferred the Republican candidate in all presidential elections except 1964. The percent supporting Republican candidates in the past six elections is as follows: 1948 (65 percent), 1952 (67 percent), 1956 (57 percent), 1960 (57 percent), 1964 (the exception, 35 percent), 1968 (57 percent), and 1972 (71 percent). In most of these elections, except for 1964, the Democrats have received about 15 percent of the endorsements.[6]

Newspaper support is a critical element in the strategy of the political office seekers. Where they are endorsed and supported by the news media, they may be encouraged to allocate radio and television funds to insure capturing the majority vote. On the other hand, they may decide to spend monies in toss-up states or areas hoping to reach potential supporters where newspapers may not have endorsed them.

In the endorsement for Nixon and McGovern in the 1972 presidential election, one week before the election Nixon had the support of 753 dailies while only 56 supported the South Dakota senator. Of all the newspapers taking part in the *Editor and Publisher* poll, Nixon received the support of 71 percent and McGovern only 5 percent; the remainder remained uncommitted or independent. The circulation of the dailies that endorsed the president had a combined circulation of over 30 million while those that supported the McGovern candidacy had slightly over 3 million. Nixon's clear dominance in editorial support was revealed in his support in large key states, states where McGovern hoped to fare well. The lopsided margins favoring Nixon were revealed in California (71–1), Illinois (39–0), Michigan (26–0), Florida (26–2), Ohio (40–1), Texas (48–1), and Virginia (21–0). The only states where more than three newspapers endorsed McGovern were in New York (30–5), Indiana (39–4), and Pennsylvania (40–3); but even in these Nixon clearly dominated the editorial support.

Although Nixon narrowly won the popular vote over Humphrey in 1968, he had over five times as much newspaper support as Humphrey. Nixon was endorsed by 634 dailies with a 34.6 million circulation and Humphrey by 146 that had 9.5 million circulation. The third party candidate, Wallace, was endorsed by only twelve dailies with a combined circulation of 159,000. In 1968 there were 250 dailies with 5.2 million circulation that were uncommitted to any candidate or adopted independent stances. Thus of the 1042 dailies reported to the *Editor and Publisher* poll, a poll that included 80 percent of the total daily circulation, Nixon had 70 percent of the endorsements compared to Humphrey's 19 percent.

An examination of the endorsements by states reveals some definite spatial patterns. Wallace was endorsed by only a dozen papers but eight were in Alabama and Mississippi. In the largest populated states, Nixon's advantage over Humphrey was very marked. The support in California was 60–12; in New York, 40–11; in Pennsylvania, 39–4; in Illinois, 38–3; and in Ohio, 35–2. In only four states did Humphrey have more than 10 newspapers endorsing him: California (12), Texas (12), New York (10), and Indiana (10). He received no endorsements from such politically important states as Michigan, Maryland, Connecticut, and Washington.

In the 1964 election between Johnson and Goldwater, however, the landslide victory for the Democrats was not reflected in the newspaper endorsements. Johnson was endorsed by 440 papers with 27 million circulation and Goldwater by 359 with slightly less than 9 million. There were 237 undeclared dailies that had a circulation of 7.6 million. Looking at the geographical pattern of support, strictly in terms of the number of endorsements, not circulation size, Johnson received no support from papers in Delaware, Maine, Nebraska, and Utah. Goldwater received no support in Washington, D.C., Hawaii, Nevada, or Utah.

In another close election, 1960, Nixon had the support of 731 dailies that had 38 million circulation while Kennedy, the winner, was endorsed by only 208 dailies that had a combined total of 8.4 million circulation. A total of 328 papers with 7 million circulation were undeclared in that year. Except for Texas, Nixon had the edge over Kennedy in endorsements in all major states: California, 65–20; New York, 50–9; Pennsylvania, 53–5; Illinois, 48–5; Ohio, 39–3; Indiana, 39–11; Michigan, 26–0; and Florida, 22–3. Kennedy's strongest support came from papers in Texas, California, Indiana, Missouri, North Carolina, and West Virginia.

Regional Journalism: Newspaper Editorials. In addition to the regional variations in support for presidential candidates, it is expected there would be differences in positions taken on key political issues. In a survey of newspapers conducted by United States Representative Bob Eckhardt of Texas in the spring of 1970, he found out that there were different editorial slants in the nation's newspapers.[7] What these reflect are variations in a region's attitudes and political culture.

One of the major issues that arose early in the first Nixon administration was whether to expand the ABM (antiballistic) system. This decision in the Senate was decided by one vote. Of the newspapers surveyed, 57 percent favored building an expanded ABM system. It was supported in all regions except the Midwest; and strongest support was in the Far West (Table 1-4). Perhaps the residents in the former area feel they are most vulnerable to nuclear attack and thus oppose the expansion of destructive military systems.

Nixon's appointments for Supreme Court vacancies aroused a great deal of controversy not only in Congress but in the newspapers and radio-television media. After having southerner Haynesworth of South Carolina rejected by the Senate, Nixon endorsed another conservative-leaning judge, Carswell of Florida. As the above table shows, the majority of papers opposed him. Those in all regions except the South opposed Carswell, and with the exception of the Florida papers the majority of southern papers even opposed him.

A volatile political issue of 1970 involved the United States invasion into Cambodia, a policy that sparked mass protests within the country taking on various forms. Approximately the same number of papers supported as opposed the president's actions. His greatest support for this military venture was in the South and West, with the least in the Northeast and Midwest where university strikes and protests were common.

The McGovern-Hatfield amendment, one of several introduced since 1968, was designed to set a definite deadline for ending the war; it was defeated in the Senate. Likewise it received little newspaper support as almost three-fourths of the papers opposed it. The strongest support for this antiwar measure was by those newspapers published in the Northeast.

TABLE 1-4   Regional Journalism: Editorial Variation–Congressman
Eckhardt's Newspaper Editorial Survey, 1970
(F = for;   A = against)

	Northeast		Midwest		South		West	
	F	A	F	A	F	A	F	A
ABM:								
Number	10	8	13	14	15	13	14	5
Percent	55.5	44.5	48	52	54	46	73.7	26.3
Carswell:								
Number	4	11	5	22	15	13	3	13
Percent	26.7	73.3	19	81	54	46	18.75	81.25
Cambodia:								
Number	7	10	11	16	15	14	14	5
Percent	41.2	58.8	41	59	52	48	73.7	26.3
Agnew:								
Number	3	9	7	13	9	17	7	10
Percent	25	75	35	65	35	65	41.2	58.8
McGovern-Hatfield:								
Number	5	7	4	15	9	14	2	12
Percent	41.67	58.33	21	79	39	61	14.3	85.7

Source: Hon. Robert Eckhardt, "Mr. Agnew, You Are Wrong About the Press," *Congressional Record*, 116 (1970), p. 37210.

CHANGES IN ATTITUDES

Women's Suffrage. Amendments to the United States Constitution demonstrate a change in attitudes and policy toward a particular group or certain issue. The amendment becomes part of the Constitution only after three-fourths of the states ratify the particular piece of legislation. As can be imagined, not all states necessarily accept proposed amendments and those that do seldom act at the same time. The ease of modern communications and greater national awareness of certain political and social issues has meant the time elapsing between the first and last state needed for ratification is remarkably short. Today thirty-eight states are needed for adoption. The almost instant action on critical proposals, such as the Twenty-first Amendment that lowered the voting age to eighteen years and was ratified in three months, indicates there is often little spatial or temporal pattern. Should all the needed states approve a piece of legislation at about the same time, no spatial or temporal pattern would be evident.

Prior to the advent of the present communications network and the political contacts of states and key politicians, ideas that confronted the national citizenry were acted upon and approved at varying rates and stages. Some states might approve specific legislation soon after it was approved in a referendum. Other states in another part of the United States might delay action by engaging in lengthy discussion prior to any enactment. Often the time elapsing between the initial adopters and the last ones was twenty-five to fifty years. The diffusion of political legislation that affected the nation as a whole was characterized by a spatial process. A certain state or group of states were the initial adopters of a proposal, such as child labor laws, prohibition, or women's suffrage. Later, states nearby or in the same section of the nation may have adopted similar legislation. Such states paved the way to an eventual constitutional amendment or the implementation of a particular social policy. Some states for religious, economic, or social reasons may never have approved or even seriously considered a piece of legislation that eventually became national law.

The Nineteenth Amendment to the United States Constitution is a case in point where a discernible spatial process is identified.[8] This granted women the right to vote in presidential elections. Wyoming was the first state to permit the suffrage of women in national elections; this was in 1869 (Fig. 1-3). Soon thereafter it was adopted by Utah, possibly because of the Mormon influence, but it was not until almost a quarter of a century later that neighboring Colorado and Idaho approved similar legislation. The origin of this innovation and its earlier acceptance in the West rather than in the Midwest and Northeast may be tied to the frontier

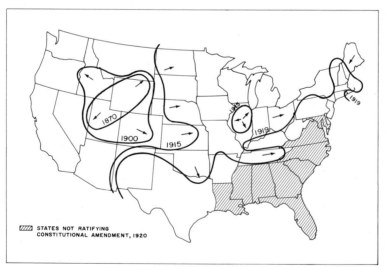

STATES NOT RATIFYING
CONSTITUTIONAL AMENDMENT, 1920

FIG. 1-3 Diffusion of Women's Suffrage. After Peter R. Gould, *Spatial Diffusion*, Commission on College Geography, Resource Paper 4, 1969, p. 68. (Reproduced by permission of the Association of American Geographers.)

settlement philosophy late last century. Individualism was a trademark of the society and this held for both men and women. In the "effete East" women were viewed in their more traditional role. The West's view is symbolized in Wyoming's state motto "Equal Rights." By 1915 most of the western states had approved women's suffrage in their constitutions. Illinois was the first state in the Midwest to grant this right. During and after World War I the suffragettes were beginning to protest and call for more equality before the law. Their activities in the streets and in the saloons were instrumental in the passage of suffrage legislation in many eastern states outside of New England, where traditional religious and family views of women held and their role in politics was viewed with dismay. This was equally true for the nine southern states from Maryland to Louisiana, a solid block that failed to ratify the amendment. Thus, this political innovation was not accepted uniformly in all sections of the nation. A barrier from New England south and west to New Mexico divided those states favoring from those not favoring this right for women.

Republicanism in the South. Other than political issues we also find that the popularity and place of a political party in a region's culture is not always received equally in all parts. This is the case of the emergence of the Republican party in the South. In a section known to insiders and outsiders as the "solid South," the Democratic party controlled all levels of the political machinery this century, save a few hard-core Republican segments in the southern Appalachians and Ozarks. The Democrats were in such predominance at the county, state, and congressional levels that the Republicans were for all intents and purposes almost outlawed. The identification of this party and its association with Lincoln did not appeal to the prevailing cultural mentality that developed in the Deep as well as in much of the Rim South. Yet to examine the political parties in the region today, a growing number of residents are voting for and identifying with the Republicans. The party has become competitive in presidential, gubernatorial, and senatorial elections. This has not been an instant development but one that has emerged slowly in the past twenty-five years.

The impression is often portrayed by politicians and by citizens outside the South that the entire region has always voted for the Democratic party at all levels. However, this is not entirely accurate as there have been some permanent flaws in the Democratic fabric, especially in the Ozarks, southwest Virginia, western North Carolina, and eastern Tennessee. Farmers in these areas were not in agreement with the lowland planters on the issues of slavery and secession. These sections of mountain Republicans have voted for Republican presidential candidates since the Civil War.[9] They have formed a nucleus for the emergence of the Republican party in the past quarter century.

The first break in the solid Democratic party strength came in the 1948 presidential election. In this race a third party, the States' Rights party, emerged whose leader, Strom Thurmond of South Carolina, represented a repudiation of the national Democratic party. In carrying four Deep South states (Alabama,

Louisiana, Mississippi, and South Carolina) he did break the solid political lock of the national party. The Republicans fared poorly in this election but the voters were offered an opportunity to express their views by voting for a candidate whom many identified with on social and economic issues. The 1952 and 1956 elections of Eisenhower illustrated a growing support for the Republican candidate. Even though the Republicans failed to carry the states, they did well in their traditional cores and in the larger cities throughout the South.[10] These urban nodes became a second locus for the acceptance of Republican candidates. In 1960, Nixon increased the strength of his party in the South. Like his predecessor, he failed to win states, but a definite strategy for the party was beginning to emerge. The "solid" South was beginning to be considered no longer so for the Democratic party. The Republicans being a minority party nationally in party registration could seize some of these states by supporting the views and attitudes of the residents. This became apparent in Goldwater's 1964 candidacy when he emphasized many of the social, economic, and political views held by white southerners. His campaign philosophy worked to the advantage of his party; they carried five Deep South states while suffering disastrous defeats elsewhere.

The 1964 election year became a landmark year for the Republicans as it demonstrated they could defeat the Democrats at the presidential level in one of their traditional bastions. Further, it showed that the party was able to engage the support of (by voting) and to identify with southern voters. The Democrats fared poorly that year, especially in the Deep South. They were losing a greater share of the large and small city vote as well as their traditional support in rural areas. By 1968 the region's political picture further illustrated the dynamism that had been growing. As in 1948, a regional third party candidate, this time Wallace of Alabama, entered the scene. His campaign rhetoric sounded like Goldwater's. He was successful in five states (Alabama, Arkansas, Louisiana, Mississippi, and Georgia). Even though the Republicans failed to win the Deep South vote then, Nixon outwardly wooed the region with his "southern strategy" engineered by the now Republican Thurmond. Ostensibly this plan was designed to encourage southern voters to support him rather than Democrat Humphrey or American Independent party candidate Wallace. Southern Republican senators and other conservative leaders campaigned in the Rim states. The effort of the Nixon Republicans was successful in that the border states carried solidified his victory. To be sure, the Wallace candidacy did prevent a repeat of the 1964 performance for the Republican party; but it did mark substantial gains outside the traditional cores and big city areas. In each succeeding presidential election the party was receiving greater support. By 1972 this was most evident. The Republicans running without a regional and third party candidate and against a Democrat that had written off the South, meant they won each state handily. They carried all states as well as almost all the counties in the eleven states of the old Confederacy. The landslide win by Nixon may be obscured by the effect of the party in the South. His victories of 70 percent or more were greater than his national average of 61 percent. The party's active support among the voters has been demonstrated by Nixon's stance on racial issues, social welfare, federal-state relations, Supreme Court nominees, and selection of southern advisers. All the while the Republicans have been gaining strength in the region the Democrats have not been nominating presidential candidates or introducing legislation favoring the majority of the region's electorate.

The diffusion of Republican support in the South is illustrated by examining the mean centers of party support for the presidential elections of 1948 through 1972 and the number of times a county has voted Republican by more than 45 percent (Fig. 1-4). In 1948 the mean center was in the traditional core area, specifically in western North Carolina. In 1952 and 1956 the center moved south-southwest illustrating that Eisenhower was beginning to gather some support from states in the Deep South. The picture remained essentially the same for 1960. However, by 1964 with the Goldwater candidacy the center of mean Republican support moved to west Georgia near the Alabama line. This southwest shift revealed the tremendous popular support the Republicans enjoyed in the Deep South. They were more successful here than in the Rim South. The election of 1968 showed a striking similarity to the 1948 election in that the mean center of Republican vote was near the 1948 node. This shows the impact of a regional third party candidate. By 1972 the political picture was again changed and Nixon's landslide was akin to Goldwater's performance of 1964 in the South. Nixon was not as successful in carrying the Deep South as Goldwater had been. Perhaps the increased black registration since 1964 or the progressive sentiments among a growing but still small number of whites may be reflected in the mean center being northeast of the 1964 node.

The diffusion of the Republican presidential vote can also be illustrated by dividing the votes since 1948 into four classes (Fig. 1-4). On a county basis a more meaningful analysis of the spatial processes and patterns can be revealed rather than the use of statewide voting analysis. A county is considered competitive with the Democrats once it has voted above 45 percent Republican. When the seven presidential elections from 1948 through 1972 are used, the patterns take on some significance.[11]

The *core* areas of Republicans parallel closely those mountain areas identified by Key.[12] They have voted for a Republican candidate at least six times. Their consistency in adhering to the Republican party has remained steadfast even in the midst of the political dynamism in the rest of the South in 1948. However, in 1964 they failed to support the Goldwater brand of Republicanism. Outside the traditional core the metropolitan areas around Nashville, Miami, St. Petersburg, Orlando, and Sarasota have voted for the GOP at least six times.

The actual birth of the Republican party is divided into three classes: *early emergence, middle emergence,* and *late emergence.* The number of times a county has voted over 45 percent Republican determines in which class it will be included. Voting in the South since 1948 has been highly unstable, especially with the 1964, 1968, and 1972 elections where party loyalty at the presidential level was seemingly up for grabs. The diffusion of the party in the past seven elections is not one that can be tied previously to a gradual Republican gain in each subsequent election.

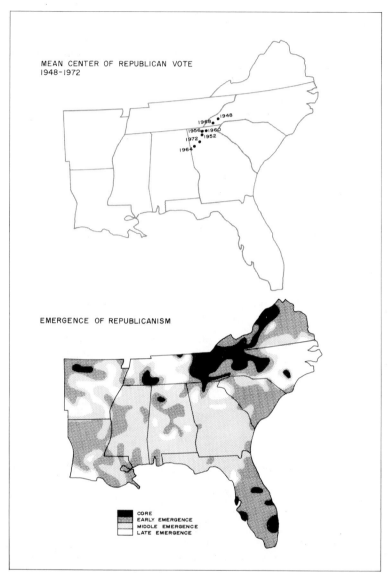

FIG. 1-4 Growth of Republicanism in the South. (After Gerald L. Ingalls, "Spatial Change in Post-War Southern Republican Voting Responses," Michigan State University, Department of Geography, Ph.D. dissertation, 1973, p. 95.)

For this reason the number of times a county has voted for the party has more meaning.

    The *early emergence* counties have voted at least three times for the GOP since 1948. The counties in this pattern are contiguous to the core and in peripheral segments of the South. Witness the dominance of this pattern in Florida, Louisiana, Virginia, and northwest Arkansas. As in the core category, the urban nodes in peripheral locations appear as outliers. Most of these counties voted Republican during one of the Eisenhower elections. Counties in the *middle emergence* category have voted for a Republican candidate on at least two occasions. Many of these cast support for Goldwater as their first Republican presidential candidate in the modern period. With the 1964 election the Republicans had gained a toehold in the Deep South. The party was no longer only competitive in the peripheral South. The *late emergence* counties have voted over 45 percent Republican in at least one election, usually 1964, 1968, or 1972. These represent the strongest anti-Republican or pro-Democratic sections of the South. These are not in the "deepest" part of the Deep South but in some peripheral locations, such as eastern North Carolina (historically solid Democratic) and central Tennessee.

The geographic emergence of the Republican party is generally one of a diffusion from the core and peripheries into the centers of the Deep South. Rim or Border states were the first to become competitive for the Republican party; the Deep South states the last. The pattern is not without some wrinkles as there are peaks and valleys representing counties that consistently are at variance with surrounding space. Political attitudes and behavior are not always uniform even within a state or a fairly homogeneous region. There are always anomalies such as the historical Republican roots in Winston County, Alabama, or a major urban center such as Leon County (Tallahassee), Florida, or a county with a large black registered population as Greene County, Alabama. Only one county, Macon County, Alabama, has not voted over 45 percent Republican since 1948 and it is smothered by the surrounding middle emergence category.

What has been treated above is the diffusion of the Republican party into the South as measured by presidential voting. The party has not been as successful in electing leading state officials throughout the region. However, since 1960 there have been ten Republican governors and senators elected from those states that have had a traditional and significant Republican element, namely, Virginia, Tennessee, North Carolina, Arkansas, and Florida. These were the first states from which the national Republican party actively encouraged Republican candidates to run for the high public offices. Within the past few years there have been Republicans running for statewide offices in all states. The Republicans are even holding primaries, a reality considered unlikely even two decades ago. The states of Louisiana, Mississippi, Alabama, and Georgia have yet to elect a Republican senator or governor but the party is gaining support in each subsequent election. At lower levels, that is, congressional races and state legislative positions, the Republicans are not enjoying as much success in their bid for top positions. The diffusion of the Republican party has come slowly to the South and at different rates; however, it is being accepted as more and more a fact of reality in dealing with the South's economic, social, and political issues. The "solid" South is thus melting more in each statewide and nationwide election.

FOOTNOTES

1. Kevin R. Cox, "A Spatial Interactional Model for Political Geography," *East Lakes Geographer*, 4 (1968), 58–76; "The Voting Decision in Intraurban Space," *Proceedings*, Association of American Geographers, 1 (1969), 43–46; and "Residential Relocation and Political Behavior," *Acta Sociologica*, 13 (1970), 40–53.
2. Americans for Democratic Action, Washington, D.C., 1972 Membership List and Chapter Listing.
3. United States House of Representatives, Committee on Un-American Activities, *The Present-Day Ku Klux Klan Movement*, Report, Ninetieth Congress, Second Session, Washington, D.C., 1967.
4. *Gallup Opinion Index*, Report 69 (March 1971), p. 12; Report 71 (May 1971), pp. 12–14, 23; Report 72 (June 1971), p. 15; Report 75 (September 1971), p. 18; Report 76 (October 1971), pp. 21–23; and Report 78 (December 1971), p. 19.
5. Governmental Affairs Institute, *America Votes*, Vol. 4 (1960), Vol. 6 (1964), and Vol. 8 (1968), Washington, D.C., *Congressional Quarterly*, 1962, 1966, and 1970. For the 1972 results see *1973 World Almanac*, New York, Newspaper Enterprise Association, 1973, pp. 42–69.
6. *Editor and Publisher*, November 5, 1960, pp. 9–13; October 31, 1964, pp. 9–13; November 2, 1968, pp. 9–12; and November 4, 1972, pp. 9–11. See also Jourdan Houston, "Candidate Endorsements," *Editor and Publisher*, March 25, 1972, pp. 7 and 18.
7. Hon. Robert Eckhardt, "Mr. Agnew, You Are Wrong About the Press," *Congressional Record*, 116 (1970), 37209–37211. See also Ben H. Bagdikian, "The Politics of American Newspapers," *Columbia Journalism Review*, March/April 1972, 8–13.
8. Peter R. Gould, *Spatial Diffusion*, Commission on College Geography, Association of American Geographers, Washington, D.C., Resource Paper No. 4, 1969, pp. 60–63.
9. V. O. Key, Jr., *Southern Politics*, New York, Vintage Books, 1949, passim.
10. Stanley D. Brunn and Gerald L. Ingalls, "The Emergence of Republicanism in the Urban South," *Southeastern Geographer*, 12:2 (1972), 133–144.
11. Gerald L. Ingalls, "Spatial Change in Post-War Southern Republican Voting Responses," Michigan State University, Department of Geography, Ph.D. dissertation, 1973. See the following for an example of the diffusion of a political party outside the United States: J. Ross Barnett, "Scale, Process, and the Diffusion of a Political Movement," *Proceedings*, Association of American Geographers, 4 (1972), 9–13. At a state scale, cities and urban counties also appear as nodes of progress in measuring reforms as in public education in North Carolina. Leonard J. Evenden, "The Diffusion of Public Educational Changes in North Carolina and the Regionalization of Progress," *Southeastern Geographer*, 9:2 (1969), 80–93.
12. Key, op. cit.

Chapter 2

PERCEPTION OF POLITICAL SPACE

Any well-established village in New England or the
northern Middle West could afford a town drunkard,
a town atheist, and a few Democrats.

Denis William Brogan

THE INDIVIDUAL'S VIEW

As the previous chapter on attitudes illustrated, not all citizens share similar views
on the political, social, and economic issues facing their state or the United States.
How a citizen views the nation's events is based on a set of regional cultural
traditions as well as the political identification of his parents, religious heritage,
social consciousness, economic status and well-being, travels and experiences outside his native region, interactions with friends, and sources of his political
information.

In a geographic context we can examine how a resident views his state in the
nation and the world and the view that a nation holds of the state. This evaluation
is not always easy to accomplish, as generalizing about a state's or region's culture,
attitudes, and adherences may be too general to be of much meaning.

27

One state that has been in the national news in the past decade is Mississippi. What concerns us here are the commonly held views of residents of that political unit. One historian cites the stated views of a candidate running for the state house of representatives in 1963 as being those reflective of Mississippians.

> I am a Mississippi Democrat with conservative political views. I supported the unpledged elector movement in 1960. I am a staunch believer in constitutional government, states rights, the southern way of life, and separation of the races.
>
> The forces of socialism and communism outside our borders are advancing and spreading rapidly over the world while within our borders, the dictatorial Kennedys, socialistic Supreme Court, politicalized federal courts, power-seizing pressure groups are gradually and certainly undermining and destroying the principals [sic] upon which this great nation was founded.
>
> Since Mississippi and the Southland has [sic] inherited the task of making the last great stand for constitutional government, states rights, individual freedom and democracy, we must cast aside our personal and political ambitions, close our ranks, unite and solidify our beliefs and convictions and advance and achieve our destiny by handing down to our children and descendants the greatest gift that one can give or receive—a free Christian, Democratic nation and world.[1]

While it is important on one hand to know how the residents of a state view the nation, it is equally worth knowing how the nation views that state. The latter can be ascertained by examining such criteria as newspaper editorials, congressional legislation, and opinion surveys. College and university students asked in the past decade to indicate their preferences for the states almost always ranked Mississippi as the least desirable place.[2] In terms of congressional legislation much that was enacted during the 1960s was concerned with improving the civil rights of blacks. There was general support nationwide for seeing that many previous injustices and inequities somehow be corrected. In this light many Americans considered Mississippi as the one state where not all citizens were able to obtain equal education, vote with impunity, purchase homes, or gain access to public accommodations. These views, in part supported by major networks and newspapers, seemed to present Mississippi to the nation as a fearful hated society of bigoted whites where blacks had no rights, the KKK was active, public officials practiced justice partially, and outside church leaders, students, and the federal government were despised. In essence such national sentiments were instrumental in making this state an undesirable and unsafe place to travel, reside, or be employed.

The Mississippi case is only one example that could be used to illustrate a nation's attitudes toward a particular state or city or the view the residents of that political unit hold in regard to a larger political order. The stereotyping that a nation's citizens retain of a city and its political image often remains long after significant events and such are difficult to erase. Although Chicago may still be considered in the public eye as a city where "bossism" reigns, it was not long ago that New York or Boston had similar images. Dallas is considered as one of the major political nodes of right-wing extremism in the United States; this in part is supported by the strength of the John Birch Society as well as being the site of President Kennedy's assassination. Some states are viewed as progressive and places where liberalism is dominant, as are Massachusetts and New York. The latter may have this image altered with a member of the Conservative party being elected to the Senate in 1970.

A POLITICIAN'S PERCEPTION OF SPACE

Introduction. A politician running for national or statewide office will develop a strategy that incorporates many elements of geography. He and his staff must consider where to make public appearances, where to spend the monies for staff and advertising, and what issues to emphasize in particular locations. As he views the citizenry in the political space that he endeavors to capture, he will be able to separate it into at least three major areas, those where he is already well known, those where he is totally unknown, and those where he is in a more or less neutral or competitive position. Such regions or states or counties or cities are grouped into these three categories, and how he perceives and groups these spaces may be based on his previous exposure to the electorate. In his attempt to capture either a party nomination in a primary or in a general election, he will have to decide where to spend the monies. They may be spent on television and radio or billboard advertising in his home state or region where he will attempt to increase his already popular support. Possibly he may try to spend monies in states where he is totally unknown in hopes that a new face and unknown image to the electorate will bring support. A third possibility is to spend those monies in competitive areas. Here he can attempt to siphon off support for the opposition or gain support from the undecided voters. A national campaign strategy incorporates geographic elements whether it be traveling or advertising in large rather than small states, or northern cities as opposed to those in the South. According to a former adviser to President Nixon, there was greater concern for how a speech or action was received in the "American Heartland" than how it was received in large northeastern cities. This was amply stated as "How does it play in Peoria."

Aside from the allocation of monies there is the issue of the personal campaign itself. In a state or national election, the candidates for senator or for president will perceive the social, economic, and political pictures differently. During a presidential election the candidates attempt to identify with the state's or region's or nation's citizenry by emphasizing and recommending legislation favorable to the majority of the voters. A national party, for example, is comprised of varying social and economic fabrics woven into a nationwide political organization. The issues stressed during a campaign are those of major note to the populace in that given city or region. During the 1972 election, Democratic party candidates oriented their public appearances to issues affecting space program cuts and unemployment in southern California, busing in Florida and in Michigan, anti-

Vietnam War statements in Massachusetts, and coal mining safety in West Virginia. One example where a popular social theme was stressed in the wrong place was Goldwater's attack on the social security system in St. Petersburg, Florida, during his 1964 campaign.

The same themes are not emphasized in all states or cities. The candidates may take even slightly different stances on the same issue in different spaces. The case of busing in 1972 provides a good example. This emotional and controversial issue has beleaguered congressmen and presidents, not to mention judges, in the past decade. During the spring 1972 primaries, Democratic candidates, of which there were many, represented different points on the ideological spectrum. They were likely to take a much harder stance on the issue in Florida and Michigan than in Illinois or Ohio. This was primarily because the candidates themselves perceived the issue as being volatile in the former two states, as indeed it was. Wallace was able to gain the greatest support for this issue in the early Florida primary in part because he was the state's neighbor. His stance on busing as well as other civil rights issues was a hard-lined position that many Americans knew and supported. This contributed to his victory in the Michigan primary, although not by the margin he won in Florida and other southern states. Candidate Wallace was so pleased with his victory in a northern state that he declared Michigan his "second home." His campaign strategy perceived the northern states in 1972 and in 1968 as an area that would support his views on race, economy, government, and society. The large blue-collar vote that he believed would carry him to victories in the northern states in 1968 never materialized.

Along similar lines the Nixon "southern strategy" of 1968 was a deliberate attempt to gain outright support from a particular region. Nixon and the Republicans realized that with Democrat Humphrey and American Independent party candidate Wallace vying for votes across the nation, the South was the one region with some vulnerability to the above candidates. The Republican objective was to gain as much ground as possible in the Border or Rim South states and possibly deflate the support for Wallace and thereby win a few crucial states. The conservative stance Nixon and his regional supporters took during the campaign on civil rights and his criticism of the Supreme Court plus the strong support from segregationist Strom Thurmond of South Carolina were distinctly to aid a regional strategy. Their perception of the area as well as their campaign strategy proved successful as Nixon's winning the Rim States from Wallace insured his election.

The Wallace and Nixon campaigns illustrate attempts to win support in areas they perceived as being competitive. Other presidential candidates may perceive their political map of the United States as having places where they have little or no chance of winning. There they may avoid spending monies and making public appearances. After the 1964 Republican convention, the liberal and eastern Republicans were highly critical of the Goldwater nomination. His views on civil rights, the Vietnam War, federal bureaucracy as well as his attacks on the "liberal eastern establishment" contributed to his unpopularity. One cartoonist perceived Goldwater's views as having the eastern seaboard sawed off the mainland (Fig. 2-

"AW, COME ON BACK—I WAS ONLY KIDDING."

FIG. 2-1 Goldwater's View of the United States in the 1964 Presidential Election. (Copyright © 1964 The Chicago Sun-Times, reproduced by courtesy of Wil-Jo Associates, Inc. and Bill Mauldin.)

1). This perception of part of the Goldwater philosophy and campaign strategy implied that the nation might be able to exist without the liberal northeast. The 1964 results demonstrated that he received almost no support in the northeast states, even in states generally perceived as being traditionally rock-ribbed Republican.

During the 1972 campaign the Democrat standard-bearer, McGovern, viewed the United States in a somewhat similar role. Since his rival Nixon had received southern support in 1968 and had made overt gestures to placate the region's citizens during his term in office, McGovern decided not to campaign there. Part of his strategy to "write off" the South was that the polls showed he had little support there (even in the Florida primary) and he was likely to garner little by further campaigning. Instead he concentrated his efforts on the major populated states in the Northeast, Midwest, and California. He believed that his previous positions on the Vietnam War, human rights and his moral rhetoric would enable him to obtain support in these states. By capturing the electoral votes in these key populated states, he hoped to win the election. The outcome of the election showed he lost all these states save Massachusetts (and the District of Columbia), although his support was stronger here than in the states where he did not campaign.

Governors and senators running for statewide office are faced with the same set of spatial decisions as presidential candidates. The major difference geographically is in the scale of their space. There are some political groups and cultures favoring their candidacy and certain key cities or counties that are essential to any statewide victory. Politicians running for state offices in California realize that Los Angeles is almost a necessity if victory is to come. The same is true for Cook County (Chicago), Illinois; Wayne County (Detroit), Michigan; and Cuyahoga County (Cleveland), Ohio. The largest city not only is important as it has the largest number of potential voters but often the turnout in such counties spells the difference between a narrow victory or defeat. As a part of the emerging Republican strategy in the South, the selection of candidates from major urban centers is considered important in their contests with traditional Democrats, some who still hail from rural and small-town areas.

The campaign strategy that a particular candidate or party adopts often reflects elements of the state's political, social, or economic geography. Most candidates have a home base or territory that they perceive as being the locus of their support. They then attempt to reach out and capture other counties and cities. In the 1971 Louisiana gubernatorial election, Democratic candidate Edwards from south Louisiana attempted to woo support of voters in the southern part of the state. A campaign committee used a clever piece of political cartography as a part of its campaign strategy (Fig. 2-2). It attempted to pit north against south Louisiana, by showing the south's lack of representation in the state house; the line dividing the two sections was more for political expediency than a genuine cultural demarcation. A more realistic divide between the two parts of the state would be some fifty miles farther south. The south with its French culture and urban-industrial economy is in contrast to the more agriculturally oriented north settled by former residents of neighboring Deep and Rim South states.

The Louisiana example illustrates a geographic strategy adopted by candi-

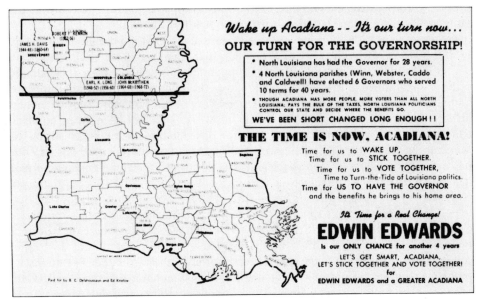

Fig. 2-2 Political Cartography in the Louisiana Gubernatorial Campaign, 1971.

dates seeking a statewide constituency. More than one politician has attempted to group a state's residents or a state's counties into readily identifiable sections. One of the more frequent examples is to divide a state into "upstate" vs. "downstate" or "north" vs. "south" categories. This is often meant to identify Republican or Democratic power bases or conservative-liberal concentrations. Examples of distinct regional philosophies exist in California, Florida, Tennessee, New York, and Illinois to name only a few. With the rural-urban migration of the past thirty years and the growth of suburbia, the "big city" vs. "rural" vote also has been identified by many party leaders. This strategy has been used to emphasize that a particular candidate is popular in the big cities and suburbs rather than in the small towns and rural areas. It is not only the perception that the individual politician himself holds of political spaces but the views and labels held by the potential voters. When most politicians campaign they attempt to separate the electorate on issues and ideological stances as well as convenient geographical units. Part of the expressed purpose behind such geographic labeling is to homogenize the electorate into categories that politicians themselves can identify.

Any elected representative, whether he be a county sheriff, coroner, senator, or president, has a spatial unit comprising his constituency. How he views that unit's population as well as their needs will influence what actions he will support or introduce in terms of policies or programs. The positions he adopts while in office will be based on his own background and experiences in addition to the support he receives from influential lobbies or individual citizens. Should he be a congressman in the United States House of Representatives who represents a rural southern biracial district where blacks have traditionally been excluded from the same political and social rights available to whites, he will have to decide on questions of education, housing, and social welfare legislation what group or groups he will be representing in his votes. The fact that there are more blacks and fewer whites in his district does not signify his support will be representing the majority of the population. He may instead vote along the lines of the financially, socially, and politically powerful elites in the district who will not fund his reelection unless he votes in accord with their views. While his district may not be granting an equal education to poor blacks, or even poor whites, or while hunger and malnutrition are rampant, or that justice by local police and judges is not administered with equity, he may not introduce or support legislation to correct such ills. Perhaps he may instead try to help wealthy cotton farmers obtain larger subsidies or get defense contracts or reclamation projects for his district.

While some representatives to a metrogovernment or a state assembly or even to the United States Senate may approach their representative spaces as mainly to satisfy a financial and social elite, there are others who do not. Instead of support for a status quo or retrenched positions, they seek new solutions to problems confronting not only their space and state but the nation as well. Their perception of problems goes beyond the bounds of their own elected space and encompasses a national sphere. This view of politics is related to the region's political culture, a theme treated in more detail in Chapter 9. Representatives from such spaces believe that problems of environmental cleanup and minority rights are not only a problem facing their space and constituency but ones that merit work with leaders in other states and nations as well. In this sense they are leaders of their counties or cities or states and their prime dedication is to improve the general welfare of all citizens, black and white, rich and poor, young and old. While in office they are affected by pressure and interest groups from all sides of the political spectrum on varying issues of environmental, economic, social, and international concern. They consider themselves as representatives of all the people, that is, a public servant in the fullest sense.

Political Advertising: Radio and Television. Within the past two decades television has become the major source of political advertising. In this regard it has replaced newspapers and radio, although not exclusively. What has happened is that advertising agencies have attempted to "sell" a political candidate to the television audience by emphasizing key personality characteristics, often over the candidate's stances on key political issues. The issues stressed as well as the type of image presented vary from region to region and one political culture to another. California is one state where television images have been particularly important in recent senatorial and gubernatorial contests.

A political party in search of popular support for the presidential–vice-presidential ticket as well as key senatorial, congressional, or gubernatorial candidates allocates a certain amount of monies for advertising. The allocation to states or regions depends on the overall campaign strategy. As expected, the large populated states, such as New York and California, with a large popular vote and electoral strength are desired "captures." States of small population or where one party is traditionally strong may not be competitive for advertising. Other states that are usually political battlegrounds, such as Illinois, Ohio, Missouri, and Texas, are places where all political parties are likely to invest heavily.

The amounts invested in radio and television advertising are different in the primary than in the general election. Heavy amounts in primaries may be attributed to a number of candidates seeking the nation's highest elected office. The general election, on the other hand, entails spending for only one set of officeholders, from presidential candidate to locally elected officials.

When data on advertising for the general election campaign of 1968 are analyzed, several distinguishable patterns emerge. In terms of radio station charges, the Republicans outspent the Democrats $6,853,115 to $4,846,246.[3] The American Independent party spent only $954,436 on radio advertising. In general the Republicans had their heaviest radio investment in the Plains states, California, three large Northeast states (Ohio, Pennsylvania, and New York), and several Border South states (Virginia, Tennessee, Florida) as well as Texas. The Democrats outspent the Republicans mainly in New England and the Midwest. In television advertising again the Republicans outspent the Democrats handily, $10,993,514 to $7,923,423. The AIP spent $807,790. The Republicans were the leading spenders in thirty-eight of the fifty states. Their heaviest efforts regionally were in the Far West, the Southwest, the South, and the Northeast states of New York, New Jersey, Pennsylvania, and Ohio.

An investigation into the expenditures for political broadcasts (radio and television) by the Republicans for the 1968 general election reveals part of the party's strategy. Large-area states with small populations are expected to have higher costs per potential voter; this holds true for Alaska, Hawaii, Nevada, North Dakota, Montana, and Wyoming (Fig. 2-3). In these states the Republicans invested much more than in the large population states of New York, Ohio, Pennsylvania, and California. The lesser amount spent in the Deep South may be attributed to the realization that this was "Wallace country" and a heavy investment with little likelihood of victory would be considered unwise.

When the primary and general election costs for both radio and television are examined for all three parties in 1968, and this in terms of winning or losing, some meaningful patterns emerge (Fig. 2-3). Republicans spent over $22 million, Democrats $15 million, and the American Independent party over $2 million. Viewed in the light of the major parties, the Republicans outspent the Democrats in thirty-five of the fifty states and in the District of Columbia. In twenty-five they spent more and won, while they lost seven to the Democrats and three to the AIP. Their heavy investment in broadcasting (radio and television) paid off in the West, Mountain and Plains states, Midwest, and Rim South states. They lost to Wallace in Arkansas, Louisiana, and Alabama. Nixon considered winning Texas, Virginia, and Florida crucial to his election. The Republicans, although outspending the Democrats, lost some key states in Texas, Michigan, Pennsylvania, and

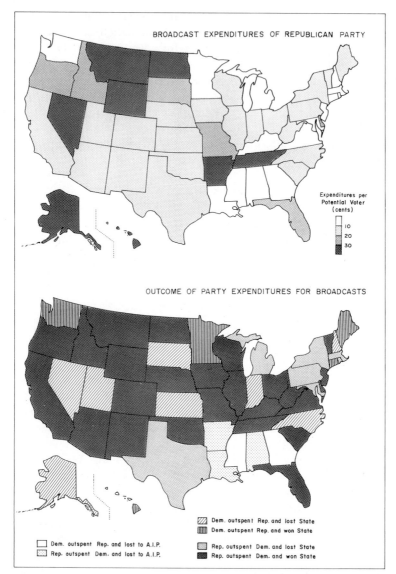

FIG. 2-3 Political Broadcast Expenditures in 1968 Presidential Election. (Federal Communications Commission, *Survey of Political Broadcasting, Primary and General Elections of 1968,* Washington, D.C., 1969.)

New York. The Democrats outspent the Republicans and won in only five states, Minnesota and Maine being two, both of which were the home states of the presidential and vice-presidential candidates. The states in which they outspent the Republicans and lost seem to indicate little by way of regional strategy, with South

Dakota, Nevada, Indiana, North Carolina, and New Hampshire being among the list. The Democrats outspent the AIP in Mississippi and Georgia but lost.

Thus the advertising of the 1968 election showed that the Republicans, although they had more monies to spend on radio and television broadcasting, implemented them into a successful strategy. Their attempt to focus on the Northeast, Rim South states, and the Midwest, Plains, and Southwest states was successful. They did not capture all the states in these regions but they did win a sufficient number to insure the necessary electoral college vote for Nixon. The Democrats, on the other hand, from an examination of the data and maps did not appear to have any broad regional strategy; this meant they captured few state and few electoral college votes even though the popular vote was close. The AIP again demonstrated its distinct sectional appeal. With fewer monies available for radio and television, it was spent primarily in states where Wallace was already in a strong position.

The 1972 presidential campaign proved to be the costliest in history, over $67 million.[4] It is estimated that Nixon spent about $45 million and McGovern $22 million, both sharp increases over the 1968 costs of $59 million for the presidential campaign. If the prenomination costs are figured and the costs of minor parties, the race in 1972 was estimated to have run about $100 million. This figures to be about five dollars for each potential voter. The total estimated cost for presidential, congressional, state, and local contests was estimated to have run about $400 million. This represents a sharp increase from the $300 million in 1968 and the $200 million four years earlier.

Personal Campaign Appearances. A political office seeker knows that in order to win an election he must consider the extent of his personal appearances. Of the many possible places available for formal or informal visits, he must decide on how many he will make and where would be the best places. Such decisions are related to other campaign policies such as available monies, television advertising, and the geographical strengths of his running mate, should he be a member of a team.

Involved in the strategy is the candidate's perception of political space, regionally and nationally. Perhaps public and private polls have shown him strong in some areas and very weak in others. Aside from the spending of monies on advertising and staff workers, he will have to devote his personal-appearance time to areas of recognized strength or in areas where an additional input (such as personal visits) may insure a close victory. What is behind a political campaign for an elective office either way is some spatial perception of the territory or political space. Candidates from large cities running for office often attempt to garner support from only one or two major cities in the state. Their decision may be to disregard entirely the small-town and rural vote. On the other hand a congressional candidate in a racially mixed district may decide on a strategy that either attempts to win support from both racial groups or he may invoke strong rhetoric and try to split their allegiances along racial lines. How he perceives the district as a whole, the varying population segments, and the major issues affecting that constituency will be reflected in the spatial facets of his campaign strategy. Should the office seeker have no or even token opposition, his strategy may be one of noninvolvement.

The personal appearances of the two major presidential candidates in the 1972 election illustrate the differing perceptions of the nation's electorate and the election itself. Nixon, ahead in polls by a substantial margin even after the Democratic convention, soon adopted a strategy of making only token personal appearances. This is revealed by his limited personal appearances from September 4 through November 7. With his commanding lead throughout most states and regions, he saw little need for becoming involved in discussing and debating national and international issues. Hence his political appearances were limited to only twelve states and the District of Columbia (Fig. 2-4). Not counting his stops to numerous small towns in northeast Ohio and upstate New York, he visited only twenty-two different cities. As the map reveals he did pay visits to a few cities in New England, the Midwest, the South, and the West. McGovern, trailing badly in the polls throughout the campaign, early adopted a strategy to concentrate his efforts on the states he believed he had the best chance of winning. These were the largest populated states. He focused his efforts on the Northeast, the eastern Midwest, the West, and Texas. At no time did he personally visit the Deep or Rim South states. Not only did he visit more states than Nixon, twenty-two as compared to fourteen, but he also visited more cities, sixty compared to twenty-two (Fig. 2-4). McGovern's visits were primarily to major population centers in key states. Often he chose to visit only one city in a state, such as Wisconsin, Montana, Oregon, South Dakota, Iowa, and Maine; frequently it was the largest one.

From these maps one element of a politician's campaign strategy evolves. Nixon, with widespread national support, saw little need for personal appearances; those few he did make were not restricted to one region. McGovern, in an effort to capture the states with the most popular and electoral votes, campaigned heavily there. He perceived little support either in the South or in the Great Plains-Rocky Mountain areas, and therefore made few or no appearances. His effort was to gain support by visiting the cities in the state that would give him the largest audiences and hopefully the best news coverage. He visited the largest states—New York, Michigan, Pennsylvania, California, Texas, and Ohio—more than once.[5]

The personal appearances and travels of the vice-presidential candidates were not identical to those of the party standard-bearers. Agnew traveled over 44,000 miles (Nixon logged over 35,000 miles) in thirty-four states and made fifty-four appearances. Shriver, the work horse of the campaign, traveled over 80,000 miles and made appearances in 200 cities in thirty-four states. His efforts were largely concentrated in the same states as McGovern's. While Nixon visited few states, Agnew made appearances in all states in the South (except Arkansas and South Carolina) as well as in the Great Plains and Rocky Mountain states, ones that McGovern had "written off." The Republican success in the South in 1968 and their expectations to win the Wallace vote led them to spend time and monies to insure support for Nixon. In this they were successful.

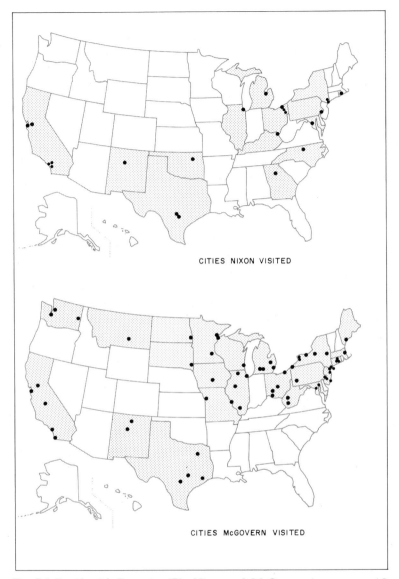

Fig. 2-4 Presidential Campaign '72: Nixon and McGovern Appearances. (Congressional Quarterly, Inc., 1972.)

VIEWS OF THE POLITICAL WORLD

The United States Perspective. The United States, being one of 148 nations in the world, holds a significant place in the mosaic of international relations.

It belongs to a number of regional organizations that are primarily defense related such as NATO, SEATO, and ANZUS, as well as economic ones such as OAS and CENTO. Also the United States is a member of FAO, WHO, ILO, WMO, ICAO, and others that are tied to specific economic and social programs of the United Nations. As a member of these regional and international organizations, the nation attempts to identify its place along with others. In so doing it represents the citizens' and the nation's philosophy in cooperative, economic, educational, scientific, cultural, or technological programs. They also provide a framework to protect the interests of American businesses abroad. Another of the major objectives of foreign contacts and interactions by treaties or formal diplomatic recognition is to protect the security of the nation. Hence the military commitments in troops or monies, treaties, and bilateral agreements with various nations throughout the world.

The locations of the major standing troops at present are perceived as places where there is likelihood of military action now or where it was once considered great. At the beginning of 1973 there were over 600,000 troops scattered throughout the world. The nearly 250,000 troops still in Western Europe were primarily there to serve as a deterrent to a Soviet invasion of Western Europe. It is indeed questionable today how much of a deterrent these troops are in the event of a possible armed conflict. Still, their stationing in bases surrounding the USSR is to be interpreted as a protection of those NATO countries as well as a demonstration of United States commitments to and interests in this part of the world.

The more than half-million military personnel sent to South Vietnam and neighboring nations in the past decade is a further index of the United States foreign policy views of the world. A part of the post-World War II philosophy that emerged in the nation's Defense and State Departments was that the communist threat to southern and eastern Asia was indeed real. The military and diplomatic leaders believed the subsequent takeover of neighboring countries by China was not a fabrication. Hence the Korean War and the Vietnam War ostensibly were fought to stem this threat. More than one military leader, foreign policy adviser, and president in the past two decades has thought the place to stop communism was in Southeast and East Asia. This view became a reality with the huge American commitment in military hardware, manpower, and bases encircling this part of the world.

Meanwhile, in other parts of the globe, the world was not perceived in the same light, even though to many Americans and foreign observers, American imperialism was not limited solely to European or Asian policies. They pointed out that the defense treaties and shipments of military arms plus clandestine activities in nations on all continents showed the United States was indeed trying to "take over" the world and make it in her image. Whether such notions are or were a myth is not a question here; however, what is important from a political geography standpoint is that this was an impression of world dominance shared by leaders of more than a handful of nations.

While the United States was heavily committed to making certain places "safe for democracy" in the past twenty years, and in this case primarily in Southeast and East Asia, there were other areas and countries where the nation kept its involvement to a minimum. Save for the landing of troops in Lebanon in 1958 during the Eisenhower administration, the United States has steered clear of direct military involvement in the hot Middle East situation. Rather than actively becoming engaged in military action, it has generally adopted a strong pro-Israeli stance by supplying them weapons during and between conflicts. More recently, the United States has attempted to play a mediator role in the conflict. For the remainder of Africa, the United States has not become involved directly in the internal affairs of the many new, emerging nations. Perhaps this is attributed to fewer direct commercial interests and colonial ties with the continent as well as a realization that the continent is not of major import in contemporary international politics.

In the case of Latin America, the United States in the past decade continued to exert its "big brother" influence on those "'neighbors" to the South. More than one president in the past century has interpreted Central and South America as the sphere of influence of the United States. Part of this perception was interpreted as a protector of the hemisphere, which meant keeping out rival or competing external (especially Russian) influences. The Cuba case is an example where the United States found that the establishment of a pro-communist state was a thorn in its side. On this island only 90 miles from mainland United States, a foreign ideology was introduced that ran strictly counter to America's perception of Latin America. The aborted Cuban invasion attempt in 1961 was designed to eradicate this communist influence and again establish a pro-American government. The 1962 Kennedy-Khrushchev dialogue over the stationing of Soviet missiles in Cuba was significant in American foreign policy. It questioned the spheres of the United States influence. The removal of the missiles and dismantling of the bases were considered a victory for the United States in its part of the world. Other brief military troop commitments into the Central American scene in the 1960s occurred in the Canal Zone of Panama in 1964 and the Dominican Republic in 1965, and were designed to prevent pro-communist takeovers of politically shaky governments as well as to preserve the United States interests in its own backyard.

The commitment of troops directly as well as military assistance, hardware, and advisers to the nations of Central and South America was designed to maintain pro-American governments. In addition, the adoption of resolutions at regional conferences such as the Organization of American States were designed to exclude from trade and diplomatic relations those nations not in accord with the major goals of United States foreign policy. In particular, this meant Cuba. The hemisphere and world political scene have changed in the past five years as many of these isolation policies have not been effective. External threats are also now considered less likely. Many western hemisphere nations that once strongly supported the blockade of Cuba have either broken the earlier agreements or are considering such actions. The election in 1970 of Marxist Allende to head Chile's government was not considered sufficient reason for overt military action by the United States. In part this may be attributed to commitments elsewhere in the world or the current unpopularity of the United States in many Latin American countries, that would only increase should there be military intervention. Furthermore, the fact that Chile is not located right in America's backyard meant that the internal affairs of Chile were not as likely to directly influence the United States.

The changing political map of the world in the past ten years has resulted in leaders and nations altering their military and diplomatic views. Where once the placement of large standing armies was considered a sufficient deterrent to military involvement, the development of long-range missile systems carrying powerful nuclear warheads makes a sizable number of troops anywhere almost meaningless. This has led some congressmen and government officials to question maintaining divisions in NATO countries. The changing political climate of China, the United States, and the USSR since 1970 has meant that many of the previous military policies and commitments to friendly Southeast and East Asian nations need to be reevaluated. If there is no apparent threat or if the threat has lessened, military and foreign policy views of that part of the world would likely be reflected in future diplomatic and military policies and programs. The sophisticated weaponry developed since the 1960s has meant that much of the former place-oriented nature of military combat and installations is now outmoded. No longer are air or naval bases needed very few thousand miles around the periphery of warlike nations. The United States maintains 2000 military bases around the world, of which over 300 have more than 500 men each, and probably this number could be reduced without endangering the security of the United States. It is argued that bases in Cuba as well as in southern Europe and South and East Asia are no longer needed. With the speed of current missiles and powerful delivery systems installed on roving submarines or bases on small Pacific islands, almost all parts of the world are equally accessible. The speed that such weapons travel in the event of attack means that a nation 3,000 miles away can be reached almost as quickly as one 10,000 miles away. Thus the mobility and sophistication of modern warfare has affected the foreign policy views of the United States government. As a result many defense pacts and treaties have lost their initial potency.

On the diplomatic scene the changing political world and the United States perception of these changes has resulted in a realization and recognition of facts and nations with which there was formerly little interaction on economic and social matters. In mid-1973 the Department of State recognized 124 nations in the world. In some nations the embassies have closed and the personnel have been withdrawn in deference to the United States views on particular international issues. Such is the case for Algeria, Iraq, Sudan, and Syria. They do not favor the United States support of Israel. In these nations only a limited staff remains. Officially, the United States does not formally recognize such nations as North Korea and North Vietnam. In the case of Cuba, the Swiss embassy handles problems relating to the United States; most of these have involved airplane hijackings. The number of diplomatic contacts has increased sharply in the past fifteen years, especially with the independence granted to many former colonies in Africa, Asia, and the West

Indies. These missions are charged with representing the United States government and its citizens on economic, social, and political concerns in these host nations.

Visits by Political Leaders. How the leaders perceive their nation or state fitting into the rest of the world is illustrated in a variety of ways. Foreign policy pronouncements, military commitments, treaty negotiations, and approval of congressional legislation reveal the position a president, or other leading official, places on their political unit in world affairs. Aside from these, a president or governor gains impressions and information about places when he travels. With the heavy schedule of activities that command the attention of high officials, they arrange carefully their travels to best serve their own state's or party's or nation's interests. Where a governor or president travels can be interpreted in part as his perception of political space. In the case of a governor, what parts of his state does he visit during the course of a year, and for a president the question is, which of the more than 100 nations does he visit? They may be nations that the United States has friendly relations with or ones with which the president would like to explore diplomatic and economic contacts. Those he decides to visit can provide him with a firsthand contact with the leaders and people, impressions that may influence subsequent policy changes and recommendations. In the same light those parts of space not visited may reveal they are not crucial to national or world interests, at least in the leader's eyes.

Two examples are provided to illustrate the perception of political leaders. The personal visits by Governor Milliken of Michigan from June 1971 through December 1972 and the international travels of President Nixon during his first term in office, 1968–1972, are used to illustrate their interaction with other political spaces. It is admitted that a leader's perceptions of political spaces are gained by other means than travels, namely through daily briefings on state or national or international relations or through reports of their personal staff, diplomatic corps, and members of legislative branches.

During the eighteen-month period mentioned above Governor Milliken visited a total of thirty-two of the state's eighty-three counties.[6] Most of his interaction was with leaders in the southern part of Michigan's Lower Peninsula where the major population clusters are located. There were more infrequent visits to the Upper Peninsula of Michigan, an area of fewer people and a greater driving distance from the capital, Lansing. He visited only five of the fifteen counties in that peninsula. Outside Michigan most·of his visits to nineteen other states were those nearby, Midwestern states whose economic and social problems were akin to those he faced. He visited only a handful of southern and western states. The governor traveled to several foreign countries on trade missions for the state in an effort to introduce Michigan manufactured products. Aside from Canada, which has a great amount of interaction with Michigan and other Great Lakes states, he visited Romania, the USSR, Belgium, England, and the Dominican Republic. The foreign travels indicate a European orientation of the state in international affairs.

It is expected that the travels of other governors would not be exactly like Milliken's. The Florida governor would probably show a preference for interacting with other southern governors as well as with the West Indies and Central and South American nations. On the other hand, a Massachusetts or New York governor may interact with both Latin America and Europe as well as with the New England and Middle Atlantic states. Perhaps the travels of a chief executive in a centrally located state such as Wyoming or Nebraska would be primarily to surrounding states rather than to foreign nations.

During his first term in office, President Nixon visited twenty-three nations (Fig. 2-5). The visits indicate the importance of three areas to United States foreign policy: West Europe, East Europe and the USSR, and South and East Asia. Outside of these, he held conferences with European heads of state in Bermuda and the Azores. The East European nations visited represented a breakthrough for a United States president. Prior to his visit Nixon had been emphasizing the need for closer cultural and economic cooperation with these nations. The visits paid to Southeast Asian nations were in part to demonstrate the continued United States "presence" in that area of the world and the commitment he felt to the nations involved militarily in the Vietnam War. The two major diplomatic plums were Nixon's extended visits to China and the USSR. The immediate and long-term effects of the accords reached with these powerful nations are likely to affect policies of the nation and world for the foreseeable future.

While the Nixon international interests and priorities can be measured in part by the emphasis on Europe and Asia, the realization that other areas were not visited may indicate they have less importance to current United States foreign policy. A visit by the president of the United States anywhere signals that nation as being of some critical economic, military, or diplomatic importance. The absence of visits to either Latin America or Africa may indicate that the president feels these are not as critical in current foreign policy as Europe and Asia. He may also feel that visits to those nations involved in sensitive international situations such as Japan and the Middle East are not in our best interests. Nixon's views on Africa and Latin America have been interpreted by leaders of nations on both continents as an indication of a lack of interest and commitment to the continents' economic, social, and political problems. This view is strikingly different from that demonstrated by President Kennedy, who had especially strong ties with Latin America as a part of his Alliance for Progress programs. The unpopularity of the United States in both developing continents may have been instrumental in the lack of a Nixon visit. It should be mentioned that his wife did represent him on a brief tour to several African and Latin American states.

Organizations' Views of the Political World. Besides the perception that individuals have about political space, political organizations and groups have views that are reflective of their credos, their lobbying influences, and their influence on the public. Political organizations are formed for a variety of reasons, as, for example, to promote international cooperation such as the United World Fed-

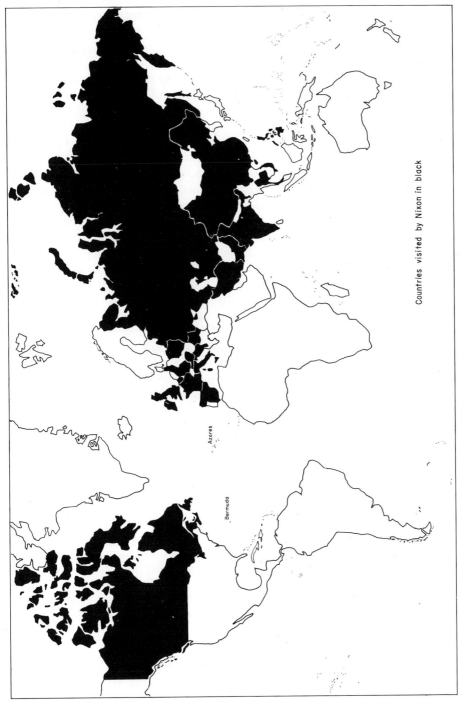

F𝜤G. 2-5 President Nixon's Foreign Travels, 1968–1972.

eralists, or to preserve America from internal and external communism, an aim of the John Birch Society. Each organization and many others have a particular view of the United States with respect to the rest of the world.

One of the most well-known conservative organizations, and one that is often labeled as a right-wing extremist group, is the John Birch Society. The organization has as one of its major goals the wish to halt the threat of socialism and communist aggression not only within the United States but in the world as well. As the various publications of the society purport and as its spokesmen espouse, America is continually being threatened by communism. The society also feels the need to warn the citizenry about this communist threat. Much of this thinking is tied to the domino-type theory where, for example, if South Vietnam or Thailand fell to communism, soon it would be the Philippines, Australia, New Zealand, Hawaii, and eventually California. Although many of its views have been ridiculed in the last decade, the society still has the support of many ardent Americans.

How the John Birch Society perceives the world's nations can be understood in part by examining and mapping the "scoreboard" data on the degree of communist influence on the economic and political affairs of individual nations. Since 1958 the society has issued annually the scores for most of the nations as well as the changes in the "communist score" since the previous year. Its earliest maps portrayed the degree of communism in varying shades of red and pink. When the 1971 data are mapped, it becomes readily apparent that most of the world, including the United States, is heavily influenced by communism (Fig. 2-6). All the East European nations, the USSR, China, North Vietnam, and North Korea had scores of 100.[7] This is not unexpected considering the society's perception of communism as being of monolithic nature. These nations have not changed their scores since 1958. In 1971 there were scores of 100 for several Latin American nations, such as Cuba and Chile and a number in North Africa and Southwest Asia. Most of the Western European nations had scores slightly above 50 percent; values were slightly higher in northern than the central portion of the continent. The United States had a 60–80 percent score indicating that the nation was more than strongly influenced by communist influences. This high score is attributed to the communist influence in the press, the education system, and changing life-styles that the society views with disfavor.

In 1971 the lowest scores or the nations safest from communism are those where there is a strong one-man dictatorial or military rule that is avidly anticommunist and often white-ruled. Therefore it is not surprising that Taiwan (10–20 percent), Portugal (10–20 percent), Monaco (10–20 percent), Mozambique (10–20 percent), Nicaragua (20–40 percent), South Korea (20–30 percent), Angola (20–30 percent), Rhodesia (10–20 percent), South Africa (30–40 percent), Paraguay (30–40 percent), and Greece (30–40 percent) had the lowest scores.

FIG. 2-6 Communism Scoreboard: John Birch Society, 1971. (Data from "Communism Scoreboard," *American Opinion*, July–August 1971, pp. 64–65, Belmont, Mass. 02178.)

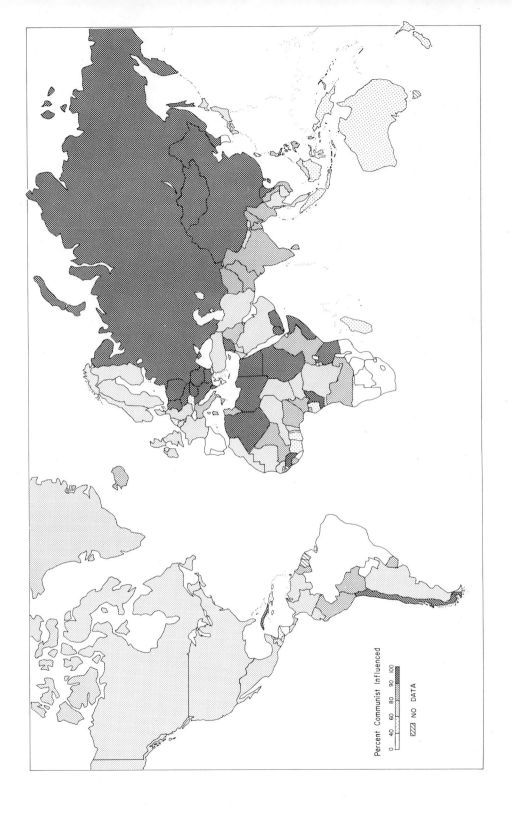

Percent Communist Influenced

0 40 60 80 90 100

NO DATA

Switzerland was also very safe from communism; its score was only 10–20 percent. Most of the developing world in Latin America and Africa had scores indicating that the communist influences were indeed strong. When the 1971 scores for the developing world are compared with those in 1958, the communist "takeover," a strong element in the society's philosophy, becomes readily apparent. Of those former colonies they had rated little or no communist influence prior to independence many are now considered strongly in that camp. With a philosophy that is vehemently anticommunist and antisocialist, it is not surprising that the world, according to the John Birch Society, is not considered safe for democracy. Most of the nations are strongly influenced by communists and are becoming more so with each passing year. The only nations the society considers safe, as no nation is completely immune from communism, are those that espouse anticommunism as an essential part of their ideology. It is worth noting the number of these nations that derive military aid and diplomatic recognition from the United States.

FOOTNOTES

1. William L. Gilbert quoted in James W. Silver, *Mississippi: The Closed Society*, New York, Harcourt Brace Jovanovich, 1964, p. 27.
2. Peter R. Gould, "Structuring Information on Spacio-Temporal Preferences," *Journal of Regional Science*, 7:2 (1967 Supplement), 259–274.
3. Federal Communications Commission, *Survey of Political Broadcasting, Primary and General Election Campaigns of 1968*, Washington, D.C., August 1969.
4. "History's Costliest Campaign," *U.S. News and World Report*, November 13, 1972, p. 20.
5. "Presidential Candidates' Itineraries, Sept. 5 Through Oct. 31," *Congressional Quarterly*, November 4, 1972, p. 2886.
6. State of Michigan, Office of the Governor, William G. Milliken, February 1973.
7. "Scoreboard," *American Opinion*, 14:7 (1971), 64–65.

Chapter 3

POLITICAL TERRITORIALITY

Heaven is no larger than Connecticut;
no larger than Fairfield County.

Bliss Carman

MAN AND TERRITORIALITY

Man the Individual. Being a social animal, man identifies and interacts with others around him. The interactions and associations may be frequent with those living in spaces very familiar to him, that is, in his immediate "home" territory, or they may be with members of a larger spatial unit. All men and women identify with members of various territorial scales whether they be the local residential neighborhood, the state, the nation, or the world. How man identifies and perceives these various spatial units socially and politically and the people in them will influence the forms and levels of interactions.

At one end of the territorial scale we find the intimate personal spaces of an individual. This facet of geography, referred to as room geography, is not of concern here however. Rather, we are concerned with the spaces man interacts with outside his place of physical residence as an understanding of them will help

49

identify and define his action space.[1] By examining the frequency and the places of interaction during a given period of time, we are able to identify a familiar space that is part of his territory. Those spaces with which he has day-by-day direct contact identify his activity space. The social and economic foci frequented for working, shopping, banking, worshipping, recreation, and visiting are those places where he is most "at home." While on a map of a city or a part of the city that territory may appear in a stellar or circular or elongated shape, it is in reality a spatial surface comprised of nodes. His perception of his territory thus may be marked by only a select number of foci in a city. As for the in-betweenness, he may be just as unknowledgeable of those places as those outside the activity space.

The knowledge of an individual's action space is filled with varying degrees of unknowns; however, they are fewer than in his activity space. He is likely to be more familiar with those spaces near his residence—the neighbor next door, and the neighborhood service station attendant and grocer—than those some distance away but still in his action space. His membership in a local church or his attendance at a Parent-Teacher Association meeting and association with friends in a daily car pool leads him to identify strongly to those with and in similar spaces. Should changes come to his life-style or his residential space, these may call for subsequent territorial adjustments. A promotion to a medium-range executive position may dictate a new set of social contacts in other parts of his city. Or the appearance of a black family or racially-mixed family may trigger latent but emotional feelings of racism. Whereas his territoriality, that is, his identification and interaction in space, may have appeared to be set, he now finds that new situations arise that conflict with his previous spatial behavior. His concern about changes in family style brought about by his interaction with a new country club set, or his children being bused across town, or his taking detours to work through blighted residential areas or his neighborhood being affected by black invasion or by an unsightly commercial development may lead him both to defend what existed and what he personally likes. He may try to oppose changes coming to his territory in whatever ways he can such as by circulating petitions, leading community drives, organizing formal protests, or possibly even running for an elective council seat.

While much of the interaction that affects an individual's sentiments about his territory is related to his and his neighborhood's overall social makeup, there are political facets that cannot be divorced from consideration. The fact that man has arranged, carved up, organized, and manipulated human spaces has affected the sentiments and reactions about territorial units. While he may live in a suburb and work in a central city, he may have decided upon that pattern because he does not want the congestion of inner city life, the substandard education system for his children, or the crimes he associates with black ghettos. He may have selected his present suburb from others because it was incorporated, that is, politically independent of the central city, and offered the public services and life-style he desired. This is in spite of a lower tax base in adjacent political units. Along with the changes affecting society in general, he may find himself faced with decisions being made that are not to his liking, but they are related to the territorial unit or units with which he identifies. A loosely defined metropolitan government may be instituted that consolidates public services and requires a tax for those working in but not residing within duly constituted limits. This decision may not be to his liking as he resents supporting welfare, education, and transportation schemes for low-income inner city residents. Being, perhaps, a second-generation foreign-born Pole or Czech, he escaped that life by a move to suburbia. If a decision were announced consolidating public schools or permitting crosstown busing to achieve racial balance, he may strive to protect his territory—his suburb—from compliance. He may even join an organization such as NAG (National Action Group) for a spell.

At the most personal level, should he find that a black or Chicano family or maybe even a Jew has moved in "down the street," he may feel his property will suffer and the neighborhood deteriorate. In the rush to avoid a market loss on his residence and fear of a rapid influx of minority residents, he may panic and sell his sacred plot of land at a loss. Although open housing has been declared such for all people, he felt relatively secure in his territorial space because of a restrictive zoning covenant his suburb designed to keep out "undesirables" and the high cost of houses in his neighborhood. Similar reactions may be evoked when duplexes or apartment complexes appear at the fringe of his neighborhood or his suburb.

Should an individual feel his territory is threatened, he has a choice to comply with those changing conditions affecting his daily life or to seek out spatial units more to his liking. In the latter course of action he may try, if he is able, to locate a political unit with a favorable tax base, a good education system (by his standards) and a strict zoning ordinance prohibiting land use for multiple-dwelling units or commercial development. Rare indeed would be the case where an individual in a metropolitan area would have his territoriality or activity or action spaces demarcated by a single political independent unit. Every social and economic interaction crosses spaces that separate variations in zoning ordinances, taxing policies, school attendance areas, water and sewage districts, not to mention many different incorporated and unincorporated political units. In some cases the differences across space may be minimal, in others they may be great especially when metropolitan interaction overlaps several county or state lines.

Man as a Group Member. At the other end of the scale of territoriality we find that groups or organizations interact in spatial units and perceive those spaces differently. Groups are formed as vehicles for expressing sentiments of identity and belonging and for stressing common goals. The programs and policies of the group members have indirect political consequences, whether they be groups comprising local zoning boards or those recommending foreign policy positions to be taken by the government of the United States.

In the same manner in which individuals define, organize, and defend their territorial units, so do groups and organizations. One facet of territoriality may be juxtaposing the political territoriality of a group over its social territoriality. This is frequently accomplished by residential and commercial zoning. This process is discussed in greater detail in Chapter 6. Suffice it at this point to mention that zoning restrictions and ordinances have been incorporated into city and suburban charters to exclude certain groups, institutions, or developments considered out of character with the government's or groups' desires. Should a given elite suburb invoke an ordinance that prohibits multiple-housing units or medium-range priced residences, the boundaries of the political unit may serve as a barrier to interaction with surrounding spaces. The *de jure* barrier in essence assumes a *de facto* consequence. Social interaction in the politically defined space may be with those individuals in the same unit or in similar social spaces in the metropolitan area. An investigation into their social interaction, work trips, and shopping behavior may reveal little or no contact with those proximate spaces. Thus the social and political space may become similar. The social spaces may be governed by the political organization that is established, being thus a spatial regulation of human behavior.[2]

While cases illustrating the above social and political territory side of behavior are far from unusual, a more common territorial example exists in many sections of cities where racially mixed groups reside in proximity. As is frequently the case, there are recognized areas where blacks and whites feel the spaces definitely "belong" to them and not others. The residents identify and acknowledge the reality of such "cores" of their territorial spaces by noting specific landmarks in their own spaces. Toward the edges of both territories are the transitional spaces where the interaction is often more with members living in the cores. This racial or class interaction is more common with those of a similar race or economic station. In many cases antiwhite and antiblack sentiments are strongest in these transitional spaces, as they represent the areas of most recent black residential expansion. The strong feelings evident in such spaces may even trigger demonstrations and possibly riots. Whites who already do not support black development see the invasion of their territory or turf as a threat. This fear may have been instigated by blockbusting attempts by black or white realtors. Whites' perception of this "territorial invasion" may be more emotional than actual, but how they act is a reflection of their desire to preserve the existing spaces. Blacks on the other hand may feel that population and housing pressures dictate the search for new spaces, and while they may not resist being the first black family in an all-white block or suburb, they know that with societal patterns operating at present, their opportunities for any housing or improved housing are most likely to be found in close proximity to existing black population clusters.[3]

Residential adjustments lead to territorial adjustments for groups just as for individuals. Whites leaving the inner city and taking up residence in the suburbs are often moving to reside in a more hospitable political and social territory. This may be interpreted to mean a space with whites and no blacks around to infringe upon him or his family or his neighborhood. Blacks see the expansion of their living spaces as opportunities for greater social interaction with the metropolitan area. The move from an inner city high-rise apartment that is totally black to a single-family dwelling at the edge of the black residential spaces that is racially mixed results in an enlarged action space and probably the activity space as well.

Development of a Nation. In addition to territoriality being characteristic of contemporary urban America, historically the notions of territoriality were ingrained in the American frontier philosophy. The movement westward was a search for land and territory (that is, space). Ideally, the more land held by an individual or by the government, often the more prestige he had. Manifest destiny itself was a spatial concept put into practice by westward settlement in the nineteenth century. With the lands acquired by treaty, discovery, direct claim, or by conquest, the adding to and filling in of the present United States space became embodied in the philosophies of presidents and the federal government's actions. In an attempt to hold these spaces from warring Indians and foreign invaders, a series of military posts and government installations were established at critical points near river junctions and mountain passes. Thus the acquisition and protection of lands belonging to the United States was not only rigidly defined but rigidly defended. Settlement spaces had political ramifications in the spatial evolution of the nation.

Beyond the limits of the United States a similar case of political territoriality can be presented by happenings in the last century and even in this one. The spread of United States influence through the hemisphere became embodied in the Monroe Doctrine. In essence this stated to other covetous foreign powers that the Western Hemisphere was the domain of the United States. Further, the United States would resist outside infringement and aggression. Later with the involvement of the nation in Europe and Asian affairs, the nation became a world power. Accompanying this rise was the acquisition of lands outright or on a treaty basis in strategic parts of every continent. This led to the spread of United States influence throughout the world and the labeling of the nation as an imperialist power.[4] Such views are certainly not without basis, as refueling stations and later naval bases, air strips, and satellite installations, not to mention missiles and manpower, were found around the edges of the nations considered hostile to the United States. Ostensibly the rationale for locating these many foci around the world was to protect the interests of the United States or its allies. Their location was to serve as a deterrent to other nations in that an attack of such bases in their host countries was indirectly one against the United States itself. It was felt that the United States was safe once these installations were in place. These miniterritorial pieces of foreign real estate were literally extensions of the United States itself around the world. As the past two decades have revealed, the nation has been very reluctant, as have been former colonial powers, to relinquish these territorial claims. There is a striking parallel between the national policies embodied in the nineteenth-century frontier mentality and philosophy and the foreign policy views of the last and even this century.

ENVIRONMENTAL SETTINGS FOR
PROTESTS AND DEMONSTRATIONS

Protests, strikes, demonstrations, riots, and guerilla warfare are examples of human behavior that occur in select spaces. Not all parts of a nation, a region, or indeed a city are equally likely to be affected by one or more of these forms. If they do not occur at random, although occasionally they may, there is some underlying set of distinguishing characteristics and circumstances that breed or incite such actions. Many of these environmental settings have a distinct spatial dimension, that is, a space where certain characteristics are in juxtaposition and are likely to result in one or more kinds of civil strife.

The realization that there are significant spatial facets of protests, riots, and guerilla warfare is attributed to the research by social and behavioral scientists in the past ten years. What their findings emphasize is that there are certain spatial and territorial notions that lead to some locales being more protest and violence prone than others.[5]

Demonstrations and Strikes. Protests, marches, strikes, and demonstrations are less violent forms of political and social involvement. These forms of action may be taken against a particular policy of an organization or government or they may be in support of needed legislative enactment or reform.

Protests and demonstrations became almost popular in the United States in the late 1960s. At first protests were mainly in the civil rights arena. They were found in cities that already had some support for the objectives outlined by black and white leaders or in large cities where the discrimination was at its worst. Cities tended to be large, located in the Northeast or California or in the South, as in Montgomery and Birmingham. More often than not university communities were the early nodes of support for minority rights as evidenced by the number and frequency of marches and other demonstrations. These also tended to be locales where the public media were influential in reaching national audiences. As the plight of Black Americans was brought more to the public fore, these forms of nonviolent action began to appear in medium-sized and smaller cities in the Northeast, Midwest, and West. They also began to be found in other large southern, even Deep South, cities.[6] It is doubtful whether protests and demonstrations in Mississippi, Alabama, Georgia, and South Carolina would have occurred on a large scale without previous support from much of the rest of the nation as well as the media. The spatial pattern of these protests suggests that there were places where protests and demonstrations were accepted first, partly because of that locale's view of society. Not all places in the United States did or would have accepted or permitted these protests at the same time. It was a combination of a hierarchical and a wave diffusion.

Cities and regions in all parts of the United States have seen public involvement in political and social action take the form of marches. In the North, it is doubtful whether workers would have organized successfully without the public support they received by strikes and outright public protests against certain practices of big businesses. Therefore new conditions that merited protesting or "taking to the streets" in the name of civil rights were not unexpected. The precedent had been set. Also many northern states had already enacted legislation that the federal government was only slowly beginning to implement. In the South groups such as the KKK had shown their muscle by marching in parades. When civil rights groups with local and outside supporters began openly protesting social conditions in the South in the 1960s, a conflict was almost inevitable. Mass protests against the traditional existing political structure meant that the society was being confronted openly with a situation that went against its grain. Workers' strikes and unions were not popular in the South, hence the passage of right-to-work legislation in most states. Nor were demonstrations promoting civil rights or protesting the administrations' policies on Vietnam popular. The South for long was considered an unpopular place to protest and demonstrate. Today this is still true in many cities, although this view is shared with many small midwest cities and towns.

The mid-1960s brought a new issue to protest, the Vietnam War. The spatial pattern of demonstrations took on appearance similar to that of civil rights. While many cities were beginning to adjust to civil rights demonstrations, the former nodes were seeing a new issue protested. Public demonstrations against the war eventually were found in most parts of the Northeast, Midwest, and West. The largest rallies and marches focused on Washington, D.C., where the administration and legislative policies were made affecting the nature of the war. Also it was a site for national press and television coverage. New York City, Chicago, Philadelphia, Boston, and Detroit were other sites for large rallies. The protests against the Vietnam War in southern cities were considered almost as unwelcome as those protesting discrimination. Strong support for maintaining the status quo on racial matters and for backing United States military involvements engendered the greatest appeal in the South. Protesting both policies did much to upset notions held previously by the region's people and leaders.

During the past three years there have been other protests and demonstrations that have evoked varying degrees of national and regional sympathy. The location of these actions again has been selective. Places that have previously had long and successful histories of political and social unrest and demonstrations seem to be the primary target. Should there also be cosmopolitan and liberal universities in or near large cities, specifically those within easy reach of a national television network or influential newspaper, they are likely to generate greater appeal. For example, the 1970 postal strikes were concentrated in large and liberal cities in the Northeast and California.[7] Protests related to women's liberation and environmental destruction are two that have occurred in the early 1970s. Marches and demonstrations in support of women's liberation or equal rights appear to be concentrated in state capitals where legislatures are in session or in cities holding beauty pageants. Both locations are considered sound places for emphasizing programs and views about abortion, welfare, child care, property settlement, and equal employment opportunities. Again not all states are equally influenced by the variety of groups protesting women's reform; witness, for example, the reluctance of some states to discuss seriously the equal rights amendment or other important women-related issues.

The environmental protests usually target a specific industry or specifically planned policy of a local, state, or federal government. Groups of citizens and officials have formed to save the alligator in Florida, halt underground nuclear testing to release natural gas in Colorado, protest the commercialization of California beaches, oppose airport construction in Chicago, and thwart nuclear power installations in New York, Georgia, and Michigan. Protests of this nature generally do not "take to the streets" as other concerns have in the past decade. This in part because of the already overwhelming popular support for cleaning up the environment. For example, the national Earth Day in 1971 was declared a time when all citizens were to discuss and reflect on matters related to saving their environments.

Riots and Guerilla Warfare. Riots and guerilla warfare, two of the more extreme forms of action against a people or an existing government structure, most often occur in places known by the participants involved. Riots by blacks during the 1960s occurred in areas of the inner city near black residences. The burnings and lootings were done to stores and establishments known by the rioters themselves. They did not venture into white suburbs, a fear shared by many white suburbanites, as these were unfamiliar territories. Rather they engaged in destructive acts and protests in those places where they lived, played, worshipped, and worked.

The riots themselves were often sparked by a seemingly random incident such as an arrest or accident. However, a certain set of circumstances often aggravated the incident into a mob action form of protest. Large numbers of people in an overly crowded and an already densely populated neighborhood where sidewalks and streets are narrow seemed conducive environments to riot beginnings and their spread. These qualities coupled with white-owned businesses, strained black-white relations, and hatred of police often triggered involvement initially by a small number of blacks. The hot summer nights were conducive to outdoor interaction and the absence of sufficient living and recreation spaces often took the form of street interactions. Demonstrating and protesting were part of the way of life in the late 1960s. The fact that the poor and the black lived in squalid living conditions did not prevent them from burning their rented complexes or places where they shopped or worked or destroying symbols of white authority.

Once the riot was in full swing, its behavior often took on spatial forms. Its origin was usually confined to selected locales in the ghetto. Not all parts of black residential areas were equally susceptible to burnings or lootings nor were all sections of white-owned stores and companies. Some white areas and installations were protected better by police and fire departments and guarded by outside National Guard troops, hence their preservation.

An example of the varying community-police relations and police jurisdiction is given as a major reason for the pattern taken by the Miami riot that broke out at the time of the 1968 Republican National Convention. The riot began in the poor black area known as Liberty City, which is partly in the city of Miami and in the unincorporated part of Dade County. It began at the edge of the unincorporated Dade County limits and quickly spread into the city of Miami portion. The two portions of Liberty City were in two police jurisdictions (Fig. 3-1). The Miami

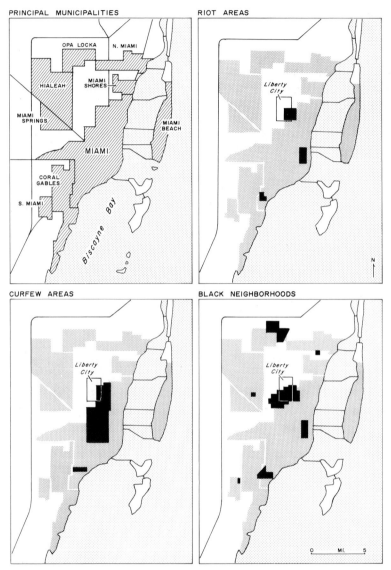

Fig. 3-1 Development of Miami Racial Disturbances, 1968. (After P. S. Salter and R. C. Mings, "A Geographic Aspect of the 1968 Miami Racial Disturbance: A Preliminary Investigation," *Professional Geographer*, 21:2 (1969), pp. 81–83. Reproduced by permission of the Association of American Geographers.)

police chief was known for his hard line on "law and order" issues and was not responsive to the many black complaints. The Dade County sheriff was more tolerant and the county also had successfully implemented police-community programs. Once the riot started it spread into the city of Miami and not into the unincorporated part of Dade County. The only reasonable interpretation for the pattern the riot took was due to the line separating the two police jurisdictions.

> The geographic delimitation of the disturbance . . . indicates that it was confined almost exclusively within the political boundaries of the city of Miami. Field investigation indicates that the political boundaries separating the unincorporated county portion of Liberty City from the city of Miami portion of Liberty City are purely artificial. No physical barriers separate the two areas. Homogeneous house types, both single and multiple type dwellings, extend well beyond both sides of the city line. Linear-type business establishments also extend on either side of the city line along NW 62nd Street. In short, a low-income Negro neighborhood has been divided, quite arbitrarily, between two local governing authorities yet, the violence, while originating on the 17th Avenue division, spread eastward and southward, deeper into the city of Miami.[8]

Guerilla warfare is a more organized form of action than riots. It involves a strategy on the part of a group or organization that desires to obtain certain demands or establish a government or insurgent state in accord with its aims. The very nature of guerilla warfare operations whether in rural or urban areas is based on the physical and human geography of the space in question.[9] In most recent cases in the United States the warfare has been associated with urban centers. However, there have been examples of guerilla warfare operations in rural areas. The Chicano protest against the federal government in the Southwest was focused in northern New Mexico, Rio Arriba County. This county and area have long been one of the most troubled spots for the federal government in their dealings with Spanish-Americans. In this very poor and isolated mountainous rural county, the Spanish traditions and heritage are probably stronger than elsewhere in the region.[10] Protests prior to 1967 against big landowners and the federal government were not unusual.

In order for a guerilla operation to be successful there must be support enlisted by members of the local area. As the leaders, probably few in number at any one time, look over the city or the ghetto, they perceive that some sections are more likely to accept them and their objectives.[11] Whether their plans be to disrupt public services in the inner city, or to murder police officers, or to set up local revolutionary governments, support for some segment of the community is needed. A base of operations is required that will insure protection from outside forces. They may select a building or residence that was previously the site of an earlier unsuccessful protest or a site that the community identifies with as being a symbol of outside oppression, killings or mass arrests being an example. For this reason a site is usually selected that is in a part of the city the participants know very well and where the police are afraid to enter. Such places are not rare in the inner city.

> The core area acts as the center of revolutionary activity in both the insurgent state and ghetto. Almost all of the militant groups have headquarters in or near

the core area. This gives the militants maximum protection while at the same time placing them in a position of maximum contact with the community for dissemination of information. This seems to be an important aspect of the Black Panthers' choice of location for their various headquarters throughout the nation. By locating in the ghetto and defending these locations so violently, they show the ghetto resident that they are there to stay and that they intend to defend the ghetto against "the white invaders" at all costs.[12]

In conducting their operations they aim to engage in actions that are disruptive to the existing authorities. Whether they are tying up vehicular traffic or shooting from rooftops, they attempt to withdraw when pursued into those spaces they know well and are accepted. Police chases on sidewalks or in patrol cars often prove futile as the guerilla leaders know their territory, particularly well at night on already dimly-lit streets. In short, the successful guerilla leader has a geography of the ghetto in his mind. They are acquainted with the stairs, basements, abandoned buildings, alleys, and rooftops much better than "outsiders." As is often the case, search attempts by the police for those responsible for destructive acts prove useless. The guerillas' success is measured by continued harassment and the enlargement of the inner city territorial base. Success comes with their acquisition of some of the spatial units and critical facilities or foci held previously by external authorities. Once they have enlarged their population base and resource base an insurgent "state" may be created. Although it is not a legally recognized state, the revolutionaries themselves may feel they represent the interests and views of the people in that territory. Furthermore, in negotiations with the formally and legally recognized government, they attempt to act as the spokesmen for the residents.

POLITICAL SEPARATISM AND TERRITORIAL IDENTITY

Minority Groups. While man interacts in large political and social spaces, there are also smaller spaces with which he most readily identifies. They may be familiar territories or turfs such as his neighborhood or maybe his personal property. These he is most likely to defend from undesirable influences infringing on his spaces. He is also likely to prevent, if possible, the usurpation of said lands and resources by others, whether it be an urban authority or the federal government. The policy of eminent domain is an example of spatial abrogation of territory. If, on the other hand, man believes that external political and social authorities (whether elected or appointed to represent his views and interests) are not engaging in actions and programs to his best interests, he may initiate attempts to withdraw from said legal compacts and structures.

With the increased social and economic attention and legislation devoted to the bringing of minority populations—Black Americans, Spanish-Americans, and American Indians—more into the mainstream of national life, there have been some predictable territorial consequences. Many leaders of movements and organizations have long recognized their inferior position vis-à-vis white society and the federal government. In their attempts to increase the awareness among their followers, they have often harkened back to former lands held by their ancestors. Not only have they demanded that certain territorial lands and waters be returned to them but that they receive reparations as well. The Spanish-Americans and American Indians especially have identified closely with their former lands. Their position is that the federal government in particular has denied them their just human rights and also their territorial rights in its land policies of last century. Treaties and other agreements were made almost unilaterally with little regard for the affected peoples and their livelihood. The former Indian and Spanish lands were subdivided and then sold to the highest bidder or awarded to the victors of open conflicts. The people who called such spaces home were also shunted off (once or repeatedly) to new reservations, some a half-continent away. These were long distances from their homes and harvesting, hunting, and burial grounds. If they were not evicted forcibly, they saw their territorial spaces severely restricted in size in each war with the government. Any opposition was quickly quelled. Attempts to obtain redress of grievances were fruitless as the regional and federal officers, courts, and agencies, even those in the Bureau of Indian Affairs, were not particularly interested in human dignity and accompanying territorial claims of Indians or the Spanish-speaking farmers. The capturing of space and the resources, human and natural, were ingredients that became embodied in the frontier philosophy and manifest destiny notions of nineteenth-century America. To the most powerful, financially or militarily, went the undemarcated lands of the poor, the nonwhite, and the mobile. Since these spaces were usually not readily identifiable on maps, and were easy to demarcate with the survey system adopted in westward settlement, financial interests, large farmers or ranchers, or the federal government were more concerned about imposing their own impress on the territory than by satisfying the claims brought by native populations.

Today, with the consciousness of these minority groups aroused, a number of legal cases have been raised in the courts about these actions and land policies of individuals and the federal government. At the basis of these claims is a request for returning certain harvesting, hunting, fishing, and burial territories that belonged to descendants of the present generation. For the most part these claims are from Indians in the Midwest and West; a lesser number are from Spanish-Americans in the Southwest. They claim that the lands were taken unfairly. In these cases the claimants have introduced documents defining the territorial limits of their tribe or nation. Even though most Indian claims were based on natural features and not the readily defined land survey system the white man introduced, they are able to present very convincing evidence in some cases for the territories and lands in question.

The Indian Claims Commission Act was instituted in 1946. It provided for a review of claims by tribes or nations against the government of the United States. Questions of fraud and mistakes involved in tribal claims as well as their review and adjudication were also within the purview of this Commission. As of October 1971, the Commission had approved the awards of $395 million. Congress has appropriated $388 million; another $50 million in claims is in various stages of appeal. These figures represent awards for 198 dockets. At present 246 others are pending before the Commission; 166 have been dismissed.[13]

The claims have come from small and large tribal councils and nations throughout the United States. The preparation of legal briefs by the parties involved includes historical, cultural, and anthropological evidence (some admittedly rather sketchy) to support the claimants. Action by the Commission and the courts is often painfully slow, sometimes involving years. Four cases that illustrate the problems involved are from Florida, Arizona, Alaska, and Ohio. In 1970 the federal government awarded the Seminoles in Florida over $12 million for the usurpation of their lands. Some of the Florida Seminoles were shipped, like other Indians, to the Indian Territory in what is now Oklahoma. Today only a very few survive. Arizona's Indian problem is partly settled now. The basic question is the areal extent of the Navajo and Hopi "aboriginal" land claims. Once this issue is resolved the Navajos are to be compensated monetarily for 25 to 30 million acres in Arizona and New Mexico. The dollar value will be based on 1868 land values. The Hopis, on the other hand, will be paid for land in Arizona; their reservation is presently within Navajo space. Their compensations will be based on 1882 and 1937 land values, for about 5 million of the 12 million acres they claim. In Alaska the tribal claims involve not only Indians but Eskimos and Aleuts as well. The overlapping and conflicting claims is a problem when mining the state's valuable resources; construction of the oil pipeline also necessitates settling these claims by federal and state authorities. The executive branch of the federal government has suggested 40 million acres in land and a $1 billion settlement to the natives, half in outright cash and the remainder in royalties for the sale of resources. The dollar appeal apparently has more appeal than the land settlement. Congress has still not reached a final decision on the claims.[14]

Indian claims to previous territorial lands have been heard in courts in several Midwest states: Minnesota, Wisconsin, Michigan, and Ohio. In early 1973, members of five Indian tribes from Michigan were awarded payments for lands taken by the federal government.[15] According to the judgment, the Chippewas, Delaware, Wyandot, Potawatomi, and Ottawa were to be paid for the area ceded by them in the Treaty of July 4, 1805, at Fort Industry (Fig. 3-2). The northern part of these lands in north central Ohio were bought for about a penny an acre. It became known as "Sufferers' Land" as it was settled by residents of Connecticut who suffered at the hands of the British during the Revolutionary War.

The most publicized case of the Spanish-Americans involves the Tierra Amarilla land grant in northern New Mexico. This land and other Spanish grants became part of the United States with the ending of the Mexican-American War and the Treaty of Guadalupe-Hidalgo in 1848. According to the treaty, the lands the United States paid for were to remain in the hands of the present occupants and were not to be bought or sold.[16] The Tierra Amarilla grant is one example of the community land grants ceded to Mexico by Spain. After the treaty was signed and westward settlement began in earnest in the 1850s and later, Anglos (especially

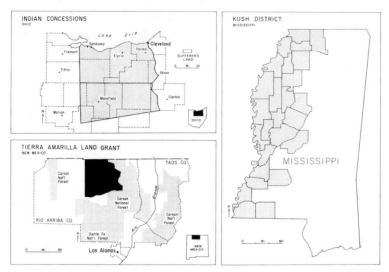

FIG. 3-2 Claims to Territory by Minority Groups. (Indian concessions, after *Detroit News*, April 22, 1973.)

from Texas) entered New Mexico, surveyed the lands, and bought them. By cheating and using very suspect surveying methods, the community land grants, identified by the Spanish survey system using metes and bounds, were gradually eroded in size and usurped by wealthy outside ranchers and the federal government. Most of these lands were acquired without financial compensation to the Spanish residents of New Mexico.

The *Alianza* of the Federal Alliance of Free City States was formed by Reies Tijerina and his followers in Albuquerque in 1963. The aim of the *Alianza* was to question the present use and ownership of lands that historically had been granted to the Spanish residents in present New Mexico. In 1966 Tijerina announced the formation of *Pueblo de San Joaquín del Rio de Chama,* an independent free city state. This was located in the area identified as the Tierra Amarilla land grant in Rio Arriba County. Part of this land is in private hands today and also in the federal government's Carson National Forest (Fig. 3-2). Once Tijerina and his followers had identified the area defining their city space, they attempted to make citizen arrests of forest rangers guarding the entrances to Carson National Forest.

During the middle and late 1960s, violence in the form of burnings, fence cuttings, cattle slaughtering, and harassment of federal and state officials became identified with the *Alianza* movement. Also the organization prepared lengthy legal briefs supporting its claims in an effort to win legal and citizen support. The attempted takeover of lands in Carson National Forest in 1966 was followed in 1967 by the violence and shooting at the courthouse "raid" in Tierra Amarilla. These were two headline items that achieved state and national attention. The *Alianza* was asking that the Spanish-American case of territories be adjudicated as they felt their rights as citizens had been jeopardized and their property had been seized unlawfully. The surveying and selling of their lands to Anglos, whom they resent, and the federal and state acquisition of Spanish lands in effect denied them the opportunity to earn a decent livelihood in northern New Mexico. This part of the Southwest has some of the poorest areas in the nation. At the root of much of their protest for a just land claim settlement was the desire to enjoy lumbering and grazing rights on adjacent federal lands, lands which the ranchers used but they did not.

While blacks do not have the historical land claims that the Indians and Chicanos do, there have been organizations claiming certain spaces. One such group is the Republic of New Africa whose major concern is the desire to form a separate state within the United States. They have asked the federal government to give to the blacks the black-populated counties of western Mississippi known as the Kush District and the five southern slave states of Georgia, South Carolina, Louisiana, Mississippi, and Alabama (Fig. 3-2). These counties and states were selected because they represent the areas where blacks have built the economy to what it is today.[17] It is argued that these states with their white control have not given blacks proper credit for their development, hence the desire for black ownership and control. Besides the request that these sites be turned over to the RNA so they can govern themselves without outside influence, the organization has asked for reparations for the way blacks have been treated in the South in the past two centuries. They have requested $400 billion. This would be used to develop the economy and society to the benefit of blacks. Although the request by the RNA will never be honored, it does illustrate an example of the identification of a group with a particular region and territory. Where the heritage of blacks is very strong even to this day, an allegiance to these former slave states has united various militant groups favoring territorial claims. Other black groups have echoed similar feelings in their call for black separatism on a much smaller scale; an example would be the Black Muslims. Rural cooperatives and small towns have been organized in the South by black groups; these are designed to serve as ties to the land and their own spaces.

Cities. While current discussions would seem to indicate that calls for separatism or redress of grievances involving territory are only heard by minority group members, it is recalled that very recently similar sentiments have been echoed by some urban leaders. There has been more than one city in the past decade that has seen the issue of a separate political status discussed. Most of these feelings are based on legislative favoritism and accompanying financial support favoring the rural or small-city sections of the state. The largest metropolitan area or areas have the most people and pay the most taxes. Therefore, they feel justified in requisitioning large sums of state monies for education, housing, welfare, sanitation, and transportation. Frequently in annual legislative sessions the leadership and fiscal battles pit New York City versus the rest of the state or Detroit versus the remainder of Michigan, or Pittsburgh and Philadelphia versus all the other parts of Pennsylvania. The financial plight facing many big city mayors and councils have led to more than one city spokesman to hint that if further support is not forthcoming, possibly thoughts regarding secession should be entertained. In their press for operating monies, many cities have seen the reluctance of state authorities to bail them out of financial messes. For this reason some large cities have established direct lobbying offices in the nation's capital.

The crux of the big city-state relations was brought to the fore by the mayoral campaign in New York City in 1969. At that time Norman Mailer and his partner Jimmy Breslin organized their campaign primarily around the theme of New York City becoming the fifty-first state. They attempted to convince the city's residents that they were paying more monies into Albany than they were receiving in services. Since the residents were being discriminated against, Mailer running for mayor and Breslin for president of City Council urged that the city secede from the state and form a city state "because the Federal government and farmers in Albany have no right dictating our life styles."[18] Whether such an action could have been legally constituted is very doubtful, however. The Mailer-Breslin ticket did represent a position in a major party (Democrat) of candidates seeking the highest elected offices in the nation's largest city. Even though Mailer finished fourth in the Democratic primary with only 41,000 votes to Procaccino's 252,000 votes, Wagner's 221,000 and Badillo's 215,000, he did bring the issue of representation and spatial allocation of a state's monies before the public. What happened in New York City in terms of a vote may signal a phenomenon that will occur in other urban-oriented states. The fact that the candidate loses is not nearly as important as the dent he can make on subsequent city-state politics.

FRIENDS-AND-NEIGHBORS VOTING

In running for office, political candidates either hope to win on the basis of being identified with a particular party that is dominant within a city, state, or region or attempt to win greater support in sections where their identity is particularly strong. Where a candidate achieves strong support in his home town or political territory and such support lessens the farther one is from that core, then it may be seen that a "friends-and-neighbors" pattern of voting emerges. The people he knows well and the problems he knows best are restricted to certain spaces. The support is greater here because the interaction is greater between the candidate and the constituents in his own backyard. It is almost as if where the candidate lives or is from is more important than his political stands. This neighborhood effect in voting is strongest where similarities in political philosophy, religion, social status, race or ethnic background are identified with one person or one party. Friends-and-neighbors voting is especially characteristic of rural states where a number of candidates vie for state offices. It exists in spaces dominated by one or more strong political parties. Although most analyses have focused on states in the South it does exist in county, congressional district, urban, and sectional voting.[19] It holds true for primaries as well as general elections.

Urban Level. In many of the nation's largest cities the contests for mayors or presidents of the city council or both become the political testing grounds for a number of expectant officeholders. Whether the races are between Republicans or Democrats or whether nonpartisan officials are running, the number and variety of candidates that vie for top offices represent the city's cultural and economic segments. It is not uncommon to have representation by blacks, East European ethnic groups, and Anglo-Saxon groups of liberal or conservative stripe in an attempt to win the party primaries. Even though an individual may know he or she has little opportunity to win the majority, he may hope to win the plurality or at least run a strong second or third. According to the friends-and-neighbors model, he banks his strength primarily on the ethnic, racial, or economic neighborhood or community he represents. It may even be the place of his boyhood residence. Even if he fails to win the nomination, he can be in a strong bargaining position with the top contender of his party or the rival one. By throwing his strength or territory to another, that is, his votes, he may affect the outcome of the general election and enhance his own political fortunes.

Probably few cities provide as good an example as New York City to illustrate the competition for mayor and city council president. All the major city political parties, Republicans, Democrats, Conservatives, and Liberals, have candidates vying for mayor. Often a candidate is supported by members of two parties. The 1969 mayoral election saw a number of candidates with varying philosophies represent ethnic, racial, and economic groups of the city. The incumbent, Lindsay, had won earlier on the Republican ticket in 1965 but not without the help of Liberals and Democrats. Since then workers' and teachers' strikes and heightened racial tensions plus the growing conservative political tone of the city and nation meant that liberal Lindsay would have to alter his campaign strategy if he hoped to win in 1969. The political, economic, and social geographies involved in trying to meld a winning combination in New York City in 1969 is described and illustrated in the March 1969 issue of *Fortune* (Fig. 3-3).

A POLITICIAN'S VIEW OF NEW YORK

John Lindsay's election as mayor in 1965, as the candidate of the Republican and Liberal parties, may have been the first step in a basic realignment of political forces in the city. Traditionally, despite a few breakthroughs by independent reformers like Fiorello La Guardia, the city has been ruled by a Democratic coalition, composed of the old immigrant, "silk stocking" liberals, Negroes and more recently, Puerto Ricans. Lindsay's victory was won in part by detaching upper- and middle-class liberals from the old coalition, and reducing normal Democratic majorities in black and Puerto Rican neighborhoods. Lindsay also profited from the growing political strength of conservative areas in Queens, the north Bronx, southwest Brooklyn, and Staten Island. While these areas gave above-average support to the Conservative party candidacy of William Buckley, as shown on the map, they also produced substantial Republican pluralities for Lindsay. Since 1965 the conservative trend in the city has continued. Lindsay's fight for a police review board in 1966 was overwhelmingly defeated at the polls; the majorities

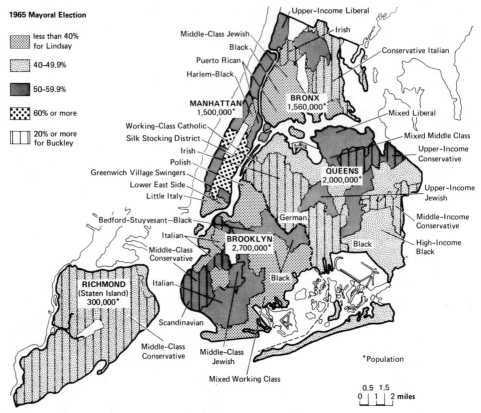

1965 Mayoral Election

- ▨ less than 40% for Lindsay
- ▨ 40–49.9%
- ▨ 50–59.9%
- ▨ 60% or more
- ▥ 20% or more for Buckley

Upper-Income Liberal

Irish

Middle-Class Jewish

Black

Puerto Rican

Harlem-Black

Conservative Italian

BRONX 1,560,000*

MANHATTAN 1,500,000*

Mixed Liberal

Working-Class Catholic

Silk Stocking District

Irish

Polish

Greenwich Village Swingers

Lower East Side

Little Italy

Mixed Middle Class

Upper-Income Conservative

QUEENS 2,000,000*

Upper-Income Jewish

Middle-Income Conservative

German

Bedford-Stuyvesant—Black

Italian

BROOKLYN 2,700,000*

Black

High-Income Black

Middle-Class Conservative

Black

RICHMOND (Staten Island) 300,000*

Italian

Scandinavian

Middle-Class Conservative

Middle-Class Jewish

*Population

Mixed Working Class

0.5   1.5
0 | 1 | 2 miles

FIG. 3-3 Politician's Map of New York City. (Tom Cardamone, *Fortune* Magazine, © 1969 Time Inc.)

against the board were heavy in the middle-class neighborhoods that he had carried the year before. In 1968, Richard Nixon carried white *working-class* areas in west Queens and the Bronx that he lost in 1960.

Lindsay's current tactic is to appeal to the liberal sentiments of middle-class Jews and the traditional Republicanism of other elements of the middle class, while holding his increased support among Negroes. The opposition coalition that seems to be forming would join conservative voters in Queens and Richmond with the remnants of Democratic machines in Manhattan, Brooklyn, and the Bronx. The great danger to the city is not so much a return to the bad old days of Tammany Hall or the muddling through of a Robert Wagner, as the formation of an essentially conservative administration that would leave the city's one and a half million blacks feeling isolated and desperate.[20]

In the June primary, Lindsay lost the Republican nomination by 5000 votes to conservative state Senator Marchi. Though Lindsay won the Liberal party's nomination, Marchi was the Conservative party's nominee. Another conservative Italian, Procaccino, who was city comptroller, captured the Democratic party nod.

The conservative nature of the city was reflected in this primary vote. Lindsay took Manhattan but not the surrounding suburban boroughs of Bronx, Brooklyn, Queens, and Richmond. His strength was among the young, affluent blacks and Puerto Ricans, although part of the minority vote went to Puerto Rican Badillo running as a Democrat. Marchi and Procaccino captured the conservative white middle-income and older voting districts. The November race resulted in the two Italian conservative candidates splitting the conservative votes and liberal Lindsay winning with a loose coalition of youth, blacks, Puerto Ricans, and liberal Democrats. His ability to win the rich and poor, young and nonwhite groups enabled him to capture 42 percent of the vote.

The New York City example could be illustrated in other cities as well. Los Angeles, San Francisco, Cleveland, and Detroit have had candidates representing the city's ethnic, racial, and economic groups run for mayor.[21] Their political and geographic strength in the final two-man race resulted from uniting groups that earlier had supported another candidate. When the contest boils down to a contest between a Republican vs. a Democrat, or a liberal vs. a conservative, or a black vs. a white, or a Catholic vs. a Protestant, the candidates ferret out those pockets or communities that they hope will expand their political support and territory beyond their own stomping grounds. The friends and neighbors pattern of support is seldom a contiguous one in cities, as it would be in states or a larger region where there is more spatial homogeneity over a larger area. The philosophical identity to crucial issues such as law and order, welfare coverage, civil rights, and government spending priorities are seldom uniform throughout the city. Political and social interaction and identity are not related strictly to distance as much as in rural areas. Also loyalty to parties and local leaders tends to be less. Support is more related to particular clusters of university students, young marrieds, high-income areas, or ethnic working-class sections.

State Level. As is often the case in state political primaries there are candidates hailing from various sections of the state. Each has his own home town and constituency. Each hopes his territorial support is strong enough either to insure a victory in the primary with a majority of votes or a sufficient plurality that will permit him to engage in a runoff. Should there be a runoff between the two top candidates, each will have to broaden his territorial base as well as political base in order to capture the necessary votes to achieve the majority and increase his support in his own bailiwick, or do both.

The 1971 Democratic gubernatorial primaries in Louisiana provide a ready example of this political model of neighborhood interaction. No less than eighteen nominees from the Democratic party vied for the office of governor; this large number was attracted because the incumbent could not succeed himself. In this strongly (almost one-party) Democratic state where regional and sectional differences are sharp and often identified with personalities and kinship, no candidate achieved 50 percent in the November 1971 primary.[22] Eight received more than 5 percent of the vote with the leader, present Governor Edwards, receiving the highest percent, 24. The results of this primary voting are revealed in the areal patterns (Fig. 3-4). Seven candidates carried more than one parish. This mosaic of voting results represented the territorial bases for several of the candidates. Almost every candidate had a home base and two or three additional parishes where his support was strongest. In the case of Edwards, his territory was the largest, encompassing eighteen parishes in French Louisiana, while Bell and Aycock carried only two each. The friends-and-neighbors model held true for the support received by Edwards, Johnston (in the northwest), Speedy Long, and Aycock. They carried their home parishes as well as several nearby. In retrospect the first primary portrays how a number of candidates vying for the top statewide-elected office hoped to gain support, namely, by capturing home bases. Their support dropped off sharply outside their home base or parish.

The runoff held in December 1971 was between Edwards and Johnston. This election provided a classic look at the north-south sectionalism that exists and has existed in statewide elections. Governors have traditionally come from north Louisiana, the area represented in the primary by Johnston (Chapter 2). Southern Louisiana, with the Acadian and Catholic vote, was represented by Edwards. In order for either candidate to gain a majority of the votes, he had to expand his area of political sympathy, that is, gain more votes in his home territory, capture more parishes, or both. It was expected that the minor candidates who won in the first primary would throw their support to either Edwards or Johnston and this would affect the voting pattern. However, this did not occur on a significant scale.

Edwards barely won the runoff with 50.2 percent of the vote; his support came primarily from what is considered southern Louisiana (Fig. 3-4). This primary illustrates the north-south cultural, religious, and political differences. In comparing the first and second Democratic primary, Edwards carried almost the same parishes but with a higher percent than earlier. Johnston expanded his territory to include most of north Louisiana. He won parishes that earlier went to Speedy Long, Gillis Long, Jimmy Davis, and Samuel Bell—all northern Democrats. Johnston also managed to carry a few parishes in southeast Louisiana.

In the February 1972 general election, Democrat Edwards vs. Republican Treen, the former won with 57 percent of the vote. This election also illustrated the primarily classic north-south political geographies in the state (Fig. 3-4). One of Edwards' major campaign planks was the dominance of the governor's chair by northern Democrats and the discrimination against the south. He was successful in using this regional appeal as his political base of support did not change drastically from the time of his initial primary victory. Democrats who voted for Johnston and other Democrats did not support their party's candidate in the general election. Edwards won by increasing his vote in his home territory and region both in the rural as well as in the major urban parishes of West Baton Rouge and New Orleans; he had lost the latter in the primaries. The size of the Republican vote for governor in February merits mention: Treen received over 480,000 votes then compared to only slightly over 9,000 he needed to capture his party's primary.

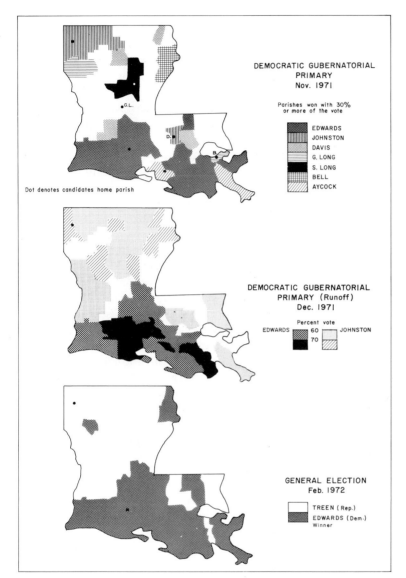

Fig. 3-4 Louisiana Gubernatorial Voting, 1971 and 1972: Friends-and-Neighbors Voting. (State of Louisiana, Secretary of State, 1971 and 1972.)

Regional Level. One salient feature of national third parties is that they tend to have a distinct regional or sectional appeal. Such a pattern would suggest that a political issue or candidate must enjoy success almost solely with the residents of that space. Outside, or the greater distance one is away from the center(s) of that space, the support dwindles.

The fate of major third parties entering the presidential races last century and this has been largely one of disaster. Their strength and identity usually have lasted only one election where they represented a protest against a particular stance adopted by the Republicans or Democrats. Their share of the popular and electoral vote has varied from a small to a significant share depending on the other candidates and their own regional support. Third parties are significant in studying American elections as they have affected the eventual winners. Their philosophies are also frequently embodied in subsequent platforms of both major parties. This usurpation has contributed to their demise. A further reason is that continued national political success requires an organizational framework that encompasses local, state, and national machinery. This is all too often lacking because of leadership, manpower, and money.[23]

In four elections this century the third-party influence has been strong. All have been significant for only one election, strong in one region, and identified with a single, dominant personality. The Bull Moose Progressive party headed by Theodore Roosevelt of New York in 1912 was responsible for helping defeat Republican Taft and elect Democrat Wilson. The party's strength was primarily in the Far West, northern Midwest, and Northeast; it won 28 percent of the popular vote and garnered eighty-eight electoral college votes. The Republicans saw similar progressive and liberal issues raised by Robert La Follette of Wisconsin in 1924. Although he was a Republican, he ran as an independent on the Progressive party ticket. He won 17 percent of the popular vote yet received only thirteen electoral votes (only his home state). His greatest strength was in the northern Midwest and Pacific Northwest and West. The strategy of his party was to deflate the Republican support for Davis in these areas and ignore the industrial Northeast and Midwest where Democrat Coolidge was strong. This strategy did help Coolidge win the election with 54 percent of the popular vote.

The two latest third-party attempts have both been launched in the South, especially the Deep South. The first was in 1948 with Thurmond's States' Rights party. This party formed after the national Democratic party convention had adopted progressive planks on civil rights, welfare, and government responsibilities. The third-party movement was ostensibly a call to the native white southerners to repudiate the Truman-Barclay ticket and support the regional political philosophies embodied in the ticket of Strom Thurmond of South Carolina for president and Fielding Wright of Mississippi for vice-president. Although this party won only 1.9 percent of the popular vote, it did garner over 1 million votes and did capture four Deep South states (Fig. 3-5). This party fared very well in the states of South Carolina, Alabama, Mississippi, and Louisiana, primarily because it was listed on the state ballots. One of the most striking geographical patterns that appears in Fig. 3-5 is the very high level of support he received and the importance of state boundaries. In the states Thurmond carried, his vote was often over 80 percent. In many counties, especially in Mississippi, the level was over 90 percent! His support in counties immediately adjacent to those four states he carried suggests the boundaries were significant. It represents the absence of his name on the ballots.

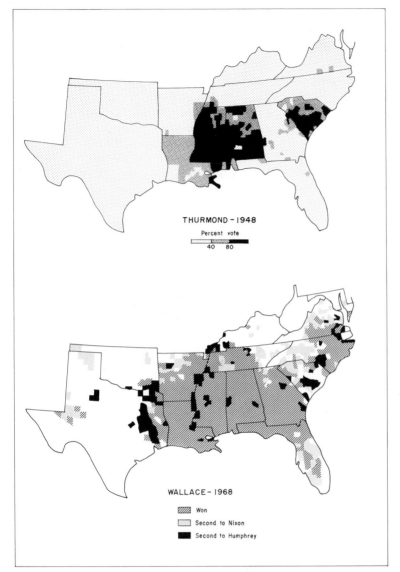

THURMOND – 1948

Percent vote

40   80

WALLACE – 1968

░ Won

□ Second to Nixon

■ Second to Humphrey

FIG. 3-5 Third-Party Support for President, 1948 and 1968. (After *America at the Polls: A Handbook of American Presidential Election Statistics, 1920–1964* by Richard M. Scammon, ed., by permission of the Univerity of Pittsburgh Press. © 1966 by the University of Pittsburgh Press. And after *America Votes*, 1968.)

Perhaps it also reveals that the geographic boundaries are also places of sharply contrasting philosophical views. Outside the South, Thurmond's party fared miserably.[24]

The 1948 election represented a turning point in the political geography of the South (Chapters 1 and 2). It not only marked the beginning of the demise of the solid Democratic South at the presidential level but the emergence of an identification with the national Republican party. Goldwater and, later, Nixon were to be the benefactors of this switch of presidential allegiances in 1964 and 1972. However, 1968 marked the appearance of another regional candidate, Governor George Wallace of Alabama. His reading of the nation and his region led him to believe that by running for president, he could win the election in his own regard or deny outright the office to one of the two major party candidates. In this spoiler role, he banked heavily on receiving strong support throughout the South and outside. Wallace organized the American Independent party that served as a vehicle for his name being placed on the ballot in all states. His position on issues involving civil rights, social welfare, universities, professors, clergymen, the Vietnam War, defense spending, and the federal government were strikingly similar to those echoed by Thurmond twenty years earlier. Throughout his campaign, Wallace traveled outside the South as he realized that a victory could not be based solely on the support of his friends and neighbors. However, the final results demonstrated that like the three other third-party candidates treated above, Wallace's party performed no differently. The AIP captured 13.5 percent of the national vote with nearly 10 million votes but it carried only five Deep South states: Georgia, Alabama, Mississippi, Arkansas, and Louisiana. This in essence was "Wallace Country." The geographical pattern of his votes was similar to that of Thurmond in many ways (Fig. 3-5). Wallace carried 578 counties in the election, all in the Southeast except a very few. He finished second to Nixon in 121 counties and second to Humphrey in 90.

The friends-and-neighbors voting model basically fits the Wallace support. The farther the counties were from his home base, Montgomery, or his home state, Alabama, the less support he generated.[25] The state boundaries were also significant in this election, especially in Tennessee and Georgia where his support was frequently 20 to 30 percent less than in contiguous counties in Alabama. In other areas of the South, the boundaries did not represent a break in his support; this is true especially for panhandle Florida and southwest Georgia, which philosophically and culturally can be considered political extensions of Alabama. Within the South, Wallace received less support in those counties with large urban centers, especially those in Rim states, and those counties with a large percent of the black population.[26] Outside the South, his support varied from about 1 to 5 percent in most counties.

The "southern strategy" of Nixon discussed in Chapter 1 did not help the third-party election chances of Wallace. Witness even the support Nixon enjoyed from Thurmond, the earlier regional third-party candidate. Perhaps a Wallace support of an anti-Nixon Republican candidate who hopes to continue winning conservative southern whites in future elections could spell the defeat or thwart the immediate plans for Republican dominance of the South's politics at the presidential level. Such a scenario may not be too unlikely. Who would have predicted the likelihood of a Thurmond endorsing a Republican president twenty years ago?

FOOTNOTES

1. Frank E. Horton and David R. Reynolds, "Effects of Urban Spatial Structure on Individual Behavior," *Economic Geography*, 47:1 (1971), 36–48. Along the political line see the following for political facets of neighborhoods: Kevin R. Cox, "The Spatial Components of Urban Voting Response Surfaces," *Economic Geography*, 47:1 (1971), 27–35; and "Residential Relocation and Political Behavior: Conceptual Model and Empirical Tests," *Acta Sociologica*, 13:1 (1970), 40–53.

2. Edward W. Soja, *The Political Organization of Space*, Commission on College Geography, Association of American Geographers, Washington, D.C., Resource Paper No. 8, 1971, pp. 20–22.

3. John S. Adams, "Directional Bias in Intra-Urban Migration," *Economic Geography*, 45:4 (1969), 302–323.

4. For a general discussion of this topic see Donald W. Meinig, "A Macrogeography of Western Imperialism: Some Morphologies and Moving Frontiers of Political Control," in F. Gale and G. H. Lawton, eds., *Settlement and Encounter: Geographical Studies Presented to Sir Grenfell Price*, Melbourne, Oxford University Press, 1969, pp. 213–230. See also C. F. J. Whebell, "Models of Political Territory," *Proceedings*, Association of American Geographers, 2 (1970), 152–156.

5. John S. Adams, "The Geography of Riots and Civil Disorders," *Economic Geography*, 48:1 (1972), 24–42.

6. Harold M. Rose, *The Black Ghetto, A Spatial Behavioral Perspective*, New York, McGraw-Hill, 1971, pp. 84–101.

7. Virginia L. Sharp, "The 1970 Postal Strikes: Diffusion with a Behavioral Twist," *Proceedings*, Association of American Geographers, 3 (1971), 157–161.

8. Paul S. Salter and Robert C. Mings, "Geographic Aspects of the 1968 Miami Racial Disturbances: A Preliminary Analysis," *Professional Geographer*, 21:2 (1969), 85. Reproduced by permission of the Association of American Geographers.

9. Robert W. McColl, "The Insurgent State: Territorial Bases of Revolution," *Annals, Association of American Geographers*, 59:4 (1969), 613–631.

10. Richard Gardner, *Grito! Reies Tijerina and the New Mexico Land Grant War of 1967*, Indianapolis, Bobbs-Merrill, 1970, p. 19.

11. Howard G. Salisbury, "The State Within a State: Some Comparisons Between the Urban Ghetto and the Insurgent State," *Professional Geographer*, 23:2 (1971), 105–112. Reproduced by permission of the Association of American Geographers.

12. Salisbury, op. cit., 109.

13. Theodore W. Taylor, *The States and Their Indian Citizens*, Washington, D.C., U.S. Department of Interior, Bureau of Indian Affairs, 1972, p. 120.

14. *New York Times Encyclopedic Almanac*, New York, 1971, pp. 149–150.

15. Luise Leismer, "Michigan Indians Will Share in New Award for 1805 Land," *Detroit News*, April 22, 1973, p. 5-H.

16. Gardner, op. cit.; and Patricia Bell Blair, *Tijerina and the Land Grants*, New York, International Publishers, 1971.

17. Robert Sherill, "We Want Georgia, South Carolina, Alabama, Mississippi, and Louisiana, Right Now—We Also Want Four Hundred Billion Dollars Back Pay,"

Esquire, January 1969, pp. 10–75 and 146–148. Also personal communication with Robert Williams, Baldwin, Michigan, February 26, 1973.

18. "Politics? The Odd Couple," *Newsweek,* May 12, 1969, p. 38.
19. V. O. Key, Jr., *Southern Politics,* New York, Vintage Books, 1949; Harold H. McCarty, "McCarty on McCarthy. The Spatial Distribution of the McCarthy Vote, 1952," Iowa City, University of Iowa, Department of Geography, unpublished manuscript, n.d., and David R. Reynolds, "A Spatial Model for Analyzing Voting Behavior," *Acta Sociologica,* 12:3 (1969), 122–131.
20. A. James Reichley, "A Nightmare for Urban Management," *Fortune,* March 1969, p. 97.
21. Roger E. Kasperson, "Toward a Geography of Urban Politics: Chicago, A Case Study," *Economic Geography,* 41 (1965), 95–107; and I. R. McPhail, "The Vote for Mayor of Los Angeles in 1969," *Annals, Association of American Geographers,* 61:4 (1971), 744–758.
22. Secretary of State, State of Louisiana, Results of November 1971 and December 1971 Primary Elections and February 1972 General Election for Office of Governor. See also various reports of the Public Affairs Research Council of Louisiana, Baton Rouge, 1971 and 1972 for analyses of the elections.
23. Edgar E. Robinson, *The Presidential Vote, 1896–1932,* Stanford, Stanford University Press, 1934; H. P. Nash, *Third Parties in American Politics,* Washington, D.C., Public Affairs Press, 1959, pp. 303–311; and W. B. Hesseltine, *Third-Party Movements in the United States,* Princeton, N.J., Van Nostrand, 1962, pp. 86–97.
24. Numan V. Barkley, *The Rise of Massive Resistance: Race and Politics in the South During the 1950s,* Baton Rouge, Louisiana State University Press, 1969, pp. 32–33, 150–169.
25. Stephen S. Birdsall, "Preliminary Analysis of the 1968 Wallace Vote in the Southeast," *Southeastern Geographer,* 9:2 (1969), 55–66.
26. Stanley D. Brunn, "The Wallace Presidential Vote in Southeast Cities," Michigan State University, Department of Geography, 1970, unpublished manuscript.

Chapter 4

POLITICAL ELITES
AND
RECRUITMENT

I come from a state that raises corn and cotton and
cockleburs and Democrats. . . . I am from Missouri.
                                    William Duncan Vandiver

Political leaders are not selected on a random basis. Rather there are certain areas, counties, cities, or sections of states that are identified with and considered promising "breeding grounds" for party leaders. This spatial selection process for recruiting contemporary elites may be based on past leaders and party factions who have their own bastions and who wish to preserve them. One way this can be accomplished is by placing their own favorite nominations before larger constituencies. Thus we find that not all parts of space, be it in a city or a state, are equally likely to have political leaders recruited and voted on by the electorate. This is well illustrated in California, where twenty-three of the thirty-three governors and twenty-eight of the thirty-seven senators have come from northern California. In 1966, for the first time, both senators and governor came from the southern part of the state.

As a political party considers nominations for key elected offices, there are certain "spaces" that are considered preferable for recruitment and others that are not seriously considered. Leaders may be recruited from a distinct part of a city or state to preserve a particular ethnic or party rule that is oriented along certain

75

philosophical lines. Where the political power traditionally lies often has much to say about future recruitment. As is often the case, competitive factions have developed within and between cities and regions. Location is not considered the only ingredient involved in recruiting political office seekers, as family wealth and name may be sufficient to override any seemingly inherent locational disadvantage. The family tradition of Kennedys in Massachusetts, Byrds in Virginia, Tafts in Ohio, and Longs in Louisiana are only a few cases where kinship ties are often the keys that unlock political doors.

The spatial selection and recruitment of party leaders are important at the urban level, where aldermen or councilmen are elected, all the way to the nominees for the presidential and vice-presidential slots in national elections. Other than those leaders elected to office, the appointment of cabinet members and justices to the Supreme Court often reflects geographical strategies. Where an elite hails from is likely to influence his perception of problems and issues facing his constituency, whether he be a chairman of a key congressional committee or a high-ranking official in charge of environmental programs in the United States Department of the Interior.

The importance of one county, Edgefield County, South Carolina, is an illustration of the role of location in the state politics of last century and this one. This is the home county of segregationist Strom Thurmond, presently Republican senator and former leader of the States' Rights party in 1948. Political analyst Sherill concludes, in examining the place of that county in the state's history, that Thurmond would be unusual not to continue in the philosophical footsteps of his predecessors.

> Edgefield was the home county of Travis and Bonham, two of the rebels who died in the Alamo; it was also the home of Chancellor Wardlaw, who wrote South Carolina's ordinance of secession; it was the home of Congressman Preston S. Brooks who, to avenge a slur on the name of U.S. Senator A. P. Butler (of Edgefield), caned to the Senate floor Senator Charles Sumner of Massachusetts and thereby helped establish the atmosphere in which reconciliation over the disputes leading to the Civil War was impossible; it was the home of Ben Tillman, who led the farmers in revolt against a state government controlled by Charleston and Columbia aristocrats with the Luciferian cry, "I had rather follow the majority to hell than these men to heaven." Edgefield County has turned out ten governors and nine lieutenant governers, most of them searing individualists. It is also the home of the state's oldest newspaper, the Edgefield *Advertiser*, whose present editor, W. W. Mims, has on at least one occasion backed up his political opinions in a sidewalk fist fight and who has advocated the establishment of a modern Confederacy.[1]

POLITICIANS AND LOCATION

Urban Councilmen and Mayors. The political power in a city is in the hands of the elected officials who propose, enact, and administer legislation and programs that govern the whole population. They are charged with allocating budget monies, establishing zoning ordinances, setting housing codes, and the administering of education, health, welfare, police, and fire services. All these programs have geographical elements at their base. How many duties and responsibilities an elected council is able to execute and how it carries them out depends in part on the members' view of the city as a whole. Where they orient their priorities and demonstrate geographic favoritism for locally or federally allocated monies and where they approve specific recommendations dealing with water quality, metro-education, or urban renewal will be a reflection of their own view of the city or of their elected constituency.

Should a city that is basically biracial in composition be governed by a council that is all white or only with token representation by minority groups, it may have little interest in focusing on problems of the inner city residents. If most of the councilmen live in white suburbia, far from the central city, their view of the inner city may be seen basically as a problem area where crime, vice, and riots are characteristic. That is, where they work is in the suburbs and their concern for the "downtown" may be seen primarily as ways to "save" it from deterioration. The space may be viewed in economic or speculative terms, that is, from a business-man's view. While education, welfare, transporation, housing, and medical care may be problems that are acknowledged, the individual councilman from a safe suburb feels detached from the residents of and from that part of the city except for commuting downtown on occasion for shopping or social events or council meetings.

Locations of officeholders and their recruitment by civic organizations and political parties may be a significant element in the political decisions that are made by a governing body in a city. High-income whites or those with a strong ethnic commitment may not look with favor on spending suburban tax dollars for curing the many ills facing poor inner city blacks or Chicanos or even elderly whites. Their solutions to crime and drugs may be to enlist more support for police man-power and equipment instead of investigating serious complaints about injustices and inequities in the education, welfare, employment, and judicial systems. The resolutions that are passed on the location of new incinerators, sewage treatment plants, parks, schools, or expressways may be basically political in nature and reflect the benefit of suburban whites while disregarding the supply/demand or cost/benefit ratios for all segments of a city. The councilmen in more than one small or large city are known to serve primarily the interests of a business or social elite, or both, and not the total citizenry. Their neglect or ignorance of problems facing the majority of the population or a sizable portion, especially if nonwhite, may indicate that their devotion is to certain powerful groups whose interests and perceptions are limited to certain favorable and not-so-favorable geographical spaces.

Councilmen and mayors may be elected at large, that is, with no com-partmentalized geographical unit as a base, or they may run against opponents in a ward system.[2] In an at-large election a candidate must express his views to the total electoral constituency, a political-city unit. These elections are seen by some blacks and inner city residents as ways to diffuse their emerging political power. If the whites leave the central city and move to suburbs that are politically independent, the blacks may be left with majority populations but with a hollow victory if jobs and monies and services are insufficient.

Besides the type of election format, there are also political party considerations. Outside the Southwest in general, Republicans and Democrats compete for control of locally elected bodies. Nonpartisan candidates, who attempt to divorce party politics from local issues, are frequent in city governments in the Southwest. Leaders of varying stances may be selected or recruited who will either serve their own party, neighborhood, or city. The representation of those that serve is not always a true reflection of the social and economic or even the political variation in the cities.

At an urban level the strength of ethnic groups is acknowledged, especially in New York, Massachusetts, Pennsylvania, Connecticut, Michigan, Ohio, and Illinois. Their rise to power was accomplished by uniting members of their group and others into a block whose strength became apparent in their consistent control of city halls, in short, clubhouse politics. One prime illustration of this is the recent Chicago mayors. The past three (Daley, Kenelley, and Kelly) were Democrats of Irish extraction who came from the Bridgeport area of the city.[3] Similar histories are repeated in other cities where Irish or Italians or East European ethnic groups had leaders who rose to power in cities in the Northeast.

From a political geography standpoint, where the elected city council members and the mayor live are important elements that are likely to reflect their views on the identification and solution of problems and issues facing the city. Location in a power sense is a reflection of perception of the knowledge of people and places and the decisions made relating to the city's social and economic problems. The power in the hands of a few conservative-entrenched councilmen is strong, as they by their actions affect the daily geographic structuring and behavior of the city's residents and its institutions.[4]

The city council members of Phoenix, Arizona, serve as a case in point. At present the mayor and city councilmen comprise a charter government group that is mostly represented by businessmen who have been or are members of the business community. They are involved in the city's and metropolitan area's growth and development. Five councilmen, including the mayor, of this quasi-nonpartisan council live in or near the Paradise Valley section of the city (Fig. 4-1). This is the area of highest median-family incomes; it also has the newest homes and the highest housing values in the city. Many of the stances taken by these councilmen are favorable to the business and commercial interests of Phoenix.

On the Phoenix city council are also two minority group members, one black and one Chicano. The black member lives in the low-income area near the Sky Harbor airport. Besides being the section of lowest incomes in Phoenix, it also has the oldest houses and a high percent of renters. The Chicano representative lives near Glendale, which is a residential area with incomes approximating the city's median.

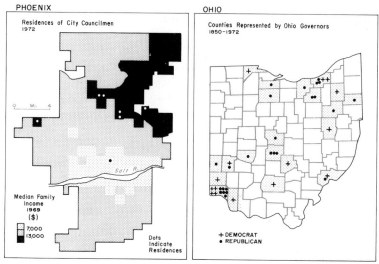

FIG. 4-1 Residential Location of Local and State Officeholders. (Phoenix City Council, Phoenix, Arizona and State of Ohio, Secretary of State, *Official Roster*, 1972.)

Governors. An individual recruited for and nominated as governor (one of the highest statewide elected offices) would likely be someone who has strong party strengths in a traditional area (rural or urban) or a candidate from a major urban node. Should the candidate have a popular political surname, this could override geographical considerations. Nor should it be considered unlikely that an individual from a small town or rural area that has little clout in state politics could be nominated or elected. However, most political party leaders and elected officials recognize the traditional power centers and regions for recruiting statewide candidates. If there was a single party clearly dominant, as in the South, winning the nomination in any Democratic primary in a major statewide race until very recently almost assured the candidate a general election victory. The gubernatorial candidate representing an urban county, the largest one in the state, for example, already has a power base that places him in an advantageous position over others. That a large number of citizens in the central city and suburbs are already familiar with his name, party, experience, and position on state issues works to his credit. Often where there is more than one major urban center in a state, the primaries of both parties become testing grounds for the candidates of both parties. In reality they may be considered competitive contests between the major urban centers as they vie for control of the leadership in the governor's mansion. Where there are regional variations in Republican or Democratic party strength as well, the candidates from urban centers take on added meaning in the recruitment of leaders and the control of the governorship. The north-south contests in California, Illinois, Florida, and Louisiana take on a tug-of-war appearance that reflects regional political factions.

The 1971 gubernatorial elections in Louisiana were basically a contest between Democratic party hopefuls. It was basically between a southern Catholic Acadian candidate and a northern rural-oriented nominee (Chapters 2 and 3). Edwards, the winner, used the north-south issue as a major campaign issue for winning both the Democratic party nomination and the general election. One of his major campaign issues was that south Louisiana, and especially Acadiana, had not been fairly represented in the statehouse, even though it has more people and pays more into the state coffers. The previous four governors had come from four basically rural parishes in the north. They served a total of twenty-eight years. His strategy was successful as he obtained regional support from southern French Louisiana and the urban parishes in the south against a Republican who won his primary with only 9732 votes.

In three large urban industrial states in the Northeast and Midwest, the dominance of very large urban centers is of note in the recruitment of governors. The state of New York has elected sixteen different governors since 1900, and seven have come from New York City. The Illinois pattern is similar with six of the fourteen different governors elected since 1900 having come from Cook County (Chicago) and two more from nearby Kankakee County. The governors from Cook County have been equally split between the two major parties. The picture of the Ohio governors elected reflects the competition between urban centers in different regions as well as that between the Republicans and Democrats. From 1850–1972 Ohio voters elected forty different governors, twenty-five Republicans and fifteen Democrats (Fig. 4-1). They came from twenty-one of the state's eighty-eight counties.[5] In general the counties represented by the governors reflect a pattern of the three main clusters of urban population, Cleveland (Cuyahoga County), Columbus (Franklin County), and Cincinnati (Hamilton County). Most of the governors have either come from these three or adjacent suburban counties. The Republicans and Democrats represented in the governor's mansion are a reflection of the strengths of each party in the state. Cincinnati is basically considered a city where both parties have acknowledged strengths. Columbus is of a Republican mold and Cleveland is usually considered the Democrats' major urban bastion. These three urban counties and the others are a reflection of the political culture and the historical developments of the state. Northern Ohio has a strong New England Yankee influence that has led to their Republican orientation in most presidential elections in the last and in this century. Cleveland is a Democratic stronghold because of the industrial work force comprised of European ethnics and blacks. Southern Ohio, and especially southeast Ohio, that rural and hilly south and southeast part of the state immediately east and south of Columbus, was settled by Border state settlers last century. This was Copperhead country during the Civil War.

Elected Black Officials. The recruitment and election of black leaders represents one of the significant political developments in the United States since 1960. This phenomenon is not restricted solely to the rural and urban South where blacks comprise from 25–40 percent of the population, but in the urban North as well. In large part the election of over 2000 blacks to various posts represents the impact of civil rights and voting rights legislation enacted since 1964. It also indicates the realization among majority whites that blacks can also be effective leaders. To blacks themselves it shows that they can achieve some political clout in decisions affecting them by using the strength of the ballot box.

That blacks can have an impact on decisions rendered and problems solved has led many local and statewide groups to engage in massive voter registration drives and to encourage blacks to run for elective offices. Even though blacks have not always been successful in winning because of mediocre support and the unpopularity of their candidate or because of low turnout, they have in the rural and urban South and urban North effectively changed the political climate of the pre-1960s. The open hostility toward blacks has ceased even in the Deep South cities and states as their power at the voting booth is being reckoned with and sought by both major parties. The rural white South and white suburban North are two areas where the place of blacks in the political process is least realized. The sentiments against blacks are not couched in the framework of the rhetoric of a decade earlier; rather it is often subtly hidden behind stances on busing, welfare, housing, and neighborhood identity.

As of 1972 there were 2264 black officials elected in the United States.[6] The present number represents an increase of 18 percent from 1971 and 35 percent over 1970. Almost one-half (1108) are city and county officials and one-third (669) of the 1972 total are school board members. The remaining are law enforcement officials (263) and members of the United States or state legislative bodies (224). Roughly half of the total were elected from the South (1073) with the Northeast and North Central states having 423 and 589 respectively. Only 179 were elected from the West.

Two states, Michigan and New York, had over 150 black officials in 1972 and seven more states had over 100: California, Mississippi, Illinois, New Jersey, Louisiana, Ohio, and North Carolina (Fig. 4-2). All the southern states have increased their number drastically since 1970; of these, now only Tennessee with forty-eight has fewer than fifty elected blacks. There were five states that did not have a black official in 1972: Idaho, Montana, Maine, North Dakota, and South Dakota.

The highest elected black officeholder in 1972 was Senator Brooke of Massachusetts. There are black representatives in the United States House from California, Illinois, Michigan, New York, Maryland, and Pennsylvania. In November 1972, a black, Andrew Young, was elected to the House from Atlanta. This was the first time this century a black representative from a Deep South state has been elected to serve in Washington. Blacks at present hold a larger number of seats in state houses. They are elected in the same large northern states cited above as well as in the South, where their numbers are increasing with each election. In the past decade black gains have been reflected in the mayors elected in several major cities, Cleveland, Gary, Newark, and more recently in Atlanta, Detroit, and Los

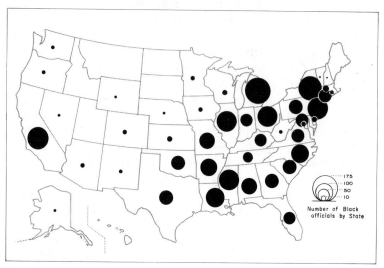

Fig. 4-2 Elected Black Officials, 1972. (U.S. Department of Commerce, *Statistical Abstract of the United States*, 1972, Washington, D.C., 1972.)

Angeles. Black mayoral gains are reflected in several small towns and medium-sized cities in the South such as Fayette, Mississippi, and Chapel Hill, North Carolina. Other than the local gains blacks have made in city councils, such as in Gainesville, Florida, and Selma, Alabama, or in school boards in Greene County, Alabama, they have had an impact on statewide races even though they lost. Recent Senate and gubernatorial races in Georgia, North Carolina, Arkansas, and Mississippi have seen blacks running in statewide contests. Their candidacy has served as a vehicle for augmenting black registration and for tempering the rhetoric of many eventual winners. White politicians recognize the political strength existing among blacks and more than one has allied himself with their problems and views and enlisted their support openly en route to a victory.

The gains made in the South are attributed to the passage of the Voting Rights Act of 1965 and the support for registering blacks by federal officials and citizens' groups and organizations. Groups such as the Student Nonviolent Coordinating Committee and the Voter Education Project of the Southern Regional Council are two examples of the many organizations, formal and informal, that have actively enlisted the support of whites and blacks from the South and North to help in registration drives. The gains were made early in the cities but later in the small towns and rural areas where registration was often made the more difficult by uncooperative local officials.

Within the 1960–1970 decade the greatest successes in black registration were in the Rim South states (Table 4-1). At the beginning of the 1960s less than one-third of all blacks were registered, but by the end of 1970, the number was over 60 percent. In fact by the latter date, the black registration figure almost equaled

TABLE 4-1   Registration of Blacks in Southern States

Item	Total	Ala.	Ark.	Fla.	Ga.	La.	Miss.	N.C.	S.C.	Tenn.	Tex.	Va.
1960:												
White	12,276	860	518	1,819	1,020	993	478	1,861	481	1,300	2,079	867
Negro	1,463	66	73	183	180	159	22	210	58	185	227	100
Percent:[a]												
White	61.1	63.6	60.9	69.3	56.8	76.9	63.9	92.1	57.1	73.0	42.5	46.1
Negro[b]	29.1	13.7	38.0	39.4	29.3	31.1	5.2	39.1	13.7	59.1	35.5	23.1
1962:												
White	12,110	884	507	1,819	1,153	935	390	1,861	481	1,300	1,840	940
Negro	1,481	68	69	182	176	152	24	216	91	151	242	110
1964:												
White	14,264	946	621	2,200	1,340	1,037	525	1,942	703	1,297	2,602	1,050
Negro	2,164	111	95	300	270	165	29	258	144	218	375	200
1966:												
White	14,310	1,192	598	2,093	1,378	1,072	471	1,654	718	1,375	2,600	1,159
Negro	2,689	250	115	303	300	243	282	282	191	225	400	205
1968:												
White	15,702	1,117	640	2,195	1,524	1,133	691	1,579	587	1,448	3,532	1,256
Negro	3,112	273	130	292	344	305	251	305	189	228	540	255
1970:												
White	16,985	1,311	728	2,495	1,615	1,143	690	1,640	608	1,600	3,599	1,496
Negro	3,357	315	153	302	395	319	286	305	221	242	550	269
Percent:[a]												
White	69.2	85.0	74.1	65.5	71.7	77.0	82.1	68.1	62.3	78.5	62.0	64.5
Negro[b]	62.0	66.0	82.3	55.3	57.2	57.4	71.0	51.3	56.1	71.6	72.6	57.0

Source: Southern Regional Council, Inc., Voter Education Project, Inc., Atlanta, Ga.; *Voter Registration in the South* in *Statistical Abstract of the United States, 1971*, Washington, D.C., U.S. Department of Commerce, 1972, p. 365.

[a] Of voting-age population.
[b] Includes other minority races.

that of the whites in the region. However, the disparity between the two groups is still great in the Deep South states in particular, where only about half of all voting age blacks are registered. Two further items merit noting: first, the white registration as a whole is also lower in the South than for the nation; and second, in two states, Arkansas and Texas, a greater percent of blacks than whites are registered.

While the increase in black registration is a major political development, it is only of significance when the blacks actively engage in the voting process. The low turnout of blacks in many local and state elections in the South has been considered one reason for the failure of a black candidate to win. The recent acquisition of the voting franchise in part accounts for the low turnouts plus the realization that voting for a candidate who shares their views can be an effective way to have some of their problems aired. The intimidation of previous generations engaging in any political activity should also not be overlooked as a reason why many poor and many rural blacks have been reluctant to vote, let alone register, against a white and for a black. Simply placing a black candidate before a majority black electorate does not insure victory as many blacks will identify and support a white candidate who may be considered the better of the two unknowns. With increasing black political awareness and participation, blacks realize that not all blacks speak for and identify with all others. Whites are being viewed in the same vein.

Southern Republican Office Seekers. The Republican party in recent years has taken an increased interest in southern politics (Chapter 1). After long being very impotent in any statewide election, the party has begun recruiting party members (some even disenchanted Democrats) to run for the Senate and governorships in particular. Even though the candidates had little likelihood of winning, especially in the early years (1950s and early 1960s), the party has been reaping success recently. In seeking viable candidates the party is looking for candidates from major urban centers or traditionally Republican areas. A candidate from such a center or area was not only assured a larger base population from his home town, if it was large in size, but a better media coverage. This strategy has been used to win Senate seats and governorships since the late 1960s. In gubernatorial races the Republicans have been more successful than in capturing Senate seats. Some of their earliest Senate victories were in traditional Republican strongholds in Rim states, such as by Tower from Wichita Falls, Texas, in 1966 and by Brock of Chattanooga, Tennessee, in 1970 and Gurney of Orlando, Florida, in 1968. Governors won in Florida in 1966 with Kirk from Jacksonville, in Tennessee in 1970 with Dunn from Memphis, in Virginia in 1970 by Holton from Roanoke, and in 1972 in North Carolina by Holshouser of Boone in the traditional Republican western part of the state. Republican candidates for governor were not winners in Arkansas, Texas, and Mississippi. In Mississippi the national party has not nominated serious challengers to incumbents. In 1970 the Republicans nominated Cramer from St. Petersburg and Bush from Houston for the Senate. Even though the Republicans lost both these races, they fared much better in United States Senate races in 1972.

They were successful in capturing seats with Helms from Raleigh, North Carolina; Edmundson from Muskogee, Oklahoma; and Scott from Fairfax, Virginia. During the same year the Republicans nominated for Senate races Thompson from Atlanta, De Toledano from New Orleans, and Blount from Montgomery; all, however, lost to Democrats.

Chairmen of Congressional Committees. Although the Congress is one of the three major branches of the federal government, it is not assumed that its 535 members (435 representatives and 100 senators) have equal political power. If they all had somewhat equal strength in national decision policies, the programs and the actions of the federal government would probably be reflected in the monies allocated to states and cities for social programs and for federal installations and institutions.

It is the chairmen of the permanent committees in the Senate and House who are in the major positions of power. Their position insures that they can steer certain actions and recommendations to floor action in their particular body. On the other hand they can also bottle up proposed and often needed legislation. Such legislation may be beneficial to the nation as a whole and to its cities. Chairmen of committees are members of the majority political party in each chamber and in the case of the 87th through the 92nd Congresses (1961–1972) all chairmen have been Democrats.

Even though the Democrats have controlled Congress from 1961–1972, the chairmen of House and Senate committees did not represent a representative cross section of the nation's states or even of population distribution (Fig. 4-3). The South was very much overrepresented by chairmen during this period, particularly in the Senate. Those states that dominate, with the exception of Washington, are all in the Southeast. No large western state such as California has had a committee chairmanship during this period; Texas has had one. The large-population states of New York, Pennsylvania, Ohio, and Illinois have had no senator heading a permanent Senate committee. On the House side, the pattern is somewhat different, although the southern states still have representatives heading the committees. New York and Texas had the largest number. Aside from the dominant position of states in the southeast quarter, there were chairmen from Pennsylvania, California, and Illinois. In terms of a cross section of states the distribution of chairmen of House committees is slightly more representative.

Beneath the patterns depicted on the maps is one major criticism of the Congress. That is its lack of familiarity and unwillingness to seriously engage in legislation dealing with national urban problems. The underrepresentation, as measured by the numbers of committee chairmen from large-population and industrial states in the East, Midwest, and Southwest, is more apparent in the Senate than in the House. A frequent assessment made of Congress is how can this branch effectively engage in serious urban legislation when members of these states are not in the chairmanship positions in the House and Senate? Chairmen mainly come from the South and many from rural states and districts. They head these key

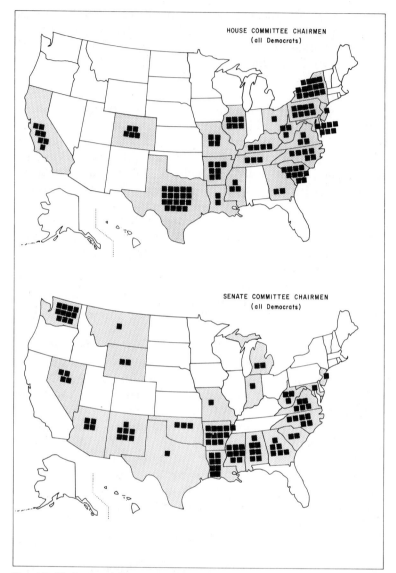

FIG. 4-3 Chairmen of Congressional Committees, 1961–1972. (*Congressional Quarterly Almanac,* 1961–1972.)

committees by reason of seniority. This is tied in part to their lack of opposition by the Republican party (as well as Democrats) in primary and general elections. In essence they represent safe political spaces. Such considerations have contributed to the same members being the head of Senate and House committees during the years under question. On the Senate side we find Fulbright and McClellan of Arkansas, Stennis and Eastland of Mississippi, Sparkman of Alabama, and Ellender of Louisiana. Outside the South, Jackson and Magnuson of Washington have headed their committees since 1960. With reference to the House, Mills of Arkansas, McMillen and Rivers of South Carolina, and Poage and Teague of Texas are southern members who served as chairmen at the beginning of each of the past six congressional sessions.

Supreme Court Justices. A total of 105 justices to the Supreme Court have been appointed by presidents since 1789.[7] The appointment of justices to this highest court is one of the critical decisions the chief executive makes as his selections can influence the direction the nation will take on issues of citizens rights, government powers, and economic controls. Therefore the states most frequently represented on the federal bench will probably have their ideals and views on social and economic issues revealed in eventual decisions.

From the appointment in 1789 of John Jay of New York as the first chief justice to William Rehnquist of Arizona appointed in 1971, thirty-one states have been represented on the Supreme Court. More than half of the justices that have served or are serving are natives of eight states (Table 4-2). The northeastern states, eastern Midwest, and Rim or Border states are the prime grounds for selecting justices. The exceeding large representation from these states is both a reflection of their large population bases, large number of leading law schools and legal firms, as well as those with an historical impact on the political development of the nation.

Prior to 1800 Maryland was the leading state. From 1801–1900 New York, Ohio, and Pennsylvania were the major states with justices appointed. Few were appointed from the South, the West, and the Midwest save Ohio. In the twentieth century, eight have come from New York and four each from Massachusetts and

TABLE 4-2   Supreme Court Justices, Major
            States Represented: 1789–1971

State	Number
New York	15
Ohio	9
Massachusetts	8
Virginia	7
Pennsylvania	6
Maryland	5
Kentucky	5
Tennessee	5
Total	60

Source: *1973 World Almanac*, New York, Newspaper Enterprise Association, p. 795.

Ohio. Three came from Tennessee and two others from each of six states: New Jersey, Connecticut, Virginia, Kentucky, Georgia, and Minnesota.

The attacks on the United States Supreme Court in the past two decades have mainly centered around constitutional decisions affecting the civil liberties of individuals and minority groups, especially blacks. The unpopularity of these judgments in the South is not unexpected, considering the traditional philosophy and rulings of many southern justices that have been at variance with the remainder of the United States as well as the decisions eventually reached by the Supreme Court itself. The dominance of the moral code and fabric of the Northeast and Midwest and the views of government, as evidenced by the recent decisions supported by justices from these states, probably contributes much to the direction society has taken and is taking at present. Were more justices appointed from the southern states, the decisions might possibly be at variance with the largest populated quarter of the nation. The absence of justices from the major populated states of the Southwest and West, especially Texas and California, is the one geographical area where the population concentration of the nation is not represented equally on the bench.

CABINET APPOINTMENTS

States of Cabinet Members. The executive branch of the federal government handles problems and issues of a very diverse nature. The president's cabinet deals with setting defense spending levels, negotiating treaties, stipulating limits on crop supports, protecting consumer rights, enforcing civil rights, maintaining price controls, and alleviating environmental crises. Individual cabinet departments are charged with solving and identifying such problems. It would be expected that when a president considers appointments to these top positions, namely, secretaries, he considers leaders with knowledge and expertise for the departments in question. In his desire to see that the problems and positions are handled effectively, he may pick elected or nonelected officials that will speak for him and his administration on policy matters and for the nation's citizens as well. Often if a president feels that he would prefer to see certain philosophies or views represented in decision making, that heretofore may have been absent, he may recommend to the Senate such individuals. This may happen in the sphere of minority representation, southern justice, labor-management relations, or environmental affairs. Those in cabinet positions are already identified with political, legal, economic, or social bases that are often apparent prior to their appointment. In like manner, their geographical location—city, state, or region—is often known as well. It may be that they are nominated for their particular position because of their regional or sectional loyalty or philosophy on matters relating to civil rights, environment, housing, financial, or international business matters.

What becomes apparent in an examination of the presidential appointees for cabinet positions is that there are distinct geographical patterns evident in the recruitment process. That is, not all members of the cabinets come from the same states or regions. Nor is the pattern basically a hodgepodge random one. In recruiting members for different positions, the state or region represented often does play an important role, although perhaps not the dominant role. However, it may be a critical element in the final decision process.

The states represented by secretaries in four key cabinet posts from 1900 to 1972 attest to the foregoing statements.[8] Of the fourteen secretaries of agriculture, all save four came from an agricultural state in the Midwest or Great Plains (Fig. 4-4). One half came from three states: Iowa, Indiana, and Missouri, all states with a heavy economic orientation towards agriculture. Six other states have been represented by one secretary. Thus, the areas with the largest concentration of farmers and those that are wealthy and successful have been represented by a leader from one of the "Farm Belt" states. For many elections the presidential candidates felt they had to carry these states or they would lose, and the selection of the secretary of agriculture was one of the most important appointments. Less is heard about this issue in an urban society and economy. Even though agricultural issues are not the paramount issue they were in national elections in the 1920s and 1930s, still presidential aspirants must be cognizant of these issues in their courting of midwestern states.

A total of twenty-five attorneys general have held office since 1900. The majority have represented states in the Northeast, especially New York and Pennsylvania. About half (twelve) have come from New York, Pennsylvania, Massachusetts, and Maryland (Fig. 4-4). The large number coming from the combined Northeast and Midwest states is a reflection of major population concentrations and the largest legal offices and law schools located around New York City and Washington, D.C. Outside the northeast quarter, only Texas, Tennessee, and Arizona have been represented. Texas, with three, is the third leading state. There may be some significance in the fact that, like Supreme Court nominees, the judicial philosophies of the president and his administration are reflected when recruiting the top lawyers to represent the government. Their training, philosophy, and experience may lead them to go hard or soft on certain labor, environmental, civil rights, or financial issues.

One of the most important cabinet posts is that of secretary of state. He is charged with the interests and the problems that arise between the United States and foreign governments. Since 1900 there have been nineteen secretaries from nine states and almost half (nine) have come from New York (Fig. 4-4). This state with its international economic, political, and business connections is recognized as the leader in its transactions with foreign and domestic concerns. In addition, it is the headquarters for international companies, the United States, and leading law and business schools. A further reflection of the industrial and commercial importance is reflected in those secretaries from the nearby states of Pennsylvania, Massachusetts, and Connecticut. Four states outside the Northeast have had a secretary: Minnesota, Nebraska, Tennessee, and South Carolina.

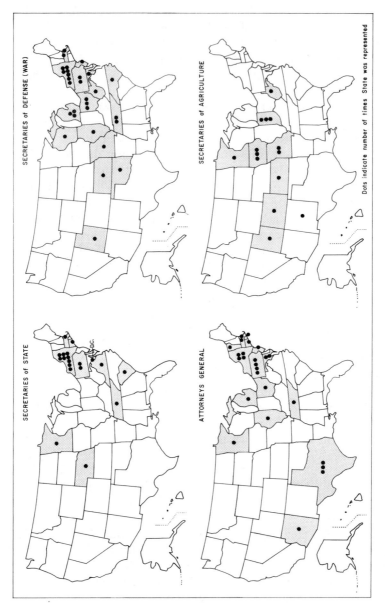

FIG. 4-4 Cabinet Members: States Represented, 1900–1972.

Clearly, the international ties of the Northeast are reflected in the choices for secretary of state. One has never represented a West or Southwest state.

There have been twenty-six secretaries of defense (or war) appointed from sixteen states since 1900. This position, again critical to national and international matters, is one of the most important in the cabinet and in the total federal bureaucracy. The industrial economies of the Northeast states produce manufacturing materials useful in peace or wartime. Clearly, this consideration is reflected in the secretaries who have served. Twenty of the twenty-six have come from five leading industrial states (Fig. 4-4): New York (seven), Ohio and Michigan (three each), Massachusetts and Pennsylvania (two each). The industrial expansion in the West and South since World War II has not resulted in represention by a cabinet appointee. Only three have come from a southern state. The economic strength and strong business and political ties have been important in the recruitment of these secretaries.

Cabinets of Kennedy and Nixon. In selecting members for presidential cabinets, leaders of the business, professional, and political worlds are usually chosen. They have certain backgrounds that recommend them for these top appointive positions. In addition, these elites by their own knowledge and experience and strengths in the several economic, societal, or political spheres represent states and major regions within the nation. It is not rare that the holder of a cabinet position was previously an elected state official, such as a governor or a federal senator or representative.

When the president considers nominations, he can weigh a number of critical factors that are important in making the final decisions. While he may consider the professional expertise or government experience as paramount, he also can weigh heavily the states these elites represent. His election may have been insured by key states or personalities in those states. Therefore, he may feel he "owes" the voters and leaders of those states some representation in his cabinet. On the other hand, he may know that to handle problems dealing with agriculture he would prefer to have a cabinet member from an agricultural state that the nation's farmers and lobbies can readily identify with on policy matters. This would seemingly be a more wise strategy than selecting a secretary from a heavy industrial state. A further reason that a president may select an individual from a particular state is to maintain his popularity or that of his party. If his philosophy is such that he views a region or a group of states as potential areas for party development, he may select leaders distinctly identified with that region's or state's philosophy and problems.

By following such geographical and political reasoning, we may see some geographical patterns to the selection of members of a president's cabinet. The two examined are the initial appointees of Kennedy in 1960 and of Nixon in 1968.[9] Kennedy's ten initial appointments came mainly from the Northeast and Midwest (Fig. 4-5). Only three came from outside: one from a Rim state, North Carolina, a state he won, and the other two from California and Arizona, both states he lost. Of the nine states these secretaries represented, Kennedy won seven. Thus it appears that the states that helped him win his close election were in part rewarded with a cabinet appointment.

Although there are some striking similarities between the Kennedy and

FIG. 4-5 States Represented: Cabinets of Presidents Kennedy and Nixon.

Nixon cabinets, there are some significant differences (Fig. 4-5). First, is Nixon's appointment of Blount of Alabama. Although Nixon lost this state to Wallace, he did receive support from several southern leaders and states that insured his election. Also as part of his party's strategy for insuring later Republican victories, he hoped that by having a cabinet member from this region, his interest in the region's problems and philosophy would be made apparent to the nation and especially to the South. Second, Nixon selected a governor from Alaska, the first time the state was represented in the cabinet. His other appointees came from the Northeast and Midwest, some being the same states from which Kennedy selected secretaries. Of the eleven states in his cabinet (the departments of transportation and housing and urban development added during the Johnson administration), Nixon won five. These were the western states of Alaska and California and three midwestern states.

When it became apparent following the 1970 midterm elections that Nixon would probably be running for a second term, the states represented in his cabinet replacements in the final two years of his first term took on a political note. Especially is this true for Connally, a former Texas governor and member of the Democratic party. His role in the administration seemed to further demonstrate Nixon's hope for receiving southern and Democratic party support in 1972. In early 1973, Connally joined the Republican ranks. Texas, being a critical state in any national election, could become a swing state in a close election. Nixon's further interest in capturing Republican support in fast-growing states was apparent in Kleindienst of Arizona replacing Mitchell of New York as attorney general. With the resignation of Hickel of Alaska as interior secretary, he picked Morton of Maryland. Already the political role of that state was known following the vice-presidential selection in 1968. Other replacements in the cabinet indicated the place of the midwestern states or "heartland" in Nixon's strategy. Butz from Indiana replaced Hardin, also from Indiana, as secretary of agriculture; and Peterson of Illinois became a replacement for Stans of Minnesota as secretary of commerce.

PRESIDENTIAL RECRUITMENT AND TICKETS

Presidential Selection. The thirty-seven presidents who have served the United States since 1789 have come from only fourteen states.[10] The geographical recruitment for these leaders is further restricted when it becomes apparent that twenty-two came from only four states and all these are in the northeast quarter of the nation. New York is the leader with seven followed by Ohio (six), Virginia (five), and Massachusetts (four). Three other states (Tennessee, Illinois, and California) have had two of their members serve as president.

Prior to 1900 the pattern of presidential selection reflected Virginia, Ohio, and New York with five, four, and four members each. Ohio did not have a presidential candidate until 1840 but it had four from then to 1900. Since 1900 there has not been any one state clearly dominating the picture. New Yorkers have been elected three times and on two occasions presidents have been elected from Massachusetts, Ohio, and California. The presidential recruitment picture from a geographical perspective reflects a strong orientation toward the major populated states, the richest industrial states, and the earliest settled ones. The West, Southwest, Midwest (except Ohio), and South have been poorly represented in the White House occupancy.

The vice-presidential representation has some striking similarities to those of the chief executives. The forty that have served came from nineteen different states. Ten have come from one state, New York. The dominance of this state in presidential and vice-presidential selection is attached to its political clout, which is basically a reflection of its industrial and population strength. New York vice-presidents were more important in winning-ticket combinations last century when nine of its ten were elected. This century only Indiana and Texas have had more than two vice-presidents elected. The overall pattern of these second-in-command leaders from Vice-President Adams to Ford reflects a favoritism toward the Northeast and Midwest. States in the South, West, and Southwest have not been successfully represented in a sizable number serving in the first or second highest elective office.

Balancing Presidential Tickets. Probably nowhere is the notion that "geography" plays a role in the recruitment and selection of politicians greater than in the presidential–vice-presidential teams nominated by the major political parties. This widely accepted view is not without substance even on the part of party politicians. Political leaders, political commentators, and the public citizenry are seen trying to match up geographical "opposites." Behind this rationale is a belief that the presidential and vice-presidential candidates must represent different constituencies and therefore different regions in order to be successful nationally. Without this broad geographical support, which is supposedly reflected in "North-South" or "East-West" or "big states vs. small states," is the belief that combinations of this nature are essential to winning. It is not only believed that these bonds in themselves will insure a national winning combination but the belief that the party strength and regulars in certain states merit placing one of their candidates before the national electorate.

In examining this notion in a political geography vein, we are interested in seeing whether there indeed has been some "geographical balance" practiced in the candidates selected by the Republicans and the Democrats. If indeed there has been, it should become apparent in an examination of the states these candidates represent. We desire to know what kind or kinds of geographical balance have been exhibited, that is, specifically what states and regions are most frequently represented by Republican and Democratic party candidates. In all likelihood, it is expected that certain states and regions are probably more frequently represented than others from previous discussion on recent presidential recruitments. Finally, in view of the traditional images and support for the two major parties, we are interested in finding out if there are any differences in the "balancing" patterns. Population shifts and ideological changes might be expected to be reflected in the teams selected.

The states represented by the presidential and vice-presidential candidates of the two major parties in this century are used to examine the notion of "geographical balance."[11] First, the Republican party tickets demonstrate a general East-West or more specifically a Northeast-Southwest axis for the nineteen elections held since 1900 (Fig. 4-6). In the elections early this century the candidates came from only three states, New York, Indiana, and Ohio. The five elections from 1900–1916 were all represented by a New York candidate, either as a president or vice-presidential candidate. This Northeast or New England and Midwest "balance" remained intact until Hoover's nominations in 1928 and 1932. His entry represented a distinct shift to the West, as he represented California and his running mate was from Kansas. The 1936 election brought back the midwestern states into the nomination picture. However, New York again appeared as the state representing candidates in the next three elections. In three of these the western stronghold of California was matched with the Empire State. In the 1948, 1952, and 1956 elections, the Republicans attempted to represent the two major population nodes by an East and West balance on their tickets. The West has been represented on all tickets since then, three times by Nixon from California and once by Goldwater from Arizona. Their vice-presidential candidates have all come from distinctly eastern states, Massachusetts, New York, and Maryland. In summary, the Republicans have shifted their geographical balance from Northeast-Midwest candidates to those representing the West and Northeast. This shift is seen as a way to hopefully capture some major populated states and regions plus have the candidates representing different philosophies and constituencies in a winning combination.

The Democratic party tickets reflect somewhat different balances (Fig. 4-7). Like the Republicans, their early nominees tended to reflect the Northeast, at least by having New York and New Jersey represented. However, Nebraska, West Virginia, Indiana, Illinois, Ohio, and Arkansas (both rural and urban states), were also represented. The combinations that were most frequent included Nebraska, Indiana, and New Jersey. With the nominations and elections of F. D. Roosevelt from 1928 to 1944, New York was represented. His vice-presidential candidates, aside from his selection of an Iowan candidate in 1940, began a shift to the South. The second slot on the ticket went to a southerner or Border state Democrat in 1928 (Arkansas), 1932 and 1936 (Texas), and 1944 (Missouri). The strength of the South was considered essential to any Democratic attempt to retain the White House. Roosevelt's pattern of combining a large industrial state and the rural South brought him and his party victories from 1928 through 1944. Subsequent presidential candidates from 1948 to 1964 continued the North-South combination. This is observed in the strategy of Truman, Stevenson, Kennedy, and Johnson. The pattern was broken in 1968 and 1972 when the party nominees came from midwestern and northeastern states. The overall pattern reflected in the party's tickets this century has been a Northeast-Midwest as well as a North-South pattern. Candidates for these two highest elective offices came from rural and urban states of the Northeast and Midwest until Roosevelt's candidacy. With his tickets and those in subsequent elections until 1968, the Democrats played a North-South

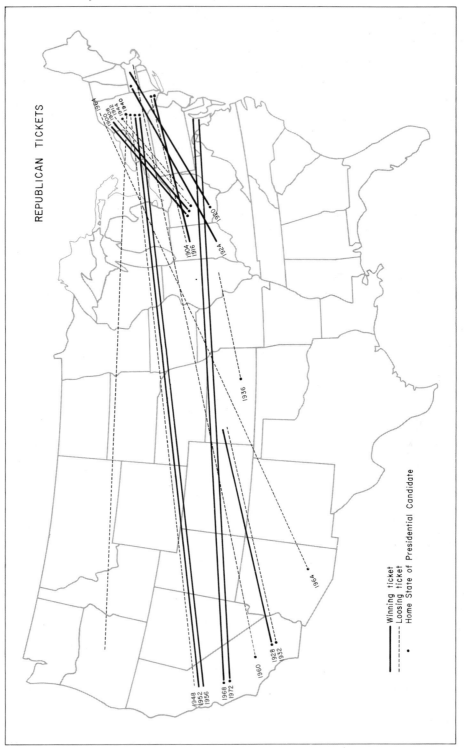

REPUBLICAN TICKETS

Winning ticket
Loosing ticket
Home State of Presidential Candidate

Fɪɢ. 4-6 Geographical Balance in Presidential–Vice-Presidential Tickets, 1900–1972: Republicans.

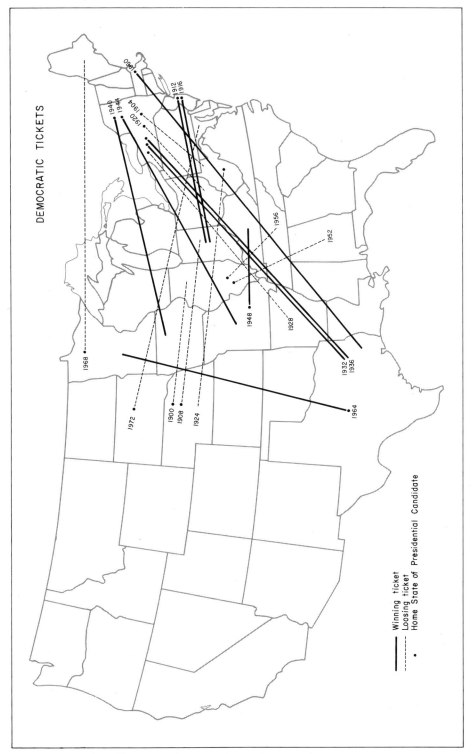

Fig. 4-7 Geographical Balance in Presidential–Vice-Presidential Tickets, 1900–1972: Democrats.

balance. In the two most recent elections the states represented took on the appearance of the party's early "balances" of this century.

In comparing the Republican and Democratic party nominations there are some striking similarities. This is especially observed in the number of candidates coming from New York and secondly from selected midwestern states, especially Ohio, Indiana, and Illinois. These seem to be key states for selecting candidates as their populations alone almost necessitate their winning for the candidate wishing to hold the White House. The contrasts between the two parties may be more meaningful in understanding the parties' ideology and notions of winning combinations. This is especially observed in the representation of California by the Republicans. In eight elections this century either a presidential or vice-presidential candidate represented this state. The Democrats have yet to nominate a candidate from this state this century. A second major contrast is the representation of the South. The Democrats have had a southerner or Rim or Border state member on their ticket in eight elections while the Republicans have yet to nominate one. The Nixon selection of Agnew of Maryland as representing a "southern" state is not considered as such here. In summary, both parties have viewed the industrial Northeast and prosperous rural and urban Midwest states as prime places to recruit or nominate presidential and vice-presidential timber. In this regard both parties were in substantial agreement early this century. Later, the Democrats used the South and southern candidates to increase the chance of winning and in the process avoided the West. The Republicans at the same time avoided the South and concentrated on the West, especially California.

What is equally as meaningful as examining those states that have been represented on the tickets since 1900 is to look into regional or state combinations that have brought victories. Consistent winning combinations are as important as losing ones. This is not to place undue emphasis on the state itself that the candidate represents. Yet presidents and vice-presidents are often nominated or selected on the basis of their state and surrounding ones which share similar views on national and international concerns. A national political party is built on sectional differences that have some underlying common social or economic denominators. For the Democrats the most successful combination has been one that has included Texas. A president or vice-president from Texas has not been on a losing ticket since 1900. (Both parties are aware of the importance of capturing this state both in the electoral and popular vote. The two most recent elections are cases in point.) Likewise, the success of a New York candidate should be mentioned even though F. D. Roosevelt was the single major candidate in four elections. Other states where a candidate has been nominated more than once and won are New Jersey, Indiana, and Missouri. Losing states for the Democrats this century are Illinois and Nebraska where on more than one occasion the candidate nominated has lost.

The Republican winning combination seems to include California. This again is due to Nixon being twice a winning vice-presidential candidate and twice the victorious presidential candidate. Ohio and New York are other winning states, and often the winning combinations early this century. The GOP has been success-ful on separate occasions in having a candidate from Massachusetts, Illinois, and Indiana; in other elections candidates from these same states were on losing tickets. Maryland has had a candidate successful twice, Agnew in 1968 and 1972. For the most part early elections were won with a New York and midwestern state com-bination and later with an East-West combination.

FOOTNOTES

1. Robert Sherill, *Gothic Politics in the Deep South*, New York, Grossman, 1968, p. 240. Reprinted by permission of Grossman Publishers.
2. Roger E. Kasperson, "Ward Systems and Urban Politics," *Southeastern Geographer*, 9:2 (1969), 17–25.
3. Mike Royko, *Boss, Richard J. Daley of Chicago*, New York, New American Library, 1971.
4. Kevin R. Cox, *Conflict, Power, and Politics in the City: A Geographic View*, New York, McGraw-Hill, 1973.
5. State of Ohio, Secretary of State, *Official Roster, Federal, State and County Officials, 1971–1972*, Columbus, 1972, pp. 98–99.
6. *Statistical Abstract of the United States, 1972*, Washington, D.C., Department of Commerce, 1972, p. 372.
7. *1973 World Almanac*, New York, Newspaper Enterprise Association, p. 795.
8. Ibid., pp. 768–772.
9. Ibid.
10. John Nathan Kane, *Facts About the Presidents*, New York, Wilson, 1959.
11. Ibid.

Chapter 5

POLITICS
AND
DECISION-MAKING

Washington is a city of southern
efficiency and northern charm.

Arthur M. Schlesinger, Jr.

Many of the public institutions and facilities that dot the map of a city, state, or nation are in that particular place because of political and geographical considerations. While there is a demand for such services, the decision of where to locate that institution or facility may not be reflective solely of economic or social considerations. The facility may appear to be in a reasonable place today; such may not have always been the case. Political power or clout in the form of an influential citizenry, lobby, politician, or organization may have been involved subtly or openly in the eventual decision regarding location. Also, regional political and rural and urban rivalries may have been involved in the competition for luring prize public facilities. Public institutions and facilities that were needed by the society, but not wanted by certain groups, may even have been forced on locations and groups with little or ineffective political influence.

An analysis of the decision-making processes behind the selection of most municipal, state, and federal institutions often reveals that a number of alternative

100

sites initially were considered. This holds true for defense installations, federal military centers, state capitals, and state prisons, as well as expressway routes, post offices, fire stations, and drug rehabilitation centers in urban areas. The final decision may have been made by one individual, or by a common vote, or even by a legislative body. Such may offset any seemingly sound economic rationale for comprehending a particular location decision.

Locational factors, whether considered in a haphazard or a serious fashion, are involved in locating any public facility or institution. Rare indeed are examples where the city or town selected or the specific route taken or land parcel purchased for locating a facility was a random event. Political forces enter the picture when the decision makers themselves examine their political space and recommend or place facilities within certain parts of it. Their awareness of the importance of that institution, the type of facility, the people directly affected, and the effects of that facility on the total population illustrate the role of politics, economics, and geography in the process. While in some cases the decision makers may reveal their spatial preferences (city, state, or national) by considering and recommending specific locations for public facilities, the final decision may represent more political than economical considerations. For example, the decision to recommend locating a proposed state capital in a central location may be turned down when another city offers free land for the capital's construction. The landing of a state or federal installation may be considered a prize if it be a military base or veterans' hospital or a university. On the other hand, the awarding of a penitentiary or a sewage treatment plant or a fire station or a missile base may not be wanted by the community, even if the politician does. However, if the people affected by the site selected are not organized or vocal, the decision makers may simply "give it" to them because no one else wants it and it needs to be placed somewhere. The leader knows that locating undesirable facilities and services in parts of space where opposition is minimal is sound geographic and political strategy.

The geography of political decisions involves the role that space plays in the decision-making process. Space is comprised of land area, resources, and people. These together represent power in social, economic, and political terms.[1] These elements of space are viewed differently by those recommending and making decisions as to where to place public services, facilities, and installations. Some spaces or areas are considered highly desirable by members of a decision-making body, be it a city council, state legislature, or congressional committee. Other spaces are not viewed in as positive a light except as locations for facilities that are considered undesirable. A city or state or federal decision-making body may look at space and attempt to "fill" it with public facilities, that is, award some (desirable or undesirable) to each section of a city, state, or nation. This is in line with disbursing public monies in the name of public facilities throughout the population. On the other hand, the same committee or commission may exercise favoritism by awarding only prize facilities and services to some parts of space and not granting any to others. Here again the political strength of the opposition political party or the powerlessness of specific groups may result in their having no public facilities and installations except maybe those that could be located nowhere else. It is significant in comprehending the knowledge of an area's and people's geography that decision makers may suggest the likelihood for selecting a particular location for a public installation solely on the basis of sound economic grounds; however, political power in the hands of a mayor, a legislative chairman, a governor, or a president may override any attempt to provide a meaningful rationale for the decision.

Competition between points or areas in space is often evident in the location of public services. In part this is true of the jobs and money and possibly prestige that an institution or facility brings. The awarding of prize or amenity facilities may go to those who are the most powerful in terms of monies, population, or political strength. Other competitive locations (that is, other parts of a city, state, or nation) may have to be satisfied with those of lesser significance or maybe none at all. In such cases it is difficult to assess the spatial dimensions of political power. It may be made more difficult because of the supposed objectivity that has taken place in the decision-making process. It is also quite possible that the decision process has had such apparent political effect that one is led to believe that certainly other more substantive considerations must have been used in selecting a particular site.

Realizing that politics does play an important role in the location of public services and facilities, a number of institutions and facilities are examined at the urban, state, and national levels. Selected examples of installations and facilities are used to illustrate the combined role politics and geography exert on the patterns of public site selections. People, land, resources, and power are all basic ingredients that are involved in public decision-making policies.

URBAN FACILITIES

A metropolitan area includes a variety of public facilities and institutions. These represent various municipal, county, state, and federal agencies (Table 5-1). The location pattern for certain of these facilities is to serve the entire metropolitan population, such as with parks, police protection, fire coverage, and post offices. These would be more numerous than those public services that would serve a more limited clientele, as for example, social welfare offices handling social security, food stamps, and unemployment compensation. On the other hand some public institutions would be limited to only a few in a large area. Airports, museums, and waste disposal sites are cases in point. The spatial patterns for public services are likely to be reflective of the demand for that particular service or facility. This is seen in the distribution of various public services in Baltimore (Fig. 5-1). While post offices and libraries would be expected to be roughly approximating a pattern similar to population density of the entire metropolitan area, federally financed day-care centers and various Office of Economic Opportunity offices are reflective of the lowest socioeconomic sections.

TABLE 5-1   Public Facilities and Offices in Major Urban Areas

Municipal	County
Schools	Court House
Day-care Centers	Jail
Police Precinct Stations	Waste Disposal Sites
Fire Houses	Hospitals and Clinics
Libraries	Morgue
Museums and Art Galleries	Rehabilitation Centers
Neighborhood Service Centers	Parks
Parks, Pools, Golf Courses	District Courts
State	Federal
Social Welfare Services	Army Recruiting Station
National Guard Armories	Navy Recruiting Station
State Liquor Stores	Air Force Recruiting Station
Highway Field Offices	Post Offices
Correctional Centers	Selective Service Offices
Community Service Offices	Social Security Administration

While public facilities are considered essential to the normal functioning of any city, where they are located often reflects internal political and geographical considerations as well as their utility. In specific instances it may be that the representative of a particular suburb on a city council or a key businessman on the planning or zoning board may eventually decide where the expressway will be routed and where the new parks will be developed. Some public facilities are strictly amenity facilities, such as golf courses, that is, they lend color and value to the residential area. On the other hand, others are considered noxious facilities. They degrade or downgrade the land values and reputation of a neighborhood or section of a city. The placement of a garbage dump or an incinerator or a fire station in a city is an example. As mentioned previously, where to place such a facility within the metropolitan area may be attributed to the powerlessness of certain residents, usually the poor. They not only lack political expertise but also frequently representation on the key zoning, planning, and governing boards.

Involved in the placement of public facilities in urban spaces are a number of spatial criteria other than the distribution of power. Among these would be the distances of a facility to an adjacent or similar one, the distance the clientele must travel, the mode of transportation needed to reach that particular facility, and lastly, the actual or expected demand for that service. It would make little sense to locate a state office giving planned parenthood information in an area of low fertility or a social security office in a youthful suburb. For this reason spatial

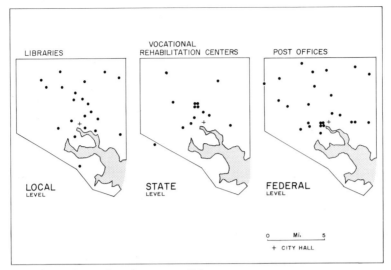

FIG. 5-1 Public Facilities Location in Baltimore.

strategies are being used to locate or even concentrate public services in optimum places. As a recent study of San Francisco has demonstrated, the search for a least cost-accessible site serving a large catchment area has been involved in the concentration of services in a single location. Even the actual site has affected the efficiency of the operation and the availability of its services to poverty neighborhoods nearby.[2]

The decisions of where to locate public facilities are not infrequently divorced from private landholdings and institutions. Museums and art galleries as an example are usually only few in number within a metropolitan area. They are usually located in the immediate vicinity of the central business district. This downtown location is considered an optimal area of maximum accessibility for the entire population as well as the clustering of adjacent facilities and institutions. Specialized municipal public institutions are often associated with other state or federal government facilities such as libraries, parks, office buildings, churches, auditoriums, and historical residences. This provides a setting amenable to locating cultural institutions.

Sports complexes and stadiums are often located adjacent to the central business district as they require easy access to the expressways that link the suburbs and downtown. Also they are located on cheaper land (if not now then at an earlier time) that is characteristic of the transitional CBD (central business district) areas. The construction of larger stadiums by municipal and state-financed bonds has either resulted in rebuilding in the downtown location or relocating in the suburbs. The high costs of downtown locations (plus possible neighborhood deterioration) and the lures of cheaper suburban lands have resulted in a number of professional teams moving outside the central city. This represents a move to the future markets. City-suburban politics are not without a major role in the decision to remain in the city or to move to a new suburban location. Examples of this are illustrated by stadiums built or being planned in Foxboro (near Boston), Bloomington (outside Minneapolis-St. Paul), Hackensack Meadows (outside New York City), and Pontiac (outside Detroit).

Similar political and economic decisions are involved in locating major public institutions, such as universities and colleges. The decision where to locate the Chicago campus of the University of Illinois was beset by the political maneuvering of Mayor Daley and several suburban communities. Initially it was proposed the campus be constructed in Miller Meadows, a county forest preserve in the suburbs. Here the land was cheap and the site was accessible for many potential commuting students. However, opposition came from various quarters so the board of trustees of the University of Illinois had to consider other sites, among them Garfield Park. Mayor Daley, hoping to draw the campus into Chicago, agreed the city would defray any extraordinary costs of other sites if the institution were located in the city limits. He pushed for a near west side location, an area that was in need of urban renewal. By employing various strategies that worked to the immediate advantage of Mayor Daley and the enhancement of his supporters, his preferred site along the Congress Expressway was chosen. The location of this institution serves as an example of how sheer urban politics and major financial interests are involved in the actual decision where to locate a major public facility.[3]

The increased social and political awareness of many central city residents since 1965 has resulted in a number of areas in cities challenging existing political forces. At issue are the decisions imposed on communities to locate a noxious facility in their neighborhood. In Philadelphia the Crosstown Expressway is one example where the local residents banded together and successfully opposed the construction of an expressway that basically was to serve suburban residents. In a nearby area of the same city the residents of Germantown were not as successful in halting the construction of a development project. When they finally learned of its construction, they were powerless to stop it (Fig. 5-2). Similar examples can be cited from other urban areas where the residents and advocate planners have had varying degrees of success in halting public service projects and recommending alternative locations or doing both. The kink in I-94 routed through Nashville is an example where land developers bought land and sold it for the Interstate. This kink is in the middle of the black area and was planned without knowledge of the local residents.[4] Additional examples can be cited from other cities where transport lines have been located to split homogeneous neighborhoods and thereby sever the cultural interaction. Airport expansion also has recently come under attack from environmental groups because of the heavy vehicular traffic and aircraft noise associated with it. Where to build city or regional airports has become a critical decision facing planners, especially with the increased demands for air services. The traffic volume merits either expanded construction at the present site or the erection of an entirely new facility. The consciences of many suburban residents have been pricked and the formation of influential citizen lobbies has made suitable construction sites difficult to find.

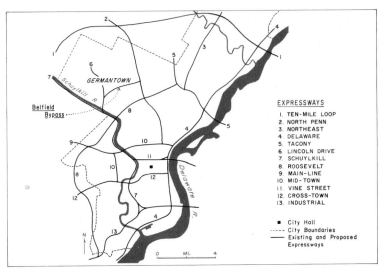

EXPRESSWAYS

1. TEN-MILE LOOP
2. NORTH PENN
3. NORTHEAST
4. DELAWARE
5. TACONY
6. LINCOLN DRIVE
7. SCHUYLKILL
8. ROOSEVELT
9. MAIN-LINE
10. MID-TOWN
11. VINE STREET
12. CROSS-TOWN
13. INDUSTRIAL

■ City Hall
----- City Boundaries
—— Existing and Proposed
     Expressways

FIG. 5-2 Proposed Transportation Routes in Philadelphia. (After Julian Wolpert et al., *Metropolitan Neighborhoods: Participation and Conflict Over Change*, Commission on College Geography, Resource Paper 16, 1972, p. 28. Reproduced by permission of the Association of American Geographers.)

The use of public monies to construct services and facilities available to the entire city or metropolitan region is frequently faced with geographical ramifications of the economic picture. Admittedly police and fire stations are essential but noise and traffic associated with them often give them a noxious label. Fumes and odors from public as well as private installations are often strong from sewage plants, garbage dumps, or incinerators. These are definitely undesirable facilities. If the city government and planners deem that an additional number of these facilities are needed, the possible sites considered will suggest something about the preferred locations for that facility. Poor black or Chicano areas may be the prime targets for placing incinerators, interchanges, and expressways. On the other hand quiet middle- or upper-income residential suburbs may be considered the best place to use monies for a new playground or municipal golf course. Even if the demand for such a facility is greater in the inner city, it may not be placed there because of suburban citizen pressure or because of the majority votes of suburban council members.

In allocating funds for the construction of public services and facilities, the point is that not all parts of urban space are considered equally in the decision processes for public facilities. Some sections of a city may be historically associated with noxious facilities, hence the feeling may be that they should still be placed there. For some urban projects there may be competition for funds, for example, urban renewal schemes. Should the monies be used in Model Cities programs to tear down low-income black housing and erect high-rise office buildings for suburban employees and executives or should new low-cost apartment buildings be constructed? In specific cases there is frequently competition within a relatively small section of a central city. Whether funds will be spent clearing a five-block area in its entirety or using the same funds for piecemeal and sporadic construction over a fifteen-block area is a decision that has spatial and usually political ramifications. In constructing amenity facilities the competition is often between suburbs. Which will be awarded the new city swimming pool and park or library or new school is one decision that often reflects basically political power and clout of individuals and groups, not necessarily current demand.

Political power is important in urban areas and is often reflected in the location of public facilities occupying small or large amounts of space. Those groups who are organized can either thwart a particular plan, most often expressways or an airport, or can lobby for a certain installation such as a park or school. Those citizens and groups by their influence affect positively and directly the development of their neighborhood and community. Those who are unorganized or poorly so often are the pawns of the planners and council. The mayor and city council are aware of the political variations of power within cities and their decisions or recommendations are often made with their geographies in mind. The spending of monies for programs and the location or relocation of needed public facilities basically involves spatial decision-making. Similar strategies also exist at state and national levels when planning the location of public facilities and institutions.

STATE INSTITUTIONS

Each state has established a number of public facilities and installations that are designed to serve its residents. These include a variety of state parks, colleges and universities, and correctional institutions. The location of these facilities becomes critical when the nature of the clientele is considered. That is, parks and public recreation sites are selected that are within easy reach of the metropolitan population as well as those with some natural beauty and pleasant environmental setting. On the other hand, the location selected for a particular facility such as a women's reformatory or mental hospital or state penitentiary may be in a small isolated town. Such a place may have been picked in order to shield the urban residents from the inmates. Often the location of institutions such as the state capital or major state university, or for that matter many other public installations as well, were made last century in response to rural or political power or both. Therefore, the site today may seem difficult to rationalize. Removing major public facilities from present locations is not an easy task. Several states have suggested relocating the state capital to the major urban center in part if not *in toto*. Florida is one example where the past decade has seen a number of legislatures suggesting the removal of the capital from its panhandle location in Tallahassee to centrally located Orlando. Major population shifts, societal demands, and economic growth have been reflected in the increase in certain public institutions, junior colleges for example, throughout a state. A number of states, such as California, Illinois, and Florida, with extensive community college systems have attempted to establish one within an approximate hour's driving time of most state residents. This strategy has led to the dispersal of public institutions to large and small, rural, isolated, and urbanized counties throughout the state. In Pennsylvania, for example, although the largest number of state-owned and operated facilities is located around Philadelphia and Pittsburgh, the smaller and isolated counties have some as well (Fig. 5-3). There are often political considerations involved in locating a park, a hospital, or a college. Any state facility or installation, whether an amenity (college or park) or of a noxious (prison) variety does bring in public monies and jobs. Many state commissions and legislatures have as one of their unwritten goals to distribute the public monies for installations and employment throughout the state. In this manner, by "filling in" the political region with public facilities, the state's citizens can reap the advantages of the money generated elsewhere in their state.

Three major state institutions are selected for an analysis of their location strategies: state capitals, the major state university, and the state prison. No matter whether the decision-making facets are examined for these public institutions last century or this or for southern or western states, the patterns are similar. Political considerations of a geographic nature often overrode any apparent sound economic or demographic rationale. Probably this is expected as these public institutions would be expected to have powerful political implications.

Capitals. The decision where to locate a state's capital was one that involved combinations of political skullduggery, rival sectional interest, and big city battles. The final decision was not always easily reached; in some cases it was made by the state legislatures, in others by a special commission, and in still others by a popular vote. Often a particular city or site was selected because it was the then or expected-to-be largest city. In many cases the decision was made to locate the capital in the approximate geographic center, whether there was a settlement there or not. This way all residents would have equal access, at least theoretically, to the central locus of state government.

A number of states especially in the eastern half of the United States considered a geographical center as a significant rationale for locating the capital. Pennsylvania is a case in point where Harrisburg finally was awarded the prize in 1812 but this was after it had been earlier in Philadelphia and Lancaster. The decision to move the capital west of Philadelphia was partly in accord with the westward movement of population as well as an attempt to remove some of the power from the eastern city. When Philadelphia lost the capital, its domination of state politics also ceased. There had been earlier attempts to remove the capital in 1784 and 1787 but both had failed until the 1799 move to Lancaster.[5]

In Ohio a central location "on the east banks of the Scioto, opposite Franklintown" was agreed on as the permanent site.[6] This site is presently

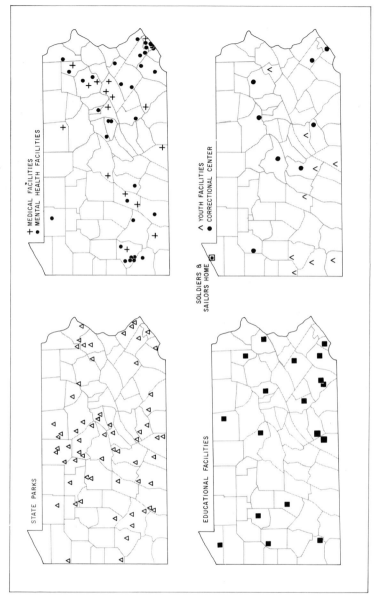

Fig. 5-3 Pennsylvania: State-Owned and Operated Facilities, 1952.

Columbus. Earlier, from 1803–1808, the capital had been in Chillicothe. When the state was founded in 1803, it was agreed that Chillicothe would only be a temporary capital. It remained there until the citizens of Zanesville petitioned for it. Legislative sessions met there from 1810–1812 after which it was again moved to Chillicothe. Finally the present site in Franklin County was approved by the legislature after a recommendation by a central Ohio county representative. Columbus became the capital in 1816. Later attempts to remove it from the present location failed.

The Michigan constitution of 1835 stated that Detroit or another city would serve as the capital until 1847. Then the state legislature was to decide on a permanent location. Detroit was the early state capital, as it was in the Michigan Territory, but of the many towns considered for the permanent location, it was not one. It was rejected because the city was considered "at the mercy of the enemy's guns in case of war."[7] In the 1847 legislature a number of cities were considered besides Detroit. They were Ann Arbor, Jackson, and Marshall. Ann Arbor was not seriously considered as it already had the state university and Jackson had the state prison. Three reports on a permanent site were debated by this governing body. One recommended the capital be located away from the Michigan Central Railroad (that ran through the southern part of the state) and not in one of the four above-mentioned cities, but in a place that would "consider the true interests of the state and the whole state, now and hereafter."[8] The second report by Pierce of Marshall favored his home town, which happened to be the site of the state land office. The third report by Goodrich of Genesee County favored a central location in the lower peninsula. He did not name a particular city, but cited the central location of Columbus, Ohio, as a rationale for a permanent site. Some considered this Lansing location as a joke as it was then an unknown wilderness. "The Lansing of war times had the advantage of being located at the geographical center of the lower peninsula, and the disadvantage of not having as yet emerged from backwoods conditions."[9] The Lansing township site was passed by the House, but southern interests attempted to defeat it in the Senate. The decision was made when the combined vote of the central and northern legislators prevailed.

There have been three capitals in Illinois, but many more locations were considered before the final site was selected. Kaskaskia was the territorial capital and was the first state capital when Illinois joined the Union in 1818. When this Mississippi River town was the capital, there were only three counties in the state. In 1820 the capital was moved to Vandalia, a town located on the Old National Road that was important in westward settlement. "In one small wagon, and at a single load, the entire state archives were transported to Vandalia."[10] Illinois then had nineteen counties. Other cities springing up around the state soon realized the importance of capturing this political plum, and in 1834 the state residents voted on six cities. The top three cities received over 7000 votes: Alton (7514), Vandalia (7148), and Springfield (7044). However, the capital did not move to the river town of Alton as the Springfield delegates, one of whom was Abraham Lincoln, at subsequent legislative sessions sought to obtain the permanent location. The General Assembly of 1837 and 1838 considered a number of cities, more hamlets than genuine urban nodes. On the first ballot, Springfield received the most votes but not enough to win as other river towns on the Wabash, Ohio, and Mississippi rivers sought the capital (Fig. 5-4). The earliest growth in the state, in the southern half, was reflected in the prospective sites. Finally, on the fourth ballot, Springfield

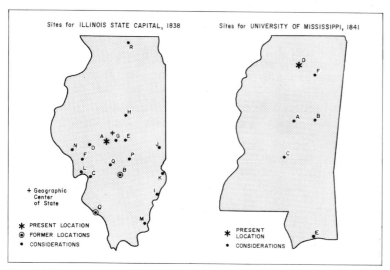

Fɪɢ. 5-4 Prospective Locations for the State Capital of Illinois and the University of Mississippi.

received the necessary votes. The state then had 72 counties; today there are 102. When the city was awarded the capital it had only about 1000 residents, but the residents did agree to donate 2 acres of ground for the capitol facilities.[11]

A central location was specifically an issue in the final decision to locate capitals in Oklahoma and Tennessee. The territorial capital of Oklahoma was in Guthrie, near the center. When the state constitutional convention met in 1906, it proposed to locate a new state capital at a place called New Jerusalem no farther than 5 miles from the geographical center of the state.[12] But the decision would not be made until 1913. It was Guthrie's aim to stall as long as possible a removal of the capital. However, Oklahoma City, its chief rival, encouraged El Reno, Enid, Granite, and Shiatook to get into the act. Part of this strategy was to encourage rivalries. The ultimate decision was made in a statewide referendum in 1910 when Oklahoma City (92,261 votes) won easily over Guthrie (31,301 votes) and Shawnee (8,383 votes).[13] Only reluctantly did Guthrie relinquish its government functions as many offices remained for several months after the election. The state supreme court even voided the election. In the midst of this post-election controversy, some state officials signed documents in both state capitals to be sure their actions were legally binding. Similarly political rivalries were also apparent in attempts to locate the Tennessee state capital in Nashville. This was seen as a central site between the two warring factions (east and west); Nashville also had advantageous turnpike and steamboat facilities that served the prosperous Nashville Basin.[14]

The decision in some states boiled down to a contest between two major cities. A popular election was held to decide the Kansas capital in 1861. Topeka, long a rival with Lawrence, won over Lawrence, Leavenworth, Emporia, and Baldwin City. Some real politicking was involved in the Kansas debate on the site selection.[15] In Wyoming only two cities were in competition for the capital. Cheyenne was awarded the government seat and Laramie the university. In Nebraska, the first state capital was at Omaha, which had been the territorial capital. Soon after statehood, Bellevue (near Omaha) contested the decision as did the powerful South Platte Democratic legislators. Lands were sold to locate the capital in the southern part of the state primarily because the South Platte area had more people. The capital commission in 1867 recommended the capital be located in the village of Lancaster but they renamed it Lincoln. The South Platte representatives objected to the name Lincoln in part because of early and strong Republican support in the Omaha area. They finally approved the new label out of sectional loyalty and were awarded the state university and state penitentiary in Lincoln as well.[16]

The mobility of early legislative sessions is illustrated by the search for the North Carolina capital. New Bern was the capital during the colonial period and remained so until 1778. The westward population movement brought about pressure for a more western location. Fayetteville, Tarboro, and Hillsboro hoped to land the permanent site. In 1781 the capital moved to Hillsboro but opposition to the city soon developed when the governor was taken prisoner by the Tories. During the ensuing years the seat of government became very transient. It met in Hillsboro again, Halifax, Smithfield, Fayetteville, New Bern, and Wake Court House. The issue was finally settled at the Hillsboro Convention of 1788 when it was proposed the capital be located at a place near the center of the state and within 10 miles of Isaac Hunter's plantation in Wake County. About half of the commission voted against the place; they considered it unsuitable for commerce. Instead they preferred Fayetteville. After still more wrangling the land was purchased in 1792 in accord with the majority's view. In the city that developed, Raleigh, the streets were laid out and named for the four judicial districts in the state, for the commissioners, the directors, and other state assemblymen.[17]

Because not all sites selected to be the seats of state government existed at the time the decision was made, dispute often arose over the name given to the city. The town of "Michigan" was used in early references to the central site that had been selected. When the state House passed on the Lansing township site it proposed "Aloda"; the Senate called the tract "Michigan." It also proposed "Okema," the Ottawa word for chief or head. A joint committee came up with "Algoma" as well as other names, Houghton, Huron, and Harrison. Finally, Lansing was chosen. The Oklahoma convention in proposing a capital recommended New Jerusalem. This would have placed it near the present town of Britton in Oklahoma County. In Texas the new lands picked for developing the state capital were named in honor of the Mexican War hero, Stephen Austin. North Carolina's capital was named for the early English settler, Raleigh. Lincoln was given to Nebraska's new capital even though the Democratic legislators objected. In this case they agreed to the name rather than risk losing the capital site.

Universities. Aside from the state capital, the state university was probably the second most important political prize a city or a region could be awarded. Similar geographical and political reasons were considered in the final sites selected. Some were decided by state legislatures and others in rather unusual and obscure circumstances, such as the decision made in Billups' Tavern to locate the University of Georgia at Athens in Clarke County. Often the rivalry between two major cities or regions in a state was settled with each receiving a major state institution. This was true for Wyoming and Kansas. The rivalry between sections of a state was intense in some states, for example, east and west Tennessee and north and south Idaho. In the eastern third of Tennessee, long the political power, the land grant establishing the University of Tennessee was given to Knoxville. Eventually the west was awarded the medical and dental schools when they were moved from Nashville to Memphis. Similar regional rivalries existed in Idaho when the north demanded the university after the capital was moved to the south. Today the major state university is in Moscow located in the panhandle while the capital is in Boise.

Some cities became the sites of the major state universities because of some rather peculiar circumstances. Fayetteville, Arkansas, voted $100,000 and guaranteed a number of buildings to locate that state's university. This town had an educational history as it was the home of Arkansas College and a seminary. Little Rock, the capital, lost out to Fayetteville when the citizens, in disgust with the governor, refused to allocate the $200,000 in necessary bonds.[18] The University of Illinois' location in Champaign County is attributed to the powerful political influence of Clark Robinson of Urbana. He was a former Massachusetts lobbyist who moved west and promoted railroads in Illinois. Benjamin Thompson in 1892 gave the state of New Hampshire half a million dollars to establish a college of agriculture on his farm in Durham. Prior to this the state university had been in Hanover.

The Mississippi state legislature decided by a vote in 1841 that Oxford would be the site for the state university. Oxford was in competition with a number of other cities or towns (Fig. 5-4). Oxford won on the sixth and last ballot by one vote over Mississippi City.[19] The North Carolina state charter stipulated that the state university be "fixing on and purchasing a healthy and convenient situation, which shall not be situated within five miles of the permanent seat of government or any other place of holding the courts of law or equity."[20] The site selected was near the geographical center of the state at a place called New Hope Chapel. Today it is called Chapel Hill.

The role of politics and economy was particularly important in the case of the Midwest where state universities and state capitals were often located in their present sites for somewhat unusual reasons. Also the specialization and prosperity of the states in question were instrumental in the rivalries that developed and the political strategies and intrigue involved in decision-making. This has been commented on by geographer Hart who states:

> The size and prosperity of the Middle Western states have fostered the growth of the cities which contain their state capitals and state universities. The two

functions are combined in Minneapolis-St. Paul, Columbus, Lansing, Madison, and Lincoln; Indianapolis, Des Moines, and Springfield are state capitals; and Ann Arbor, Champaign-Urbana, Columbia, and Lafayette are state university towns. The growth of such places to metropolitan size is ironical, because our forebears hoped to protect the weakest and most susceptible members of society (legislators and students) against the snares and temptations of the wicked and sinful city by locating the capital and the state university as far away from it as possible in a setting of rural purity. Jefferson City, Iowa City, and Bloomington have managed to retain their nonmetropolitan status, but many of their denizens seem to find this no special cause for jubilation.[21]

Some major state universities are presently located in the capital city as the above quote indicates. Outside the Midwest the major university may be located in the state's largest city which may or may not be the state capital, such as the University of Hawaii in Honolulu (capital), the University of New Mexico in Albuquerque, the University of South Carolina in Columbia (capital), the University of Utah in Salt Lake City (capital), the University of Washington in Seattle, and the University of Rhode Island in Providence (capital), and the University of Vermont in Burlington. While it might appear to be sound strategy to place the major state university in the largest city, there are ample examples where the major campus is in a small city and perhaps even isolated part of the state. Often such decisions reflect the political and economic power of early agricultural or mining interests in legislative bodies. Some of these today are primarily university towns, for example, Fayetteville, Arkansas; Boulder, Colorado; Storrs, Connecticut; Gainesville, Florida; Athens, Georgia; Moscow, Idaho; Urbana, Illinois; Bloomington, Indiana; Iowa City, Iowa; Lawrence, Kansas; Orono, Maine; College Park, Maryland; Oxford, Mississippi; Amherst, Massachusetts; Durham, New Hampshire; Chapel Hill, North Carolina; University Park, Pennsylvania; Vermillion, South Dakota, and Morgantown, West Virginia. Numerous other examples of public colleges and universities in these states and others can be cited where the education facility is the major raison d'être for that city today.

Prisons. State prisons and penitentiaries (and even prison work camps which can still be found in some southern states) tend to be located in one of three sites, the capital city, the largest city or a large city for that state, or in a small town. Frequently the small towns are isolated from the major population clusters. Thus safety of the majority of the population is assured. The advantage of locating the prison in the state capital was that trained personnel could be attracted and also that other related state institutions and facilities were often located there. The concentration of the prison and the capital in the same location also helps the city to be identified as a distinct governmental node for that state's residents. Examples where the two are combined include Ohio (Columbus), Nebraska (Lincoln), North Dakota (Bismarck), Idaho (Boise), Tennessee (Nashville), Oregon (Salem), New Mexico (Santa Fe), Missouri (Jefferson City), South Carolina (Columbia), Virginia (Richmond), and New Jersey (Trenton). Some states have these two functions and major state universities in the same city.

Prisons are also found in large cities in some states, often but not necessarily the most populated. This is observed for the state of Michigan (Jackson for southern and Marquette for northern Michigan), Rhode Island (Warwick), Illinois (Joliet), Indiana (Michigan City), Maryland (Baltimore), South Dakota (Sioux Falls), and Alaska (Ketchikan). Some smaller cities where penitentiaries are found are in Iowa (Ft. Madison), Oklahoma (McAlester), and Wisconsin (Waupun).

The view shared by some early legislators and citizens, most often those of powerful political and social and economic clout, was that prisons and similar "obnoxious" institutions should be in small towns in isolated parts of states far from the city population. This is apparent in the prisons in Georgia (Reidsville), Kentucky (Eddyville), Florida (Raiford), New York (Attica), Wyoming (Riverton), Montana (Deer Lodge), Vermont (Windsor), and Maine (Thomaston). Many of these are not only some distance from major urban centers but are located on minor state roads. Smaller towns near larger ones, such as in West Virginia (Moundsville) near Wheeling and Connecticut (Somers) near Hartford, are other examples of strictly prison towns.

FEDERAL INSTITUTIONS AND INSTALLATIONS

The federal government with its varied programs and policies has established a number of institutions and facilities that are designed to either serve the entire population, such as veterans' hospitals, or a specific group, such as Indians. The spatial pattern of federal facilities may be spread randomly throughout the nation as is the case of nuclear power installations, spread uniformly with respect to the population distribution as is true for federal hospitals, or concentrated in a particular region or group of states such as military training centers. Some of the same strategies used in locating certain state prisons and correctional institutions are illustrated in the sites selected for federal installations. For example, small isolated towns are the sites of some federal penitentiaries (Lewisburg, Pennsylvania, and Marion, Illinois), federal reformatories (Alderson, West Virginia), and the national leprosarium (Carville, Louisiana).

National parks and national monuments are most numerous in the western states primarily because of the large amounts of federally owned land. This made it possible to set aside rare and prize scenic, geological, and unique biological environments. Twenty-five of the thirty-eight national parks are in the western half of the nation; over half (forty-two) of the eighty-two national monuments are in Arizona, New Mexico, California, and Colorado.

The actual reasons behind the location strategies for certain federal institutions and installations may be economic or environmental, but political favoritism exhibited by government leaders and committees and lobbies to a district, state, or region may be the primary reason. Political considerations were doubtless paramount in the location of the National Aeronautical and Space Administration's manned space flight center going to Houston, Texas. This multimillion dollar enterprise being awarded to Texas was considered the enticement that led Lyndon Johnson to agree to serve as President Kennedy's vice-presidential candidate in the 1960 election. If the center had not gone to Texas, it would probably have gone to the Goddard Space Center in Maryland. Other examples where politics have been important in the construction of federally sponsored facilities were in the laying of railroads last century, such as the routes chosen across the Rocky Mountains.[22] Often the routes selected and cities linked were more tied to who held the land for speculation and to local or state political clout than strictly economic considerations or terrain limitations. The present-day rail network nationally and regionally is characterized by examples of routes that today seem unrealistic. Many of the cities that were the beads on these strings are not important economically today. The interstate highway system laid out since World War II is another example of a system that was not originally destined solely to serve as a vehicle for rapid economic development or to facilitate cross-continental access to prime tourist and recreation states. Local and state politicians, together with land speculators (often one and the same), were often responsible for the specific routes taken, the cities linked, and the number of interchanges. A primary purpose of the interstate system was designed to help the Department of Defense move men and matériel to locations anywhere in the nation in case of an emergency. Both the railroads of last century and the highways of this one have helped tie the nation's space together. This is one of the goals of government projects, that is, to establish federally financed projects throughout its space that can make the nation a more compact unit for settlement, economic, or defense purposes.

Often the location of a federally financed project involves the consideration of a large number of possible sites. Such is the case with the awarding of a $375 million atom smasher to the hamlet of Weston, Illinois (350 population) in December 1966 by the Atomic Energy Commission. One of the major reasons given for this choice was the proximity of adjacent science institutions, such as Argonne National Laboratory in nearby Lemont, and major universities in the Chicago area. Initially more than 200 localities in forty-six states were considered. The attraction of trained professionals and technicians and the multimillion dollar payroll stimulated the competition for this federal installation. The final list of six sites included Weston as well as Brookhaven, New York; Ann Arbor, Michigan; Madison, Wisconsin; Denver, Colorado; and Sacramento, California. One major reason given for selecting a Midwest site was that the region's scientists and politicians had felt slighted in the nation's share of atomic facilities.[23] Other reasons given for selecting this hamlet 30 miles west of Chicago were the proximity to a major transportation hub, flat terrain, inexpensive land, and plenty of water. When it was announced that Weston had been selected, the community quickly passed a fair housing ordinance in order to be in accord with federal housing guidelines. Just how much politics played in the selection of the Illinois location is difficult to determine except it bears mentioning that of the six states involved in the final consideration, only Illinois was to have a Democratic governor beginning in January 1967.[24]

In an effort to assess some of the political strategies behind locating federal installations and institutions, a select number are treated. Among those examined are the nation's capital, Indian reservations, containment camps, military institutions, national defense installations, and various nuclear projects.

Site of National Capital. The influence that a major institution, such as the national capital, has on a particular region and the nation is dependent partly on the historical and cultural development during the time of its selection. This image even carries forward to the present day. Washington, D.C., being in an area of historical importance to the development of the United States, early acquired an influence that was more akin to the Middle Atlantic States and New England than states along the Atlantic coast immediately to the south. The views of independence for the nation shared by the early legislators and their views on the rights of men and the limits and role of government early gave the nation a philosophy based on morality, equality, and justice. These views prevailed in later times. The earliest settlers as well as those that came after the Revolution lent further support to the progressive philosophy that was emerging.[25]

Before 1800, Congress met in eight cities: Baltimore and Annapolis in Maryland; Lancaster, Philadelphia, and York in Pennsylvania; Princeton and Trenton in New Jersey; and New York City. Some of these same cities (as well as Boston, Massachusetts; Williamsburg, Virginia; Wilmington, Delaware; Reading, Pennsylvania; Newport, Rhode Island; and Kingston, New York) were hopeful of landing the site for the emerging nation's capital. Discussions on the site ultimately boiled down to northern vs. southern interests, especially among Virginians. Prime locational considerations were a site somewhere between New Hampshire and Georgia (the settled area) that was on a navigable waterway and that provided easy access to the Alleghenies and beyond. Northern representatives did not wish to locate the capital in a slave-holding state; they were opposed mainly by supporters favoring a site in Virginia. Madison, Jefferson, and Washington all promoted a site on the Potomac River, which was finally approved in 1790 by the acquisition of land from Maryland and Virginia. This was only supported after Jefferson received enough votes for the federal government to assume the state war debts in exchange for a southern site for the capital.

Today, Washington, D.C., is considered on the southern margin of the progressive quarter of the nation. It retains, even as it did early, a strong ideological image probably akin more to New York, Boston, and Philadelphia than to Norfolk, Raleigh, Atlanta, or Charleston. Yet it retains an image that blends the cultural and social geographies of more distinctly identified regions to the north and south. The representatives and senators coming to cosmopolitan Washington from all sections of the nation are not beyond being influenced by the prevailing philosophies of the city itself.

At issue here is the effect of the site for the federal capital and the surrounding area on the decisions rendered by the Congress. Ideally the nation's capital represents a political no-man's land or a political node where all parts of the nation's philosophy are merged. Yet the place carved out to be the national seat of government is not isolated; it occupies a place within a larger space, namely, a political region, that has its own cultural and political heritage. This is reflected in the view of many government employees and spokesmen and the molders of public opinion. If the nation's capital were ever moved to another location, a thought expressed not infrequently, such as St. Louis or Chicago or Denver or Houston or Atlanta or Los Angeles, the political philosophy of that area would doubtless be reflected in the views expressed in the decisions reached by Congress or the Supreme Court as well as the news media coverage of legislative actions on the economy, society, and international politics. The location of the nation's capital on the eastern seaboard and the historical development of the nation also illustrate the closer social, economic, and military ties to Europe than Latin America or Asia.

Indian Reservations. The federal government's decision to place Indians on reserved lands last century had strong underlying political as well as social motives. Distinct geographical locations and environments were apparent in the lands set aside for these native Americans. The location of present-day reservation spaces compared to the original tribal territorial claims (that once approximated 2 billion acres) reveals that besides their lands being drastically shriveled in area, they were pushed and placed on lands considered undesirable for white habitation and development by Washington and state and territorial officials. Today, Indians occupy lands only about 3 percent the size of their original lands. The Indians, not having a voice in the land they claimed, were at the whims of often unconcerned but powerful military and smooth-talking government officials. All too often decisions made in distant Washington were made by officials unfamiliar with said lands. The reservation sites selected for the peaceful as well as the warlike Indians were hot, dry, and rocky and in uninhabited and isolated parts of the West. Their distant location from whites was to insure that mingling with them would be at a minimum. Frequently the Indians were found to be occupying valuable agricultural and mineral land. They were moved and then moved again en masse, often against their will, to new locations that would insure a life of poverty would continue and that spirits would be debilitated. Nearly 400 separate treaties have been made with Indian nations, some more than once, in the past two centuries. They were broken almost as soon as they were made.

The Indian population today is approximately 800,000, less than 1 percent of the total population.[26] Nine states have over 20,000. Arizona and California have the most with over 90,000 each followed by New Mexico with 72,000 and North Carolina with 44,000. The states of Washington, South Dakota, New York, Montana, and Minnesota have between 20,000–35,000 Indians.

Indian reservations vary in size from twelve that are over 1 million acres to many less than 1-square mile (Fig. 5-5). Of the 56 million acres of reservation land, the largest reservations in area are in the western states. The largest, both in area and number of residents, is the Navajo reservation in northeast Arizona with

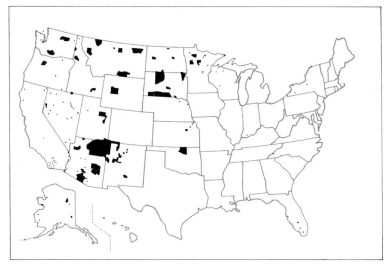

FIG. 5-5 Indian Reservations. (U.S. Department of the Interior, *National Atlas of the United States*, Geological Survey, Washington, D.C., 1970.)

almost 14 million acres and 120,000 population. Many of these large units have only a small population. The second largest reservation is Pine Ridge in South Dakota with slightly over 10,000. Ten other reservations have between 5,000–10,000 Indians (Table 5-2). Of the 245 Indian reservations located in thirty states, the leading states with numbers of reservations are California (65), New Mexico (25), Washington (22), Nevada (21), Arizona (16), Minnesota (11), and Wisconsin (10).

Their present location in rural areas has contributed even to this day to their culture of poverty and their isolation from the mainstream of American life. The location on these reserved lands far from the major national and even state population clusters has meant the residents have become more and more separated from the changes that are occurring in society. Those Indians who have traveled to cities, such as Denver, Minneapolis, Phoenix, and Los Angeles, for a brief period have found the "world" a place very different and often not to their liking. For this reason and others, many young Indians have returned to the rural reserves as the place of solitude. The federal policy to restrict their livelihood to certain pieces of undesirable real estate has made it very difficult to earn a living from agriculture. The Soil Conservation Service of the Bureau of Indian Affairs estimates that of the 56 million acres of Indian reservation lands today, 14 million are critically eroded, 17 million severely eroded, and 25 million slightly eroded. Most of these lands are in scrawny grasslands and dissected terrain. Some are even leased to white ranchers as these are federal lands. Indians farm presently only about 6 percent of their land and most of that dry-farm agriculture is lacking in water for irrigation.[27]

Political forces were involved in the federal government's removal and

TABLE 5-2   Largest Indian Reservations in Population

State	Reservation	1969 Population	Land Area (acres)
Arizona	Navajo	119,546	13,989,212
South Dakota	Pine Ridge	11,151	2,778,000
Arizona	Gila River	7,555	371,933
South Dakota	Rosebud	7,181	978,230
North Dakota	Turtle Mountain	7,037	70,240
Washington	Yakima	7,010	1,095,236
Montana	Blackfeet	6,220	906,441
Arizona	Papago	6,216	2,855,240
Montana	Ft. Peck	6,000	964,864
Arizona	Ft. Apache	5,885	1,664,872
Arizona	Hopi	5,846	2,472,254
New Mexico	Zuni	5,128	407,247

Source: U.S. Department of Commerce, *Federal and State Indian Reservations: An EDA Handbook*, Washington, D.C., Economic Development Administration, 1971.

dispersal of Indians in the past two centuries. If specific Indian tribes and nations were on valuable fishing, hunting, or agricultural territory, they were either displaced by treaties or forcibly evicted by the military, often in accord with state or congressionally approved legislation. Indians were almost always moved to lands that were worse than those that they occupied originally. Even these spaces gradually decreased in size with the actions of greedy land developers and ambitious government officials.

The classic case in American history of mass Indian removal was engineered in the 1830s when the federal government in accord with southern states moved the Five Civilized Tribes from Florida, Georgia, Alabama, and Mississippi to Oklahoma Indian Territory. The Choctaws, Cherokees, Creeks, Chickasaws, and Seminoles were forced to move because the states and covetous white developers wanted their lands. The federal government had made treaties with these nations to preserve their claims but it also authorized "exchanges" of land. The Indian Removal Bill passed in 1830 by Congress initiated these wholesale land exchanges. When the states failed to honor Indian claims to lands in their states, the Indians were shipped or sent or marched to the then unwanted desert lands farther west. The removal of these civilized tribes to Oklahoma is one of the sorriest human stories in the nation's history.

The Oklahoma settlement and resettlement story is repeated throughout the history of the Great Plains, West, and Southwest.[28] The political and military maneuvers used to evict Indians often saw them transported across half a continent and during the winter season. Moves more than once were not uncommon for many nations during the 1830–1870 years. Such wholesale removal efforts from original Indian-claimed lands are behind the grievances of various Indian groups today. Some are attempting to air the grievances by preparing lengthy legal briefs to win hopeful court approval and others are engaging in more militant actions such as the takeovers at places like Alcatraz, Wounded Knee, and abandoned military posts.

Japanese Containment Camps. The major example of removal and relocation of groups in this century involved the Japanese-Americans in World War II. Soon after the bombing of Pearl Harbor in December 1941, the West Coast population began to develop a fear of further Japanese sabotage and destruction, both from within and without. The Japanese, in California especially, had an impact on the economy that went back to the last century. They had been instrumental in laying railroads and in developing some of the state's prize agricultural lands. However, once the fear of Japan and the Japanese-Americans was instilled, it intensified and the resulting hysteria diffused to nearby coastal Oregon and Washington. Mayors, civic leaders, and even state officials such as then attorney general of California, Earl Warren, were fearful of the destruction that the first- and second-generation residents might bring to power installations, airports, railroads, and the cities. The Tolan Committee developed as one of its goals to identify the location and property of all Japanese residents.[29]

It was the Tolan Committee that recommended evacuation of the West Coast Japanese, a project that when accomplished sounded strikingly similar to the Indian removals engineered by the federal government last century. The Japanese descendants, about 70,000 who were United States citizens, were taken without legal petitioning of their grievances and with little or no provisions to sixteen Assembly Centers in the West and Southwest. Thirteen of these Assembly Centers were in California and the remaining three in Oregon, Washington, and Arizona. Most of these reception centers were racetracks, fairgrounds, livestock pavilions, or abandoned CCC (Civilian Conservation Corps) camps. From these reception centers they were removed to ten War Relocation Centers in 1942 (Table 5-3). These ten sites were located in very isolated sections of western states and in places that had unusually inhospitable desert environments. In these containment camps over 100,000 Japanese-Americans lived in very crude living quarters until the termination of the war.

Military Institutions: Academies and Training Centers. Soon after the Revolutionary War, Commander in Chief Washington and other generals realized the need for a school or academy devoted specifically to the training of personnel for the nation's army. Land armies were considered the backbone of the nation's defense against Indians and outside aggressors. Congress in 1777 adopted a measure creating such a military academy. A site then had to be selected. One that received early and popular support was West Point on the Hudson River in New York State.

TABLE 5-3 Relocation Centers for Japanese-Americans During World War II

Place	State	Capacity
Manzanar	California	10,000
Tule Lake	California	16,000
Poston	Arizona	20,000
Gila River	Arizona	15,000
Minidoka	Idaho	10,000
Heart Mountain	Wyoming	10,000
Granada	Colorado	8,000
Topaz	Utah	10,000
Rohwer	Arkansas	10,000
Jerome	Arkansas	10,000
	Total	119,000

Source: Allan R. Bosworth, *America's Concentration Camps*, New York, Norton, 1967, p. 120. Copyright © 1967 by Allan Bosworth.

To General Washington this was one of the key fortresses during the Revolutionary War; few other sites were even given serious consideration. A historian in commenting on the selection of this site states:

> The West Point site was singled out for its economy and convenience; its buildings had been maintained and a small garrison was maintained there after independence had been won. The choice was a fortunate one, because the isolation of the spot, its rugged natural beauty and its historic associations all made positive contributions to the development of the Academy.[30]

The United States Military Academy was established there in 1802.

The earliest navy training operations were conducted in conjunction with the armed forces. Some training was performed at an asylum in Philadelphia. The War of 1812 showed to the president and his key generals the importance of naval power for the protection and security of an emerging continental and eventual world power. The need for a specialized academy for training personnel for specific naval tasks received support from Congress but it was not until 1845 that an academy was formally established. The then secretary of navy, George Bancroft, who had been the founder of the Round Hill School in Northhampton, Massachusetts, made the decision to locate the academy in Annapolis. In writing about the selection process, a naval historian comments that:

> Some opposition to the school resulted from rivalries for its location in particular places. The Military Academy was in the North, and in Congress there had been

a feeling that the Naval Academy should be located in a southern state. The Maryland legislature had previously petitioned Congress to establish the Academy in Annapolis. By 1st June, Bancroft had decided upon Annapolis. . . .[31]

The air force did not have its own academy until 1955. The decision to locate in Colorado Springs was made by secretary of the air force Harold Talbott. This site and others had been recommended to him by a specially created commission. Initially 365 proposals were considered, but after careful scrutiny the list was reduced to seven sites. Other than the Colorado Springs site, the commission recommended Camp Beale, California; Madison, Indiana; Charlotte, North Carolina; and three sites in Texas at Grapevine, Grayson, and Randolph Air Force Base.[32] The full Senate and House committee hearings on the creation of the academy contain the dialogue between Secretary Talbott and various representatives about the criteria he considered in selecting a site. Aside from locating the academy in a place where pilot training could be conducted, the secretary was interested in a small community, about 10,000 population, near a larger city where the enlisted men and families of the personnel could participate in recreation and community activities.[33] Several senators, especially Senator Lyndon Johnson of Texas and Senator Richard Russell of Georgia, both on the Senate committee, requested their states be given serious consideration. However, political considerations were apparently not involved in the secretary's final decision. At one stage in the hearings, Senator Russell queried the secretary about the selection process:

> Senator Russell: Is it contemplated that there will be any regional or geographic limitation put on as to whether these sites will be considered that have been submitted?
> Secretary Talbott: No, I don't believe so. I think some may automatically—if you consider Limestone, in northern Maine, for example, where we have had such terrific snows all winter; it just eliminates itself. Other than that, I don't think there is any limitation.[34]

Finally, Talbott decided upon the present site near Colorado Springs. The bill that Congress passed creating the establishment of an academy specified that the final site would be made by the secretary himself after reviewing the recommendations of the aforementioned commission.

In summary, the military academies were created when Congress felt that specialized training for naval or air force operations was necessary for the nation's defense and security. The sites selected for the three major academies involved historic and regional (geographic) considerations. Such were apparently more important in the final site selection than overt political pressures from congressmen or presidents or even generals and admirals.

Military training centers seem to reflect more political influence than other installations for the army, navy, and air force. In part this is because there are more and also the influence of individual congressmen needs to be considered. The political ties come from being on the key House Armed Services Committee where seniority has brought many southern representatives in the past several decades to either head the committee or be among its high-ranking members. In 1972, of forty-eight primary military training centers, thirty were located in the South. The leading state was Texas with ten; South Carolina, Florida, and Alabama each had three (Fig. 5-6). Outside the South, California is the leader with seven.

These centers for the training of military personnel are political plums for any senator or congressman as they contribute to his political prestige regionally as well as contributing financially to the economy of local areas in his state. The spillover effects of military installations are often substantial even though they are primarily restricted to the immediate area surrounding the base. Many of these bases are foci of "wealth" in otherwise poor rural areas. Aside from the regional and political strength of such congressmen as L. Mendel Rivers of South Carolina and Carl Vinson and Richard Russell of Georgia, the South offers an amenable year-round physical environment that enhances the training of army, marine, naval, and pilot personnel. Certainly one of the better examples of political influence exerted in locating military facilities is that of former Congressman L. Mendel Rivers of Charleston, South Carolina. As former chairman of the powerful House Armed Services Committee, his district had an air force base, coast guard base, army depot, marine barracks, naval base and shipyard, and a veterans' hospital.

A pleasant climate coupled with a variety of terrains and some sparsely inhabited and inhospitable segments enhances the training in southern states and California. In some areas the physical environment is such that training for tropical warfare is best gained at bases located in Georgia, South Carolina, Florida, and Alabama. Such were considered simulations for the conditions expected in Vietnam, Laos, Cambodia, and Thailand.

Parris Island, South Carolina, near Beaufort, proved a successful location for training marines because of its isolation from the mainland and a varied tropical terrain of marshes and tidal flats. This entire facility as it now stands was developed from scratch. The marine corps facility in Quantico, Virginia, was developed after the Philadelphia Naval Yard proved too small. As one writer has commented on the marines' needs:

> A tract having suitable terrain of both artillery and infantry was essential, and it was desirable that it could be readily reached by transport vessels. Such a supposedly suitable area was found at Quantico, Virginia, about 40 miles below Washington on the Potomac River.[35]

Both bases at Parris Island and Quantico became important training centers for European campaigns by the time of World War II.

Defense Installations. As a part of the national defense system, missiles are placed in crucial locations that will protect the nation as well as be in a position to retaliate in case of an emergency. The actual location of strategic missile sites suggests that several geographic considerations were involved in the air force bases

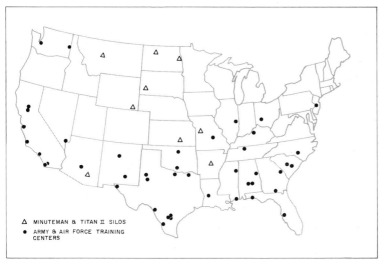

Fɪɢ. 5-6 Military Training Centers and Missile Bases. (U.S. Department of Defense, 1971.)

specifically designated to handle long-range land-based missile systems. Minuteman missile locations and Titan II silos are found in nine locations.[36] Their pattern suggests the importance of an interior continental location and a very sparsely populated area (Fig. 5-6). Strategic missile sites that are deep in the interior of North America suggest they would receive ample warning time from peripheral continental warning stations such as from the DEW (Distant Early Warning) network on the northern borders of Alaska and Canada. In the event of a missile strike aimed at one of these missile locations or a major industrial-population node, there would be ample time to launch antimissile missiles or other warheads against the enemy. Attacks from aggressors would be much easier if the bases were located on the East or West Coast. The number of sites in the northern half of the United States suggests the attack would most likely be expected from a nation hurling missiles over the North Pole region and across Alaska or Canada, or across both en route to the major populated areas.

In May 1972, President Nixon signed an agreement with the Soviet Union restricting the building of the Safeguard ABM (antiballistic missile) installations. The treaty stipulated that each nation was limited to only two such installations. One was to be in the area of the nation's capital. Originally the United States had planned to build two, one in the Washington, D.C., area and the other at Grand Forks, North Dakota. However, later the Department of Defense decided to construct a Safeguard ABM facility only at the North Dakota location.[37] In location terms, Grand Forks is located approximately in the center of the North American landmass. Further, it is not near a major population center. The reason for deciding on this site was in part because of its location advantages in the event of a first strike as well as the fact that construction was already under way when the treaty was signed.

A sparsely populated and continental interior location are two primary geographical considerations that are apparent in the location of military facilities other than strategic missile sites. The NORAD (North American Air Defense Command) established in Cheyenne Mountain, Colorado, is another example. This subterranean city and defense post near Colorado Springs exercises control of the air defense system for the United States and Canada. The stable geologic structure of this part of the continent was an additional ingredient that influenced this location.

Similar criteria were used to select the small town of Park Falls, Wisconsin, as the initial site for Project Sanguine. The construction of this grid of underground communications antennae (100 by 70 miles) in Chequamegon National Forest (federally owned land) was to provide an instant communications network to all the nation's strategic military forces around the world, especially nuclear submarines. The reason for this defense installation being built in northern Wisconsin was its location in the middle of the United States-Canada landmass, making it least vulnerable to an attack on the continent. Also, the subsurface layer of dense rock in which the network was to be cased was satisfactory. The absence of major mountains nearby that tend to disrupt signals further made the site advantageous as well as its distance from industrial and heavily populated areas. While some of the area's residents initially expressed concern about what this facility might do to the natural environment, there was support for its construction in the congressional district that bordered the one held by Congressman Melvin Laird. He was secretary of defense when Project Sanguine was announced in 1969. In time the defense department had to abandon this Wisconsin site·in view of the protests of environmentalists, area residents, and state politicians. The chief concerns were the effect construction would have on the natural vegetation and the effect of radio signals on the local wildlife. Other sites had to be considered and one in Llano County, Texas, immediately northwest of Austin, apparently had the inside track as the subsurface geology fit the project, the population is sparsely distributed, and the residents were friendly. According to Congressman Fisher, whose district includes the county, "Down there, we are very conscious of the needs of the military. If Sanguine is in the natural interest, we would welcome it."[38] Probably sentiments about patriotism are involved in the final sites selected for major defense installations. However, this site was also abandoned due to local protests. By late 1973, sites in northern parts of Michigan, Minnesota, and New York were being considered.

Nuclear Testing, Stockpiling, and Dumping. Once the United States embarked on a program of manufacturing nuclear weapons, the decision had to be reached early where tests could safely be conducted. In the late 1940s the specific location for such testing aboveground or underground was not as critical as at present. The earliest testing was done on small government-owned or leased isolated Pacific Islands, or in the Yucca Flats testing grounds west of Las Vegas, Nevada. This state was selected for its sparse population and great distance from major population nodes (where radiation dangers from contamination might be high) and because the federal government owns most of the land. Similar reasons were behind using the White Sands proving grounds in New Mexico and the rocket and atomic laboratories of Los Alamos. When the federal government owned these lands, it meant permission from residents would not have to be obtained or that political protests could largely be discounted. In the early days of atomic testing there was general support for the development of nuclear weapons systems and little political concern about the actual sites themselves.

Since the 1950s, the proliferation of nuclear weapons and the possible resulting holocaust from the host of nations having adequate delivery systems have resulted in international disarmament conferences calling for the elimination of aboveground testing and the reduction of nuclear material production for military purposes. Furthermore, the environmental concerns of the past five years have questioned the safety of conducting even underground testing. This is not to mention the protests questioning whether tests are indeed necessary for the nation's security. Nevada, Colorado, and islands in the Aleutian chain off Alaska have been the sites for the most recent underground explosions. In these areas the concern was expressed by politicians and citizen groups that high levels of radioactive materials being emitted into the atmosphere would impose harmful effects on man, animals, plants, and the soil. The decision where to conduct such testing in safety and without protest has been primarily one to find places where the United States owned or had rights to the use of land. Many foreign governments have become increasingly skeptical of nuclear weapons testing and especially so in the light of environmental concerns and the belief that it further indicates a global military strategy. For such reasons remote locations far from major population centers have been selected, as in the Aleutian chain. Also, such places are less likely to attract opposition. Still, environmentalists from various parts of the United States and Canada, earth scientists, and some political leaders protested the 1971 decision to explode a five megaton H-bomb under Amchitka Island in the Aleutians. Their concern over the damage to the local flora and fauna as well as resultant earthquake damage in already earthquake-prone Alaska led them to question the necessity and timing of such an explosion. After legal battles had proved futile, the tests were conducted with little apparent damage to the physical environment.

An additional concern that has developed with the onset of nuclear power is what to do with the residual material that is produced at the same time. This atomic residue is worthless but highly radioactive. For example, the short- and long-term effects of "hot earth" on resident populations and agricultural land have been expressed recently in Grand Junction, Colorado, and Hanford, Washington. The problem the Atomic Energy Commission still faces, and probably one that many states and cities developing nuclear power installations will face, is what to do with this hot material. Because it is dangerous but worthless, the government searches for suitable locations to dump it. The public has become aware of this problem in the past year as environmentalists and politicians have tried to prohibit these nuclear "garbage" dumps from being located in several places. One site the AEC considered was Lyons, Kansas, a small middle western town of 5000 inhabitants about 50 miles northwest of Wichita. Lyons was selected as a dump site as it had deep abandoned salt mines that would act as a shield against possible radioactive leaks. Also the geologic stability of the area made it a likely candidate. Possibly this town was selected as it was far from major population centers and also political and environmental protests. If such was the case, the AEC was not successful as the town was able to get the commission to withdraw it from consideration as a dump site. Other likely places that may be considered for these atomic waste dumps may have characteristics similar to Lyons. It would seem that locating dumps in places far from possible radioactive damage to large numbers of people would indicate that sparsely populated portions of the South and mountain West would be seriously considered. The government decision to place waste materials in drums and sink them off the Florida east coast in the early 1970s drew protest from environmentalists and legislators who envisaged possible damage to the state's beaches, a major economic asset for the state. However, their protests proved useless except to arouse further the public's awareness of the dangers of atomic waste materials.

FOOTNOTES

1. Kevin R. Cox, *Conflict, Power and Politics in the City: A Geographic View*, New York, McGraw-Hill, 1973, pp. 71–104.
2. Paul D. Marr, "Functional and Spatial Innovation in the Delivery of Governmental Social Services," in Harold M. Rose and Harold McConnell, eds., *Perspectives in Geography 2: Geography of the Ghetto: Perceptions, Problems, and Alternatives*, De Kalb, Illinois, Northern Illinois University Press, 1972, pp. 225–238. See also Lawrence A. Brown et al., "Day Care Centers in Columbus: A Locational Strategy," Columbus, Ohio, Ohio State University, Department of Geography, Discussion Paper 26, 1972.
3. Roger E. Kasperson, "Toward a Geography of Urban Politics: Chicago, A Case Study," *Economic Geography*, 41 (1965), 95–107.
4. Julian Wolpert et al., *Metropolitan Neighborhoods: Participation and Conflict Over Change*, Washington, D.C., Commission on College Geography, Association of American Geographers, Resource Paper No. 16, 1972, pp. 27–43. See also Anthony J. Mumphrey and Julian Wolpert, "Equity Considerations and Concessions in the Siting of Public Facilities," *Economic Geography*, 49 (1973), 109–121.
5. Sanford W. Higginbotham, *The Keystone in the Democratic Arch: Pennsylvania Politics 1800–1816*, Harrisburg, Pennsylvania Historical and Museum Commission, 1952, pp. 333–335.
6. Daniel J. Ryan, *History of Ohio*, New York, Century History Company, 1912, pp. 147, 182, 427–449.
7. Charles Moore, *History of Michigan*, Chicago, Lewis, 1915, p. 412.

8. Henry M. Utley et al., *Michigan*, New York, Publishing House of Michigan, 1906, Vol. III, p. 291.
9. Moore, op. cit.
10. Randall Parrish, *Historic Illinois*, Chicago, A. C. McClurg, 1906, p. 311.
11. Ibid., pp. 303–317.
12. Gaston Litton, *History of Oklahoma*, New York, Lewis Historical Company, 1957, p. 525.
13. Ibid., p. 526.
14. Stanley J. Folmsbee et al., *Tennessee: A Short History*, Knoxville, University of Tennessee Press, 1969, pp. 205–206.
15. G. Raymond Gaeddert, *The Birth of Kansas*, Lawrence, University of Kansas Press, 1940.
16. James C. Olson, *History of Nebraska*, Lincoln, University of Nebraska Press, 1955, pp. 86–91 and 290–291.
17. Hugh Talmage Lefler and Albert Ray Newsom, *North Carolina*, Chapel Hill, University of North Carolina Press, 1963, pp. 243–345.
18. John Gould Fletcher, *Arkansas*, Chapel Hill, University of North Carolina Press, 1947.
19. Robert Lowry and Wm. McCardle, A *History of Mississippi*, Jackson, Mississippi, R. M. Henry, 1891, p. 424.
20. Lefler and Newsom, op. cit., p. 248.
21. John Fraser Hart, "The Middle West," *Annals, Association of American Geographers*, 62 (1972), p. 278. Reproduced by permission of the Association of American Geographers.
22. American Geographical Society, *The Golden Spike: A Centennial Remembrance*, New York, American Geographical Society, 1969.
23. "For the Midwest, A Scientific Plum," *U.S. News and World Report*, December 26, 1966, p. 6.
24. "Illinois, Near the Tree," *Time*, December 23, 1966, p. 21.
25. Wilbur Zelinsky, A *Cultural Geography of the United States*, Englewood Cliffs, N.J., Prentice-Hall, 1972, passim.
26. U.S. Department of Commerce, *Federal and State Indian Reservations: An EDA Handbook*, Washington, D.C., Economic Development Administration Handbook, 1971.
27. Stan Steiner, *The New Indians*, New York, Dell, 1968, p. 163.
28. Ralph K. Andrist, *The Long Death, The Last Days of the Plains Indians*, New York, Macmillan, 1970; and Vine Deloria, Jr., *Custer Died for Your Sins*, New York, Macmillan, 1970.
29. Allan R. Bosworth, *America's Concentration Camps*, New York, Norton, 1967.
30. Sidney Forman, *West Point*, New York, Columbia University Press, 1951, p. 3.
31. W. D. Puleston, *Annapolis, Gangway to the Quarterdeck*, New York, Appleton-Century, 1942, p. 50.
32. United States House of Representatives, Committee on Armed Services, *Full Committee Hearings on H. R. 5337, To Provide for the Establishment of the United States Air Force Academy, Hearings, 1953–54*, Eighty-third Congress, Second Session, No. 50, p. 3028.
33. United States Senate, Committee on Armed Forces, *United States Air Force Academy, Hearings, 1954*, Eighty-third Congress, Second Session, 1954, p. 29.

34. Ibid.
35. Clyde H. Metcalf, *A History of the United States Marine Corps*, New York, Putnam, 1939, p. 455.
36. U.S. Department of Defense, *Annual Report for Fiscal Year, 1968*, Washington, D.C., Government Printing Office, 1971.
37. "What the Treaty with Russia Does to U.S. Defenses," *U.S. News and World Report*, October 2, 1972, pp. 32–33.
38. "Defense: Wisconsin Gets Wired for Sound," *Business Week*, April 26, 1969, pp. 116–117, and "The Citizens vs. Project Sanguine," *Business Week*, August 12, 1972, p. 114.

Chapter 6

ORGANIZATION
OF SPACE

Legislators represent people, not trees or acres.
Chief Justice Earl Warren

Once man has acquired a piece of space, whether by exploration, conquest, or treaty or grant, some system is required that will separate it from adjoining spaces and segment it for purposes of internal organization and administration. At least this need for some spatial order is characteristic of the Western view of space where claims are made and lines are drawn on maps that divide and further subdivide that space into a numerous variety of units. At one end of the scale are the boundaries and lines that separate the nation from its contiguous neighbors while at the other extreme are lines placed on maps and demarcated in space that define personal property. Whether a survey system may have been adopted that uses simple geometry, that is, latitude and longitude coordinates, or features in the physical landscape, the objective is to facilitate the operations transacted within those macrounits or microunits by developing some spatial order of organization. These lines on maps are usually without observable consequence on the physical and cultural landscapes; yet often individuals, groups, and even political units attach emotional and moral feelings to these political or personal territorial units.

131

People may identify strongly with their state and know that it is different or maybe better from surrounding states because it has a different color on maps and globes they use. Many view spaces like Huck Finn who told Mark Twain as they were flying over the Midwest in their flying boat, he knew he was over Indiana as it was pink on his map and Illinois was green. Others identify their political space by street address or their elite suburb such as Grosse Pointe. They prefer to give that location than Detroit as it is likely to evoke a more positive response from listeners. Furthermore, when questions of personal property are involved, the residents assume this space is their personal domain. (This notion has already been treated in Chapter 3.)

Man has segmented and divided space for political purposes into so many units that problems have resulted in its administration and organization. From one political space have come other political spaces, some evolving into permanence, others dissolving and being reorganized. One of the reasons for the variety of political organizational schemes observed in the United States is that groups viewed, settled, and surveyed spaces in different ways. For example, there has been a lack of uniformity in the survey systems adopted. These were originally designed with varying degrees of success in settling rural areas; however, they were not as useful in organizing metropolitan regions. Few efforts have been successful to organize and administer the plethora of government units for the sake of efficiency. While one city may have accepted some form of consolidated metropolitan government, another city nearby, perhaps even contiguous in the same or adjacent state, may have found such a task impossible to achieve for political and legal reasons. Even with metropolitan organizational structures, there are often unincorporated suburbs that choose to remain outside a larger authority. On a map these units appear as holes in the metropolitan fabric, as for example, Highland Park and Hamtramck in the Detroit metropolitan area or Bexley in Columbus, Ohio.

In recent years the question of reorganizing political space has become a topic that county, city, state, and national leaders have begun to face. Such thoughts and schemes are not left to the utopian planners or radical politicians. The interdependence of man and his space with other men and other spaces often attains national and regional dimensions, as well as within the state or a city itself. This has signaled the need for consideration of alternative forms of administering and organizing these political spaces that handle public policies and services. Inequities in taxes, educational standards, criminal sentencing, and environmental quality ordinances, to name only a few, are frequently based on the boundary lines drawn by developers, planners, and politicians several decades earlier. Even the states find themselves losing much of their former identity at a time when regional and national programs and planning schemes disregard these supposedly defined boundaries placed in space last century and earlier. Even the ownership and utilization of property, once considered a most sacred right of all Americans, has lost much of its personal quality. In urban and metropolitan schemes that consider the use and misuse of spaces, the owner finds that he no longer can use or sell his piece of space, be it a farm or a residential plot, according to his own personal whims. More and more property is being considered as just another item of transaction in a service-oriented urban society.

The ways in which man segments and organizes his spaces for political purposes is a reflection of his own societal views or those of a particular group. While a general system may be adopted by society for segmenting space, whether based on geometrical coordinates or natural features or some combination, the actual division of space into the multitude of units can take on many forms. This is to say that by organizing space to satisfy his goals for organization and administration, man can also manipulate space. This can be performed by gerrymandering to help a political party or a specific urban development program or can involve enacting zoning policies to preserve a segment of space from certain external groups or noxious land uses. The manipulating of space illustrates that the spaces are not organized with the total society and its general welfare in mind. More often than not the manipulation of spaces, and the people and resources within them, are designed to retain in power a certain select group or to protect a certain group from being affected by undesirable groups or commercial and industrial enterprises. Once these shenanigans are exposed by a watchful public or opposition group they may be terminated, as in the case of excessive gerrymandering and malapportionment. However, both still occur but not as blatantly as earlier. In the case of zoning practices outlawing blacks or other minority groups from purchasing properties, once the United States Supreme Court stated restrictive clauses were unconstitutional, many cities and suburbs with such clauses, whether in the South, North, East or West, felt they lost an important exclusionary social protection right. Whereas earlier each city with such ordinances considered it could establish zoning restrictions different from its surrounding neighbors, the court ruling in effect placed all cities on an equal footing. That open housing became available in all spaces did not mean that blacks and other groups would flood to all-white suburbs or that zoning would be halted. The immediate result of the legislation and court rulings has been little black movement to suburbia. Zoning still occurs, with other rigid housing requirements being set, or by restricting severely the types of commercial and industrial developments for the given political unit.

ESTABLISHMENT OF POLITICAL SPACES

Land Survey Systems and Settlement. When the earliest European settlers were living on the East Coast, they soon realized the need for establishing some system for demarcating spaces for their farms, towns, and states. It was understandable that they would adopt a practice similar to what existed in Europe itself, namely, a system that used straight lines and natural features. The organization of towns in New England was based on varying-sized political units that were formed by straight lines. Beneath these were the farms that used various man-made features such as rivers, tree lines, mountain peaks and gaps, as well as roads and fence rows to delineate spaces.[1] This unsystematic reference system based on geometry and natural features was used in the original thirteen counties. In the Middle Atlantic states and the trans-Allegheny sections of Tennessee and Kentucky the metes and bounds system was used to organize counties. This is illustrated in the counties formed in Virginia, where rivers and access to water were a primary basis for the counties organized, and in Pennsylvania where the mountain ridges and valleys were used (Fig. 6-1). Problems arose in the colonies along the Atlantic that used the metes and bounds system. Rivers changed courses, fence rows were removed, trees felled, rocks moved and man-laid stakes were stolen or misplaced. Family, city, and even state controversies and armed battles, at times intense and lengthy, were the result of utilizing this particular survey system.

With westward settlement, beyond the Appalachians, politicians realized that another system needed to be implemented. With the Land Ordinance Act of 1785 a system was adopted based on meridians and parallels. This was first used in the principal states of the Northwest Territories. This cadastral system used elements of simple geometry and straight lines to set up newly settled lands for occupancy. The impact of this rectangular survey system affected the political, economic, and social organization of the entire region in question. The basic unit of this system was the township, a 6-by-6-mile spatial unit. Square-sized farm parcel sizes (40, 80, 160, 320, and 640 acres) were formed.[2] Streets, counties, and states had patterns that achieved a certain regularity. The outgrowth of this geometrical order in rural areas was a mosaic of checkerboard squares of varying sizes imprinted on the natural landscape. Once this system was adopted as national policy it was imprinted over flatlands, where it fit ideally, as well as over hilly land and water bodies. Homestead laws of 1862 and 1909 also specified the sale of lots in 160- and 320-acre plots. The federal government even tried to get the Indians to assimilate into the American system by passing the Dawes Act of 1887. This broke up their communal lands and settled them on 160-acre plots. This allotment scheme was very unsuccessful and was ended by the Wheeler-Howard Act of 1934.

A county outline map of the United States reveals the impress of these two land survey systems on the flatlands of the West Texas High Plains and mountainous eastern Wyoming (Fig. 6-1). For the nation as a whole, small irregular-shaped and sized counties appear roughly in the eastern third and geometrical-based lines, straight lines predominant, exist in the remainder. In the main this holds true for state boundaries as well as those for counties, even though straight lines formed the same state borders for some early colonies. Some colonial cities were also laid out in a rectangular fashion. There are many examples within each state where straight lines and the checkerboard pattern are often disrupted by a dominant natural feature, such as a river or a water divide. These provided convenient border limits. In general the later a state or territory was permanently settled the fewer the counties created. For example, Georgia, Iowa, and Washington are all of approximate equal size (55,000–65,000 square miles) yet they have 159, 99, and 39 counties respectively.

The survey system of square and rectangular units for farms, townships,

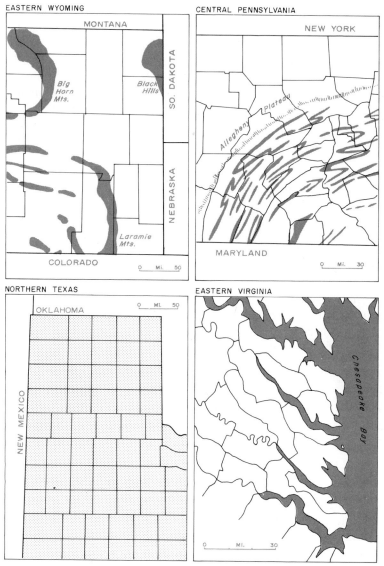

FIG. 6-1 County Outline Patterns in Selected States. (U.S. Department of the Interior, *National Atlas of the United States*, Geological Survey, Washington, D.C., 1970.)

counties, and states may appear to be pleasing as it is precise, logical, and orderly. This is partly because of the Western "container" view of space that finds a symmetry based on lines and straightness and squareness appealing and attempts are made to "fill it" by some systematic surveying scheme.[3] This survey system was not incorporated without some basic problems. Two that were especially perplexing to the surveyors, settlers, and politicians were the laying of this rectangular grid system over varying terrain and over previous territorial claims. It seemed to make little sense to carve out farm lots or mining claims, or for that matter even counties or states, in a terrain composed of hills, dissected plateaus, and mountains. Such a system may have been effective in helping settle and politically organize the flat Midwest states of Iowa, Indiana, and Kansas, but it made less sense when utilized in hilly lands in Wyoming, Colorado, and New Mexico. In such cases prominent landscape features such as mountain peaks, river divides, and channels would seem to have been favored over a system that attempted to arrange spaces solely on right angles. As a result, combinations of the above are evident in the present boundaries in several western states.

The second problem and one that was equally thorny involved juxtaposing any congressionally approved survey system with existing territorial claims. More specifically, the concern was using the metes and bounds system and the township and range system over original claims, either of other governments, Spanish or French, or on Indian lands. Once these lands became part of the territory of the United States, the survey systems already adopted elsewhere in settled areas were used to arrange and organize the spaces. This became a perplexing problem when the original residents of such spaces found their lands taken from them, in part because they were not powerful enough in a military sense to thwart the western expansion or because their mother country lost a war and hence their jurisdiction over said spaces. Also the issue became controversial when the native residents could not specifically identify their tribal lands and territory. The western settler was interested in permanent location and organization of space, not temporary. The geometrical view for surveying lands was easy and was exact, criteria that could not be applied with ease to the often inaccurate, haphazard, and ambiguous claims on lands granted by a Crown Government, or to an Indian nation's hunting and fishing territories. In cases in Florida, Texas, and New Mexico, the rectangular grid was simply superimposed over the Spanish land grants after scheming and greedy farmers, ranchers, and politicians usurped these spaces. While the political organization appears currently intact with the system imprinted last century or this, problems from the early surveys remain. More than one problem of a political, cultural, and legal nature has arisen historically and now more recently, questioning the abrogation of original Spanish or Indian claims by an external authority, namely, individual states or the federal government.

Just as there are variations in the schemes used to define and delimit the political organization for the states and counties in the United States, so are there differences in the way space is divided and carved up for political purposes within cities (Fig. 6-2). In some the pattern for electing city officials follows a pattern similar to the rectangular land survey system, that is, with an orderly and eye-appealing system of square blocks formed by the intersection of straight streets at

FIG. 6-2 Urban Political Districts. (After maps showing political districts, from *America Votes*, vol. 7, 1966, pp. 42, 185, 149, and 268.)

NEW ORLEANS WARDS

DETROIT WARDS

NEW YORK CITY ASSEMBLY DISTRICTS

Southern
LOS ANGELES
COUNTY
ASSEMBLY DISTRICTS

right angles. Other cities have shapes different in the central city and suburbs. Various manipulative schemes are frequently used by urban politicians in an attempt to either gerrymander out particular ethnic groups or racial groups or do the same for opposition political parties in order to give other spaces greater political strength than they might generally be expected to have.

Creation of Political Spaces. The original claims to new territories seldom are permanent as new and more settlers arrive who demand their spaces either be added to existing organizational units or that new ones be created. Particular religious, cultural, economic, as well as political motives develop that call for some representation separate from the mother country or from a colony with which they were originally identified. Such reasons were behind the creation of the thirteen original colonies. Although their desire for independence was a unifying thread, the states that formed were founded for a variety of reasons. Rhode Island, for one example, was a spatial refuge from religious and political persecution. Pennsylvania likewise desired religious freedom within its bounds. Massachusetts, on the other hand, with its puritanical view, drove independent-minded settlers elsewhere.

As the eastern seaboard became more populated in the seventeenth and eighteenth centuries, the population spread away from these initial commercial nodes to the rural areas in the interior. Here agricultural interests developed as did some small urban nodes. The increased distance from the original political nodes necessitated the creation of additional governmental units. This was seen in Virginia where the eight counties or shires created in 1634 proved insufficient to handle the colony's growing population as well as the movement farther west. This plus the feeling that a resident should not be more than a day's journey from a political node led to more counties being created.[4]

It was not only local governmental units that were in demand with the growing and dispersing population, but states as well. Maine, for example, was originally part of Massachusetts and Delaware part of Pennsylvania. These states were organized formally in 1820 and 1787 respectively. With settlement beyond the Alleghenies, a number of states laid claim to these then-unsurveyed lands. This led to conflicting claims, some that were not formally resolved until the following century. Claims for statehood were based on a feeling of second-class citizenship of the residents in part of a territory, as well as their having the required population base to merit joining the Union.

The present states of North Dakota and South Dakota represent a division of the Dakota Territory in 1889. Initial settlement in what is presently southeast South Dakota concentrated the political power there but when mining and agricultural interests developed farther north and west, so did new streams of population. Bitter rivalries developed between the southern part of the territory and the northern part, especially when the territorial capital was moved from Yankton to Bismarck in 1883. The territorial rivalries were really three, southeast Dakota Territory, the Black Hills mining interest, and the railroad interests in what is presently North Dakota. The location of the capital in Bismarck represented a victory for the northern and railroad interests over those in the south who could not agree on a capital relocation. The support for separate states along the forty-sixth parallel developed soon thereafter. Bitter struggles for the location of institutions within the territory resulted in a duplication of sets of mental hospitals, penitentiaries, universities, and agricultural colleges being built. Statehood finally came to the territory in 1889. Pierre was selected as the capital of the newly created southern state because it had a more central location and a former governor held valuable property there. Bismarck remained the capital of North Dakota.[5]

Political forces at the regional, usually North vs. South, as well as at the party level, Democrats vs. Republicans, were also involved in the order of admitting states. If the Republicans were in power they wanted few new states created last century that would be pro-slavery as well as enhance the strength of the Democratic party. Compromises were often reached in Congress between the parties to admit a northern and a southern state at the same time, for example, the admission of Maine as a free state in 1820 and Missouri as a slave state in 1821. Arkansas (1836) and Michigan (1837) were another regional trade. This particular legislation known as the Missouri Compromise banned slavery in all states north of Missouri's southern border. The admission of Kansas as a free state in 1867 was not without a bloody internal battle between the proslavery and antislavery forces. Such political considerations cannot be divorced from an examination of the states created and the timing of their admission into the Union. Outside of those states admitted in the 1700s, there has been a fairly regular pattern to the number admitted (Table 6-1). Even the threshold population necessary for petitioning for statehood was waived on occasion; Nevada became a state in 1864 with less than the specified limit because of the support it gave President Lincoln in votes and the North economically during the Civil War. The last states to enter the Union were those with a very sparse population, Oklahoma in 1907 and Arizona and New Mexico in 1912. Alaska and Hawaii, also with very small populations, were admitted as recently as 1959. The likelihood of other states being admitted in the foreseeable future is rather dim, except possibly for Puerto Rico. However, its present Commonwealth status has distinct economic privileges that make its political status not amenable to immediate change.

TABLE 6-1   Admission of States to Union

Year Entered	Number
Before 1800	16
1801–1825	8
1826–1850	7
1851–1875	6
1876–1900	8
After 1900	5

States were not formed or admitted to the Union with complete support on the part of their residents. Cultural and economic forces within a state or territory have often taken on political dimensions that have resulted in competition for leadership in the area's organizational framework. In some states the sectional interests were so strong that they petitioned for separate statehood either in an existing legislature or to Congress. To the political geographer examining the political organization of the United States these issues of sectionalism are important not only for the proposed political unit but because these rivalries have remained in some states to this day.

One of the earliest cries for statehood was in the trans-Allegheny area of present-day West Virginia. With westward settlement in this area continuing into the latter part of the eighteenth century, the settlers felt isolated from the eastern political domination of Pennsylvania and Virginia. They proposed the state of Westsylvania in 1776 and requested that they be admitted as the fourteenth state to the Union. The bounds of this proposed state would include part of the present-day lands as well as parts of adjacent Kentucky and Pennsylvania (Fig. 6-3). Much of this was in the Vandalia land claims. However, these trans-Allegheny counties remained part of Virginia until 1863 when they withdrew from the pro-slavery state, formed their own constitution, joined the Union, and supported the northern causes during the Civil War.

In Tennessee, the west and east have long been at odds on the location of

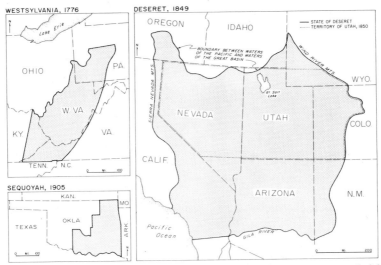

Fig. 6-3 Proposed States. (Redrafted with permission from a map compiled by E. R. Varner in *Utah Historical Quarterly*, 8 (April–October 1940), opposite p. 65. And after Charles H. Ambler and Festus P. Summers, *West Virginia: The Mountain State*, second edition © 1958. Reprinted by permission of Prentice-Hall, Inc., Englewood Cliffs, after U.S. Department of the Interior, *National Atlas of the United States*, Geological Survey, Washington, D.C., 1970.)

public institutions as well as on the disbursement of public funds. These political differences derive from the varying cultural backgrounds and economic orientation of the two halves. In 1841–1842 separate state movements were introduced calling for a west Tennessee state of Jacksonia and an east Tennessee state of Frankland. The placing of Nashville as the state capital in the middle of these warring sections represented a compromise that did not favor one region over the other. These regional rivalries had political overtones that continue to this day, as evidenced by state party leadership and voting patterns.[6]

At the time of statehood discussion in present-day Oklahoma, there was support by citizens in the Indian Territory portion to form an independent and separate state of Sequoyah (Fig. 6-3). In 1905 a convention was called, a constitution adopted, and delegates elected to present the case in Washington for a state separate from Oklahoma Territory. The proposed constitution was submitted to the residents of this forty-eight-county area of Indian Territory and ratified. However, the Washington climate, being Republican at the time, did not favor adding two separate states. This would have meant four more Democratic senators and more representatives from the same party, a concession Congress was unwilling to grant. Thus the proposed state of Sequoyah was never brought to fruition, although the impetus for the separatist movement did demonstrate the political organization and support for those identified with the Indian Territory.[7]

At times, other than political reasons motivated settlers to form a particular state such as in Utah where the Mormons proposed the state of Deseret (Fig. 6-3). It was the desire of these pioneers to form a political unit that would exemplify the social and economic standards characterized by their religion.

One state where sectionalism has remained strong since initial settlement is California. When the state was admitted in 1850, the internal political differences did not recede. The northern counties, around the San Francisco region, were settled first by residents from the Northeast and Midwest in contrast to the southern part where farmers from the South and border states comprised the majority. These contrasts in culture as well as economic orientation and political philosophy contributed in part to the regional variations. However, it was also attributed to the second-class status perceived by California's southern counties that led to their support for separating and forming either an independent nation or at most a new territory. Southern California felt justified in this claim as it was taxed more heavily than the more populous north and lacked the economic advantages (railroads and ports) and services that were enjoyed by those residents farther north, especially those agricultural and mining interests in the Central Valley and Sierra Nevada and the economic enterprises focused in San Francisco.

The grievances grew to the extent that a plan was introduced into the state legislature in 1859 for the formation of a new state with San Luis Obispo County as its northern boundary. Plans already had been proposed in the early 1850s for a separate Pacific Republic. This new territory would be named Colorado. The plan was submitted to the voters in the proposed territory and handily approved. However, it never received additional support from Congress as the Civil War had begun. The nation and Congress showed little concern for the internal problems in this first noncontiguous state and for creation of a Pacific Republic, especially since many of those in the proposed state were sympathizers for the South. They also disregarded support for this measure by the California legislature, governor, and voters of the region.[8]

The sectionalism that was present at the time of statehood and during the Civil War has prevailed since. Measures for separating the state that have been introduced in the legislature since 1960 reveal these northern and southern rivalries remain. These have centered most recently in the representation in the state assembly and state senate. Cleavages have become rural vs. urban as well as north vs. south. Northern California especially around San Francisco and Oakland dominated state politics from 1848–1929. They maintained their grip on the legislature even when the southern part had a larger population. This was accomplished by the reapportionment of congressional and legislative districts to their advantage and devising an election scheme based on number of representatives per county. There are only ten counties in what is identified often as southern California.[9]

One of the first tasks that any newly created state faced was to form a county unit of organization. In some states, California, for example, the number initially approved when the state joined the Union in 1850, eighteen, was not the number initially adopted, twenty-seven. As the state grew in population and economic strength, especially in the agricultural and mining and port areas, there were demands for more new counties. Within the next half century, thirty-one more were added. The major increases were in the years immediately following statehood; from 1851–1854 three were added per year. The last county formed was Imperial County, which separated from San Diego County in 1907. The greater number of counties in the northern half of the state contributed to the early dominance of the region's strength in state politics, a dominance in the state legislature that continued into the twentieth century.[10]

A similar situation existed in Arizona where the number of original counties (four: Pima, Mohave, Yuma, and Yavapai) because the basis for carving out other counties. An earlier county, Pah-Ute, which once was part of Mohave County, became known as Arizona's "lost county" because Congress gave it to Nevada in 1866.[11] Maricopa County was carved out of Yavapai and Pima in 1871; Phoenix became its county seat. Pinal was originally part of Yavapai, Pima, and Maricopa counties. Additional counties were created in 1879, 1891, 1899, and the last, Greenlee County (bordering New Mexico) in 1909. This county was originally part of Graham County, which was once part of Pima and Apache; Apache was created in 1879. This political maneuvering brought about little change in the state's territorial boundaries but did internally as the number of counties increased from the original four to the present fourteen.

An inspection into the county arrangements within a state reveals a variety of political and settlement reasons which are often behind the number, size, and shape of a state's organization. Often a state legislature would create counties prior to settlement, as was the case in west Texas, where fifty-four counties were created in 1876. These checkerboard patterned counties (Fig. 6-1) did not function in a political sense immediately as each county had to wait until 150 farmers were registered before formal organization could take place. Most of their land transactions were handled until then by counties in the eastern part of the state which had the necessary population. There are even cases where a farmer in Fisher County registered his dog as Bill Purp in hopes of expediting the county's formal organization.[12]

In Nevada the sixteen counties today range in area from two less than 1000 square miles to one over 270,000. The largest ones are in the eastern half of the state. The smallest are in the area near Carson City in the west because of the influence of a single individual. When state capital locations were being discussed, an enterprising lawyer from Carson City, William Stewart, wanted the permanent location in his hometown. However, other representatives also hoped to land the prize but Stewart received the necessary votes by promising those who supported him that they could have county seats located in their counties. The result showed his regional support, a clustering of very small counties in the western part of Nevada.[13] The early legislature created one county in the northwest part of the state, Lake County, which later had its name changed to Roop County. Later, however, it was absorbed by Washoe County "because it lacked sufficient population to function properly."

Political rivalries and sectional differences in North Carolina accounted for the changing political map in the late 1700s and early 1800s. The political and economic power had long belonged to the eastern part of the state, also the area of greatest population initially. In the state house of commons, each county had one senator and two representatives. The east had more counties, controlled both houses, and elected its officials. In short it dominated the state's politics. By 1830 the western counties had a larger population but were unable to control the state government. They tried to increase their strength by creating new counties but the east would either defeat such proposals or create new ones of its own. From 1776 to 1833 eighteen new counties were created in the west and fifteen in the east. The rivalry between these two sections continued until the west threatened secession. The west tried in vain to call a constitutional convention but was unsuccessful until they finally enlisted some support from the Cape Fear representatives by agreeing to support their request for a removal of the state capital to Fayetteville. Raleigh had burned in 1831. Even though the eastern representatives were unsuccessful in relocating the capital, the support they gave the west did enable a constitutional convention to be called in 1834.[14]

Political problems in settling the United States, whether in individual states or territories, were not limited to these macrounits. Frequently they were concerned with counties, their formation, their areal extent, and the county seat location. All were important in the political organization and power that developed at the local level. Territorial, state, and national problems to many early settlers were not of prime concern in their daily lives. They were more concerned with the location of the land office, the preservation of local law enforcement, and the hopeful landing of a railroad near their lands and their settlements. In western Washington the value of property near county seats was realized.[15] The political representatives in state or territorial legislatures were important to the agrarian population as it was their responsibility to see that local education, economic, and judicial interests were preserved from adjacent states, foreign countries, or Indians.

Counties were often created from existing counties in the Midwest and West, especially as more people "filled in" the spaces and they petitioned for their own political bases of power and organization. In southeastern Washington, Grant County was created in 1909 to border on Douglas, Lincoln, Adams, and Franklin because of the settlers' demand for a unit of "more serviceable size and convenience."[16] This triggered competition for the county seat, especially for those on railroad lines. The "urban" places of Ephrata, Wilson Lake, Quincy, Soap Lake, Wheeler, and Warden all desired the seat. Ephrata was finally awarded the prize.

Often intense and bitter rivalries developed over the location of county seats. Charges of fraud, impropriety, theft of records, and even open bloodshed and warfare were not unusual last century, especially in the frontier days of the "wild" West. There is recorded the "Spink County War" in South Dakota in which the territorial militia was called out to end disorder that resulted in the moving of the county seat from Ashton to Redfield.[17] Another story from the same area involved the county seat records being taken in the dead of night by force by the winning county seat or in the case of Hamlin County, Dakota Territory, where Castlewood simply "moved the capital" at night from Spaulding. County wars were not unusual in the frontier West; for example, the famous Lincoln County war in New Mexico was between political and economic rivals whose power went beyond the county limits.

Frequently a county seat was changed, not only by vote of citizens or theft of records or violent means but merely by a simple reorganization of the space. When this occurred, it would result in severe population and economic decline for the earlier political node. This situation is illustrated in Iowa by the passing of Homer. Homer was the original county seat of Risley County, which was an important settlement node in the northcentral part of the state.

> Far back in the early fifties [1850s] Homer shone as a bright star on the western horizon. It was the best known town in northern Iowa, probably because the land office was located there. Toward this embryo city the people of the eastern states wended their way, by whatever method of locomotion was available.[18]

A weekly stage ran from Des Moines to Homer by way of Boone and many new settlers passed through and homesteaded nearby. By the mid-1850s the only other settlements in the county, then changed to Webster County, were Fort Dodge and Webster City (then Newcastle), both almost insignificant in numbers. It was not long before the two above centers began to increase in population and economic strength. They pressed for both a change of the county seat and separate counties.

Homer was in the geographical center of its county, however; and when the two new counties were created by the state legislature, Fort Dodge and Webster City competed for the seats for these two new counties and were successful. Fort Dodge became the county seat for its newly created county, Webster; and Webster City became the seat for the second new county, Hamilton County. Risley County ceased to exist as did Homer, as this political maneuvering intrigue "dealt a death blow to the town of Homer, which soon passed into history."[19]

There is still alteration of political spaces. Boundary claims are even now being settled that have been in question for over a century between states or between the United States and its neighbors (Chapter 7). In the past twenty-five years, two new counties have been carved out: Los Alamos, New Mexico, from Santa Fe and Sandoval counties in 1959. This small unit serves as the focus for government testing of atomic materials and systems. The second, Menominee County, Wisconsin, was created from Oconto and Shawano counties in 1961 as an independent political unit instead of the reservation it once was. Of course, probably the prime example of political carving was withdrawing of land from Maryland and Virginia for the nation's capital in 1791. A total of 69¼ square miles was taken from Maryland, 31¾ from its southern neighbor.

ADMINISTRATION OF SPACE

The Nation. The United States is composed at the macrolevel of fifty states. They have a total of 3,615,122 square miles and 203,235,298 people according to the 1970 census. States vary widely in area in square miles as well as in numbers of inhabitants. The largest state in square miles is Alaska with over 566,000 followed by "giant" Texas with slightly over 262,000 square miles. Altogether twenty-eight states have over 50,000 square miles (approximate size of Alabama) with a total land area of 2.9 million square miles. At the other extreme are nine states, not counting Washington, D.C., with less than 10,000 square miles. These are, with the exception of Hawaii, part of the early settled colonies. Their combined land area is almost 60,000 square miles. All could fit into the present state of Georgia with room to spare.

The number of counties in each state varies greatly. This, in part, is attributed to the period of settlement, particular survey system or systems used to arrange the counties, and the forms of government. All states have counties except Louisiana, which has parishes. Texas has the largest number with 245 and Georgia the second most with 159. The former has used a rectangular land survey system, except in part of east Texas, while the latter adopted the metes and bounds system. Five other states have 100 or more counties, Kentucky (120), Missouri (114), Kansas (105), Illinois (102), and North Carolina (100). These six states have 945 counties, almost one-third of all those in the nation, 3,049. Their combined land area is over 615,000 square miles, about one-sixth of the total or the size of Alaska and Alabama together. On the other hand, eight states have less than fifteen counties: Delaware (only 3); Rhode Island and Hawaii (5 each); Connecticut (8); New Hampshire (10); and Arizona, Massachusetts, and Vermont (14 each). With the exception of the larger Arizona, these states have a combined total of seventy-three counties and a total area of slightly over 40,000 square miles, about the size of Virginia.

Aside from the wide variances in area, there are likewise substantial differences in the population of states. There are six states according to the 1970 census that have more than 10 million population (California, New York, Pennsylvania, Texas, Illinois, and Ohio); another six have over 5 million. These dozen "mege-states" have 120 million-plus people, roughly 60 percent of the total for the entire United States. Smaller states in numbers of people are also in evidence; fourteen, including Washington, D.C., have fewer than 1 million and four have less than 500,000: Nevada, Vermont, Wyoming, and Alaska. These "ministates" have only 9 million, less than 10 percent of the nation's total and a number equal to the present population of Ohio.

The county has historically been the focus of local government power in much of the United States. As mentioned previously, there are presently 3,049 counties. This does not include the Independent Cities in Virginia that increase with each decennial census. There were thirty-two in 1960 and thirty-eight in 1970. This is the major reason for the variations in total number of counties from one decade to the next. If one divides the 3,049 counties into the over 200 million inhabitants in the nation in 1970, this would average out to 65,000 people per county. However, this is nowhere near the statistical average for most counties. There are seventy-five counties that have over 500,000 and twenty-three that have over 1 million population. The twenty-three have a total of 43 million people (one-fifth of the nation's total), more than the combined state populations of California and New York. While the political impact in voting or decision-making is now in the hands of those county units with the large populations, there are 874 counties that have fewer than 10,000 population each in 1970. In fact, twenty-four counties had less than 1,000 people. Texas has most of these miniscule counties, 106 with less than 10,000 people. Nebraska has the most counties with fewer than 1,000 people, six, followed by Nevada, Montana, and Colorado with three each. The concentration of these small counties in the western half of the United States is in part a reflection of the large areal units and lack of intensive agricultural economies.

Counties, like states, vary widely in area. If the Alaskan Census Divisions can be considered as counties, there were twenty-three in the United States with over 10,000 square miles. Fifteen of these were in Alaska alone. The Upper Yukon Division has over 84,000 square miles, which is larger than the state of Kansas. Altogether four Alaskan divisions have over 50,000 square miles each. In these could be placed all the 245 counties of Texas. Outside of Alaska, San Bernardino County in southern California has the largest area, over 20,000 square miles. Within its boundaries could be placed Rhode Island, Delaware, Connecticut, New Jersey, and half of Massachusetts and still have some room left. At one time San Bernardino had a larger area than at present. Other large counties in the West were

Coconino, Arizona, and Elko and Nye, Nevada, each with over 17,000 square miles. There are large-sized counties in Arizona, California, and Wyoming that have over 10,000 square miles.

Large-sized counties may appear to be important because they occupy large sections on maps; however, there are numerous small-sized ones as well that are much more important in a political sense at state and national levels. Sixteen counties, excluding the Virginia Independent Cities, have less than 100 square miles. Some of the smaller ones are New York, New York (23 square miles); Bristol, Rhode Island (25 square miles); and Arlington, Virginia (26 square miles). In the main these small units are located in the northeast quarter of the United States, especially in the central cities. The Independent Cities in Virginia are just that; in 1970 there were thirty-eight and thirty-six had less than 100 square miles. In fact, fourteen had 5 square miles or less.

Organizational Hierarchies. The public services that are demanded by the population of counties, cities, and states as well as the nation are handled at a variety of levels in the organizational and administrative hierarchy. These agencies arrange the spaces in such a manner that, theoretically at least, the execution of their duties is handled effectively. In many cases each political unit, such as a city, has any number of specialized districts that overlap. City agencies, such as fire, police, education, water, irrigation, recreation, cemetery, and sanitation, have specific districts where their work is coordinated and either centralized or decentralized throughout the metropolitan area. This is illustrated by city council and school districts serving the city of Houston (Fig. 6-4).

Overlapping these are the county units of government that are numerous in

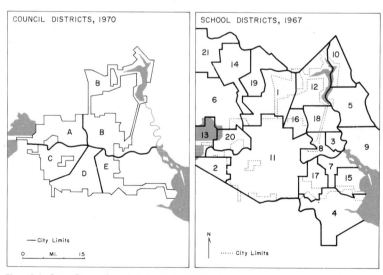

FIG. 6-4 City Council and School Districts in Houston. (City Planning Commission, Houston, Texas.)

any large metropolitan area. These boundaries may become important in city planning and city services if there are substantial differences between them, as in the case of zoning, law enforcement, or environmental protection. Above these are the state districts that may be different for each agency or branch of the state government. Nebraska is a state that has a fairly even population density except for the Omaha and Lincoln nodes, yet a number of state agencies have carved up the state in various fashions to handle specific duties (Fig. 6-5). Although there is some underlying similarity in those illustrated, rarely do they coincide either in number or in areal extent.

Finally, there are the various federal agencies connected with the departments that have organized the nation into a number of regions or districts. At the national level the Federal Reserve Bank Districts and the Post Office ZIP areas illustrate how the spaces are carved up and allocated for particular departments (Figs. 6-6 and 6-7).[20] In other agencies the number of regions for federal agencies and departments varies from three or four to over fifteen.[21] Again as at the lower levels of the hierarchy, rarely do the departments have similar regional patterns for delimiting national space.

The political hierarchy of the United States may be likened to a quilt that has many small patterns overlaid with increasingly larger patterns. Some of the patterns may overlap but often at the microlevel imperfections in the order exist. As stated in the earlier portion of this chapter, the township in the Midwest or town in New England was the lowest rung on the political ladder. In 1967 there were 17,105 townships.[22] These units mainly handled problems relating to schools, roads, safety, and other basic public services. They elected public officials, disbursed public funds and held meetings. The town meeting in New England or in the Grange Hall or township school in the rural Midwest were the original seats of power in rural America. From these many services moved to the county court house. In the main, their impact has declined as counties and states have absorbed their duties and organizational responsibilities.

The next rung of the ladder was the county, the major political and organizational element in the rural settlement and expansion of the United States. The counties increased in number, as did their political power and organization. As was discussed, two of the major political battles that developed in the formation of states and territories were the creation of counties and the awarding of county seats. These foci of political concentration were responsible for handling the major legal problems that arose, whether it involved land registration, judicial hearings, or the election of representatives to the state legislature. Counties in this century, like the townships, have seen many of their functions curtailed as a more streamlined and efficient way of handling services was developed at the state level. It should not be forgotten that in many rural areas of the South, Midwest, and West the population of many counties has been reduced, yet still they are important for handling the local political problems. The allegiance of residents to rural county seats for solving their local problems is strong, even though their political power has been eroded with reapportionment.

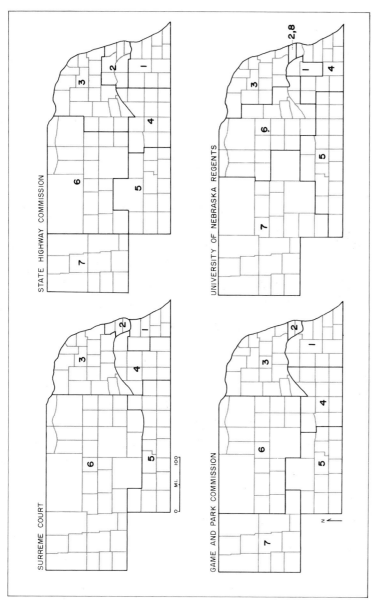

FIG. 6-5 Organizational Framework for State Services in Nebraska. (*Nebraska Blue Book,* 1970.)

The next order in the political fabric is the state. The fifty states today are the major political units that comprise the United States. States that developed during the agrarian era of the last two centuries gradually assumed many of the economic, political, and social functions that were heretofore the domain of the

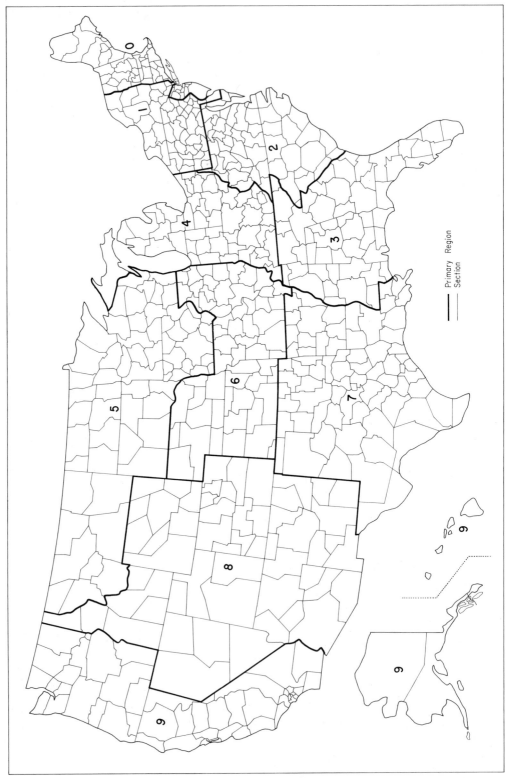

FIG. 6-6 ZIP Areas: U.S. Postal Service. (U.S. Department of the Interior, *National Atlas of the United States*, Geological Survey, Washington, D.C., 1970.)

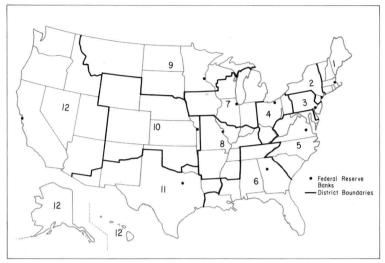

Fig. 6-7 Federal Reserve Bank District. (U.S. Department of the Interior, *National Atlas of the United States*, Geological Survey, Washington, D.C., 1970.)

counties. At the same time that the states themselves were becoming the major governmental unit for treating problems within the confines of their borders, they began to lose some of their political importance. The national concern for uniform policies governing civil rights, welfare, education, housing, and environmental protection has left the states playing a lesser role than earlier. National goals implemented by national programs have been occurring in the past four decades; these have superseded many state plans. Thus the boundaries that once served to separate states solving the same problem but in a different fashion are functional as states are now handling them alike.

Even though the major political unit within the United States is still the state, there has been an attempt to identify economic areas that have similar problems that may not be restricted to existing state boundaries. A prime example of this would be the five Regional Commissions and Appalachia that have been identified (Fig. 6-8). These commissions were formed under the Public Works and Economic Development Act of 1968.

> The basic goal of each commission is to bolster the economy of a region through comprehensive, long-range planning and the coordination of available resources on the local, State, and Federal levels.[23]

Altogether the nearly 1000 counties in these six regions encompass parts of twenty states. In some cases, as in New England, whole states are included, while in others a select number of counties are included. Congress supported various programs and

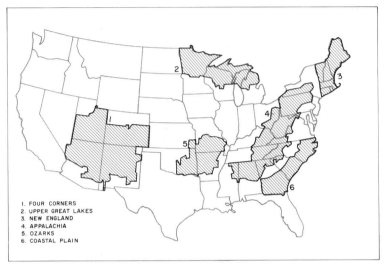

1. FOUR CORNERS
2. UPPER GREAT LAKES
3. NEW ENGLAND
4. APPALACHIA
5. OZARKS
6. COASTAL PLAIN

FIG. 6-8 Federal Regional Commissions. (U.S. Department of Commerce, Economic Development Administration, 1970.)

activities to the tune of $23 million in fiscal 1970 and nearly $5 million from the Department of Commerce for planning and technical assistance.

REORGANIZATION OF SPACE

Spaces that have been delimited and demarcated remain as such with varying degrees of flexibility. Those political units, such as townships, counties, and states, were imposed on the physical and cultural landscapes before many of the current political and governmental operations were implemented. Once man found that he could not nor wanted to live in isolation, interdependence developed between man and society. This led to various plans and systems of organization being implemented to satisfy his social, economic, and political desires. He set up cities, suburbs, school districts, and legislative districts. As the economic and social changes took place, such as a shift from rural to urban occupations, population movements to cities, and increased need for public-service coverage (safety, education, and general welfare), the original organizational frameworks themselves were called into question. Some he desired to change, for example, annexing adjacent lands into a city to bring in added revenues and provide more comprehensive services to a larger population base. Others he was less reluctant to change, perhaps even feeling cautious about merging with a large city for fear of dominance and loss of exclusiveness and unique identity. In political terms, reorganization was both supported by those who felt they were legitimately being denied a power and organizational base for solving their problems and opposed by those who fought any relinquishing of their political clout.

The reorganization of political space has not been accomplished without rivalries and hassles between groups, cities, political parties, and even regions. County reorganization and consolidation has met with varying degrees of success in Connecticut, Florida, North Dakota, and Oregon. In 1973 a bill introduced but defeated in the Oregon Senate proposed reorganizing the present thirty-six into eight new ones. Support for examining the organizational structure of public services and political districts has been far from unanimous in any political unit whether it be for local zoning ordinances, school busing plans, metrogovernment consolidation, or gerrymandered legislative districts. As a result many plans for reorganizing and rearranging political spaces have led to court hearings and often lengthy court battles. Some eventually awaited a Supreme Court ruling.

Reapportionment. One of the major political plans calling for reorganization was the manner in which states elected members to Congress and their own state houses. The landmark Baker vs. Carr decision by the United States Supreme Court in 1962 formed the basis for the congressional districts to be elected on the basis of population. In essence the decision rendered that representatives are to be elected on the basis of population, hence the one-man–one-vote system, not on the basis of what were termed geographic factors such as acres or trees. The initial impact of this and subsequent decisions meant that most states during the 1960s had to reapportion their legislative bodies in line with guidelines of nearly equal population, compactness, and contiguity. Each of these was violated, and in some cases grossly, by districts in more than one state.[24]

The House of Representatives is fixed at 435 members by the Constitution. Ideally each district should have approximately an equal number of residents sending a representative to Congress. However, before reapportionment in the 1960s, and even now, this is not always the case as members are sent by differing numbers of inhabitants in the states. This is because districts are not permitted to cross existing state lines. District plans are approved at state levels.

In the past sixty years there has been a large increase in the number of persons each congressman represented. In 1910 the districts averaged 211,000; this increased to 465,000 by 1970. By the year 2000 the average constituency is estimated to number about 625,000; most of these will be urbanized clusters or nodes. Districts in the more rural parts of the United States will increase in size (area) substantially from what they already are.

Even though the average population per district was 465,000 persons in the present Ninety-second Congress (203 million divided by 435 seats), the sizes on a state basis exhibited great disparity. First, the average district population does not apply to Alaska, Wyoming, Vermont, Nevada, North Dakota, and Delaware as they have less than this figure or they do not have enough to qualify for two members. The Constitution provides for each state to have at least one representative. These six states have slightly over 2.5 million inhabitants, the approximate population of Iowa, which also sends six members.

The states that had the average district population less than the 465,000 figure were rural as well as urban. Some of the smallest average district populations were in large rural states: South Dakota (333,000), Montana (347,000), and Idaho (357,000). Even Ohio (427,000), Pennsylvania (437,000), Wisconsin (442,000), and New York (444,000) had district sizes smaller than the national average.[25] By the same token, states such as Arizona, Florida, Colorado, Utah, and California had districts averaging over 525,000. The largest averages were in Arizona with 591,000 and Florida with 566,000. For the nation as a whole the variances in district sizes were found in the North, South, East, and West in rural as well as urban states. What these disparities indicate is that the congressmen represent quite differing numbers of people. Some represent a population much less than the 465,000 average and others represent more.

Prior to the redistricting from the 1970 census, there was also a great variance in district populations within the states. This subject is treated below under the subject of malapportionment. In an ideal sense after each census each state was to establish district populations of approximate equal numbers. However, due to political manipulations and political power of certain rural areas, especially state assemblies, the variance between the largest and smallest districts was often great. Also, redistricting was not always done. The greatest discrepancies prior to the 1970 redistricting plans were in California, Nebraska, Maryland, Illinois, and Minnesota (Table 6-2). In other words, there were still intrastate contrasts even after redistricting in the 1960s. For over half the states the variance now is less than 1 percent.[26] Often to complete this assignment, and have a small variance, some shrewd boundary drawing and political maneuvering had to be utilized to meet the approximate equal-population requirement.

When the 1970 census figures were released and utilized in the redistricting of states, four, Hawaii, Maine, Nebraska, and New Mexico decided not to redraw their boundaries. Those six states who were entitled to one representative or did not have sufficient population for two congressmen did not have to engage in the legislative and legal hassles that accompany redistricting. As mentioned previously, they are already entitled to one representative, even though their population is less than the nation's average per district and they may be growing at less than the nation's average. The latest redistricting attempts have reduced major variances in the population sizes between the largest and smallest districts from previous plans even though gerrymandering might still be applied (Table 6-2).

Even though Supreme Court rulings have not permitted wide population discrepancies between the largest and smallest congressional districts, a February 1973 ruling allowed a wider difference for state electoral districts. Virginia's 16 percent discrepancy in population for the house of delegates' districts was upheld by the highest court.

Another thorny problem that raises its head in the redistricting process is the population variances among states. Each state is granted a specific number of members for the forthcoming decade based on its population, and it is up to the

TABLE 6-2   Variance in Redistricting, 1970
(range of largest and smallest districts)

State	Variance	
	After Redistricting (percent)	Before Redistricting (percent)
Michigan	0.0026	35.9
South Dakota	0.013	10.0
Georgia	0.020	3.2
Florida	0.10	53.4
Colorado	0.12	47.6
Nebraska	0.12	55.9
New York	0.15	0.15
Rhode Island	0.16	87.1
Maine	0.24	19.6
Ohio	0.46	0.46
Missouri	0.50	38.1
Virginia	0.67	50.9
New Mexico	1.24	1.24
Illinois	1.32	64.6
Minnesota	1.39	64.1
Massachusetts	1.60	35.9
California	1.65	106.3
Pennsylvania	2.23	54.2
Texas	4.99	54.4
South Carolina	8.17	21.4

Source: © *Congressional Quarterly Weekly Report*, July 8, 1972, p. 1663.

state courts and legislatures to decide which political plans will be implemented. This not infrequently results in one party redistricting to its advantage, often with the court decision rendered by justices elected from the same party. The realization that all redistricting needs to be done within the confines of state boundaries results in some major variations in population averages between states. In the present Congress, twelve members are elected from Florida (6,789,000) and fifteen from New Jersey (7,168,000). The average population per district varies from 566,000 in Florida to 477,000 in New Jersey. By the time of the next federal census the population probably will be greater in the Sunshine State as it is one of the more rapidly growing states. Such discrepancies are behind moves to have a national census of population every five years as well as the concern that voters in one state have an advantage over those in another. Another case is that of the Connecticut and Oklahoma delegations, each currently with six members, the former state with 3,032,000 (505,000 per representative) and the latter with 2,559,000 (427,000 per representative). With such variations it would appear that a national average would be more closely met and the variances between the largest and smallest districts reduced if there were 435 districts drawn on a basis other than being confined to set political boundaries, namely, the states. Probably state boundaries mean little in variation in legislative action and stands taken by present elected officials. The line happens to be a politically fixed historical limit that merely served as a convenient organizational scheme for electing representatives in rural America. Variations in economic issues, social legislation, and international sentiments are rarely separated by state lines, especially where urban orientation and regional interdependence are replacing state units.

Population changes have brought changes in the membership in the House of Representatives. In the past twenty years the greatest gains have been in the South (Florida) and Southwest, and the losses in the Northeast and Midwest. New York, once the largest state and therefore the one entitled to the largest delegation, has seen its strength drop from forty-three to thirty-nine members. California, by contrast, has watched its representation increase from thirty to forty-three in the same period. Similar decreases have been occurring in the members elected from Pennsylvania (30 to 25), Massachusetts (14 to 12), and West Virginia (6 to 4). Increases not as dramatic as California's but equally as important since 1950 are seen in Florida (8 to 15), Arizona (2 to 4), and Texas (22 to 24). The membership in Illinois, Indiana, Michigan, Ohio, and New Jersey, all large-population states, has remained essentially the same in the past two decades. In the past decade alone, six states picked up a total of twelve seats, five going to California and three to Florida (Fig. 6-9). By contrast, ten states lost twelve seats, two each lost in New York and Pennsylvania.

If the population patterns continue for the next three decades, and there is little reason to suggest otherwise, the gains will be in Florida, Texas, and California. The West, which currently has seventy-six members or 17 percent of the total, will increase possibly to ninety-seven or 22 percent of the 454 members by the year 2000. By then, California alone may have as many as fifty-nine representatives in Congress. Florida is expected to account for most of the increase in the South's representation. It will likely have the fourth largest delegation behind California, New York, and Texas. The remainder of the South, especially the Deep South, will see its strength reduced, except possibly for Virginia. The northeastern and midwestern states, especially those large urban ones, New York and Pennsylvania, will gradually see their numerical strength in Congress eroded. The same seepage will be seen in the more rural Midwest, Plains, and Mountain states. As was mentioned above, many of these may be reduced to a single delegate.

The reapportionment and redistricting issues raise some questions about

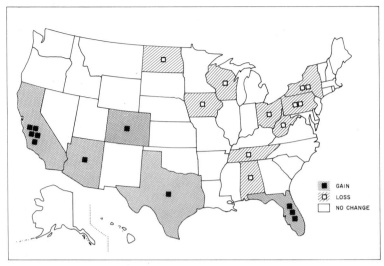

FIG. 6-9 Membership Changes in U.S. House of Representatives, 1960–1970. (U.S. Department of Commerce, *Statistical Abstract of the United States, 1971*, Washington, D.C., 1971.)

congressional constituencies and representation in a national decision-making body. One is how long the constitutional provision will remain that each state shall have one representative. Already there are six and the number may increase to twelve by the time the 1980 census is available, if population trends continue. Likely candidates for losing one of their two seats are South Dakota, Montana, Idaho, New Hampshire, Rhode Island, and Maine. While the impact in the House would be felt in only twelve states with twelve members, a rather small number in the 435 total, the effect would be greater in the United States Senate. Here the policy of electing two senators per state, regardless of population, not only works to the advantage of the rural states in the South and West but those that are gaining population at less than the national average rate. If one counts the six states that currently have one representative and add those six that may be reduced to one in the next decade, this will result in twelve representatives but in twenty-four senators out of 100! This would mean twenty-four senators coming from states that altogether have less total population than the state of New Jersey, which only elects two senators. These ministates (in population) definitely have an advantage and do play a major role affecting the directions of national decision-making.

At the state level, the recent congressional redistricting in Washington is used as an example to illustrate how different political parties have adopted spatial strategies primarily to serve their own gains. The state legislature was commissioned to devise a plan that would be in accord with the constitutional guidelines of having only minor population variations, compactness, and contiguity. The Senate, controlled by the Democrats, passed a reapportionment plan favoring them, and the House, where the Republicans had a majority, passed a plan enhancing their party. After a year of deliberation in which the plan of neither party was accepted, the First District Court commissioned a geographer, Richard Morrill of the University of Washington, to redistrict the state's congressional and legislative districts.

The court laid down criteria for defining the districts. They were as follows: a maximum of only 1 percent deviation (±684 inhabitants) in numbers; maintenance of the integrity of counties and cities insofar as possible; a prohibition of unnecessary irregularity and sinuosity; the following of natural geographic boundaries to the extent possible; unity of character, that is, not splitting Indian reservations and much of the Seattle "central area" (black ghetto); plus the practical criterion of changing the existing pattern as little as needed to meet these existing criteria.[27]

There are some definite differences in the sizes and shapes of the three plans (Fig. 6-10). Each political party attempted to either keep or gain control of the legislative chambers. The location of incumbents is shown on the maps as well as the gerrymandering involved to retain the seats of these members of both parties. The Republican wedge plan around Spokane eliminates central Democratic control. District 13 places two incumbent Democratic senators together, while preserving a Republican in District 9. The part of District 15 shifted south to the Columbia River sacrifices a Democrat to a rural Republican in Yakima County; two Democratic senators are in District 39, parts of which are almost unreachable. The districts are arranged to sacrifice perhaps two Democratic senators.

The gerrymandering devices and manipulation of space are also found in the Democratic plan. In Spokane the Democrats wiggled the figures to get all Democrats. District 13 goes almost halfway across the state from suburban Seattle to beyond Moses Lake. In the Seattle suburbs the Democratic plan attempts to whittle down the Republican strength, even though the Democratic areas there are losing strength. Districts 12 and 13 are additional examples of excessive gerrymandering.

In the Court-approved Morrill plan, the basic geographic criteria outlined by the court were applied in redistricting the state. When these criteria are used the resulting plan as expected would be different from that designed to serve partisan advantages. In a state as diverse in its population distribution, natural features, and present county-boundary structure, some irregular-shaped congressional districts are expected. Yet the Morrill plan does not have the glaring spatial violations seen in the Republican and Democratic proposals.

The increase in black consciousness, registration, and voting in the political arena has resulted in only a dozen black congressmen being elected to the House of Representatives. In Congress blacks nowhere approximate their percent of the national population, about 11 percent in 1970, as many state legislatures have carved districts in such a fashion that it is difficult for them to run competitive races. For example, if congressional districts in Mississippi ran north-south instead of east-west, undoubtedly one or two blacks would be elected. In 1970 there were fifty-nine districts where blacks were more than 30 percent of their population (Fig. 6-11). In the main these are found in two locations, the South and in the central sections of large northern cities. Only ten of these districts had over 50

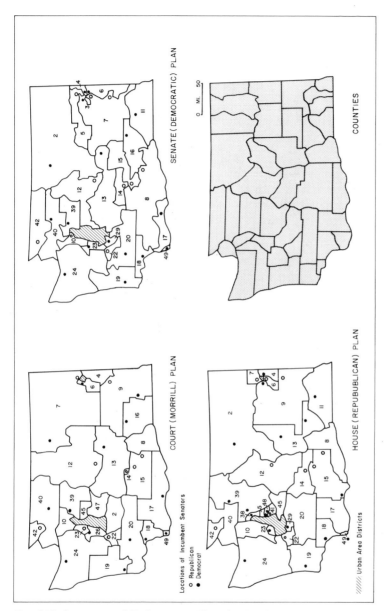

FIG. 6-10 Congressional Redistricting Plans for Washington. (After Richard Morrill, "A Geographer in Redistricting Land," Seattle, University of Washington, Department of Geography, 1972, unpublished paper.)

percent black population and twenty had over 40 percent. Percents much lower often preclude the election of blacks. Possible increases in the number of black representatives may come from reorganizing the district boundaries to grant them a

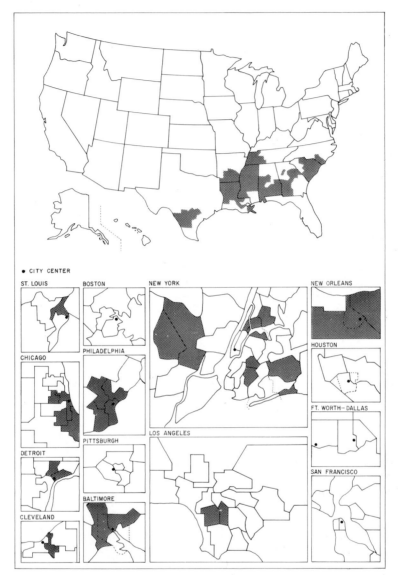

FIG. 6-11 Black Congressional Districts. (U.S. Department of Commerce, *Congressional District Data*, Districts of the 92nd Congress, Washington, D.C., 1971.)

greater share of the district population instead of splitting them up between several surrounding districts. However, this would take state-approved legislative and court approval. On the other hand a high voter registration and turnout in predominantly black districts may bring victory for black officeholders or for those whites espousing the concerns facing black Americans.

Metropolitan Reorganization. The population increases in the larger urban areas in the past twenty-five years have resulted in some basic political problems in organization and administration. Especially is this true for the manner in which revenues are collected and services rendered to residents. Problems in lack of monies and ineffective levels of public services have led to various forms of organization and reorganization being attempted. Historically, the most frequent way of solving problems was to annex adjacent unincorporated territory into the metropolitan limits. In this way cities hoped to keep pace with political and social problems that accompanied rising population. However, in many cases, this soon proved an unwise tactic in that within and surrounding many metropolitan areas independent suburbs developed their own political organization and provided their own services. These local governments did not want to be absorbed into a larger political unit so they organized and incorporated specifically for reasons of maintaining separate residential, racial, commercial, and education standards for residents in their political space.

The result of metropolitan development has led to a myriad of local government units, each often operating differently and independently on the varying political and social problems. This has not been accomplished without problems for the central city and autonomous suburban communities. The central cities have found that they are going bankrupt because the middle- and high-income residents departed for the suburbs. This condition put an added strain on the minority groups and older immobile whites who remained, in part because social and economic conditions do not facilitate their absorption elsewhere. High costs for education, welfare, housing, police, sanitation, and transportation are only a few of the critical problems central cities face because of the existing political organization.[28] One of the more frequent cries of central city politicians and planners is that suburban whites use the central city for employment, enjoyment, and shopping but fail to contribute to its basic services. Suburbanites in effect take their money earned in the central city and spend it elsewhere in their own independent suburbs. Some cities have applied a low tax rate on noncity residents.

Suburbs may be politically independent and detached but they are not immune to problems of a governmental nature. Few are the problems in cities or suburbs that are restricted solely to distinct political limits and types of urban developments. Education may be improved in the suburbs over the central city but the property taxes might be higher. It costs a small suburb more per capita to retain its own police force, fire department, schools, and sanitation services than if it were consolidated with adjacent suburbs or the entire metropolitan area. However, economic savings are not always of foremost importance to local residents as they seek to identify personally with "their own" police force, schools, and city council. This personal attachment is one element that is important to local political units; the residents feel that they are more and better protected by local police and better represented by local zoning boards and city councils than if they were amalgamated with others.

Problems that metropolitan areas face are more than simply related to the number of independent local governments, of which now there are estimated to be over 70,000.[29] One of the basic problems involves the multiplicity of districts that handle various branches in the government hierarchy. Aside from the township, county, metropolitan, and state levels of administration, there are school, health, police, fire, zoning, and housing districts. These cut across differing social and economic groups, not to mention varying political divisions. As one political geographer has remarked along these lines: "Looking over a set of maps showing the political boundaries of American cities becomes a revealing exercise in geopolitical science fiction!"[30] This myriad of organizations is one basic reason that varying attempts at consolidation and reorganization are more often heard now than earlier by politicians and planners at all levels of government. The need for defining, delimiting, and supplying metropolitan spaces with the variety of public services demanded in the most effective and efficient manner is one of the major problems facing contemporary America. If it goes unchecked, it may trigger such complex political, economic, and social problems that cities will become unmanageable and ungovernable. Cries of such about New York City and Los Angeles have already been uttered by politicians and social critics.

Figures from a 1967 report on local governments in the nation's metropolitan areas illustrate the dilemmas and complexities facing urban administrators.[31] Local governing units include those that are strictly political as well as those that handle education, health, police, fire, sanitation, water and other public services within political parcels. The number of local governing units varies widely within population size classes and regions as well (Table 6-3). It is not only that large SMSA's have many local governments but so do medium-sized and small ones. Problems remain whether they are 50, 250, or 500 in number and whether they are in the Northeast, South, or West. There is little pattern to the numbers in the SMSA's except the headaches that result everywhere from the large number of units so often geographically fragmented, separated, and organized that needless duplication and inefficiency result.

In order to solve some of the political organization problems, several policies have been adopted with varying degrees of success throughout the nation. One is to simply annex the land that is already adjacent to the city, not only the present built-up area but spaces beyond as well. However, this may not be easy if there is city and county competition for territorial space, as is the case in Virginia.[32] The policy of incorporating land for long-term anticipated growth has been used by some western cities that are the single foci in space and have plenty of room for uninhibited expansion. Even extraterritorial space has been annexed in line with generous incorporation laws. Houston and Oklahoma City are examples.

A number of metropolitan areas have at least tried to handle political administrative problems effectively by having the city and county boundary coincide. Some attempts even date to last century. In effect, city-county consolidation is designed to prevent the further Balkanization of political space and bring in all local government units into a single major political unit. This is carried out to provide uniformity in public services for the entire area and hopefully services that

TABLE 6-3   Local Governments in Selected SMSA's

Large SMSA's			Small SMSA's		
	1970 Population	Govt. Units		1970 Population	Govt. Units
New York City	11,528,649	551	Phoenix	968,487	116
Los Angeles-Long Beach	7,032,075	233	Columbus, Ohio	916,928	127
Chicago	6,978,947	1113	Hartford	816,737	67
Philadelphia	4,820,915	876	Sacramento	800,592	213
Detroit	4,202,784	242	Syracuse	635,946	191
Boston	3,375,396	146	Honolulu	629,176	4
San Francisco-Oakland	3,109,519	312	Salt Lake City	557,635	64
Washington, D.C.	2,861,123	84	Nashville-Davidson	541,160	32
Pittsburgh	2,401,362	704	Jacksonville	528,865	13
St. Louis	2,363,745	474	Richmond	518,317	7
Baltimore	2,071,947	27	Flint	497,950	97
Cleveland	2,064,194	207	Tulsa	475,264	107
Houston	1,985,031	214	Harrisburg	410,626	200
Newark	1,856,556	207	Wichita	389,352	137
Minneapolis-St. Paul	1,813,647	220	Mobile	376,390	30

Source: U.S. Department of Commerce, Bureau of The Census, *Local Government Finances in Selected Metropolitan Areas and Large Counties, 1969–1970*, Washington, D.C., U.S. Government Printing Office, 1971, p. 3.

are cheaper and more efficiently handled. Consolidation may also be used to deflate the political power of a central city and increase the potency of the suburbs. Racial issues may have played a role in Jacksonville's merger with Duval County in 1968. The black population of the county was increasing and probably eventually would have elected a majority or nearly so of the council had not the merger been approved by the county's voters. Such consolidation schemes are only one way that organizational progress has been made. In a number of cities, these schemes have been defeated at the polls, as in Albuquerque, Tampa, Memphis, and St. Louis. Similar metrogovernments have been developed in Davidson County-Nashville, Tennessee; and Marion County-Indianapolis, Indiana. In the latter case, it is called Unigov. A variety of other metropolitan experiments have been attempted with varying successes.[33] At a regional level, the successes have been less spectacular, as is the case for SEMCOG (Southeast Michigan Council of Governments), which strictly operates in an advisory capacity for local governments. The Dade County-Miami, Florida federation developed in 1957 represents another perspective to the attempted solution of political and organizational problems facing big cities. Local governments in the county still retained some powers such as police, while others such as tax collection and land-use planning were transferred and integrated into a more centralized authority, namely, Dade County authorities. This gradual and piecemeal approach to consolidating political spaces has not been without political and community problems. In Michigan SEMCOG (Southeast Michigan Council of Governments) has been attempting to coordinate governmental efforts in seven counties and 210 townships and communities. To date it has been only partly successful.

The major regions of successful or at least attempted political organization at the metropolitan level have been in Florida, the Southwest, and West. Cities in these rapidly growing areas are still often spatially detached in a manner that permits ready consolidation schemes. That is, coalescing of a half-dozen large cities is rare; often only two or three are dealt with within any reorganization. The economic expansion in these urban areas, a dynamic construction industry, land speculation, unchecked zoning, nonpartisan politics, and already lax state or city laws on growth and organization encourage various ways to solve urban problems. Thus the period of a nation's urban development probably has much to say about a city's ability and interest to engage in metropolitan reorganization of space. The contrast between the older urban Northeast and newer Southwest is readily seen. As one author has commented on this metropolitan problem:

> To further complicate matters, a variety of things can happen to redefine the regulatory jurisdictions in the fringe no man's land. Unincorporated areas can be annexed by adjacent municipalities, or new municipalities can be carved out of unincorporated territory if they meet certain set state requirements as to size and density. Developers, landowners, and affected residents can then engage in an elaborate coalitional struggle to define who regulates what terrain. Boundary manipulation on the metropolitan fringe is a great American urban pastime, played with particular adroitness and sophistication in the growing metropolitan areas of Florida, California, Michigan, and Texas.[34]

MANIPULATION OF SPACE

The spaces that delimit the varying political units in the nation or in a particular metropolis are of differing sizes and shapes. Some of these are such because they adhere to what early surveyors and planners considered to be natural and legitimate means of organizing political spaces. Thus, when river channels or mountain divides or significant vegetation types were used to lay out county or city boundaries, irregular shapes were certain to result. These apparent wiggles were straightened out in subsequent boundary drawing by using straight lines often in areas where earlier natural features had been used.

As man began to see the political significance attached to boundary drawing and the organization of his spaces, he realized that there were many different approaches that could be used to accomplish the same goals. That is, while he may have been concerned with locating a new school or drawing a city council district, just how he proceeded to carry out these tasks often took on political significance. A school would not have to be located equidistant from all children's residences, even though such optimal planning may be desirable in organizing urban school districts. Neither would the same criteria have to be used to locate other schools, as he may let political and social influences outweigh strictly economic considerations. In other words, spaces can be arranged in many differing ways. Man can manipulate spaces for political and social uses to serve his party's political advantage or that of his social group. Just how many spaces are needed in a city or nation, what sizes and shapes they acquire, and what changes are made in line with societal advancement and population alterations are reflected as he organizes spaces.[35] There are three major manipulations of space that are illustrated in the political organization and administration of the nation and its cities. They are malapportionment, gerrymandering, and zoning. They often exist in conjunction at varying levels of the political hierarchy.

Malapportionment. One way of manipulating political space to the advantage of a particular party or group is to apportion the representation in some such way that they are not equated fairly with others. That is, some spaces have more residents than others but they all elect the same number of congressmen or state legislators. This procedure may or may not include gerrymandering schemes. The Supreme Court in its 1962 Baker vs. Carr decision, the one-man–one-vote issue, was triggered by glaring differences in population size of districts sending representatives to Congress. While a few states had population variances between districts that were minor, there were many more that had 10 or 20 percent or more. In some cases, the variations in district population were almost ludicrous. They were not restricted to only rural or urban states or the South or North. They occurred throughout the nation.

The differences in sizes within a state ranged from 236,000 to 635,000 in Alabama (that is, each elected one representative); 303,000 to 553,000 in Pennsylvania; 216,000 to 952,000 in Texas; 374,000 to 540,000 in Kansas; 375,000 to 483,000 in Minnesota; 257,000 to 410,000 in Idaho; and 319,000 to 690,000 in Connecticut. The percent of the districts that deviated by more than 15 percent also varied markedly from ten of fifteen in New Jersey, four of four in Arkansas, six of seven in Maryland, and twenty-four of thirty-eight in California. Deviations less than that amount were found in Maine, North Dakota, Wisconsin, and several other states.[36]

One of the major reasons for court testing of reapportionment schemes was the ignorance and laxity with which states had carried out the task. Decennial censuses did not always result in an examination of the population changes as they might be reflected in new forms of district drawing and representation. Prior to the landmark Supreme Court decision, the last redistricting in Idaho was in 1911, in Louisiana in 1912, in Montana in 1917. Other states were equally tardy in carrying out this responsibility; in South Dakota, Colorado, Rhode Island, Connecticut, Georgia, and Alabama it was 1931. Some states did redistrict in 1951 and 1952 but had not before the Baker vs. Carr decision; these include Maryland, Ohio, Oklahoma, Tennessee, and Virginia.

Publicizing the number of people who elected a representative to Congress revealed in many cases that the protectionist politicians were frequently from the rural and sparsely populated parts of a state. They were not working on legislation favoring the urban areas, often where half to two-thirds of the population lived. Suburban and central city areas quite legitimately felt slighted as their votes counted much less. Such were the bases for cries of reapportionment and numerous and lengthy court battles eventually led to a redistricting of most states.

The issue of overrepresentation and underrepresentation can be amply illustrated by figures from several states. In Michigan in 1963 the state had nineteen representatives elected from a population of slightly less than 8 million. The average population per district was 435,000. Four districts had populations within 10 percent of this figure. However, wide variations existed; one representative from the rural Upper Peninsula was elected from a district of only 177,000 (59 percent less than the state average) and another from the rural north had a district of only 241,000 (45 percent less). On the other hand, the rural overrepresentation was countered by urban underrepresentation. Three districts in the Detroit area had 803,000 (85 percent above the state average); 690,000 (59 percent above); and 665,000 (53 percent above) residents. For the state as a whole, three predominately suburban districts averaged 719,000 and eight mainly rural districts averaged only 340,000. Two mixed districts averaged near the state average.[37] These figures illustrate how less than a majority of the state's population, by organizing the district designs, could by boundary manipulations elect more than a majority of the state's delegates to Congress.

Patterns similar to those in Michigan were exhibited in the election of congressmen from Florida, where the rural Democrats from the panhandle had smaller population bases than in the urban south but elected more members than if the districts had been about equal in population. The average district population was 413,000; two Florida representatives came from rural districts with only 237,000 and 241,000 residents. The Miami portion of the state was carved up into districts of 476,000; 507,000; and 666,000 residents. Extremes in variation existed in Florida even though six of the twelve districts had variations of less than 10 percent. Massachusetts had all its twelve districts within 12 percent of the state average while adjacent Connecticut had variations approximating 40 percent from the state average for three of its six districts. Maine had both its districts only 4 percent from the state average while Maryland had districts ranging in size from 711,000 in Baltimore to 243,000 on the eastern shore. Colorado had ranges from 654,000 for Denver suburbs to only 196,000 for the west and Grand Junction area.

Malapportionment was not only characterized by districts sending representatives to Congress but by state legislatures as well. Some states elected one of their two legislative bodies on the basis of population numbers and the other on the basis of area. This triggered similar arguments that have been raised with respect to the United States House and Senate. While one branch is elected on the basis of population, the other is on the basis of area. Area usually was interpreted to mean counties; and this meant each county could elect one state senator, for example, whether it had 6,000, 60,000, or 600,000 people. Thus, prior to state reapportionment a minority of a state's counties in population could theoretically control one branch of the state legislature, and often they did. It was the rural and small-town sections that retained their traditional power in this manner. For example, prior to redistricting, the state senate in Alabama was controlled by 25 percent of the population. In Florida the figure was 12 percent, in South Carolina 24 percent, and in Virginia 38 percent. Outside the South, values were similar, as in Illinois it was 29 percent, in New Jersey 19 percent, in Maryland 14 percent, in California 11 percent, and in Nevada only 8 percent. Similar discrepancies existed in the lower houses of government for many states.[38]

At a regional level the malapportionment patterns take on striking contrasts. In the South, the most heavily overrepresented sections before reapportionment for the states' senates were those rural areas that were losing population such as west central Tennessee, southern South Carolina, and panhandle Florida (Fig. 6-12). These spaces had politicians who retained powerful positions in their state senates primarily because they did not reapportion and did not lend support to competitive challenges. The advantages they enjoyed were at the expense of the urban areas in most states. For example, the Birmingham, Jackson, Atlanta, Chattanooga, Columbia, Jacksonville, Tampa-St. Petersburg, Orlando, Ft. Lauderdale, and Miami areas all were underrepresented before reapportionment in this legislative body.[39] Once reapportionment occurred the variations within as well as between these states were reduced sharply.

Malapportionment was a cry that urban leaders and politicians uttered in

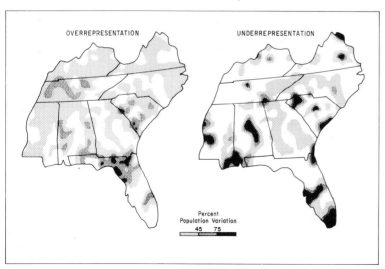

Fig. 6-12 Malapportionment in States' Senate in the South. (After D. O. Bushman and William R. Stanley, "State Senate Reapportionment in the Southeast," *Annals*, 61 (1971), pp. 654–670. Reproduced by permission of the Association of American Geographers.)

the late 1950s and the early 1960s. They felt that the inequities behind their selection and election of state and national delegates were depriving them of a voice in influencing and determining policy for their more populous regions. Financial needs and discussion and solution of urban problems heeded their call for reapportionment. It was understandable that rural or small-town dominated legislatures or both were reluctant to reapportion the state along lines that would lead to lessening their political influence. They had built up their political power by altering their district lines as little as possible (if at all) to ensure their reelection and thereby control over state policies and developments. This is one way that chairmen of House committees were elected (and still are but to a lesser extent) year after year, that is, by protecting their political base by either not altering the outlines or by gerrymandering to insure victory. While the legislatures were dominated by these pork barrelers, they were responsible for helping to upgrade the economy of their districts by building roads (many rural areas in the South and Midwest are very over-roaded at present) and by bringing in federal funds for dams, veterans' hospitals, colleges, military installations, and other government institutions. Yet they did neglect the problems and people in urban areas, even when more people lived there. This is exemplified in California where the regional schisms discussed earlier took on the rural-urban flavor as well. Northern counties continued to dominate the state senate until the 1962 Supreme Court decision forced reapportionment. This brought about a change in the course of state politics, from a north to a south dominance. Originally the representatives of both houses were based on population. Yet the legislature failed in 1921, 1923, and 1925 to reapportion on the basis of the 1920 census. Northern interests, dominated by the Farm Bureau, Grange, and San Francisco Chamber of Commerce, supported a 1926 general election that embodied a plan whereby no county could elect more than one member to the state senate and no senator could represent more than three counties. Thus, northern control was insured for the next thirty-five years as the ten southern counties with 60 percent of the state's population could elect only ten senators while the north had thirty.[40]

Gerrymandering. Another manipulative device to serve to the advantage of a political party or group is gerrymandering. This practice involves forming advantageously shaped districts to insure the election of a congressman or state legislator or city councilman. Gerrymandering is suspected when the shape of districts is severely distorted from an ideal compact shape. Many districts take on an appearance similar to former Representative Emmanuel Celler's of New York City, whose district "looks like somebody threw a shoestring on the map."[41] The origin of the term "gerrymander" is attributed to a Massachusetts governor, Elbridge Gerry, who signed into law a district in Essex County, which when certain animal features were added to its shape, looked like a salamander; hence, the coining of the term "gerry-mander."

While gerrymandered space in the form of grotesque sizes and shapes is attributed to rural politicians, such as the "bacon strips" districts developed by

North Carolina legislatures to sap Republican strength in the western part of the state, it is characteristic of powerful urban politicians as well.[42] Nor is this strategy limited to one major party or one region of the United States (Fig. 6-13). Gerrymandering may take place in other forms than the weird shapes usually associated with it, as it is any way that district lines are drawn to insure more representation than expected. Republicans or Democrats, blacks or whites, central cities or suburbs can be deprived of their political potential by arranging political districts into wedges, rectangles, or nondescript shapes. The United States Supreme Court has never specifically handled the question of gerrymandering, just how much is permissible, probably because measuring it would be difficult. It has ruled in its various reapportionment decisions that districts were to be compact and contiguous and equal in population.[43] Yet there have been and are still ample examples where each is still violated by state legislative plans that have the approval of state courts.

Political scientists have identified five different types of gerrymandering.[44] The first is the *stacked* type; this is the type depicted in Fig. 6-13 in which grotesque shapes are the result of politicians seeking out pockets of party strength. If the districts were arranged in another shape, they might face stronger opposition and candidates may even lose. The second type, labeled *excess vote*, concentrates the opposition in a few districts. Planned landslide victories or "overkills" occur as a result of the majority party giving the opposition political party or minority population some token representation by insuring it can capture a seat or position with a margin of 75 percent or more. This political manipulation and maneuvering was once used by rural pork barrelers as a way of maintaining their control but giving some representation to large urban areas. It has also been applied in cities where the whites "give" the blacks a district or two that black candidates win by 85 to 95 percent. The third type of gerrymander that has been identified is called the

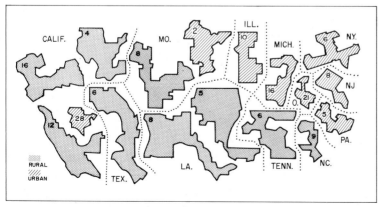

Fɪɢ. 6-13 Gerrymandered Congressional Districts. (U.S. Department of Commerce, *Congressional District Data*, Districts of the 91st Congress, Washington, D.C., 1968.)

wasted votes pattern. In this case the majority political party arranges districts in such a way that the opposition votes are wasted on losing candidates. This pattern actually dilutes the opposition's strength. The gerrymandering pattern illustrating this type of districts looks like urban "bacon strips" or pieces of pie that give the suburbs all or almost all the power and none to the central city. This attack almost insures that candidates from the central city are certain to lose. Pork-barrel power was also insured by diluting urban strength in this manner. *Racial* gerrymandering comprises the fourth type and simply uses any one of the above three types to insure that the blacks, Chicanos, or any racial or ethnic group that has a political power base is gerrymandered or districted out of its potential stronghold. This has been one of the more frequent types of manipulation used by urban politicians to diminish the central city's majority black population. That central cities in the South and North have about 40 percent black population yet few black councilmen or congressional representatives are often linked to this type of gerrymandering. The fifth and the final type is labeled the *silent* gerrymander, silent as the pattern for the district does not change with population changes. This particular type is often called "barnyard politics," as more pigs than people are associated with rural barons who maintained their power base year after year and decade after decade, even while they had less and less of the state's population. As mentioned above, the permanence of these districts for thirty or forty years was one of the reasons reapportionment was carried out in the 1960s.

The juxtaposition of geography and politics in the redistricting process is well illustrated in North Carolina. Here the task involved the issues of malapportionment and gerrymandering. The initial redistricting posed several problems for the state legislature as members came from districts that were drastically different in numbers of people as well as shapes. Most of the types of gerrymandering described above applied to the state. Any plans prior to the accepted final 1967 version attempted to preserve the eastern dominance, to return incumbents, and to gerrymander out Republicans. Once the final plan was approved by the court some of the districts had peculiar shapes even though the populations were similar. The Democrats, much to their disappointment, were not successful in forming districts to insure Republican defeats, as four were elected in 1968.[45]

Gerrymandering is a spatial manipulation that is usually attached to the voting districts of congressmen, state legislators, and urban officeholders. Yet the manipulation of political space can be used in organizing and administering public services in a metropolitan area. The organization schemes of various agencies such as police, fire, selective service, sanitation, education, and health are handled by geographic divisions within a city. These spaces have to be divided in some such way that will insure their delivery to the area's residents. Among the various proposals for the geographic division of space that a city adopts, some may favor the central city and others certain suburbs. The issue of gerrymandering enters the picture when there have been deliberate attempts to favor certain suburbs or parts of a city over others. For example, the various plans for organizing Detroit's school districts can involve gerrymandering and excess manipulation depending on whether integration or local community control is sought.[46] Police and fire protection are other examples where the districts may be constructed to protect and save prize commercial and industrial locations rather than older and poorer areas. In other words, some spaces, by their organization, are overserviced and others are underserviced. When local control of the draft boards was involved in the selection of young men, there were often districts that saw the suburbs and central cities linked. In this way a draft board was able to have a certain pool of low-income blacks from areas that it might decide to induct the quota from instead of from certain favored high-income white suburban areas. Health districts and sanitation zones are other examples where the demand for medical care and trash pickup are not always suited to acute daily and weekly demands of the population. Political manipulation of spaces organized for handling urban services can by some cautious boundary drawing favor certain spaces and peoples over others. It may be that opposition party strongholds or low-income areas or both are spatially discriminated against because they did not favor a particular candidate or bond issue. Quite possibly planners and politicians know their protests may be few and ineffective.

Zoning. Another form of changing the form and uses of space, with political strings attached, is done by zoning. Some of the earliest municipal zoning ordinances were incorporated in the first several decades of this century, as they dealt with commercial and industrial expansion and the health of cities.[47] In effect, zoning was considered an acceptable way to help alleviate some of the urban land use problems. In the past several decades, the last in particular, the term and process have taken on a pejorative connotation as local governments have developed restricted clauses that prohibited the movement of blacks or the invasion of polluting industries or expanding shopping centers. These political divisions have attempted to control their own territorial development and composition by incorporating such clauses in their charters.

The major objective of zoning is to establish a set of legal policies and guidelines that will help direct the social and economic development of certain spaces. It is thus very beneficial in planning as a city can direct and influence its industrial and commercial expansion, residential development, and recreation spaces. In large part zoning helps give and make an image for a city or suburb. Zoned lands approved by nonpartisan zoning boards have given some order to the metropolitan planning process. It has specified types of building codes and space requirements and has ordered patterns to industrial, commercial, and residential developments. These regulations for the use of space have prohibited haphazard arrangements and uses of urban space. Politics is involved when these restrictions apply to certain spaces either within a total urban area or in select parts. The developers are required to conform to certain public standards, such as setting aside part of a housing development for schools and parks. Zoning is thus not without its time and space considerations. While rigid zoning may be characteristic of some northern cities, policies and boards in southern and western cities have often adopted less stringent stances (if any at all) in urban development.

Other than for cities and industries and commercial developments, the art of zoning has taken on a high degree of importance to individuals. Many individuals view the ordinances they have enacted in their city or suburban charter as ways to insure their domains are preserved. They are just as concerned about what goes on in their space as immediately outside. Protecting their suburb from minority group members or low-income groups or multiple-dwelling units is served by attempting to include restrictive covenants in their city charter. Likewise they would not favor adjacent political spaces being zoned for night clubs or X-rated movie houses. These give the spaces an unsavory image. Private property is also involved in the zoning game, as individuals are very concerned with how their personal space can and will be used. Social and economic changes in the past three decades especially have changed property from a piece of public domain that could be purchased and used for the individual's whims to its context within a larger political space.[48] Cities and states have already adopted varying land use policies that rigidly govern the present and potential uses of personal and community spaces.

Within an urban area zoning has been utilized in a variety of ways to devise and organize the spaces to the advantages of certain individuals or groups. In California are a number of examples where cities in the Los Angeles area have developed for specific industrial or commercial purposes, for example, Commerce, Irwindale, Vernon, Industry, and Walnut. Other parts of cities here and elsewhere have developed specifically along street lines to locate noxious industries, to isolate blacks, or to permit gambling and other illicit activities.[49] Zoning policies assume that different criteria are applied to develop the land uses in a metropolitan area, be they for residential (single- or multiple-family), industrial (light or heavy), commercial (shopping or strip development), or recreation (parks or night clubs). The diversity of zoning policies by local governments within a metropolitan area is another major problem facing reorganization and consolidation schemes.

Recent examples where the spaces have been zoned to accommodate specific purposes are in the Black Jack area of St. Louis and the dairy cities in Los Angeles. Black Jack, Missouri, achieved national recognition in 1971 when the residents of this middle-high-income area north of St. Louis objected to a multiple-family dwelling unit plan being built to serve low-income residents. At first the community was unincorporated but when the Park View Heights project was nearing a reality, the suburb quickly incorporated and adopted a zoning regulation prohibiting the construction of homes for more than one family. Although the open housing law of 1968 declared unconstitutional housing clauses with restrictive racial specifications, this case provided a legal test for housing developments and restrictive clauses. Residents of Black Jack stated their reason for incorporating was strictly economic not racial.[50]

Another example where the manipulation of municipal spaces has resulted in some peculiar land use patterns is the incorporation of three dairy cities, Dairyland, Dairy Valley, and Cypress in the Los Angeles city limits. These cities were of early import to the metropolitan area as they supported it with fresh milk. With the demand for more milk and subsequent pressure on the lands in the surrounding southern California metropolitan areas, these three cities incorporated in the mid-1950s. Their strict zoning policies were designed to develop and insure a competitive milk position vis-à-vis northern California and thereby also thwart attempts to purchase lands for residential speculation. As the city increased in population these remained "islands of agriculture amid a growing metropolis."[51] In 1960 these cities comprised 18 square miles, 75,000 cows, and only 6,000 people.

Additional political factors are responsible for these specialized communities.[52] Even though the cost for producing milk is lower in northern California, state laws governing the price of milk make southern California competitive. Through political pressures and favorable zoning policies, the Los Angeles area receives milk from the immediate area and nonperishable dairy products such as cottage cheese and cream from the north. A rather unique state law provides that any area with more than 500 people and the consent of the majority of the land-holders can incorporate into a city status and establish its own zoning ordinances and local property taxes. In this way the dairymen in the Los Angeles area were able to unite and create these dairy cities; land was zoned exclusively for agriculture and the tax assessments made in line with such land use. Speculation for residential land use, alluded to previously, was not permitted or practiced in these cities, even though it was on immediately adjacent lands. In this regard, Fielding, who analyzed this political role comments:

> . . . Because of state control of milk pricing in California, sufficient incentive is not provided for milk distributors to obtain milk from the least-cost producing districts. This political factor is the most important element explaining the location of dairy production in the Los Angeles milk market.[53]

Other examples of peculiar zoning policies can be cited for urban areas. High-income suburbs, often to preserve their exclusiveness, have adopted policies governing the lot sizes, variety of building materials, and housing designs. At times some even become amusing such as the "shadow law" in Palm Springs, California, that states no house shall cast a shadow on another. This restricts the size and orientation of the house as well as the property. Equally as interesting are restrictions placed on "For Sale" signs in Coral Gables, Florida, or the manicuring of lawns and shrubbery. Zoning is a political maneuver that does manipulate and govern the changes in urban space. The fact that the restrictions are not uniform within a metropolitan area leads to economic and social patterns that affect an individual's and city's or suburb's interaction with adjacent spaces.

FOOTNOTES

1. William D. Pattison, "The Original Plan for an American Rectangular Land Survey System," *Surveying and Mapping*, 21 (1961), 339–345; Norman J. W. Thrower, *Original Survey and Land Subdivision*, Chicago, Rand McNally, 1966, pp. 1–14; James E. Vance, Jr., "Areal Political Structure and Its Influence on Urban Pat-

terns," *Yearbook*, Pacific Coast Geographers, 22 (1962), 40–49; and Raymond E. Murphy, "Town Structure and Urban Concepts in New England," *Professional Geographer*, 16:2 (1964), 1–6.

2. Alfred J. Wright, "Ohio Town Patterns," *Geographical Review*, 27 (1937), 615–624; Hildegard Binder Johnson, "Rational and Ecological Aspects of the Quarter Section," *Geographical Review*, 47 (1957), 330–348; and John Fraser Hart, "Field Patterns in Indiana," *Geographical Review*, 58 (1968), 450–471.

3. Edward W. Soja, *The Political Organization of Space*, Washington, D.C., Commission on College Geography, Association of American Geographers, Resource Paper No. 8, 1971, pp. 9–11 and David Harvey, *Explanation in Geography*, London, Edward Arnold, 1969, pp. 191–229.

4. William Edwin Hemphill et al., *Cavalier Commonwealth. History and Government of Virginia*, New York, McGraw-Hill, 1952, pp. 50–51.

5. J. Leonard Jennewein and Jane Boorman, *Dakota Panorama*, Sioux Falls, Dakota Territory Centennial Commission, 1961, pp. 187–195 and 363–373.

6. Ted Klimasewski, "Analysis of Spatial Voting Patterns: An Approach in Political Socialization," *Journal of Geography*, 72 (1973), 26–32.

7. Gaston Litton, *History of Oklahoma*, New York, Lewis Historical Publishing Company, 1957, pp. 495–498.

8. Walton Bean, *California, An Interpretive History*, New York, McGraw-Hill, 1968, pp. 176–177; Herbert Phillips, *Big Wayward Girl, An Informal Political History of California*, New York, Doubleday, 1968, pp. 16–21; and Ralph J. Roske, *Everyman's Eden. A History of California*, New York, Macmillan, 1968, pp. 300–302.

9. Royce D. Delmatier et al., *The Rumble of California Politics. 1848–1970*, New York, Wiley, 1970, p. 211.

10. Rockwell D. Hunt and Nellie Van de Grift Sánchez, *A Short History of California*, New York, Crowell, 1929, pp. 463–464 and 643–644.

11. Madeline Ferrin Paré, *Arizona Pageant, A Short History of the 48th State*, Phoenix, Arizona Historical Foundation, 1965, pp. 211–213.

12. Rupert Norval Richardson, *Texas, The Lone Star State*, New York, Prentice-Hall, 1943, p. 383.

13. James W. Hulse, *The Nevada Adventure. A History*, Reno, University of Nevada Press, 1969, pp. 101–102.

14. Hugh Talmage Lefler and Albert Ray Newsome, *North Carolina*, Chapel Hill, University of North Carolina Press, 1963, pp. 332–338.

15. D. W. Meinig, *The Great Columbia Plain, A Historical Geography, 1805–1910*, Seattle, University of Washington Press, 1968, p. 360.

16. Ibid., pp. 447–448.

17. Jennewein and Boorman, op. cit., p. 193.

18. Bessie L. Lyon, "The Passing of Homer," *Palimpsest*, 3 (1922), 384.

19. Joseph A. Swisher, "The Location of County Seats in Iowa," *Iowa Journal of History and Politics*, 22 (1924), 358. See other numbers of the same volume for fascinating and amusing histories behind county seat locations.

20. Ron Abler, "ZIP-Code Areas as Statistical Regions," *Professional Geographer*, 22:5 (1970), 270–274.

21. *National Atlas of the United States*, Washington, D.C., U.S. Department of the Interior, Geological Survey, 1970, pp. 278–294.

22. *Statistical Abstract of the United States, 1972,* Washington, D.C., U.S. Department of Commerce, 1972, p. 408.
23. U.S. Department of Commerce, *Economic Development Administration, Fiscal 1970. Jobs for America,* Washington, D.C., Government Printing Office, 1970, p. 34.
24. Congressional Quarterly Service, *Representation and Apportionment,* Washington, D.C., 1966.
25. *Statistical Abstract of the United States, 1971,* Washington, D.C., U.S. Department of Commerce, 1971, p. 358; and "Redistricting Report: Few Changes for Either Party," *Congressional Quarterly Weekly Report,* July 8, 1972, pp. 1661–1664.
26. *Congressional Quarterly Report,* ibid., p. 1663.
27. Richard Morrill, "A Geographer in Redistricting Land," Seattle, University of Washington, Department of Geography, 1972, unpublished paper, pp. 5–6. See also his "Ideal and Reality in Reapportionment," *Annals, Association of American Geographers,* 63 (1973), 463–477.
28. Kevin R. Cox, *Conflict, Power and Politics in the City: A Geographic Perspective,* New York, McGraw-Hill, 1973, pp. 27–69.
29. Harold M. Mayer, *The Spatial Expression of Urban Growth,* Washington, D.C., Commission on College Geography, Association of American Geographers, Resource Paper No. 7, 1969, p. 5.
30. Soja, op. cit., p. 46.
31. U.S Department of Commerce, *Local Government Finances in Selected Metropolitan Areas and Large Counties, 1969–1970,* Washington, D.C., Government Printing Office, 1971, pp. 1–5.
32. John D. Eyre, "City-County Territorial Competition: The Portsmouth, Virginia Case," *Southeastern Geographer,* 9:2 (1969), 26–38.
33. Soja, op. cit., pp. 48–49; Cox, op. cit.; and John C. Bollens and Henry Schmandt, *The Metropolis, Its People, Politics, and Economic Life,* New York, Harper & Row, 1970, pp. 279–372.
34. Oliver P. Williams, *Metropolitan Political Analysis, A Social Access Approach,* New York, Free Press, 1971, pp. 70–71.
35. These various aspects are treated in Bryan H. Massam, *The Spatial Structure of Administrative Systems,* Washington, D.C., Commission on College Geography, Association of American Geographers, Resource Paper No. 12, 1972.
36. Howard D. Hamilton, ed., *Legislative Apportionment. Key to Power.* New York, Harper & Row, 1964, p. 131.
37. "CD [Congressional District] Count: 203 Rural, 50 Suburban, 103 Urban, 79 Mixed," *Congressional Quarterly Weekly Report,* September 20, 1963, p. 1649.
38. Hamilton, op. cit., pp. 6–7.
39. Donald O. Bushman and William R Stanley, "State Senate Reapportionment in the Southeast," *Annals, Association of American Geographers,* 61 (1971), 654–670.
40. Delmatier et al., op. cit., p. 211.
41. "How the Census Shapes the Vote," *Business Week,* November 28, 1970, p. 46.
42. V. O. Key, Jr., *Southern Politics,* New York, Knopf, 1949, p. 226.
43. Congressional Quarterly Service, op. cit.
44. Andrew Hacker, *Congressional Districting. The Issue of Equal Representation,* Washington, D.C., Brookings Institution, 1963, pp. 40–70; and Douglas M. Orr,

"The Persistence of the Gerrymander in North Carolina Congressional Redistricting," *Southeastern Geographer*, 9:2 (1969), 39–54.

45. Orr, ibid.
46. Michael A. Jenkins and John W. Shepherd, "Decentralizing High School Administration in Detroit: An Evaluation of Alternative Strategies of Political Control," *Economic Geography*, 48 (1972), 95–106; and Cox, op. cit., pp. 105–131.
47. Two useful books on zoning are Richard F. Babcock, *The Zoning Game*, Madison, University of Wisconsin Press, 1969; and Seymour Toll, *Zoned Americans*, New York, Grossman, 1969.
48. John E. Cribbet, "Changing Concepts in the Law of Land Use," *Land Use Controls*, 1 (1967), 21–54.
49. Norman Williams, Jr., *The Structure of Urban Zoning*, New York, Buttenheim, 1966, pp. 23–227, discusses various types of zoning with legal documentation.
50. "Fixing the Odds in Black Jack," *Time*, April 26, 1971, pp. 19–20.
51. Gordon J. Fielding, "Dairying in Cities Designed to Keep People Out," *Professional Geographer*, 14:1 (1962), 16.
52. Gordon J. Fielding, "The Los Angeles Milkshed: A Study of the Political Factor in Agriculture," *Geographical Review*, 54 (1964), 1–12.
53. Ibid., p. 9. For another California urban zoning peculiarity in Los Angeles see Howard J. Nelson, "The Vernon Area, California—A Study of the Political Factor in Urban Geography," *Annals, Association of American Geographers*, 42 (1952), 177–191.

Chapter 7

BOUNDARIES
AND
INTERACTION

Morality knows nothing of geographical
boundaries or distinctions of race.

Herbert Spencer

In dealing with the organization of spaces, the previous chapter focused primarily on how and why man has established certain types and scales of spaces. Less emphasis was given to the actual separating of space. This involves boundaries, their delimitation (that is, what methods are used to define the boundaries), and demarcation (the actual manner in which boundaries are identified in space). Boundaries are important to the political geographer examining the United States as they reveal the way in which the nation has been pieced together like pieces in a multicolored jigsaw puzzle. Furthermore, boundaries are important in that their presence is reflected in varying degrees of human behavior. This is true for some state as well as international boundaries.

Even a cursory examination of boundaries in the United States reveals they are of different length and shape. Some follow parallels and meridians as in much of western United States; others follow river channels and mountain divides. The

177

boundaries of some political units enclose that space in basically rectangular fashion, whereas any number of states have peculiar shapes or parts of their boundaries that seemingly defy rational explanation. State, county, and township boundaries appear fairly intact, in that changes have been few in the past decade. Legal limits of cities and metropolitan areas have changed with growth and expansion into neighboring townships (or towns), counties, or even into more than one state.

By the very nature of outlining a state's or nation's territory, there have been disputes over specific spaces. Claims often resulted from hastily conducted surveys or inaccurate measures. These disputes were involved in some of the earliest settled areas of the United States and continued even into the twentieth century. It was not until 1973 that the courts decided on the state boundaries for Michigan and Ohio in Lake Erie. Establishing the final boundaries for states and the United States and its two neighbors was settled by compromise, sometimes, however, after legal battles or minor military campaigns. The definite "lines" marking where one state or nation ended and another began became important in land settlement claims, port or river access, and mineral lode rights. State and federal claims to lands such as the Great Salt Lake remain undecided at this time. The rights to the mineral salts are at the basis of the controversy.[1]

In terms of human behavior, boundaries can be viewed in a number of ways. The boundary may be permeable, that is, crossing from one political space to another does not alter an individual's daily or weekly social or economic travels.[2] This is the case for most boundary crossings within cities and states in the United States. Impermeable boundaries would present a barrier to the individual. There may be few legal entry points, as along the United States-Mexican border, or the person may consider the border interrogation as an element likely to give "the border" and the neighboring foreign nation some significance. The transportation lines crossing international borders indicate whether the separating line disrupts or attracts interaction. As one example, along the United States-Canada boundary rail networks in both nations are separated by the forty-ninth parallel; it acts as a divide whereas it does not for primary and secondary quality roads.[3]

While boundaries may appear fixed on maps as well as in space, the significance of them changes. Township, county, and state boundaries once were important in the social and political organization of the nation. With rapid communication and the increasing mobility of the nation's population, lines separating these spaces are diminishing in importance. This is not to imply that all spaces are alike as man still can construct and enact zoning, industrial, social, or criminal legislation that differentiates one political unit from another. Metropolitan boundaries in particular have not remained the same, as the incorporation of political units of varying size, shape, and complexity into a homogeneous political city has been fraught with many problems. Behind such difficulties have been calls for some reorganization or restructuring of political spaces that will provide a way to alleviate the urban concerns arising from boundary designs.

Even in the international sphere boundaries have lost much of their earlier importance. Air power and satellite development have reduced the separate de-marcation of air space for the United States, Canada, and Mexico. The evolution and development of a nation's political, social, and economic programs with its neighbors is seen in the lessening of border tensions, especially when land and air space is involved. This is in part true for ocean space as well, although the fishing and mining claims in territorial waters of bordering nations may present legal problems in the future.

In the discussion below the focus is on the development of the United States and the role boundaries have played in shaping the individual states and the nation. The international boundaries are similarly examined. Aside from the role of boundaries in the organization of political units, the ways in which these affect human behavior are treated. As will be seen in the unfolding discussion, while some places may be only "lines on a map," in other parts of the nation and especially in international boundaries, behavior reflected in shopping and communication varies with the presence of "the line."

DELIMITING THE NATION'S POLITICAL UNITS

Evolution of Boundaries. The present boundaries for these units were not imprinted on the physical and social surface overnight. They represent more than two centuries of man's defining and delimiting space at various levels. From the unspecified Indian claims to the original charters and grants of acquisition to France, Britain, Spain, and Mexico, the political spaces have been delimited. The original coastal settlements along the Northeast underwent change as the gradual westward movement of the population took place. Original companies establishing political bases in New England or the Middle Atlantic found that disputes arose between them. This resulted in some boundaries being fixed early as the Maryland-Pennsylvania line. Some states were formed from other states, as Kentucky from Virginia Company lands and Delaware from Lord Baltimore's Maryland grant. Settlement beyond the Alleghenies into the Northwest Territories and Louisiana Purchase lands resulted in many vast territorial claims for Michigan, Arkansas, Nebraska, and Iowa. As the numbers of residents moving west increased and some permanency of settlement developed, minimum population requirements were met for admission to the Union. Political maps for most of the last century changed every decade as territorial claims first increased in size then later decreased with new states being formed.[4] Boundaries marked spaces that were easy to delimit, such as the grid system used in much of western United States. Disputes over territories developed with foreign nations; some were settled amicably, others not so, as with the Mexican War, after which the United States acquired huge chunks in the Southwest. Demarcating and defining political space were important to the evolving nation for individual homesteading schemes as well as for the confines of the entire political organization, from townships to states. Often the process was easy as there were few legal substantiations to Indian claims that were considered accurate or necessary to consider in laying out and selling newly acquired "public" lands. Politicians and surveyors sitting in the nation's capital or in territorial capitals or in overseas locations often learned later that what may have appeared as clear descriptions resulted in ambiguous demarcation. Colonial North Carolina is a case in point where the ambiguous wording in the colonial charters led to over a century of controversy with her neighbors.[5] Furthermore, with westward settlement in the seventeenth, eighteenth, and nineteenth centuries, the shape of the present state gradually evolved (Fig. 7-1).

One example where a state was created from other territories and states is Idaho. Originally it was part of Oregon Territory and then Washington Territory (Fig. 7-2). When these territories became states, the lands left over became part of Idaho Territory. Montana's western boundary was fixed once it joined the Union. In economic orientation and cultural ties, contrasts that had developed earlier deepened between the panhandle and southern Idaho. At one time the panhandle even threatened secession and formation of a state of Lincoln. Even though these plans were never carried out, they do represent the sectionalism that developed within the state for internal improvement funds, the state capital, and the state university. At the base of much of the internal diversity with Idaho was the way in which the state was created. A geographer who has investigated the problem has commented on the salient historical developments:

> This completes the evolution of Idaho's outline. The changes occurred mostly at the request of other states and territories. Like a remnant of cloth from which the desired pieces were cut, Idaho's shape possesses neither logic nor beauty—it has been called a "geographic monstrosity."[6]

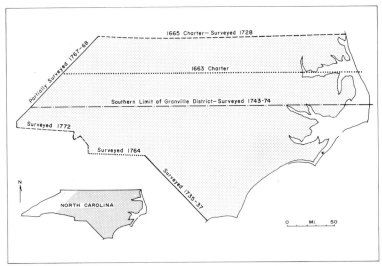

Fig. 7-1 Evolution of North Carolina's Boundaries. (After H. R. Merrens, *Colonial North Carolina in the Eighteenth Century*, Chapel Hill, University of North Carolina Press, 1964, p. 30.)

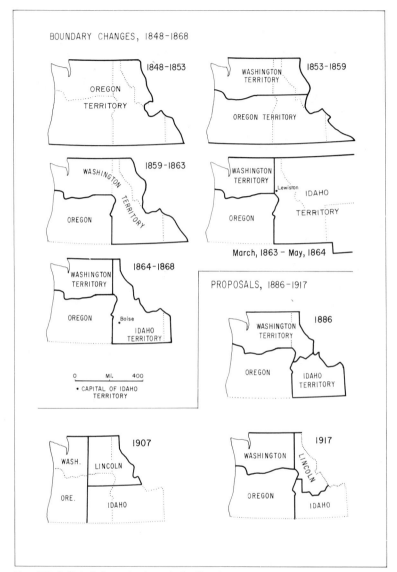

BOUNDARY CHANGES, 1848-1868

1848-1853
OREGON TERRITORY

1853-1859
WASHINGTON TERRITORY
OREGON TERRITORY

1859-1863
WASHINGTON TERRITORY
OREGON

March, 1863 – May, 1864
WASHINGTON TERRITORY
Lewiston
IDAHO TERRITORY
OREGON

1864-1868
WASHINGTON TERRITORY
OREGON
Boise
IDAHO TERRITORY

0   MI.   400
• CAPITAL OF IDAHO TERRITORY

PROPOSALS, 1886-1917

1886
WASHINGTON TERRITORY
OREGON
IDAHO TERRITORY

1907
WASH.   LINCOLN
ORE.   IDAHO

1917
WASHINGTON   LINCOLN
OREGON   IDAHO

Fig. 7-2 Political Organization of the Pacific Northwest. (After B. E. Thomas, "Boundaries and Internal Problems of Idaho," *Geographical Review*, vol. 39, 1949, p. 100. Adapted, with permission. Copyrighted by the American Geographical Society of New York.)

When controversies developed between states they were often based on minor territorial claims such as access to rivers or the proper parallel or meridian to be used. Settling disputes was important; when states were formally organizing themselves for admittance to the Union, their boundaries had to be fixed. When different surveys defined a territory's boundaries differently, the situation was solved by adjudication, new surveys, or in some cases even minor military border skirmishes. Politics was also involved in choosing which surveys were to be accepted by the territorial officials and which ones were to be recommended to Congress.

A major exception to the small amounts of territory being "fought for" and awarded by states was the Michigan-Ohio claims to the "Toledo Strip." The two states had differing claims, both of which had some validity, for this important western Lake Erie site. Michigan claimed the mouth of the Maumee River as its southern boundary in 1816. However, Ohio claimed the same land (eight miles wide on the east and four miles on west) when it entered the Union in 1803. Congress, President Jackson, and the neighboring states of Illinois and Indiana all had a hand in trying to settle this ticklish question. The two states involved claimed this 468 square mile strip at various times by holding courts and encouraging settlement. The inability to agree on Michigan's southern boundary delayed its admission into the Union until 1837. The question was finally settled with Ohio being granted the strip and Michigan receiving what is now the Upper Peninsula. Michigan Territory had already included the eastern third of the peninsula. Residents of the Upper Peninsula were not wholeheartedly in support of joining the rest of Michigan. They wanted to form the territory of Huron as they felt Detroit and the Lower Peninsula would 'neglect them.[7] It is interesting that similar sentiments are still heard today. Examples of similar political settlements involving territorial claims can be cited for most states in the past two centuries.

Some state boundary lines were much more than east-west or north-south lines on a map. They affected national settlement patterns and regional identities and the entry of states and territories into the Union. Three examples of political boundaries that had regional and national ramifications were the Mason-Dixon line, the Missouri Compromise, and the Oregon Territory limits.

The Mason-Dixon line between Maryland and Pennsylvania traditionally has served to separate the North from the South. Even though this 230-mile line completed in 1768 was to separate the lands of William Penn from Lord Baltimore, it remained important in the Civil War. Present-day politics may have resurrected this regional boundary as seen in President Nixon's vice-presidential selection coming from Maryland in 1968. Nixon's strategy was to capture border and southern states en route to the White House, and while many Americans might not consider Maryland a southern state, it does have a cultural and political heritage that gives it a transitional flavor.

Last century the southern boundary of Missouri, lat. 36° 30' N, became a line separating the admission of slave-holding states to the Union. According to the Missouri Compromise of 1820, Congress decreed that slavery was prohibited north of this line. Southern states formally brought into the Union after that date were "matched" by a free state in the North.

The presidential election of 1844 involved the settling of United States and British claims in the Pacific Northwest. At issue was the northern limit of the Oregon Territory. President Polk ran on the slogan "Fifty-four-forty or fight," which showed his desire for a formal boundary limit. Also, it involved the evolving nation's territorial claims. After the election, negotiations between the United States and Britain led to an agreement based on the forty-ninth parallel, in essence continuing the boundary westward that already was used in separating the Canadian and American Great Plains. This 1846 treaty stated the international boundary was to follow the forty-ninth parallel west to the middle of the channel separating Vancouver Island from the mainland, south through the Juan de Fuca Straits and into the Pacific Ocean.

Morphology of Political Units. Boundaries in space result in political units acquiring a variety of shapes. The shape of the nation, state, or city may have political consequences that affect its political organization and administration. Shapes as related to an effective government were of greater concern when interaction and communication were less. States that have great breadth and little width may have been settled by varying groups who later amalgamated into one political unit. Problems often arose in the form of sectionalism. Such would hold true for Tennessee where the Appalachians, Highland Rim area, and Delta counties have been at odds on more than one political issue in the past century. North Carolina is another where the three marked physical regions, Coastal Plain, Piedmont, and Appalachians have differing political and social ideologies. California is another example. Often the physical distance separating these groups led to the development of separatist movements. Some were successful as in West Virginia being formed from Virginia. Distance even today can still be a hindrance to political development, distances that are in part due to the shape of the state. For example, from Key West to Pensacola, Florida, the distance is 813 miles; from Beaumont to El Paso, Texas, 828 miles; from Brownsville to Amarillo, Texas, 788 miles; from San Diego to Yreka, California, 760 miles; and from Detroit to Ironwood, Michigan, 611 miles. Granted that the distances are large, but it is also the cultural and political differences that exist at various "ends" of these states that make them tied more to adjacent states than the one in which they are politically included. This interaction is especially difficult in those states that are physically separated, Michigan and Virginia. The Upper Peninsula is more tied economically to Wisconsin than Lower Michigan and Virginia's eastern shore is tied more to the Maryland part of the shore.

Political geographers have regarded the ideal shape for a political unit as a circle. If the population were concentrated evenly and the capital in the center, all parts would theoretically be equally accessible. The surveying methods in which states were created in the eighteenth through the twentieth centuries allowed no circular states. Only northern Delaware has an arc for its boundary. This marked the northern boundary of the Duke of York's land, an arc based 12 miles from New Castle.[8] More frequently, geometrical methods used to delimit states left a number that were squares or rectangles. Most of these are found in the western half of the United States. States that have a square or fairly square shape include Wyoming, Utah, Colorado, Arizona, and New Mexico. Rectangles bounded by specific meridians and parallels are more common, as in North and South Dakota, Kansas, Oregon, Montana, and Nebraska. Some have one border of the state marked by a river or mountain range that disrupts it from being a perfect rectangle. Even states that appear almost "perfect" in space—that is, a square or rectangle—were not always initially delimited in that manner. In Wyoming, had not Congress granted the Wyoming Territory a part of Idaho Territory in 1868 "to maintain its symmetry," it would have not been the shape it is at present.[9] The Texas and Oklahoma panhandles do not exactly jibe because the official Texan boundary was made to coincide with the west fence of the XIT ranch.

Geometry was used to demarcate states in the western half of the nation. Natural or physical features were used more in the East, although not exclusively. Major transport arteries or barriers such as the Mississippi and Ohio rivers and the Appalachian system helped shape the present boundaries of at least fifteen states. The combination of surveys results in states having a variety of shapes, some being very small and compact in size, for example, the earliest settled states in New England; long and narrow states as in Tennessee and North Carolina; rectangles with panhandles or river borders for Alabama, Mississippi, and Indiana, or rather amorphous shapes as in Maryland and West Virginia. The shapes of many states illustrate the desire for direct access to the oceans or lakes or major rivers. Examples of this include the Erie Triangle purchase by Pennsylvania, the Gulf ports established in Mississippi and Alabama, and the importance of the Missouri-Mississippi river system to interior states.

A state outline map of the United States reveals a number of peculiar appendages that are explained by some fascinating historical and cultural developments. Often some group or individual wanted to be included in said state rather than another, so the final boundaries may have been adjusted. Or it may be that survey lands "forgot" some territory. One of the most striking features on an outline map is the number of states with panhandles. Some are long and narrow and quite large as in Oklahoma, Idaho, and Florida. Others are somewhat smaller such as in Maryland and West Virginia. Utah, Nebraska, and Texas all have panhandles that are quite large and stubby. Minipanhandles can be found in Missouri, Alabama, Mississippi, and New Mexico.

The Idaho panhandle remains from the controversy over present lands in the northern part of the state last century. This has been alluded to above. The western boundary of the panhandle was delimited for Washington in 1863 and the eastern boundary for Montana the next year. This "in between space" became a zone of competition between Montana miners and eastern Washington agriculturalists. The panhandle represented a buffer between the two jealous neighboring states and a problem to southern Idaho as well, as the economic and cultural orientations were much different.[10]

The Oklahoma story is somewhat different in that the present panhandle was not desired by any state. When the state boundaries for neighboring Kansas, New Mexico Territory, and Texas were created, this left an unclaimed rectangle of about 5700 square miles (larger than Connecticut) in between these three states. It was really a space without a government until it became part of the Oklahoma Territory. Originally it was not within the territory as the western boundary of these lands was fixed at the 100th meridian. As one historian has commented, "It simply became a lost orphan in the Great West."[11] In the western settlement where land claims were important, this rectangular plot was overlooked in search for more valuable lands farther west.

Three other states with rather unusual shapes in the sense of a number of projections and indentations are Missouri, West Virginia, and Maryland. The Missouri "boot," that appendage in the extreme southeast, is included in Missouri because of one individual, J. Hardeman Walker. He owned a plantation near Caruthersville, a Mississippi River town south of lat. 36° 30′ N parallel that became the southern boundary for Missouri. Walker along with support from several river towns in the immediate vicinity had greater sentiment at the time to the northern river center, St. Louis, rather than Arkansas Point to the south. These settlers petitioned to be excluded from Arkansas, where they naturally belonged. This meant that for the smaller area, Missouri's southern boundary became lat. 36° N and the St. Francis River the western border of the boot.[12] The northern panhandle of West Virginia represents the land between the Ohio River and the western boundary of Pennsylvania, which was agreed on by Pennsylvania and Virginia in 1784. The eastern panhandle includes two counties, Jefferson and Berkeley, that West Virginia wanted to include in its state in order to maintain control over the Baltimore and Ohio Railroad. Virginia fought the inclusion of these counties, however, and Congress finally sided with West Virginia, even though there were Virginia supporters within their bounds.[13] Maryland's shape follows the early territorial claims Lord Baltimore received on the eastern shore to the narrow panhandle in the west that is bounded by the Potomac River (in one place less than two miles) and the Pennsylvania border, the famous Mason-Dixon line.

Just as there are different shapes for the states, so are there for the counties (Fig. 6-1). Elongated shapes as in Virginia demonstrate the importance of access to the ocean or Chesapeake Bay or both for the early county governments. Similar elongated shapes characterize parts of those states within the Appalachian system. Ridges and river channels were used to delimit these minor units. The flat Midwest best reveals the use of the township and range system. The counties in Kansas and Iowa, for example, are arranged in almost a perfect checkerboard fashion. In Iowa fifty-nine of the ninety-nine counties have between 460–660 square miles; in Kansas 45 of the 105 have between 720 and 920 square miles. Many of these are squares and have their county seats located in the geographical centers, a pattern that holds true for many state capitals as well.

As stated in the previous chapter, counties evolved with the growth and expansion of a state. There were instances where counties were formed from existing ones. Subdividing and further subdividing were not unusual. In some states, counties even engaged in legal and armed battles. The famous Hatfield-McCoy feud represented a county battle between Pike County, Kentucky (pro-Union) and

Logan County, West Virginia (pro-Confederate) in the 1880s. Local law enforcement was almost nil in both counties as the two clans engaged in open warfare. Even the United States Supreme Court got involved in the political affairs at these counties, mainly because Pike County officials entered Logan County and abducted members of the Hatfield clan.[14]

Political space to the traveler is demarcated by road signs (sometimes attractive) to the state he is entering. Frequently this is immediately preceded by a public advertisement for the state he is departing, thanking him for his presence and hoping for a quick return. The boundaries do not usually serve as places to stop, reduce speed, or alter particular forms of behavior unless there are specific reasons. Truck traffic carrying interstate commerce frequently has to check in at stands near the borders. Some travelers do take advantage of special gas prices, liquor stores, and illicit activities in state border locations. Similar experiences may exist in crossing county lines. For most observant travelers, they are made aware by a small sign as they pass from one county to the next or from one city into another. In essence the lines mean nothing as the boundaries between these political units are completely permeable. County lines may make a difference if one lives in a "dry" county and wants to purchase liquor in a neighboring one. Also tax rates and insurance rates may be lower in adjacent counties; this may influence one's decision where to build a new home or locate a branch of his company. Town or township lines are generally not marked on the landscape.

THE INTERNATIONAL BOUNDARIES

Establishment and Demarcation. Just as states within the United States developed their present size and shape due to population expansion, military conquest, and resource rivalries, so have the boundaries separating the nation from Mexico and Canada. Although these boundaries may appear as natural today because of their permanence, this stability has not always existed. Disputes between the United States and its neighbors went into the twentieth century, especially in establishing the permanent Canada-Alaska boundary. Prior to that, controversies dating from the eighteenth century arose over the St. Croix River along the Maine-New Brunswick boundary to the Oregon Territory and forty-ninth parallel issue last century.[15] The forty-ninth parallel in particular was established in two different periods. The section from Lake-of-the-Woods in Minnesota to the Rocky Mountains (then called Stony Mountains) was established separating United States and British interests in 1818. The westward extension to the Strait of St. Georgia was fixed in 1846 after the "fifty-four-or-forty" fight alluded to above. The entire length of the United States–Canada boundary is 3987 miles. The Alaska-Canada boundary is 1538 miles. The entire boundary is marked by a series of straight lines, even in rivers as turning point monuments on shore mark the spaces of the two nations.

The United States-Mexico border also has evolved from the Spanish and

Mexican claims to the lands that are now within the United States. The Treaty of Guadalupe Hidalgo in 1848 following the Mexican War established the Rio Grande as part of the space separating Mexico and the United States. The Gadsden Purchase from Mexico in 1853 rounded out the western boundary dividing the two nations. The United States bought the land in order to permit construction of the Southern Pacific railroad. Most of the disputes have been over specific changes in river channels in the Rio Grande or the irrigation rights to the Colorado River. The length of the international boundary from the Gulf of Mexico to the Pacific Ocean is 1933 miles.

The delimitation of international boundaries has also resulted in its share of political oddities. One such is the Point Roberts, Washington, area, a small piece of land south of the forty-ninth parallel in the Strait of Georgia. This tiny bit of United States real estate is approachable by land only through Canada. This exclave has developed as a summer resort community serving Canadian rather than Washington residents. Its physical isolation from the mainland has brought it closer economically and socially to Canada.[16] The forty-ninth parallel did not continue westward into the Pacific Ocean as it would have split Vancouver Island, an early and important Canadian commercial node. Another exclave is found in the Lake-of-the-Woods area separating Minnesota and Manitoba. Like the one in the Washington area, it can only be approached by land through Manitoba. The Minnesota "neck" represents the early belief that the Mississippi River originated in the Lake-of-the-Woods area. Finding the origin of this river was important for settling United States and Canadian claims in the late eighteenth century.

The most recent boundary settlement between the United States and Mexico involves the completion of the 1964 American-Mexican Chamizal Convention Act. The El Chamizal section of the Rio Grande separating El Paso and Ciudad Juárez had been a political problem confronting the two nations for over a century. The Treaty of Guadalupe Hidalgo of 1848 established the middle course of the Rio Grande or the section south of New Mexico to the Gulf as the official boundary. The problem that developed soon thereafter was that the course of the river channel changed often due to flooding. This created a number of cutoffs leaving the political territory of each nation not always easy to identify. In most parts of the river where there were cutoffs, each nation exchanged approximately equal parcels of land from time to time according to the Banco Treaty of 1905. The river had cut about 10,000 acres from the United States and 18,000 acres from Mexico during these times. No problems were created in these early years as the lands were remote and contained no valuable agricultural, industrial, commercial, or urban lands. The section known as El Chamizal in particular became a problem as early as 1869 when the Mexican government questioned whether the lands in this part of the river (598 acres) actually belonged to the United States because of a southward shift of the river. What the new river channel had done was to add that land to the United States. In 1895 Mexico laid first claim to the El Chamizal but the United States view was that the land belonged to it, as a result of the normal processes of river erosion and deposition. To reduce the flooding that at

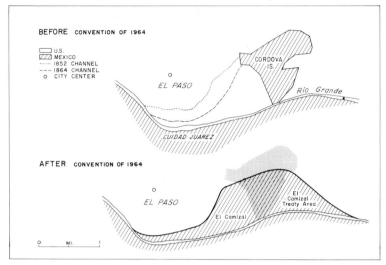

FIG. 7-3 El Chamizal Boundary Dispute. (After J. Hill, "El Chamizal: A Century-old Boundary Dispute," *Geographical Review*, vol. 55, 1965, pp. 513 and 517. Adapted, with permission. Copyrighted by the American Geographical Society of New York.)

times became serious, a diversion of the river was carried out in 1899 that created a Mexican political bridgehead, called Cordova Island, in the El Paso area (Fig. 7-3). This "island" belonged to Mexico but the international boundary went around it.

Finally in 1910 both nations agreed to arbitrate the El Chamizal problem. Canada was the neutral member of the team. The majority of the commission voted that the area between the 1852 and 1864 channels belonged to the United States and the land between 1864 and 1911 channels was Mexico's (Fig. 7-3). Even though both nations had agreed initially to accept the decision of the commission, the United States refused to accept it. It felt the commission's task was to decide on the entire tract. Further, the United States felt that the 1864 flood, one of the more serious, did not carve a new channel and, additionally, it could not even be located precisely. The Mexican government felt the land should be turned over to her, but it was not until Kennedy became president that the United States honored the commission's decision. The act cited above was signed by President Kennedy and President López Mateos in Mexico City in August 1963.

Once the treaty was signed there were still problems to be solved between the two nations as Cordova Island and El Chamizal were utilized by the city of El Paso as well as by industrial, commercial, and residential developments. The problem with the island was that it was a bottleneck to east-west transportation and communications in El Paso. It really impeded the growth of both cities as Ciudad Juárez only had entry through a narrow connection at the island's base. Also the industrial and agricultural interest in El Chamizal had to be compensated. The railroads owned the industrial lands and the University of Texas the agricultural lands. Those residing in the area also had to be relocated. Mexico had no such problem in the northern part of the Cordova Island, the 193-acre section ceded to the United States by the treaty. The land was vacant. According to the 1964 agreement the United States ceded 823 acres known as El Chamizal to Mexico and the United States received the northern part of Cordova Island. A combined International Boundary and Water Commission was created in the agreement and was to construct a new channel and relocate the six bridges.[17]

International boundaries are demarcated in a number of ways. At the international crossings into Mexico and Canada entry stations are found on bridges on the Rio Grande, over the Great Lakes, and over the St. Lawrence. The traveller is aware he enters another nation by signs in Spanish, English, or French (if in French-speaking provinces) indicating a border crossing is ahead. At such places the traveller may be asked his citizenship, state of birth or residence, destination, and length of travel in Canada or Mexico. Similar questioning is conducted when crossing any of the number of land entry stations. Plates on bridges mark the actual boundary between the nations. On land a series of monuments or markers indicates the boundary. Often monuments appear along roadsides or in open fields. Forested lands between Canada and the United States are marked by a 20-foot cleared swath. This practice was introduced by former Alaska Governor Riggs who was also on the Boundary Commission from 1935–1945. He believed "A cleared vista is an essential element of a well-marked boundary."[18] International boundaries are also marked by reference markers in lakes and rivers. A series of lighted buoys and steel spars and lighted towers is used on the St. Lawrence, Great Lakes, and in the Washington-British Columbia waters. Stone monuments with turning points and angle markings are found along some shorelines. Along the entire 5500 mile United States-Canada border there are over 8000 references, monuments, and marked points on land and water.

Economic Patterns. The transportation network on each side of the international boundaries reveals something of the interaction levels between spaces on each side. Along the United States-Canada border, particularly in the western half of the boundary, the rail and highway networks of both nations run in an east-west direction. In fact, they almost parallel one another in this area of homogeneous physical terrain. The forty-ninth parallel has been labeled by one geographer as a classic example of an artificial boundary.[19] The rail pattern is more offset by the international boundary than is the highway pattern. Many links almost reach the border, but few actually cross it.[20] Few major highways run in a north-south direction. From International Falls, Minnesota, to western Alberta there are only five major roads that cross the boundary. The Trans-Canada Highway and United States Route 2 essentially run parallel to the forty-ninth parallel, often less than 100 miles apart in an area of flat plains. Along the United States-Mexico border the road pattern is more striking. United States highways 80, 90, 277, and 83 hug the border from southern California to Brownsville, Texas. Immediately to the south of the border, there is no cluster of highways, except for the extreme eastern border with Texas. The road network in this part of the United States is like that near Canada, running east-west. Across into Mexico there are few major roads that run north-south. Along this nearly 2000-mile border there are only eight major crossing points and most of these are in extreme southern Texas or in southern California. The rail patterns are essentially the same. The pattern of these transport networks affects the degree of intercourse between the nations involved and the residents living in the spaces adjacent to the boundaries. Whether the individuals crossing the border into Mexico or Canada are actually overcoming barriers, the rail and highway networks of the United States have been constructed to "fill in" the spaces and tie the east and west parts of the nation together rather than promote ready commercial ties to the neighbors to the north and south. There are cases where the Canadian Pacific railroad was permitted to construct a route from Montreal through Maine to New Brunswick, and where the Michigan Central railroad built a route through southern Ontario to connect Detroit and Buffalo.

Another example where the United States-Canada international boundary represents distinct economic patterns is in the agricultural activities in the Great Plains section. This is an area that has a similar physical base and cultural development. Economically it is one of the major wheat areas of North America, a crop valuable to the economy of both nations. Whether it is destined for regional or national or international markets, its dominance is not reflected by the forty-ninth parallel (Fig. 7-4). However, secondary and tertiary crops reflect the government policies of the nations involved. Barley is more important to United States farmers

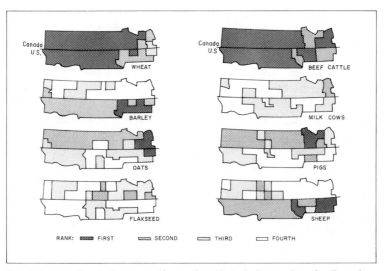

FIG. 7-4 Agricultural Patterns Along the United States–Canada Boundary. (After Henry J. Reitsma, "Crop and Livestock Production in the Vicinity of the United States–Canada Border," *Professional Geographer*, 23:3 (1971), pp. 218–219. Reproduced by permission of the Association of American Geographers.)

as it is related to the wheat allotment programs where acreage is restricted. Oats are more valuable to Canadian farmers as it is tied to their greater agricultural self-sufficiency and livestock needs. Flax is important primarily in the Mennonite-settled areas of Canada. Similar agricultural patterns appear when livestock densities are measured on both sides of this international border. The density of beef cattle, the dominant animal, is not affected by the forty-ninth parallel. Milk cows, however, have a pattern that reflects each nation's supply areas for dairy products. Milk in Canada is produced to supply the Winnipeg area; the dairy lands in the United States are farther south in Minnesota and Wisconsin. Hogs have a higher density in Canada because they are related to oats and the diversified farming endeavors. They are unimportant in the United States. Sheep, on the other hand, are found in greater numbers in the United States than Canada because the United States government subsidizes wool production by the National Wool Act of 1954. Basically the contrasts in agricultural livelihood on each side of the border reflect the governments' roles in agriculture, alternative and competing producing areas, and market destination. To some extent the cultural-settlement pattern is important.[21] These variations in crop and livestock patterns and farm size are reflected by a boundary that passes through a basically homogeneous environment.

BOUNDARIES AND BEHAVIOR

The delimitation and demarcation of political boundaries result in a variety of forms of behavior for residents living in the immediate area as well as for those some distance away. Boundary behavior will be reflected in the perceptions, attitudes, and forms of interaction if there is some special significance attached to the political space immediately beyond the border itself. Otherwise boundaries are likely to have no meaning. While the behavior may take on particular note in the vicinity of an international boundary, there are cases even in the United States where state boundaries separate differing social and economic environments. Unless boundaries are purely functional, that is, only administrative as for police or fire or water districts, there is likely to be some significance attached to the ways in which they affect individual and group behavior. Many boundaries in a city or state do not result in differing behavior for those who move across these during the course of a day or week. On the other hand, suburban limits or state lines may affect a resident's decision where to live because of lower property taxes, where to purchase major household commodities because of lower sales taxes, or where to find certain types of recreation that are outlawed within his own space. More than one Floridian has seized upon opportunities to obtain quick blood tests just inside southern Georgia, or a Wisconsin resident to purchase colored margarine in northern Illinois, or a Californian to obtain an instant divorce in Nevada, or a New Yorker to obtain cheaper cigarettes in New Jersey. Even county lines become important in liquor purchases, especially with the number of dry counties still found in the South. Individuals in nearby states or even farther away know that the boundary actually acts as a point separating different political spaces and that the "world" is different "on the other side." Movement between most cities and states is free and unlimited; there are literally any number of crossing points where states or cities with different environments can be entered. Although the entire state or city may have these different conditions, the boundary becomes important as it is the first place where the individual is affected by the new environment.

Distance from a boundary may be reflected in how the individual views it, especially if the boundary acts as a barrier to interaction. This is true for the international boundaries. A person crossing into Canada may feel different than entering Mexico. If there are few points of entry that are rather distant from one another and if there are special gates or search procedures involved in crossing into adjacent space, the perception and interaction assume a different character than if it were permeable. Of course, what one individual may consider a barrier, another may not. Boundary-crossers have different views of the border than those never crossing it. Those citizens regarding the boundary as a barrier may even reside along the boundary but not perceive the immediately adjacent spaces as friendly, for they live a long distance from an entry point. In other words individual shopping, working, and recreation behavior is likely to be affected by the nature of the boundary itself. In a study of shopping behavior of residents along the New Brunswick-Maine border, the Canadian residents revealed they had more knowledge of opportunities for shopping in their own provinces but perceived the opportunities greater across the border.[22] If an international boundary is basically impenetrable or perceived as such, it is likely to result in distorted action spaces for those residents in the area immediately adjacent to the crossing points. In an examination of marriage partners in Vancouver, it was shown that even though Tacoma, Seattle, and Bellingham were closer than Toronto, Winnipeg, and Montreal, fewer grooms came from United States cities. The international boundary was indeed a powerful influence on social intercourse.[23] On the other hand, television watching of both Canadian and Washington stations was enjoyed by residents on both sides of the international boundary (Fig. 7-5). Distance from the boundary as well as the television reception area influenced the amount of national television watching.[24]

Often impressions about political spaces take on a perception that applies for the entire state. In other words, crossing the border immediately brings into focus feelings about the entire political space. Northern residents from Illinois or Michigan traveling to the South for winter or summer vacations may be aware of previous racial and social tensions as they enter and leave southern states. They may feel somewhat tense when entering Alabama or Georgia, conditions that may stop immediately when they arrive at the Florida border. The significance of such boundaries is likely to affect a person's perception of social justice, as well as his travel habits within a certain state. It may also influence where to spend monies for lodging and eating. More than one Northeast or Midwest liberal has viewed the boundary separating states such as Alabama and Florida or Georgia and Florida in social and political terms. Outside of Florida he felt uneasy in his travels as he viewed possible threats of KKK activity, police ticketing cars with out-of-state

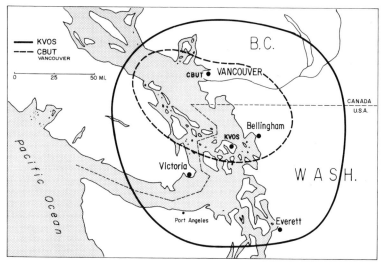

Fig. 7-5 Television Coverage Along the Washington–British Columbia Boundary. (After J. V. Minghi, "Television Preference and Nationality in a Boundary Region," *Sociological Inquiry*, 33 (Spring 1963), p. 71.)

license plates, or small-town speed traps for certain Deep South states. Possibly he endeavored to travel straight through these states to avoid spending monies to support what he considered racist politicians and political practices. However, once inside Florida he felt more secure, not in part probably because of the free orange juice offered at the entrance station, but because of the myriad billboard advertisements that whetted his appetite for a Florida vacation. Even though the political and social culture is basically alike on both sides of these state borders, once inside the Sunshine State the northern tourist felt more "at home." Local residents living in the border area do not perceive the boundary in the same manner, although marriage rates are higher along the border in south Georgia than north Florida.

Similar behavior is often exhibited along international borders. The significance attached to "the border" will be related to the distance an individual is from the crossing as well as how frequently he enters the foreign country. For many United States citizens, entering Mexico or Canada brings out some forms of behavior that are not found when state or city political boundaries are crossed. In the first place, the citizen is in a foreign nation and this means he is subjected to the political and social policies of another political unit. The feelings that are exhibited when crossing the border may remain while traveling or living in any part of that foreign nation. This is in spite of the fact that language may be similar, as is true for English throughout most of Canada. Entering Canada or Mexico is not like entering Pennsylvania from Ohio. There are customs stations and entrance stations where the individual is asked where he is going, how long he will be traveling in the nation, and what is the purpose of the travel. For the most part international border crossing is a brief operation but it may on occasion involve searches of self and car and belongings. Such are likely to lead to some sort of barrier perception for the crossing point and the nation itself.

It is possible that entering Canada brings out different feelings than entering Mexico. For most United States citizens there is no basic change in the cultural, language, and social and economic environment that is observed or felt once Canada is entered. It is viewed by many travelers as just like another state. On the other hand, when Mexico is entered, the transition to a different human background becomes apparent immediately. Road signs, poverty, and cultural changes exhibit a sharp contrast from what the cultural and social landscape was in adjacent Texas, New Mexico, Arizona, or California. No formal passport or travel visas are required to enter Canada, provided the stay is rather short. In Mexico one can travel fairly unrestricted for 15 miles beyond the border. However, if one goes beyond, another checkpoint is encountered. This free zone of travel may not present problems to the United States citizen as no formal passport is necessary. Beyond this zone, another brief interrogation session and more formal travel authorization is required for those wishing to continue southward. Boundary residents residing on the United States side as well as citizens from other states realize the importance of purchasing certain items in Mexico or Canada. Canadian and Mexican stores selling jewelry, paintings, handcrafts, as well as liquor do a land-office business primarily because they cater to United States citizens crossing the border just to purchase such items and then return as well as those leaving the foreign nation after more extended travels and stays.

Just as individuals view the international boundaries as places where the advantages are often greater than in their individual state or the United States, so do groups such as major industrial and commercial concerns. The international border has become an important consideration in the location of certain types of industries owned by United States companies. Boundary cities and states in Mexico or Canada have become the sites for branches and subsidiaries of United States concerns in order to take advantage of lower labor costs or production costs. Furthermore, these help the economic health of border regions and the foreign nation as a whole.

Along the United States-Mexico border are over 300 firms employing over 30,000 workers and doing $500 million worth of business in Mexican border cities. The Mexican government has granted special compensation, such as the importation of raw materials and equipment in-bond and duty-free for companies located within a 20-kilometer strip in Mexico. This is provided their production is exported. This program has stimulated the growth of Hong Kong-type industries, such as electric goods, electronics, textiles, and food processing in United States cities with neighbors immediately across the border. Twin-city economies have developed in a number of these cases, as in Tijuana-San Diego, Mexicali-Calexico, Nogales (Mexico and Arizona), Ciudad Juárez-El Paso, Nuevo Laredo-Laredo, and Matamoras-Brownsville. The Mexican cities and their states have been among the most rapidly growing sections of the nation, in part because of the higher wages provided by these border industries. This industrial input has been in addition to their tourist trade, which has expanded in recent years. The United States interest in seeing this program develop has been supported by American companies financially establishing some of these concerns and by the same companies or branches purchasing their products under special provisions outlined in favorable United States tariff legislation. American businesses have realized the advantageous position of locating border-industry plants in Mexico, for if the same commodities were produced within the United States, they would be more expensive for the consumer.[25]

The United States-Canada boundary is also reflected in the industrial patterns found particularly in Ontario. In the mid-1960s, the level of foreign (namely, United States) ownership, investment, and direction became a major concern to citizens and politicians in several provinces. The greatest investment is in those areas immediately adjacent to heavily industrialized parts of the Midwest and Great Lakes. Branch plants of United States-controlled industries are most heavily concentrated in southwestern Ontario. Fewer externally controlled plants and firms are found away from this "economic shadow" zone in southern Canada.[26] United States manufacturers have seized upon the opportunities made available early this century to help develop the Canadian economy by setting up business branches. These "border" investments are heaviest in the production of automobiles and parts, chemicals, rubber, and electrical goods, all examples where Michigan, Illinois, Ohio, Pennsylvania, and New York have already excelled. Their expansion into neighboring Canada has stimulated the Canadian economy but likewise benefited the corporations headquartered within the United States.

FOOTNOTES

1. Deon C. Greer, "The Political Geography of the Relicted Lands of the Great Salt Lake," *Journal of Geography*, 71:3 (1972), 161–166.
2. John D. Nystuen, "Boundary Shapes and Boundary Problems," *Papers, Peace Research Society (International)*, 7 (1967), 107–128.
3. Roy I. Wolfe, "Transportation and Politics: The Example of Canada," *Annals, Association of American Geographers*, 52 (1962), 183.
4. U.S. Department of Interior, *National Atlas of the United States*, Geological Survey, Washington, D.C., 1970, pp. 140–141. The evolution of political spaces in the West is described and illustrated in Donald W. Meinig, "American Wests: Preface to a Geographical Interpretation," *Annals, Association of American Geographers*, 62:2 (1972), 170–172.
5. Harry Roy Merrens, *Colonial North Carolina in the Eighteenth Century*, Chapel Hill, University of North Carolina Press, 1964.
6. Benjamin E. Thomas, "Boundaries and Internal Problems of Idaho," *Geographical Review*, 39 (1949), 101.
7. Willis Frederick Dunbar, *Michigan: A History of the Wolverine State*, Grand Rapids, William B. Eerdmans, 1965, pp. 307–316. For a geographical and legal examination of the Michigan-Wisconsin border problems see Lawrence Martin, "The Michigan-Wisconsin Boundary Case in the Supreme Court of

the United States, 1923–1926," *Annals, Association of American Geographers*, 20:3 (1930), 105–163; and "The Second Wisconsin-Michigan Boundary Case in the Supreme Court of the United States," ibid., 28:2 (1938), 77–126.

8. Edwin N. Griswold, "Hunting Boundaries with Car and Camera in Northeastern United States," *Geographical Review*, 29 (1939), 355.

9. Thomas, op. cit., 101.

10. Ibid.

11. Gaston Litton, *History of Oklahoma*, New York, Lewis Historical Company, 1967, p. 414.

12. Frederic Arthur Culmer, *A New History of Missouri*, Mexico, Missouri, McIntyre Publishing Co., 1938, pp. 140–142.

13. Charles Ambler and Festus P. Summers, *West Virginia, The Mountain State*, Englewood Cliffs, Prentice-Hall, 1958, pp. 251–253 and 316–317.

14. Ibid., pp. 317–318.

15. John W. Davis, "The Unguarded Boundary," *Geographical Review*, 12 (1922), 586–601.

16. Julian V. Minghi, "Point Roberts, Washington: The Problem of an American Exclave," *Yearbook*, Association of Pacific Coast Geographers, 24 (1962), 29–34.

17. J. Hill, "El Chamizal: A Century-Old Boundary Dispute," *Geographical Review*, 55 (1965), 510–522.

18. A. F. Lambert, "The United States-Canada Boundary," *Surveying and Mapping*, 28 (1968), 31–39.

19. Stephen B. Jones, "The Forty-Ninth Parallel in the Great Plains: The Historical Geography of a Boundary," *Journal of Geography*, 31 (1932), 351–368; and "The Cordilleran Section of the Canadian-United States Borderland," *Geographical Journal*, 89 (1937), 439–450.

20. Wolfe, op. cit., pp. 183–184.

21. Hendrik J. Reitsma, "Crop and Livestock Production in the Vicinity of the United States-Canada Border," *Professional Geographer*, 23 (1971), 216–223; and "Areal Differentiation Along the United States-Canada Border," *Tijdschrift voor Economische en Sociale Geografie*, 63 (1972), 2–10.

22. David R. Reynolds and Michael L. McNulty, "On the Analysis of Political Boundaries as Barriers: A Perceptual Approach," *East Lakes Geographer*, 4 (1968), 21–38.

23. J. Ross Mackay, "The Interactance Hypothesis and Boundaries in Canada: A Preliminary Study," *Canadian Geographer*, 11 (1958), 1–8.

24. Julian V. Minghi, "Television Preference and Nationality in a Boundary Region," *Sociological Inquiry*, 33 (1963), 65–79.

25. C. Daniel Dillman, "Brownsville: Border Port for Mexico and the U.S.," *Professional Geographer*, 21 (1969), 178–183; and "Commuter Workers and Free Zone Industry Along the Mexico-U.S. Border," *Proceedings*, Association of American Geographers, 2 (1970), 48–51; and Federal Reserve Bank of San Francisco, "Factories on the Border," *Monthly Review*, December 1971, pp. 212–216.

26. D. Michael Ray, *Market Potential and Economic Shadow*, Chicago, University of Chicago, Department of Geography, Research Paper 101, 1965. And his "The Location of United States Manufacturing Subsidiaries in Canada," *Economic Geography*, 47 (1971), 389–400.

PART II

PATTERNS AND ORGANIZATION

Chapter 8

GEOGRAPHY
AND
THE LAW

You cannot legislate against geography.
Sir Wilfred Laurier

In an examination of laws in the United States, there are definite geographic dimensions. Laws enacted affecting individual and group behavior and actions are not the same in all states or indeed even within the same counties or cities. The manner in which various cultures have identified a problem and codified it in some framework has resulted in a multiplicity of interpretations for the same issue. Equally as significant in a geographical analysis is the manner in which laws are interpreted when convictions and punishment are meted out by courts and judges. What may be a petty crime in one location (city or state) may be a serious one in an adjoining political unit or one in another part of the United States. Uniformity or standardization in the interpretation of crimes or for that matter even basic human and social welfare issues with legal regulations are often found wanting. Changes are frequently difficult to obtain even within individual cities and states. Rulings by higher courts are seen as ways to bring some uniformity to the legal interpretation of contemporary societal issues; however, their enforcement often

199

takes on a distinctly geographical flavor as the past decade has revealed in the handling of civil rights issues.

Laws are formal enactments that are ostensibly designed to set the framework within which individuals and groups can operate according to acceptable societal standards. The concern from a political geography framework lies in the realization that these acceptable forms of behavior have a distinct spatial character. Local political units may not be able to purchase certain books or see certain movies because of a judge's rulings. States have established grounds for marriage or divorce that may be totally at odds with a bordering political unit. Even at the national level the Constitution has been interpreted differently in the Northeast than in the South, even though the wording of specific amendments is to insure equal rights for all citizens. At the international level, laws governing immigration and favored trade treatment illustrate various legal arrangements.

In an ideal sense each citizen has what might be termed "spatial rights," which are defined in a political and social geographic context. Each American supposedly can live, work, and travel where he wants. However, this is far from reality as the past two decades have vividly demonstrated. This is in spite of laws on the books stating equality of races and sexes. Some citizens enjoy spatial mobility and rights that others do not for reasons of cultural or class restrictions. Differences exist between a *de jure* interpretation and a *de facto* interpretation of laws. Minority groups in particular have recognized that they have been denied equality in education, voting, employment, public accommodations, and justice. Many of the race and class barriers were erected by certain cultural elites or groups that enacted legislation affecting residents differently in those spaces. These were legitimized even though the United States Supreme Court interpreted human rights and societal situations differently. It was expected that when local, state, or regional interpretations of individual and group behavior were in conflict with a Supreme Court ruling, a certain amount of strong rhetoric or subsequent lengthy legal maneuvering would likely result.

Because of the various cultures settling the United States in different times and in different sections, the mosaic of laws on the books today was certain to result. The initial settlers in New England were interested in the individual and his independence from church and state. Therefore it was not surprising that these states have taken the lead in provisions regarding separation of powers and civil liberties. While these states may be labeled progressive in some spheres of human behavior and interaction, they are not in all, as the religious influence has often impeded reforms in birth control dissemination and abortion legislation. The southern states, often viewed as conservative in legal interpretations, were settled later and by groups whose economic orientation and social patterns were different from the Northeast. The agrarian society and economy, in large part influenced by blacks, developed a political and legal philosophy that favored elites and separated races and classes. It was not unexpected that as the United States evolved into one formal political unit differences in the interpretation of laws and individual and group behavior would be at odds. This especially came to the fore when a Supreme Court ruling in effect erased local, state, or indeed even regional interpretations. These rulings in effect set the tenor for the nation, although their execution is still performed at state and local levels. That is, the speed and diligence with which the "law of the land" is carried out rests with the state and local courts, judges, and legal officers.

The discussion below concentrates on geographical variations in laws at various levels in the United States and on some spatial considerations of the administration of justice. While there is much that could be examined about geography and the law, the focus here is on the diverse ways in which political units at various levels of the hierarchy interpret the same situation or condition. Not only do they vary within the United States in the way laws are established but in the ways penalties are assessed and the judicial process executed. A geographical appraisal of laws suggests that there is more diversity than uniformity, even in a nation that is losing much of its regional distinctiveness. Legal reforms are difficult to attain at the state or national level, as they basically relate to specifically bounded political spaces. Establishing uniform policies for sales taxes on liquor purchases or the qualifications for judges or for penalties for auto theft seem equally as difficult to attain as the setting of highway speed limits, the fining of environmental polluters, the licensing of barbers and beauticians, or the setting of maximum sentences for first-degree murder. Laws as they serve to protect peoples and spaces are not readily altered unless by a higher authority, and even then the reaction to change is not always performed easily, quietly, or in concert with the newly established ruling.

GEOGRAPHICAL VARIATION IN LEGAL INTERPRETATION

The hundreds of laws that are on the books in the United States serve to illustrate that individuals and groups are subject to the interpretations of many political units during a week, year, or lifetime. What may be a lawful activity in Nevada may be unlawful in Utah or what may be the minimum jail sentence for burglary in Arkansas may be much higher in neighboring Louisiana. Local conditions may permit an individual to sell certain pornographic books in San Francisco but perhaps not in San Fernando. East Lansing, Michigan, is the home of Michigan State University. Students, professors, and city residents can purchase *Playboy* and other girlie magazines in community newscenters within East Lansing but not at stores in adjacent Meridian Township. There township officials have taken these off the shelves. Legal hearings were still going on in late 1973. How much we pay for a major household item will depend on the state sales tax. If we crossed into an adjacent state the initial cost of the item may be the same but the sales tax less. Illinois residents travel into Indiana to take advantage of the lower state tax. These are just a few examples illustrating that where a person is in space affects what laws or set of laws will govern him. There are local, state, and national regulations that cover most forms of behavior. Where these are in agreement the problems are few, but more often than not they are in conflict. This results then in confusing litigation that often impedes speedy and impartial justice.

In view of the geographical diversity in laws, specific examples at the local, state, regional, national, and international levels will be investigated. Laws are place-oriented; that is, they were or are designed to cover the residents and their activities in specific spaces or places. The reason for the myriad of laws, often ludicrous in modern eyes, is that the developers of these laws interpreted the situations and behaviors to the satisfaction of the cultural "norms" of the majority or of elite groups.

Local Variations. Communities and counties have established their own standards by their heritage, by popular vote, by favorable court rulings, or a ruling elite defining what is permissible. This has resulted in acceptable behaviors in certain spaces and unacceptable forms even in contiguous cities or counties. The sales of alcoholic beverages in the South are marked by laws that are interpreted with apparent randomness. A northerner driving from north Georgia to south Georgia crosses counties that are completely dry, beer and wine only, and completely wet. It is almost as if you want to purchase a drink, and cannot in the county you stopped in for gas or a meal, just wait ten minutes (as counties are small in area) and you will be in a wet county. In Arkansas a tourist going from east to west encounters wet and then dry counties (Fig. 8-1). This mosaic pattern predominates in other Deep and Rim South states. There are even cases in North Carolina, Louisiana, as well as in Arkansas where there are wet cities in dry counties. Local political decisions governing the sales of alcoholic beverages are at variance even in a section that is basically fundamentalist and conservative.[1]

Retail sales of liquor and other items are governed in many cities by a set of "blue laws." These are especially popular in the New England and Northeast states as they prohibit the sales of retail items on Sundays. In New York the state blue law goes back to 1778. However, its enforcement is not uniform. Currently, Long Island residents can be fined, sentenced, and even property confiscated for disobeying the law, even if it involves car washes. Meanwhile in neighboring New York City, many retail stores are open on Sunday. There are also "fair Sabbath" provisions that permit shopowners to operate Sundays provided they observe a religious day at another time. This proviso mainly serves the large Jewish population of New York City.[2] Baseball fans are aware of these laws affecting the termination of weekend games in Philadelphia.

The religious heritage in New England seems to have created a number of other local court rulings and laws. The popular expression "banned in Boston" meant that certain books, movies, or other entertainment was not welcomed even in liberal Massachusetts. Local standards have been an issue in a number of court hearings since 1965 involving the sales of specific books or showing of certain movies. In June 1973, the U.S. Supreme Court in an antipornography ruling stated

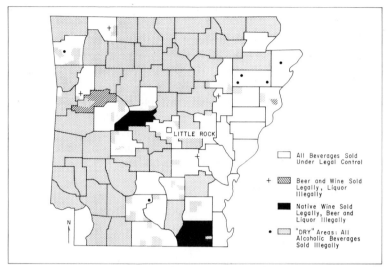

FIG. 8-1 Wet and Dry Counties in Arkansas. (State of Arkansas, Department of Alcoholic Beverage Control, 1973).

that local judges could decide "community standards." This is resulting in court cases by owners of book stores and movie houses. Local citizens, groups of parents, clergy, and judges in the past have endeavored to prevent certain books from being placed in school libraries or to prevent showing of what are termed sexually explicit and morally degrading films. The earliest judgments were rendered against foreign books and films, but later they protested American publishers and filmmakers. The cultural composition of a city does play a role in the types of entertainment available. Movie producers and their distributors are aware that while "Deep Throat" or "The Godfather" or "Last Tango in Paris" or "Guess Who's Coming to Dinner" may not be popular (that is, long-running) in parts of rural New England, the Deep South, or the Great Plains, others that have appeal to families and patriotism such as "Green Berets" or "The Music Man" or "Mary Poppins" enjoy greater success. The ratings of movies also change depending on the audience. What may be considered suitable as a PG (Parental Guidance) for an urban audience may become a G (General) in another part of the nation. This is to attract a larger clientele. Local options are seen in other forms of entertainment as well, such as in the construction of gambling houses or betting on horse or dog races.

The social development of spaces was often carried out under a set of regulations and guidelines that were to insure preservation of the locale. Housing codes and restrictions were set up to prevent multiple-family dwelling units from being erected or to preclude the sales of property to certain groups, as to blacks, Jews, or Spanish-Americans. The belief was that by placing such restrictive clauses in city charters, preservation of local spaces would be maintained. Court rulings since 1960 have thrown out most racial clauses, even though attempts to obtain favorable court rulings on social and economic exclusiveness are still heard. Zoning, as mentioned in Chapter 6, was used as one measure to maintain "community standards" on the social composition of a neighborhood or city.

Restrictions on the mobility of minority groups were placed in formal housing contracts and in city charters. This practice was found not only in the South as northern cities enacted similar pieces of legislation. In southern cities, formal codes were unnecessary as many blacks simply "knew their place" and this was "on the other side of the tracks" or "out of town." More than one Deep and Rim South state had laws, *de facto*, specifying that blacks had to be "out of town by sundown." To be found in town after that time endangered one's self and property. It is not surprising that blacks or other discriminated-against minority groups, for example, Jewish residents in large cities, sought out spatial refuges where local laws did not affect them or where they could enact their own governing structures. Local laws are often tied to the political territoriality of individuals and groups, a topic treated at greater length in Chapter 3.

Environmental regulations have been established at all levels of the political hierarchy since 1968. Although political ramifications of the environment are treated in Chapter 12 specifically, suffice it to say at this point that local governments (cities and counties) have taken steps to alleviate some of the crises. Patchwork political patterns result from such endeavors as one suburb's attempt to restrict industrial expansion and pollution levels only to find an adjacent political unit with a completely different set of guidelines. Frequently, these local, state, and national regulations are at variance. Regulations on noise levels, smoke tolerances, and water quality that are locally based are only a small step to the solution of the major problem. However, they do provide a framework for broadening the base for handling environmental concerns at the state and national levels.

Laws also exist at local levels with reference to methods of financing the needed government services. Taxing of corporations and individuals is the major source of revenue. Some cities assess a local income tax that along with state and federal revenues adds to the city's coffers. Levels of tax assessment vary from city to city and also within cities. The property tax is one of the major sources of revenues for local communities. The concern of this issue to the public has been the high rate and the resulting inequities in public education in particular. This topic is discussed at greater length in Chapter 11. At the root of problems of the local property tax matter is its use for financing public education, especially when the tax level varies within a city and is often directly related to the local educational quality. Various state and local districts have become involved in legal hassles in the past few years in an attempt to erase inequities and devise needed tax reforms.[3]

State Variations. Just as there are variations at the local level, so are there at state levels. Regulations affecting many issues involving human behavior and interactions are almost as numerous as the number of states. Each state in its initial constitutional development and subsequent changes has established laws governing its residents and its spaces. In some cases the specific wording of laws was taken from another state or from the Constitution. At other times, the interpretation was unique to the state itself. Changes in laws, in interpreting the laws and the conditions in a modern light, also vary with the states. Some states are more progressive, new forms of legislation being supported and passed whereas in others the same issues may never even be discussed.

Progressive legislation in the past decade is reflected in certain Northeast, northern Midwest, and Western states. In the main, response to contemporary societal issues was seen in earlier legislation affecting individual liberties and the separation of powers. The cultural climate for such legislative advancements is built on a heritage that stems from the days of initial settlement (Chapter 9). For example, nine states in early 1972 that have lowered the age of majority to eighteen or nineteen years were Michigan, New Mexico, Tennessee, Illinois, North Carolina, Vermont, California, Washington, and Wisconsin. By late 1973 the number had increased to forty-three. This law, an outgrowth of the Twenty-sixth Amendment to the United States Constitution permitted this age group to own property, make wills, execute contracts, and marry without parental consent.[4] No-fault auto insurance is now available in New York, Delaware, Massachusetts, Connecticut, New Jersey, Florida, and Michigan. A progressive piece of legislation involves compensating the victims of crimes. Seven states now have such provisions on the books: Massachusetts, California, Nevada, New York, Hawaii, Maryland, and New Jersey. Civil servants can strike in Pennsylvania and Hawaii. Maryland still retains a motion picture censorship board that passes judgment on those films seen in the state. Florida, Washington, and Illinois have passed "sunshine laws" whereby the sources of the political campaign funds are to be revealed to the public. Even now there is a federal bill being reviewed that would allocate public money for campaigns.

Variations in the requirements for voting and the stipulations for marriage and divorce are critical societal issues that have received national attention recently. In the arena of voting, there was a hodgepodge pattern at the state level until the March 1972 Supreme Court ruling that wiped out all requirements for residency.[5] The arguments presented for maintaining a minimum period before being eligible to vote were to prevent fraud and to insure that the voter had some time to gain knowledge of local issues. Numerous states had enacted laws preventing newcomers or "carpetbaggers" from engaging in meaningful political activities (voting and office seeking). Lengthy residency requirements preserved local and state residents and interests from new migrants. Prior to the above ruling, fourteen states had residency requirements of less than one year. These were mainly urban-industrial states in the northeast quarter of the United States (Fig. 8-2). New York and Pennsylvania required only ninety days, the fewest of any state. The others required six months. The pattern for county eligibility represented a wide variety of patterns with little regional or sectional homogeneity, except that the longest time required

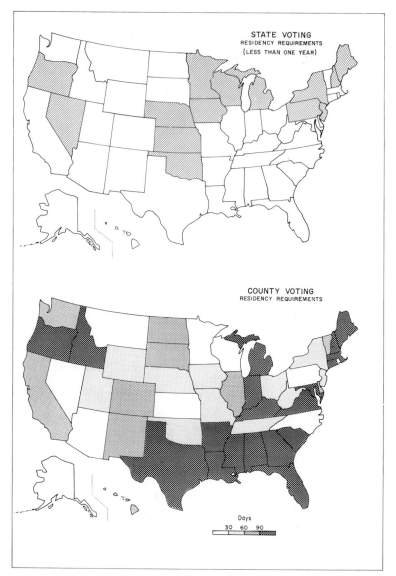

Fig. 8-2 Voter Residency Requirements. (U.S. Department of Defense, *Voter Information 1970*, Washington, D.C., 1970.)

was in southern states (Fig. 8-2). This may be interpreted as a way to protect the traditional political system. Certainly a lengthy period would tend to discourage political involvement. Outside the South, a six-month period was required for county voting in Idaho, Kentucky, Maryland, Michigan, and Rhode Island. The remainder of the states showed a variation from thirty days in Arizona, forty in Ohio, ninety in California, and four months in Utah. In view of these lengthy requirements needed for establishing residency, the Court felt a thirty-day registration period before an election was sufficient time to be eligible to vote. It was estimated that this ruling would add 3 to 5 million new voters in the 1972 elections. Even though the specific residency requirements were struck down, the individual wanting to vote must prove he is a legal resident of the state and locale in question.

Another major topic of legal concern in recent years has been the issue of marriage and divorce. In view of their importance in contemporary society, some uniform legal interpretation may be expected. However, this is far from the case. Marriage is easier to attain, just like divorce, in some states than in others. Common-law marriages are recognized in Alabama, Colorado, Georgia, Idaho, Iowa, Kansas, Montana, Ohio, Oklahoma, Pennsylvania, Rhode Island, South Carolina, Texas, and the District of Columbia. Age requirements vary from state to state. Four states as of July 1970 did not require a blood test (Minnesota, Maryland, South Carolina, and Nevada). Washington only requires an affidavit filed by the male. The length of waiting period after applying for a license also varies widely. There is apparently no significant pattern or uniform rationale (Fig. 8-3). A total of twenty-two states require no waiting period, one state (South Carolina) requires twenty-four hours, two (Arizona and Maryland) require forty-eight hours, sixteen require three days, one (Connecticut) requires four days, and six require five days (Wisconsin, Montana, Ohio, Maine, New Hampshire, and Minnesota), and one state (Oregon) seven days! Such a crazy quilt pattern represents varying local and state and regional interpretation. An accurate appraisal seems to defy sound reason. In terms of age required to marry, again there is wide variation. Each state sets up its own laws. Minimum ages for men and women vary depending on whether parental consent is required. There were sixteen different sets of age requirements existing in 1970; only some are illustrated in Fig. 8-3. For parental consent most states require males to be twenty-one. Lower ages are permitted in the South for males and females. Perhaps southern society feels boys and girls develop faster and are better able to partake in family life.[6]

In divorce, likewise, there are wide differences in state laws. The possible reasons given for divorce within states range from adultery, cruelty, drug addiction, impotence, and nonsupport to several states (Michigan, Iowa, and Georgia) that have a no-fault rule, that is, an agreement reached between consenting adults that the marriage be annulled. In other states, such as California, Texas, Florida, and Oklahoma, the marital contract can be easily voided. The length of residency needed for termination of a marriage varies widely from state to state from over one year for seven states (three are Northeast states where the Catholic legislatures and Puritan heritage may have attempted to discourage divorce) to less than a year in several western states (Fig. 8-3). In these western states where society has historically been more open, the recent population growth and resulting social instability together with experiments in living (cohabitation to communal living) may have been instrumental in pushing through legislation that made divorce legally less difficult. Of course, the state of Nevada with its six-week residency requirement is an example of a state that has made divorce a major business

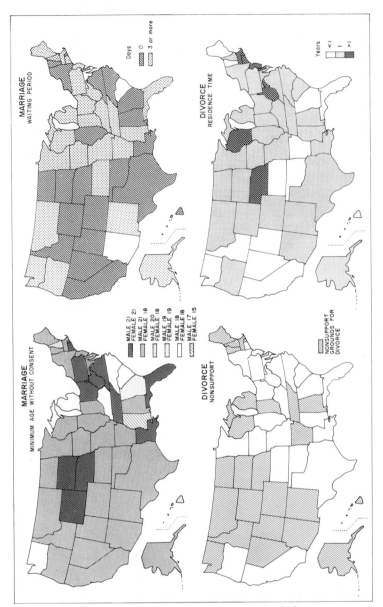

FIG. 8-3 Marriage and Divorce Requirements: American Style.

enterprise. And, if one does not like Reno or Las Vegas, he or she may travel to Sun Valley, Idaho, a state with the same residency period.

The grounds for divorce vary widely, almost in as many ways as the marriage stipulations. Nonsupport is acceptable grounds in many western and New England states and several in the Deep South and Midwest (Fig. 8-3). Again there is little uniformity in the pattern. Drug addiction is considered acceptable grounds, especially in the Southeast states and others in New England and the Midwest. The diversity in laws illustrates the role cultural, religious, and political groups have played in developing the requirements for marriage and divorce within individual states. Often with changes in society there are attempts to modernize some outdated laws; however, this is difficult when touchy social issues are at stake. This is in spite of successful reforms proposed and adopted even by neighboring states.

In addition to the many geographical variations that exist at the state levels for social behavior and institutions, it is important to illustrate that economic discrepancies also are found. These are important if purchases of major and minor items are made. States support their programs by enacting general sales taxes; these are far from uniform across the United States. They range from 2 percent for three states, Indiana, Nevada (which also has a one cent county tax), and Oklahoma to Pennsylvania with 6 percent and Connecticut with a whopping 6.5 percent state sales tax![7] Most states have a 3 percent tax, as fifteen do, or a 4 percent, as eighteen enjoy presently. There is little regional or economic uniformity to the state taxes as Arkansas and Massachusetts both have 3 percent, Alabama and New York both have 4 percent, and Mississippi and New Jersey both have 5 percent.

To further supplement state revenues, a number of states have state income taxes. State gasoline taxes vary from five cents per gallon in Hawaii, Missouri, and Texas to eight cents or more for sixteen states, again revealing no pattern. Twenty-six states have a seven cent tax.[8] Another major item purchased in states is liquor. State taxes on a gallon of distilled spirits show wide variation. Seven states (Colorado, Kansas, Kentucky, Maryland, Nebraska, Nevada, and New Mexico) charge from $1.00 to $1.99 per gallon. At the other extreme, the tax per gallon is $3.50 or more in Alaska, Florida, Georgia, Minnesota, Oklahoma, and Tennessee. Moonshining states do not seem to enjoy any special privileges for spirit purchases.[9] Taxes likewise vary in purchases of a barrel of beer from less than $1.00 in Maryland and Wyoming to over $12.00 in Alabama, Mississippi, North Carolina, and South Carolina—states with dry or partially dry counties. Lower taxes seem to be prevalent in the urban-industrial states in the Northeast, perhaps due to the cultural heritage and taste for beer.[10] The higher taxes in the South may also be tied to the states favoring prohibition of alcoholic beverages.

Even in the sphere of elected public officials there are different policies in the states. While all states elect higher officials such as governors, senators, representatives, and various secretaries, at the lower echelons the number and variety elected are far from uniform for the nation. For example, in Michigan drain commissioners are elected and in Texas railroad commissioners are voted on by the electorate. Local prosecutors are elected in forty-five states and are appointed in five. In twenty-nine states they are elected on a county basis and in twelve on the basis of existing judicial districts.[11] There is no uniform pattern to the local law enforcement officials. County sheriffs are elected in forty-seven states, constables in thirty-eight, and coroners in twenty-six. Sheriffs are appointed in Nassau County, New York (Long Island), and in Dade County, Florida (Miami).[12] Judges are appointed by the governors or another body or are elected by the voters on a partisan or nonpartisan basis, the method depending on the particular state in question. Partisan elections characterize the South and Southwest, nonpartisan the Plains and Mountain states. For most legal positions the residence, legal training, salaries, and retirement of officials exhibit wide variation from state to state.

State medical boards and agencies have established a series of laws and guidelines governing the health of individuals. With each state setting its own laws, it is not surprising that wide variations exist. An individual wishing to donate his body or organs to science will find that compliance with his state laws is not always easy. Even the degree of experimentation with human subjects exhibits ample variation. Should an individual wish to have acupuncture practiced on him to relieve his aches and pains, Nevada is currently the only state sanctioning such. Euthanasia (right-to-die with dignity) legislation has been discussed in the past few years in Florida and Wisconsin. The treatment of other medical problems such as drug addiction and disease control or commitment to correctional institutions varies from state to state, often with little similarity in contiguous states.

Regional Laws. Laws are not enacted by regions per se but by groups of states within a particular section of the United States. Such laws are designated "regional" as they may reflect a set of conditions existing in those spaces that are not found in other spaces. Probably the best example of such enactments are those instituted by the South to separate the whites from the blacks. States had passed almost without opposition a set of laws that pertained to the voting, education, and public accommodation of the black citizens. In short, the civil rights and liberties for blacks were not the same for whites in this region. Poll taxes and literacy tests were two blocks designed to preclude black involvement in politics. Separate housing developments, schools and colleges, parks, and medical facilities were established for each of the races. While such laws were on the books for states from Virginia to Texas, the integration of blacks and whites in the education system was stifled in northern states by carefully constructed district boundaries especially in large metropolitan areas. Public accommodations, voting, and public office seeking were much more attainable in the Northeast and Midwest. Many of the barriers to black involvement in American life that were erased by Supreme Court rulings in the 1950s and 1960s had earlier been passed by state legislatures from Minnesota to Massachusetts. This does not imply that problems did not arise here with reference to open housing and cross-district busing.

Right-to-work laws are concentrated particularly in the South. Such legislation is a reflection of the agrarian heritage in the region and the strong sentiments against industrial unionism. In most of the states the percent of the employees belonging to unions is very low compared to the industrial states in the Northeast and Midwest (Table 8-1).

The legislation that is proposed and eventually put into law at a regional

TABLE 8-1   Southern States with Right-to-Work Laws
and Percent Union Membership

State	Membership
North Carolina	7.5
South Carolina	8.6
Mississippi	13.8
Texas	13.9
Florida	14.4
Georgia	16.6
Virginia	16.6
Arkansas	19.0
Tennessee	19.4
Alabama	20.1

Source: *Statistical Abstract of the United States, 1971*, Washington, D.C., U.S. Department of Commerce, 1971, p. 233.

level represents a combination of economic, social, and religious views of the total population or at least of those in leadership positions. The religious and often puritanical heritage of certain New England and nearby northeastern states has been responsible for strong views on Sunday observance (blue laws), birth control information dissemination, abortion, and divorce reform. Many states with a Catholic dominance have been reluctant to advance new causes or repeal antiquated legislation. Similarly the strength of the Baptists and other fundamentalist groups in the South have supported prohibition and fought the teaching of evolution in schools and the legalization of gambling.[13] In the West, the frontier philosophy of openness and flexibility is seen in politics as well as in the social arena. California as the leader has experimented with various forms of education and life-styles. The open-ballot system in the state permits almost any issue to be submitted to a referendum from capital punishment to coastline development or lettuce boycotts. Even though many of the issues are not approved, the independence of party and ideology reflects a participation in legal enactments found in few other places in the United States.

National Laws. Laws protecting the nation as a political unit and its citizens are enacted by approval of three-fourths of state legislatures in the case of constitutional amendments or by decisions handed down by the Supreme Court. Whether the eventual law is an outgrowth of a group of states (often regional support reflected) passing legislation or by a single case originating in Virginia or Vermont, the final decision has a nationwide impact. That is, national decisions rendered about open housing, jury selection, voter residency, and environmental rights apply to citizens regardless of race, religion, or national origin in all parts of the United States. Ideally, such is the case for most of the decisions reached by the highest court, but the 1950s and 1960s have shown that interpreting a decision is not always followed the same in Wisconsin and South Carolina or Oregon and Louisiana. The classic cases involving school desegregation and integration of public facilities were not without lengthy legal rhetoric and violence in many Deep South rural areas as well as urban centers.

While laws affecting the nation's citizens may appear to be against a particular region or group of citizens, such is not intended to be the case. The reason for national interpretation of critical societal issues is to protect all citizens, a provision in the Constitution. It is expected that when three-fourths of the states approve an amendment to the Constitution, whether it be granting all citizens the right to vote (Twenty-fourth Amendment passed in 1964) or the current equal rights amendment under discussion, it is also expected that some states or states within a political region will not be in total support of the constitutional revision. However, national laws as such are intended to protect the life and rights of all citizens in the United States, whether the elected state officials and representatives supported the revision or not. It almost goes without saying that some Supreme Court decisions will be easier for the states and lower echelons of the political system to administer. Erasing voter residency requirements can be accomplished with relative ease at the local or state level. Decisions rendered about cross-district busing, abortion legalization, the abolition of capital punishment, and impositions on environmental violators are not accepted uniformly or with ease in all parts of the nation. Not infrequently have local or state organizations and governments implemented challenges to Supreme Court decisions. One of the latest attempts is a move afoot in some state legislatures to invoke capital punishment for air hijacking and the killing of public officials, police, and fire fighters. Challenges to court decrees are not unique to this decade as contemporary interpretations of social, economic, or political issues are often the outgrowth of earlier court tests at lower levels.

International Laws. The laws of a nation are not restricted to the framework governing the events and processes within its political bounds, but in its interactions with other nations. Legal limits of a nation's land and water boundaries are relatively easy to define. When specific air limits are outlined, the task is much more difficult.

The land boundaries separating the United States from Mexico and Canada are discussed in the previous chapter. A variety of monuments, turning point markers on land, and forest clearings separate the legal limits of the nation. In a legal sense, the United States-Canada boundary has been described as a place in the movies "where the sheriff abandons his horse and leaps to a sled pulled through the snow by a team of huskies. . . ."[14]

The United States in 1966 extended its offshore boundary from a 3-mile limit to a 12-mile limit primarily to protect the nation's fishermen from other nations. Several major fishes consumed by the American public (haddock, flounder, tuna, halibut, mackerel, and cod) are caught outside this limit. This meant that

American fishermen, already at a disadvantage with modern Soviet and Japanese trawlers, faced severe competition. Other fishes such as salmon, shrimp, menhaden, lobster, and king crab are caught within the 12-mile limit.[15] The concern over defining the legal limits of a nation's waters is much more than preserving spaces for national fishing grounds. Mining underwater resources whether petroleum or natural gas or sulphur and some newer lighter minerals are reasons for laying rather specific geographic boundaries to the ocean bed. Strategic and defense reasons are other significant reasons for claiming and controlling underwater areas. The near future may usher in additional reasons for delimiting the areal extent, horizontal and vertical, of the ocean's waters, especially if undersea farming and underwater settlements are established. Already it seems likely that conflicts between nations over ocean territorial claims are not far off. Seizures of foreign fishing vessels or spy ships within territorial waters have already heightened international tensions and stressed the lack of common agreement between pact member nations as to the adjudication procedures.

The offshore boundary questions on occasion involve the geographical domain of states and those of the federal government. When they are in conflict, legal hearings have been held to determine the claims. Probably the most noted state-federal controversy involved the actual jurisdictional limits of individual states and the federal government in the Gulf of Mexico. Petroleum and natural gas finds in offshore lands led states to extend their lands beyond the three-mile territorial limit. States in believing these lands belonged to them granted concessions and received royalties from mining operations within these waters. A Supreme Court ruling prohibited an extension of said territorial lands for Alabama, Mississippi, and Louisiana but approved an extension to nine miles for Florida and Texas waters. The Texas Territory was extended as it represented an interpretation of Spanish claims to land when the state was admitted to the Union. Florida's case rested on a statement in its revised constitution that read the boundaries of the state were three leagues from land. In fact, the Florida waters question is still in the courts.[16] Beyond the legal limits of state and federal seas, ocean waters can be used for fishing, mining, or intelligence purposes by any nation. Surveillance of the water boundaries by the coast guard or air force or patrolling submarines and radar installations is not without problems. The occasional capture of a Cuban or Soviet fishing boat in territorial waters attests to this reality.

The complexities of air and water jurisdictional limits were illustrated by Pacific Southwest Airlines, an intrastate California carrier that was in violation of federal laws. The problem arose when the flight patterns from San Diego to Los Angeles to San Francisco passed twice from state space to United States air space. By virtue of the fact that its patterns were more than four nautical miles offshore on two occasions, the PSA became subject to interstate rather than intrastate carrier regulations.[17] The obvious solution to this situation would be to plan routes with more land connections that would not necessitate high seas travel (Fig. 8-4).

The space programs and explorations by various nations in the past decade have seen a growing concern for discussing and solving some national and inter-

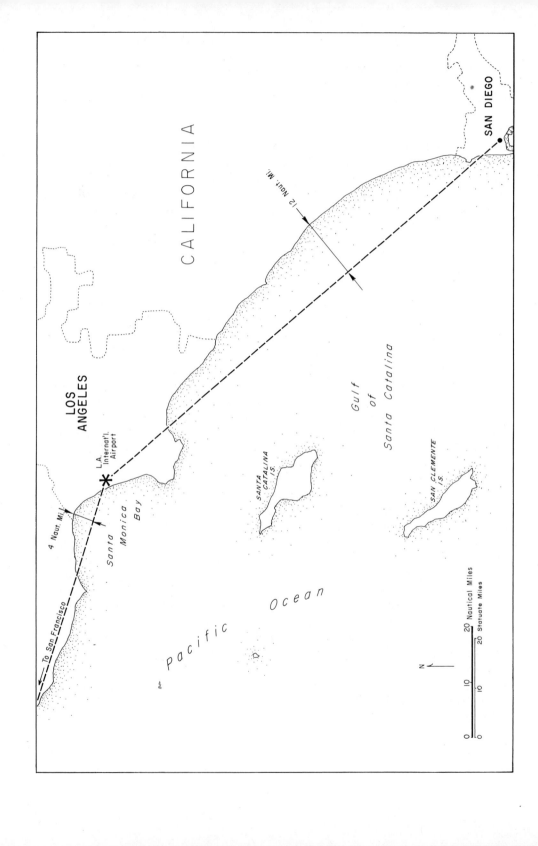

national legal problems connected with airspace. One major concern has been the actual definition of a nation's territorial airspace. The United States, like other nations, has set certain legal limits to its own space by permitting the landing of foreign aircraft such as from the Soviet Union only at certain points. Unfriendly nations are not free to transport cargo or passengers to every major city. Furthermore, their flight patterns are restricted. A ticklish legal point that has not been resolved is where does a nation's airspace end and outer space begin. Outer space is usually considered in international law like the high seas.

While flight patterns for United States commercial airlines may be restricted in flying into or over certain nations, as in the case of Cuba, satellites from the United States or any nation are relatively immune from international sanctions. They may be for weather, economic, biological, or security purposes but the specific intent of some may be unknown and their incursion difficult to detect. Questions about the legal facets involving the access and passage of aircraft and satellites, and the registration, nationality, liability, and safety elements of satellites in particular have prompted international discussions. The Space Law Treaty approved by the United Nations General Assembly in 1962 is a step in the direction recognizing the political and legal facets connected with the exploration and exploitation of outer space for military, civilian, or environmental purposes.[18]

The United States also establishes laws governing the admittance of immigrants. While immigrants, that is, persons from other nations admitted for purposes of taking up permanent residence, have become an important part of the nation's development, actual restrictions were not placed upon their entry until this century. Prior to 1920 there was only a qualitative limitation placed on numbers entering. The 1921 Immigration Act placed a quantitative number on those entering; it was 3 percent of the number of people born in that country who were residing in the United States as reported in the 1910 Census of Population. This quota applied to East European nations. In 1924 a new quota was instituted, being 2 percent of the residents in the United States from that country counted in the 1890 census. Subsequent ceilings were placed on the number of immigrants admitted, 150,000 in 1929 and 158,000 in 1967. The most recent immigration laws went into effect in 1968 when the numbers allocated to each nation "which were not used were transferred to an immigration pool and made available to preference immigrants who could not obtain visas because the quota for their country was exhausted. The allocations from the pool and from existing numbers could not exceed 170,000."[19] The direct result of the immigration laws has meant a large number of eastern Europeans entered the United States early this century. The Cubans represent the largest number of recent immigrants; special political cor-

Fig. 8-4 Flights of Pacific Southwest Airlines over California. (Redrafted from Figs. 10 and 11 in F. J. Hortig, consulting engineer, "Jurisdictional, Administrative, and Technical Problems Related to the Establishment of California Coastal and Offshore Boundaries," in *The Law of the Sea: Boundaries and Zones*, ed. by Lewis M. Alexander, Columbus: Ohio State University Press, 1967. Used by permission of the author, the editor, and the publisher.)

siderations in their homeland have been behind their settlement in south Florida in particular. Without laws governing the number of persons from other nations entering the United States, peculiar and particular social, economic, and political problems arise. Low-paid foreign laborers, namely, migrant workers (*braceros*) have been banned from agricultural operations much to the chagrin of some fruit and vegetable farmers in the Southwest. Highly specialized professionals such as doctors and scientists, who represent a brain drain from their own nations, are also carefully screened prior to their admittance into the United States. The present immigration laws are structured in such a way that persons of varying backgrounds and nationalities can apply for entry. Whether and when they are in fact admitted depend on their meeting the qualifications for entry.

The United States has established a rather intricate set of tariff laws that govern the trade patterns and policies of this nation vis-à-vis the rest of the world. Tariff regulations are designed to protect farmers and industrialists in the United States from unwise and unfair international competition. The levels of duty imposed on varying foodstuffs and manufactured goods are constantly subject to revision as they reflect internal and international economic changes. Monetary crises in major trading blocs and internal agricultural failures or industrial shutdowns are equally as significant in influencing the tariff levels set that reflect supply-demand conditions. The latest agreements on tariffs and trade are embodied at the international level in GATT (General Agreement on Tariffs and Trade). The agreements were ostensibly designed to have tariff concessions between member nations. In effect the liberalization of restrictions, which occurred in the Kennedy round of talks, covered several thousands of agricultural and manufactured commodities and were designed to promote an easing of international trade. Many results of these rounds of international talks have resulted in most-favored-nation clauses.

Tariff levels are set in a dollar and cent amount for literally thousands of items that enter the United States from over a hundred nations.[20] Furthermore, the levels set in one year are seldom identical to previous years. Specific tariff levels are set for animal and dairy products, wood and paper, textile fibers and products, chemicals and related products, nonmetallic and metallic products and hundreds of other miscellaneous products.

One example of the quotas allocated for supplying the United States market involves various agricultural commodities. According to the Agricultural Adjustment Act, specific amounts have been established for certain dairy and animal products, and certain plant materials.[21] Cheeses and cheese substitutes are mainly to come from northern European countries and Italian-type cheeses from Italy, Australia, and Argentina. Cotton quotas were set for import restrictions for nations in Africa, Latin America, and Asia (Table 8-2). Agricultural products being subject to climatic and biological considerations as well as consumer tastes are among the items of most concern to the nation's farmers. Sales of American wheat to the Soviet Union and likely sales to the Republic of China in the future will be among the international legal agreements affecting the United States.

TABLE 8-2   Cheese and Cotton Tariff Quotas, 1968

Cheese and Substitutes for Cheese Containing or Processed from Edam and Gouda Cheese		Cotton, Not Carded, and Not Otherwise Processed: Staple Length Under 1⅛ Inches	
Nation	Quota (in pounds)	Nation	Quota (in pounds)
Denmark	514,000	Egypt and Sudan	783,816
Ireland	99,000	Peru	247,952
Netherlands	51,000	India and Pakistan	2,003,483
Norway	110,000	China	1,370,791
West Germany	154,000	Mexico	8,883,259
Other	17,000	Brazil	618,723
		USSR	475,124
		Argentina	5,203
		Ecuador	9,333
		British East Africa	2,240
		Indonesia and Neth. New Guinea	71,338
		Other	44,881

Source: United States Tariff Commission, *Tariff Schedules of the United States, Annotated* (1972), Washington, D.C., U.S. Government Printing Office, 1972, TC Publication 452, pp. 575 and 587.

GEOGRAPHY AND JUSTICE

Just as there are varying state interpretations of the same social institution such as marriage or the requirements for certain elected officials, so are there differences in the penalties for crimes. States in their early formation established the degree of punishment that should be meted out for felonies and misdemeanors. Cultural heritage coupled with the role of law and government resulted in some regional similarities but more often an interpretation that was unique in itself. Resultant state laws exhibited little similarity even with adjacent states. While laws governing those residents within a state may have been acceptable when the population was fairly immobile, the mobility of law violators has geographical ramifications that impede ready and impartial justice. From the criminal's standpoint, this point is amply illustrated by Grodzins:

> The individual criminal has become mobile. He may flee or fly across state boundaries, and he can plan a robbery in one state, execute it in another, dispose of the loot in a third, and look for sanctuary in a fourth.[22]

A criminal cognizant of existing laws and the legal climate knows that penalties for certain crimes, whether speeding, auto theft, burglary, drug pushing, polluting water, or homicide, are not alike in all states. Some states and their courts are more concerned with the social conditions and consequences of the crime whereas others adopt harsh punishment standards as ways to discourage the recurrence of crimes. As the above quote indicates, boundaries play an important role in the administration of justice. City, county, and state boundaries frequently set off different interpretations of laws. When criminal acts involve political units with varying laws, problems can result in the ensuing legal process. State boundaries were important lines during days of prohibition, gun-running, and gangland warfare. If the criminal act was performed in one state, the lawbreakers knew that if pursued by the police or government officials, a quick retreat "across the border" placed them in safe territory. The significance of state boundaries in the interpretation of laws and the administration of justice is not limited solely to last century. The Mann Act passed by Congress in 1910 stated it was a violation of the law to transport a woman across a state line for immoral purposes. In the late 1960s Congress enacted legislation stating that a person could be convicted of breaking a law if he crossed state lines with the intent of carrying out a riot. This became the grounds for the Chicago Seven trial following the 1968 Democratic Convention. Probably an even more ridiculous example was the arrest of persons serving alcoholic drinks to Amtrak passengers in dry Kansas in 1971. This situation involving the state boundaries of Kansas reached absurd proportions when airlines announced they would not serve drinks when they flew over "Kansas skies."

The geography of justice involves the varying penalties stipulated for the same crime and the legal processes themselves. There are definite areal variations in the time prior to appearance in court and the sentencing periods as well. While many of these contrasts are identified at the district court level, state variations exist as well. Again the state as a political unit can become an important element in the legal process prior to sentencing. Frequent are cases where an individual under indictment is not permitted to travel in certain states. For example, Jimmy Hoffa could not travel in all states when he was awaiting trial during the early 1960s. The wife of Clifford Irving (author of supposed biography of Howard Hughes) could not travel outside New York and Connecticut while she was awaiting trial in February 1972. Similarly Russell Means, a militant Indian leader, was arrested in Los Angeles in April 1973, as he was not permitted to travel out of South Dakota where he was awaiting trial.

In the same way that the social and political heritage are an integral part of the legal constructs for a state, likewise such heritage is a part of the administration of justice. Persons convicted for similar crimes in Montana, Maine, and Mississippi are not always likely to receive the same sentence. Judges with training and experience in their home districts or regions are often likely to interpret the law in the light of the region's philosophy. When such conditions operate, as indeed they do, the severity of punishment for a minor or major crime displays definite geographical consequences. These variations are found on a regional basis and within a state as well. Cosmopolitan urban nodes may be expected to reveal more views in concert with contemporary society than distinctly rural areas. The latter may interpret violations the same way as judges and juries did twenty-five or fifty years ago.

An additional element in the geographical process of justice involves the place for trials. Ideally an individual tried for a crime would be expected to have an equal likelihood for a fair hearing no matter where the hearings were set. However, this is not the case as criminals and their lawyers know that where a particular trial is held may influence the jury selection and decision as well as the actual sentencing. Some places are likely to be more favorable to certain forms of societal behavior than others. For example, individuals cohabiting the same residence or smoking marijuana are more likely to be punished with a light sentence or none at all in a university town, even though both conditions are considered a crime in the state. An appearance before a judge or jury in a small town or rural environment may lead to harsh and lengthy sentences even within the same state as the above college community.

The discussion below dwells on these three facets of justice, that is, the geographical variations in penalties, the convictions, and trial settings. Lack of uniformity on a state basis results in individuals being subject to the legal framework of that particular location. One of the concerns of the political geographer is that shifting an individual to another location within the same state or to another state in the United States may result in an entirely different interpretation of laws and administration of justice. The conditions may be more favorable or more stringent to the individual.

Penalties. The punishments for four crimes are selected for detailed examination. They are the penalties for first-degree murder, states with capital punishment for rape, jail sentences for marijuana, and the jail sentences for general lewdness. Even though these penalties are grouped for mapping purposes into four or five classes, it is more often the case that there may be as many as thirty, forty, or perhaps even fifty different penalties. Violators can receive a combination of jail or fine sentences depending on the state and the severity of the crime.

One of the penalties that has been under attack in recent years is capital punishment. Twelve states had abolished this as a form of punishment prior to the Supreme Court decision in June 1972. These states in the main were progressive states that stressed individualism and had a moral tenor to criminal laws enacted. The states were Alaska, Hawaii, Iowa, Maine, Michigan, Minnesota, North Dakota, Oregon, Rhode Island, Vermont, West Virginia, and Wisconsin. New York and New Mexico, in addition to North Dakota, Rhode Island, and Vermont, retained capital punishment for a number of crimes such as treason and piracy. Since the Court's decision, a number of states that had not abolished capital punishment have proposed legislation favoring capital punishment for airplane hijackers and persons convicted of murdering certain public servants such as police and fire fighters. The Supreme Court ruled that capital punishment for murder or rape, when jury-imposed, was cruel and unusual punishment.

Prior to this ruling, the maximum penalty for first-degree murder varied widely from state to state. As stated above, Midwest and some Northeast and New England states that had abolished capital punishment had lifetime sentences. Other states had death by electrocution, lethal gas, and hanging (or shooting in the

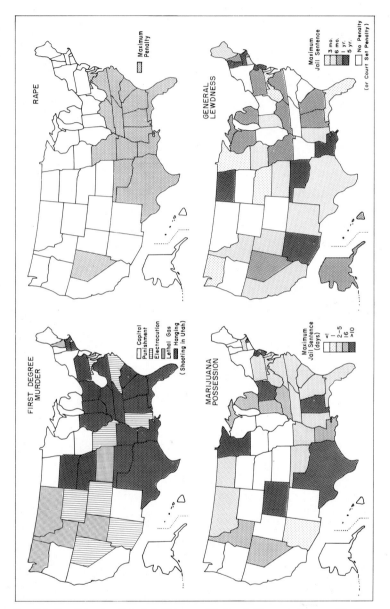

FIG. 8-5 Penalties for Selected Crimes. (National Commission on Marihuana and Drug Abuse, 1972. And data from Richard Rhodes, "Sex and Sin in Sheboygan," *Playboy*, August 1972, pp. 188–189. © 1972 by *Playboy*. Used with permission.)

case of Utah) on the books. There appears to be little semblance of what might be termed significant regional patterns (Fig. 8-5). Hanging is found in some of the states where violence historically was considered an acceptable way of settling differences. The line of reasoning is confounded by its practice in New Hampshire and Delaware. Electrocution was the maximum penalty for first-degree murder in the largest number of states and particularly in the Midwest and Southeast. The pattern of death by lethal gas exhibited little areal homogeneity. Many of those individuals convicted of first-degree murder awaited the Supreme Court ruling. Some had remained on death rows for several years as 1967 marked the last year of an execution in the United States.

Even though there were no uniform patterns allowing for criminals convicted of first-degree murder, as exceptions occurred in states with similar political and social traditions, there were more distinct patterns for penalties for other crimes. For example, prior to the Supreme Court ruling, capital punishment was the maximum penalty for rape in sixteen states, especially the southeastern states where criminal violence is high and the law is often administered partially-to blacks and the poor (Fig. 8-5). This strong penalty illustrates a regional philosophy that historically has stressed social separation of the races, a strict interpretation of laws, strong fundamentalist religious views, and the preservation of an agrarian and traditional society. Together these conditions meant that acts of violence not condoned by the ruling white elites were severely punished. Many of these cases involved blacks, who were on death rows at the time of the 1972 landmark decision.

One of the most controversial issues that the public, legislatures, and courts have been facing recently is drugs. The questions about sale, possession, and prescriptions are of concern as is the classification (felony or misdemeanor) and imposition of penalties. The most popular drug that has been discussed and debated is marijuana. At the root of the question is not simply whether it is a felony or misdemeanor to be in possession of the drug, but whether it is harmful and addictive. If it is harmful, at what levels is it so; and if it is illegal, what is a meaningful penalty for the user and pusher. A number of national organizations and commissions have attacked the issue and studied it from all facets. The result in a legal framework is reflected in its present status in society, and that is one of complexity and confusion.

There is no uniform pattern of laws governing the person convicted of possessing marijuana. In fact, few states had similar laws in the early 1970s (Fig. 8-5). Although the map illustrates the maximum jail sentences a resident of a state can receive for possessing marijuana, there are many more than five legal interpretations and patterns. State-to-state variations even with very recent changes in state laws still exist to minor and major degrees. In Michigan the sentence for possession of marijuana is a short jail sentence of not more than ninety days; and in Utah, South Carolina, and Iowa it is not to exceed six months.[23] All these states are classed in the same pattern on the map. Stiffer sentences are imposed for possession in Indiana (not more than ten years) and Rhode Island (not more than fifteen years). The stiffest penalty is life imprisonment, which can be imposed in Texas for possession (the minimum penalty is two years if convicted). Other states that call for heavy maximum sentences for possession are New York and Colorado (fifteen years). Many states have a fine that can be imposed as well. Needless to say there are separate penalties for being convicted a second and third time, possessing the drug for sale, selling it, and selling it to minors. With the social significance attached to this drug, it would seem in order that some legal agreement needs to be reached as to its safety and a more uniform set of penalties. In the past years a number of states and cities have revised their criminal codes in dealing with marijuana, some lightening the sentence as in Ann Arbor, Michigan (once a $5 fine), and others calling for tougher legislation against the pusher, as in New York.

The final criminal act that is treated in this discussion is the jail sentence for general lewdness. This is one of a series of consensual sex offenses that states have classed along with adultery, cohabitation, fornication, and crimes against nature that have rather specified fines or jail sentences or both.[24] Penalties as in the marijuana possession situation described above exhibit little regional or sectional homogeneity. The maximum penalty for being convicted of lewdness in 1972 was five years, which was on the books in seven states. In other states there is no specified sentence (Fig. 8-5). Fines vary from $25 in Maine to $5000 in Rhode Island and Oklahoma. Most state laws have a certain amount of flexibility in the fine or jail sentence. Similar inconsistencies in other consensual sex offenses are found in the nation's fifty states. For example, persons convicted of adultery pay a $10 fine in Maryland while in Michigan an individual can receive up to four years in jail or a $2000 fine or both. Different penalties exist for men and women in Hawaii. Even though many of these laws on the books reveal rather stiff and seemingly unreasonable jail sentences or fines, individuals are often not convicted of these crimes, especially in New England and in the South (two regions with harsh sentences). Changing social conditions and moral codes have demonstrated in many cases the dated interpretation of consensual sex offenses. In New York City only two individuals have been convicted of adultery and none for fornication in the past fifty years. Another smaller city, Sheboygan, Wisconsin, has a much higher investigation rate; in 1971, a total of 118 cases of sex offenses were reported.[25]

Convictions. Once an individual has been arrested for committing a crime, his appearance before a judge or jury may result in his being cleared or being sentenced. The rates for those cleared of arrest after being charged with an offense may be suspected as being similar in all parts of the United States; however, such is not the case. The *Uniform Crime Reports* of the Federal Bureau of Investigation give the percent cleared by arrests for nine geographic divisions of the census and for the varying kinds of crimes.[26] The variations, some of which would be expected to vary from year to year, are more reflective of the social climate and heritage of the regions themselves. That is, what may be viewed as a harsh crime in the South or West may not be in New England.

TABLE 8-3   Percent Cleared by Arrest, Rank by Geographic Divisions
(1 = least cleared; 9 = most cleared; T = tied percentages)

Crime	Percent Cleared by Arrest	Geographic Divisions								
		New England	Mid-Atlantic	East North Central	West North Central	South Atlantic	East South Central	West South Central	Mountain	Pacific
Total Crimes	21.0	1	9	7	6	5	4	8	3	2
Crime Index	20.1	1	2	6T	6T	8	5	9	3	4
Violent Crimes	47.6	6	1	4	2	5	9	8	7	3
Property Crimes	16.1	3	2	7	8	6	1	9	4	5
Murder	86.5	1	3	4	5	8	9	7	6	2
Manslaughter	80.9	2	4	8	3	9	1	7	6	5
Forcible Rape	56.4	8	5	3	6	7	9	4	1	2
Robbery	29.1	5	1	8	2	3	4	7	9	6
Burglary	19.4	1	2	7	9	3	6	8	4	5
Larceny, Total	18.4	2	1	8	7	5	3	9	6	4
Auto Theft	16.9	2	1	5	9	7	3	8	6	4
Aggravated Assault	64.9	8	4	1T	5	7	9	6	3	1T

Source: U.S. Department of Justice, Federal Bureau of Investigation, *Crime in the United States, Uniform Crime Reports—1970*, Washington, D.C., 1971, pp. 110–111.

The ranking of the major classes of crime is used as one index to measure the variations in spatial justice (Table 8-3). In 1970, in 21 percent of the cases, the individual was cleared. However, this percent cleared varies widely by geographic divisions (regions not entirely homogeneous in social behavior) and for the varying crimes. What these rankings illustrate is that the chances of being cleared after an initial arrest vary with the geographic division and for the crime itself. In other words, location seems to influence the likelihood of later being convicted and sentenced.

For violent crimes as a group (murder, manslaughter, forcible rape, robbery, and aggravated assault), the Middle Atlantic, West North Central, and Pacific states had the lowest percents cleared while the South and West (West South Central, East South Central and Mountain) had the highest percents cleared. For property crimes (burglary, larceny, and auto theft) the Northeast is low but the Midwest and West South Central divisions are highest.

When specific types of crime are examined for those cleared by arrest, New England, the Middle Atlantic, and the Pacific states appear to have the fewest cleared by arrests. Perhaps this is a reflection of morality, that is, a concern with fair and impartial justice. On the other hand, for both violent and property crimes the West South Central, East South Central, and South Atlantic states appear almost consistently to have the largest percents cleared. Maybe this reflects an ineffective judicial system or perhaps an overcautious police force. There are examples of specific geographic divisions that are high for certain crimes; for example, the West North Central is high in those cleared by burglary and auto theft charges and low for those arrested for robbery and manslaughter. Similarly, the East South Central has low percents of arrests cleared for manslaughter, larceny, and auto theft and has high percents cleared for murder, forcible rape, and aggravated assault. The Mountain region ranks low for those cleared for forcible rape and high for robbery. Exact reasons for the differences between geographical divisions as well as for specific classes of crime are difficult to assess without greater knowledge of the social and legal climate for smaller units.

If an individual is not cleared after an initial court appearance, that is, he is charged with violating some law, the legal machinery again takes on a geographic dimension. It may be assumed that these court procedures involving arrests, convictions, and sentencing operate uniformly throughout the United States or even within districts. Indeed, they do not. There are discrepancies between and within districts and states as local standards and judicial views on crimes and criminals exhibit seemingly little uniformity. If the differences are sufficient, it would indicate that the system of justice is administered and interpreted with impartiality. Factors depending on the criminal act, the place and timing of the trial, and the judge or jury hearing the case may lead to an indictment or exoneration based strictly on geography.

A recent presidential task force has commented on varying facets of spatial injustices. While most states have maximum fines or jail sentences for criminal acts, the actual decision reached by a judge could be completely different if the same individual were tried in an adjacent state. In Wisconsin, for example, there are sixteen variations in the statutory maximum terms of imprisonment for felonies on a first conviction. Oregon has 1143 criminal statutes containing 466 different types and lengths of sentences. In Colorado a person convicted of first-degree murder must serve ten years before being eligible for parole while a person convicted of a lesser degree of the same offense must serve at least fifteen years. The same state has a statute stating destruction of a house by fire is punishable by a maximum twenty-year imprisonment while destruction of a house with an explosive carries a ten-year maximum. In California a person who breaks into the glove compartment of an automobile to steal the contents is subject to a fifteen-year maximum sentence. If he stole the car, he would face only a ten-year term. It is no wonder that such inequities are behind attempts at statewide and national legal reform.[27]

The discrepancy often enters right into the courtroom. Admittedly a certain amount of difference is bound to exist, due to local standards and an individual judge's view of the case and criminal; but, "the problem of disparity arises from the imposition of unequal sentences for the same offense, or offenses of comparable seriousness, without any reasonable basis."[28] In the federal system the average length of prison sentences for narcotics was eighty-three months in the Tenth Circuit but only forty-four months in the Third. During 1962 the average sentence for forgery ranged from a high of sixty-eight months in the Northern District of Mississippi to only seven months in the Southern District of the same state. Auto theft, a common crime throughout the nation, brought sentences averaging forty-seven months in the Southern District of Iowa to only fourteen months in the Northern District of New York. In a 1966 study of the Detroit Recorders Court that covered a twenty-month period, where sample cases were distributed equally among judges, one judge imposed prison terms upon 75 to 90 percent of the defendants he sentenced while another did on only 35 percent of those he sentenced. One judge consistently imposed prison sentences twice as long as the most lenient judge. This report adds that "Unwarranted sentencing disparity is contrary to the principle of even handed administration of the criminal law."[29]

To illustrate further various forms of judicial behavior, data on case load, trial period, and sentencing are examined on a district court basis. An attempt is made to observe if there are certain areas or districts that enjoy legal advantages over others. Although detailed data are available on a state basis, the ten district courts and District of Columbia were used for purposes of elucidating macropatterns. First, to the political geographer, it is readily admitted that the court districts are not regions reflecting similar population size, social, economy, cultural or political homogeneity (Fig. 8-6). The strange sizes and shapes of some districts leave much to be desired when significant regional comparisons are attempted. While the First District comprising New England is fairly homogeneous (except for the inclusion of Puerto Rico) and the Fifth representing the South is fairly so, including within the same district the states of Tennessee and Michigan or including the Pacific Southwest, Northwest, and Alaska and Hawaii in District 9 does seem to be

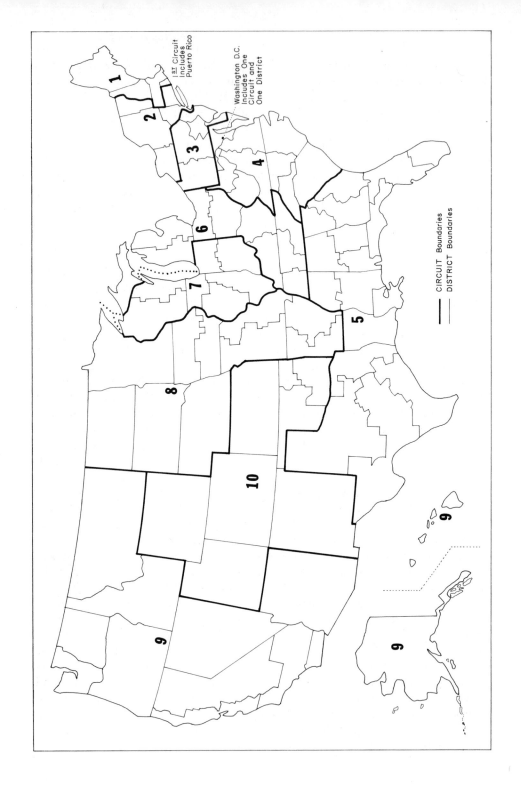

1

ST Circuit
Includes
Puerto Rico

2

Washington D.C.
Includes One
Circuit and
One District

3

4

6

7

5

8

10

9

9

9

CIRCUIT Boundaries
DISTRICT Boundaries

a rather unwieldy regional grouping. Another example is including Arkansas with states in the Northern Plains. It is realized that the outlines of the districts are for administrative purposes; however, the legal hierarchy may be important in cases heard at the various levels. At this juncture regional philosophies are likely to enter in the judicial processes.

Within the past few years, the issue of case load per judge has arisen as it is felt the large loads on some judges in some districts were hampering a continuous flow or due process of justice. For example, in 1965 in the District of Columbia Court of General Sessions four judges had to process the preliminary stages of 1,500 felonies, 7,500 serious misdemeanors, 38,000 petty offenses, and an equal number of traffic cases. In Atlanta in 1964, three judges of the Municipal Court disposed of more than 70,000 cases.[30] Using the 1970 district court data it was observed the case load varied markedly for criminal and civil cases. First, in dividing the cases into these two categories, civil cases were most common in Districts 1, 6, 3, and 8. Criminal cases were most common in District Court 9, in fact, in 40 percent of those heard. In terms of the weighted case load per judge, the heaviest load was for those judges in District 1 where thirteen judges handled 332 cases. Four districts, 2, 3, 5, and 9, had an average of six or fewer cases per judge.[31]

Involved in the case load is the number of judges able to hear the charges. The time interval the case is pending can be used to measure if an efficient and speedy judicial process actually is in operation. Cases pending six to twelve months were most common in District 9 where 40 percent were within this time period. The District of Columbia and Districts 1 and 3 had less than 15 percent of the cases pending this amount of time. More frequent were cases with fugitive defendants that were over one year. In several districts the percent over twelve months was such that the backlog prevented a speedy legal process, District 9 having 80 percent pending one year or more; District 10, 74 percent; District 8, 73 percent; and District 7, 63 percent.

The median length of time also varied depending on whether a jury or non-jury trial was held. For non-jury trials the median length varied from eighteen months (District 2) to fifteen months (District 3 and the District of Columbia) to a six-month wait in District 10. Jury trials also showed wide contrasts from a thirty-four-month wait in District 3 to a nine-month wait in District 5, 8, and 9.

Lack of sectional or regional uniformity was exhibited in the forms of sentences meted out to those convicted in 1969. Of all those sentenced in the district courts and in Washington, D.C., the harshest sentences were handed out to those in the District of Columbia. Nearly 60 percent of those sentenced were given prison sentences over five years. The lightest sentences, that is, those with less than a year and a day, were for criminals in Districts 2, 6, 4, 8, 10, and 3; the percents varied from 16 percent for the Second and Sixth Districts to 10 percent for the Third. Not all persons sentenced were given prison sentences as some were placed

Fig. 8-6 Federal Judicial Court Districts. (U.S. Department of the Interior, *National Atlas of the United States*, Geological Survey, Washington, D.C., 1970.)

on probation. An individual had a better chance of being placed on probation in District 3 than in any other as 52 percent were given such. The length of the probation period also showed regional contrasts, often with a pattern that was difficult to interpret. Probations of less than twelve months were most common in District 1, where almost one-quarter were given sentences within this period. Light sentences of this tenure were rare in District 4, 5, 6, 10, and 8 where 10 percent or less were given less than one year. Probation periods from one to three years were more common in District 6 (71 percent), District 8 (70 percent), and District 10 (66 percent).

Significant district differences also appeared in the length of imprisonment (Table 8-4). When the prison sentences are divided into categories from six months or less to over ten years, some crude consistencies emerge. Light sentences, less than six months, are most common in District 3, 10, 8, 6, and 2. The heaviest sentences, those from three to four years, are in District 10, 8, 4, and 3. Ten-year or more sentences tend to be fewer in some of the same districts that had the lightest sentences. Exceptions appear as in District 3, 5, and 9. District sentences did not always follow the national averages. District 5 and to a lesser extent District 1 paralleled rather closely the national averages for the different prison terms. Frequently districts approximated the national average for one span but not for others. In summary, district values did not seem to exhibit marked similarity or consistency for most prison stays.

Locational Settings for Trials. The place a criminal trial is held may influence the conviction and the type of punishment meted out. In a jury trial, members selected from the community in question are thought to reflect the standards and philosophy of that particular location. Because lawyers for the prosecution and defense are aware that community and societal views of crimes and certain groups of citizens (blacks, students, or foreign-born Americans) vary from place to place, they will attempt to have the trial occur in a location most favorable to their case. Persons arrested for a criminal act in one location may be tried within that same location or the lawyers may argue for a change of venue. This is in reality a request that the court case be heard in another location primarily as it is believed the individual cannot receive a fair trial in the place of the crime. Local sentiments against the crime coupled with media-influenced opinion may preclude a fair hearing and selection of an impartial jury.

The selection of jury members from the local community may determine the execution of an impartial trial. If all members selected for a jury in South Carolina or Mississippi investigating charges of police brutality toward a black leader were whites from rural areas, the prevailing racial sentiment of the region may render a fair hearing impossible. More than one all-white jury in the South has automatically disenfranchised resident blacks of rights already enjoyed by members of the white community. It is not surprising, therefore, that civil rights lawyers in the past twenty years have carefully picked cases that could be tried in southern cities and metropolitan areas. Here the legal climate, itself a term with geographical

TABLE 8-4 Length of Prison Sentences in District Court Regions

Region	Total	1–6 Months		7–12 Months		13–24 Months		37–48 Months		61–120 Months		121 Months Plus	
		Number	Percent	Number	Percent	Number	Percent	Number	Percent	Number	Percent	Number	Percent
Total	11,535	1,655	14	1,118	10	2,041	18	1,952	17	1,038	9	577	5
1	203	28	14	32	16	34	17	22	11	13	6	10	5
2	791	50	6	101	13	201	25	96	12	89	11	35	4
3	370	10	3	30	8	64	17	60	16	47	13	38	10
4	1,012	78	8	99	10	220	22	180	18	74	7	81	8
5	3,099	555	18	304	10	663	21	416	13	258	8	78	3
6	1,219	72	6	147	10	263	22	177	15	100	8	121	10
7	624	54	9	51	8	127	20	96	15	77	12	42	7
8	634	35	6	50	8	109	17	139	22	56	9	23	4
9	2,861	744	26	232	8	278	10	554	19	260	9	114	4
10	722	29	4	72	10	82	11	212	29	64	9	35	5

Source: Administrative Office of the U.S. Courts, *Federal Offenders in the United States District Courts, 1969*, Washington, D.C., 1971, pp. 148–149.

dimensions, was considered more diversified and tolerant of more contemporary views of racial matters. Similar views are expressed regarding students convicted of smoking marijuana. A college town or big city is preferred for a hearing as opposed to a small isolated county seat location.

Legal counsels for many civil rights and environmental groups carefully select cases that they have a good chance of winning. In part their choices reflect the location of the hearing. A random jury selection from a city, state, or region with favorable philosophies to the case in question, or for that matter even hearings before certain judges and in certain districts, may give the organization an edge in any eventual jury indictment and ensuing judicial decisions.

The federal government has also become involved in grand jury investigations in the past few years, some of which have had a distinct geographical and legal character. The "Chicago Seven" trial following the 1968 Democratic Convention in that city was an attempt to prove carefully laid riot plans were involved in the street melee. The defense argued that their clients could not receive a fair trial in the city because of the sentiment against the seven, the protests, and the views of Mayor Daley, the local media, and citizenry as well. At one stage during the trial the defense even argued that the judge was exhibiting partiality in his actions against certain defendants. To the political geographer interested in law, the question arises whether the defendants would have been indicted on various counts had the trial been held elsewhere.

The case of Father Daniel Berrigan and the "Harrisburg Eight" was held in the Pennsylvania capital city. The eight were charged by the federal government with planning the bombing of defense installations in Washington, D.C., and the kidnapping of then-presidential advisor, Professor Henry Kissinger. In their search for a trial location, the federal government selected Harrisburg. This rather small isolated city in a conservative part of Pennsylvania had a low Catholic population and a rather strict constitutional judge. All these were considered advantageous to the prosecution's case; however, the jury dismissed almost all charges against those brought to its attention.

There are other cases, past and present, that can be cited where the location of the trial probably influenced the final decisions reached by the judge and jury. Angela Davis was tried on murder, conspiracy, and kidnapping charges in Santa Clara County (in San Jose), California. The defense hoped to have the trial in San Francisco, a place where it was felt she would receive a fair trial. Santa Clara County was not considered a hospitable location; however, she was not indicted. The grand jury convening in Tarrant County, Texas, in 1972 involved the "Fort Worth Five," a group of New Yorkers, Catholics, and Irish-born members who were sympathizers of the militant Irish Republican Army. They were charged with gunrunning to Northern Ireland. The likelihood of support for such activities would certainly be much different in Fort Worth than it would be in Boston or New York City. The 1973 "Pentagon Papers" trial in Los Angeles represented a location with strong patriotism and previous pro-Nixon sentiment. If the federal government had picked Philadelphia or even Miami, the trial may have taken different turns, but the case was thrown out due to Watergate-related developments.

Skillful lawyers for organizations or the federal government or for that matter even for individual clients acknowledge the importance of geography or place location for a hearing and trial. Whether the case involves a practice found nationwide such as cross-district school busing, water pollution, consumer protection, or racial zoning, the particular city, state, or district judge may have an important bearing on the eventual judgment. The observation among legal groups that justice is not administered the same in all parts of space is behind the attempt to have the initial hearing or the trial itself in a place most favorable to the client. The client in this case may be an individual, a particular group, or even the nation's citizens.

LEGAL AND ADMINISTRATIVE REFORM

The national awareness of crucial social problems in the past decade in particular has been noted in Supreme Court decisions. In probably no other ten-year period in recent history has the nation's highest court taken on and rendered judgment on so many issues involving civil liberties and rights. Existing local or state laws governing legislative reapportionment, voter residency requirements, welfare coverage, school desegregation, civil disobedience, literacy tests, fair trials, capital punishment, and abortion were only a few of the many concerns that were discussed. National guidelines or conditions were interpreted that applied equally to individuals in sparsely populated western states and central cities in parts of the Northeast. Furthermore, these decisions were for all citizens regardless of race, creed, socioeconomic status, or national origin. The executions of said judgments were not without the erection of local and state barriers that attempted to circumvent Supreme Court rulings, as in school desegregation or capital punishment.

Individual and group rights are still being challenged in courts and legislatures at the present time. One of the best known that is currently under discussion is the equal rights amendment to the Constitution. The United States House of Representatives in 1971 and the Senate in 1972 passed legislation permitting equal rights for all regardless of sex. Since then states have been discussing this proposed twenty-seventh amendment. As of May 1, 1973, thirty of the necessary thirty-eight states have ratified the proposal; seventeen have failed to ratify it and three were still debating it. Most of those states that have endorsed this measure are identified as having progressive or liberal orientations in the arena of civil rights (Fig. 8-7). However, there are exceptions to this generalization. The measure failed to be ratified by the necessary three-fourths of the states in 1973 but the states have until 1979 to ratify the 1972 congressional vote. In large part this issue has been supported by women's liberation groups who see existing state statutes discriminating against them in career openings and advancements, salaries, and legal protection.

The case involving the equal rights amendment is but one of several pieces

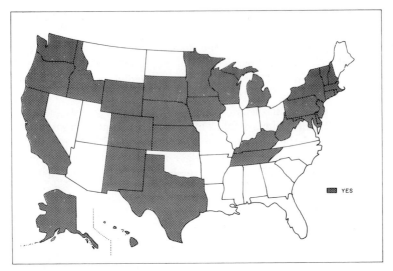

FIG. 8-7 Status of Equal Rights Amendment, May 1973.

of legislation currently being discussed in many of the state legislatures. The national concern for matters relating to human resources and development are not being restricted to only a handful of states. Rather, congressmen and state legislatures and even local officials in Florida are discussing some of the same issues as those in Maine, Washington, and California. Probably the current environmental concerns best illustrate this situation. Dealing with air or water or noise pollution is not a matter that relates to county or state boundaries. Similarly the protection of the environment, the resources in an energy crisis, and the definition of an individual's environmental rights are issues paramount in agricultural and urban-industrial states. The convening of local officials and state leaders to discuss regional and national issues is seen as an attempt to provide uniform guidelines and policies for current social and economic problems.

National concerns and discussions about current issues have been instrumental in reducing the passage time for amendments to the United States Constitution. The Twenty-sixth Amendment, permitting eighteen-year-olds to vote, required slightly more than three months for the necessary states to ratify the congressional resolution. From the above discussion about variations in legal interpretation of similar institutions and practices and the different penalties and judicial systems, it is often easier to introduce legislation on new problems than to alter existing measures. The state laws and statutes that govern the age requirements for marriage, the professional training for medical practitioners, and the purchasing of property and others were frequently implemented at the time of state formation with little regard to adjacent states. That is, local and state governing bodies dealt with problems of life and property, and to alter these into a more uniform national legal system may be difficult to attain. Even in such minor areas as the examination for a driver's license, states do not agree as to the content and reapplication procedures. The need for some lessening of these and other inequities is discussed at greater length in Chapter 13. What appears from a legal standpoint at present is a number of crosscurrents governing the behavior of citizens. National decisions are handed down on matters involving voter residency and fair trial procedures but not on equally important concerns as state statutes determining welfare requirements and approved medical practices. Local political units enter the complex picture when residency and taxing levels are not alike even in similar adjacent spaces. While it is admitted that certain legal duplications and inconsistencies have been outlawed or eroded, some still continue. American Indians, as an example, are under the aegis of federal or state or tribal authorities, depending on where they reside. South Dakota and Utah Indians are under the jurisdiction of all three levels while tribal and federal levels administer to those in North Dakota and Wyoming. At present there are forty-five states with state jurisdictions, sixteen with federal, and fourteen with tribal jurisdictions.[32]

The geographical interpretation of laws is one concern of reform-minded politicians and legal planners but so is the administration of justice. The election requirements of public officials, case-load volume, period prior to trial, correctional programs, and actual sentencing are all elements involved in discussions recommending improvements in the legal system. All too many of these are still tied to local and state laws. While an administration of justice that operates the same in all states is probably a long way off, at least legal experts are beginning to consider alternatives to the present system. The chief justice of the supreme court of Minnesota in commenting on the statewide defender system stated:

> There is probably no single system that can be devised that is ideal for every state in this country. Our states differ in population, in congestion, in size, and in many other respects, and obviously, what is best for Minnesota (if we have the best) may not be the best for New York or California.[33]

Local and state considerations as a part of any administrative framework were echoed by the National Advisory Council of the National Defender Project, which stated:

> The system adopted by a particular jurisdiction should be designed to fit the geography, demography, and development of the area. . . .[34]

In order to accommodate the societal problems facing cities, counties, and states, a number of proposals have been made and programs implemented. The Arkansas-Mississippi and Arkansas-Tennessee Boundary Compacts have been developed to coordinate criminal matters near the Mississippi River. The New England State Police Compact provides for central criminal records and emergency assistance among the six state police forces. Another example is the Waterfront Commission Compact between New York and New Jersey enacted in 1953 to coordinate state efforts and check organized crime in the New York Port area.[35] The cooperation effort also extends to more local levels in the case of certain police functions. Lake County, Illinois, performs communications services to twenty localities within its confines. The cities of Chicago, Des Moines, Philadelphia, Milwaukee, and Wichita offer police training programs to surrounding suburbs. These intergovernmental cooperative efforts even extend to Chicago and Philadelphia, offering crime laboratory services to neighboring governments.[36]

The enforcement of laws being tied to local or state officials can and does result in impartial justice, as has been pointed out above. The number of prosecuting officers varies widely from state to state and from county to county. Problems result at local and state levels when there is a lack of coordination and similar interpretation of said crimes. The President's Commission on Law Enforcement and the Administration of Justice recognized the geographical nature of legal administration when it stated in regard to coordination that:

> A local prosecutor is usually the product of the community which he serves. He is locally elected and is likely to be responsible to his constituency. Most important, since marked variation in the crime problem and in community resources may exist from area to area within a state, he is in a position to adjust prosecutorial policy to local conditions.
>
> But division of the prosecutorial function and lack of coordination among local offices within a single state is also likely to have deleterious consequences. A strict enforcement policy in one county may simply divert criminal activity into neighboring areas. A community's effort to deal with crime will be limited if criminal groups can operate from a nearby jurisdiction with relative impunity. This may be seen in large metropolitan areas where prostitution, gambling, and bootlegging become exceedingly difficult to suppress when they are operated from a nearby haven.
>
> Our traditional notion that the criminal law will be applied within a state with a reasonable degree of uniformity is weakened by a fragmented system of prosecution. Prosecutors exercise enormous discretionary authority within their jurisdiction. They decide whether to prosecute and for what offense; they decide whether to negotiate a plea of guilty and on what terms.[37]

It becomes quite clear from such discussions that the legal framework suffers from a lack of consistency at local and even state levels. The responsibilities are tied to intergovernmental structures encompassing local, state, and federal levels. Jurisdictional problems involved in criminal justice are not infrequently geographical problems. A 1971 report on the criminal justice system in dealing with the intergovernmental nature of this problem stated that: "The state-local system must be geographically adequate." This means that "a government must encompass a large enough area and population to insure that criminal justice functions will be performed with at least a modicum of technical expertise."[38] As it now exists state government plays the major role in Alaska, Connecticut, Rhode Island, Delaware and Vermont while local government is more involved in Michigan, Illinois, California, New York, Massachusetts, and New Jersey. Problems become greater when there is little or no coordination between the numerous political units in a metropolitan area. Criminal activities are mobile but the present legal systems covering such actions are often without the intergovernmental and extraterritorial police power that are necessary for an effective system of justice.

The streamlining of justice to bring it more in tune with the nature and needs of society involves more than police reorganization systems. It also involves the handling of cases in the local and state courts. Only recently have Texas and Oklahoma proposed doing away with the two state supreme court systems. Effective justice is behind these moves. In like manner the qualifications for judges and the extent of a state's correctional programs merit attention. Too frequently are individuals in state correctional institutions treated differently, again depending on the state commitment to such cases and their response to much-needed reforms. It seems likely that legal and administrative reforms will erase some of the geographic discrepancies affecting individuals and groups as local, state, and federal leaders and agencies discuss the interpretation of laws and the execution of justice in a modern light.

FOOTNOTES

1. John Fraser Hart, *The Southeastern United States*, Princeton, N.J., Van Nostrand, 1967, Fig. 6, "Alcoholic Beverages."
2. Guy Halverson, "Should You Wash Your Car on Sundays?" *Christian Science Monitor*, April 14, 1973, pp. 1 and 13.
3. Clyde E. Browning, "The Property Tax and Public Policy: A Neglected Opportunity for Geographic Research," *Proceedings*, Association of American Geographers, 5 (1973), 35–38.
4. Guy Halverson, "U.S. Youth Refocuses Activism," *Christian Science Monitor*, February 12, 1972, pp. 1 and 3; and George B. Merry, " 'Early-adulthood' Statutes Spreading," ibid., October 3, 1973, p. 4.
5. Department of Defense, Office of Information for Armed Forces, *Voter Information 1970*, Washington, D.C., Government Printing Office, 1970.
6. *World Almanac 1971*, New York, Newspaper Enterprise Inc., 1971, pp. 18–21.
7. Advisory Commission on Intergovernmental Relations, *State and Local Finances, Significant Features and Suggested Legislation, 1972 Edition*, Washington, D.C., U.S. Government Printing Office, 1972, p. 179.
8. Ibid., p. 291.
9. Ibid., p. 295.
10. Ibid., p. 297.
11. Advisory Commission on Intergovernmental Relations, *State-Local Relations in the Criminal Justice System*, Washington, D.C., Superintendent of Public Documents, 1971, p. 112.
12. President's Commission on Law Enforcement and the Administration of Justice, *Task Force Report: The Courts*, Washington, D.C., Superintendent of Public Documents, 1967, pp. 77–79.
13. Donna R. Clifton, "Political Expediency States 'in Line at Gambling Window,' " *Christian Science Monitor*, September 8, 1971, pp. 1 and 3.
14. A. F. Lambert, "The United States-Canada Boundary," *Surveying and Mapping*, 28 (1968), p. 31.

15. Lewis M. Alexander, "Geography and the Law of the Sea," *Annals, Association of American Geographers*, 58 (1968), 178.

16. Louis de Vorsey, Jr., "Florida's Seaward Boundary: A Problem in Applied Historical Geography," *Professional Geographer*, 25:3 (1973), 214–220.

17. F. J. Hortig, "Jurisdictional, Administrative, and Technical Problems Related to the Establishment of California Coastal and Offshore Boundaries," in Lewis M. Alexander, ed., *The Law of the Sea: Offshore Boundaries and Zones*, Columbus, Ohio, The Ohio State University Press, 1967, pp. 231–234.

18. Irwin L. White et al., *Law and Politics in Outer Space: A Bibliography*, Tucson, University of Arizona Press, 1972, pp. 14–24.

19. *Statistical Abstract of the United States, 1972*, Washington, D.C., U.S. Department of Commerce, 1972, p. 87.

20. United States Tariff Commission, *Tariff Schedules of the United States, Annotated (1972)*, Washington, D.C., U.S. Government Printing Office, 1972, TC Publication 452.

21. Ibid., pp. 571–582.

22. Morton Grodzins, *The American System*, Chicago, Ill., Rand McNally College Publishing Company, 1966, p. 93. Reprinted by permission.

23. National Commission on Marihuana and Drug Abuse, *Marihuana: A Signal of Misunderstanding*, Washington, D.C., Superintendent of Public Documents, 1972, vol. 1, Appendix, pp. 552–557. See also "Penalty for Simple Possession of Marijuana (First Offense)," *Playboy*, November 1970, p. 67.

24. Richard Rhodes, "Sex and Sin in Sheboygan," *Playboy*, August 1972, pp. 188–189.

25. Ibid., p. 129.

26. U.S. Department of Justice, Federal Bureau of Investigation, *Crime in the United States, Uniform Crime Reports, 1970*, Washington, D.C., 1971, pp. 110–111.

27. President's Commisssion on Law Enforcement . . . , op. cit., p. 15.

28. Ibid., p. 23.

29. Ibid.

30. Ibid., p. 31.

31. These district data were taken and calculated from the Annual Report of the Director of the Administrative Office of the United States District Courts, 1970, *Reports on the Proceedings of the Judicial Conference of the United States, Washington, D.C., March 16–17, 1970, and October 29–30, 1970*, Washington, D.C., U.S. Government Printing Office, 1971, pp. 220–325. See also, Administrative Office of the U.S. Courts, *Federal Offenders in the United States District Courts, 1969*, Washington, D.C., 1971.

32. Theodore W. Taylor, *The States and Their Indian Cultures*, Washington, D.C., Department of Interior, Bureau of Indian Affairs, 1972, p. 177.

33. Advisory Commission on Intergovernmental Relations, *State-Local Relations in the Criminal Justice System*, op. cit., p. 223.

34. Ibid.

35. Ibid., p. 87.

36. Ibid., p. 153.

37. President's Commission on Law Enforcement . . . , op. cit., p. 75.

38. Advisory Commission on Intergovernmental Relations, *State-Local Relations in the Criminal Justice System*, op. cit., p. 10.

Chapter 9

POLITICAL CULTURES

In America, the geography is sublime, but the men are not.

Emerson

The United States is comprised of political cultures whose numbers, areal importance, and political impact vary markedly. Some such as the New England "Yankee" influence developed and have not been affected by other cultural stock. Texas, on the other hand, has midwestern, Spanish-American, Deep South, and even European elements, each with a definite social and political impact. While the original settlement influences of diverse racial and ethnic groups may have diminished, the cultural impress on the political system has remained. Regional and sectional differences in national as well as state politics remain in spite of government programs and laws affecting a region's citizens. Frequently those initial ethnic and racial contrasts that have disappeared or coalesced in the political and social arena have been replaced by rural-urban or central city-suburban political cultures. In some cases economic ties have replaced social ties in the evolution of a political culture. The mobility of Americans in all states and in all regions has affected the political character and culture of the nation, often by erasing local and sectional adherences to a particular political ideology and culture and thereby helping to create a national awareness of contemporary issues. Examples can be found of voter realignments in suburbia, the South, and the Southwest that have strengthened the existing political culture and have seen it altered by an infusion of new population segments with different views on politics and society. The lack of major contrasts in the major national parties today illustrates their attempts to appeal to cultural groups of varying ideologies throughout the nation. This is in spite of visible efforts to capture voters in prime target regions, be they midwesterners, southerners, or New Englanders.

That political cultures exhibit distinct geographical characteristics comes as no surprise. Whether they are examined in Colorado or Connecticut or South Carolina or South Dakota, even the most casual observer of the American political scene realizes that political cultures have somewhat of a distinct regional character. Being that the present culture is deeply rooted in the state's or region's history, there are elements such as views of government and the rights of citizens that are embodied in state mottos, the state constitution, the popularity of regional songs (such as "Dixie"), and even the current legislative matters under consideration. The views of its elected representatives, at city or congressional levels, the responsiveness of the state's elected bodies, and the citizen's participation in the government processes are not identical throughout the nation. Variations in public participation in government can be measured by voting or recruitment, by the formation of laws protecting citizens, by assessing the representatives themselves or state houses in the light of responsiveness to contemporary issues, and by the agents of change that operate within political space. Using these and other indices states or parts of states can be grouped into regional political cultures.

Regionalizing political cultures is difficult especially when there are often overlapping ideologies in space. Even in an area as politically homogeneous as New England, the Great Plains, or for that matter the South, there are distinct differences. Macropolitical regionalization schemes often hide significant and rather distinct political cultural differences between northern and southern New England, northern and central Great Plains, and Rim and Deep South. The problem becomes more compounded when states themselves are used in classifying and regionalizing America's political cultures. Racial, ethnic, and cultural contrasts at a state level exist within Ohio, Florida, Michigan, Texas, Mississippi, California, and Virginia to name only a few.

This geographical examination of political cultures focuses on several major themes in an attempt to portray the varying character that exists at various scales throughout the United States. Initially elements of a state's iconography, that is, its images and symbolism, are considered important as they often rather reveal subtle but salient cultural facets that were important in early political development. These have remained as such to the present. This political heritage sets the basis for examining specific facets of the political environment at the regional and state level. The climates for the development of political extremism are treated as are the political party strategies, insofar as they focus on cultures. State legislatures are assessed as are congressmen in an effort to ferret out cultural variations in the political system. Following these discussions will be an analysis of political regions and political philosophies at the national and regional levels.

IMAGES AND SYMBOLS

As each state has evolved and developed it has acquired a set of traditions and common concerns that have become identified with its culture. These elements have tied together diverse groups of people into the common identity associated with that particular state. Each state has its own iconography; that is, unifying symbols or bonds that are not completely like any other political unit. The state nicknames, place names, mottos, emblems, holidays, monuments, songs, and even advertising on license plates represent a special significance and identity. They give each state a uniqueness that is shared by all residents within those political bounds, whether they are conscious of it or not.

The names of states often reveal the heritage of the native inhabitants, outstanding physical features, names of prominent individuals, and directional orientation. Names of Indian tribes or nations were behind the formal labels given to Indiana, Illinois, Iowa, the Dakotas, and Delaware. Spanish names are the basis for Florida, Colorado, New Mexico, and California. States bearing the same names as rivers hold true for Ohio, Mississippi, Missouri, and Arkansas. Names of individuals are behind the names for Washington (first president) and Pennsylvania (William Penn). Besides these major political unit labels, names of early historical settlers or leaders were given to state capitals: Baltimore, Maryland; Austin, Texas; and Raleigh, North Carolina. Some states were given directional labels, often indicative of a splitting up of an original territory, for example, North and South Dakota, North and South Carolina, and West Virginia.

Whether the name of a state was decided by the original settlers or by legislatures or popular vote, these names have remained significant on the political landscape. Even if the states have lost or are losing much of their original distinctiveness, names of political units even in modern society reveal something of the original cultural heritage. County names themselves group into several distinctive geographical patterns. Just as for states, the names given to these minor political units by the settlers and legislatures reveal the imprint of original cultural groups or the names of prominent individuals associated with their own heritage. In a very crude sense, county names are grouped into those with a Spanish base, an Indian label, and those named after presidents of the United States (Fig. 9-1). Spanish names, not unexpectedly, are dominant in the Southwest, especially in former Mexican-controlled spaces in Texas, Colorado, New Mexico, and California. Fewer names appear in Arizona and Nevada. In the main these counties parallel the areas of heaviest Spanish-surname population at the present time. Indian names were given to counties most notably in the northern Midwest (the states of Iowa, Wisconsin, Minnesota, and Michigan), and New York. These were spaces dominated by a number of major tribes and nations. Eastern Oklahoma also has a

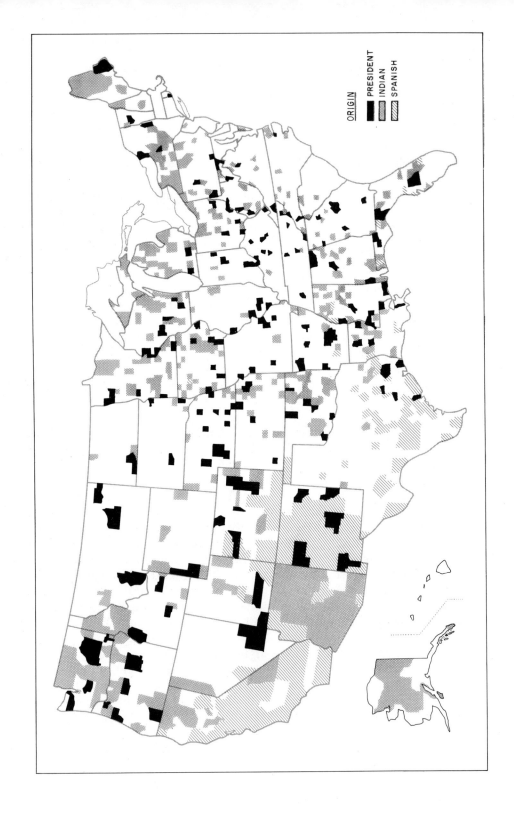

concentration, this portion the former Indian Territory that once petitioned for statehood (Chapter 6). Lesser numbers of Indian-derived county names appear in Florida, Arizona, and the Pacific Northwest states. Scattered names in the South attest to the lands the Indians occupied prior to their march westward. Indian-Eskimo names are apparent in Alaska especially in the panhandle section.[1]

If the original settlers and elected representatives did not adopt labels or names of the occupants they found in these spaces, frequently they named counties after American presidents.[2] A total of 186 counties, roughly 6 percent of all counties, are named after twenty-three presidents. The distribution of these presidential-county names are scattered evenly throughout the nation. The leading states are Nebraska (with eleven counties named after presidents), Iowa and Arkansas (nine each), Mississippi and Oklahoma (seven each). Ten states have six each. The pattern in failing to reveal any marked regional concentration illustrates that the settlers moving west in the 1700s and 1800s identified with certain major presidents, regardless of whether they agreed in total with their programs and policies. The presidents with the most counties named in their honor are Washington (thirty-one), Jefferson (twenty-six), Jackson (twenty-two), Madison (nineteen), and Lincoln (sixteen). There is even some regionality to the states having counties honoring these five presidents. Washington and Jefferson counties are in the eastern half of the United States (save New England), the southern Great Plains, and Pacific Northwest. Madison counties are primarily in the eastern half of the nation. Jackson counties are in midwestern and southern states, areas of his popularity. Counties honoring President Lincoln are in the western half of the nation, representing states formed after the Civil War. The South has no counties honoring this Illinois president except Arkansas and Mississippi. County names in the Pacific Northwest reveal the presidents and leading statesmen who engineered the Lewis and Clark expedition and the subsequent Louisiana Purchase in 1803. Noted individuals or terms important to specific ethnic or cultural groups were behind the Dutch county names in Michigan and Indiana, French names along the Great Lakes and Louisiana, royalty labels in coastal Virginia, and Confederate leaders in the South. Descriptive features (lakes, hills, valleys, glaciers, woods) in the physical environment were given to these minor political units, often when it appeared that almost no other legitimate label was readily available.

Another important element in a state's heritage is the state motto. There is, surprisingly enough, some striking regionality to mottos (Table 9-1). The original framers of the state constitutions attempted to embody their new state's philosophy in a single simple short phrase. The mottos of New England states emphasize liberty, justice, freedom, and independence, all important elements in the earliest years of colonization. A number of midwestern and especially agricultural states

FIG. 9-1 Origins of County Names. (After George R. Stewart, *American Place Names*, New York, Oxford University Press, 1970. After J. N. Kane, *Facts About the Presidents*, first edition, New York, Wilson, 1959, pp. 300–301. Copyright © 1959 by Joseph Nathan Kane.)

TABLE 9-1   State Mottos and Nicknames

State	Motto	Nickname
Alabama	We Dare to Defend Our Rights	Cotton State
Colorado	Nothing Without Deity	Centennial State
Georgia	Wisdom, Justice, Moderation	Peach State
Idaho	Let It Be Forever	Gem State
Kansas	To the Stars Through Difficulties	Sunflower State
Maine	I Direct	Pine Tree State
Michigan	If You Seek a Pleasant Peninsula, Look About You	Wolverine State
Montana	Gold and Silver	Treasure State
New Mexico	It Grows as It Goes	Land of Enchantment
North Dakota	Liberty and Union, Now and Forever, One and Inseparable	Sioux State
Rhode Island	Hope	Little Rhody
Texas	Friendship	Lone Star State
Washington	By-and-by	Evergreen State
West Virginia	Mountaineers Always Free	Mountain State
Wyoming	Equal Rights	Equality State

Source: 1973 *World Almanac*, New York, Newspaper Enterprise Association, 1973, pp. 721–749.

have mottos containing the words people, rights, independence, equality, and progress. Several southern states identified with the Confederacy have mottos that stress defending rights. God and Deity are part of the mottos adopted by Arizona, Colorado, Florida, Connecticut, and South Dakota. Finally there are some states whose mottos do not seem to identify with a cultural group or philosophical or moral theme.

Each state has an official set of plants and animals that are also a part of its iconography. However, not all the fifty states have the same kinds or the same number of these state symbols. All states and the District of Columbia have a state bird, tree, and flower. A total of forty-seven states have state songs; there is none in Connecticut, District of Columbia, New Jersey, and Pennsylvania. Four states have a state fish, Alabama the tarpon, Alaska the king salmon, Oregon the chinook salmon, and Wisconsin the muskellunge. Six states have a state animal, these mainly being mountain and forested states, Colorado the mountain sheep, Kansas the buffalo, Oregon the beaver, Vermont the Morgan horse, Wisconsin the badger, and West Virginia the black bear. Finally there is one state with a state gem, Idaho (star garnet). In recent years some states seemingly have gone to extremes with "stateness" as Ohio legislating tomato juice as its state drink!

Nicknames are additional ways that citizens within a state and the nation identify and associate various images and events (Table 9-1). All states have nicknames except Alaska and the District of Columbia. The nicknames can be classed into six groups. Twelve states have one that relates to plants, trees, flowers, or crops. Seven states have attached a name that relates to an animal. In addition five states carry a mineral label, six ones with a major physical feature, and nine that are considered symbolic. There are ten states whose nicknames are basically nondescript.[3]

More often than not the nicknames for a state are used to advertise a particular feature characteristic of the state. In this way they connote certain images to those residents outside its borders. License plates are one such way of conveying such impressions. For example, Alabama plates contain a slogan "Heart of Dixie," while Arkansas plates are labeled "Land of Opportunity" and New Hampshire's "Live Free or Die." Often license plate slogans are meant to serve as free advertising for the state's amenities, such as Florida's "Sunshine State," Georgia's "Peach State," Michigan's "Great Lake State," Arizona's "Grand Canyon State," and Hawaii's "Aloha State." Sometimes the slogans are nondescript as Ohio's 1973 plates with the "Fasten Seat Belts?" slogan. Besides these mottos or slogans, some states identify the counties of the state by name as in Kentucky or by number as in Florida and Iowa. A person with such a knowledge of the state's geography is readily available to identify with the driver whether he finds him in an adjacent state or a national park or a city in another part of the United States.

A further way of examining a state's political and cultural heritage is to look at the observance of legal or public holidays. In a technical sense these are not set national holidays as such as each state has jurisdiction over its own. These are set by legislative or executive decree. However, nationally most states observe the federal legal public holidays, but even here there are variations.[4]

Federal legal public holidays are New Year's Day, Memorial or Decoration Day, Independence Day, Labor Day, Columbus Day, Veterans Day, Thanksgiving, and Christmas Day. Most states observe Lincoln's birthday as February 12, except Alabama, Arkansas, Florida, Georgia, Hawaii, Illinois, Iowa, Maine, Massachusetts, Mississippi, Nevada, New Hampshire, North Carolina, Ohio, Oklahoma, South Carolina, Tennessee, Texas, and Virginia. In Illinois and Oregon, it is the first Monday in February and in Arkansas, it is Memorial Day. Memorial Day as the last Monday in May is a legal holiday in all states except Mississippi and South Carolina. Columbus Day, the second Monday in October, is observed in most states except Alaska, Maine, Mississippi, New Mexico, Nevada, Oklahoma, Oregon, South Carolina, South Dakota, Virginia, and Wyoming.

Some states declare a number of other days legal or public holidays. For example, January 19 is Robert E. Lee's birthday and is a holiday in Arkansas, Florida, Georgia, Kentucky, Louisiana, Mississippi, North Carolina, South Carolina, Tennessee, and Texas. In Alabama and Mississippi it is the third Monday in January. Patriots' Day (always the third Monday in April) is observed in Maine and Massachusetts. Confederate Memorial Day is observed on various days in April, May, or June in most southern states. Flag Day is a legal holiday in Pennsylvania.

Many states have declared the day of their independence as a legal holiday. Bunker Hill Day, June 17, is observed in Boston and Suffolk County, Massachusetts. Town Meeting Day is always the first Tuesday in March in Vermont and April 22 is Arbor Day in Nebraska. A number of other holidays are honored for individuals or birthdays of noted persons such as Huey P. Long's birthday in Louisiana on August 30.

Major events and landmarks in a state's or a region's history are further examples of culture that carry an imprint from initial settlement periods to contemporary societal impressions. Revolutionary War statues, memorials, and historical landmarks in the New England area attest to the importance of this struggle from the mother country. The importance of this war is exemplified by specific features in the cultural landscape erected or set aside by these first settlers or subsequent generations.[5] By and large their distribution reveals the sites of early confrontations and negotiations (Fig. 9-2). The views of the individual and government that developed in the late 1800s have remained a part of the political culture to this day.

Military conflicts and campaigns have also played a key role in the political culture and philosophy associated with the South. Civil War battles are marked by many state landmarks as well as by national cemeteries. Thirty of the nation's eighty-four national cemeteries are in only four states, Virginia (fourteen), Kentucky (eight), and Tennessee and North Carolina (four each). Four other southern states have three each, Arkansas, Louisiana, Missouri, and Texas. Altogether there are fifty national cemeteries in the southern states.[6] The South's steepage in military history, attributed in large part to its defeat in the Civil War,

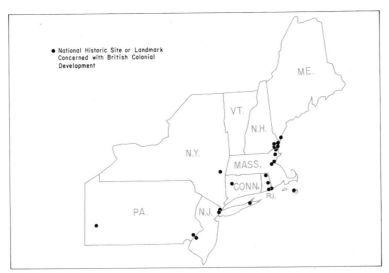

Fig. 9-2 Colonial Memorials in Northeast States. (U.S. Department of the Interior, *National Atlas of the United States*, Geological Survey, Washington, D.C., 1970.)

has elements that remain today. Probably more than any other single region the South favors stronger military and defense postures. This is seen in its support for defense appropriations and installations, not infrequently tied to congressmen on key committees, and its support for a stronger foreign policy. An overrepresentation of top army personnel such as generals and green berets is also a reflection of the region's residents and their leaders and of the glorification of the military in society and politics.

POLITICAL ENVIRONMENTS

The culture that has developed in a state or region is reflected in the political settings for certain events and practices. States and regions with a representative form of government and decision-making at the local level often have a similar degree of politics at the state level. Town meetings in New England and Grange Hall assemblages in the Midwest, both important structures for local involvement in politics, have been carried into the practices, debates, and subsequent legislation by elected members to state houses. In like manner, the lack of group political participation has been associated with the South, at local or state levels. Much of this sentiment is still observed today with the political matters being the responsibility of the "court house gang" or traditionally favored social and economic elites. The frontier philosophy of independence and lack of strong political party identity have contributed to a climate in the West where nonpartisanship is characteristic. In large part this has been reinforced by the migration of citizens from the Midwest, East, and South and by the internal mobility within the region itself.

Political climates and environments develop in space and these reflect both the heritage of the state or region and the internal changes that are taking place. To be sure, symbols and images are an important part of the culture and climate of a region but so are the voluntary organizations, politically related lobbies and pressure groups, and the radio, television, and newspaper media. These may either reinforce existing political attitudes and views or be involved in altering certain facets of the society. In other words, measuring and assessing a political segment of space involve a consideration of previous as well as contemporary developments. The effectiveness of organizations, lobbies, and major networks seldom is restricted to one particular political region. Rather they have an impact on regions with varying shades of political background and opinion. In some areas their views may strike a note accordant with the political region as a whole while in other cases their positions may appeal only to big cities or selected occupations or racial groups. Furthermore, the timing of significant politically related programs and events varies in space. What may have been an acceptable form of political action or politically expedient legislation in Massachusetts in 1964 may not have become acceptable in parts of Montana or New Mexico until 1970. The complexities of politics at local, state, regional, and national levels are probably best illustrated in an organizational

framework when the Republicans and Democrats attempt to fashion party platforms and select major leaders from diverse cultural ranks. Legacies from previous
campaigns and administrations are molded with the contemporary posture of the
nation in efforts to devise successful strategies, strategies that preserve cultural
variations as well as cut across differences. In the discussion below selected environmental aspects are treated in this light, specifically the cultural settings spawning
the development of political extremism, current reflections on national political
party strategies, and the assessment of state legislatures and congressmen.

Political Extremism. Organized political behavior of the extreme right and
left within the past decade is not found in all parts of the United States. Rather it
is concentrated in particular pockets or nodes and regions having distinguishing
characteristics that are conducive to the formation of very conservative or very
liberal philosophies. During the 1960s both ends of the political spectrum enjoyed a
fair amount of success by backing certain legislative issues and supporting national
political candidates. Names of organizations, such as the John Birch Society,
Student Nonviolent Coordinating Committee, and Americans for Democratic
Action, all labeled extremist, were household words. Their leaders, publications,
advertising, and stances on political issues jettisoned them into the national political limelight. Their support was evidenced by the formation of new chapters,
increased membership rolls, lobbying efforts at local and national levels, and in
office seekers openly advocating their support. However, their focus and support
was not found uniformly in all regions. This suggests that certain social and
economic characteristics are associated with extremist political behavior at the left
and right.[7]

Extreme right-wing activity is concentrated primarily in the states of the
South and West, states that are undergoing the most rapid population and social
changes (Table 9-2). In the South (rural and urban) most right-wing extremism
has been associated with civil rights actions of the federal and state governments.
Most particularly, this is equated with the Ku Klux Klan and the use of white
citizens councils. California, especially southern California, Texas, and peninsular
Florida have witnessed the flourishing of extremist organizations whose support was
also based on a number of foreign and domestic policies. Other states such as
Arizona, Utah, Idaho, Colorado, Washington, and Oklahoma have seen a lessened
development of right-wing activity. The southern California and Dallas, Texas,
areas are two of the major foci for the John Birch Society and the Christian Anti-
Communist Crusade, the latter headquartered in Long Beach. Other organizations
such as the Minutemen (membership low in 1973) and the American Council of
Churches are strong in the rural and urban Southwest. The popularity of these
right-wing organizations during the 1960s in this part of the United States can be
documented by the size of the membership rolls, the number of chapters, hours of
radio broadcasts, circulation of reading materials, open support for congressmen,
and their involvement in local and state politics. Other more readily observed
characteristics in the political landscape such as the popularity of flying the Ameri-

TABLE 9-2   Distribution of Rightists by Census Regions (percent)

Region	National Population	Wartenburg and Thielens Study	McEvoy Study	McNall Study
California	8.8	33	30	34
Other Far West	6.8	9	11	9
South	30.7	29	29	22
North Central	28.8	18	19	19
Northeast	24.9	11	10	16
Unknown			2	
Totals	100.0	100	100	100

Source: Data for the Wartenburg and Thielens Study and the McEvoy Study from Hannah Wartenburg and Wagner Thielens, Jr., "Against the United Nations: A Letter Writing Campaign by the Birch Movement," New York, Bureau of Applied Social Research, Columbia University, 1964, mimeographed report; and James McEvoy, "Letters from the Right: Content-Analysis of a Letter-Writing Campaign," Ann Arbor, Mich., The University of Michigan, Center for Research on Utilization of Scientific Knowledge of The Institute for Social Research, 1966, mimeographed report.

can flag and the once-common "Save the Republic: Impeach Earl Warren" or "Martin Luther King Is a Communist" billboards or "Support Your Local Police" bumperstickers provide some measure of right-wing popularity in a local area.

To the political geographer the reasons behind such spatial concentrations of right-wing political activity deserve analysis. The development of such activities is not difficult to associate with the South as it is here that the blacks and whites have lived side by side for generations. Changes in the laws affecting the heretofore disenfranchised blacks in voting, education, housing, employment, or accommodation would lead more than one militant or even complacent white southerner to join right-wing groups. Upsetting the traditional mores led to local, state, and sectional efforts to stymie racial progress. The incorporation of some of these views was even channeled into right-wing third-party goals. Flowering extremism took place in Southwestern states that are having the greatest population increases and those where population turnover and associated changes in life-style are most evident. In the case of suburban southern California, vast numbers of Americans move and become a part of a political space that initially they know little about. In their desire to be accepted by their friends and community, and at the same time seek out an acceptable life, they may adopt the political behavior of the existing area. They may acquire political views related to a larger political unit, that is, the United States, rather than be bothered about the local community. They may find that they can share feelings about national social programs or foreign policy with their friends and neighbors who come from all over the United States. Their involvement may become rather intense. Being that they are already residing in a suburb or town where almost everyone else has a similar socioeconomic status and length of stay and where local bonds are not well developed, a broader allegiance and identity may enable the person to fit in his new-found political world. Often in such environments, the political party system is poorly organized and structured. It is not surprising that nonpartisanship is popular at the local levels in the Southwest. The wide-open nature of the political system almost encourages grass-roots political involvement. In the absence of a formalized party structure at the local level and a stable political organization, background ties of rural or small-town life, fundamentalist religion, region, ethnic group, as well as occupation may encourage supporting activities of the right wing. When organized they may form the local political base of a national party and receive recognition as Goldwater's following did in 1964. Such organizations of the extreme right are not looked on with disdain in many parts of the West and Southwest as they are in the Midwest and East. In Dallas, for example, the *Dallas Morning News* provides a readily acceptable platform for right-wing organizations. The wide-open nature of the political and social milieu has made it possible for extremist activities to be an acceptable political form of behavior. Groups demonstrating an undying support for Americanism and a philosophy tying together religion, economics, society, and politics are not considered completely deviant in a regional political context. What seems as aberrant behavior to citizens in other parts of the United States is not for these Southwest states or portions of others. Rightist views of a Communist threat (once national and world-wide), opposition to social welfare programs, big government, and racial progress are just as different (and often as difficult to comprehend) for many other Americans to support as is the ridiculing of the Supreme Court, a militant stance on Vietnam, and a request for United States withdrawal from the United Nations and vice versa. More often than not their views in advertising or publications are espoused by political office seekers they support, whether for local school boards fighting sex education, or presidential candidates Goldwater in 1964 or Wallace in 1968. These groups are attempting to find order and meaning in American religion, economy, society, and politics. The combination of these spheres in a single philosophy appeals to those urban and rural Americans who are uprooted and moving to an already dynamic social environment. Even within the South and Southwest the peak of extremist activities seems to enjoy greater support around military bases, defense installations, and defense-related communities where retired military and science-engineering personnel reside than in adjacent spaces.

Political behavior of the extreme left at the national level is most often associated today with "the liberal East" or with California. Even though the East as a region may exhibit some striking similarities in its support for popular protests such as grape or lettuce boycotts or for a political candidate such as McGovern or for a particular piece of liberal legislation or for radical politics, it cannot be labeled properly as extremist at the left. One valid barometer that can be used to measure recent extreme liberal or radical behavior is the events occurring on a college or university campus and community. However, even here the political attitudes and activities are far from similar in the East. In general most colleges and university campuses and communities are more liberal in social or economic or political views than surrounding communities or counties. Such is not unusual as the environment is conducive to new forms of involvement and commitments, often of even a short duration. Once students leave their testing periods in this unique social and political environment they may once again take on the political and social behaviors of their parents. In measuring political activity of the extreme left by such measures as the initial protesting against free speech, civil rights, communist speakers, the Vietnam War, or Cambodia incursion, certain campuses stand out above all others. The University of California at Berkeley, Harvard-MIT, Princeton, Columbia, Wisconsin, Michigan, and Ohio State have been identified as the foci for extremist political behavior.[8] Whether such protests by marches or sit-ins or demonstrations or riots are carried out by a few or many is not a central point here, rather it is how larger society views the activities. The university or community or both have sanctioned or accepted such protests as acceptable forms of political behavior. In like manner to the right-wing extremism treated above, such behaviors and actions may be viewed as extremist by those outside the city and region. Inside they are considered an acceptable response to political issues.

On campuses and in university towns where extreme left-wing political activities and radical programs are found, there has traditionally been support for liberal causes and programs. Major universities are considered nuclei for international teams of scholars who attract students from more than one particular state. Some of the major centers for radical actions are major state-supported universities where citizen political involvement has been traditionally active in state and local government. Pennsylvania, Massachusetts, New York, California, Michigan, Wisconsin, are cases in point where an open political system is a part of a state's heritage. Many of the earlier nodes of socialism and communism especially in cities in the Northeast and California where East European ethnics concentrated and strikes occurred have been foci for more recent radical political behavior.[9] Early cities important in the organization of trade unions that supported leftist views were New York, Philadelphia, Chicago, Minneapolis, Cleveland, St. Louis, and San Francisco. Protests and demonstrations during the 1960s in the name of civil rights or the Vietnam War are not new to residents of states where social and labor organizations (automobile, steel, coal, and longshoremen) have often expressed their views or requested their demands in a similar vein. The cosmopolitan nature of the faculty and of a student body (domestic and foreign students) plus a history of concern for national and international affairs appears conducive to the formation and organization of unorganized as well as organized forms of extremist political behavior. Large- and medium-sized state and private universities offer students a wide variety of social, political, economic, and religious clubs and chapters that they can identify and associate with. The student on such a campus may take up, like his counterpart in the right-wing community or region, the "cause" of individualism, freedom, and brotherhood by belonging to an organization calling for a lettuce boycott, prison reform, black studies, abortion clinics, sexual freedom, or environmental cleanup.

Aside from the half-dozen or more liberal foci for political extremism, there are others further down the hierarchy. In the main these colleges and universities are in the Northeast, Midwest, or in California and Washington in the West. While many Americans may desire to group all colleges and universities into one mode of political behavior, they simply cannot be classified this easily. It takes time and an organization to develop political protest and for the action or views to diffuse to other universities. Some parts of the Mountain, Great Plains, and southern states (except black colleges) have been relatively immune from radical activities. What may be extremist at Princeton in 1964 may be considered as such in a small Nebraska or Georgia or Montana college in 1972. The issue may be the same but the perspective of that issue in a national light may be different. In the 1970s other than the Vietnam War and other international military engagements, protests for women's rights, a cleaner and safer environment, and ending Watergate-type corruption in government appear to be the concerns of many Americans. While there may be widespread sentiment for such issues, activism may be generated from large cosmopolitan campuses and colleges in large cities. Should open protests for abortion or environmental preservation or the impeachment of President Nixon become more acceptable, there may eventually be other environments that will see such liberal demonstrations. Clearly, social environments are important in examining and assessing various forms of political extremism. Whether the behavior be of the extreme right or left, there are historical roots and contemporary developments that contribute to its presence.

Political Party Strategies. The development of the two major political parties, and even third and fourth parties, has been associated with a political cultural base that is usually fixed on one or more political regions. These regional settings contain large numbers of potential voters or ideological claims or both that are incorporated into the building of a national party organization. For a successful campaign effort, whether at a national or state level, elements of the political regions are molded into party platforms and even into the representation of candidates placed before the electorate.

Both the Republicans and Democrats have been identified with specific political regions and political cultures. Democrats have been linked for the past thirty or forty years (and even longer in some parts of the United States) with labor, ethnic groups, the poor, liberals, and white southerners. Regions where they traditionally held sway were the South and Northeast. Even if their strength was not uniform in the northeastern quarter of the nation, cities where labor and ethnic voters dominated gave them strength. The South's support for the Democratic party goes back to Reconstruction and mainly was of an anti-Lincoln and anti-Republican sentiment. Within this mixture of peoples and ideas and regions, the Democrats molded a national party that enjoyed a great measure of success until the mid-1960s.

The Republicans likewise formed a national party that attracted farmers, industrialists, businessmen, and middle-income and middle-class Americans. Their strength in the Farm Belt, suburbia, and the rich states was noted in their party philosophy and recruitment of major party leaders (Chapter 4). States in rural New England, the Midwest, Great Plains, and West were considered settings that embodied the Republican views on domestic and foreign policy.

Social and economic changes in the nation in the past twenty and particularly the past ten years have altered the political system. Population shifts not only to suburbia but to the Southwest and West have brought about political issues and problems that both major parties did not face earlier. The social, economic, and political gains of minority groups, especially black Americans, since the 1950s have seen shifting of a whole region's allegiance to a national party. Rising income and educational standards of second- and third-generation ethnic group members have seen some lessened importance of ethnic status and the development of more class awareness. The involvement of the nation in issues such as civil rights, the Vietnam War, and environmental quality are bringing about a greater consciousness of political and social problems that disregard traditional regional boundaries.

Within the light of these changes, the political party system of the nation is undergoing some subtle and some drastic changes. The rise of third-party movements in the South in 1948 and 1968 and the role they played in national politics helped signal the end of the "Solid South" for the Democratic party (Chapters 1 and 3). When a major political party can no longer count on one regional cultural setting for its automatic support, there is evidence of a shifting of the residents' identification. This is made apparent by another political party attempting to make inroads and usurp some of the issues that led to the dissatisfaction of the voters. The Republican party's "Southern Strategy" in 1968 was an obvious attempt to reap success from traditional Democrats (Chapter 1). It reached its greatest success since 1952 with Nixon's strong showing in the South (Deep and Rim) in 1972. Thus, what appears to have occurred in the South in recent times at the presidential level is the Republicans adopting some views of traditional white Democrats. The philosophy of Nixon, and Goldwater before him, was conservative in nature, but popular in view of the Democratic party's support for liberal and black voters.

Further Republican strategies have been outlined in Kevin Phillips' *The Emerging Republican Majority.* This Nixon strategist envisioned the Republicans becoming a majority party by seizing and retaining control of two political geographical regions, the Heartland and the Sun Belt. Using the historical and recent cultural impress on the geography of the United States, Phillips sees this emergence represented in the 1968 presidential election.

> The geography of Richard Nixon's 1968 victory indicates that the great American Heartland—the insular and interior core of the United States—has abandoned the Civil War-ingrained loyalties that divided politics along an extension of the Mason-Dixon line. Because tradition no longer keeps the Arkansas, Kentucky, and New Mexico countryside Democratic while the Dakota, Kansas, and Michigan countryside is Republican, the vast American interior is drawing together as the seat of a conservative majority. For years the Northeast has dominated

national politics as Heartland power split along Civil War lines, but now new sociological forces are dividing the Northeast and uniting the Heartland.

As a result of this trend, the Heartland—the land of Methodist church suppers, mile-high mining camps, county fairs, steamboats round the bend, cattle drives, waving wheat, Park Forest, Middletown, German biergartens, Polish polka parties and elm-lined Main Streets, U.S.A.—is shaping up as the mainstay of a new political era. To define the Heartland with more geographic than socio-political precision, it includes every state without a coastline or seaport, save Vermont, and reaches from the Appalachians to the Rocky Mountains. Together these 25 states cast 223 of the 270 electoral votes needed to elect a President of the United States. In 1968 Nixon carried 21 of the 25 Heartland states. Kindred areas like the Outer South and Southern California (heavily settled from the Heartland) provided the additional margin of victory.[10]

Besides the Heartland being the key to successful Republican dominance, as Phillips observed in 1968, the second important geographic region was the "Sun Belt." This coastal strip of states from Charleston-Savannah-Jacksonville west to southern California is undergoing population changes that are drawing in more potential electoral votes. It is the growing conservative nature of this "Sun Belt" that will lead to a majority party status for the Republicans. The focus in presidential elections is on Florida, Texas, Arizona, and California and it is these states rather than the liberal Northeast that will determine future presidential victors. As Phillips has described: "The Sun Country is America's new settlement frontier, and like other frontiers of the past, its politics are nationalistic, anti-intellectual and ethnocentric."[11] Much of the conservative nature of state and local politicians comes from inherently traditionally political regions but also from the infusion of residents from the Heartland and South. The epitome of future conservative Republicanism is probably best exemplified in southern California.

While the future success of the Republican party may well be in those conservative Heartland and Sun Belt regions, there are other social and behavioral scientists who view the political scene in a somewhat different light. Scammon and Wattenberg view the focus on presidential elections in the future as those states with large metropolitan centers.[12] This would indicate the importance of California, to be sure, but also of the Northeast. Large liberal states and cities in the Northeast were not considered as basic to future Republican strongholds; Phillips was willing to downgrade their roles. The basic strategy according to Scammon and Wattenberg is to concentrate the strategy on a region called Quadcali. The authors illustrate their geographic strategy as follows:

> If one draws a *quad*rangle from Massachusetts to Washington, D.C., to Illinois, to Wisconsin, and then adds in *Cali*fornia, it includes a majority of Americans. Where Americans live, they vote. Where a majority of them live and vote is where Presidents are elected.
>
> In all, 266 electoral votes are needed to win. It is estimated that Quadcali will comprise about 300 electoral votes after the 1970 census.

Of the sixteen states in Quadcali, all but one (Indiana) are either Democratic or close—the Republican margin of victory being no higher than 4.5 percent and usually slimmer than that. In a tidal year, all those close states can drop like a row of falling dominoes—the familiar image. Carry Quadcali—win the election. Lose Quadcali—lose the election. Split Quadcali close—and it will be a close election that no book can tell you about in advance.

So there you have it: Middle Voter. A Metropolitan Quadcalian, middle-aged, middle-income, middle-educated, Protestant, in a family whose working members work more likely with hands than abstractly with head.

Think about that picture when you consider the American power structure. Middle Voter is a forty-seven-year-old housewife from the outskirts of Dayton, Ohio whose husband is a machinist. She very likely has a somewhat different view of life and politics than that of a twenty-four-year-old instructor of political science at Yale.[13]

Thus, we find that political analysts of the American scene perceive the environments in somewhat different lights when assessing future presidential politics. In essence Phillips has zeroed in on conservative political areas where he believes the Republicans can offset the numerical strength of the Northeast. Scammon, Wattenberg, and Phillips recognize the importance in future politics of California and certain "border" states such as Illinois, Indiana, and Ohio. Within the cultural and political settings of these and other states the major parties will attempt to identify support for future elections.

Assessing State Legislatures. The political environments of states are revealed in the organization and behavior of respective state legislatures. The accountability of elected members, the willingness to openly debate controversial issues, and the effectiveness of the entire legislative operation are ways that states can be assessed. When a state is compared with all others, whether on a particular piece of legislation or on a rating as to the representativeness of its members, it stands to reason there will be states with high, middle-range, and low ratings. The concern here in analyzing the areal character of the states is whether there is consistency in the various ways states are assessed.

While there are many examples of state legislation that have attracted national prominence since the formation of the nation, the past fifteen years have ushered in more than a score of sufficient note. Debates and discussions and subsequent legislation pertaining to school desegregation, equal employment, open housing, capital punishment, abortion reform, environmental protection, model cities, mass transit, church-state relations, women's rights, voter qualifications, and reapportionment are only a few. In each of these and subsequent pieces of legislation there are state senates and houses of representatives that discussed and instituted legislation before others. This is to say that some individual legislatures were considered in the forefront of particular issues.

In a recent study by a political scientist on eighty-eight innovations in the United States, distinct patterns in the acceptances of new programs were found.[14]

The larger, wealthier, industrial states, that is, those in the Northeast and Midwest, tended to adopt new programs before the smaller, less developed states (Fig. 9-3). Of further note was the role of cities in the consideration and adoption of new programs at the state level. An examination of the correlational values leads to the conclusion "that New York, California, and Michigan adopt new programs more rapidly than Mississippi, Wyoming, and South Dakota, primarily because they are bigger, richer, more urban, have more fluidity and turnover in their political systems, and have legislatures which more adequately represent their cities."[15]

Within certain political regions, there are recognized pioneers or leaders in the innovation of political programs and social goals, whether they be in the spheres of civil rights, medical licensing and certification, employment standards, or tax reform. California, Massachusetts, Michigan, New York, and Colorado are "seen as regional pace setters, each of which has a group of followers, usually within their own region of the country, that tend to adopt programs after they have led the way."[16] Contacts between leaders of local, state, regional, and national levels lead to the diffusion of information about programs affecting the states' general welfare. These communications networks existing between mayors, governors, or agency heads lead to interaction with officials in states having similar social and political backgrounds as well as like economic problems. The more rapid adoption by state governments of some programs today than fifty or twenty-five years ago attests to the greater amount of interaction between states and the national awareness of major problems. The establishing of environmental agencies and legislation is a case in point.

To illustrate the state and regional differences in the acceptance of one significant piece of legislation, the reapportionment issue is examined. Specifically,

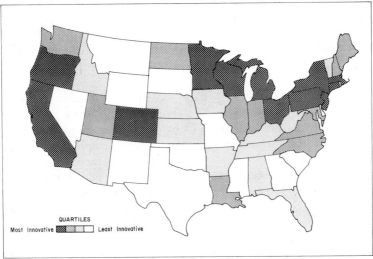

Fig. 9-3 Composite Legislative Innovation Scores. (Data from J. L. Walker, "Diffusion of Innovations Among States," *American Political Science Review*, vol. 68, no. 3 (September 1969), p. 883.)

the states that supported the Dirksen amendment are discussed. Senator Dirksen's proposal was seen in response to the one-man–one-vote ruling the Supreme Court made in regards to apportionment. His amendment was specifically designed to have one house of a state legislature elected on some other basis than population. This was interpreted to mean "geography," which usually related to political divisions or square miles. One representative from each county, irregardless of its population, would certainly have given a different representation in an elected state house than a plan based on equal population. By getting the necessary two-thirds of the states to approve his amendment, Dirksen hoped a constitutional convention would be called to formally consider the reapportionment question. It would stand to reason therefore that the states with a small population would probably favor calling such a convention, as on important issues each state would have one vote. Inasmuch as the rural states and small populated states felt the brunt of the Supreme Court ruling, it was understandable that many would file petitions supporting the Dirksen amendment. The first states filed petitions in 1963 and others continued until 1969.[17] Even though the actual count of states passing the amendment approximated the necessary number for a constitutional convention, legal delays and contests would have postponed and even rescinded the legislation passed in many states. Liberal states and mainly urban states, such as New York, Pennsylvania, Connecticut, Massachusetts, Michigan, and California, never supported the amendment (Fig. 9-4). In the main the first states to approve two separate reapportionment schemes were mainly large-area states with small populations in the West and South. In the middle and late 1960s even some progressive Midwest states joined the effort.

In 1971 a Citizens Conference on State Legislatures assessed the strengths

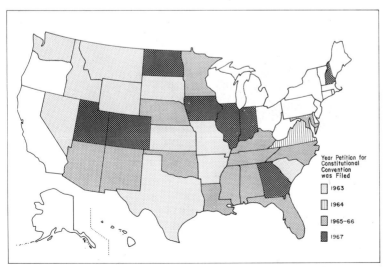

Fig. 9-4 States Supporting Dirksen Amendment. (Data from © *Congressional Quarterly Service Weekly Report.*)

and weaknesses of legislatures. They were rated on the basis of how functional, accountable, informed, independent, and representative they were. Furthermore, each state was given an overall rating on the basis of the criteria utilized. This effort was designed to measure the capacity of each state legislature for effectively handling and executing the problems it faces, insofar as it is governed by its own structure, practices, and policies.[18]

California, New York, Illinois, Florida, and Wisconsin are the five highest states in the overall ranking (Fig. 9-5). Northern Midwest states as well as Alaska and Hawaii are also included in the top ten. The ranking of these legislatures is of interest in that what are frequently designated as liberal or progressive states are not all ranked high; for example, Massachusetts is twenty-ninth and Pennsylvania is twenty-first. Likewise some conservatively oriented states have rather high rankings; Oklahoma is fourteenth and South Dakota is seventeenth. Southern states comprise the lowest rankings, although not exclusively as Indiana, Montana, Arizona, Delaware, and Wyoming appear near the bottom. Patterns of regional uniformity appear in the Midwest and South, but two states with similar political cultures may have drastically different rankings; examples are Idaho (eighteen) and Montana (forty-one), or Ohio (sixteen) and Indiana (forty), or Maryland (twenty) and Virginia (thirty-four).

Areal patterns for the five specific criteria used to assess the legislatures in general support the patterns depicted in Fig. 9-5. The most informed state legislatures are in the Midwest, Florida, New York, and California; the least are in the Rim and Deep South states including Texas. The most representative states are in the eastern Midwest, New York, Connecticut, as well as in the Southwest (save Arizona) and California. The least so are in the South and northern Plains and Rockies. Interestingly, Pennsylvania and New Jersey also ranked low. The most

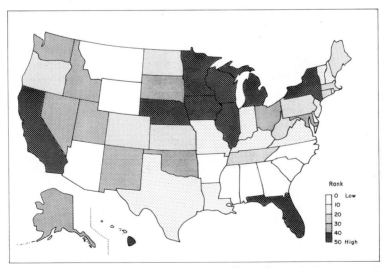

Rank

0 Low
10
20
30
40
50 High

FIG. 9-5 Overall Rank of State Legislatures. (Data from © *Congressional Quarterly Service Weekly Report.*)

independent state legislatures had a pattern that included California, South Carolina, New York, Wisconsin, Illinois, Alaska, and Hawaii. The states of Vermont, Indiana, Alabama, Texas, and Wyoming all ranked from forty-one to fifty according to this criterion. In essence this areal pattern showed little meaning. Functional state legislatures marked states in the Midwest, Northeast (although not New England), West, and Florida. Southern states were the least so. In general, the accountability of the state legislatures had a similar pattern.

Ratings of Congressmen. A number of organizations, some with definite political stakes and others with public service in mind, annually rate the performance of individual congressmen. This is often done in order to identify the stances (usually voting record) of a particular senator or representative with respect to the organization's stated goals and objectives. Among the organizations that are involved in calculating a performance score or consistency index are the AFL-CIO, the Friends Committee on National Legislation, the Americans for Democratic Action, and the Americans for Constitutional Action. The rating is based on the congressman's vote on what are considered critical pieces of foreign and domestic legislation enacted or discussed during the recent session. The issues may involve defense budget allocations, expansion in public welfare schemes, model city funds, votes on foreign policy issues, or treaty negotiations. On the basis of the specific organization objectives each member of congress is given a score; he then can be compared with others in his own state or his region. In essence an index or rating provides an organization's perception of congressional voting behavior for the nation. High scores are given to those that are most in tune with the organization's objectives. Therefore, it is expected that not all ratings nor indeed the perceptual maps of all organizations would be identical.

The consistency index for representatives in the second session of the Ninety-first Congress (1970) as measured by the Americans for Constitutional Action may be used to illustrate if meaningful areal patterns can be discerned. It is expected that areal similarities would reflect some underlying social and political threads. This nationally recognized organization is nonpartisan and nonprofit and ostensibly concerned with the preservation of the Constitution. As it envisages its goals, the organization supports foreign military operations but not foreign aid, defense allocations, monetary reforms that indicate sound fiscal responsibility, and employee relations favoring the businessman. The ACA is not generally disposed to favoring increased monies for social welfare as this is not in line with a strict interpretation of the Constitution.

In the session of Congress under discussion, each member was given a cumulative consistency index rating. The rating was based on the individual's performance with respect to nineteen issues (Table 9-3). On a number of stances the ACA views were counter to legislation passed by the House of Representatives. Basically the ACA rating is considered an index of conservative voting. High scores, that is, nearing 100, indicate almost total agreement with the organization's goals whereas a low score signifies the representative has little in common with objectives of the Americans for Constitutional Action.[19]

TABLE 9-3   Issues Forming Bases for Index Rating by Americans
for Constitutional Action, 1970

Issues in U.S. House, 2nd Session, 91st Congress	House Vote	ACA Stance
1. Passage of Foreign Aid Bill	202–162	NAY
2. Product Promotion Jointly by Employer and Employee	190–186	NAY
3. House Upholds Nixon Veto on Labor HEW Appropriations	226–191	NAY
4. Defense Facilities Securities Bill	274–65	YEA
5. Reduction of Labor HEW Appropriations Funds	189–206	YEA
6. Criminal Laws for District of Columbia (no-knock)	294–47	YEA
7. NASA Funds	229–105	NAY
8. New Federal Welfare Program	243–155	NAY
9. Increasing the Federal Debt Limit	236–127	NAY
10. Lowering Voting Age to 18	272–132	NAY
11. Override Veto of Medical Facilities Construction	279–98	NAY
12. Establishment of National Development Bank	216–112	YEA
13. Freedom-of-Choice School Plan	191–157	YEA
14. Cooper-Church Amendment (tabled)	237–153	YEA
15. Right-to-Work	227–159	YEA
16. Federal Subsidies for International Travel Commission	174–208	NAY
17. Federal Subsidies for Agriculture (limit)	212–171	NAY
18. Override Veto of Education Appropriations	289–114	NAY
19. House Upholds President's Veto of HUD	204–195	NAY

Source: Americans for Constitutional Action, *ACA Index, 2nd Session, 91st Congress, 1970,*
Washington, D.C., 1970.

As the organization looks at Congress it perceives that some pieces of legislation are basically in tune with its objectives while others are not. When the scores for representatives are grouped and mapped, another image of the candidates and the House emerges (Fig. 9-6). Some sections and regions of the nation have representatives elected whose basic voting pattern corresponds closely with ACA views. Particularly is this true in the Deep South, rural Northeast, rural Midwest, and Great Plains-Rocky Mountain area. The weakest support is found in the urban districts. In the main this is true for almost all parts of the United States. Representatives from the largest cities in California, New York, Ohio, Pennsylvania, Wisconsin, Minnesota, Michigan, Missouri, and Florida did not rate high on the consistency index. Even representatives in urban districts in the Rim or Border South did not have scores as high as those in surrounding districts. The support for ACA measures, as evidenced by these scores on nineteen issues, appears to come from rural or small-town America whether north or south, east or west.

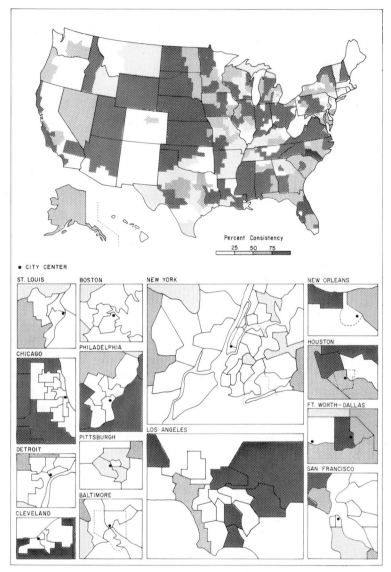

FIG. 9-6 Americans for Constitutional Action: 1970 Rating of Members of the House of Representatives. (Data from *1970 ACA Handbook.*)

REGIONAL POLITICAL PHILOSOPHY

The Regionalization Process. Even a casual examination of the political scene in the United States suggests that indeed not all states or sections share similar views about political issues and the role of government and the individual in the political processes. What is behind such sentiments is the recognition of distinct political regions that can be identified, measured, and analyzed. Political geographers are interested in defining and delimiting such regions and understanding the variations that exist.

In seeking to identify regional political cultures some of the initial questions to be asked are the criteria or political traits, characteristics, or measures used to segment space. This is especially a delicate problem as cultural boundaries seldom have any finiteness; rather, differences tend to blur the edges. As indicators we could use several individual measures, such as the elements of a state's or region's iconography or its consistency in presidential voting, ideological orientation of elected officials or government spending levels, or the patterns of politically related voluntary associations. However, better than basing a region's philosophy on any one measure would be a regionalization scheme that included a large number of elements.

In delimiting political regions or political cultural areas the scale of the analysis is an important consideration. Political scientists and sociologists have tended to use states; however, this level of analysis often proves unsatisfactory when it is realized there are strong political, cultural, and ideological differences within states.[20] For example, Ohio has both a southern (Border state) influence in the Southeast and a Yankee (New England) influence in the Northeast. Similarly the state of California has a northern part settled by midwesterners and northeasterners and a southern California section settled by Spaniards and southerners. Both regions are distinct in their cultural development and have divergent views about state and national politics. Other examples of intrastate variations exist in Texas, Illinois, Florida, North Carolina, and New York. Therefore, it appears that state boundaries may be unsatisfactory limits to use to delimit regional political philosophies. Precise boundaries are difficult to draw especially when attitudes, views, and ideologies are involved that affect diverse groups, even groups occupying the same space. It is generally agreed that the South has definite views about federal involvement in state issues, but is a drawing of the South to include the Border states an accurate philosophical region? The consideration of Kentucky as a Border state, and Maryland and Delaware as not (which have some distinct southern elements), is often an attempt to label political thought on the basis of existing boundaries. Even within the South itself, for example, the Appalachian parts of Virginia, Alabama, Tennessee, Georgia, and North Carolina have regional voting patterns and regional philosophies at variance with other groups and classes in their respective states. There is always some fuzziness or arbitrariness involved in drawing boundaries and especially those where cultural impress, attitudes, and behavior are involved. Political cultures overlap and what may appear as a fairly homogeneous political region at one level becomes a highly complex pattern at another level. Thus even though a boundary line separating distinct political ideologies or cultures may appear on a map, it should not be interpreted as having a definite beginning or end at that point, whether it be a state line, following a physiographic feature, or the areal extent of a dominant ethnic group.

In the process of delimiting space into distinct political cultural regions elements of similarity are sought. For example, in delimiting New England as a political cultural region, it is assumed, all other things being equal, that there are more elements of similarity between those segments of space (towns, counties, or states) than with other parts of the United States. It may be that in looking at spending priorities of state budgets, the views of local government, the evolution of the two-party system, political elites, and the question of reapportionment, the northern rural Republican New England states (Maine, Vermont, and New Hampshire) have more in common with Nebraska and Kansas than with southern urban Catholic New England comprised of Massachusetts, Rhode Island, and Connecticut. However, as a contiguous political unit New England does have a definite political character that is different from any other political region. In looking at the subject of federal involvement (or interference) in state politics, another key element in regionalizing political cultures, it may be that residents of Arizona may have more in common with Mississippi than any political cultural region delimited in the Southwest. The emergence of urban-based state governments that came as a result of reapportionment has revealed that large-population states and cities in the Midwest, the far West, the Northeast, and the South often have much more in common than with surrounding rural political units. The need for advisory and financial assistance in the arenas of housing, welfare, transportation, and education have transcended regional political philosophical developments and united these disparate points into a homogeneous political mass that has some striking political orientations and similarities.

Behind the development of any political culture and political region is a host of related and interrelated considerations. The initial time frame of settlement, the location of that settlement, the group or groups responsible for early settlement and subsequent occupancy all are behind the evolution of that region's political and cultural thought. As groups increased their numbers and their degree of permanence they established their views on the individual and the system of government, from local to national levels. This codifying process in the United States was usually based on the heritage of the dominant population group or the philosophies of ruling elites. Laws, organization, and the political processes were often changed and amended with the influx of new settlers who introduced their own views of the individual, state, and nation in the political processes. The results of such mixtures of people and varying political thought have continued from the eighteenth-century settlement on the Atlantic seaboard to the development of the continental interior and far West last century, and even to the current migration streams to the South and Southwest. Even though the current political ideology and culture of a region may appear static today in some sections, states, and locales, the actual identification of that culture represents a lengthy tradition of individuals and groups attempting to mold a political philosophy. This was designed to be in basic agreement with their views of society, the economy, and the body politic. With the technological, social, and legal changes affecting the United States, political cultures and political regions are best considered as layers of a cake that are constantly undergoing dynamism. This is probably best represented in the philosophical changes in the South and Southwest regions where northerners or New Englanders or midwesterners are having an impact on the traditional party and political structures.

Once distinctive political traits and indicators have been identified in the United States and in specific sections or regions, the question arises with reference to labels for such cultural groups. One is tempted to use labels such as "conservative" with reference to the South, or "liberal" with reference to the Northeast. However, conservative New England is not the same as conservative Deep South and liberal Atlanta is not the same as liberal Hartford. Such ideological labels are not very acceptable in regional discussions. Another label that might be considered is party identification. Republicans in North Carolina may have little in common with those in Kansas and the same for Democrats in Massachusetts and Mississippi. Therefore in a regional discussion, party identification does not represent an accurate classification of a political culture. States could be grouped together (as has been done by political scientists) that have some similar political culture, and labeled as Upper Middle West, Frontier, South, and West. However, such directional classifications fail to reveal political cultural variations in their titles. The labeling of a political culture, with all of its peculiarities and distinctiveness, does present somewhat of a dilemma when criteria involving nationalities, voting, partisanship, government spending, apportionment, local autonomy, and political leadership are used. The tendency may be to adopt philosophical, party, and geographic labels that must be interpreted with a degree of circumspection. When southern conservative rural Democrats are seen to have more in common with midwestern rural Republicans than urban New England Democrats, such labels lose much of their meaning.

Political Cultures. The best detailed discussion of political cultures within the United States has been by a regional political scientist, Daniel Elazar.[21] In his examination of the "political geology" of the nation's cultures, he has identified three major political cultures. They are individualistic, moralistic, and traditionalistic. They all have nationwide proportions in that through time their impact has not been restricted to only one section; rather there are offshoots that reach from coast to coast. Even though the three may be considered as distinct layers throughout the nation's political space, the three both blend (overlap) in some spaces and in others primarily occupy a large part of a particular section. Furthermore, in mapping these cultures, Elazar disregards state boundaries and realizes the covariation and fusion of these cultures in some cities and sections of states (Fig. 9-7). The labels of these cultures are meant to be basically descriptive and not meant to explain historically or politically the contemporary political culture.

The *individualistic* political culture, as the term implies, basically emphasizes those areas where private concern and private initiative are important in the political culture; community intervention and involvement are limited. A democratic order of government is favored and one that operates strictly for utilitarian

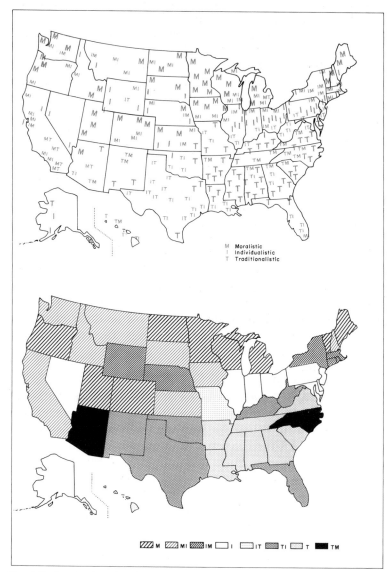

FIG. 9-7 Geography of Political Cultures. (After Daniel J. Elazar, Copyright from *American Federalism*, Second Edition, by Daniel J. Elazar. Copyright © 1972 by Thomas Y. Crowell Company, Inc. With permission of the Publisher.)

purposes, that is, one that handles the functions of the people. Politicians elected to office in these sections are expected to offer a high quality of service for the public. There is a tendency to believe that politics are "dirty." Officeholders are expected to serve themselves by status and economic rewards and serve those who supported them. Favoritism and party regularity are of utmost importance. Elected officials are to give the public what it wants rather than institute new programs unless, of course, there is overwhelming demand. The individual as an officeholder in this public-directed culture and the individual as a private citizen are both important in this culture. According to Elazar this political culture is found mainly in the Middle Atlantic, the central midwestern states, and parts of the West and Great Plains. It is frequently found in conjunction with the moralistic political cultural areas.

A *moralistic* political culture is the second type identified and as the term implies it emphasizes the society as opposed to the individual. The commonwealth idea of government is stressed by its members; here politics is important as it is one aspect leading to a good society. Politics devoted to the public good and the public interest is paramount. The world of politics and the issues politicians consider is the concern of every citizen hence the participation of nonprofessionals in many aspects of political life. The government is seen as an institution with a moral obligation to promote a good life for all citizens. Elected politicians in the moralistic culture adhere less to their individual loyalties or strict party lines. Party lines are not that rigid in considering citizen issues; thus party labels have less meaning. Frequently there is a shifting of parties on crucial issues. Nonpartisanship also is characteristic of this political culture. This political culture is dominant in New England, Middle Atlantic, the northern Midwest states, the northern Plains, the Mountains, and the West. Although it is most commonly associated with the individualistic political culture, it does occur with the traditionalistic culture in the Appalachian area of the South.

The *traditionalistic* political culture adheres to a view of politics, society, and economics that is reflective of a preindustrial social order. It is characterized by an old precommercial attitude where social and family ties are more important than individual advancement and where a good government to its citizens meant limited involvement. Politics is viewed as the concern of a small powerful elite who "inherited" the right to govern by social or family ties. Individual citizens were not nor were they expected to be active in politics. Political parties were of minimum importance because they permit a degree of openness that was contrary to the existing social order, namely, an elite order. Politicians elected based on family backgrounds or prestigious social positions played not only a conservative or traditional role in government but more a custodial role in executing political decisions. They are not likely to institute new programs, unless pressured from the outside. In addition its political leaders are strongly antibureaucratic, as such a system of state or federal bureaucracy interferes with the "fine web of interpersonal relationships." The regionality of this culture is very strong, occurring especially in the southern states, the Border states, and the Southwest. It also occurs in the southern parts of Illinois, Indiana, Ohio, and in West Virginia.

The formation of these political cultures represents the impress of various cultural groups on specific cities, sections, and territories. The mixture of varying European ethnic and racial groups, the differential historical migration streams, more recent rural-urban migration, and technological advancements affecting the nation's people all have contributed to the evolving political cultures that have developed.

Behind the basic patterning of the political cultures are three broad migration currents. These differ as to their timing on the nation's space, their cultural composition, and locational orientation. What is worth noting at this juncture is that the initial cultural imprint either at the time of early permanent settlement or at the time of formal political organization, such as creating a state, has remnants that still exist.[22]

The first broad cultural pattern represents the settlement in New England, the Great Lakes, and later the Pacific Northwest. The Puritan and Yankee settlers were responsible for early political thought that centered in New England. To these early settlers religion was an important part of their life as it involved moral issues such as education, abolition of slavery, and politics. Subsequent New England settlers who moved to the northern Midwest states mixed mainly with northern Europeans, especially Scandinavians. Both groups shared similar views of society and government, namely, that of establishing progressive political and societal schemes. With the movement of these settlers westward last century, their progressive political views became associated with parts of the northern Plains, northern Rocky Mountains, and Pacific Northwest including northern California.

The second major cultural current began with the original settlers in the Middle Atlantic states. These came mainly from England and the Germanic spaces of central Europe. Some mixed with those northern Europeans to form pluralistic political cultures in states such as Pennsylvania and Ohio. To these settlers individualism in politics, society, and personal philosophy was very important, a trait that was reflected in the movement of those Middle Atlantic settlers and their descendants to the central Midwest, the Great Plains, and territories farther west.

The third major stream was associated with the southern states where the economy was based primarily on agriculture rather than industry or commerce. The system of agriculture developed here was a plantation-centered form that incorporated slavery, an ingredient strictly against the grain of the citizens and states to the north. This landed-gentry system stressed social elites and family structure rather than the individual in society. Furthermore, it subjugated large numbers to a less-than-human status in society and politics. Such a philosophy was not only engendered by the southern states from Virginia and Kentucky south to east Texas, Louisiana, and northern Florida but by the southern parts of Ohio, Indiana, and Illinois. In these latter states the political culture is far from homogeneous as some threads of all three migration streams are still evident in the political processes and social systems.

These three broad migration streams were mainly instrumental in the development of regional political thought last century. However, even though their influence remains strong today, as is evident in national voting patterns and views of the federal government, there have been other areal shifts that have occurred and that are also behind the political cultures existing today. There has been a strong migration from rural areas to cities in the Northeast, the Midwest, the South, and the West since the early 1900s. Sizeable numbers of southern, eastern, and central European immigrants settled in the first few decades in northern and the Northeast cities. Blacks moved from the rural South to the urban North particularly following the 1930s and 1940s. Central city residents in the nation began moving to the suburbs en masse following World War II. Recently there has been a movement of whites, young and old, rich and poor, moving from urban and suburban northern cities to those in the South and Southwest. This has accounted for the skyrocketing growth rates for many large and medium-sized cities and for new towns. Some of these new migrants assimilated easily into their new communities and became a part of the prevailing political ideology, as in the case of right-wing extremism in southern California. Others retained their identity such as university enclaves of northerners in the urban South. These movements have complicated the picture of regional political ideology and cultures in some cities and states. In essence, it has added layers to the political cake, layers that frequently fail to blend with the existing cultures. Thus, the political culture for the nation is in a fluid condition for many cities and states. Even at the regional level this fluidity is exemplified in the South and California. The gradual assimilation of citizens with diverse political culture backgrounds is partly reflected in the present dynamic state of American politics. As stated previously in the discussion of political party strategies, the migration of people from central city to suburb or from North to South is affecting the regional and national planning of both major political parties.

An examination of these three political cultures on a state basis reveals some basic changes are occurring (Fig. 9-7). The most populous political culture in 1970 was the T/TM/TI combination found in sixteen states that had over 58-million people (Table 9-4). Both the M/MI and I had over 51-million residents. That the political party strategies focus on the South and Southwest as opposed to the

TABLE 9-4   Populations of the Cultural Groupings by State, 1940–1970[a]

Political Culture[b]	Number of States	Total Populations (in millions)			
		1940	1950	1960	1970
M/MI	17	30,998	38,113	47,751	51,413
IM	6	13,479	23,936	27,149	29,678
I	9	34,491	38,748	45,969	51,183
IT	2	3,785	3,955	4,320	5,447
T/TM/TI	16	39,947	45,167	52,915	58,436

[a] Cultural groupings as of 1970, Alaska and Hawaii included in 1960 and 1970.
[b] For purposes of overall analysis, it is possible to combine the eight points on the continuum in Fig. 9-7 into five categories.
Source: Daniel J. Elazar, Copyright from *American Federalism*, Second Edition, by Daniel J. Elazar. Copyright © 1972 by Thomas Y. Crowell Company, Inc. With permission of the Publisher.

Northeast and Midwest is borne out by the population changes. As Elazar points out these population figures do not reveal whether the population increase in these regions is reinforcing established political cultures or is incorporating new elements into it. Phillips sees the Sun Belt states (some in the TM, MI, and TI categories) becoming Republican and in a conservative vein. Nor does the table reveal if the changes that are occurring in the moralistic cultural group are the result of the individualistic political culture or the result of social and economic changes in the individualistic states. The continuation of recent population trends to urban areas and to the peripheral (South and Southwest) may herald the emerging pattern of new political cultures or some substantial modifications of existing ones. The level of migration, the attitudes of the immigrants, the prevailing political cultures, and the social and economic changes occurring in cities and their respective regions may result in the emergence of new patterns. These may lead to the formation of national rather than regional cultures.

Toward a National Political Culture? In light of the social and economic changes that have taken place especially in the past fifteen years, the question is often posed as to the formation of a political culture that embodies all citizens. A good case can be presented for the development of such a culture considering the prominence of a few television networks and newspaper wire services, the dominance of metropolitan newspapers, the upgrading of economic wages and consumer considerations, and the increased federalism in the past decade. These coupled with the national legislation gains in the spheres of civil rights, housing, education, consumer protection, and environmental quality may lead some citizens, social scientists, and even political party strategists to see the emergence of a national political culture.

Whether indeed a national political culture is emerging is best illustrated by examining what political and social changes are taking place at the different levels of the hierarchy. If local and state and sectional interests are found to be engaging in similar pieces of legislation or voice similar views about federal funding and federal interpretation of laws or guidelines, the previous contrasts in county, state, and sectional levels would likely be lessened. In a number of recent studies of political attitudes, social indicators, and governmental programs and spending, differences that existed in the past appear to remain in spite of the national awareness of issues at all levels in the past decade.[23] Sectionalism or the division of areal states into distinct political areas that are different from surrounding spaces "is seen as the nucleus of an area's culture or economy against the larger national interest."[24] The most widely quoted political cultural region that embodies district sectionalism is the South.[25] Other examples can also be cited, such as New England, the Midwest, and the Rockies, all of which have some distinguishing political cultural trademarks that separate them. Those political and social elements, that at an early time identified those political regions or sections with a particular regional philosophy, seem to have remained to this day.

Even though there are intraregional differences, still these sections have some readily identifying characteristics.[26] In the Northeast, the northern New

England states (Maine, New Hampshire, and Vermont) are mainly rural, Protestant, and Republican. In southern New England and in large part the remainder of the Northeast, Catholics and immigrant groups are important in the political process. Two of the trademarks of the region are the local political autonomy and the role of ethnic groups in a competitive political framework. In contrast, the South has a low political participation rate and a government administration with more state house control. Again, single-party dominance has been characteristic until recent Republican successes yet the philosophy has retained a conservative posture vis-à-vis the remainder of the nation. The Rim or Border South does not have a political climate similar to the Deep South as here there has been more competition, historically as well as at present. Differences remain in the Midwest and far West, even with the passage of social and political legislation since 1950. The varying ethnic and racial and economic groups have given the Midwest a philosophy that has brought about rivalries and competition at varying levels—rural-urban, north-south (splits in Ohio and Illinois as examples), Republican-Democrat, and ethnic-racial. With the later settlement in western states, political and cultural contrasts still did not disappear completely, although nonpartisan politics is important and at times political competition is intense. The federal involvement in the settlement, land purchases, and resource development all gave the region a character that differs from others.

The political culture of the United States continues to reflect the social heritage of the original settlers and the changes in the economy and in society that have taken place since then. Because all states or sections were not settled by the same peoples at the same time and for the same reasons, state constitutions, local autonomy, and individual roles in the political processes are not expected to be the same. It is also unlikely that they would ever become identical, although some differences may be disappearing. There are states that historically were more important in the sectional philosophies that evolved last century. These pioneers continue to remain paramount in contemporary political legislation in their respective region. Even in terms of national legislation, some states and regions have had a greater impact on bills introduced and the passage of subsequent legislation. While at one time the strength of the "farm bloc" was considered basic to the passage of certain congressional legislation, the term now applied is the strength of "urban coalitions." Regional philosophies as embodied in congressional voting continue to remain on particular issues. Proposals calling for political reform are more likely to receive rural and urban support in the moralistic and individualistic states than the traditionalistic. However, on other issues such as busing sectional voting may not exist, as northern legislators at times band with southern representatives.

FOOTNOTES

1. George R. Stewart, *American Place Names*, New York, Oxford University Press, 1970.

2. Joseph Nathan Kane, *Facts About the Presidents*, New York, Wilson, 1959, pp. 300–301.

3. *1973 World Almanac*, New York, Newspaper Enterprise Association, 1973, pp. 721–729.

4. Ibid., pp. 359–360.

5. Various historic landmarks are depicted in *National Atlas of the United States*, Washington, D.C., U.S. Department of the Interior, Geological Survey, 1970, pp. 146–147.

6. *1973 World Almanac*, ibid., pp. 508–509.

7. A good comprehensive reader on right-wing extremism is Robert A. Schoenberger, ed., *The American Right Wing: Readings in Political Behavior*, New York, Holt, Rinehart and Winston, 1969.

8. George J. Demko et al., "Student Disturbances and Campus Unrest in the United States: 1964–1970," in Melvin Albaum, ed., *Geography and Contemporary Issues: Studies of Relevant Problems*, New York, Wiley, 1973, pp. 533–541. Related facets of disturbances and demonstrations are treated in Chapter III, "Political Territoriality."

9. Various cities and states are mentioned in James P. Cannon, *The First Ten Years of American Communism*, New York, Lyle Stuart, 1962, pp. 245–310; and in his *The History of American Trotskyism*, New York, Pioneer, 1944.

10. Kevin P. Phillips, *The Emerging Republican Majority*, Garden City, Doubleday-Anchor Books, 1970, pp. 290–292. Copyright © 1969 by Arlington House, Inc., New Rochelle, New York. All rights reserved. Used with permission.

11. Ibid., p. 442.

12. Richard M. Scammon and Ben J. Wattenberg, *The Real Majority*, New York, Berkeley Publishing Company, 1971 pb., p. 70. Reprinted by permission of Coward, McCann & Geoghegan, Inc. Copyright © 1970 by Richard M. Scammon and Ben J. Wattenberg.

13. Ibid., pp. 70–72.

14. Jack L. Walker, "The Diffusion of Innovations among the American States," *American Political Science Review*, 63 (1969), 880–899.

15. Ibid., p. 887.

16. Ibid., p. 893.

17. "33 States Ask Congress for Constitutional Convention," *Congressional Quarterly Weekly Report*, August 1, 1969, pp. 1372–1373.

18. "The States: Are They Ready for Revenue Sharing?" *Congressional Quarterly Weekly Report*, June 25, 1971, p. 1398.

19. Americans for Constitutional Action, *The ACA-Index, 2nd Session, 91st Congress, 1970*, Washington, D.C., 1970.

20. For discussions on political regionalization and cultural facets of regions see Daniel J. Elazar, *American Federalism: A View from the States*, New York, Crowell, 1972; Ira Sharkansky, *Regionalism in American Politics*, Indianapolis, Ind., Bobbs-Merrill, 1970; and Norman R. Luttbeg, "Classifying American States: An Empirical Attempt to Identify Internal Variations," *Midwest Political Science Quarterly*, 15 (1971), 703–721. The topic of territorial separatism, exemplified in the history of various states, is a fascinating area for political cultural studies. It has only been touched on by C.F.J. Whebell, "A Model of Territorial

Separatism," *Proceedings*, Association of American Geographers, 5 (1973), 295–298.

21. Elazar, op. cit., pp. 93–102.

22. Ibid., pp. 103–126; Sharkansky, op. cit. and Wilbur Zelinsky, *A Cultural Geography of the United States*, Englewood Cliffs, N.J., Prentice-Hall, 1973, pp. 44–47.

23. Norval D. Glenn and J. L. Simmons, "Are Regional Cultural Differences Diminishing?" *Public Opinion Quarterly*, 31 (1967), 176–193; and Samuel C. Patterson, "The Political Culture of American States," *Journal of Politics*, 30 (1968), 187–209.

24. Sharkansky, op. cit., p. 165.

25. For studies on regional political cultures of states and regions see Thomas C. Donnelly, *Rocky Mountain Politics*, Albuquerque, University of New Mexico Press, 1940; V. O. Key, *Southern Politics*, New York, Knopf, 1949; Russell B. Nye, *Midwestern Progressive Politics*, East Lansing, Michigan State University Press, 1951; Duane Lockard, *New England State Politics*, Princeton, N.J., Princeton University Press, 1959; Frank H. Jonas, *Western Politics*, Salt Lake City, University of Utah Press, 1961; Gabriel A. Almond and Sidney Verba, *The Civic Culture*, Princeton, N.J., Princeton University Press, 1963; John H. Fenton, *Midwest Politics*, New York, Holt, Rinehart, and Winston, 1966, and his *Politics in the Border States*, New Orleans, Hauser Press, 1957; Herbert Jacob and Kenneth N. Vines, eds., *Politics in the American States*, Boston, Little, Brown, 1965; Frank Munger, *American State Politics*, New York, Crowell, 1966; and Raymond E. Wolfinger and Fred T. Greenstein, "Comparing Political Regions: The Case of California," *American Political Science Review*, 63 (1969), 74–85.

26. Sharkansky, op. cit., pp. 167–177.

Chapter 10

ELECTORAL
GEOGRAPHY

*When the average voter steps into the booth he
registers the prejudice of the allegiance bred by a
mix of geography, history, and ethnic reaction
which stems from a past he knows only murkily.*

Kevin Phillips

The response of individuals and groups to elected political representatives or to important social issues is measured by the patterns of voting. The results of such voting when examined at a precinct or national scale seldom reveal complete areal similarity in the response. Rather, the response varies from little to great support for a candidate or a particular issue within a congressional district, a metropolitan area, a state, or a political region. For the political geographer the election results are of importance in that the variation in the patterns can be analyzed in conjunction with particular social, economic, or political cultural characteristics. The manner and degree to which particular facets of the population vary with voting results aid in comprehending the attitudes and behaviors of groups, whether they be a particular occupation class or ethnic group.

Electoral results are one of the major ways, besides polls and editorial

271

commentaries, to ferret out the reaction of people to key social and economic issues facing cities and the nation. They also provide barometers for important office-holders at local and national levels. The degree of success a particular referendum enjoys or a potential high-office seeker receives is measured in the light of salient indicators of the population in question. Projecting the results of a piece of urban legislation or state voting to another city and state is often tied to the characteristics associated with its passage or defeat elsewhere. This reasoning also holds true when the support for a national political candidate is projected. Should he receive working-class support in one locale or region, it is often suggested his voting appeal may be similar in another location.

In analyzing the results of voting response at various scales, the investigations may focus on the behavior of individuals or of groups. Political surveys concentrate on the social, economic, and political behavior of selected individuals and from such attempt to account for the sentiments of groups. In other words, survey research efforts attempt to measure how income level, occupation, religion, age, sex, and race reflect the attitudes of individuals to certain pieces of legislation and politicians. The spatial and behavioral facets of voting response surfaces are treated in Part I. Notions involving how neighborhood interaction, proximity to dissimilar economic groups, scaling of political identity and association, and perception of issues and politicians are ingredients that survey analysis would relate to the attitudes of individuals. Thus one level of voting analysis could relate to survey results of individuals.

A second type of analysis of electoral geography focuses on the patterns of the resultant votes. That is, in what manner can the results be classified or grouped and to what characteristics of the population can the outcomes be related. These efforts in concentrating on group behavior relate specific social, economic, and political criteria of aggregates to the votes. The varying income categories, major occupation types, and age cohorts are related to the response surfaces or voting patterns for political units, be they precincts, counties, congressional districts, or states. These ecological associations, as they are termed, examine the associations or covariations of units rather than individuals as holds true for survey analyses. The aggregate vote of a particular political unit, such as the support for an urban referendum or for a particular candidate, is associated with selected social and economic facets of the residents in that unit of political space.

Investigations into voting patterns are usually of either a survey or an ecological nature. Combinations of both analyses would likely lead, if properly executed, to a thorough treatment of the behavioral processes and resultant patterns themselves. Inasmuch as many social scientists, and political geographers among them, do not incorporate both levels of analyses, a word of caution in the interpretation of voting results in a spatial context is in order. As was stated above the results of surveys conducted apply to those individuals and those of similar backgrounds. This is assuming the sample has been carefully selected and properly administered. Such sample results of individuals whether in a central city location or a suburb or a small town cannot be applied to characteristics of a particular geographical unit. That is, survey results of suburbanites cannot be used to associate selected group characteristics of residents in a particular suburb or in other suburbs. Very simply this is stating that survey results are inappropriate when a specific political geographic unit is considered for examination. In like manner, ecological analyses, that is, those voting studies focusing on patterns within a city or state, cannot be attributed to specific individuals. Using aggregate results to define the behavior of individuals leads to committing what is termed the "ecological fallacy." For example, an urban political geographer wishing to examine the areal variation in the support for the city financing of additional recreation land may find support higher in the suburbs than the inner city. He may then select certain social and economic characteristics such as the percent of homeowners, median income of white-collar employees, and fertility level to relate to the demand for more park and playground space. While there will likely be positive associations between these variables and the precinct voting pattern, only group levels of analyses can be made. One is not free to say that because a high correlation exists between the vote and fertility that a certain individual in a suburb with a large family supported the referendum. The fallacy that results is the juxtaposing of ecological and survey results.

In the discussion below the elections treated at varying scales are examined by using the ecological approach. The lack of sufficient behavioral data having spatial dimensions is a primary reason. Furthermore, most of the political geography contributions to the study of elections have been carried out using patterns. The areal associations of select social and economic characteristics to the voting pattern have been the most frequent types of analyses performed. Combinations of cartographic and statistical analyses of voting have been carried out in a number of cities and states. In many ways these pattern analyses can be likened to a series of cartographic or visual overlays. Maps depicting levels of black population or poverty levels or urban population densities or education levels are superimposed on the voting map.

Areal variations exist in the ethnic population, major occupation types, age cohorts, and income strata within a city, state, or nation. These social and economic facets can be associated with the voting for a particular party, issue, or candidate. When cartographic or ecological analyses are performed, they provide insight into the geographic nature of the voting response in question. However, in addition to select social and economic characteristics that are frequently measured with voting patterns, the question arises as to the importance of certain spatial facets. That is, are there specific geographical or spatial facets that might likewise be incorporated into voting studies that might not be included in studies by other social and behavioral scientists? These would relate to how space might be reflected in the voting patterns. One such facet relates to distance. Social and spatial distance from a particular group may influence the vote of individuals and groups. For example, white suburbanites may be more likely to support park and playground space for inner city blacks than those whites living in the same spaces as blacks. Also urban and suburban counties in a state would more likely favor using highway funds for mass transit than would rural areas some distance away. Distance is important in measuring the support for political candidates. The friends-and-neighbors model discussed at the city, state, and regional levels in Chapter 3 illustrates how support dwindles for a candidate the farther one is away from the "home base."

The level of interaction in a spatial sense may also be reflected in the response of individuals and groups to particular issues and candidates. Strict geographical contiguity or proximity does not signify interaction and association. Rather the opposite may exist. The presence of blacks and European ethnics in large Midwest and Northeast cities in similar geographical spaces does not automatically bring about social and political interaction. This is also true for Spanish-Americans, blacks, and Indians in a metropolitan area. How this interaction may be reflected in a voting pattern is illustrated by substantially different support for referenda and office seekers. Very high support may be tied to one group and in immediately adjacent precincts or wards, very low support may exist. Major islands or sinks for a particular party or individual politician are often associated with an appeal or lack of it to one particular social or economic group or to a particular environment, such as urban nodes.

Voting patterns have taken on a renewed interest in the political geography literature in the past decade.[1] While sister disciplines such as political science and political sociology have traditionally treated votes as they relate to class and party, it has been only recently that many of these methods and findings have been surfacing in the geographic literature. Particularly is this true for investigations at levels other than the national and state scale. Political geography studies contributing towards an understanding of national (presidential) elections have been limited either to major journals or recent textbooks.[2] Regional analyses have been performed by several geographers.[3] More frequent have been those treating voting results of political parties within a state.[4] The study of congressional voting patterns is limited to date to a single geographical reference.[5] Votes within urban areas are only beginning to be the focus for geographic investigations.[6] There are a host of studies awaiting geographic inquiry at all scales, from local to national. An understanding and appreciation of the issue, party, or candidate in question and as these relate to critical social, economic, and political cultural variations will aid in supplementing knowledge about the geographical nature of elections.

In an attempt to illustrate the variety and types of elections that await inquiry by geographers and others, a number are selected for scrutiny. Examples of partisan and nonpartisan votes are used as well as voting results at different levels. The four most recent presidential elections and recent critical congressional votes illustrate the diversity of support for parties, individuals, and certain issues. The variations are associated with salient features of the social and economic landscape. These also provide a backdrop within which to examine the membership in the United States House of Representatives and the Senate. States have offered a number of referendums to their electorate especially in the past decade. Four critical issues in four different states are used to analyze voting variations at this level. That most voters live in urban areas is not surprising, yet the voting results in cities await more geographical analysis. Again, a series of referendums in four cities are selected to identify significant variations in their responses to contemporary issues.

While an examination of the voting results provides meaningful insight into the nature of the region and the voters, the actual mechanics in the voting processes are important. Specifically an understanding of the public involvement in voting can be documented by the levels of participation. In the same way that not all parts of a city or state or the nation vote alike, nor do they participate at the same level. This involvement in the political or voting process can be measured by the levels of registration and the voter turnout on election days. The geographical nature of both these measures exhibits distinct areal differences within cities, within states, and within regions. To date political geographers have ignored this important ingredient in the election process. A major reason for its importance is that participation reflects the political cultural and environmental setting of the space (city or state or region) in question. Also the realization that wide variations exist suggests that political involvement is far from uniform throughout the nation. Many are the referendums and the candidates that have lost because of the turnout level. Had it been even a slight percentage higher, different social measures may have been adopted and different politicians would be making decisions for the citizenry. The importance of turnout and registration is such that it is treated here within the context of electoral geography.

NATIONAL PATTERNS FOR PRESIDENTS

Presidential elections since 1960 have displayed little nationwide uniformity in party allegiances. There have been close elections, 1960 and 1968, landslide elections, 1964 and 1972, and the strong influence of a third party, 1968. In the midst of these dynamics there have been elections when the Republicans were so soundly defeated (1964) that they were written off by some students of politics for the next generation in American history. The same has been said for the Democrats in 1972 when their loss left them in disarray and destined for oblivion for the immediate future. Such predictions have not held true nor are they likely to. Probably the only truism that remains in this period of changing allegiances and alteration of party philosophy is that both the Republicans and Democrats will remain vying for the top elected spot and will have varying degrees of success. The period of single-party dominance, at least in the White House, is doubtful for several continuous elections. Rather the changes occurring in the South, the Southwest, and the suburbs are likely to be the focus for political aspirants of both parties. The directions these areas will take in the future party-wise or ideology-wise cannot be predicted with complete certainty today.

Elections have been analyzed and described by historians, pollsters, political scientists, journalists, and commentators. Geographers and in this case political geographers have not devoted much space to the votes for presidential candidates or parties nationwide. To be sure, there are exceptions, but in political geography textbooks the topic has been by and large ignored.[7] Other social scientists, namely, political scientists and sociologists, have considered this one of the major emphases of their discipline. While these analyses are useful in examining the particular issues and personalities in each presidential election and the national voting results, these are of minimal utility when areal variations are considered. For the geographer interested in presidential elections, the questions of where the candidates received their support and why these spaces voted as they did are the most crucial. It almost goes without saying that a candidate and party do not receive the same level of support throughout the United States, which in itself suggests that issues of urban-rural residence, race, income, and occupation are behind the varying levels of support.[8]

Among the various approaches that can be used to analyze presidential elections on a national basis are those utilizing preelection and postelection survey results. However, in the main, these are not especially useful for geographic investigations as they are basically not spatially specific enough to permit meaningful analyses. In addition, often published studies fail to give additional socioeconomic characteristics and political characteristics of those surveyed at particular locations. Usually the tabular results group the support for candidates and parties by macroregions such as the South, the West, or the Midwest, rather than focusing on the particular locational considerations for the votes. Another approach that can be considered when treating recent elections involves the major political issues (foreign and domestic) that were critical to the election in question. These then could be handled with respect to particular candidates and parties. While such ingredients are useful in a thorough analysis of presidential elections, they are often not place-specific. In other words, support for a particular foreign policy action or domestic legislation may have widespread national appeal. Such does not imply that sectional interests and philosophies are not involved in the party platforms and political campaigning of particular candidates. Even the most recent elections have catered to special sectional and ethnic interests such as civil rights programs in the South and the ethnic blue-collar voters in the industrial North or the agricultural interests in the Midwest.

The four most recent presidential elections, 1960 through 1972, are considered on a macrogeographic basis. The major areas of support for each party and candidate are examined on the basis of states and counties carried. While there are some similarities underlying the voting in the elections, there are some significant contrasts that appear in a political geographical analysis. An investigation into the actual reasons why a particular state or particular county voted as it did in any election is frequently difficult if not impossible to assess. Using the general indicators of residence, race, occupation, income and party may not be satisfactory to handle a single political unit's voting behavior. Rather than attempt an exhaustive analysis of each election throughout the United States, the emphasis is on the general areal patterns and specific socioeconomic and political cultural characteristics that will aid in comprehending the geographic results.

In a partial attempt to account for some of the variations existing in particular counties, a number of special-type counties are investigated with respect to the 1972 election. Specifically, counties examined are those that have a large urban population, a large Spanish-surname and black population, a large number of senior citizens, university populations, and those receiving large amounts of defense contracts. Counties in these categories are examined to determine if the vote for Nixon was greater or less than the national average.

The 1960 election pitting Kennedy (Democrat) from Massachusetts vs. Nixon (Republican) of California was won by the former but by only slightly over 100,000 votes out of more than 68 million votes. The popular vote was closer than the number of states, electoral votes, and counties carried by either candidate (Table 10-1). On a state level Nixon carried all states in the western half of the United States save Texas, Nevada, and Hawaii. Kennedy carried all the eastern states except those in northern New England (traditionally Republican), those East Central states of Ohio, Indiana, Kentucky, and the Rim states of Virginia and Florida. Kennedy also lost Iowa and Wisconsin to Nixon. The greatest support for Democrat Kennedy was in the traditionally Democratic South, Texas, the Northeast, and the large industrial states of Michigan and Illinois (Fig. 10-1). As the table and map illustrate, Nixon carried more states and more counties, but lost out in the important electoral college vote. On the county level Kennedy won those in the southern half of the United States and major urban nodes in the northern half. Of the fourteen largest Standard Metropolitan Statistical Areas in 1960, the Democrats won all ranging from 50.2 percent in Los Angeles-Long Beach to 61.9 percent in Detroit. This pattern of capturing key urban counties in major states is a phenomenon that appears in later presidential elections, most especially in 1968. A candidate who can capture the metropolitan vote of New York, Chicago, Los Angeles, Philadelphia, and Detroit can go a long way to winning the state's electoral support. The 1960 election represented a victory for the traditional Democratic areas in the South and for those urban Democratic strongholds in the North. Nixon and the Republicans won the more sparsely populated and rural parts of the United States.

The 1964 election was the first of two landslides that have occurred within the past decade, the other being 1972. Incumbent Johnson (Democrat) of Texas was almost assured victory when the Republicans nominated Goldwater of Arizona. Civil rights programs were being developed and legislated during this time which had the support of Johnson and much of the nation except in the South where opposition by Goldwater was received warmly. The militaristic posture of Goldwater in regard to the ensuing Vietnam War was in sharp contrast to the campaign strategy of peace-loving Johnson. In many senses the electorate envisioned a clear distinction between the two candidates in terms of social legislation, foreign policy, and quality of leadership. The popular vote and the results of the electoral vote and that of the states and counties carried revealed the much more popular support for Johnson (Table 10-1). By all proportions Johnson swamped Goldwater by taking 61 percent of the popular vote. The vote was so overwhelming against Goldwater that he won only six states, five in the Deep South (South

TABLE 10-1   Results of Presidential Elections, 1960–1972

Election	Candidates	Popular Vote (in thousands)	Percent	Electoral Vote	Electoral Percent	States Carried	States Percent	Counties Carried	Counties Percent
1960	Kennedy (D)	34,227	49.7	303	56	23	46	1255	40
	Nixon (R)	34,108	49.5	219	41	27	54	1873	60
1964	Johnson (D)	43,130	61.1	486	90	45	88	2311	74
	Goldwater (R)	27,178	38.5	52	10	6	12	819	26
1968	Nixon (R)	31,785	43.5	301	56	32	63	1873	60
	Humphrey (D)	31,275	42.7	191	36	14	27	696	22
	Wallace (AIP)	9,906	13.8	46	8	5	10	561	18
1972	Nixon (R)	47,042	60.7	517	96	49	96	3001	96
	McGovern (D)	29,072	37.4	17	4	2	4	130	4
	Schmitz (AIP)	1,081	1.4	0	0	0	0	0	0

Sources: "Vote Cast For President, 1900 to 1968," *Statistical Abstract of the United States, 1972*, Washington, D.C., U.S. Department of Commerce, 1972, p. 358; Government Affairs Institute, *America Votes*, vol. 4 (1960), vol. 6 (1964), vol. 8 (1968), Washington, D.C.; and 1973 *World Almanac*, New York, Newspaper Enterprise Association, 1973, pp. 42–69.

Carolina, Georgia, Alabama, Mississippi, Louisiana) and his home state. Johnson won 90 percent of the electoral votes and over 70 percent of the counties. The only areas where he did not fare well were in the Deep South (notice state boundaries delimiting candidate support) and parts of the Plains and mountain West (Fig. 10-1). Even in these latter regions where Goldwater conservatism was

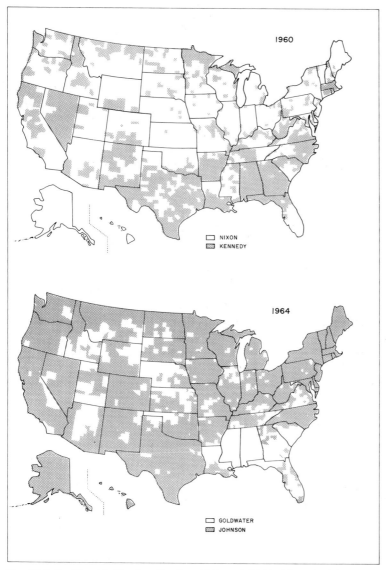

Fig. 10-1 Presidential Election Results: 1960 and 1964. (*America Votes*, 1960 and 1964.)

popular, the Republican candidate did not win any state. The Republican void is best illustrated in the Northeast where he had almost no support; in fact, he failed to carry a single county in eight states. Part of the Johnson landslide is illustrated by his nationwide support, except in the Deep South, in the rural as well as the urban areas. He carried the twenty largest SMSAs in 1964 by margins from 55.7 percent for Cincinnati to 82.2 percent for Providence-Pawtucket-Warwick, Rhode Island. The big-city support was in the East, Midwest, and West. Of the thirty largest SMSAs, Goldwater managed to win only San Diego (50.3 percent), Atlanta (50.1 percent), and New Orleans (51.4 percent).

The year 1968 included a new twist to presidential politics with the introduction of a third party that potentially could have had a serious impact on the choice of the next president. The development of the American Independent party headed by George Wallace of Alabama represented the first time in twenty years a third party could play a spoiler role in American politics. Wallace, long known to Americans for his opposition to civil rights programs, was hopeful of achieving victory or at least blocking Nixon and Humphrey, Democratic party candidate from Minnesota, from an outright victory. Politics in 1968 was fluid to say the least with a nation beset by the assassination of two national figures, student unrest, riots and protests by blacks, crime and permissiveness, the unpopularity of the Vietnam War, an incumbent president's decision not to rerun, and the deteriorating quality of urban life. Into this political year were cast three national figures, Humphrey, the vice-president under Johnson, Nixon, a previous two-term vice-president and 1960 presidential campaign loser, and Wallace, a regional candidate with many negative views on social conditions. The volatility of the year was illustrated by the party conventions and the changing support of all candidates in national public opinion polls. The closeness of the race was reflective of the divisions among races, ages, philosophies, and sections that existed. The Nixon victory was close only in the sense of the popular vote as he nosed out Humphrey by a mere half-million votes of the nearly 73 million votes cast (Table 10-1). His victory margin percentwise was only slightly over 43 percent. Wallace was able to drain support away from both candidates, particularly in the southeast quarter. Nixon carried thirty-two states and lost only five Deep South ones to Wallace and eight to Humphrey. In addition Nixon lost Texas (as he did eight years earlier), Washington, Hawaii, Michigan, and the District of Columbia to candidate Humphrey. On a county basis, the map reveals that most of the nation was Republican as indeed it was with Nixon taking 60 percent of all counties (Fig. 10-2). The Nixon support was mainly in the western half of the United States, save Texas, the Midwest and Northeast except for major cities, and the Rim South. As has been mentioned in previous chapters, Nixon attempted to capture some of the Wallace strength with his southern strategy. In these endeavors he was successful, as without victories in North Carolina, Virginia, Florida, and Tennessee the election outcome may have been entirely different. The support received by Wallace was primarily akin to Thurmond's in 1948, that is, a regional support. Outside his home territory his support was low. Humphrey's support can be attributed to his home state (Minne-

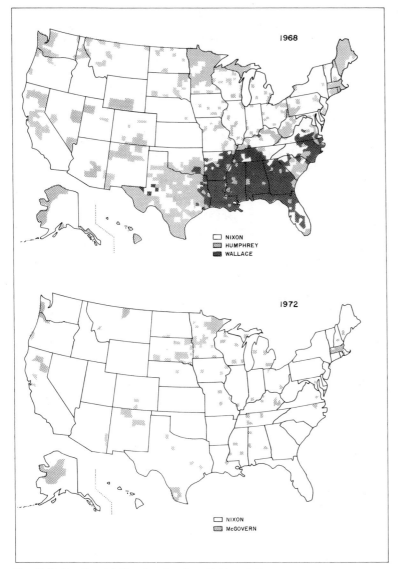

Fig. 10-2 Presidential Election Results: 1968 and 1972. (*America Votes,* 1968 and 1973 *World Almanac.*)

sota) and that of his vice-presidential candidate (Muskie from Maine), politically liberal areas in southern New England and northern California. Some of the counties Humphrey won in the South were those with high black populations. The closeness of the Nixon-Humphrey vote is in large part attributed to the success enjoyed by the Democratic standard-bearer in metropolitan areas. Humphrey won all the ten largest SMSAs except for Los Angeles-Long Beach, which went to Nixon. Furthermore, Humphrey won fifteen of the largest twenty and seventeen of the largest twenty-five. The metropolitan votes he lost were primarily in southern California and in Texas. By capturing only a very few counties in large urban states, as in New York, Pennsylvania, and Michigan, Humphrey won the state's electoral votes. The crucial nature of large urban areas in close elections is viewed in the light of this election. The Humphrey strategy of concentrating on major urban population nodes almost assured him a popular election victory.

The 1972 presidential election had reminiscences of 1964 especially with the incumbent, in this case Republican Nixon, almost assured of victory once McGovern was nominated by the Democrats in Miami. McGovern of South Dakota was known to many Americans for his long-standing criticism of the Vietnam War. This view plus his liberal stances on defense cuts, abortion, welfare reform, and his replacing the initial vice-presidential selection did not engender widespread national support. Nixon on the other hand was an incumbent, which in itself was an advantage. Also he was making efforts to wind down the Vietnam War, nominating conservatives to the Supreme Court, and wooing Wallace and conservative voters by his stands on busing, radicals, and major newspapers. Throughout the campaign Nixon enjoyed a role Johnson had in 1964, that of an appearance of stability and aloofness that did not necessitate direct comment or dialogue with his Democrat opponent. While Nixon did not achieve the winning percentage that Johnson did against Goldwater (60.7 versus 61.1 percent) he did amass a far greater percent of states and counties carried (Table 10-1). With the eighteen-year-old vote in 1972, Nixon did have a larger popular vote than Johnson. He succeeded in winning all states except Massachusetts and the District of Columbia. This virtual shutout of McGovern was reflected in the counties won by Nixon (Fig. 10-2). The McGovern counties number only 130; the only easily identifiable areas of his support were in Massachusetts, South Dakota and Minnesota, and scattered counties throughout the remainder of the nation. He failed to carry a single county in fifteen states and in thirteen he carried only one. Support for McGovern beyond the national average was evident in the Northeast, northern Midwest and West Coast states. Nixon had over two-thirds of the voters' approval in the Deep South and some Border South states. The third-party candidate, Schmitz of California representing the American Independent party, further showed the regional appeal for these minor party nominees. Even though he won only 1 percent of the national vote, he won more than that in the western states, Idaho (9 percent), Alaska (7 percent), Utah (6 percent), Oregon (5 percent), Montana and Washington (4 percent each), and California and Arizona (3 percent each). This standard-bearer for Wallace did not fare well in the Deep South except for Louisiana (5 percent).

A major change in the 1972 election was the Republican support for the president in large cities. In the previous three, the Democrats had won almost all the largest metropolitan areas. This year of the fifteen largest populated counties in the United States, Nixon won nine. Of these, five were by less than his national vote of 61 percent. McGovern was concentrating throughout his campaign on the major cities in key states. He did have partial success here but not to the degree he had hoped or the level of his predecessors. The urban counties he won were primarily in the Northeast, especially those containing Detroit, Philadelphia, Boston, and three boroughs (New York, Kings, and Bronx) in the New York City area. Nixon's successes in the large counties were less than the national average except for Orange and San Diego counties in California, Nassau in New York, and Harris County (Houston) in Texas.

While large urban counties are but one example of counties that frequently exhibit a similar voting profile, there are other types of counties that could likewise be examined. It is expected that an investigation into various types of counties such as the poorest, the richest, those with the largest number of young voters, or those containing major government installations, would show similar voting behavior. This is assuming that the counties in question can be identified as having a single homogeneous population segment (such as senior citizens) or a dominant government-related economy. Even though the results for presidential candidates may not be equal to the individual's national performance, their averages may appear deviant in regards to the particular state. Just as support for a presidential candidate in major and even minor urban centers is different from the surrounding rural areas, so counties containing a large university or college community are expected to have a voting pattern that is distinct.

The preferences of newly enfranchised young voters were studied during Campaign '72 with both political parties openly soliciting their support. The party and ideological bent of these young citizens were unknown, and with the constitutional amendment passed lowering the voting age from twenty-one to eighteen (except for Georgia and Kentucky which already had a lower age), it was hoped their involvement in the national political process would be significant. Polls taken by the United States Bureau of Census soon after the election showed that slightly less than half of the young people eligible to vote actually did so.[9] The one environment where political activities had been especially high in the past decade was the college or university community. It was expected that the generally more liberal orientation and preferences of counties with a large university or college affiliated population would have a larger vote for McGovern than Nixon in 1972. To almost all college students and faculty McGovern was the more liberal candidate and the one who espoused some popular campus issues such as ending the Vietnam War, openness in government, and a more realistic stance on marijuana, abortion, and amnesty for draft evaders. Nixon was viewed as a more moderate or possibly moderate to conservative candidate.

When the voting results for 1972 were studied for university or college counties, the Nixon support was usually less than his state average. In the Northeast and Midwest states his support in some counties was less than a majority, that is, he lost them to McGovern. Liberal university counties containing the University of Michigan (Washtenaw County), University of Iowa (Johnson County), University of Wisconsin (Dane County), University of Massachusetts (Hampshire County), and not surprisingly the University of South Dakota (Clay County) all supported Democrat McGovern. In other states Nixon support was less than the state average in counties with Indiana University (Monroe County), University of Wyoming (Albany County), University of North Carolina (Orange County), University of Kansas (Douglas County), University of Florida (Alachua County), and the University of Colorado (Boulder County). Even in some Deep South states the Nixon support in counties with the major state universities was less than his state average; this holds for the University of Georgia (Clarke County) and Mississippi State University (Oktibbeha County). In most of these counties Nixon's support was from 5 to 10 percent less than the state average.

Three other special types of counties also exhibit some similar underlying voting behavior. They are those with a large black population, a large Spanish-surname population, and those with a large percentage of older residents. First, the blacks have been voting heavily for Democratic candidates since the Kennedy election in 1960. The strides in the civil rights field accomplished during the Kennedy and Johnson administrations have led to almost bloc voting for the Democratic standard-bearers. Nixon particularly, with his southern strategy of 1968 and his obvious attempts to woo white southern voters, especially those that had Wallace leanings, did not endear the blacks who were registering and voting in ever-increasing numbers. His Supreme Court nominees and his stands on busing, equal employment, and civil liberties also led blacks to vote against him. Of the ten counties with the largest percent black population in 1970, only four voted for Nixon in 1972 (Table 10-2). While this table does not give the percent of the blacks who were registered or who voted, it does reveal the low level of support Nixon received in these counties. Many of these are very poor and very rural counties in Deep South states.

For reasons similar to the voting behavior of black Americans, the Spanish-surname populations voted against President Nixon and the Republicans. The Democrats have long had a successful corner on minority groups, including those of Mexican and of Puerto Rican descent. The largest areal concentrations of the Spanish-surname population are in the Southwest, especially in Texas, California, Colorado, New Mexico, and Arizona. In these states were the counties with the largest percent of residents with a Spanish-surname in 1970. Nixon managed to win five of the top ten counties and four of these by a narrow margin (Table 10-2). Thus most of these very poor and rural counties voted for Democrat McGovern rather than the Republican candidate. Other than these Spanish-surnamed Americans living in the Southwest, the Puerto Ricans in New York City and Cubans in Miami need to be treated briefly. Those Puerto Ricans in New York City have voted in a liberal and Democratic manner in recent elections. Cubans in Miami have been voting in large numbers beginning in 1968. They tended to vote less Democratic and more Republican than the residents they replaced. Also the conservative flavor of Cuban voting appears in their stronger support than the county for candidate Wallace in 1968.[10] The stronger foreign policy advocated by the Republicans plus the Democratic Bay of Pigs debacle appears to underlie part of their more conservative philosophical outlook and support for Republicans.

While Nixon did not fare well in counties with major universities or a large

TABLE 10-2   Nixon Vote in Special Types of Counties, 1972

	Black Counties			Spanish-Surname Counties	
Location	Percent Black	Percent Nixon	Location	Percent Spanish	Percent Nixon
Charles City, Va.	83.0	31	Starr, Tex.	98	43
Macon, Ala.	81.7	33	Mora, N. Mex.	95	51
Greene, Ala.	75.4	30	Jim Hogg, Tex.	92	94
Jefferson, Miss.	75.3	44	Zapata, Tex.	92	48
Claiborne, Miss.	74.9	43	Maverick, Tex.	90	51
Hancock, Ga.	73.8	81	Taos, N. Mex.	86	42
Tunica, Miss.	72.8	61	Webb, Tex.	86	42
Wilcox, Ala.	68.5	86	Guadalupe, N. Mex.	85	52
Holmes, Miss.	68.2	48	Duval, Tex.	84	16
Talbot, Ga.	68.0	65	Rio Arriba, N. Mex.	82	46

	Old-Age Counties			Prime Military Contracts	
Location	Percent Over 65 Yrs.	Percent Nixon	Location	PMC Per Capita, 1968	Percent Nixon
Charlotte, Fla.	35	76	Orange, Fla.	$497	79
Pasco, Fla.	32	72	Jackson, Miss.	326	90
Manatee, Fla.	30	80	Cobb, Ga.	243	85
Pinellas, Fla.	30	70	Hancock, Tenn.	234	82
Sarasota, Fla.	29	80	Tarrant, Tex.	224	62
Hamilton, Tex.	27	72	Independence, Ark.	191	65
Citrus, Fla.	26	74	Winnebago, Ill.	187	60
Elk, Kans.	26	78	Clinch, Ga.	176	83
Mills, Tex.	26	74	St. Louis City, Mo.	157	38
Llano, Tex.	25	74	Eau Claire, Wis.	154	52

Source: *Federal Outlays, Fiscal Year 1968; 1970 Census of Population;* and *1973 World Almanac.*

black or Spanish-surname population in 1972, he did much better in those with sizable numbers of older Americans. Of those counties with the largest percentages of senior citizens, that is, those with residents over 65 years, Nixon very handily won all. Whether these were in Texas or Florida, the two areas with largest percent of older Americans, almost three of every four voters supported the president (Table 10-2). Possibly the moderate to conservative image Nixon created plus the indecisive positions of McGovern on several issues left many older Americans with little opportunity but to endorse the incumbent. When three-fourths of the voters in these special counties voted for Nixon at these levels, it suggests that he received support across the socioeconomic spectrum. Maybe even the issues of the preservation of tradition and Americanism were important in these retirement counties.

President Nixon in 1972 also received strong endorsement from counties with a large defense outlay. Military spending and priorities were a point of difference between the Nixon and McGovern campaigns. Nixon was an advocate of a strong defense posture and was in favor of committing needed funds for present security as well as future defense needs. McGovern on the other hand had long been a critic of high military spending levels and the priorities the Nixon administration had set for the nation. He was in favor of recommitting defense monies to other categories of need. For many citizens, especially those in defense- and space-related industries, a McGovern victory would not only result in their possible unemployment but would be a weakening of America's defenses. If the ten leading counties receiving the highest prime military contracts per capita in fiscal year 1968 are examined, all went for Republican Nixon in 1972 except for one (Table 10-2). His support in some of these government-defense-related counties was from 60 to 90 percent! Clearly these counties did not favor the candidacy of McGovern. While McGovern's views may not have been the sole reason for the overwhelming support Nixon received, it cannot be argued that government-related counties and areas fail to recognize the bread and butter issues as well as national party platforms.

These are only a few of the special types of counties that exhibit some striking patterns of voting for presidential candidates. Others could be selected such as those with high-income suburban populations, with declining central city or rural populations, with particular ethnic groups, or with a particular economic base be it agriculture or industry or tourism. The selection of the above example serves to illustrate that a national voting surface for a presidential candidate is comprised of some states and regions where he does better or worse than the national average but likewise of minor peaks or depressions that can be associated with particular population or economic characteristics of a smaller unit.

CONGRESSIONAL VOTING

In each session of Congress there are hundreds of bills and resolutions that are passed by one or both chambers. These run the gamut of issues ranging from consumer protection to national security and from civil rights legislation to creation of national parks and shrines. The support for these measures can be examined within a geographic framework, namely, what variations in the vote existed and what underlying elements are related to it. To be sure, there are almost as many different voting patterns as there are members in the Senate and the House of Representatives. Votes can be examined in the light of political party support, ideological lines (that is, conservative vs. liberal), support for presidential views, and in line with the ecological characteristics of a congressman's district. It is expected that the manner in which a member of Congress votes will represent his own personal stance or those he represents or both. On critical issues his decision may be only supported by a part of his constituency, such as labor or minority groups or special interest groups such as major industrial concerns within his district or state.

A geographical treatment of congressional voting would attempt to ferret out the underlying conditions and circumstances that result in the areal variation. With 435 representatives and 100 senators voting on a particular piece of legislation it is often difficult if not impossible to discern why an individual congressman voted as he did. Thus analyses are often reduced to examining more salient facets such as urban vs. rural orientation, political culture of the district or state, or party alignments. In this manner the results of the voting can often be interpreted. Lest the descriptive analyses of congressional voting be considered as easily comprehended, the behavior of individual legislators needs to be taken into account. While most urban districts in the South may vote in like manner on a key civil rights proposition, there may be districts whose representative will not vote in tune with his counterparts elsewhere. It may be that he has opposition to the particular item for entirely personal (not political or philosophical) reasons. The same can be illustrated for Plains senators who may not all vote in like manner on key agricultural legislation. In other words the voting of senators and representatives may not always follow in neatly contrived party or regional voting packages.

The vote rendered by the Senate or House or Representatives on issues varies from unanimous support, or nearly so for some pieces of legislation, to close margins. Senate votes are often decided by six votes or less and in the House crucial votes may be by margins of fifteen to twenty. When close votes are examined they would likely lead to the emergence of significant geographical variations. Such are the cases discussed below. Votes on bills or resolutions are cast in the "yeas" vs. the "nays," however, actual voting tallies are more often than not more complicated. While there are members who vote "yes" or "no," there are others who are "paired for" or "paired against" a particular issue. In addition, there are some who were "announced for" the bill and others who were "present, not voting" and those who were "absent."[11] Thus combining the votes for analyses into two groups, the yes-voters and the no-voters, does reflect the varying stances adopted by individual congressmen.

Among the myriad of bills, resolutions, and amendments voted on by the Senate and House of Representatives in the past five years, examples of what are considered key legislation are identified for analyses. Within the Senate the votes on the Haynesworth Supreme Court nomination, the antiballistic missile system, electoral reform, and an end-the-war amendment are considered. Other votes that had major significance to the development of domestic and foreign policies involved appropriation authorizations, employment guidelines, environmental protection, and the confirmation of key government personnel. In the House side, two bills are examined, one involving the authorization of funds for continued development of the supersonic transport and the second, a controversial busing measure.

Other major pieces of legislation also emerged from the House of Representatives in the past five years such as on gun control, prayers in public schools, defense allocations, welfare reform, and consumer protection. The particular votes selected for analysis were close votes and ones that are considered crucial pieces of legislation in that their impact influenced or directed subsequent national policies.

House of Representatives. During a particular session of Congress thousands of measures are introduced. Only a fraction even get released from committee hearings where they are voted on the floor. For example, in 1969–1970, in the Ninety-first Congress, over 26,000 measures were introduced and of these nearly 1,000 were enacted.[12] Of those bills that are voted on, the votes may be supported by both Democrats and Republicans, or by both conservative- and liberal-leaning representatives, and by members from all parts of the nation. For example, on most bills related to the defense budget, environmental protection, creation of federal parks, the votes are heavily favored by all representatives. A geographic analysis of such bills would reveal little difference between parties, regions, or rural-urban constituencies.

The importance of the environment as a political, social, and economic issue has seen the introduction of legislation proposed and enacted affecting the daily lives of all Americans. An examination of the many bills introduced would reveal that many passed by lopsided margins, such as the creation of new federal agencies. One bill that aroused the attention of conflicting interest groups was the funding used to support the development of a supersonic transport (SST). Environmentalists, industrialists, and legal experts were concerned with the fate of monies to continue development of this plane. Although funds for SST development had been allocated in previous congresses, the appropriations in the Department of Transportation budget for fiscal year 1971 aroused a great deal of interest. An amendment was introduced in 1971 to delete the appropriations for SST development, an amendment not supported by President Nixon. The vote was close but the amendment was adopted 216–203.[13]

A cartographic analysis of the vote in the House reveals that the urban areas, especially in the Northeast, Midwest, and to a lesser extent in California, voted for the amendment (Fig. 10-3). Representatives from these states were concerned about sonic booms and the subsequent damage to individuals, wildlife, and building construction in these densely populated areas. Conservation groups were likewise at work in these and other states to help defeat this amendment. Support for development of the plane came mainly from those states and sections of states such as Georgia and Washington that depended heavily on the aerospace industry for their economic livelihood.

Civil rights legislation within the last decade was marked by the interest of the courts and legislative bodies as to the rights of all citizens as specified within the United States Constitution. The legislation involving voting, open housing, job equality, and certainly education all have been landmark actions. Probably in no area more than education has the problem of civil rights legislation been so drawn out and laden with controversy, political craftiness, and legislative

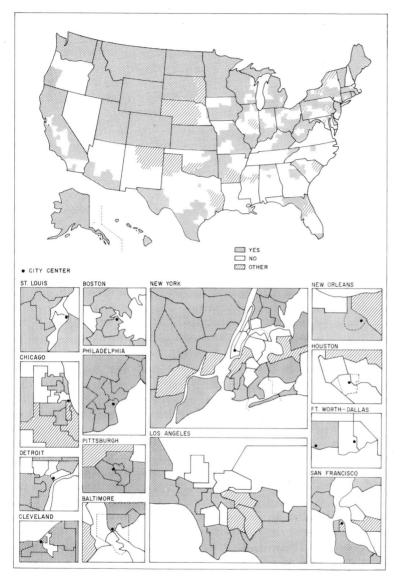

Fig. 10-3 U.S. House Voting: Support for Supersonic Transport, 1971. (Data from © *Congressional Quarterly Service Weekly Report.*)

ineffectiveness. In recent years the question Congress has been asked to face repeatedly is the issue of busing. The busing of students to achieve racial balance or equal educational opportunity has been a source of a great deal of misinterpretation and confusion. With the more conservative mood of the nation in dealing with civil rights matters in recent years, busing has come to be an emotional issue to northern and southern representatives. One of the most recent attempts to deal with this issue was an amendment to the Higher Education Act of 1972. Among the items included in this bill, passed in June 1972, was a provision granting funds for school desegregation and postponing the implementation of court desegregation orders requiring busing. This was adopted by the House by a 218–180 vote.[14] Both Republicans (89–76) and Democrats (129–104) supported this measure, although the northern Democrats supported it more (109–44) than their southern

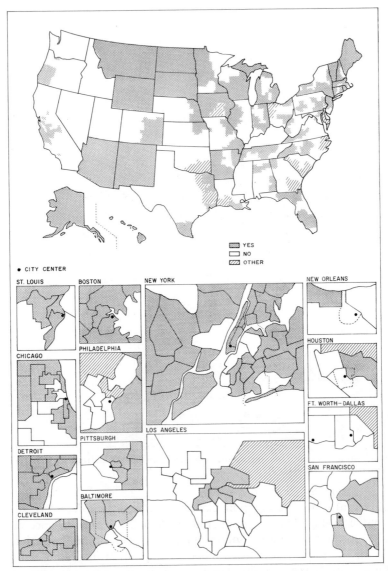

FIG. 10-4 U.S. House Voting: Antibusing Measure, 1972. (Data from © *Congressional Quarterly Service Weekly Report.*)

counterparts (20–60). In terms of the geographic examination of the vote, the South as a region had a uniform pattern opposing the legislation except for support in a few urban centers (Fig. 10-4). Many of the cities and non-urban districts in the Northeast, Midwest, and West with Democratic representatives supported the measure (Fig. 10-5). A number of pro-civil rights legislators stated they did not like the busing provisions but supported the legislation to avoid jeopardizing federal

FIG. 10-5 Composition of the U.S. House of Representatives, 1970–1972. (Data from © *Congressional Quarterly Service Weekly Report.*)

programs. Congressional members of the Black Caucus, namely from the inner city portions of northern metropolitan areas, did not support this legislation as they felt it was a setback for an integrated society.

United States Senate. Soon after Nixon was elected president in 1968 he had the opportunity to nominate a Supreme Court justice to replace the seat made vacant by the resignation of Justice Fortas. During his campaigning Nixon had openly criticized the Supreme Court and particularly the "Warren Court" for not adhering to what he believed was a strict interpretation of the United States Constitution. Thus he promised, if elected, to fill vacancies with "strict constructionists." To many Americans this meant a justice that had particular appeal to southern and conservative voters.

The first nominee Nixon submitted for Senate confirmation in 1969 was District Court Judge Clement Haynesworth of South Carolina. The fact that this candidate was from the South and from South Carolina led many political leaders to assume this selection was part of his "southern strategy" of 1968 and in partial gratitude for the support the southern states gave him. To some politicians, it was believed Nixon had agreed with Senator Strom Thurmond, of the same state, to put forward such a candidate. It was obvious to the media and various congressmen that this was indeed a payoff to Thurmond for his personal help to Nixon in carrying certain southern states in 1968, without which he may not have won the presidency. Judge Haynesworth's record was closely scrutinized by the Senate, especially in regard to his ethical impropriety and participation in cases where financial interests were in apparent conflict of interest. His nomination was opposed by both labor and civil rights leaders.

The final vote on his confirmation was close, 45–55, with the result that he failed to receive the necessary majority vote.[15] A total of 26 Republicans and 19 Democrats voted for him with 17 Republicans and 38 Democrats against. An analysis by party and ideology reveals the vote was more on conservative-liberal lines than strictly party affiliation. Conservative southern Democrats joined conservative and moderate Republicans in support while northern Democrats and liberal Republicans voted against the nomination. On a geographical basis both senators from the Northeast, Midwest, and Northwest states opposed his nomination (Fig. 10-6). His support came solidly and not surprisingly from the southern states. Split votes were noted in key states, especially Texas, Illinois, and California, states that had one conservative and one liberal senator in 1969.

The issue of the level of and categories within the Department of Defense budget is an annual issue in the Senate as well as in the House of Representatives. Introduced are numerous bills calling for increased appropriations for existing programs as well as for new ones to preserve the nation's security. Most military funds in Congress are approved by wide support, party-wise, ideology-wise, and region-wise. In the Nixon administration the 1969 vote on funds for an antiballistic missile system (ABM) was considered one of the most important defense issues to arise in recent years as it enlarged the nation's missile programs and capabilities. An

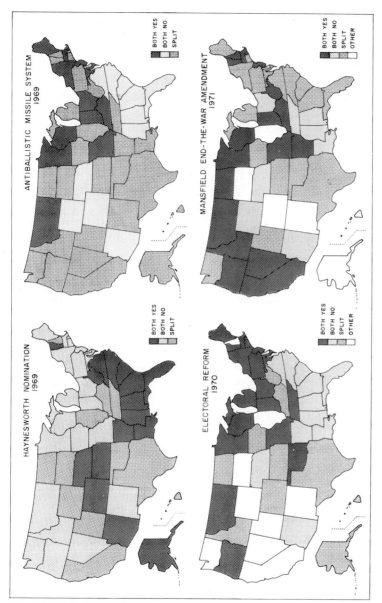

Fig. 10-6 U.S. Senate Voting. (Data from © *Congressional Quarterly Service Weekly Report*.)

amendment to the Military Procurement Authorization Act was proposed to prevent funds from being used on Safeguard (ABM) while allowing development of other antiballistic missile or weapons systems. The major outcry for this ABM was the high cost to the taxpayers plus the genuine utility of such a system in line with the then-current state of United States military preparedness and the international calls for international arms reduction. The Senate vote on the amendment was tied 50–50 but was broken when Vice-President Agnew voted "No," hence it was defeated.[16] Most of the Republicans voted in line with the Nixon administration (14–29) that called for a defeat of this amendment but the Democrats voted in favor of slicing funds (36–21). The northern Senators (31–7) voted differently than their southern counterparts (5–14) (Fig. 10-6). On a state basis, two patterns of the vote emerge. First, the Southeast states favored funds for developing this system, a pattern not unexpected in view of their defense-related economies and presence of members on key Senate committees. Also the South usually favors a hard line taken on most foreign policy and defense issues affecting the nation. Both senators from the several Northeast and Midwest states voted for the cutting of funds; in other states in the same regions one senator voted for and the other against the proposal. A meaningful geographical interpretation for the remainder of the nation poses numerous problems.

The 1968 presidential election, especially with the strong showing of a third party, raised a number of questions about the processes and procedures involved in the election of presidents. Not only was the question of the possible spoiler role for a third-party candidate considered a distinct possibility but the need was expressed for electoral college reform. The Senate took up the issue of reform once Congress convened after the election. Various plans were proposed and introduced that hopefully would receive presidential support as well as that from both parties and varying points on the ideological spectrum. At the root of much of the reform thinking and legislation was an overhaul of the existing system, a system that even though admittedly ineffective, was still strongly supported by senators. The outcome of months of hearings was a motion to invoke cloture (cut-off debate) on a constitutional amendment that would abolish the electoral college and substitute instead a direct popular election of presidents. This measure was rejected by a 54–36 margin (two-thirds necessary to invoke cloture) in September 1970.[17] Thus it failed by six votes even though a majority of Republicans (21–18) and Democrats (33–18) supported it. Northern Democrats supported cutting off debate by a wide (30–2) margin, while southerners (3–16) opposed it. This pattern of strong southern rejection to abolishing the college is revealed in a cartographic representation of the vote (Fig. 10-6). What is noteworthy in this vote is that the senators from the South stand out as a clear homogeneous regional block (Fig. 10-7). Supporting electoral reform, as many expressed it, would alter one of the basic tenets of the Constitution. In these states and this region a preservation of existing political and social tradition is considered important in political matters. Also many of these states are still heavily influenced by rural areas which gives them strength if the election were thrown into the House of Representatives where each state would have one vote. The urban states in the North and Midwest where political competition is keen were those basically in support of electoral reform. The western half of the United States did not exemplify any clear pattern on this particular Senate vote.

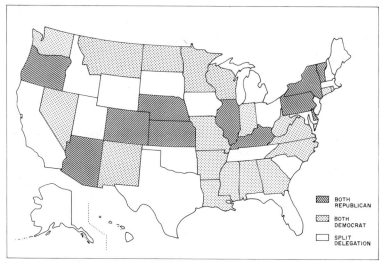

FIG. 10-7 Composition of the U.S. Senate, 1970–1972. (Data from © *Congressional Quarterly Service Weekly Report.*)

The United States Senate in the past few years has attempted to play an important role in the construction of foreign policy. Even though it has been by and large ineffective in its attempt in both the Johnson and Nixon administrations, it has seen fit to hold hearings on issues related to Vietnam, defense appropriations, troop deployment and withdrawals, the Cambodian incursion, and Indochina bombings. The resentment of being left out of some crucial foreign policy decisions has resulted in attempts to pass legislation aiming to restrict the powers of the president on foreign policy matters. Within the past few years a number of amendments were introduced to set a specific deadline for ending the Vietnam War. After numerous attempts to successfully pass such an amendment, one was finally passed in September 1971. Labeled the Mansfield Amendment to End the War, it was tacked onto the Senate defense procurement bill. The measure declared it the policy of the government that a withdrawal of troops from Indochina would be completed within six months after enactment of this defense bill, the withdrawal being dependent only on the release of the United States prisoners of war by North Vietnam and North Vietnam allies.[18] The amendment was adopted 57–38, a negative vote in this case supported President Nixon. The Republicans voted against it (15–27) while the Democrats favored it (42–11). Northern Democrats supported it (33–2) and surprisingly among the southern Democrats it was tied (9–9). The vote in this bill did not have any strong regional patterns as senators, many of whom were conservative as well as moderate in their positions, were growing weary of the long-drawn-out conflict and were hoping to end the United States involvement. Therefore, many who had earlier opposed such an amendment now supported it (Fig. 10-6). The split votes in the South and Plains states reveal different stances than earlier support for such amendments. Still support was concentrated in New England, the Midwest, and far West while opposition was concentrated as expected in several Deep South states, states which consistently have supported strong United States military policies in Indochina and elsewhere (Fig. 10-7).

STATE NONPARTISAN ELECTIONS

Aside from the public officials elected in state elections, many voters are also asked to express on the same election day their views on one, two, or more nonpartisan issues. Frequently referendums are held on issues that failed to win legislative approval hence citizen groups and lobbies hope for particular action by an expression of the electorate. In other cases voting may be done on politically related issues such as creation of state departments or organizations or amending the Constitution. These may be stipulated in the state charters as needing the approval of the electorate. The concern here is the nature of issues placed before the voters that basically have a nonpartisan ring. In the past decade and the recent years in particular residents of a number of states have been asked to express their sentiments on some critical social and economic issues. There are examples where states have placed on the ballot issues of parochial aid to education (Maryland), property tax to finance public education (Oregon), prayer in schools (Florida), abortion (Michigan), environmental cleanup (New York), and coastal development (California). In these and other cases the views of the majority were considered either as the basis for the direction of particular policies and programs or as the framework for subsequent court testing. California, in particular, the state with more propositions on the ballot than any other, has seen the stands taken by the majority of the electorate on issues of capital punishment and open housing not held up by the state supreme court.

To illustrate the expressions of the voters on critical nonpartisan votes, four are selected from as many different states. They are the 1972 vote on daylight saving time in Michigan, the Colorado vote on the proposed 1976 Olympic games, the 1964 vote in California on open housing, and finally the straw vote in the 1972 Florida primary on busing. In each case the areal variation in these votes is examined in the light of the diverse social and economic environments within the states. Depending on the vote in question, the resultant pattern may be related to urban areas or black populated areas or income levels or the political cultures within the states.

Residents of Michigan have voted on a number of rather controversial issues in the past few years. Among them were proposals dealing with aid to parochial schools, abortion reform, and, as just mentioned, daylight saving time. It may appear unusual that the issue of whether the state should go on daylight saving time (DST) would generate much thought and difference of opinion. However, it has as evidenced by a narrow defeat (1490 votes out of 2.8 million cast) in the 1968 general election calling for a change to DST and subsequent defeats in the state legislature. Michigan was one of several states, others being Hawaii, Arizona, and Indiana that have not always gone on DST during summer months in recent years. The fact that Michigan was on a different time than surrounding states created problems for transportation and communications services and for employees commuting to metropolitan areas in adjoining states. Many residents favored the extra daylight hour as it gave them more time for outdoor recreation activities. However, not everyone supported the increased daylight period. Farmers in particular were vocal in opposition. Others thought that the voters had no right to tamper with "God's time."

The November 1972 vote was passed with 55 percent of the electorate favoring the state changing to daylight saving time during the summer months. The turnout was higher than four years earlier. The areal pattern of this vote still revealed differing opinions and showed some interesting variations throughout the state (Fig. 10-8). Only twenty-one of the state's eighty-three counties supported the measure yet these had most of the voters. The major contrasts in voting were between the Upper and Lower peninsulas. The greatest support came from metropolitan southeast Michigan—the Detroit metropolitan area—where the referendum was approved by over 60 percent of the voters. Other urban counties in the southern half of the Lower Peninsula supported the measure. Among them were Saginaw, Grand Rapids, Lansing, Jackson, and Kalamazoo. These urban islands stand out as outliers surrounded by an ocean of rural opposition. The extra daylight hour for recreation and leisure activities probably accounts for much of the support for DST in urban areas. In a state where recreation is a major industry and the outdoor activities popular in summer, the extra hour of daylight had special appeal to residents of big cities. The Upper Peninsula stands out as an area of very low support. In six counties there was less than 20 percent support for the measure. The only county to favor the state going on DST was the easternmost county. This part of Michigan is tied more economically and socially to northern Wisconsin and especially the Green Bay area than it is to Detroit and southern Michigan. The farmers generally opposed the change of time because it would upset their farm schedule; for them the extra hour would be a dark one in the morning and would delay their getting into the fields because of the dew that still might preclude early operations. It was also argued that the time change would upset the timing mechanism for livestock feeding. Extreme southwest Michigan also did not favor the time change. These few counties contain a large number of commuters who daily are employed in the northern Indiana and Chicago area. The times in both Michigan and adjacent Illinois were the same when the former was not on DST and the latter was. However, a change in the Michigan time would result in orienting a day's life to two different timing systems.

The voting pattern on this referendum in the state revealed a peculiarity that is distinctive to Michigan's position in the Eastern time zone. The state being in the extreme western part of the Eastern time zone automatically gives it almost an extra hour of daylight that residents in New England and the extreme Northeast do not enjoy. The farther west one resides in Michigan the more of that extra

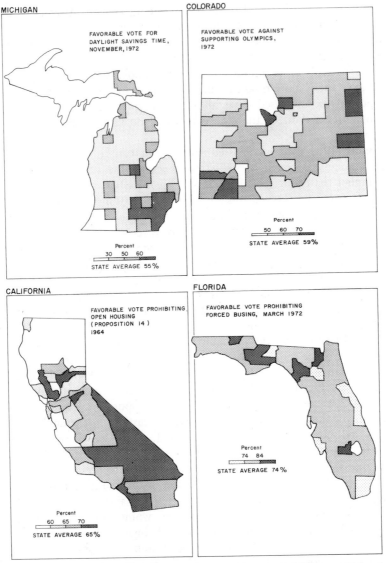

Fig. 10-8 State Nonpartisan Voting Results. (States of Michigan, Colorado, California, and Florida Boards of Elections.)

daylight period he enjoys. A change from standard to daylight time would mean that the residents in the western part of the state who were employed or had the majority of their interaction with an adjoining state in a different time zone, would have a confusing daylight-darkness schedule. The map in part illustrates the change in voting pattern from east to west. Counties in the extreme eastern part supported the measure by over 60 percent while those in the southwest and Upper Peninsula, conscious of their position in the Eastern time zone and their interaction with Illinois or Indiana or Wisconsin, gave less than 30 percent or less than 20 percent in the Upper Peninsula. After this election delegates of the four westernmost Upper Peninsula counties petitioned to the United States Secretary of Transportation to request that these counties be permitted to remain on standard time. This would place them during the summer on the same time as Wisconsin. After deliberations this request was granted.

Voting on environmental issues has been a new ingredient in the referendum scene. States have asked their voters to express their views on financing new projects or creating new agencies to come to grips with some of the problems the citizens and industries are facing. Examples where state referendums on environmental issues have achieved national attention are few but one that stands out is the November 1972 vote by Colorado residents on financing the 1976 Winter Olympic games. The international commission charged with selecting sites for the winter and summer games that year had picked sites near Denver. However, due to the heavy financial costs incurred in organizing and operating these games, the residents of Colorado were asked to support a referendum prohibiting the state from levying taxes and creating loans for the development of the games. As the day of election approached it became clear that the supporters of the wording in the referendum were the conservationists and environmentalists who foresaw irreparable damage being done by developers to the vegetation, wildlife, and scenic areas in the state. On the opposite side were land developers and commercial interests who envisioned the games as a way to aid the state's economy, not only for the immediate future but for long-term international tourism and athletic programs as well. To many citizens in the nation the vote symbolized the willingness of the voters of a scenic state with much natural beauty to favor preservation of the natural environment or to permit land development interests to reign.[19]

When the votes were counted, the referendum passed with 59 percent favoring the proposal. In other words, the majority did not support levying taxes and making loans available to finance the 1976 games. A total of fifty-seven of the state's sixty-three counties voted yes. Even though almost all counties had a majority favoring the wording of the referendum, there was some measurable areal variation of the vote within Colorado (Fig. 10-8). The strongest sentiment against financing the games, that is, these counties with the largest "yes" votes, were the urban counties. In the main their vote was above the state average, Denver having 60 percent; Colorado Springs, 60 percent; Greeley, 63 percent; Pueblo, 69 percent; Boulder, 72 percent; and Durango, 73 percent. The large urban complexes in the Denver vicinity, where the games were scheduled to be located, did not favor financing this international event. In these cities in particular the conservation and environmental groups were among the strongest in the state. They viewed the games as bringing in outside developers that would destroy much of the natural beauty in the immediate area. Furthermore, the games would usher in a host of commercial developments that would draw in thousand of tourists but would leave lasting damages on the cities and communities involved. Opposition leaders to the games also realized that the financial costs were very dear and would not in all likelihood be recovered in the near future. Cities hosting recent Olympic games have attested to the heavy financial outlay required.

The major similarity underlying those counties favoring the Olympic games were those of small and sparse population. These were as a rule distant from the major urban nodes in the state, particularly in the northwest. Quite possibly the residents of these rural counties envisioned the games as one way to help upgrade their economy. Issues of pollution, overpopulation, overcrowding, uncontrolled development, and commercialism that were important to residents of Denver, Boulder, and Colorado Springs are not of paramount interest to many small-town residents or those in rural areas. On the contrary they might welcome the interest of outside developers in their communities and scenic areas in the hopes they would be more than compensated with better paying and permanent employment.

As was mentioned previously, California voters, more than those of any other state, express their views on a variety of social issues by means of referendums. In recent years the electorate has been asked to express its feelings with respect to marijuana, capital punishment, pornography, lettuce boycotts, mass-transit funds, higher education, and environmental protection. Of all the controversial issues voted on by Californians in the past decade, one that was very important at the time (mid-1960s) dealt with open housing. The reason this vote and several others have been considered crucial is that California voters according to some political and social analysts represent a valid cross section and barometer of national public opinion. The reasoning is such that approval of a particular issue by state's voters may eventually lead to its adoption in other states and eventually perhaps even by Congress.

In the early 1960s open housing nationally was considered a hot and touchy political issue. By 1964 Congress approved its first massive civil rights legislation, but open-housing legislation was not approved until four years later. When California residents were asked to express their views in 1964, the referendum supporting open housing was soundly defeated. The state average for the fifty-eight counties was 65 percent favoring the prohibition of open housing. Later the state Supreme Court stated that the regulations prohibiting open housing were unconstitutional. Still, the vast majority of citizens were soundly against granting housing opportunities equally for all groups in society. In only one county, Modoc in the extreme northeast part of the state, was the referendum defeated, that is, the nays outnumbered the yeas. The largest support for this measure was in Mono County (on the Nevada border) and in Orange County (south of Los Angeles) (Fig. 10-8).

Although almost two of every three voters expressed views prohibiting open housing in the state, the voting patterns reveal some geographic variations that basically reflect much of the current cultural differences.[20] In the main the northern half of California voted less than the state average and the southern half greater. Southern and northern California have distinct political differences that have been alluded to in earlier chapters. Counties in southern California, that is, the southern third of the state, voted over 70 percent in favor of the proposition while those in the north, areas near the Oregon and Nevada borders, voted almost

55 percent in favor of prohibiting openness in housing. The north-south differences in the state as evidenced in this vote also exist in the voting for governors and senators in the past decade. The northern part of the state is consistently more liberal and progressive in its voting than conservative southern California. The seven southernmost counties of southern California are almost always at variance with those located north of San Francisco, except for a peculiar conservative pocket at the north end of the Central Valley. Migration streams with contrasting geographical orientation and dissimilar nineteenth-century settlement patterns are carried over into the contemporary views Californians express in voting on social referendums and for candidates as well. The north-south or liberal-conservative measurement is illustrated time and again with reference to the issues and candidates. In a highly predictable fashion the southern part of the state votes consistently on this and other nonpartisan issues more in a conservative direction than the state average and the northern part votes in an opposite pattern. This consistency in voting behavior remains even with the post-1950 migration to all parts of the state. Apparently the migrants from all parts of the United States have basically solidified rather than altered measurably the prevailing political philosophy in these respective political regions.

Of all the civil rights legislation debated and approved in the past decade, education seems to have been the target of the greatest number of attacks. Most other issues involving the rights of minority group members are related to this single issue, be it housing patterns, employment patterns, job training, or the overall quality of urban life. Whereas in early years the focus of education was on dual educational standards and systems, the issue of late has zeroed in on busing. The busing of students to achieve integration or racial balance or improved learning has become an emotional issue that has confounded presidents, congressmen, governors, mayors, and the lives of many individual citizens. At the root of the problem is a desire to achieve a better education system for all groups, realizing that the blacks, Chicanos, and Indians have not enjoyed the same benefits of education as some whites. The question is not simply whether a better education for all is a desired national goal, but rather in what ways can this be accomplished most effectively and peacefully. Proponents and opponents of busing have voiced concern as the best ways to tackle the underlying problems and inequities that result. While racial sentiments are probably the basis of much opposition to cross-district busing, it is apparent that concerns of child safety and neighborhood control can be equally as important.

In the past several years the Congress, state legislatures, and the courts have become involved in the constitutionality of busing. Some citizen groups have been formed ostensibly to lobby or to protest certain decisions, such as the National Action Group (NAG) headquartered in Pontiac, Michigan. The complexities of the issue are made more difficult by the fact that the arguments cannot be placed easily into two separate camps. Public opinion polls have indicated that although nationwide the populace disapproves of busing, they do favor equal education for all Americans.

In March 1972 Florida voters were given an opportunity to voice their sentiments about school busing. This was the first state where the residents were able to express their feelings in a referendum. The vote was held in conjunction with the Florida presidential primary. The presence of Alabama governor George Wallace running in the Democratic primary, who is almost a favorite son in some parts of the state, did much to arouse the electorate's feelings about the busing issue. Even though Floridians knew their vote would probably not be legally binding, the nature of the straw vote was such that it could be considered an indicator of support for this controversial issue in a not-so-southern state. President Nixon also had not clarified his views on busing prior to the election as he seemed interested in awaiting and evaluating the Florida results. Soon thereafter he did issue a statement on the subject that was basically in opposition to busing.

Of the more than 1.5 million votes cast, over 74 percent were in favor of prohibiting forced busing. This is not surprising considering the national sentiments against the forced (usually meant court-ordered) busing of students. While it might be expected that all sections and counties voted alike on this issue, there were some definite geographic variations (Fig. 10-8). At the outset it needs to be mentioned that all counties favored prohibiting forced busing. The weakest support came from Alachua County (home of the University of Florida) with 52 percent; the largest came from Holmes County (near the Alabama border) with a vote of 91 percent. The latter county, a panhandle county, borders on Alabama and is considered definitely a part of "Wallace Country."

The least support for the forced busing came not altogether surprisingly from some of the urban counties. Those counties with colleges or a large number of nonnative Floridians had less than 74 percent support. This list of cities includes Tallahassee, Gainesville, St. Petersburg, Sarasota, Daytona Beach, Miami, and the Cape Kennedy space complex in Brevard County. Other cities were above the state average, such as Pensacola, Tampa, Orlando, and Jacksonville, the last definitely considered a southern city. The most solid support for a measure that would prohibit the forced busing of students came from north Florida, especially in small and sparsely populated counties that are very rural and very poor. These also have the largest concentrations and populations of blacks in the state. In the same Florida counties in 1968 Wallace received his strongest support.

URBAN NONPARTISAN VOTING

Residents of cities vote for mayors, councilmen, judges, sheriffs, and various commissioners. They also vote on a variety of issues that are usually of a nonpartisan nature. Among the more frequent issues that the electorate is asked to express views on are school financing and funding particular projects for the city such as library construction, water and sanitation systems, recreation improvements, and public office buildings. There have also been particular topics of a controversial nature that urban citizens have voted on such as urban renewal, fluoridation of water, open housing, school busing, and the Vietnam War. What makes these nonpartisan votes of interest to the political geographer is the attempt to find sound explanations for the varying expressions of support. Of particular note in such analyses is the realization that areas of the central city or the suburbs are not always associated simply with Republican or Democratic party registration or socio-economic levels. In other words, voting on a particular issue such as ending the Vietnam War or limiting a city's population or funding the construction of a jail or a library is not always explained by the same socioeconomic reasoning that can account for a politician's or party's support.

The lack of geographic research and even social science research on non-partisan voting in urban areas prompts a treatment of the general topic. In addition, the overriding importance of many of these issues to urban development, such as financing schools and environmental cleanup, suggests that the geographical bases of support or lack of it be examined. Four different nonpartisan votes that are somewhat of a critical nature throughout the United States are selected to illustrate the areal variation and the reasons for these differences in four cities. The votes analyzed are the 1966 urban renewal vote in Charlotte, North Carolina, the Youngstown, Ohio school bond votes in 1968 and 1969, the open housing vote in Flint, Michigan in 1968, and the 1972 vote in Boulder, Colorado on restricting building heights. In each case the variation of the vote in each city is examined and related to salient socioeconomic characteristics of those areas in question.

Among the municipal programs instituted in the 1960s was the Model Cities program associated with the Department of Housing and Urban Development. Ostensibly these programs were designed to help cities deal with their housing, transportation, and downtown commercial problems. Federal monies were involved in financing a variety of urban projects. Cities desiring such funds had to request monies for specific programs. The initiative was either taken by city governing boards or in some cases by a referendum. A number of cities throughout the nation placed this issue of urban renewal and urban redevelopment before the electorate. Defeats were not uncommon and often the victories were only by the narrowest of margins. While federal support for urban schemes might be thought to be unanimous, it was often far from this as many voters were reluctant to support federal projects that did not benefit them directly. In addition, urban renewal projects were often tied to either upgrading the housing quality of inner city blacks or making their relocation and mobility possible. Black riots and demonstrations did little to encourage the support of such programs by whites. Finally, there was some objection to these programs as they further illustrated the federal bureaucratic machine. Like many other social welfare projects, they were not popular because by the very nature of the system prevented the root problems from being effectively solved. Support was most often from local businessmen and downtown developers who reviewed such programs as vehicles for stimulating the economy and image of the central city. Also many citizens of varying ideologies and political persuasions supported the notion of Model City neighborhoods and urban renewal in the hope that some of the housing, transportation, and social issues of the city, especially as they affect minority groups, would be corrected and ameliorated by federal revenues and local cooperation.

Charlotte, North Carolina voted on urban renewal development programs in December 1969. This was the second time the voters had approved such a referendum, the first being in 1966. The vote in 1966 was narrowly approved, by 51 percent but the 1969 vote was supported by 64 percent of those voting. The primary urban renewal project in Charlotte focused on an area near the central business district called the Brooklyn district. This was an area of blight that along with several other sections near the downtown was in need of upgrading.

Support for urban renewal programs did not come equally from all parts of the city (Fig. 10-9). In general a northwest-southeast band of support that included the city center was surrounded by a suburban area of nonsupport in the east and west. An examination into the geographic variation in the vote revealed that those census tracts containing a large percent of white working-class population did not support the referendum.[21] By and large these are in the peripheral areas that appear as weakly supporting urban renewal. Their backgrounds plus their possible fears of black invasion may have contributed to their rejection of the idea and specific programs. Black areas supported urban renewal en masse. Of those census tracts that had over 80 percent black population in 1960, their support on this referendum was by 70 percent or more. Blacks voted yes on the referendum regardless of their income, occupation, or housing status. Most blacks are concentrated and reside in the northwest and central parts of Charlotte, almost in harmony with the areas of highest support. A high favorable vote for urban renewal that is immediately contiguous to precincts of very low support suggests the sharply contrasting voting patterns of the blacks and whites. For the city as a whole, there was a positive relationship between a favorable vote and socioeconomic status. In the southern part of Charlotte where the highest status areas are located the referendum carried, often by slightly more than the majority. By contrast, areas of the lower socioeconomic strata in the west and north fringe did not support federal funds or programs being used for downtown urban renewal.

Another very popular concern of urban residents in the past few years has to do with school financing. The issue involves a host of problems related to urban education such as the level of facilities, salaries, construction, class size, and number of holidays. The problem has become so critical in some cities that strikes have been called resulting in extended sessions. In other cases programs themselves have been curtailed and personnel released for lack of funds. Today education problems would rank among the major ones confronting mayors and city councils. Citizens become irate when they see their tax monies increased, salaries for teachers inflated, teachers unionizing, riots and disruption occurring, and the general quality of education not up to their expectations. More often than not cities have seen their school levies and bonds defeated because of a "revolt" by taxpayers. They voice not only the criticisms cited above but also the belief that the basis for financing urban education, namely, a property tax, is unjust and unsatisfactory. Some recent court decisions have been in agreement with this observation.

Youngstown, Ohio attracted national attention in November 1968 when the voters defeated the levying of school bonds for the sixth consecutive time. The education picture became so dismal that schools in the city were closed soon

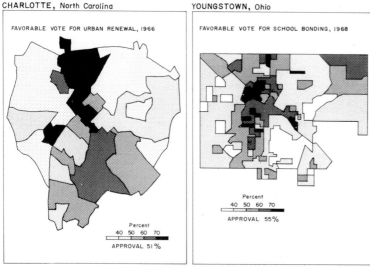

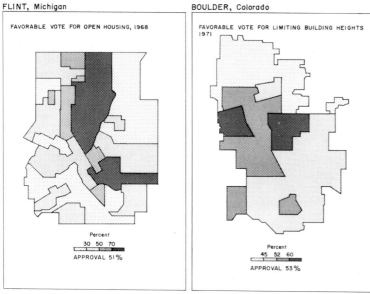

Fig. 10-9 Urban Nonpartisan Voting Results. (Cities of Charlotte, Youngstown, Flint, and Boulder Boards of Elections.)

thereafter until the start of the new calendar year. Cutbacks in programs, unionization, and the waste of funds seem to have contributed to the electorate's negative attitudes. The November 1968 vote was 48.7 percent in favor, the largest support the referendum had enjoyed up to that time. The residents finally succeeded in passing the education funds in a May 1969 referendum.[22]

Most of the support for the requisite school bonds came from the central part of the city, more precisely a north-south band, and from the northeast quarter of Youngstown (Fig. 10-9). The main opposition to the levies was in the wards containing large percents of foreign-born population and in the lower working-class neighborhoods. Often these were the same residents, especially in the west and southeast parts of Youngstown. As political scientists have pointed out, often these groups exhibit little "public regardingness." Their primary loyalties are to their own particular group and there is little support for broadly based public services, of which education is one.[23] It might be expected that middle-class elements in the community as a group would favor the school levies, however, they did not. The only group that favored the passage in sizable numbers was the black population; this group resides north and south of the central business district and in the northeast quarter. Additional support came from some areas of older residents who live near the downtown and from some middle- and high-income groups.

When the referendum finally did pass, it was attributed in large part to the turnout. The positive vote was only slightly higher than in November 1968 but the negative vote was 5000 less. The 55 percent victory was attributed to the negative voters staying home. The opposition for this issue even in the May vote was still found in the foreign-born and working-class wards and precincts. The greater across-the-board support came from the more prosperous residents, the older residents, and the blacks. These combinations plus somewhat stronger support from the middle-income residents of Youngstown resulted in the approval of additional levies. It is not surprising that wealthy families supported the levy as they are able to most afford the additional tax burdens plus they generally exhibit a public regardingness philosophy. Blacks who in general support public service programs likewise often vote in a bloc. It is rather unusual to find that older residents would favor school levies. Maybe those in Youngstown are interested in the image of the city and desire to see a viable community, this in spite of the realization they do not have children in the public schools.

As stated above with respect to California, one of the most controversial pieces of civil rights legislation debated and finally approved in the 1960s dealt with open housing. Blacks had for long been restricted in the buying, renting, and selling of properties by *de facto* or *de jure* housing classes approved by developers or city councils. The issue became paramount in the national eye when other legislation on education and public accommodations had been passed by Congress and found to be constitutional by the United States Supreme Court. The riots and demonstrations in the mid-1960s further focused on the plight of the blacks regarding living space and the quality of urban life. Prior to congressional approval of open-housing legislation in mid-1968, a number of cities in the North placed the issue on the ballot. Flint, Michigan in February of that year became the first city to pass such a referendum.[24]

The victory in Flint was won by the narrowest of margins, 20,170 for to 20,140 against. This vote came after the mayor had resigned from the city council in protest against the city not approving open housing. This vote was surprising considering that approximately 20 percent of the population is black and the city is a strong union town heavily oriented toward automobile manufacturing. A large percent of the working class in Flint is comprised of whites with a southern heritage. It was expected that these combinations would heighten racial tension and lead to a sound defeat of the referendum.

Support came from the blacks and from some middle- and high-income whites. The blacks voted as a bloc as they realized the overriding nature of this issue. Blacks in Flint live in two major clusters. The area north of the central business district is a low-income section called the Buick neighborhood, as it is near the Buick plant. The second area is the Thread Lake or Oakwood-Lapeer Park section in the southern and eastern part of Flint. It is a residential area of middle-income black families. Both areas voted overwhelmingly in favor of open housing. Although statistical correlations were not significant in relating the vote to income or education levels for whites in Flint, some middle- and high-income precincts and wards did approve its passage. Black-white support was apparent in the backing the referendum received from a number of organizations such as the NAACP, Urban League, AFL-CIO, ACLU, League of Women Voters, and two local organizations, Friends of Fair Housing and HOME (Housing Opportunities Made Equal). The greatest opposition came from the low-income white areas of working-class populations, for the most part in places immediately adjacent to the blacks. This is especially true in the northeast and the southern parts of the city. In these same wards and precincts George Wallace running as the American Independent party candidate in 1968 garnered from 25–33 percent of the vote, much more than the 11 percent he received from Flint as a whole.

As in the Youngstown case just described, turnout was also critical here. The narrow victory for open-housing supporters was achieved by a combination of high turnout in some black precincts and wards, up to 60–70 percent, and low support (less than 40 percent in some) in white lower income sections. Thus the combination of blacks turning out in large numbers and voting as a bloc plus the support of some middle- and high-income whites accounted for the very narrow victory.

With the increased attention on environmentally related matters by the federal and state governments, private companies, and citizens themselves, a number of cities have submitted a variety of referendums to the electorate. These have included measures to limit the size (numbers) of the city, to expand the development of parks and recreation lands, to preserve scenic areas, and to finance environmental programs. Votes on such issues are expected to increase in the next few years. Another issue that has surfaced in a number of cities, particularly in the western states, is a limitation on the building heights. One such case is Boulder, Colorado where in November 1972 the referendum limiting the height of new buildings was approved.

Of the more than 21,000 citizens who voted on this measure, 53 percent approved it. Support for the limitations was not unanimous as the variation ran from 39 percent in one northern precinct to 70 percent in a central business district precinct. Boulder is a fairly homogeneous suburb of Denver, mainly with a middle- and high-income and a highly educated citizenry that is politically and socially attuned. Still, however, there were some measurable differences throughout the city on this vote (Fig. 10-9). The central business district and the university-oriented precincts near the center of Boulder not surprisingly endorsed this limitation. It is many of these same sections of the city that are politically liberal and most conscious of environmental issues. The northern part of Boulder gave less support for this environmental referendum. These are mainly areas of mixed residential types, some older homes, large lots, plus trailer court developments. A number of retired persons live in these precincts. Perhaps they do not envision the seriousness of ecological issues as much as those in the university areas or those suburban middle-class areas in southern and southeast Boulder. Fairly homogeneous residential developments may have prompted those residents in the south and southeast to encourage the incorporation of environmental schemes for the city. As a rule the income and education levels for most of Boulder are above the average of Denver proper. The University of Colorado faculty and students plus skilled personnel with various federal government and private companies have contributed to an environmental consciousness that characterizes the city of Boulder and its council. It is worth noting that on the same ballot as this building limitation was a measure calling for ZPG (Zero Population Growth). This was defeated.

VOTER REGISTRATION AND TURNOUT

Aside from the areal voting patterns for political offices and for partisan and non-partisan issues, one other major theme merits consideration in electoral geography. That is the levels of political participation evidenced within cities, states, and the United States. While it comes as no surprise that counties, congressional districts, and states seldom if ever all vote alike on a similar piece of legislation, it should equally not be expected that the levels of political participation would be the same throughout space. Political participation in this context is measured by the turnout (actual number who voted with respect to the possible number who are eligible) and registration (number of eligible voters who are actually and formally registered). Variations in both of these are expected to exist in view of the mobility of many Americans who are ineligible to vote until certain residency requirements have been satisfied as well as the political consciousness of particular political cultures. As was demonstrated in the previous chapter, the moralistic and individualistic philosophies stress public involvement of citizens vs. the traditionalistic culture that leaves politics basically to a select elite. The consciousness of a population that has been limited in its involvement heretofore, as is true for the black and Spanish-surname populations, and the importance gained by voting is not actualized within a short period of time. The realization of strength and power gained at the voting booth is still an intangible political ingredient to many young, middle-aged, and older Americans. Their cynicism regarding political parties being basically alike and similar sentiments about politicians in general lead many not to participate in the voting process. These reasons coupled with the frequent difficulty involved in registration and voting, whether it be the use of computer cards or the time of the year, further contribute to varying levels of participation.

With regards to many democratic nations of the world, the United States turnout in top-level elections is low. Since 1960 the percent of the population casting votes for presidential elections in the United States has declined with each succeeding election: 1960, 63.1 percent; 1964, 61.8 percent; 1968, 60.7 percent; and in 1972, down to 55.6 percent. A partial reason for the lower turnout rates is attributed to the lack of uniform residency requirements (even though partially resolved with the 1972 Supreme Court decision), the mobility of voters, plus a general lack of confidence and resulting apathy in the American political system. To such reasons must also be added the difficulty in registering, whether it be young citizens or poor or overseas Americans. Turnouts in Australia, New Zealand, France, Netherlands, West Germany, and other nations are higher because there is compulsory registration and compulsory voting. In these the turnout ranges from 80 to over 90 percent. The voluntary nature of American politics, whether by registering or voting, is evidenced by the heavier levels of citizen turnout in certain areas than in others. Were some voting practices implemented in the United States, new and different voter alignments may result.[25] What is especially significant to a social scientist analyzing electoral behavior in recent history is that when only six out of every ten or five of every ten eligible voters actually do vote, an interpretation of the vote's meaning is difficult to assess. Clearly when only about half the eligible voters do not engage in this form of political process, the reasons merit investigating as do the varying levels of participation. It would appear that if ample discrepancies in participation exist within a city, state, or nation, reform measures would seem in order with the aim of encouraging a higher turnout and possible enlightened awareness of citizen involvement in the political process.

The two latest presidential elections and the 1970 midterm congressional elections are first examined on a state basis. Following this discussion variations within the Northeast states are investigated on a county level in regards to the 1972 elections. As was stated above the political climate in 1968 was heightened especially with the rise of a third party from the South. The candidacy of Wallace did much to augment the voting rolls not only of new white Wallace voters who had not voted for president in recent elections but of newly enfranchised blacks as well. Even though the national turnout for 1964 and 1968 was similar, fantastic differences occurred in the South. For example, the percent casting votes for presidential elections went from 36 percent to 57 percent in Alabama, from 34 to 53 percent in Mississippi, and from 47 percent to 54 percent in Louisiana. The levels in Arkansas, Georgia, Florida, and Tennessee remained almost the same.[26] Even though the southern states did increase their turnouts, still on a nationwide basis the southeast quarter stands out as having the lowest levels of participation (Fig. 10-10). The highest turnouts are in the sections with the moralistic and individualistic political cultures. Party competitiveness and involvement appear to be evidenced in voting in presidential elections. Traditional single-party dominance in the South and the involvement of political elites in politics plus previous barriers to registration and

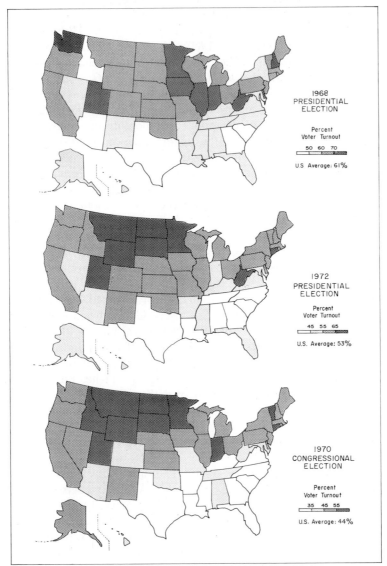

FIG. 10-10 Voter Turnout Levels: 1968, 1970, 1972. (U.S. Department of Commerce, *Statistical Abstract of the United States*, Washington, D.C., 1971; and *1973 World Almanac*.)

voting, such as poll taxes, literacy tests, plus personal intimidation, help account for the lower levels. Prior to black registration drives, often one-third of the population or less voted for presidential elections in Deep South states.

Even though the turnout was lower in 1972 than in 1968, there was a larger number of voters registered nationwide. For the most part the number of registered voters was higher in 1972, mainly because of the lower voting age.[27] As in the case of the number of eligible voters who actually voted (being low in the South and selected western states) these same also had the lowest registration levels. Selected states are listed for 1968 and 1972 in Table 10-3. The highest levels of registration, over 90 percent, are found in certain New England states and those in the northern Plains plus Rocky Mountains. It thus appears that the political involvement on the part of the residents in a particular region is portrayed in their registration as well as in the actual voting process. Where registration is low, turnout tends to be low as in the southern states and where the level of formal registration is high, these same voters turn out in significantly large numbers in presidential and off-year elections.

TABLE 10-3   Registration Levels for Selected
States, 1968 and 1972

State	Percent Registered	
	1968	1972
Alabama	68.7	79.9
Arizona	59.7	76.7
California	58.6	74.8
Florida	81.5	82.3
Idaho	75.4	88.6
Illinois	84.1	85.0
Louisiana	70.9	79.4
Maine	88.8	89.1
Michigan	78.1	84.1
Montana	70.5	87.8
Nevada	63.6	72.6
New Hampshire	85.4	93.1
New York	70.5	74.4
North Carolina	69.2	71.1
Oregon	74.4	86.1
South Dakota	90.0	92.6
Utah	95.3	98.1
Vermont	85.3	95.3
Virginia	62.3	69.0

Source: The number of registered voters by state for both years was obtained from the State Boards of Elections. The number of inhabitants over twenty-one years and over eighteeen years were used to calculate the percent of voting age population registered in 1968 and 1972.

The 1972 presidential election saw only slightly more than half of all eligible voters cast votes. As four years earlier, the South had the lowest turnouts, in some cases lower than in 1968 (Fig. 10-10). The basic pattern of high turnout in moralistic and individualistic states was reflected in 1972. The highest turnouts were in South Dakota (71 percent), North Dakota (70 percent), Montana and Utah (both 69 percent) and Minnesota (67 percent), all states with historical roots emphasizing cooperative government structures and political involvement.[28] The states with a moralistic flavor have slightly lower turnout rates than those where individualism was important in early settlement and continues to be.

The midterm congressional elections in 1970 illustrate an areal pattern similar to both election years (Fig. 10-10). However, the major difference is in the percent casting votes for a member of the United States House of Representatives. Although the national average was 44 percent, again a value lower than 1966 and 1962, the variations from state to state are very marked.[29] Low values existed in Louisiana (18 percent) and Kentucky (22 percent) to the highest in South Dakota (60 percent), Montana (61 percent), and Utah (64 percent). Even in primarily large urban states such as New York, Pennsylvania, Ohio, Michigan, and Illinois, slightly less than half of the population cast votes. Large sparsely populated rural states in general tend to participate at slightly higher levels than densely populated urban-oriented states. Whether this is strictly a reflection of the political culture or the ties of the western states to federal programs, as many are dependent on the national government (a topic treated in the following chapter), sound answers are at times difficult to come by.

Just as there were geographical differences between the states in 1972, there were also contrasts in the registration and turnout of particular groups. While there were an estimated 140 million eligible voters in the election, only 76 million or about 55 percent actually voted. The registration figures were higher, 72 percent.[30] It is estimated that 87 percent of those who did register actually voted. Among whites the percent was higher, 76, than for blacks, 66, nationwide. For white-collar workers the rate was 83 percent compared to only 69 percent for manual workers. College graduates who registered voted at a rate of 81 percent compared to only 49 percent for those with less than four years of education.[31] The 1972 election was significant in several spheres, one that it was the lowest turnout since Truman's victory in 1948 when only 53 percent of eligible voters actually voted. Not only is it noteworthy that nearly half the eligible voters failed to vote in 1972 but nearly 29 million registered voters failed to cast ballots.

In an effort to look more closely at the geographical nature of voter registration and turnout, the 1972 registration levels and presidential vote are discussed by looking into the variations in nine Northeast states (Fig. 10-11). First, the registration level in these states is very high, over 75 percent in most states.[32] Yet there are differences in that process, from registration levels over 90 percent especially in rural northern New England to less than 60 percent in central Pennsylvania. The high levels are characteristic of those sections where local politics (town meetings) are popular and interest and awareness of political events is high. Also there is a

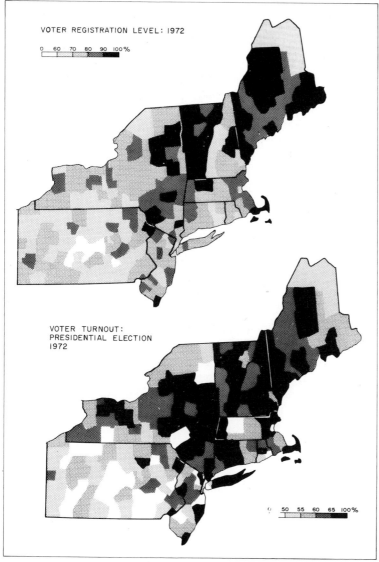

Fig. 10-11 Voter Registration and Turnout Levels in Northeast States. (States of Maine, Vermont, New Hampshire, New York, Massachusetts, Connecticut, Rhode Island, New Jersey, and Pennsylvania Boards of Elections.)

suggestion that small sparsely populated counties especially in the northern part of the Northeast have higher levels of registration. The lowest areas, especially in Pennsylvania, are associated with some of the poorest and most economically distressed counties. In addition, these are losing population. Granted there are other counties with similar environments outside of Pennsylvania but they do not have such low levels of registration. In examining voter registration with reference to urban counties, no clear pattern emerges. Pennsylvania's two largest urban counties, containing Philadelphia and Pittsburgh, have higher registration levels than surrounding areas. This is also true for Buffalo. For the largest urban areas in the Northeast the central cities have lower registration levels than surrounding suburban counties. For example, the difference between central city New York City and Boston vs. the suburbs is 10 to 15 percent.

The interstate and intrastate variations in registration also exist in the percent that turned out to vote for president in 1972 (Fig. 10-11). Basically the turnout map mirrors that of registration except that the ranges are greater. In some Pennsylvania counties slightly more than 40 percent of the eligible population voted compared to over 90 percent for the same in Massachusetts. The reasons suggested for the differences in registration also hold true for the turnout variations. Clearly there are differences in the political participation from New York to Pennsylvania and even within those and neighboring states. Central cities have lower turnouts than do the immediate suburban areas; again possibly income and race as they are related to the political processes are important. Population change is not entirely related to turnout levels as counties in the Northeast with declining or slowly growing population exhibit both low and high turnouts. Even within a small state such as Connecticut or New Jersey there are differences in the turnout levels. While social scientists have tended to emphasize voting results and neglected registration and turnout in their studies, it is hoped that the questions raised by examining these maps will stimulate added research. Political geographers have yet to examine the areal consequences and determinants of voter registration and turnout either within a city or a state or in the nation. The above is only a crude attempt to incite further study.

FOOTNOTES

1. The two best statements on electoral geography are J. R. V. Prescott, "The Function and Methods of Electoral Geography," *Annals, Association of American Geographers*, 49 (1959), 296–304; and Kevin R. Cox, "The Voting Decision in a Spatial Context," in Christopher Board et al., eds., *Progress in Geography, vol. I, International Reviews of Current Research*, London, Edward Arnold, 1969, pp. 81–117.

2. Studies of presidential elections on the national level by geographers are indeed rare. For example, see John K. Wright, "Voting Habits in the United States, A Note on Two Maps," *Geographical Review*, 22 (1932), 666–672; and Robert M. Crisler, "Voting Habits in the United States," *Geographical Review*, 42 (1952), 300–301.

3. Regional voting studies are likewise few. Stephen S. Birdsall, "Preliminary Analysis of the 1968 Wallace Vote in the Southeast," *Southeastern Geographer*, 9:2 (1969), 55–66; and Stanley D. Brunn and Gerald L. Ingalls, "The Emergence of Republicanism in the Urban South," *Southeastern Geographer*, 12:2 (1971), 133–144.

4. Geographical analyses of state voting patterns have been a more common theme for unpublished thesis and dissertation research. Still, however, published efforts are few: Robert M. Crisler, "Republican Areas in Missouri," *Missouri Historical Review*, 42 (1948), 299–310; Kennard W. Rumage, "Some Spatial Characteristics of the Republican-Democratic Presidential Vote in Iowa, 1900–1956," *Iowa Business Digest* (Winter 1960), 17–21; and Ted Klimasewski, "An Analysis of Spatial Voting Behavior: An Approach in Political Socialization," *Journal of Geography*, 72:3 (1972), 26–32.

5. The single geographical reference on congressional voting patterns is Howard R. Smith and John Fraser Hart, "The American Tariff Map," *Geographical Review*, 45 (1955), 327–346.

6. Political geography studies dealing with political party performance in cities include Pierce F. Lewis, "Impact of Negro Migration on the Electoral Geography of Flint, Michigan, 1932–1962," *Annals, Association of American Geographers*, 55 (1965), 1–25; Roger E. Kasperson, "Toward a Geography of Urban Politics: Chicago, A Case Study," *Economic Geography*, 41 (1965), 95–107; Paul S. Salter and Robert C. Mings, "The Projected Impact of Cuban Settlement on Voting Patterns in Metropolitan Miami," *Professional Geographer*, 24 (1972), 123–131; and I. R. McPhail, "The Vote for Mayor of Los Angeles in 1969," *Annals, Association of American Geographers*, 61 (1971), 744–758. Nonpartisan studies by geographers are cited below.

7. Aside from the studies by Wright and Crisler cited above, geographers have ignored national presidential election results. Even two very recent political geography texts, not readers, have only a handful of pages devoted to the topic: Norman J. G. Pounds, *Political Geography*, New York, McGraw-Hill, 1972, pp. 235–239; and Harm J. de Blij, *Systematic Political Geography*, New York, Wiley, 1973, p. 325. The latter does contain Birdsall's article on the Wallace vote of 1968.

8. Political scientists have published numerous articles and books on recent American elections. Probably the best single statements of each election are those published by political scientists at the University of Michigan. Philip E. Converse et al., "Stability and Change in 1960: A Reinstating Election," *American Political Science Review*, 55 (1961), 269–280; "Electoral Myth and Reality, The 1964 Election," *ibid.*, 59 (1965), 321–336; and "Continuity and Change in American Politics: Parties and Issues in the 1968 Election," *ibid.*, 63 (1969), 1083–1105. Two standard books on American elections that are of use to political geographers are A. Campbell et al., *The American Voter*, New York, Wiley, 1960 and V. O. Key, Jr., *The Responsible Electorate: Rationality in Presidential Voting, 1936–1960*, Cambridge, Belknap Press, 1966.

9. "Many Youths Failed To Vote," *Christian Science Monitor*, January 10, 1973, p. 7.

10. Salter and Mings, op. cit.

11. In *Congressional Quarterly Weekly Report* the votes are recorded as follows: record vote for (yea), paired for, announced for, record vote against (nay), paired against, announced against, and the all-inclusive category of not voting, voted "present," and did not announce.

12. "U.S. Congress, Calendar of the U.S. House of Representatives and History of Legislation," *Statistical Abstract of the United States, 1971*, Washington, D.C., U.S. Department of Commerce, 1972, p. 355.

13. "House Deletes SST Funds From Transportation Funds Bill," *Congressional Quarterly Weekly Report*, March 19, 1971, p. 599. The vote is recorded in

"CQ House Votes 12–16," *Congressional Quarterly Weekly Report*, March 26, 1971, pp. 729–730.

14. "House Action Clears Higher Education Anti-Busing Bill," *Congressional Quarterly Weekly Report*, June 10, 1972, p. 1371; and "Higher Education Amendments of 1972," *Congressional Quarterly Weekly Report*, June 17, 1972, pp. 1500–1501.

15. "Senate Rejects Haynesworth Nomination to Court," *Congressional Quarterly Weekly Report*, November 21, 1969, pp. 2310–2311; and "Senate Turns Down Haynesworth Nomination," *Congressional Quarterly Weekly Report*, November 28, 1969, p. 2430.

16. "Nixon Wins Senate ABM Battle by One-Vote Margin," *Congressional Quarterly Weekly Report*, August 8, 1969, pp. 1432–1435; and "Senate 50–50 Tie Vote Signals Administration Breakthrough as It Wins the Safeguard ABM Battle on a Series of Narrow Votes," *Congressional Quarterly Weekly Report*, August 8, 1969, p. 1471.

17. "Senate Refuses to Cut Off Debate on Electoral Reform," *Congressional Quarterly Weekly Report*, September 18, 1970, pp. 2239–2340.

18. "Senate Reaffirms Support for Vietnam Withdrawal," *Congressional Quarterly Weekly Report*, October 2, 1971, pp. 2048–2051; and "CQ Senate Votes, 206–211," *Congressional Quarterly Weekly Report*, October 2, 1971, p. 2059.

19. Monty Hoyt, "Turn Down Olympics! Denver Just Might," *Christian Science Monitor*, November 2, 1972, p. 7.

20. Raymond E. Wolfinger and Fred I. Greenstein, "The Repeal of Fair Housing in California: An Analysis of Referendum Voting," *American Political Science Review*, 62 (1968), 753–769; and Robert M. Pierce, "California's Enduring Political Regionality: Patterns and Processes in Voting Behavior," East Lansing, Michigan, Department of Geography, Michigan State University, MA thesis, 1971, pp. 49–52.

21. Wayne L. Hoffman, "A Comparative Analysis of Two Urban Non-partisan Referendums: A Factor Analysis Solution," Gainesville, Florida, University of Florida, Department of Geography, Ph.D. dissertation, 1970, pp. 66–102.

22. Stanley D. Brunn, Wayne L. Hoffman, and Gerald H. Romsa, "The Defeat of a Youngstown School Levy: A Study in Urban Political Geography," *Southeastern Geographer*, 9:2 (1969), 67–79; and "The Youngstown School Levies: A Geographical Analysis in Voting Behavior," *Urban Education*, 5:1 (1970), 20–52.

23. M. Parenti, "Ethnic Politics and the Persistence of Ethnic Voting," *American Political Science Review*, 61 (1967), 717–726.

24. Stanley D. Brunn and Wayne L. Hoffman, "The Spatial Response of Negroes and Whites Toward Open Housing: The Flint Referendum," *Annals, Association of American Geographers,* 60 (1970), 18–36.

25. Richard L. Strout, "The 'Stunning' Drop in U.S. Voters," *Christian Science Monitor*, April 21, 1973, p. 16.

26. "Percent of Population Casting Votes—States: 1960 to 1970," *Statistical Abstract of the United States, 1972*, Washington, D.C., U.S. Department of Commerce, 1972, p. 375.

27. "Many Young Voters . . . ," op. cit.

28. *Congressional Quarterly Guide to the 1972 Elections*, Washington, D.C., Congressional Quarterly, Inc., 1972, p. 60. This valuable source gives voting and population data as well as information of candidates, issues, and parties.

29. "Percent of Population . . . ," op. cit.

30. "That Low Turnout," *New Republic*, November 25, 1972, p. 9; and "The Party, and the Voter Turnout," *Christian Science Monitor*, November 25, 1972, p. 14.

31. Strout, op. cit.

32. County registration figures for 1972 were derived from the Boards of Elections for respective states. The 1970 Census of Population for these states provided the county populations over eighteen years in 1970.

Chapter 11

GOVERNMENT PROGRAMS

The total influence [of the military establishment and
industrial complex]—economic, political, even spiritual—
is felt in every city, every state house, and every
office of the federal government.

Dwight D. Eisenhower

One of the major responsibilities of any politically organized unit, whether a
township in Maine or the federal government headquartered in Washington, D.C.
is to provide services to the citizens in those spaces. These may be kinds that reach
all the residents such as postal service or perhaps only those reaching a specific
segment of the populations such as dairy farmers or those over sixty-five. Whatever
the case may be, there are distinct programs of the national, state, and local
governments that affect the economic viability and social development of distinct
political units. Not all parts of political space receive identical programs or even the
amounts of support for the same programs. Economically depressed areas of the
nation and the inner city are examples where there have been efforts by the federal
government and state governments to assist with critical problems. Even in these

cases there are variations in the types and programs and levels of financial support that affect distressed areas.

The variations in the kinds of programs and the levels of financial support are found in local, state, and federal government organizations. The particular programs that exist often depend on the political culture's views of government involvement in solving problems and the financial and administrative support available. Local areas' most crucial needs are to provide for the education, recreation, health, and safety of the city's residents. Whether they accomplish these broad services with local and state support is not an issue here, however, the aim of local units of government is to provide a certain level of services to the population within its limits. States also have a responsibility to their citizens to take care of the general welfare of their businessmen, children, farmers, unemployed, prisoners, and mentally ill. In short, their duties are to provide a level of support for all the residents. Even at the federal level, congressional leaders and members of the executive branch realize their responsibility "to promote the general welfare" of all the nation's citizens, regardless of race, creed, color, religion, or national origin. This broad philosophy has been imbued in federal programs involving agricultural extension support to farmers through the Department of Agriculture, loans to businessmen through the Small Business Administration, and broad national programs under Medicare and the Social Security Administration. While many of the programs are concerned with national goals and objectives, such as with highways or education, others relate to particular areas, such as subsidies to cotton farmers or defense contracts to aerospace industries. The varying levels of federal support to state and local governments are best exemplified with the grants-in-aid programs and the revenue sharing schemes, the latter only begun in 1972. Federal programs are also devised to utilize and develop publicly owned lands. Other than monies and programs specified for state and local areas, the United States government also engages in various international programs. Three of the major assistance programs are those under the Foreign Military Sales Act of 1968 whereby foreign nations can purchase military hardware or benefit from various foreign aid programs and the Peace Corps program. In the discussion below various local, state, and federal programs are examined insofar as they reflect areal variations in policies or levels of support.

FEDERAL PROGRAMS

Areal Impact of Decisions. Political decisions about programs affecting the United States are for the most part decided in Washington, D.C. by Congress or the president. Thus the plans and programs affecting the nation's lands, resources, and peoples are made in one locale. Yet the impact of these decisions goes far beyond the metropolitan center on the Potomac River. A program with national ramifications such as increased social security payments affects Alaskans, Alabamans, and Arizonians alike. Civil rights legislation insofar as it dealt with public accommodation, education, employment, voting, and housing was designed to affect the advancement of all minority groups in the nation, even though it was realized at the outset that programs and enactments would not affect all regions alike. Most of the bills and acts passed by Congress were designed to bring the South in concert with the remainder of the nation. For this reason federal programs dealing with educational policies affected Deep and Rim South states more than those in New England or the Midwest. Such regional differences existed until busing became an issue, as this affected northern, southern, and western cities. The same national impact was realized with the policy of open housing.

The impact of economic programs frequently affects a particular region or segment of the economy. This is true, for example, with an increase or a decrease in funds for international wars or for space exploits. When contracts for such projects are authorized by Congress, companies in cities such as Houston, Boston, Orlando, Seattle, Dayton, Philadelphia, and Los Angeles compete. Likewise, when cuts in production are made some cities and areas, such as those above, are affected. Other cities and states are little affected by cuts in the space or military budget. A similar contrast in federal policies can be illustrated by sales of wheat to the USSR in the summer of 1972. Farmers in the Midwest and Plains are interested in the immediate and long-term gains to be made by selling grain to the Soviet Union or possibly even China. Prices go up for such products when there is an anticipated demand as does acreage devoted to those grains. Market fluctuations are likely to affect the economy and livelihood of these agricultural-oriented states rather than industrial centers in the Northeast.

One economic program with wide national ramifications in the past few years has been the wage/price controls exercised on labor unions and businesses. Ostensibly the rationale for these government-watched controls was to stem rising inflation characteristic of recent years. These and other federal pronouncements, however, did not affect the economic livelihood of all locales at the same rate at the same time. While rising construction costs may be tempered by wage/price controls and affect the rapid building in south Florida, it is doubtful that similar programs would affect slower rates of construction in parts of Minnesota or Nebraska. While large eastern cities may be affected by cutbacks in the allocation of energy fuels or by ceilings on steel prices, the effect on the selling price of agricultural commodities in Midwest states is not likely to be related to wage controls or even guidelines imposed on big labor unions. That is, economic policies and programs implemented to affect the nation affect sectors of the economy and regions differently.

Policies of the federal government insofar as they have varying geographic impact are not limited to the nation's economy. They may also be reflected in facets of the nation's foreign policy. As a prime example, the sale of arms to Israel is a frequent request that is granted by both Democratic and Republican administrations. Support for maintaining the power balance in Israel, along with the plight of Soviet Jews, are issues that generate more appeal in New York City and the northeast coast than in the South and Rocky Mountains. Farmers and ranchers in these latter regions are more concerned about trade negotiations with members of the European Economic Community than with defending Israel. The normalization of United States-China relations started and engineered by President Nixon in 1972 probably engendered more support on the West Coast (probably San Francisco in particular) than in the Midwest or New England. The Asian economic and cultural orientation of the Pacific coast states will be enhanced by increased diplomatic and economic gestures to China. Other examples could also be cited where statements by the president or key senators have greater appeal in some cities and regions than others. Support for the Irish Republican Army is probably higher in Boston than in any other city in the United States, and for overthrowing the Castro regime in Cuba Miami would certainly be the locus of such support. Verbal and financial support diminishes rapidly away from these population concentrations of Irish- and Cuban-Americans.

Those residents living in the vicinity of international borders are often affected by changes in policies between the member nations. Farmers in he Southwest, as an example, were opposed to terminating the *bracero* program, under which Mexican-Americans were permitted to work as cheap labor in harvesting fruits and vegetables. When this ready supply of unskilled cheap labor was cut off, it forced many farmers in Texas and California to either employ unemployed Americans (at higher wages) or consider mechanization. In the Southwest today some Mexicans are permitted to cross the international border and work in fields and industries. However, they must be formally authorized to do such. A further development between the governments of Mexico and the United States that has definite areal implications is the use of the Colorado River. Controversies have arisen between California, Arizona, and Mexico over the amounts of water to be used for irrigation and power in both nations. Jealousies as well as justified uses for these international waters for agriculture, industry, power, and homes are behind the discussions and agreements. Along the United States-Canada border, mutual problems affecting the residents involve fishing limits of each nation and the strong economic position of American businesses in cities across the border. With air and water pollution becoming critical international legal issues recently, the states and provinces bordering the Great Lakes have been the focus of attention. Programs and conferences calling for understanding the effects of fishing, shipping, dumping, and air polluting have been undertaken by both governments.

Should the national government become involved in a dispute of major proportions with a neighbor, the effect of ensuing actions leads to definite geographic variations. Probably the best case of such an event in the past decade is the aborted 1961 Bay of Pigs invasion of Cuba and the 1962 Cuba missile crisis. The former suggested the likelihood of a major regional, that is, Caribbean, confrontation while the latter had international ramifications. In both cases the impact of these events was greater on Florida than any other state. What had been a time for healthy real estate developments and continual immigration was suddenly stifled by these events in a foreign neighbor only ninety miles away. In short the state went into an economic recession because of the actions and plans executed at the national level. These military buildups in Florida and surrounding states had little or no impact on the daily lives and economic livelihoods of residents in Washington, West Virginia, Wisconsin, and Wyoming.

National Social Programs. Under various departments and agencies the federal government provides aid to families with dependent children, aid to the permanently and totally disabled, old-age assistance, medical care, unemployment benefits, manpower programs, summer youth employment, surplus food commodities, and food stamp programs. These are only a few of the many available to individuals or groups designed either to satisfy particular personal needs or to institute programs concerned with employment.

The major social services are those connected with the Department of Health, Education, and Welfare. Specifically those concerned with Medicare, old age, survivors and disability insurance—commonly known as Social Security programs—are those reaching from Washington, D.C. to citizens in all states and counties. There are 637 district offices with 211 branches and 98 metropolitan branch offices where information can be obtained about such programs. The Medicare program is a form of health insurance for the aged; at present over 20 million persons are enrolled. Individuals receiving benefits under the varying Social Security programs receive a stipulated amount from the government depending on their age, previous income, marital status, number of dependents, and physical condition. At present the payment levels in the different categories are the same throughout the nation. That is, there is no geographical variation in the monthly payments to the widow at age sixty whether she lives in Maine, Mississippi, Minnesota, or Montana. In this respect social benefits under these Department of Health, Education, and Welfare schemes are standardized. For retired citizens this means that with their payments being the same in all states and cities, many elect to live in warmer climates where living costs and conditions are more desirable than in northern states.

Programs involving Aid to Dependent Children (ADC) and Old-Age Assistance and Aid to the Permanently and Totally Disabled are conducted by the states in cooperation with the Department of Health, Education, and Welfare. Payments to individuals and families are not the same for all counties and states as each establishes its own standards. The variance between states is especially marked in the low ADC payments in the southern states and high levels in New York, California, and other urban-industrial states (Fig. 11-1). Differences within states also exist with the urban counties frequently having higher payments. In part this situation acts as a magnet to potential welfare recipients within states as well as to major metropolitan areas such as New York, Newark, Detroit, and Chicago where the payments are much higher than in Atlanta, Birmingham, Houston, Savannah, and Memphis. These higher costs have created a heavy tax burden on these cities and states. Even though the data in Figure 11-1 are from 1960, the areal variations exist in roughly the same degree today.[1]

Two additional social benefit programs with national scope are associated

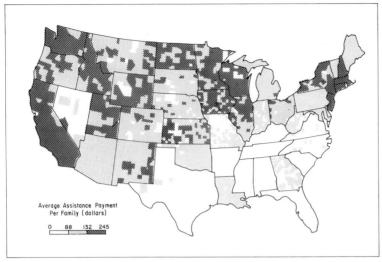

Fɪɢ. 11-1 Aid to Dependent Children, 1960 Support Levels. (U.S. Department of Health, Education, and Welfare, 1963.)

with the Department of Agriculture. These deal with the distribution of surplus food commodities and the newer food stamp programs. Both of these are programs designed to increase the food consumption of low-income families. The older Direct Commodity Distribution program, begun in the 1930s, distributed surplus foods to poor families. One of the major criticisms of this plan was the limited choice of foods available plus the costs incurred in storing the foods and administering the program. The Food Stamp Act of 1964 has been replacing the older program by issuing food stamps to individuals and families based on income and number of dependents. As this program is designed, it enables the individual to purchase what foods he desires, using the existing retail system.[2] The value of the food stamps issued, like the social security payments, is the same throughout the United States. That is, a family of four with an income below $4000 cannot obtain more food stamps in South Carolina than Pennsylvania.

Successful implementation of the food programs is administered by the United States Department of Agriculture in cooperation with state and local officials. Local public officials can institute such programs and will have a great deal to say in determining whether low-income families indeed are to benefit. In more than one county in the rural South the food programs affect only a small number of families. This in spite of a large number of families in the poverty class and the county being designated a hunger county.[3] Local and state efforts are important in the degree to which the food stamp programs are available. In 1968 there were still a large number of counties that did not have either federal food program (Fig. 11-2). These were not restricted only to the poverty areas in the South as large sections of the western half of the United States did not participate. The importance of state boundaries on Fig. 11-2 suggests that possibly state efforts in Virginia,

FIG. 11-2 Counties Without Federal Food Programs, 1968. (Federal Outlays, Fiscal Year 1968.)

Florida, Missouri, Kansas, and Texas discouraged participation in these social programs. Regional political philosophy in some areas does not favor federal government involvement in group welfare programs. Rather the belief of many citizens in the individualistic political culture is such services that benefit low-income groups are not a responsibility of the national government. However, since the late 1960s with the discovery by legislators of severe malnutrition and extreme poverty conditions in many parts of the nation, food programs have been expanded. At present most counties have offices that administer one or the other federal food program. Even though these services may be available in almost all counties and cities, this does not imply the level of participation. Problems still remain in the actual knowledge of such programs, the formal application for participation, the element of personal pride involved, plus local intimidation from some farmers whose tenants would benefit from them. There is more than one place in the nation where politicians and citizens feel that programs upgrading the health of individuals and groups under various social welfare schemes are opposed. Government "handouts" for food and unemployment and aid to dependent children are held in more disfavor than medical care and Social Security benefits. What many critics fail to realize is that they directly benefit from other government programs such as Federal Housing Administration loans or tax breaks for investment or even agricultural subsidies.

Grants-in-Aid to States. Programs of assistance to states have been one of the major responsibilities of the federal government in the past two decades. It has been during this period that agencies and bureaus have been established within the varying departments to funnel monies for specific programs. Federal aid to states is not a totally new innovation as during the Revolutionary War military aid was given to the colonies and during the last century federal funds helped set up schools in the Northwest Territories and colleges by the Morrill Act. Federal-state programs began to take on serious proportions with the various social welfare schemes instituted in the 1930s, especially for public works and highways. By the late 1960s the federal government had become deeply involved in education, urban development, and antipoverty programs.

The increased commitment of the federal government is illustrated by the skyrocketing increase in the budget devoted to various programs. In 1927 the per capita federal aid was $2. This increased to $9 per capita in 1948, $79 in 1968, and $119 in 1970.[4] In absolute amounts the federal aid to state and local governments grew from $2 billion in 1939 to $15 billion in 1965, and from $24 billion in 1970 to $39 billion in 1972.

The sharing of federal revenues is undertaken with varying schemes. Some of the funds the federal government acquires from the states and local governments are returned with "strings" attached. That is, monies are returned for specific programs having rather rigid guidelines that must be followed. These are termed conditional grants and have been the more frequent uses of federal monies. Grants under this broad category may be formula grants (that is, allocated on the basis of formulas involving population, income level, and taxing ability), matching grants (where each level of government contributes a specific amount to a project or program such as highways), or project grants (for specific projects as for demonstration purposes). The second broad category of grants are those labeled "unconditional." These are monies disbursed to states, counties, cities, and townships that can be used for any purposes. The revenue sharing program started in 1972 is designed to share some of the federal monies with these levels of government.[5]

The importance of these federal programs to a political geographer is that the level of assistance varies from state to state whether under the grant programs or with the newly implemented revenue sharing program. Furthermore, these areal patterns can be associated with social and economic characteristics of particular states and regions. In 1970 the aid per capita varied from $535 in Washington, D.C. to only $68 in Indiana. Variation exhibited just as much latitude on a state basis when particular programs are examined.

Prior to an analysis of the geographic variations in the federal aid to states for specific programs, the basic reasons for the granting of such assistance need to be treated. One is to help states themselves to increase expenditures for particular programs, to actually subsidize particular programs of national interest (highways), to help those states that are unable financially to meet state and federal standards, and to encourage groups, public and private, to tackle problems they may have neglected. Federal disaster aid is also granted those individuals and areas that suffer from calamities, flood, drought, hurricane, and snow damage. The federal support also is designed in part to help equalize the state and local tax burdens on services that are needed, as for highways and education.

Behind these government programs are certain federal objectives that apply to all citizens such as education and public assistance. Hence support is granted to help bring to certain national standards those states unable to foot the bills themselves. This usually results in the richest states supporting the poorest states. In reaching the decision of what amount of support to grant to a state or area for a specific program, economic rationale and not political favoritism are major considerations. However, the political factors may be suspected when aid is granted to a key committeeman's home state or section that granted the winning party or president support in presidential and off-year elections.

When discussing federal programs and federal-state relations in the light of granting financial support for specific programs, it is expected that the flows of monies will vary from state to state and region to region. The development and funding of areal problems is not without precedent, especially in regards to the development of the Tennessee Valley Authority schemes in the 1930s. More recently the regional approach to solving problems has been recognized in programs designed to help the states comprising the "farm bloc," Colorado River irrigation, Appalachia, and Great Lakes pollution. The states involved in these various programs have realized that they are unable themselves financially or administratively to identify and solve their problems. Hence the federal government's decision to help them with grants of varying types. Thus it is not surprising that when considering particular programs there is geographical variation in the flow of monies to states and areas. The leading categories of federal aid in fiscal year 1970 were for public assistance, highways, education, antipoverty, food distribution, urban development, and public health.

The average total per capita grants in the United States in 1970 was $119.[6] However, this average had little meaning when the ranges of values are examined. Nine states had payments of less than $90 per capita and five states and the District of Columbia had a per capita figure over $180 (Fig. 11-3). If the general guidelines of federal programs are adhered to, namely, equal treatment for equals, then the rich states with their larger resource bases would be expected to be supporting the poorer states. In part this was true as the map shows. In the main the more prosperous states in the Northeast and Midwest received the smallest amounts of aid, however, Nebraska cannot be considered a rich state. On the other hand, the poorest states, in particular those in the southeast region were not receiving the largest amounts per capita for all programs.[7] By contrast, the largest and highest payments went to some poor states (Alabama and Mississippi) but also to some large sparsely populated western states (including California) that are not among the poorest in the nation. Thus it appears that the pattern of aid was not uniform but that there were regional consistencies.

The largest percent of the budget granting assistance to the states was for various public assistance programs. The national average of $37 per capita again was not a good indication of the various state averages. Seven states received less than $20 per capita (Indiana the lowest with only $10 per capita) to four states that had over $50 (California the highest with $73) (Fig. 11-3). The dollar assistance in such a program is a reflection of the cost of living as well as the cooperative efforts

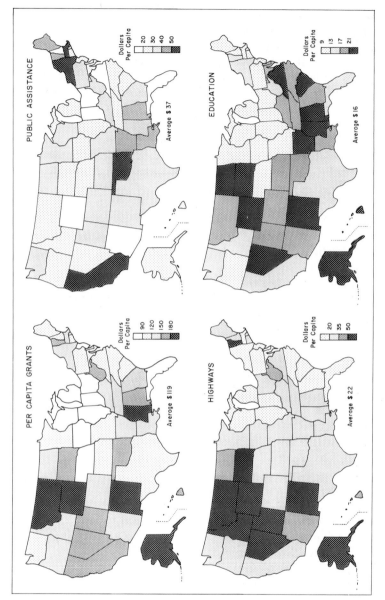

Fɪɢ. 11-3 Federal Grants-in-Aid to States, 1970 Program Levels. (Data from © *Congressional Quarterly Service Weekly Report.*)

of local and state officials to participate in such federal programs. The high welfare systems of New York and California together with higher living costs than in many other states is well known. The large number of low-income persons in such areas as northern New England and the Deep South is acknowledged and the federal government's programs are designed to reach such people. The whys behind the low values in Indiana, Ohio, New Hampshire, Wyoming, Arizona, Virginia and Florida may be attributed to local unwillingness to participate actively in such federal programs. It may be that group-type welfare assistance is not popular. Most of these states do have sizable numbers of low-income blacks, Chicanos, whites, or senior citizens. Most of the remainder of the nation had values closely approximating the national average.

Highways, especially federally funded interstate highways, have been a major part of the national budget since 1956. In this cooperative federal-state venture the federal government contributes 90 percent of the costs. With the joint funding it is expected that states with large areas and smaller populations would have difficulty in meeting their costs. Smaller states with large and dense populations and also with less difficult terrain would likely be the states with the federal highways system already completed. In 1970 the average highway aid was $22 per person, however, this value varied from a high of $133 in Alaska and $111 in Wyoming to $10 each in Florida and North Carolina (Fig. 11-3). The states receiving the lion's share of highway aid were those in the mountainous West, again those states with an insufficient population base to finance these networks. Wealthy and smaller states with large population bases in the Midwest and Northeast had the lowest assistance grants, this to be expected as most highways have been completed.

The federal role in education, elementary through university, has been an arena of greater funding in recent years as well as increased controversy. Involved have been the desegregation of schools, the withholding of federal funds, busing programs, and lessening of support for certain forms of higher education. Ostensibly, it is expected that the states that can afford their own school system would not be as likely to have need for substantial federal assistance. On the other hand, poor states would be expected to be major recipients of such aid. In 1970 the average per capita was $16, this varied in states from a low of $9.69 in Nebraska to over $76 per person in Alaska and Washington, D.C. (Fig. 11-3). The map of federal aid reveals several significant areal patterns, one being the larger amounts to the Southeast states, states that are acknowledged to have the lowest national educational standards. Behind these patterns may be political motives, especially in the South, an area the Nixon administration considered critical to his reelection in 1972. The South in 1970 did not have the distinct pattern of lowest levels as it did in 1965.[8] It may be that the Nixon administration granted more federal aid to southern schools in hopes of receiving support at the polls later or more aid may be granted as local and state officials see little need for continuing to become involved in legal cases involving education. Perhaps there is also widespread belief in the South that education systems will only get improved by continued federal assistance. The second large area with higher than average support represents large sparsely populated and dispersed rural population areas in the Plains and Mountain West in addition to Alaska and Hawaii. The high fixed costs of an education system in such states precludes the states footing the total education bill. The lowest federal support is in the states that not only can most easily afford their own system but in states that have a strong well-developed system at present. This includes the Northeast and Midwest states. The reason why Nebraska receives such a small amount of federal aid may be attributed to strong local or state support or an unwillingness to accept federal monies. States receiving federal monies also must submit to federal guidelines in education as well as in other programs.

Revenue Sharing. A new and innovative federal program was begun in 1972 called General Revenue Sharing.[9] Basically it is a sharing of federal revenues from income tax receipts with state and local governments, revenues that can be used for any program or project. These unconditional allocations of monies are in contrast to those grant programs just treated. The United States Treasury sent out checks to over 60,000 state and local governments in late 1972. These totaled over $5.3 billion. By the end of this five-year program in 1976, the payments are expected to total over $30 billion.

The amount of revenues shared with each state and local government is based on several key social and demographic criteria. When these are considered, geographic variations in the amounts received are the result. For states, the proportion of nation's population in each state is considered as well as the state's tax effort and its per capita income. Additional criteria that can also be considered are the percent of the population residing in urban centers and the proportion of the state revenue coming from state income taxes. Whether a state decides to consider the three or five-factor formula in determining its allocation depends on which will be more beneficial. Within states the revenues are to be divided approximately one-third to the state government and one-third to county and other government units (cities and towns and townships) within each county. By the end of the first year in operation state governments are to receive nearly $1.8 billion and local governments $3.5 billion.

Under the conference agreement reached by the House and Senate, as each branch used different criteria to calculate the amount of revenue sharing funds, the states of New York with over $591 million and California with over $556 million received the most dollars.[10] The next five leading states, all large in population, received between $200 to $275 million each. They were Illinois, Pennsylvania, Texas, Michigan, and Ohio. Twelve states received between $100 to $199 million each. A total of seventeen states received less than $50 million. The smallest amount of revenues in a dollar amount were shared with the state and local governments in Alaska ($6 million), Wyoming (nearly $10 million), Nevada ($11 million), and Vermont, New Hampshire, and Delaware (all approximately $15 million). Both Alaska and Hawaii received an additional stipend from the federal government because of the higher cost of living and their separation from the rest of the nation.

Just as the dollar amounts varied from state to state, so did they with reference to cities. New York City received by far the largest amount of any city, over $247 million. This is more than six other major cities received altogether, Los Angeles ($35 million), Chicago ($69 million), Philadelphia ($43 million), Detroit

($36 million), San Francisco ($19 million) and Washington, D.C. ($23 million).[11] As these figures illustrate the dollar receipts are not always related strictly to population size, however, in general there is a positive relationship between size of the city and the amount of shared revenues. Seventeen cities received over $10 million for the first year and 106 received over $1 million. Small amounts, less than $500,000, were paid to small cities such as Carson City, Nevada ($61,000); Pierre, South Dakota ($66,000); Minnetonka, Minnesota ($154,000); Martinsburg, West Virginia ($154,000); and Laramie, Wyoming ($215,000).

Because of the nature of the revenue sharing program, cities have almost unlimited possibilities for using these funds. Some such as Detroit, in a financial bind, planned to use its nearly $37 million to take care of needed public services such as park repair, sanitation projects, and maintaining regular city library hours. In the West some cities are using these monies to purchase air conditioning systems for courthouses, install sidewalks, and engage in other capital improvements. While large cities are faced with an ever-present perplexing problem of trying to obtain more monies, their dilemma appears to remain even after receiving monies under this new sharing program. Small towns and rural counties, which benefit from this program as well, are often faced with what projects and services are really needed. That is to say, townships and small towns often are hard pressed to devise ways to spend these monies. Rural townships in Illinois basically handle highways and in Michigan they are responsible for police and fire protection. Some townships in central Michigan planned to spend their amounts, which vary from $15,000 to over $60,000, on purchasing new patrol cars or fire equipment, hiring more secretaries or policemen, buying dictating equipment, installing fire alarm systems, renovating the jail facilities, or blacktopping roads. Burlington, Vermont, as another example was to receive almost $1 million which is about a 19 percent addition to its $6 million budget for general city government. The city spends about that amount ($6 million) on its school system but these revenue funds cannot be used for school operations. Instead the city planned to use $160,000 to help start construction on an ice rink and bath house, $225,000 to develop a more modern traffic light system downtown, $44,000 for new voting machines, and $33,000 on new musical instruments and uniforms for the city band.[12]

To illustrate the effects of this revenue sharing scheme on one area, the Southwest region is selected. Using the threefold criteria, the variation in per capita revenues varied markedly within five states: Texas ($22.10), Oklahoma ($23.00), Arizona ($27.30), New Mexico ($30.90) and Louisiana ($33.60). Three were above the national average of $26.10. In absolute amounts Texas received over $247 million while New Mexico obtained slightly over $31 million. Within these states the amounts received by the cities varied in absolute as well as per capita (Table 11-1). The cities received less than the national average for the largest cities in the United States partly because of the threefold formula used. The Northeast states had larger revenues when the fivefold formula was used to calculate allocations. Southwest cities per capita allocations did not even closely approximate the state averages. In Texas, for example, the eight largest cities contain over half the state's

TABLE 11-1   Revenue Sharing Allocations to Major Southwest Cities, 1972

City	1970 Population (in thousands)	Allocation	
		Total	Per Capita
Houston	1233	$15,015,942	$12.18
Dallas	844	11,707,710	13.87
San Antonio	654	8,570,932	13.11
Fort Worth	393	4,600,536	11.71
El Paso	322	5,478,268	17.01
Tucson	263	4,437,180	16.87
Austin	252	2,899,086	11.50
Corpus Christi	205	3,185,662	15.54
Shreveport	182	3,778,106	20.76
Lubbock	149	1,925,472	12.92

Source: Edward E. Veazey, "Revenue Sharing Funds Assigned to Capital Projects in Southwest," *Business Review*, Federal Reserve Bank of Dallas, April, 1973, p. 10.

population but they received, again because of the formula used, slightly over a fifth of the state's allocation and less than a third of local government monies.[13]

Inasmuch as the program does not specify how the monies are to be spent, cities in the Southwest are using them for a variety of purposes. Houston plans to use its $26 million (the first year's allocation) on street and sewer improvements and building a new solid-waste disposal plant. Additional projects are a new court building, a renovation of city hall, and purchase of park and recreation lands. In Dallas the $18 million to be received through mid-1973 is designed to cover operating expenses, capital expenditures (repairs and renovation of public buildings), and pay interest on bonds already sold. Other cities in the Southwest plan to use these federally shared revenues on various special projects.

The program, even though less than a year in operation, has already stirred up controversy. Most particular it is the large cities that feel they are not receiving a fair share of these revenues. In short, they find that funding capital improvements and meeting operating budgets are still dilemmas that remain. The intergovernmental transfer of funds leaves them with less than they desire for education, transportation, health, welfare, safety, and recreation services. Big cities complain when they are in desperate need for more monies and they see small counties and cities dreaming up plans on how to spend their gifts. Since the program ideally has no restrictions, although there are some such as monies cannot be used on federal matching-fund projects, it poses problems when vital services must be planned. The budget directors in the major cities are unsure just how much to plan for these shared revenues as the life of the program may expire in 1976. Planning long-range uses for temporary monies, plus monies that will vary in amount depending on the formula used, can result in financial headaches just as great as before the program started.

Economic Programs. Economic decisions that are made without political considerations and ramifications are becoming rare these days. National guidelines and laws governing interstate commerce, wage scales, investment loans, subsidies, tax breaks, and fair employment practices are becoming just as much a part of companies with international expansion plans as those contemplating moves to a small rural town outside Chicago, Portland, or Atlanta. The importance of political and governmental programs and policies in economic decisions has been significant for several decades, however, each year the ties between the two spheres are becoming closer. Economic geographers by and large in their discussions of decision making have ignored political realities, except for select passing references. By the same token political geographers have tended to bypass this important topic, preferring, it seems, to leave it to the domain of the economic geographer. The importance of this subject is such that an examination of the topic in general is warranted as well as some specific examples of the political and economic ties.

Whether the agricultural or industrial sector is considered, influences of federal government policy have played a key role last century and this in all regions of the nation.[14] Aside from such programs as the grants-in-aid and revenue sharing schemes treated above, specific economic developments are attributed to actions endorsed by the executive or legislative branches. Among the more frequently cited cases are the steel plant developments encouraged in western states before and after World War II. Decentralization away from the industrial heartland in the Northeast was desirable for defense reasons. Also such programs proved wise with the burgeoning population that has occurred in the West and Southwest since 1950. Military and space contracts helped develop the economy of much of this part of the nation. As it also turned out, the dependence on the federal government became substantial. The awarding of military contracts and location of army, navy, and air force bases and institutions helped develop the economy of some cities and portions of states that by themselves generated little vitality. This is probably best exemplified in the South where senators and representatives on key committees often used their positions to funnel monies and projects into their own states or districts. The association of Representative L. Mendel Rivers and Charleston, South Carolina is one of several examples that is often cited.

Programs beefing up the local economies also exist within the agricultural realm. Most especially crop subsidies to major producing areas reached such proportions that dollar limits were finally imposed on the amount an individual producer could receive. The allotment programs whether for cotton, wheat, or tobacco affected the regional economic health of those states producing sizable amounts for national or international consumption.[15] The production of some agricultural items is still tied to certain federal programs, without which the economic health of specific areas would be drastically affected. Sugar is a case in point where the price subsidies granted to beet and cane producers encourage its production. Cane farmers in Florida, Louisiana, and Hawaii are protected from cheaper sugar cane entering the United States. Rice production is a further example of a minor crop nationally but one whose growers have protection by national regulations. In the livestock arena sheep and wool production is governed by certain acts of Congress. American ranchers are protected from foreign mutton and wool entering the national market except under rather specific restrictions.

Not all programs are tied to particular industries or crops. Some aim to handle a variety of economic matters about a region. The most recent and popular example of such a policy has dealt with Appalachia. During the early and mid-1960s the federal government in cooperation with state and local governments from New York to Alabama undertook a series of programs that dealt with this economically depressed area. Federal antipoverty programs were established to provide an economic uplift to the area. Highway construction, job training, recreation development, and investment lures were only a few of the schemes that were designed to upgrade one of the largest and most acute areas of poverty. Numerous were the federal, state, and local reports issued and agencies developed during the 1960s. The outgrowth of this and other regional economic efforts in New England and the Ozarks eventually led to economic policies for the central parts of cities. Housing, education, transportation, recreation, and public health programs were implemented again on a broad basis to provide economic incentives to residents of those cities and interested developers from the outside. Economic and social investments in urban renewal, Model Cities neighborhoods, projects such as Headstart, drug clinics, and vest-pocket parks were all examples of federal monies that were aimed at identifying and solving problems of a miniregion, namely, the central city.

Economic assistance in the form of favorable tax treatment and investment loans also held true for business transactions with possessions of the United States or other nations. The favorable position of American industries in border areas of Mexico and in Canada has been treated in Chapter 7. Similar tax breaks exist for those industrial concerns that have helped develop the Virgin Islands watch industry and the industrial and tourist developments in Puerto Rico. In the case of the Virgin Islands, a group of tropical islands with a poor resource base, special tariff legislation was enacted in 1954 that encouraged the assembly of watch parts. The impact of this industry has been for the United States market to rely more on those watches assembled in the Virgin Islands and less on traditional importers such as Switzerland.[16] In the case of Puerto Rico tax concessions were granted to American businesses desiring to locate on the island. The success of Operation Bootstrap has helped change the island's dependence on tropical agricultural commodities to one where industrial development and tourism are major ingredients in the economy. In tourism especially the Commonwealth Government through its financial programs and advertising promotion was mainly responsible for the rapid growth in investments during the 1950s. Important particularly were tax exemptions granted to large hotel facilities.[17]

In order to specifically illustrate the scale and areal impact of various federally funded projects and programs, three different topics are treated. They are the crop subsidy payments administered by the Department of Agriculture, prime military contracts from the Department of Defense, and space contracts under the aegis of the National Aeronautical and Space Administration. These provide a picture of the levels of federal projects within the nation for particular ingredients of the economy. As is observed from this analysis, some portions of the United States and of certain states are tied heavily to specific programs. On the other hand there are some states and portions of the nation that have benefited little from those programs investigated.

The federal government has been actively involved in the agricultural sector of the nation's economy since the Homestead Act of 1862. Most notably have been the programs implemented in the 1930s and later years that involved production quotas, price supports, soil bank programs, and subsidy levels. Programs involved major crops such as wheat and cotton as well as less important ones such as sugar beets and cane and tobacco.[18] Ostensibly the role of the Department of Agriculture was to maintain supply-demand conditions that were favorable to the nation's farmers. In recent years various programs have come under attack by congressmen especially from urban areas and various citizens groups. The complaints have dealt with the exceedingly large payments to a few selected rich farmers and corporations, the presence of poverty and hunger in rural America, and the spending priorities of Congress.

In particular, the direct payments of subsidies to farmers has become a major issue with the dollar amounts doubling alone from 1964 to 1968 (nearly $3.5 billion). Most of these subsidy payments were to the largest cotton, wheat, and feed grain producers. In 1968 alone a total of 261 producers received $100,000 or more; a year later the number jumped to 353.[19] Only a handful of farmers received the lion's share of the subsidies in 1968: J. G. Boswell Company of Kings County, California ($3.0 million); Giffin, Inc., of Fresno County, California ($2.7 million); and South Lane Farms also of Kings County ($1.1 million). Four other concerns in Kings County, California (Salver Land Company); Fresno County, California (Vista del Llano Farms); Bolivar County, Mississippi (Delta and Pine Land Company); and Maricopa County, Arizona (Farmers Investment Company) all received over $500,000 each in direct payments. These were cotton producers; individual wheat and feed grain farmers generally received less than $150,000.[20]

Not unexpectedly the largest payments in 1968 for crop subsidies went to the areas where production was the highest. This is particularly true for cotton in the Mississippi Delta, Carolina Piedmont, Texas High Plains, Rio Grande Valley, and the Central Valley of California (Fig. 11-4). In Kern and Fresno counties, California over $20 million in crop subsidies were paid to farmers and corporations in each county. On a per dollar subsidy per square mile the leading county was Sunflower County, Mississippi with over $13,000 per square mile. Twelve counties, ten in Mississippi, had subsidy amounts of over $7,500 per square mile. Sunflower County is the home of United States Senator James Eastland, whose plantation

Fig. 11-4 Cotton Direct Payments, 1968 Levels. (Federal Outlays, Fiscal Year, 1968.)

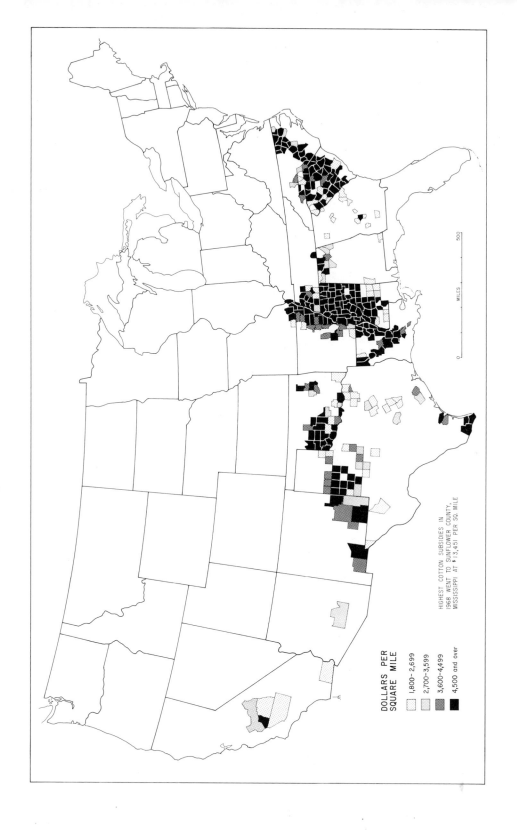

DOLLARS PER
SQUARE MILE

1,800 - 2,699

2,700 - 3,599

3,600 - 4,499

4,500 and over

HIGHEST COTTON SUBSIDIES IN
1968 WENT TO SUNFLOWER COUNTY,
MISSISSIPPI AT $13,451 PER SQ. MILE

MILES

0   500

received over $146,000 in 1968. Although his plantation was given national recognition for the payments he received, it is worth noting that thirteen farmers in Mississippi received larger amounts that year.[21]

More than one analyst of the American economy has remarked about the political relations that affect specific government programs and policies. This situation has been illustrated in the case of congressional committees affecting agricultural policies.[22] One economist in discussing the programs of direct payments has stated that resistance to dollar limitations, now set at $55,000 per crop instead of unlimited sums per individual that existed in 1968, comes from "a rim of states from Hawaii-California–South Carolina which hold key positions on congressional agricultural and appropriations committees."[23] This pattern of committee representation and crop subsidies per district can be examined by measuring the presence of a representative on the House Committee on Agriculture and the direct payments received by farmers in his district (Fig. 11-5). An analysis of this relationship reveals that there indeed was a strong relationship. Of the thirty-four committee members, twenty had districts that received over $4 million in fiscal year 1968.[24] Some districts received payments primarily for one crop such as cotton while for others it was for wheat and feed grains. Four districts, District 1 in Arkansas, District 18 in Texas, District 1 in Mississippi, and District 18 in California received between $30–60 million in payments. All these were primarily cotton areas. The greatest support for wheat payments went to District 1 in Kansas ($96 million) and District 2 in North Dakota ($54 million). The eighteenth district in Texas, the sixth in Iowa, and the first in Kansas received the largest amounts for feed grains, from $20–26 million in each. Congressman Dole of the first district in Kansas in 1968 had the district with the largest amount of crop

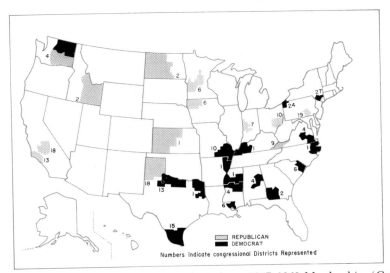

Fig. 11-5 U.S. House Committee on Agriculture, 1967–1968 Membership. (Congressional Index, 90th Congress, 1967–1968.)

support, over $117 million. Congressman Price, who represented Texas's nineteenth district received the second largest amount, over $102 million for cotton, wheat, and feed grain farmers. In total over $600 million was received by congressional districts whose representatives were on the important House agricultural committee. This represents almost one-quarter of the total payments for the three leading crops. Of the ten leading districts receiving subsidies in 1968, five had members on the House committee. Furthermore, twelve of the leading thirty districts had either a Republican or Democrat on this key congressional committee.

That there is a direct relationship between membership on the House Committee on Agriculture and the level of direct payments received illustrates that the cotton, wheat, and feed grain producers are represented and protected by influential representatives. Even on the key Cotton Subcommittee are found representatives from the prosperous cotton lands in Arkansas, Mississippi, Missouri, Texas, and California.[25] This situation is equally true for those members on the Livestock and Feed Grain Subcommittee.

It has been the huge outlays to select farmers and many who live in poor sections of the nation that contributed to changes in the level of support. This sentiment was in part behind the Agricultural Act of 1970 that called for a payment limitation of $55,000 per crop to an individual producer. This passed both houses of Congress in large part with members from the urban districts in the Northeast, Midwest, and California voting on one side and the South, Plains, and Rocky Mountain representatives on the other.

A further issue in the discussions on budget items in the Department of Agriculture was the rural poverty conditions that existed in many of the same areas as those receiving large subsidies, especially for cotton. As was described above, some counties had no federal food programs in 1968 or if they did, the dollar amounts were very low. For example, in 1968 a total of seventy-seven counties in the Mississippi Delta Region received over $235 million in cotton direct payments but only $25 million for the food stamp program or food distribution services. In particular areas of high subsidy levels, acute poverty and hunger conditions existed in the Missisippi Delta and Piedmont areas of the Carolinas.[26] For example, in 1968 Mississippi County, Arkansas, received over $12 million for direct payments for cotton but only $625,000 for food stamp bonus coupons in a county that had 29 percent of the population with incomes below the poverty level in 1969; it was also categorized as a hunger county. In Lynn County, Texas, in the same year over $9 million was received in direct payments but no federal food dollars in a county where 23 percent of the population was below the poverty limit in 1969. Similar situations existed in other counties, not only in the South but Plains, Midwest and West as well.[27]

Military contracts supported by the Department of Defense are one of the major sources of revenue for selected states and counties. The awarding of these contracts either for supplies necessary for standing armed forces or for supplying international military ventures becomes critical when the sums are sizable. It was during the years of the Vietnam War that the defense outlays reached immense proportions. One of the major years of this overseas involvement was 1968; the Defense Department's budget that year reached over $78 billion or almost 43 percent of the total federal budget. Among the items necessary for carrying out this war were food, uniforms, munitions, missiles, airplanes, various land transportation vehicles, plus electronic and radar communication devices. Simply supplying material for defense needs in 1968 totaled $23 billion. Another $7 billion was devoted to research and development contracts.

When appropriations demanded by the national government reach such staggering financial levels, it becomes obvious that there will be intense and competitive bidding among industries producing airplane engines, rifles, uniforms, or radar equipment. Not unexpectedly the contracts also take on geographical ramifications. The result of the awarding of contracts signifies that some states and cities stand to benefit from these programs while others will not. The leading states receiving the largest amounts of prime military contracts that supplied material were some major historically important industrial states in the Northeast and Midwest plus Texas and California (Table 11-2). California alone received over 12 percent of the supply contracts and almost one-third of all research and development contracts.[28] Clearly only a select group of states in the Northeast, Midwest, South, Southwest, and West benefited from defense contracts. The impact be-

TABLE 11-2   Leading States Receiving Prime Military Contracts: Supply and Research and Development, 1968 (in thousands of dollars)

Prime Military Contracts: Supply		Prime Military Contracts: Research and Development	
State	Amount	State	Amount
1. California	$ 3,211,214	1. California	$ 2,155,978
2. Texas	2,915,260	2. Massachusetts	567,624
3. Connecticut	1,981,501	3. New York	484,415
4. New York	1,804,095	4. Texas	428,919
5. Pennsylvania	1,310,098	5. Ohio	399,722
6. Ohio	1,133,769	6. Florida	264,347
7. Missouri	1,069,408	7. Georgia	253,880
8. Indiana	857,512	8. Pennsylvania	238,018
9. Massachusetts	855,766	9. Washington	226,521
10. Illinois	710,341	10. Maryland	188,738
U.S. Total	23,010,943	U.S. Total	6,467,178

Source: *Federal Outlays, Fiscal Year 1968, Compiled for the Office of the President by the Office of Economic Opportunity*, Springfield, Va., Clearing House for Federal Scientific and Technical Information, National Bureau of Standards, 1969 and 1970.

comes increasingly localized when the contract dollar amounts are examined on a county basis. A total of thirty-seven counties received over $100 million in supply contracts in 1968; the largest amounts were for Los Angeles, California ($1,851,-000), Tarrant, Texas ($1,597,000), Hartford, Connecticut ($977,000), St. Louis City ($955,000), and Nassau, New York ($748,000). Four states, California, Texas, New York, and Ohio had four counties each that received over $100 million each and two states, Connecticut and Pennsylvania, had three each. In total only nineteen states had at least one county that received over $100 million.

When the dollar amounts are treated on a per capita basis, a few select metropolitan counties, not all large in population, emerge as the major beneficiaries of these defense-supply contracts (Fig. 11-6). Orange County, Florida ($497), had the largest amount followed by Jackson County, Mississippi ($326); Cobb County, Georgia ($243); Hancock County, Tennessee ($234); and Tarrant County, Texas ($224). Altogether sixteen counties received over $100 per capita in prime military contracts in 1968. Thirty-one more received from $50 to $99 and 176 more over $10 per person. Those counties receiving the largest dollar amounts either on an absolute or per capita basis were often the production nodes for one or two major companies such as Lockheed Aircraft near Atlanta, McDonnell Aircraft in St. Louis, Martin-Marietta Corporation in Orlando, and General Dynamics in Fort Worth.[29]

Another major program that was financed by the federal government was the space program during the 1960s. Placing men on the moon was only one of several projects that the Kennedy, Johnson, and Nixon administrations supported. Others included satellite and rocket projects, telecommunications networks, and various projects involving remote sensing and radar imagery. Prior to the cutbacks in the space program in the late 1960s, a number of states and cities were heavily dependent on these federal contracts. Of the total $3.6 billion budget for contracts underwritten by the National Aeronautical and Space Administration in 1968 almost half went to firms in California, and to those primarily in the southern part of the state.[30] Many of the same companies that produced items for the Department of Defense also received space contracts. Especially is this true for the Los Angeles and San Diego areas. In fact, Los Angeles received over $1.3 million in NASA contracts in 1968, more than three times the second-ranked Nassau County, New York ($398 million); and third-ranked Brevard County, Florida ($312 million). After California the next six leading states receiving space contracts were New York ($441 million), Florida ($298 million), Louisiana ($231 million), Texas ($217 million), Alabama ($186 million), and Maryland ($124 million). Together they did not receive as much monies as California. Contracts were awarded for producing particular equipment items needed in space projects as well as constructing launching pads and equipping monitoring stations.

In this examination of defense and space contracts the prominent position of California is most apparent. For supplying materials needed by the Department of Defense, engaging in research and development projects for the same department, and for producing items needed for the various NASA programs, it received

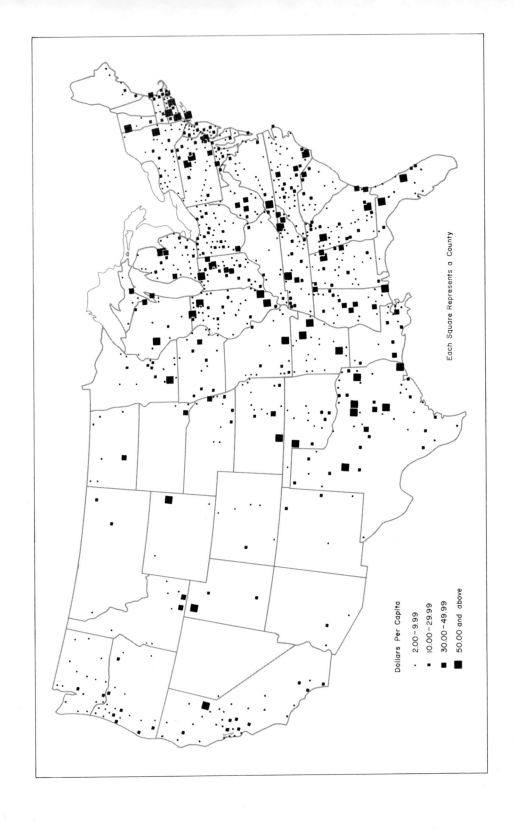

Each Square Represents a County

Dollars Per Capita

.   2.00 – 9.99

▪   10.00 – 29.99

■   30.00 – 49.99

■   50.00 and above

nearly $8 billion, nearly one-quarter of the total received by all states.[31] Quite literally this largest state might be considered a "contract state." The next leading states receiving contracts for these categories had nowhere near the California levels. Texas received slightly over $3.5 billion and New York nearly $2.7 billion. The overdependence of southern California in particular on federal contracts is revealed when congressional discussions involving cutbacks in the Department of Defense and National Aeronautical and Space Administration are echoed in Washington, D.C. When these become a reality, the dependence is felt by higher unemployment rates and subsequently economic recessions. Similar miniregional recessions have occurred in major cities such as Seattle and Orlando in the past five years as well as in many small areas that have had federal outlays cease or be reduced considerably by phasing out military bases or halting construction of particular space projects.

Public Lands. The United States was formed by acquiring lands by conquest, purchase, or exploration during the eighteenth and nineteenth centuries. Once these lands became part of the United States, portions of them were granted to states that were formed and also sold to groups and individuals for settlement and economic uses. Still there remain over 761 million acres, about one-third of all land, that are owned by the federal government. These are used for various forest, recreation, and institutional purposes.

From 1781–1867 the United States acquired nearly two billion acres of land and water for an estimated $85 million. The largest amounts added to the nation's space were the Louisiana Purchase in 1803 with over 523 million acres, the Alaska Purchase in 1867 that included over 365 million acres, and the Mexican Cession purchases in 1848 that totaled over 334 acres of land. Smaller land purchases were the Red River Basin and the Gadsden Purchase in 1853. The most expensive acquisition was the Louisiana Purchase, $23 million, only $8 million more than the Gadsden Purchase, a piece of land in the Southwest, only 3 percent as large, bought from Mexico fifty years later.[32]

During the past 120 years the federal government has disposed of nearly 1.1 billion acres. Of this 328 million acres have been granted to states for a variety of purposes such as supporting common schools, reclaiming swampland, constructing railroads, supporting institutions (universities, hospitals, asylums) and other purposes. Public lands have also been granted or sold to homesteaders (287 million acres), railroads (94 million acres), veterans as military bounties (61 million) and various other objectives such as reclaiming desert lands and planting trees. Probably the most noted of these public land programs are those involving homesteading in the prairies, plains, and mountains in the western half of the United States. The original Homestead Act of 1863 was designed to offer productive agricultural lands at a low cost thereby encouraging the settlement and development of the interior. Initially lands could be purchased for $1.25 an acre after the individual had estab-

Fig. 11-6 Prime Military Supply Contracts, 1968 Levels. (Federal Outlays, Fiscal Year, 1968.)

lished a six-month residence tenure and cultivated part of the lands. In subsequent homesteading acts, larger amounts could be purchased at somewhat higher costs. It has been estimated that over a million families received title to nearly 250 million acres of public domain lands.

The railroads purchased lands and worked to connect the West Coast states with the midsection and the East Coast. Transcontinental railroads such as the Union Pacific, Southern Pacific, and Northern Pacific obtained valuable lands in a checkerboard pattern for a twenty-mile path on either side of the tracks that snaked westward. These purchases by corporations helped develop cities and towns as well as agricultural and mining lands in the vicinity of the actual rail lines. Even today these lands granted to railroads are important in the economic livelihood of several western states.

Of the 761 million plus acres still owned by the federal government, the largest amount, 474 million acres, is under control of the Bureau of Land Management. Forest lands amount to 186 million acres and these like the BLM lands are primarily in western states. Other lands that are owned by the government are associated with various agencies such as the Fish and Wildlife Service, Bureau of Reclamation, Bureau of Indian Affairs, United States Army, and Atomic Energy Commission (Table 11-3).

Federal lands as a percent of state land are highest in the West. The largest amount of such lands is in Alaska where the federal government owns almost 97 percent of all the state.[33] In four other states, the federal government owns over 50 percent: Nevada, 86 percent; Utah, 66 percent; Idaho, 63 percent; and Oregon, 52 percent. Six other states, again all in the western half of the nation, have from one-third to one-half of their lands owned by the federal government (Fig. 11-7). The majority of lands in the West are under the jurisdiction of the Department of the

TABLE 11-3   Major Public Land Areas, 1970

	Millions of Acres
Total Acreage Owned by Federal Government	761,300,913
Department of Interior	540,354,156
Bureau of Land Management	474,138,908
Fish and Wildlife Service	27,970,197
National Park Service	24,412,105
Bureau of Reclamation	8,751,141
Bureau of Indian Affairs	5,033,850
Department of Agriculture	186,917,063
Forest Service	186,500,409
Defense Agencies	23,434,292
Atomic Energy Commission	2,117,220

Source: U.S. Department of the Interior, Bureau of Land Management, *Public Land Statistics, 1971*, Washington, D.C., Government Printing Office, 1971, pp. 11–13.

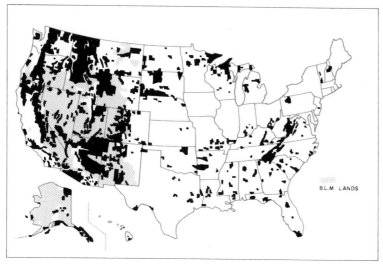

Fig. 11-7 U.S. Public Land. (U.S. Department of the Interior, *National Atlas of the United States*, Geological Survey, Washington, D.C., 1970.)

Interior and the Department of Agriculture. Under the former department are the Bureaus of Land Management, Reclamation, Indian Affairs, Mines, and the Fish and Wildlife Service and the National Parks. The United States Forest Service is presently under the jurisdiction of the Department of Agriculture. The specific lands that are owned and controlled by the federal government are grazing lands, national forests, national parks, Indian reservations, Atomic Energy Commission test sites, and various military installations. The number and amount of land devoted to these and other uses varies from state to state. The major reason for these large holdings in the western half of the nation represents the lands acquired by the federal government under major treaties and cessions. In an effort to maintain proper conservation and utilization of some lands national forest and wildlife refuges were established. In like manner areas of distinct natural and scenic beauty were set aside as part of the National Park system.

In the eastern half of the nation, federal lands are much less represented. Five states have less than 1 percent of their lands owned by the federal government and in fifteen other states this figure is less than 4 percent. Aside from the major acreages devoted to national forests, national parks and monuments and wildlife refuges, there are numerous military bases and federal institutions that occupy miniscule portions of land.

Problems remain in the ownership and utilization of said lands, some of which are carryovers from last century. Conflicts occur particularly in the West where ranchers, timber, and mining companies desire greater use of these public lands. Such lands are leased to individuals and corporations for grazing livestock and select timber cutting and mineral exploration, yet these lands remain in control of the federal government. The dependence of a state's economy can be tied heavily to the uses and restrictions placed on farmers and miners, especially in a state such as Nevada.[34] Problems such as irrigation, grazing allotments, land tenure, procurement of credit, plus the intermingling of public, railroad, private, and Indian lands remain. Similar controversies exist between the government and businessmen and conservationists in regard to the exploitation of essential minerals, the demand for outdoor recreation facilities, the adjudication of Indian lands, and the establishment of military testing sites.

In short the multiple uses, management, and administration of these federal lands are behind the many cases individuals, corporations, and states are making. The controversy involving the construction of the Alaskan pipeline is one further example of the political considerations that are investigated by environmentalists, major petroleum companies, Indians, and the state and federal government. Also the desire by major lumbering concerns to increase timber cutting on federal lands is seen by some observers as one way to help supply the construction industry with needed materials, thereby hoping to lower actual costs. Natural gas companies with their underground explosions in Colorado in 1973 are hoping to test the feasibility of obtaining cheap and large supplies of this energy source. Similar arguments are heard by petroleum companies wanting to drill in offshore areas. Claims by some Indian groups to lands acquired illegally are further testing the actual lands, rivers, and lakes taken last century. Coupled with these pressures on the federal government for new and different uses, management, and ownership of these public lands are minor concessions of said lands to states for parks and recreation developments. Even though the acreages are small, they do illustrate that public lands are still being transferred to states and purchased by individuals.

STATE AND LOCAL PROGRAMS

Revenue Sources. Just as the federal government collects revenues from individuals and businesses to use for operating as well as sharing with states, so do state and local governments. If a particular state or region finds that it is not able to generate a sufficient amount of funds for carrying out particular services and functions, it relies on the federal government to supply monies in the form of grants-in-aid (whether conditional or block grants) or in the form of revenue sharing. The same procedure operates at the state and local government levels where funds are disbursed to lower units in the political hierarchy.

Prior to the intergovernmental transfers in 1969, the total general revenue for all fifty states and the District of Columbia amounted to almost $115 billion. Of this, $19 billion came from the federal, $50 billion from the state, and $46 billion from local governments. The operating levels for states did not all reflect the national pattern of 17 percent federal, 43 percent state and 40 percent local origin. Some states were heavily dependent on the federal government for a large part of their general revenue, such as Alaska, Washington, D.C., and small and sparsely populated states such as Wyoming, Vermont, New Mexico, and West Virginia. In others, namely, Delaware and Hawaii and Louisiana, the state government represents the source of over half the revenue generated. Local levels are important for generating monies in the District of Columbia, Nebraska, and New Jersey. The total general revenue from all three sources is related to the population of the state, with California having over $15 billion and New York over $14 billion. The smallest amounts were for Alaska with $294 million and Wyoming with $279 million.

On a per capita basis the variation between states for the general revenue sources was considerable. The national average for federal government was $95 in 1969 but twenty-eight states had per capita figures above that amount.[35] The highest were those mentioned above that were heavily dependent on the federal government for supplying monies for needed services: Alaska ($393 per capita), District of Columbia ($285), and Wyoming ($261). The lowest were some southern states which have tended historically to veer away from the federal government as a source of financial support, Florida ($66 per capita), South Carolina ($67), North Carolina ($68). Two other states were also low, New Jersey ($62) and Ohio ($70).

Levying taxes was an additional way to generate monies for the state and local governments. For all taxes the national per capita average in 1969 was $380. The heaviest taxing states were New York ($576 per capita) and California ($540). Ten other states, Hawaii, Nevada, Massachusetts, Wisconsin, Michigan, Wyoming, Maryland, Washington, Minnesota, New Jersey, together with the District of Columbia, taxed each person from $400 to $499. Four southern states had the lowest taxes per resident, Mississippi ($242), South Carolina ($225·), Alabama ($224), and Arkansas ($221).

One of the more popular sources of generating revenues was the property tax. In 1969 the average tax per capita was $152. Taxes from this source were highest in California ($249); New Jersey ($227); New York ($221); and, strangely, South Dakota ($204). The lowest were in Alabama ($36), South Carolina ($49), Arkansas ($58), and Louisiana ($60).

Expenditures. Once the states and local governments have collected revenues, they allocate them to a variety of education, public welfare, health, highway, and other programs for the inhabitants. Inasmuch as not every state has the same amount of monies available nor the same status of supplying these services, it is not surprising that the per capita allocations would differ. Regional philosophy about government spending and government responsibility also enter the picture. It is expected that whether the citizens and their elected leaders view the allocation of monies as providing for the better social and economic well-being of the public or only for a limited group, that such thinking would be reflected in the priorities and spending patterns for particular programs. Variations in the amounts allocated on a per capita basis would likewise be expected to vary depending on the amount of total monies collected from the local and state government. Should funds not be large or sufficient, transfer payments from the federal government may aid in supporting some vital services. With meager or sufficient resources, still the budget directors and agency officials need to devise a strategy for funding the various agencies at certain levels.

Four programs are used to illustrate the geographical variations in per capita spending levels within the states and the District of Columbia. They are expenditures for public welfare, highways, education, and the average monthly payment for aid to dependent children (the amount per family). These illustrate that regional variations exist just as in the grants-in-aid programs of the federal government.

Public welfare expenditures vary widely from state to state as is expected considering living cost differentials. Especially are north-south contrasts marked. Nationally the states and local governments spent $60 per capita for various public welfare schemes for their citizens in 1969.[36] The figures ranged from a low of only $20 for Indiana to a high of $141 for Massachusetts (Fig. 11-8). Six states spent less than $30 per capita and eight plus the District of Columbia spent over $60. Besides Massachusetts, New York and California spent over $100 per person for various forms of assistance, both examples of states that attract residents from all parts of the United States. The highest amounts of public welfare aid are not only in states that are the wealthiest and where the living costs are highest as in the Northeast and Midwest but where the prevailing political philosophy is such that group programs for the total citizenry are considered the responsibility of state and local governments. Exceptions of course appear such as Indiana, which is a unique state philosophy-wise in the Midwest. Individualist political culture is still strong. Louisiana and Oklahoma, both with rather large portions of poor people and poverty counties, do spend more than might be expected on welfare programs. Florida with its large number of poor whites and blacks and retired citizens might be expected to have a well-developed system providing public welfare, however, such is not the case as evidenced from the map. The low spending per capita in most southern states is not only attributed to the lower living costs but also to the lack of extensive programs supported by state governments that reach citizens who are in need of such assistance.

For highways, state spending likewise varies geographically with an average of $74 per capita in 1969. Five states averaged over $130 per capita on their road system with the largest amounts (over $200 per capital) in Alaska and Wyoming and the smallest in Georgia and Florida with $52 and $53 respectively. It is difficult to make a great deal of meaning from this pattern (Fig. 11-8). One regional spending pattern that emerges is the low state expenditures for the Southeast states in particular. Their spending may reflect the existing conditions of their roads, some very good state roads and others very poor. It is difficult to discern from this pattern of spending whether the amounts represent the upkeep on existing roads or the planning and construction of new systems. The latter situation probably is the case in the states with large underdeveloped areas, as in Alaska, Wyoming, and Montana. In these states road construction costs would also be expensive and the tax burden per individual resident would be higher. Also in southern states where seasonality is not a major factor in road construction, this would help reduce costs.

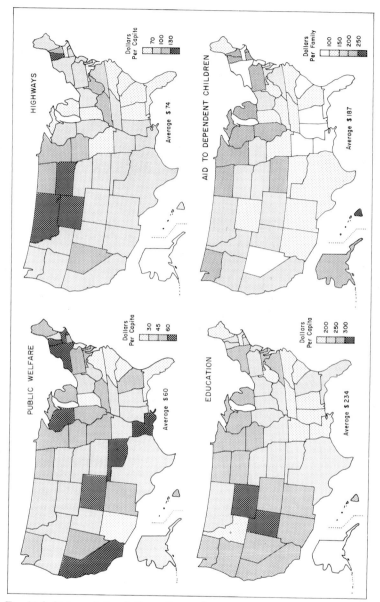

F<small>IG.</small> 11-8 State and Local Expenditures for Public Services, 1969. (U.S. Department of Commerce, *Statistical Abstract of the United States, 1971,* Washington, D.C., 1971.)

As discussed above, regional variations in the quality of education are revealed in varying amounts of federal aid received in states. Likewise, an examination of state and local spending shows major contrasts. The southeast states spent the lowest amount per student in 1969, with the lowest being Arkansas with $157 per capita. Eight of the eleven states that averaged less than $200 per capita were in the Southeast (Fig. 11-8). It was some of these same states that had higher than average federal support. The priority of education in a state's budget is reflected in the wealthy states in the West, Midwest, and Northeast, and those states that have historically stressed public education for all citizens. The largest amounts per capita were found in Alaska and Wyoming where fixed costs for education are high and in Utah, a state whose Mormon influence stresses uniform high quality education. These three spent over $300 per capita. The map does reveal some anomalies, for example, the low per capita spending in Idaho and in Massachusetts, the latter possibly attributed to parochial school support.

One of the most important state programs that is administered by state agencies in cooperation with the federal government is the financial assistance granted to families with dependent children. The ADC payments as they are discussed above (Fig. 11-1) do vary within the United States on a county level because of living costs but also the varying state levels set for such aid. It is recognized that even today states with large segments of their population in the poverty group still do not reach all those who might qualify. Partly this may be attributed to the state's political outlook toward public assistance programs as well as the residency requirements set up and the delivery of social service systems. In 1970 seven states had average monthly payments for ADC per family of less than $100, and six of the seven were in the Southeast (Fig. 11-8). The lowest level was only $46 in Alabama.[37] By contrast the surrounding states spent 50 to 100 percent more on families with dependent children and some which had equally large percents of residents below the poverty level. The highest payments were found in the states with a higher cost of living, a larger resource base, a larger urban population (attracting families especially from the rural South), and a state philosophy that was concerned with providing adequate welfare coverage. Thus it is not surprising that most of the states are above the national monthly payment of $187 per family. The largest payments are in New York, New Jersey, Massachusetts, and Hawaii, all with more than a $250 payment per month. Again peculiarities of state governments, their unwillingness to contribute financially significant sums to such programs, may account for some of the anomalies, such as Indiana, Delaware, and Nevada.

Metropolitan Programs. The importance of government programs takes on an important light when metropolitan areas are considered. It is not only that they are important because of large numbers of inhabitants but because of the financial problems incurred in the delivery of vital services to its residents. In a recent report on the financial structure of the seventy-two most populous metropolitan areas, it stated over half (52 percent) of the nation's population lived in them. They had over 12,800 units of local governments (16 percent of all local governments in the United States) which ranged in number from four in Honolulu to over 1,300 in the Chicago SMSA.[38]

During the 1969–1970 year, almost two-thirds of all the general revenue for these areas was derived from locally imposed taxes, especially from the property tax. The remaining third of the revenue came from state governments. Little (less than 4 percent) came from the federal government. On a per capita basis the amounts of general revenue varied markedly from $795 in the New York SMSA to $198 in the Honolulu SMSA. In general the highest amounts tended to be in New York and California metropolitan areas (over $500 for most) and the lowest in the South and Southwest (from $250–$400 per capita). When the sources of revenue are divided into local vs. state and federal categories, some significant variations appear. Local monies are a major part of metropolitan budgets for cities in Texas, such as Dallas and Houston (78 percent); Honolulu (85 percent); some Ohio cities, Cincinnati (81 percent) and Akron (77 percent); and some in New Jersey, namely, Paterson-Clifton-Passaic (80 percent); and in Massachusetts, Boston (76 percent). By relying mainly on local tax sources they receive little from federal and state sources. More than one city government in the South and Southwest has rejected federal outlays not because it does not need the money but because it means strings are attached. Also prevailing political attitudes are not strongly in favor of federal government intervention in local matters. Needless to say this philosophy is not the same elsewhere in the United States, as intergovernmental revenues (state and federal government) account from 40 to 50 percent of the total revenues in metropolitan areas in New York, California, Delaware, Virginia, and Minnesota.

In terms of expenditures in these seventy-two metropolitan areas, by far the largest outlay went for education. Almost 43 percent of the monies went for construction, equipment, land purchases, and staffing. Other major categories that were funded were public welfare (10 percent), health and hospitals (6 percent), police protection (5 percent), highways (5 percent). In the same way that state and local government spending efforts varied from one state to another so did the per capita amounts for these vital services. A sample of selected cities and their per capita outlays for local schools, public welfare, health and hospitals, police protection, fire protection, and parks and recreation are depicted in Table 11-4. Contrasts exist between the metropolitan areas of major regions, Northeast vs. South, and also somewhat in relation to size. The level of revenues generated, the economy of the metropolitan area, the priorities set on services, the existing structure, and governmental philosophy of providing sound education systems or efficient police administration or a year-round recreation program all play a role in the per capita dollar amounts allocated.

School financing probably more than any other expenditure is a problem facing the budgets of metropolitan areas. At issue is meeting the educational demands for the central city and suburban sections and an equitable basis for collecting revenues for this and related services. Although differences in educational standards and quality within metropolitan areas have long been recognized, it has been only recently that the disparities have been identified and programs initiated to attempt a correction of such geographical differences. That the central city has a

TABLE 11-4   Local Government Expenditures for Services in Selected SMSA's, 1969–1970 (per capita)

SMSA	1970 Population	Local Schools	Public Welfare	Health and Hospitals	Police Protection	Fire Protection	Parks and Recreation
Birmingham, Ala.	739,274	$116.62	$ 3.00	$14.22	$12.16	$ 8.22	$ 5.82
Phoenix, Ariz.	968,487	188.09	.03	16.74	20.78	8.10	9.59
Los Angeles-Long Beach, Calif.	7,032,075	186.85	117.09	34.98	35.27	16.36	17.63
San Jose, Calif.	1,064,714	244.04	67.22	36.40	24.23	13.52	14.68
Denver, Colo.	1,227,529	181.02	35.18	20.41	14.83	10.09	13.58
Jacksonville, Fla.	528,865	142.87	2.75	17.77	15.73	10.00	7.20
Miami, Fla.	1,267,792	176.39	3.37	29.86	23.70	11.14	19.65
Atlanta, Ga.	1,390,164	198.71	5.34	42.07	13.56	10.26	7.28
Chicago, Ill.	6,978,947	171.92	12.50	15.85	32.48	11.46	20.11
Indianapolis, Ind.	1,111,173	170.16	17.66	32.69	13.70	8.20	6.36
Louisville, Ky.	826,553	170.64	5.47	27.02	17.86	8.85	7.61
Boston, Mass.	3,376,286	170.06	12.35	23.82	24.70	23.78	7.47
Flint, Mich.	497,950	248.90	7.71	73.01	16.04	8.02	9.13
Omaha, Nebr.	542,646	167.93	32.88	16.19	14.46	9.77	7.31
Newark, N.J.	1,856,556	199.14	60.85	20.69	31.64	19.90	14.03
New York, N.Y.	11,528,649	227.45	162.96	77.47	52.47	20.52	16.78
Columbus, Ohio	916,228	151.72	15.46	7.22	21.79	11.42	10.12
Dayton, Ohio	850,266	168.10	12.82	7.63	14.90	8.30	8.11
Tulsa, Okla.	475,264	138.76	.62	5.12	11.51	10.38	5.80
Harrisburg, Pa.	410,626	206.15	12.36	.79	7.45	3.00	4.65
Philadelphia, Pa.	4,820,915	187.04	14.99	13.89	24.93	8.52	11.76
Knoxville, Tenn.	400,337	147.09	4.02	8.58	11.75	11.17	12.77
Dallas, Tex.	1,555,950	145.75	1.14	19.00	17.70	11.10	14.91
Houston, Tex.	1,958,031	154.38	1.25	16.78	16.08	11.53	4.51
Salt Lake City, Utah	557,635	184.99	.03	6.31	12.02	6.47	13.28
Richmond, Va.	518,319	185.76	42.42	3.92	16.09	14.05	8.34
Seattle-Everett, Wash.	1,421,869	228.94	.06	24.24	18.91	10.83	23.56
Milwaukee, Wis.	1,403,887	195.02	42.12	40.07	28.91	13.48	22.35

Source: U.S. Department of Commerce, Bureau of the Census, *Local Government Finances in Selected Metropolitan Areas and Large Counties, 1969–1970*, Washington, D.C., 1971.

higher pupil/teacher ratio, inferior classroom settings, higher absenteeism, accompanied by a lower pupil expenditure compared to many suburbs is not surprising. For example, in Los Angeles the pupil/teacher ratio is 27 and the pupil expenditures is $601; these figures for Beverly Hills are 17 and $1192. Similar discrepancies exist between Detroit where the pupil/teacher ratio is 31 and expenditure is $530 compared to high-income Grosse Pointe where the values are 22 and $713. Such differences between the central city and suburb are not restricted to West Coast or Midwest cities as they exist in the Northeast as well. For example, in New York City the pupil/teacher ratio is 20 and the expenditure per pupil is $854 compared to Great Neck's values of 16 and $1391 respectively.[39]

Geographical differences in per pupil expenditures and pupil/teacher ratios are based on areal variations in the property tax collected on a per capita basis. In a recent study of the metropolitan financial structures of the thirty-seven largest SMSAs, twenty of the thirty-four cities that had educational tax data published for the central city and outside the central city had a higher tax rate per capita in the

TABLE 11-5   Education Taxes for Central City and
Outside Central City for Selected
SMSA's, 1966–1967 (per capita)

SMSA	Central City	Outside Central City
Northeast Region		
Boston	55	108
Buffalo	40	55
New York	90	139
Philadelphia	51	85
Midwest Region		
Chicago	65	104
Indianapolis	78	98
Detroit	50	95
Kansas City	86	66
Cincinnati	79	69
Cleveland	81	112
South Region		
Miami	62	62
Atlanta	56	55
New Orleans	39	10
Houston	41	99
West Region		
Los Angeles-Long Beach	100	100
San Francisco-Oakland	85	127
Seattle	85	53

Source: Advisory Commission on Intergovernmental Relations, *State and Local Finances, Significant Features 1967 to 1970*, Washington, D.C., Nov. 1969, pp. 68–69.

latter area.[40] The differences were found in metropolitan areas in all regions of the United States. They existed for large and small metropolitan areas and in some cases the disparities in the taxes collected were considerable (Table 11-5). During this same year, 1966–1967, in which the educational taxes were higher outside the central city, the overall tax rate was higher on a per capita basis in the central cities of thirty-two of these metropolitan areas. The residents of the central city support more than education; they also finance the welfare, police, fire, health, and transportation services for the metropolitan area. Although it is recognized that in many cases the central cities residents outnumber those in the suburbs, still they find it difficult to support often even acceptable levels of these vital urban services. Herein lies one of the dilemmas facing metropolitan government, namely, funding necessary services in an equitable and efficient fashion. More than one central city official has bemoaned the suburbanites using central services daily but contributing little financially to support them.

In education the discrepancies in property tax levels as they are related to geographical variations in quality and standards have become the focus of legal and budgetary attention.[41] Several states, among them California and Michigan, have recognized that the inequities in financing public education lead to some students having better opportunities for education than others. This is based solely on the present property tax method of financing public education. A 1973 United States Supreme Court decision stated that the property tax was an acceptable way to finance education in a state or city. Still, however, a number of legislators and citizen groups are pushing for property tax relief for supporting public education as well as other vital public services. It is expected that moves to continue for financial reform will be heard by metropolitan areas and large-population states.

INTERNATIONAL PROGRAMS

The United States maintains a number of military, economic, and social programs with various regions and nations in the world. These dollars spent in the form of grants or loans or the selling of military hardware exhibit geographical variations. That not all nations receive foreign aid or Peace Corps volunteers or military support comes as no surprise to the citizen or the social scientist. For the political geographer interested in the international relations of the United States the concerns are what amounts of assistance are available to what nations for what specific programs.

In 1970 the total economic and military assistance granted to foreign nations was nearly $2.5 billion.[42] Nearly two-thirds was military aid in the form of hardware, tanks, planes, and weapons. Sales for these items are included under the Foreign Assistance Act and the Foreign Military Sales Act. The increase in weapons sales to other nations has increased markedly in the past few years, so much so that the effect of such actions is called into question. In 1972 the United States sold $3.4 billion in arms and in 1973 the amount was expected to reach $4 billion.[43] The major nations receiving arms in the past have been South Vietnam, South Korea, Taiwan, and Turkey, all nations that the United States considered valuable allies. Recently the United States has turned to selling instead of giving them to some South American nations and Israel. In mid-1973 negotiations for sales were underway with several Mideast nations, especially Iran, Kuwait, and Saudi Arabia.

Besides the economic assistance programs described below, the United States financially supports international agencies and contributes to development loans. In 1969 the total investment to international development agencies such as the International Bank for Reconstruction and Development and the Inter-American Development Bank totaled $184 million. Development loans to Near East and South Asia, Latin America, East Asia, and Africa totaled $682 million. The major regions receiving these monies were Near East and South Asia and Latin America, each with approximately $280 million. To show the changing commitment of President Nixon to Latin America, the loans amounted to $468 million in 1966.

Foreign Economic Assistance. Foreign aid in the form of economic assistance in 1970 amounted to almost $1.7 billion for both loans and grants.[44] Most of this, over $818 million, went to Asian countries, especially in support of the Vietnam War. Almost 20 percent of all the economic assistance dollars went to South Vietnam ($308 million) and over one-third (nearly $585 million) went to South Vietnam, India, and Pakistan. Both Latin America and Africa received far less than Asian countries, in fact more went to India than to all of Africa.

That most economic assistance is granted to a small number and select group of nations is not surprising. Frequently the dollars granted to help finance transportation routes and facilities, agricultural projects, and construction of dams or institutions are to the same nations that are friendly either to United States or Western geopolitical interests. Of the thirty-nine nations that received aid in 1970, the largest share of the assistance went to two or three major nations in each of the developing continental regions (Fig. 11-9).

In Asia, aside from South Vietnam, both India and Pakistan are the chief beneficiaries. It has long been a policy of the United States government to maintain friendly political and military relations with the Indian subcontinent. Even though the relations were strained during the Pakistani War in late 1971, the United States was concerned about supporting both the developing economies of Pakistan and newly formed Bangladesh. This in part was to prevent outside, especially Soviet influence, from acquiring a greater toehold in the subcontinent. Three other Asian nations that have traditionally had a significant role in the United States foreign policy also received sizable amounts of foreign aid; they are Korea, Turkey, and Thailand. Since World War II, Taiwan has received over $2 billion in grants and credits, however, it presently is not dependent on foreign aid. It is apparent in an investigation of economic assistance programs to Asia that peripheral and key geostrategic nations are the chief beneficiaries of various programs. This partly is a reflection of United States foreign policy interests in Asia, that is, of

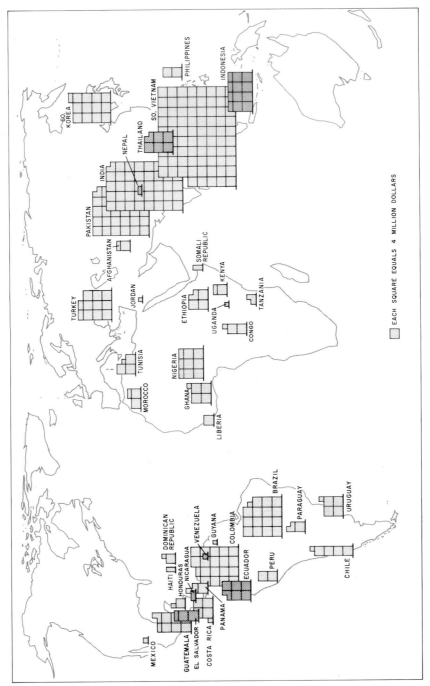

FIG. 11-9 Foreign Economic Assistance, 1970. (U.S. Department of Commerce, *Statistical Abstract of the United States, 1971*, Washington, D.C., 1971.)

a policy of containment. This in the most elementary terms meant investing in and supporting governments and economies in select key nations.

Economic programs to Latin America became a popular theme of President Kennedy's Alliance for Progress that was operational in the early 1960s. In the main this program was designed to demonstrate a hemispheric commitment by the United States to help solve key social and economic problems. Internal political changes both within the United States and in Latin America itself changed the political scene by the late 1960s. Most noted were the frequent changes of government that brought military coups or regimes to power. Also the nationalistic stances taken by these leaders more than once resulted in nationalizing United States interests or jeopardizing United States investments. For these and other reasons, such as the alliance of some nations with Cuba, interest by the Nixon administration cooled toward the region. This is observed in the amount of economic assistance to Latin America, which was nearly $378 million in 1970. As in Asia, over one-third the aid went to two nations, Colombia ($74 million) and Brazil ($61 million). Both, especially the latter, are recognized as major economic powers on the continent. It is worth noting that Argentina did not receive a million dollars in assistance in 1970 and Chile received only $17 million. The military leadership in Argentina and election of a Marxist in Chile may have led to the commitments for that year. Other than these two economic grants (even though small in comparison to Brazil) Venezuela and Mexico received little economic assistance. Although it may be expected that the level of economic assistance is related to the level of economic development, this is not always the case. Brazil and Mexico are both examples of nations with large and relatively prosperous economies yet the former received substantially more assistance from the United States government in 1970. Brazil had long been recognized as the megapower in Latin America and to maintain friendly military and political relations with this nation the United States helps invest in various economic programs. Both Chile and Peru are nations with sizable resource bases, yet because of their Marxist leanings (prior to the overthrow of Allende in 1973), overtures to Cuba, and nationalization of United States interests, were instrumental in little economic aid being granted in the early 1970s. The sentiment of representatives and senators is often expressed that the United States has no business in helping these nations develop if they are going to treat the United States unfairly. Such expressions illustrate the close ties of the United States foreign military and economic policy in Western Hemisphere relations.

Assistance to Africa demonstrates some key geographical and political considerations. Only eleven nations received over one million dollars of economic assistance in 1970 and over one-third went to Nigeria. As Fig. 11-9 shows, five nations stand out as getting the lion's share. Besides Nigeria they are Ghana, Ethiopia, Tunisia, and Morocco. The pattern reveals the support for major economic producers on the continent, both presently and in the future. This is especially true for Nigeria and Ghana both which have promising economic potential. The other nations that reap the benefits of the United States foreign economic aid are those that have long been friendly to the United States and have table governments. This it true for Ethiopia, Morocco, and even Tunisia. Even though the military interventions in Africa by the major world powers have been limited in the past decade, the United States usually counts on some of these nations as being its military allies. This is in addition to the friendly relations with the Republic of South Africa. Two further patterns emerge when treating the economic assistance to Africa in 1970. One is the void for Arab nations in North Africa. Outside of Tunisia and Morocco, both not in the same ideological camp as Libya and the United Arab Republic, aid was not granted nor requested. This is ostensibly because of the United States support for Israel. The second pattern is the almost complete absence of aid to some of the poorest nations in Africa. In 1970 outside of the Congo (Kinshasa, now Zaire), Liberia (long-established ties to the United States), and East African nations, almost no assistance was available. In part this can be attributed to the small populations of these ministates, but also because their importance to United States foreign and domestic policy is not great. Since many are former British and French colonies, perhaps the view is that these mother nations should support their economic development. Also the distance from the United States to Africa probably also plays a role in the decisions rendered about amounts and kinds of assistance. With increased congressional criticism of foreign assistance programs, it may be viewed a better investment to support backyard nations, namely, those in Latin America rather than those in Africa. This rationale was not applied in the case of Southeast Asia where invest-ment there was designed to thwart China and communism from reaching other parts of Asia.

In large part the United States position in the developing world acquired different roles in treating the three continental blocs. While in Asia the foreign economic and military policies were to contain the USSR and China and thereby thwart communism, in Latin America it became vital to protect United States interests in the Western Hemisphere. Africa was considered in a military light as a neutral continent with United States support to select nations designed to offset Soviet investments. The views that presidents and congressmen have about a particular continent or region or even individual nations will depend on its political, military, and economic importance to total United States foreign policy.

Peace Corps. Besides the granting of foreign aid to developing nations, the Peace Corps program is an additional expression of the nation's commitment to the less-developed areas and nations of the world. Before an individual nation receives Peace Corps volunteers the host nation must request persons for specific purposes. Over 8000 individuals were serving in the Peace Corps as of late 1971.[45] Not all nations ask for or are supplied with these volunteers and trainees. Those who do participate are involved in a host of tasks ranging from teaching in schools, organiz-ing agricultural cooperatives, planning towns and settlement schemes, or working in hospitals as interns or nutrition experts. The services of the Peace Corps members are in high demand and represent a different interest and investment than foreign aid programs. More often than not foreign aid schemes have definite political or military ramifications. Peace Corps programs are basically nonpolitical and nonmili-

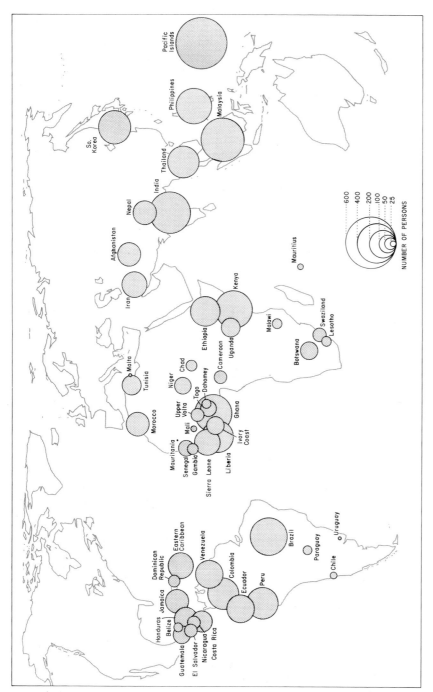

Fig. 11-10 Destinations of Peace Corps Trainees and Volunteers, 1971. (Office of Staff Placement, Peace Corps, 1971.)

tary and are viewed as investments by the United States in helping the host nations identify and solve some of their basic economic and social problems.

Whereas the foreign aid in recent years has only gone to a rather select number of nations and those primarily in South and Southeast Asia and less in Latin America, the United States has supplied Peace Corps volunteers and trainees to more nations. As of September 1971 there were one or more volunteers in fifty-five nations. By far the largest number at that time were in South and Southeast Asia and the Pacific. Malaysia and India alone had over 400 at that time and the Philippines, Micronesia, and Korea had over 300 each. Africa was represented with almost 2500 volunteers and trainees. Most of these were in selected East and West Africa nations (Fig. 11-10). Even many of the ministates and some of the poorest in the continent had Peace Corps personnel helping with various agricultural, urban, health, and education problems. The United States interest and commitment to the Latin American region, attested to in part by foreign aid programs, is also illustrated in the Peace Corps investment. Whereas the foreign aid was mainly to continental Latin American nations, the Peace Corps program affected the Central American nations and selected islands in the Caribbean. Almost one-third of all volunteers in late 1971 were in Brazil, Peru, and Colombia. There were almost 500 in the five Central American nations and over 400 in the Caribbean.

In comparing the maps depicting United States foreign aid and the Peace Corps volunteers, the contrasts in these two international investment programs become apparent. While military and strategic reasons seem to underlie the heavy foreign aid expenditures in South and Southeast Asia, a different set of policies appears to be involved in the Peace Corps efforts. The same nations that receive the most foreign aid are not those receiving the largest number of volunteers and trainees. In no region is this more apparent than in Africa, a continent that most major world powers have steered clear of major military involvements in recent years. Latin America, possibly because of its proximity to the United States and being a Western Hemisphere neighbor, definitely has an important place in the foreign relations of the United States. Foreign aid seems destined for a select group of nations, primarily large and potentially powerful ones, while Peace Corps volunteers and trainees are present in numerous small nations as well. The varying political perceptions of the United States as revealed in these financial and personnel commitments to other nations is partly tied to the views of presidents and congressmen who recommend and implement international policies. Political issues may be paramount in most cases but the social and economic considerations are likewise related to these development endeavors.

FOOTNOTES

1. County levels of assistance for Old Age Assistance, Aid to Families with Dependent Children, and Aid to the Permanently and Totally Disabled are given in tabular and map form in U.S. Department of Health, Education, and Welfare, *Public Assistance in the Counties of the United States, June 1960*, Washington, D.C.,

Welfare Administration, Bureau of Family Services, Division of Program Statistics and Analysis, November 1963.

2. Two good statements on the food stamp and food distribution programs are W. F. Upshaw, "The Food Stamp Program," *Monthly Review*, Federal Reserve Bank of Richmond, November 1968, pp. 8–9; and R. Johnston, "Food Stamps and the Banks," *Monthly Review*, Federal Reserve Bank of San Francisco, October 1970, pp. 191–195.

3. The initial report on recent hunger conditions in the nation was by the Citizens Board of Inquiry, *Hunger, USA*, Boston, Mass., Beacon Press, 1969. Geographical aspects of hunger and poverty are discussed by Richard Peet, "Poor, Hungry America," *Professional Geographer*, 28 (1971), 99–104.

4. "Federal Aid: Funds to States Up 19 Percent in 1970," *Congressional Quarterly Weekly Report*, July 9, 1971, pp. 1486–1491.

5. *Special Analyses of the United States Government, Fiscal Year 1973*, Washington, D.C., U.S. Government Printing Office, 1972, p. 249.

6. The dollar aid to each state for fourteen largest programs in Fiscal Year 1970 is given in "Federal Aid: Funds to States . . . ," op. cit.

7. The federal aid programs in the South are treated by Clyde E. Browning, "Uncle Sam in the South: Federal Outlays to Southern States," *Southeastern Geographer*, 11:1 (1971), 62–69.

8. Stanley D. Brunn and Wayne L. Hoffman, "The Geography of Federal Grants-in-Aid to States," *Economic Geography*, 45 (1969), 236–239, examines the expenditures in 1965. There have been increments in expenditures for most programs and some regional shifts in allocations as well.

9. Executive Office of the President, Domestic Council, *The History of Revenue Sharing*, Washington, D.C., U.S. Government Printing Office, 1971.

10. "Revenue Sharing: House-Senate Agreements Filed," *Congressional Quarterly Weekly Report*, October 7, 1972, pp. 2630–2631.

11. "Congress Clears Nixon's Revenue-Sharing Plan," *Congressional Quarterly Weekly Report*, October 14, 1972, p. 2702.

12. Dick Frazier, "Revenue Sharing: Where Did It Go?" *The State Journal* [Lansing, Michigan], March 22, 1973, p. B–6; and Lee Hickling, "Revenue Sharing Works Badly at Extremes," ibid.

13. Edward E. Veazey, "Revenue Sharing Funds Assigned to Capital Projects in the Southwest," *Business Review*, Federal Reserve Bank of Dallas, April 1973, pp. 8–11.

14. A recent study has demonstrated how northeastern cities, especially New York City, enhanced their economic position during and after the Civil War. By contrast the South never was able to effectively recover. Andrew F. Burghardt, "The Economic Impact of War: The Case of the Civil War," *Journal of Geography*, 72:6 (1973), 7–10.

15. Data on direct payments for crops are derived from *Federal Outlays, FY 1968, Compiled for the Office of the President by the Office of Economic Opportunity*, Springfield, Virginia, Clearing House for Federal Scientific and Technical Information, National Bureau of Standards, 1969 and 1970. These data report the federal government's impact (by dollar amount) by state and county for each federal program. They provide a wealth of information for the geographer inter-

ested in particular programs such as defense contracts, space contracts, transportation projects, antipoverty grants, and many others.

16. F. E. Oxtoby, "The Role of Political Factors in the Virgin Islands Watch Industry," *Geographical Review*, 60 (1970), 463–474.

17. Robert C. Mings, "The Influence of the Commonwealth Government on the Growth of the Puerto Rican Tourist Industry," *Memorandum Folio, Southeast Division, Association of American Geographers*, 18 (1960), 153–159.

18. Several geography studies have discussed the role of the federal government in agriculture. Among them are David C. Large, "Cotton in the San Joaquin Valley: A Study of the Government in Agriculture," *Geographical Review*, 47 (1957), 365–380; William A. Imperatore, "Effects of Federal Contracts on the Basic Geographic Characteristics of Cotton Production in Georgia," Athens, Georgia, University of Georgia, Department of Geography, MA thesis, 1963; Leslie Hewes, "The Conservation Reserve of the American Soil Bank as an Indicator of Regions of Maladjustment in Agriculture with Special Reference to the Great Plains," *Wiener Geographische Schriften, Festschrift*; Leopold B. Scheilde, N4, 24–29 (1967), 331–346; Karl B. Raitz, "The Government Institutionalization of Tobacco Acreage in Wisconsin," *Professional Geographer*, 23 (1971), 123–126; and James S. Fisher, "Federal Crop Allotment Programs and Responses by Individual Farm Operators," *Southeastern Geographer*, 10:2 (1970), 47–58.

19. "Farm Bill Makes Superficial Cuts," *Business Week*, August 15, 1970, p. 22.

20. *Congressional Record*, March 26, 1970, p. E2536. See also "Farm Subsidy Payments Run Into Millions of Dollars," *Congressional Quarterly Weekly Report*, June 12, 1970, p. 1545.

21. Individual farmer receiving over $25,000 in payments in each country in 1968 are listed in *Congressional Record*, March 26, 1970, 2536–2579.

22. Charles O. Jones, "Representation in Congress: The Case of the House Agriculture Committee," *American Political Science Review*, 55 (1961), 358–367.

23. A. Paulsen, "Payment Limitations: The Economic and Political Feasibility," *American Journal of Agricultural Economics*, 51 (1969), p. 1241.

24. Using the data for direct payments that are available on a county basis, the counties in a representative's legislative district were listed as was the total amount received by each county in FY 1968. In most cases the districts in these rural areas coincided with county lines, however, in those districts with divided counties, maps of current land use were used to determine the payment allocation per district.

25. *Congresssional Index, 90th Congress, 1967–1968*, New York, Commerce Clearing House, Inc., 1968.

26. Stanley D. Brunn and James O. Wheeler, "Spatial Dimensions of Poverty in the United States," *Geografiska Annaler*, 53 (1971, Series B), 6–15.

27. The dollar amounts for food distribution services and food stamps allocated to each county are listed in *Federal Outlays, FY 1968* . . . , op. cit.

28. Defense contracts for prime military supplies and for research and development are also published in *Federal Outlays, FY 1968* . . . , op. cit.

29. Geographical aspects of the defense industry are treated by Walter Isard and Eugene W. Schooler, "An Economic Analysis of Local and Regional Impacts on Reduction of Military Expenditures," *Papers, Peace Research Society (International)*, 1 (1964), 15–44; Gerald J. Karaska, "Interregional Flows of Defense-

Space Awards," *Papers, Peace Research Society (International)*, 5 (1966), 45–62; and M. Polovitskaya, "The Geography of Research and Development in the United States," *Soviet Geography: Review and Translation*, 11 (1970), 784–796. Political aspects of defense contract awards are discussed by James Clodfelter, "Senate Voting and Constituency Stake in Defense Spending," *Journal of Politics*, 32 (1970), 979–983; and Stephen A. Cobb, "Defense Spending and Foreign Policy in the House of Representatives," *Journal of Conflict Resolution*, 13 (1969), 358–369.

30. *Federal Outlays, FY 1968 . . . ,* op. cit.

31. Geographical aspects of the aerospace industry are treated by David C. Weaver and James R. Anderson, "Some Aspects of Metropolitan Development in the Cape Kennedy Sphere of Influence," *Tijdschrift voor Economische en Social Geografie*, 60 (1969), 187–192; and Guy Jalabert, "Les industries aerospatiales aux États-Unis," *L'Information Géographique*, 35 (1971), 25–46. Industrial dependence on government contracts is discussed in H. L. Nieberg, *In the Name of Science*, Chicago, Ill., Quadrangle Books, 1966, pp. 184–199.

32. U.S. Department of the Interior, Bureau of Land Management, *Public Land Statistics, 1971*, Washington, D.C., Government Printing Office, 1971, p. 10. Geographical and historical discussions of public lands are treated by Marion Clawson, *Uncle Sam's Acres*, New York, Dodd, Mead, 1951; and *America's Land and Its Uses*, Baltimore, Md., Johns Hopkins Press, 1972.

33. *Public Land Statistics, 1971*, op. cit., pp. 4–6.

34. Glen D. Weaver, "Nevada's Federal Lands," *Annals, Association of American Geographers*, 59 (1969), 27–49. The public and private problems, arising in the Los Angeles area are well documented in Rodney Steiner, "Reserved Lands and the Supply for Space for the Southern California Metropolis," *Geographical Review*, 56 (1966), 344–362.

35. "General Revenue of State and Local Governments—Origin and Allocation, by States: 1969," *Statistical Abstract of the United States, 1971*, Washington, D.C., U.S. Department of Commerce, 1971, pp. 405–406.

36. Ibid., p. 407.

37. "Public Assistance-Expenditures, by Source of Funds, and Monthly Payments to Recipients, 1960–1970," ibid., 294.

38. U.S. Department of Commerce, Bureau of the Census, *Local Government Finances in Selected Metropolitan Areas and Large Counties: 1969–1970*, Washington, D.C., 1971. Various social, political, and economic facets of metropolitan areas are treated in parts of Chapter Four of Kevin R. Cox, *Conflict, Power, and Politics in the City: A Geographic View*, New York, McGraw-Hill, 1973, pp. 71–104.

39. These figures are derived from a table cited in U.S. Commission on Civil Rights, *Inequity in School Financing: The Role of the Law*, Washington, D.C., 1972, Clearinghouse Publication No. 39, p. 51.

40. Advisory Commission on Intergovernmental Relations, *State and Local Finances, Significant Features 1967 to 1970*, Washington, D.C., November 1969, pp. 68–69.

41. Three recent articles in Federal Reserve Bank publications handle some of the current problems in metropolitan school financing: "Paving the School District's Bumpy Fiscal Road," *Business Review*, Federal Reserve Bank of Philadelphia,

October 1971, pp. 8–11; Stephen F. LeRoy and Peggy Brockschmidt, "Who Pays the School Property Tax?" *Monthly Review*, Federal Reserve Bank of Kansas City, November 1972, pp. 3–13; and Anita A. Summers, "Equity in School Financing: The Courts Move In," *Business Review*, Federal Reserve Bank of Philadelphia, March 1973, pp. 3–13.

42. "Foreign Economic and Military Aid Programs: 1948 to 1970," *Statistical Abstract of the United States, 1971*, Washington, D.C., 1971, p. 762.

43. Dana Adams Schmidt, "More Nations Buying Weapons From U.S.," *Christian Science Monitor*, May 29, 1973, pp. 1 and 4.

44. "Foreign Aid—Commitments for Economic Assistance Under the Foreign Assistance and Predecessor Acts: 1948 to 1970," *Statistical Abstract of the United States, 1971*, Washington, D.C., 1971, pp. 763–764.

45. Office of Staff Placement, Division of Personnel, Reports and Special Studies Branch, Peace Corps, *Monthly Summary of Peace Corps Volunteers and Trainees as of September 1971*, Washington, D.C.

Chapter 12

POLITICS
AND THE
ENVIRONMENT

Pollution, politicians, and power
do indeed a strange brew make.

Anonymous

The protection of the environment and the quality of life have long been recognized as concerns of wildlife groups and social organizations. It is only recently, however, that the issues have attained political significance. This occurred when there was concern about present and future energy sources, excesses of air and water pollution, the degradation of scenic natural areas, the destruction of wildlife, and more recently the value placed on human life. Even though government agencies and departments at local, state, and national levels have been interested in such problems for more than fifty or seventy-five years, an integrated and interdependent approach to the environment has by and large been ignored. Examples of programs dealing with soil and water conservation, radiation levels, national parks, and public health have been in effect for much of this century. The crucial nature of these and other issues did not take on a significant air until the severity of the environmental issues for man and nature was recognized.

Once issues relating to environmental quality achieved national importance, as evidenced by public opinion polls and the vast number of new groups of concerned citizens that were formed, political actions began to follow. First, the federal government that long had been rather complacent in identifying, handling and financing problems dealing with air and water, energy resources, and the quality of human life began to take a genuine interest. Dated acts passed late last or early this century were either used as a basis for challenging the actions of industrial polluters or were the framework for developing more recent legislation. Acts and amendments dealing with air, water, pesticides, radiation, wildlife, and noise have been introduced and approved by both the United States Senate and House of Representatives. The federal government in realizing the need for immediate actions founded agencies such as the Environmental Protection Agency in 1970 and established a Council on Environmental Quality whose responsibility is to issue an annual statement on the nation's environmental status.[1] It was soon realized after the federal government became involved that consolidating agencies and bureaus was essential to efficiency and uniformity as there were all too many overlapping programs in a half dozen different departments. For example, National Oceanic and Atmospheric Administration (NOAA) established in 1970 consolidates both the former Weather Bureau and Coast and Geodetic Survey.

While administration was a key to the national government's commitment to the problems of dealing with the environment, financing cleaning up the environment was necessary if the conditions were to change. This resulted in substantially increasing the budgets for environmental programs and for engaging in cooperative efforts with states and local governments. The effect of federal monies has been felt especially in the construction of municipal water treatment plants. Other than in water pollution the federal government has been involved in problems related to airport noise and location, critical radiation levels, auto emission levels, and public land management.

States and local governments have likewise been taking a much closer look at their lands, vegetation, wildlife, water and air, and levels of life, particularly in cities. Some states, especially those in the New England, Middle Atlantic, and Great Lakes regions have had legislation on the books related to environmental quality and protection before the federal government. Some states in these regions served as innovators for recent legislation passed about radiation levels, pesticide damage, water quality standards, and class action suits against violators. Cities such as New York, Chicago, Los Angeles, and Philadelphia have been in the forefront of much legislation related to noise levels, air and water quality standards, and concerns related to the physical space for humans. Although states and local governments likewise have long had programs related to the protection and preservation of the environment, their impact and influence often has been little because of insufficient monies and trained personnel. With recent federal legislation that calls for states meeting set standards for air and water quality, monies have increased for environmentally related projects and problems.

Problems are certain to arise, as they do, once the different levels of government become involved in handling emissions from power plants and industries into interstate waters. Even though there are national standards set for pollution levels in air and water, until all states meet them, differences will remain and legal challenges will be taken to courts. Cases involving conflicting local government guidelines and regulations on noise levels, smog levels, water pollution, and land use plans already exist. When such cases cross state lines or international boundaries, the legal webs become especially complex. Environmental law, especially those facets relating to political geography concerns, are certain to arise in cases involving states suing other states, local governments suing states, and citizen groups suing specific industries, states, and even the federal government. A number of legal contests have arisen over the programs dealing with growth and development of a state or city.

Already environmentally related organizations and specific individuals are playing a definite role in political facets of the environment. Cases in Alaska, California, Colorado, Michigan, New York, Florida, indeed in most states, have been presented by national or regional environmental groups to question specific projects related to wildlife protection, power plant construction, coastal development, and uses of public lands. Other than in the legal arena groups at the local and national levels have pushed for congressional legislation and the placing of environmental issues on the ballot. That much credit is due to the efforts of such groups for the passage of specific bond issues relating to funding specific projects or the state amendments on environmental rights almost goes without saying. The political clout of groups either on local city councils or state legislatures in rating congressmen on environmental issues, and even in financially working for the election of select individuals, demonstrates that the environmental interests have taken a greater role in handling concerns than simply protecting a forest or preserving certain wildlife species.

The importance of environment, ecology, and politics is a topic that has seen much discussion, legislation, protest, and analysis in the past five years in particular. Biologists, urban and regional planners, government administrators, industrialists, popular writers, and numerous social scientists have examined various facets of the problem. Political geographers have also begun to contribute to this topic, even though there is much that still can be researched and written.[2] The aim of this discussion is to tie together some notions of how the themes of environment, politics, and geography are interrelated. It may be argued that a treatment of some facets especially as they relate to government programs, legal arguments, financing projects, citizen response either in organizations or in voting processes, ideally merit inclusion in earlier chapters. Although there is merit in this argument, it is felt that with the contemporary importance of this topic, which has acknowledged political ramifications of a geographic nature, it deserves discussion as a separate unit. For the political geographer interested in the relations between politics and the environment the issues of differing response to critical issues (as measured by legislation or innovative programs or environmental voting), the jurisdictional problems at different levels, the financing of projects, and the overall quality of life are significant topics. As these relate to geographical variations in attitudes and organization they attain importance to the political geographer examining the quality of life and the protection of the environment in cities, states, regions, or the entire United States.

GEOGRAPHICAL DIMENSIONS OF ENVIRONMENTAL QUALITY

Scale of Problems. Analyses into the areal patterns of environmental pollution and deterioration are probably the best examples to illustrate how meaningless the present political organization actually is when problems need to be solved. Air and water pollution as well as high levels of noise or radiation are not confined to a specific political unit such as a county, city, or state or even international borders. Rather they cross spaces of progressive and conservatively oriented states, manufacturing and agricultural states, rich and poor states, rapidly growing and declining states, and those with dense and sparse populations. The same rationale holds true when metropolitan areas are examined; the various pollution sources are not restricted solely to one income, racial, occupational, or residential development. Central cities and suburbs are affected even if they cross county and state lines.

Water pollution levels are not uniform throughout the United States. Not unexpectedly the degree of pollution follows river basins, which know not political organization schemes that overlay them (Fig. 12-1). The greatest levels of stream miles polluted are in the Northeast (44 percent), Northern Plains (39 percent), and Central States (37 percent). The lowest levels are found in the Southeast (23 percent).[3] A further categorization of pollution levels reveals that 38 percent of the watersheds in the Northern Plains and 36 percent in the Northeast are predominantly polluted. That is, over 50 percent of stream miles are polluted. The leading regions of extensively polluted water (20–49.9 percent) are the Pacific Coast (59 percent), Northeast (56 percent), and Central and Southern Plains (both 52 percent). The Southeast stands out as the major region with the lowest levels of water pollution.

The pollution of local and state and interstate waters is derived from a number of sources. Municipal, agricultural, and industrial wastes, pesticides, phosphates from laundry detergents, chemicals, metals, and toxic materials all have contributed to the pollution of waters. By far the major source of organic water pollution is the waste material from industries. Secondly, municipal and agricultural wastes are most important. Even in examining the key sources of pollution, there are some salient geographical patterns. Along the Pacific Coast and Plains states, agricultural pesticides, fertilizers, and wastes are the major causes. In the Central states municipal wastes are the major contributors and in the Northeast and Southeast it is the industries that add the greatest wastes to the waters. Even though the Environmental Protection Agency has stated the BOD level (biochemical oxygen

Fig. 12-1   Water Pollution Levels. (Council of Environmental Quality, 1971.)

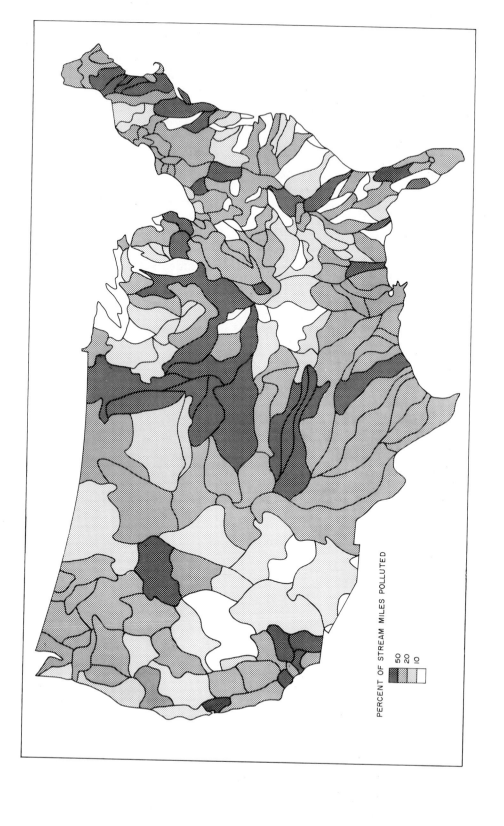

PERCENT OF STREAM MILES POLLUTED

50
20
10

demand), the amount of oxygen used in five days by biological processes involved in stabilizing organic matter, has remained fairly constant in recent years, the overall quality of the nation's waters has deteriorated. This is attributed to accelerated eutrophication, increased discharges of toxic materials, and greater deposition of sediments. Pollutants are derived from the variety of sources stated above. In about one-third of all waters the pollution levels fail to meet federal water quality standards. Less than 10 percent of all waters are unpolluted or moderately so.

Just as the quality of the nation's waters varies within and between states and regions, so do the levels of air pollution. Two major regions stand out as having the highest pollution potential levels of air pollutants. They are in the West, especially California, and in the Appalachians (Fig. 12-2). This figure is based on routine forecasts of air pollution potential (FAPP). The areas with the highest frequency have a high frequency of high pressure systems as well as temperature inversions. The area with the lowest level of air pollution potential is in the middle of the United States that includes the western Midwest and Great Plains to the Rocky Mountains.[4]

Polluting the air can come from a variety of sources, the key ones being emission of materials from automobiles and from industries and power companies. Even with the slight decline in air pollution levels in the past few years the automobile still is the single greatest source. Other than industrial wastes being emitted in the air from cities in the North and South, there are noxious materials being aired from municipal incinerators and local backyard burning. Forest fires also add to the pollution levels in some regions.

Part of the areal patterns for air pollution are based on the prevailing

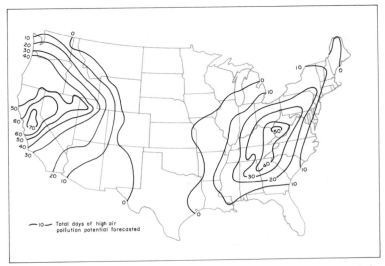

Fig. 12-2 Frequency Air Pollution Potential Levels. (U.S. Department of the Interior, *National Atlas of the United States*, Geological Survey, Washington, D.C., 1970.)

atmospheric conditions and the climate of a city or region. Stagnant high-pressure cells off southern California as well as in the central and southern Appalachians for much of the year preclude the upward movement and free flow of air out of the source regions. Unique topographic conditions, especially for cities in valleys, where temperature inversions occur, can trap auto emissions and industrial pollutants.

Variations in air pollution exist within cities as well as within states. The specific pollution content that is monitored for a city as well as parts of a city will depend on the location of such devices. Clearly the reading in the central part of a city would vary from that in a residential suburb. The level of pollution depends on the location of industries as well as the heaviest concentrations of vehicular traffic. Not infrequently these are both located in the central parts of cities. In Chicago, Illinois, and Gary, Indiana, the highest levels of sulphur dioxide and particulate matter are near the central business districts of both cities. They both are associated with the areas of lowest incomes. The relationship between the physical environment and social and economic environment has long been identified as more than a coincidental association. Especially in the past decade has the geographical variation in social and economic health been related in central cities to the quality of life as affected by physical processes.[5]

Metropolitan variations in pollution are not limited to the quality of air that is breathed. It also exists with reference to the nature of other hazardous sources such as noise. Noise in particular has been found to have distinct geographical patterns that relate to the frequency and direction of flight patterns. With the growing population of metropolitan areas, greater use of plane travel, and the production of larger and louder planes, the areal patterns would be expected to expand. This has been treated in a recent examination of the noise pollution levels affecting the Boston area and eastern Massachusetts (Fig. 12-3). Similar noise cones especially from sonic booms have been predicted for the densely populated northeastern quarter.[6] The congressional debate on the supersonic transport legislation in 1971 was opposed by big-city representatives from the Northeast who as part of their case envisioned a sonic boom stretching from Massachusetts to the central Midwest. Industrial, construction and vehicular noise from automobiles and trucks also add to the exceedingly high noise levels in the central part of cities. It is mainly the inner city that is affected by the deteriorating quality of life. This includes levels of garbage, trash, junk, and litter, all of which are highest in this location. Abandoned housing, unsound structures, and dwellings infested with rats are not rare. Lead poisoning cases are highest in these locations. The patterns of pollution and facets of human life are portrayed in geographical patterns within cities. In the main, the inner city has the most undesirable, unhealthy, and stressful environments.[7]

Diversity of Problems. Few have been the counties, cities, and states that have not been affected by an increasing number and diversity of pollution problems and concerns related to environmental quality in the past few years. They have run the gamut from the location of sewage treatment plants, the sites for landfills, the

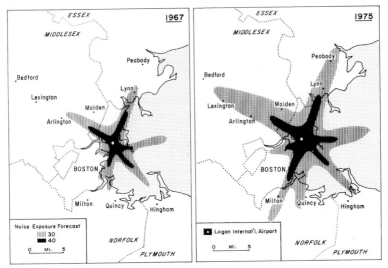

FIG. 12-3 Noise Pollution Levels in the Boston Area. (After Gordon M. Stevenson, Jr., "Noise and the Urban Environment," in Thomas R. Detwyler and Melvin G. Marcus et al., *Urbanization and the Environment: The Physical Geography of the City*, Belmont, Calif., Duxbury Press, 1972, pp. 216 and 217.)

placement of nuclear reactors, the private uses of public lands, the location of regional airports, the legal jurisdiction on improving water quality, the bases for land use planning, to the national funding for proposed supersonic transports and pipelines. Environmental groups, politicians, administrators, and professionals (biologists, urban and regional planners, social scientists, medical and legal practitioners) have all worked at local, state, national, or international levels to cope with the problems. Likewise they have been concerned with the immediate and long-term implications of their findings and recommendations. Cities and states that long had little or no particular interest in environmental concerns have found that executing studies and implementing policy are becoming more a part of their responsibilities to their citizens. To some extent this urging has come from the federal government's greater involvement in the past decade but it has also come from the recognition of what is transpiring in other states and the increasing nature of cooperative efforts. Also citizen action in the form of study groups or affiliation with national organizations has stimulated the importance of environmental issues at all levels of the political hierarchy. Much of the impetus for recent legislation and court tests has been derived from the recognition that the environment as an issue is a national issue and not one of importance only to residents in California or Wisconsin or in the Southeast states or to big-city areas. In short residents in various geographical settings are affected by the nature of projects, legal cases, laws, and funding relating to the protection of the environment and improving of the quality of life.

One of the more nationally identified environmental clashes has been the proposed Trans-Alaskan Pipeline. The proposal entails constructing an 800-mile pipeline from Alaska's North Slope to the port city of Valdez on the Gulf of Alaska. With the shortage of economically recoverable oil reserves in the "lower forty-eight," the higher costs of foreign petroleum, and the tremendous reserves along Alaskan Arctic coast, the need for such a pipeline seems plausible. Construction of the proposed pipeline was halted by various environmental and legal groups arguing about the potential ecological damage to the flora and fauna of Alaska, the likelihood of increased seismic activity, and the Indian and Eskimo land claims. As of early 1974, construction is still stalled even though it has been approved by Congress. When the pipeline is completed, the actual location of its route takes on political dimensions.

The enlargement of existing airport facilities or the location of new regional airports have been the subject of consideration by environmentalists, urban planners, and politicians in most states with large urban nodes. That the problem is a genuine one that demands some solution in view of the increase in passenger and freight traffic in the past five years almost goes without saying. Among the specific concerns are whether to build new facilities or to simply add on to existing ones. The tendency has been recently to build new regional airports some distance away from major population concentrations. In such places they would be safe from large residential areas where high noise levels and crash probabilities would affect a greater number. Nature groups have fought such proposed sites as the Everglades as the locus for the Miami jetport. Alternative sites that have been considered are lake or ocean airport platforms in Lake Michigan for Chicago and in the Atlantic Ocean for New York City and Miami. The political ramifications are often paramount in the final decisions reached about where to build new facilities, although citizens groups have been successful in requesting hearings on such expansion and even collecting damages from those directly affected by high noise levels near airports.

Power plants have become another focus for environmentalist actions and legislation. The concern is not only the air pollution or thermal pollution of waters that may exist but the possible leakage of radioactive materials. The potential damage from power plants has been raised in the Four Corners area (where Colorado, New Mexico, Arizona, and Utah juxtapose), the Calvert Cliffs area on Chesapeake Bay, the Sea Islands off the Georgia coastline, and nuclear power plant construction sites in Michigan and New York. In the last two states conservation groups have been involved in lengthy legal entanglements; construction was even halted on the New York project.

Another issue that has achieved prominence in the nation's eye has been the utilization and preservation of scenic and biologically unique environments. Hardly a decade ago organizations and groups at the local or national level would not have had an opportunity to have their case heard in the courts or even given support by the public. Today the situation is indeed different and environmentalist groups have successfully blocked or altered considerably the actions taken by industries and governments whose plans would misuse the physical environment. Although examples such as the Alaskan pipeline and Miami jetport are basically to protect the environment, other cases exist that illustrate the proper use of areas for public recreation. The Hell's Canyon on the Snake River was basically to protect an area of unique beauty and wildlife from flooding and to use for power developments. Similarly, the Florida Barge Canal was finally halted not only because it was not really needed but because it was destroying the beautiful and wild Oklawaha River. Recreationalists and environmentalists have worked to prevent rapid residential development and commercialization of national parks and forest preserves. The controversy in New York with reference to the Adirondacks is an example of the lines that are drawn in dealing with a unique natural area. In fact when national monuments and parks, scenic areas, and wild rivers are discussed in Congress, the opposing forces usually are environmentalists vs. the developers. Political considerations in the form of the specifying geographic dimensions of the proposed area, the issuing of permits for power plants, and the financing of particular projects often accompany the legislation.

Although it is often forgotten in examining environmental issues and crises, political considerations are of paramount importance.[8] The jurisdiction of the area where a crisis occurs or where proposed development is planned may result in overlapping and conflicting authorities. Such is the case when oil spills exist in California, Louisiana, Texas, or on interstate waters. Taking any environmental polluter to court usually involves violations of local, state, and federal laws. Whether it be with respect to strip mining, airport noise levels, nuclear power plant locations, industrial discharges into water or air, or uses of land, the cases involve airsheds and river basins and ordinances in cities and states, not to mention laws enacted by the federal government. Most states are faced with environmental legislation that affect a host of problems. While air and water pollution have traditionally been their most crucial concerns, pressures from citizen groups and the federal government in the past decade have called for enacting legislation to deal with land use, noise levels, pesticide amounts, strip mining, solid waste, and toxic materials. To aid in meeting the environmental problems, a number of states have asked for voter approval of environmental bond issues and as well as introduced legislation protecting the resources and establishing a set of environmental rights.

HISTORY OF GOVERNMENT INVOLVEMENT

Federal Level. Prior to the mid-1960s most legislation concerning environmental matters was enacted by states and local governments. They were in charge of setting limits on air and water pollution and for policing their actions. Outside of the national health and safety concerns associated with radiation levels, the federal government had a policy of noninvolvement or limited involvement. Even though legislation was passed relating to air and water quality levels before 1965, the federal government's position was to help finance projects to states and local governments by means of grants-in-aid. However, since 1965 not only have funds for environmental protection and research increased but Congress has approved legislation giving the federal government regulating powers over air, water, noise, and other levels. This switch from a basic policy and philosophy of limited regulatory powers to the establishment and enforcement of quality acts has contributed probably more than any single facet to the national awareness of environmental problems.

In order to understand and appreciate the legislation that has been passed by Congress in the past two years, legislation affecting all citizens in all states, a brief history of the federal government involvement is warranted.[9] Air pollution was identified as primarily a state responsibility with the initial law in 1955 entitled Air Pollution Control—Research and Technical Assistance. As the title indicates, funds for research were granted to states and cities especially to aid them in reducing pollution levels and for setting standards. The initial direct federal involvement was a part of the Clean Air Act of 1963 when the state was still the prime focus for setting pollution standards. Furthermore, this act encouraged regional cooperation and aided such efforts by financial outlays. The Air Quality Act of 1967 brought the federal government directly into the national limelight. Regulating control policies were established as well as certain air quality standards and the framework for enforcement. Subsequent amendments have spelled out auto emission guidelines.

Water is the second major environmental problem. It is important from a public health, industrial, residential, and recreational standpoint. The earliest federal legislation was the Rivers and Harbors Act of 1899, which basically prohibited dumping waste materials into navigable waters. This nineteenth-century law has been used in the past few years to bring violators into court. Public health standards, especially as they relate to drinking water, became part of the Public Health Services Act of 1912. This act also dealt with the pollution menace to navigable lakes and streams. One of the major industrial polluters has been oil; this led to the Oil Pollution Control Act in 1924. It basically provided a means to combat oil discharges that caused damage to marine life, recreation facilities, and docks and harbors. Unfortunately, especially in later years, this law affected only coastal waters. The first federal involvement in water quality in general was a part of the Water Pollution Control Act of 1948. The problem of water pollution was recognized and financial support granted to states and cities. State policing was still important and remained so until the Water Pollution Control Act of 1961. It replaced the 1948 one that expired in 1956. The 1968 act laid out the federal controls over interstate waters and assumed greater federal regulatory powers. Still, financial assistance was granted and intergovernmental handling of water problems was recommended. The crucial nature of water was recognized by congressional legislation from 1965–1970. In 1965 the Water Quality Act was passed that stated it was a national policy to regulate the quality of the nation's waters. The Federal Water Pollution Control Administration was created under the Department of Health, Education, and Welfare. It aided in the construction of sewage treatment plants and in continuing research on water quality. The Clean Water Restoration

Act of 1966 authorized funds for the construction of water treatment facilities and also helped set standards for interstate waters and for states. Since then states have been developing programs that are in line with federal guidelines. The Water and Environmental Quality Improvement Act of 1970 basically outlined federal juris- dictional responsibilities and geographical limits in matters relating to the nation's waters. It also strengthened the federal government's position in dealing with oil polluters and the regulation of hazardous substances. The Council of Environ- mental Quality was created as a part of this 1970 bill. More far-reaching legislation on the federal government's role in water quality was passed in 1972 legislation.

As in the case of air and water quality, the regulations affecting solid waste and noise were left to states and local government. However, with the increased volume of trash and garbage and the destruction of nonreturnable and nondispos- able packaging materials, the federal government found itself involved. The national scale of this problem was recognized in the Solid Waste Disposal Act of 1965 that became a part of the Clean Air Act. It proposed research into ways to reduce waste and dispose of solid wastes. There were no regulatory provisions in the act; it did, however, make available grants-in-aid. Various states have enacted pro- grams and policies relating to the disposal of solid wastes in the past few years. Noise levels that are dangerous to individuals were ignored by the federal govern- ment in large part until legislation passed in 1972. States and local governments were considered in a better position to hear concerns voiced about industrial, residential, and vehicular noise levels considered dangerous to human health. The first step in national involvement was the Walsh-Healy Amendment in 1969 that set decibel levels for industrial noise on projects with government contracts and industries dependent on such. Research on the problem was funded by various agencies such as the National Aeronautics and Space Administration, the Public Health Service, and the Federal Aviation Administration. The noise levels around airports were such that cities and individuals have been petitioning to Congress for federal action. Success was achieved in 1970 with the Airport and Airway Develop- ment Act that authorized the secretary of transportation to consult with other government agencies on environmental problems relating to new airport systems, their location and impact. As stated previously, the 1972 legislation did represent a major step forward in this area.

The single exception to environmental problems on the part of the federal government dealt with radiation levels. With the development of nuclear power for military or industrial or, later, consumer use, the problem of radiation was con- sidered so critical that national regulatory controls were established by the Atomic Energy Act of 1946. An amendment in 1950 called for cooperation of all states with the national government on problems relating to radiation protection and the destruction of waste materials. The levels that are dangerous to human health are of vital importance as the dependence on nuclear power as a major fuel source is envisioned as a very likely occurrence by the year 2000.

Only in the past few years has the federal government taken measures to deal with issues involving environmental health. The production and uses of pesticides as they may endanger humans, wildlife, and vegetation has been behind the Federal Insecticide, Fungicide, and Rodenticide Act. This and subsequent legislation have resulted in more stringent testing and labeling of major pesticides and similar toxic substances (to humans and animals) as well as bans on the sale of some such as DDT. Lead paint as it relates to lead poisoning is a problem particularly in the inner city. In 1971 a Lead-Based Paint Poisoning Prevention Act was passed that basically aims to investigate the nature of the problem and to ban use of lead-based paint on federally owned or financed projects. Solid wastes as they present a danger to air and water pollution as well as visual pollution, that is, littering the landscape, are additional areas where the federal government is becoming involved in health matters. The increases in waste materials and suggested recycling measures are being researched. Noise pollution as it relates to industrial, transportation, or household levels has been a problem recognized by the executive and legislative branches. The passage of legislation by the 1972 session of Congress did represent the first attempt to actually identify some problems and recommend some abatement procedures.

In terms of agencies to administer programs the federal government created the Environmental Protection Agency in late 1970. This single agency was to serve as the major intergovernmental unit responsible for environmental matters. Prior to the establishment of EPA concerns about air and water pollution, wildlife management, public land use, pesticides, transportation noise, radiation levels and many other problems of regional and national concern were handled within existing Departments of Agriculture, Commerce, Defense, Health, Education and Welfare, and Interior, and Transportation. Within these departments there were various agencies responsible for handling rather specific problems. As an example, within the Department of Interior, agencies handled stream erosion on public lands, forest cutting, grazing lands, Indian reservations, national parks, and fish and wildlife. A proposed Department of Energy and Natural Resources has been recommended to handle all agencies dealing with land, air, energy, public lands, and resources.[10]

State Level. In examining the response of states to problems dealing with the environment, there are some programs that are similar, again due in large part to federal government guidelines, and others where differences are substantial. Some states are definitely innovators when it comes to developing new agencies, funding environmental projects, or enforcing the state's "rights" to protect and preserve the environment. New York, Illinois, Pennsylvania, Rhode Island, North Carolina, and New Mexico are among the states that have either passed an "Environmental Bill of Rights" or have received approval by the electorate to protect the natural resources. Citizen suits can be brought against industries and developers in Connecticut, Minnesota, Massachusetts, and Michigan. Protection of the environment and challenges to potentially damaging uses are authorized in California, Montana, Washington, Delaware, and Puerto Rico.

Some states have formed new agencies to handle environmental concerns or have reorganized existing state agencies. New York transferred most of the agencies that dealt with pollution and resource management into a new Department of Environmental Conservation. Washington consolidated its agencies into a Department of Ecology. Illinois by its environmental act passed in 1970 transferred some agencies and created in addition three new ones: Pollution Control Board, Environmental Protection Agency, and Institute for Environmental Quality.

While the legislation of new measures deals with the environment and the establishment of new agencies or the reorganization of existing ones represents advances in the areas of protection and preservation, probably dollar commitments illustrate one of the most positive steps any state will take. Clearly the funding for environmentally related projects, whether by legislative actions or passage of bond issues by public referendums is on the rise. Whether the funding is measured by funds or in manpower, the increase is substantial for water and air pollution control agencies. From fiscal year 1971 when state funds for water pollution agencies were $31.2 million they increased to $44.2 million for the following year. For air pollution control agencies the dollar values from state and local funds were $47.3 and $56.8 million for the same years.[11] These do not include state and local funds allocated for municipal sewage treatment plants which totaled $2.17 billion in grants and loans in 1971. This substantial increment in dollars for air and water control agencies does not represent an equal commitment from each state or each region (Table 12-1). Water quality expenditures were highest in the Northeast and especially the Middle Atlantic states of New York, New Jersey, and Pennsylvania. Almost 60 percent of the dollars were spent by nine states, even though they have only one-quarter of the nation's population. These are some of the most industrially oriented states in the nation, however. Air quality, if dollar allocations can be considered an index of the problem, is most important to the three Middle Atlantic states and five Pacific states of Washington, Oregon, California, Alaska, and Hawaii (Table 12-1). It is worth noting that relatively small amounts are spent in the Rocky Mountain states, to be expected in view of small populations, and in the South. Even though 30 percent of the nation's population lives in these sixteen states in the South, the expenditures for air and water quality control programs are considerably below similarly populated areas.

In general each year reveals that states are taking a greater involvement in environmental matters as evidenced by more strict regulations on air and water quality. Under the Clean Air Act, the EPA has worked with a number of states to bring them in line with federal air quality standards. As of May 1972 fifty-four states and territories had adopted emission standards, limitations, and other standards in compliance with national standards. However, only thirty-three states had authority to require stationary sources to install emission monitoring devices and report such results to the states. Another facet of the Clean Air Act involved the emission from new automobiles. California alone was permitted under the regulation to have stiffer standards. Still, not all states have complied with the specifics of the act; only twenty-one states have motor vehicle inspection.

Water quality is the second major activity that state agencies are concerned with, especially as it affects the standards in water quality, waste disposal, sewage

TABLE 12-1   State Government Expenditure for Water and Air Quality Control, by Region and Geographic Division, Fiscal Year 1969–1970 (thousands of dollars)

Region and Geographic Division	Water Quality		Air Quality	
	Total Expenditure	Average Per State	Total Expenditure	Average Per State
Total (50 states)	$157,088	$ 3,141	$22,767	$ 455
Northeast (9 states)	92,557	10,284	6,343	705
New England (6 states)	30,760	5,127	1,175	196
Middle Atlantic (3 states)	61,797	20,599	5,168	1,723
North Central (12 states)	26,073	2,173	2,685	224
East North Central (5 states)	23,231	4,646	1,961	392
West North Central (7 states)	2,842	406	714	102
South (16 states)	19,880	1,243	6,538	409
South Atlantic (8 states)	11,767	1,471	4,309	539
East South Central (4 states)	1,759	440	1,218	305
West South Central (4 states)	6,354	1,589	1,011	253
West (13 states)	18,578	1,429	7,211	555
Mountain (8 states)	1,606	201	1,238	155
Pacific (5 states)	16,972	3,394	5,973	1,195

Source: *Council on Environmental Quality, Third Annual Report,* 1972, Washington, D.C., Government Printing Office, 1972, p. 161.

treatment systems, and cleanup operations. As of April 1972, only eight states did not have standards that were approved under federal law; they were Alabama, Georgia, Illinois, Louisiana, Michigan, Mississippi, Ohio, and Tennessee. All states had some form of monitoring water quality yet not all states had similar legislation on the books for controlling water pollution by industries or municipalities. Thirty-one states had a permit system controlling water pollution by their municipalities and thirty-five had a similar system for industries. Arizona, Connecticut, Hawaii, Indiana, Kansas, Louisiana, Maine, Mississippi, Nevada, Nebraska, New Hampshire, New Mexico, North Dakota, Vermont, and Wyoming did not have a permit system. Some states had permits for industries only such as Delaware and Minnesota while others had permits only issued to municipalities as in Arizona and Washington.

Besides air and water quality, a number of other consumer protection and environmental protection measures have been enacted by the states. Phosphates in detergents are regulated in six states: Florida, Indiana, Minnesota, New York, Connecticut and Maine. Thirty-two states now have laws governing solid waste and in twenty-five states permits for such disposal are issued. Florida, New Jersey, Oregon, Nevada, Illinois, and Vermont are states that have taken the lead in dealing with trash, garbage, throwaway beverage containers, and junked vehicles. The dumping of sewage or industrial waste into the ocean was instrumental in New Jersey and Rhode Island prohibiting such actions by recent legislation. Antinoise legislation has been heard more in the past two years. New York, Connecticut, Massachusetts, California, Illinois, Vermont, Michigan, and North Dakota have been in the forefront of legislation dealing with vehicle noise (automobiles, airplanes, trucks, and more recently off-road recreational vehicles). Radiation, its level, potential damage to environmental health, and place in a state's energy picture, has become important in several key states. Maryland, Minnesota, Oregon, Michigan, Ohio, Vermont, Wisconsin, and New Mexico have been among those attempting to assess the environmental impact of higher levels and increased uses of nuclear power. Finally, pesticides, their registration, regulation, advertising, and penalties for misuses, have been the target of legislation in Delaware, California, Alabama, Texas, Utah, New Hampshire, Michigan, New Jersey, North Carolina, and Georgia.

Local Level. Local governments cooperate with federal and state agencies governing air, water, solid waste, radiation, pesticide, and other programs. To supplement these a number of cities have enacted environmental measures to handle problems within their own jurisdictions. For this reason even though there is intergovernmental cooperation, often local government regulations and guidelines are more strict or at least at variance with the state and federal agencies. This is true for air and water pollution, noise levels, and solid-waste programs. New York City's Environmental Control Board in the first half of 1971 handed down twice as many fines for air pollution violations as the city's criminal courts. Realizing the severity of air pollution in New York City, the city has even devised emergency procedures to close streets and restrict automobile use during crises situations. Los Angeles, having recognized the severity of the smog problem, enacted strict auto emission limits that led to the eventual federal regulations. Water pollution measures have mainly dealt with dumping of wastes, the establishment of quality standards, and multiple-use plans for a city's water. San Diego and Los Angeles have developed boards to deal with all facets of water quality. In Seattle a eutrophic lake was restored for recreational purposes. Chicago has devised plans for handling overflow sewage by underground tunnels.

Most cities have carried out programs and the construction of solid-waste treatment plants in cooperation with federal and state monies. Still problems remain in cities as to the location for these facilities. Even the location of sanitary landfills becomes a problem that is likely to affect neighborhood development, industrial expansion, not to mention possible alteration of drainage patterns and sediment deposition. Some cities and counties adopted rather strong measures about phosphate levels in detergents that were on occasion not in harmony with proposed state legislation.

In noise levels, cities not unexpectedly, have taken the lead in establishing decibel levels and restrictions on uses of certain types within cities.[12] Although it is estimated that as many as 2000 communities have noise control laws, it is doubtful that these laws are enforced readily. Especially because many noise-polluting sources bring money and jobs into a city, prosecutors have felt reluctant to test the noise levels of major industries. The past three years have seen large cities and suburbs either update their existing laws or adopt new ones to handle this environmental concern. Chicago with 1971 legislation adopted an ordinance that specifies the levels of noise emission that are permitted. New York has introduced a Quiet Community Program that enforces standards as well as conducts noise research. Other cities such as Memphis, Boston, Washington, D.C., Urbana (Illinois), and Minneapolis have adopted ordinances. Cities in California such as Beverly Hills, El Segundo, Torrance, and Alhambra appear to be among the national leaders in this important arena.

Noise levels are not only restricted to airplanes and airports, but also to construction, industrial and commercial concerns, land vehicles, internal building noise, and household appliances. Funding and research at federal levels has been increasing in the past few years, especially now that the 1972 Noise Control Act passed in Congress. Many communities in response to the severity of the noise problem have asked for greater federal control over the high decibel levels for residential developments surrounding airports. Such hearings have led to citizen concerns in the location of newly proposed airports. Authority for such matters rests with the Department of Transportation and its Federal Aviation Administration. The legislation protecting citizens was outlined in the Airport and Airway Development Act of 1970.

Other than airport noise, ordinances affecting vehicle noise levels have been enacted in a number of cities. Decatur, Illinois and Madison, Wisconsin have horn-blowing ordinances. Salt Lake City prohibits excessive vehicle noise in quiet zones. Beverly Hills, California prohibits repair or testing vehicles in residential areas if it discomforts residents. In three cities, Missoula, Detroit, and Minneapolis, motorcycle noise levels are set. Construction ordinances have been passed by a number of cities. In Portland, Oregon, noise-producing equipment is prohibited from 6:00 PM to 7:00 AM and in Toledo, Ohio, from 9:00 PM to 6:00 AM. Emergency situations are permitted. As mentioned above noise legislation exists in New York City and Chicago. Industrial and commercial noise ordinances have been restricted to blowing steam whistles except at the beginning and the end of working days, outlawing excessively loud machinery, and regulating use of outside speakers. Residential noise legislation also has begun to appear on the books in a number of cities. In the main it relates to the use of domestic sources such as radios, television sets, air conditioners, and power lawn mowers. White Plains, New York, is one example where use of fans, air conditioners, lawn mowers, and chain saws are prohibited when they disrupt the peace of the community's residents. Similar laws exist in Memphis. Ceilings on noise levels from such sources have been set in Torrance and Alhambra, California. The result of such noise legislation is illustrated by new federally supported construction which must be approved by the Department of Housing and Urban Development. Interior building noise levels are being involved in the establishment of building codes. It is hoped that such policies will not prohibit construction in noisy parts of central cities.

POLITICAL RESPONSES TO ENVIRONMENTAL CONCERNS

Recent Federal Legislation and Funding. The ninety-second session of Congress was most successful in approving various bills regarding the protection of the environment. Measures were established in 1972 by both houses that set precedents for federal involvement in water pollution, ocean dumping, coastal zone management, marine mammals, pesticide control, and noise control.[13]

By far the most important piece of legislation passed was the Federal Water Pollution Control Act Amendments of 1972; these were passed over President Nixon's veto. It authorized over $18 billion to aid states in constructing waste treatment plants and an additional $2.75 billion to reimburse communities that had built such at their own expense earlier. The bill authorized loans to small businesses for water pollution control and for continued research efforts. Another of the amendments set a national goal of eliminating all pollutants from being discharged into United States waters by 1985 and to make such waters safe for fish, wildlife, and recreation by 1983. The Environmental Protection Agency was authorized to administer a new pollutant discharge program. State programs had to be approved by the EPA which could take over control if states failed to meet the federal standards.

Another of the major ingredients in this water control legislation was the requirement placed on industries to use the "best practicable" technology for treating any discharges into United States waters by mid-1977. By 1983 such industries will have to install the "best available" equipment. The bill also set criminal penalties between $2,500 and $25,000 a day, or a year in prison, or both for violators. Second offenses had stiffer fines and sentences. Citizens with interest in protecting the environment will be able with this most recent legislation to sue polluters, the federal government, and the Environmental Protection Agency.

The Ocean Dumping bill banned the unregulated dumping of waste materials into oceans and coastal waters. The waters covered are those that are part of the nation's territorial limits. The basis for legislating such dumping was to protect human health, the marine environment, and economic potential of such waters. The transporting and dumping of chemical, biological, radiological, or radioactive wastes out to sea was prohibited and enforced with stiff fines ranging up to $50,000.

Another piece of legislature that dealt with waters was the Coastal Zone Management bill. Ostensibly it was concerned with the management, use, protection, and development of United States coastal zones. Coastal waters included under this bill were bays, sounds, lagoons and estuaries, the Great Lakes, and adjacent shorelines such as tidal areas, salt marshes, wetlands, and beaches. The bill authorized $186 million to go to states to help them develop programs in line with federal guidelines. The importance of such lands were vital considering that three-fourths of the nation's population lives in coastal states and population growth is most rapid now in these areas at the edge of the nation's land peripheries.

Marine animals, their protection and banning of products, were covered under the Marine Mammal Protection Act. It set a moratorium on killing most animals as well as a ban on importing animal products. As the legislation was enacted it covered seals, sea lions, whales, porpoises, dolphins, sea otters, manatees, walruses, and polar bears. The act did not prevent the killing or capture of all marine animals as some are necessary for scientific research and zoos. Others are needed for economic livelihood, as ocean mammals by Alaskan Indians, Aleuts, and Eskimos. The seal harvest in the Alaskan Pribilof Islands was to continue for one year under the administration of the Commerce Department.

Pesticide legislation continued in 1972 with congressional passage of the Federal Environmental Pesticide Control Act. It stipulated that all pesticides had to be registered with the EPA, which would also regulate their usage. It went far beyond a simple labeling of chemicals in pesticides that had been incorporated in the 1947 Fungicide and Rodenticide Act. Other than some rather rigid requirements for registering pesticides the act stipulated that the federal government could be authorized to pay indemnity to pesticide manufacturers and retailers whose products were declared a hazard and needed to be removed from the market.

Another environmental topic discussed above that has attained greater importance in the past three years deals with noise levels. The Noise Control Act of 1972 was the first federal legislation that was specifically concerned with reducing detrimental noise levels. The bill authorized the setting of noise emission standards on commercial products and transportation equipment, motors, engines, electric or electronic devices. The EPA is also to propose noise standards for aircraft, but the final authority rests with the Federal Aviation Administration. It is estimated by the EPA that noise subjects some 40 million citizens to hearing damage or other mental or physical health hazards and that some 64 million Americans live in homes affected by aircraft, traffic, or construction noise.

Even with these landmark environmental bills passed, other issues are still being considered by either one or both houses. In 1972 both the Senate and House of Representatives failed to pass tough legislation on such important topics as toxic chemicals (such as sulfur dioxide) and strip mining. Discussions on these as well as on other problems of population numbers, the energy crises (that became acutely evident in late 1973), public land utilization, and international environmental issues remain as topics awaiting congressional action.

Federal involvement in the environment in the financial arena takes place within a number of departments and agencies. The single major agency devoted to handling the multifaceted environmental concerns is the Environmental Protection Agency. Even yet there are aspects of air and water pollution, public land management, toxic materials, recreation spaces, waste treatment, and energy reserves that are within the overlapping domains of Departments of Agriculture, Commerce, Defense, Transportation, and Interior.

In terms of budget outlays for pollution control and abatement activities, the EPA has the lion's share of monies available. Its budget jumped from $718 million in 1971 to an expected $1544 million for fiscal year 1973 (Table 12-2). Most of these dollars are used for helping state and local governments construct municipal sewage treatment facilities. Appropriations for such construction were only $214 million in 1969 but by 1972 they had already reached $2 billion. By 1977 about 146 million Americans are expected to be served by secondary sewage treatment facilities, a rapid increase from the 91 million in 1969. Other than the EPA budget, monies to control and abate pollution increased in the Departments of Defense, Atomic Energy Commission, Transportation, Agriculture, Interior, and Commerce. Altogether federal monies devoted to pollution control and abatement for all agencies have increased from $685 million for a 1969 estimate to an expected figure for 1973 of $2.44 billion, this being more than a threefold increase.[14]

Although the EPA budget accounts for over 60 percent of the federal funds allocated, and these as mentioned are primarily for municipal sewage treatment facilities, some of the research projects of other departments are impor-

TABLE 12-2   Pollution Control and Abatement Activities,
by Agency (in millions of dollars)

	Outlays		
Agency	1971 (actual)	1972 (estimate)	1973 (estimate)
Environmental Protection Agency	$ 718	$1,287	$1,544
Defense—Military	82	130	235
Atomic Energy Commission	122	136	154
Transportation	22	56	79
Agriculture	67	107	139
Defense—Civil	7	50	56
Interior	45	87	82
Commerce	20	26	30
General Services Administration	2	2	5
National Aeronautics and Space Administration	25	30	29
National Science Foundation	9	11	15
Other Agencies	31	53	72
Total	1,150	1,975	2,440

Source: *Special Analyses of the United States Government, Fiscal Year 1973*, Washington, D.C., Government Printing Office, 1972, p. 298.

tant. The Department of Defense receives funds to devise ways to reduce pollution from industrial production facilities, military bases, naval vessels, aircraft, and jet engine test facilities. Also research monies are available to develop new methods for disposing of wastes. The Atomic Energy Commission receives funds to study air pollution of radioactive materials as well as the effects of ionizing radiation. Thermal radiation in lakes, streams, and estuaries is an additional research project engaged in by the AEC. Crop pesticides and fertilizers and disposal of animal wastes are projects studied by the Department of Agriculture. Because the Forest Service is within this department, problems of stream pollution and erosion have been studied. The Department of the Interior is particularly concerned with the pollution from facilities in national parks as well as recommended wise usage of natural resources, especially gas and oil. Finally the Department of Commerce provides grants for waste treatment plants as well as conducts the monitoring and establishment of air and water standards. These are a part of the duties of the National Bureau of Standards. Other agencies are also involved in performing research on a variety of projects such as the National Aeronautics and Space Administration, the General Services Administration and the Corps of Engineers.

Public Referendums. A number of cities and states have asked their residents to support environmental measures. Among the state proposals are those calling for bonds to finance cleaning up the air and water or buying lands for recreation as well as those to support particular projects. In 1972 voters in four states supported environmental measures. California voters approved a Coastal Zone Conservation Act that in essence ended the haphazard development that had been occurring on the state's shores. As a result of the passage, a commission was to be created that could veto any new development along the shores. State real estate interests and oil companies opposed this zoning referendum. In Colorado, as was discussed in Chapter 10, the voters failed to approve the financing of the 1976 Winter Olympic Games. High costs to residents in the state plus the likely damage to the natural environment led voters to oppose the games being held in Denver. Florida voters approved bonds amounting to $240 million for purposes of buying prize environmental lands in the state plus purchasing lands for outdoor recreation. Probably the largest environmental bond issue to be supported in recent years was the 1972 issue by New York voters. Residents approved $1.15 billion to be used for cleaning up the air and water in the state.

Similar state bond issues were approved in 1970. Alaska residents okayed $11 million for water and sewer projects and $2.3 million for park and recreation facilities. Illinois passed a $750 million bond issue for controlling water pollution. Maine passed a $4 million bond issue to be used to control oil spills, Nevada passed a $5 million issue for parks, and Washington voters approved $40 million for recreational facilities and $25 million for water pollution control in 1970. Not all states saw their bond issues win approval as Rhode Island voters turned down a $3.1 million issue for sewage projects. Washington residents, although they supported two bond issues, did not favor establishing a five-cent deposit on soft drink and beer containers. California voters did not approve the use of gasoline taxes for air pollution studies and mass transit development. This was in 1970.

The environmental importance to some states and their citizens is illustrated by referendums calling for an amendment to the existing state constitution, as was approved by Virginia and Rhode Island voters in 1970. Both have devised an "Environmental Bill of Rights" outlining the protection of the environment and the rights and responsibilities of individuals with respect to its use.

Cities have placed a number of environmental issues before the electorate, mostly involving bonds for public projects such as water treatment facilities, sewage plants, and parks and recreation lands. In cities that have had rapid population increases in the past decade or two, a number of citizen groups and councils have been concerned about the effects of unrestricted growth on the city and environment. Limitations on the construction of new buildings or residential development restrictions have been placed before a number of voters. Most such votes have been in California and Colorado cities and more recently discussions on such have been held by Florida communities. Not all referendums have been successful. As was discussed in Chapter 10, Boulder residents approved a proposal in 1971 to limit the height of downtown buildings to 55 feet. Voters also approved a plan to purchase and develop green belt spaces. San Francisco residents have twice defeated a proposal to limit the height of downtown buildings to thirteen stories. Already there is a 40-foot limit in most residential areas. Laguna Beach, California has limited the height of buildings in the city limits to 36 feet. Likewise voters in Santa Fe, New Mexico, have approved an ordinance requiring all new construction in the heart of the city to conform to the old Pueblo style and if it is above 35 feet, there must be setbacks. Elsewhere a 65-foot limit is in force. Similar height restrictions have been approved by voters in Lincoln City, Oregon; Highland Park, Illinois; and Telluride, Colorado. In this last ski resort community of only 500 people, no A-frame houses are permitted as there must be sidewalls on all houses constructed.

Population densities and numbers have been other issues that are stirring community interests in California, Colorado, and Florida. City councils and various environmental groups are becoming increasingly aware of the problems to city services and the natural environment that result from unplanned and unrestricted growth and development. Boulder, Colorado, one of the more environmentally conscious cities in the United States, submitted the issue of a population ceiling to its voters in November 1971; however, it was turned down. Yet other cities are discussing the same problem. Boca Raton, Florida, a middle- to high-income residential community north of Miami submitted the same question to its voters in November 1972. Here voters approved placing a ceiling on 40,000 dwelling units—houses, multiple dwellings, and condominiums. This theoretically would place a population limit of 100,000 on this present city of 40,000. After that number has been reached, supposedly no further building permits would be issued.

Organizational Impact. The popularity of the environment issue in society is also illustrated by groups and organizations of a formal and informal nature that are concerned about environmental protection and the quality of life. Although there have long been nature and conservation-oriented groups concerned with protecting endangered species and unique natural niches, these have received a new life recently. This has been true especially for those that are interested in learning about and appreciating the natural environment, but true also for those interested in preserving it by political and legislative means. This renewed interest is exemplified by a 33 percent increase for the five largest environmental organizations that have national affiliations from June 1970 to June 1971. These five are the National Wildlife Federation (700,000 associate members), the Sierra Club (135,000 members), the National Audubon Society (75,000), the Wilderness Society (70,000), and the Izaak Walton League (50,000).[15] Others that have been active are Friends of the Earth and in legal challenges the Environmental Defense Fund.

Although these national organizations are concerned with such projects as protecting unique vegetation areas and preserving rare fauna, the interest on the part of several has become political-environmental instead of educational-environmental. Actions by one or more national groups have been behind the opposition to continued construction of the Cross-Florida Barge Canal, the appropriations for supersonic transport development, private misuse of public lands, and government damming of scenic canyons in the West.

Efforts in the political arena are not restricted to national organizations and their local chapters. It was estimated that in 1971 there was as many as 3100 environmental organizations in the United States. This does not include the large number of civic, church, or school groups or even local chapters of national organizations. The 1971 Conservation Directory of the National Wildlife Federation lists over 250 national and regional organizations of varying sizes and nearly 400 state environmental groups. It is not surprising that this number of local, state, and national groups when involved in an environmental issue can have a significant impact. Citizen groups were especially popular during the Earth Day 1970 observance. Many groups have organized, with or without a national organization's support, and focus on a single project. Challenges were made either by marches, debates, or even bringing suits against an oil refinery location in Maine, nuclear power plants in Michigan, strip mining in Arizona, a dam on the Delaware River, road cuts through North Carolina forests, hydroelectric facilities in Wisconsin, and planned residential development in California. Numerous are the other cases where a locally formed civic group became involved in very local issues such as landfill sites, freeway or expressway routes, industrial noise pollution, or park projects.

Environmental organizations have become directly involved in state and city elections and in the funding of certain environmentally planned projects. These groups have financed campaigns to inform the public about the candidates' views on significant environmental issues and to arouse the critical importance of such to those of varying incomes, ideologies, and political parties. Recent statewide successes on bond issues in California, New York, Florida, and Colorado are examples where environmental organizations can take credit for the passage of critical referendums.

Financial contributions to congressmen are a part of the philosophy of the League of Conservation voters. In 1970 the League endorsed and helped finance the campaigns of twenty-two politicians; seventeen won. In the 1972 election thirteen were supported with donations from $1,000 to $16,000 and seven won. Altogether over $70,000 was donated to politicians and various state groups.[16] The League's major goal in 1972 was to defeat the powerful chairman of the House Interior Committee, Congressman Wayne Aspinall (Democrat from Colorado). He was defeated in the primary, probably in part because of the energies of the League of Conservation Voters and other groups such as Environmental Action.

Besides financial contributions environmental organizations such as the League of Conservation Voters endorse candidates. In 1972 it endorsed fifty-seven gubernatorial and congressional candidates and forty-three won.[17] Only four of the twelve House members (commonly referred to as the "Dirty Dozen") Environmental Action hoped to defeat won; these had poor records on environmental legislation. Specific votes on environmental legislation in both the Senate and House of Representatives are used by the League to measure a score for each congressman. Of the nineteen environmental votes used in 1971–1972 the highest ratings were given to both senators from Massachusetts (Kennedy and Brooke), Wisconsin (Nelson and Proxmire), New Jersey (Case and Williams), Minnesota (Mondale and Humphrey), and California (Cranston and Tunney). These senators also come from some of the more environmentally conscious states as evidenced by new programs to finance projects and protect the environment from unwise use and development.

Locational Decisions. The location strategies affecting environmentally related projects are assuming a greater political character. No longer are the routes for interstate highways, interchanges, power plant sitings, sanitary landfills, and recreation lands planned solely with economic considerations as the primary factors. Rather, social and environmental considerations are playing an important role insofar as they affect the quality of life of residents directly and the impact of changes on the physical and natural environment. This policy shift has meant that the strategies involving the location of public-owned or used facilities are being subjected to political pressures and policy-making agencies. The implementation of such projects is handled under a variety of programs administered by various governmental agencies, bureaus, and departments.

Environmental policy considerations regarding location have attained critical importance within the past few years. In the main this is a reflection that without adequate urban and regional planning for the location of such facilities as highways, power plants, pipelines, and parks that damage to some environmentally critical areas may continue unabated. The indirect results may not only lead to the destruction of wildlife, marshlands, coastal lands, scenic rivers, and unique vegetational areas but to eventual damage of other segments of the natural environment. In short it is realized that the environment is an intricate interdependent system that is closely tied together, land-water-air and man-animals-plants. Besides the recognition that unregulated planning and growth will continue to upset the delicate ecological balances, there is a growing appreciation for preserving and protecting the environment. This means that man's existence depends on both preserving a physical and natural environment suitable for habitation as well as for aesthetic purposes. Although this notion is not a new one, as it has long been recognized by conservation organizations and natural resource agencies, the political ingredient is recent. Politicians and government agencies that in the past were considering the location of hydroelectric dams or nuclear power plants from an economic utilization point of view are now forced to consider the impact of such projects on the environment. Similarly is this true for the location of interchanges and expressway routes in metropolitan areas. No longer is the construction viewed strictly in technological terms. Now the projects consider the effect on the residents directly and the land use picture for the metropolitan area.

It stands to reason that when political considerations enter planning of publicly owned and used facilities, controversies will develop. The cases provide opportunities for environmental groups to challenge government-sponsored projects and programs. This situation has occurred on a number of occasions within the past few years. Recreation developers collide with environmentalists and environmentalists with highway agencies and power plant corporations with both state and local governments and with citizens' lobbies. That decision making is no longer ignoring the views of environmentalists has led groups to challenge a number of potentially damaging projects and land uses in state and federal courts. The outcome has led either to the abandoning of a particular project or a consideration of alternatives that are within environmental guidelines stipulated by the states or the federal government. For example, the controversy over southern Lake Michigan for steel plant expansion, harbor facilities, open space, and prize recreational lands has involved various political jurisdictions and industrial and citizen groups for over a decade.[18]

Major controversies have developed relating to the location of federally funded highways. Interstates are now prohibited from splitting or cutting through public parks unless meaningful alternatives do not exist. That the influential Federal Highway Administration is being faced with charges from environmentalists is a very recent and significant development. Cases involving proposed interstates through parks in San Antonio and Memphis have resulted in lengthy court battles. Especially was this true for the Breckinridge Park and Olmos Basin parklands in San Antonio. As of mid-1973 it appeared that an alternative route would not have to be selected as Congress approved the plan favoring the highway interests. Such did not appear to be the case in the Overton Park in Memphis where an alternate expressway will probably have to be devised. Highway location planners are now finding that they must consider the residents affected by these federally funded projects. As was pointed out in an earlier chapter on decision-making strategies, all too often projects that were considered undesirable or noxious were placed in the poorest sections of cities where political organization and power were considered ineffectual. That this situation is changing is evidenced by inner city groups organizing to oppose highway routes and interchanges in their neighborhoods. When these groups cooperate with environmentalists they can potentially thwart projects as they did in the Foothill Expressway in Alameda County east of San Francisco Bay.

Controversies over the location of highways are not limited to cities. They also arise over planned routes through national parks and environmentally critical areas. It has almost been a truism that federal highway agencies and programs were not especially concerned with preserving or protecting an environment. Even though with the National Environmental Policy Act of 1970 environmental considerations are to be a part of strategies, examples where highway interests have lost out to environmental groups in the mid-1970s are rare. Two examples where the highway developers have not had their way are in the proposed expressways splitting Franconia Notch State Park in New Hampshire and in the Big Cypress Swamp in Florida. In the New Hampshire case a compromise expressway plan was approved that prevented dividing this environmentally unique park and in Florida the governor in 1973 announced that the proposed interstate going through the swamp would have only one access point.

Probably the single most publicized environmental issue in the past five years has been the proposal to construct an Alaskan pipeline. The basis of this issue is primarily one of location. That there are large reserves of petroleum, estimated at 20 billion barrels, on the North Slope and that the United States needs cheap and large quantities of petroleum at present are both given.[19] The problem is how to transport this large supply to the areas of greatest demands. Ocean tankers through the Northwest Passage and routes through Canada have both been considered but not in a serious vein. Rather the oil companies desire to construct a pipeline through Alaska to the Gulf of Alaska and then ship it southward. Another proposal had the pipeline through Alaska and Canada (Fig. 12-4). Politics and environmental issues entered the picture soon after the 1969 discovery. The proposed 800-mile pipeline route through Alaska was opposed by environmental groups such as the Environmental Defense Fund, Wilderness Society, Friends of the Earth, and many others. Their objections were that the proposed route crossed areas of frequent earthquake activity and unique wildlife habitats. The impact of constructing such a pipeline in an area of permafrost without adequate and effective prior land use planning would result in possible additional destruction to the environment. Many interests in Alaska favor the pipeline construction as they desire to see the economic boom that will accompany such a project. Environmental groups and Aleuts, Eskimos, and Indians in the same state do not totally favor such a project unless adequate compensation for lands is forthcoming and the environment is protected. In spite of these arguments Congress approved its construction in the fall of 1973. This was after the Supreme Court had backed a lower court ruling blocking the project.[20] When construction will begin is difficult to discern, but any right-of-way proposal will have to contain a well-documented environmental impact statement.

In Alaska and in other states there are decisions involving the uses of public

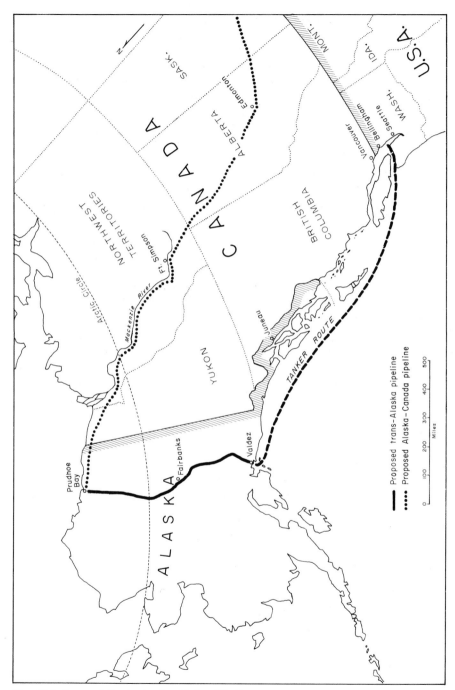

Fig. 12-4 Proposed Routes for the Alaskan Pipeline.

land. Where water needs are considered for recreational and municipal purposes, there are decisions to be made involving their utilization and management. In local areas where the conflicting interests exist, the eventual decision made about the use of a facility may depend on the perception of the problem from the politicians involved. Their perception may differ from that held by the public directly affected. A mayor or city council may perceive an environmental crisis the same or differently; the policies implemented may reflect strictly personal biases or favored development interests. This problem is characteristic of local politicians who may operate with only partial knowledge of key environment decisions.[21]

The decisions to be made about the utilization and protection of the environment are not restricted to local politicians and community interest groups. They also exist in the recommendations to be made on federally funded projects and the management of public lands. Again water and recreation resources are two key facets of the environment that the federal government has a direct input in policy recommendation and making. The various government agencies in the departments of Interior, Agriculture, and others are responsible for recommending the construction of dams, the draining of waste lands, the levels of agricultural intensity, the unwise destruction of forest or mineral lands, and the wisest use for national parks and wilderness areas. Problems arise when federal programs are not in harmony with public views. This places the political implications of the protection and preservation of public lands squarely in the public eye. At times the federal programs have not been primarily concerned with the views of individuals and groups about environmental matters and have instead implemented their agency policies. Highway development and airport location are two prime examples where either citizens' protests were ignored, or if they were considered, did not seriously affect positions taken by various agencies.[22]

The recent or renewed interest in states and the federal government in the environmental ramifications of highway and airport location, oil and gas pipeline construction, mining, and recreation interests has not been associated with the location of power plants. As stated above, it has been a national policy to insure that the location of these power installations using radioactive materials were in areas of low population numbers and density. This was in large part as a safety precaution against humans, vegetation, and wildlife. The early Atomic Energy Commission power reactors in sites such as Oak Ridge, Tennessee and Richland, Washington are cases in point. With the development of nuclear power as a significant energy source, the decisions involving the location of these installations have confronted state and local governments. Some states, sensing the serious nature of potential damage due to radiation leaks into the air or of thermal pollution, have introduced measures to regulate the industry. Minnesota, Maryland, and Oregon have all issued water use permits containing the limits on radioactive effluents that power companies with nuclear reactors can emit. Other states, such as Ohio, New Jersey, and Michigan, have called for studies on the environmental damage of lands in the vicinity of nuclear power plants.

The potential environmental hazards associated with nuclear power reactors would appear to dictate a location away from major populated areas. The actual sites approved by the Atomic Energy Commission would ideally be in places where the potential damage to the population would be minimal and where the physical environment would be suitable for such construction. Although there are examples of existing and proposed nuclear reactors in sparsely populated locations, the federal government in cooperation with local and state officials has seen fit to place reactors near most of the nation's largest cities. In California, for example, most of the proposed reactors are located in the densely populated southern third of the state and in the vicinity of existing fault lines.[23] Such locations would appear to be unwise from an environmental point of view considering the already heavy air pollution levels existing in that part of the state (Fig. 12-5).

It would appear that with the greater environmental consciousness of the public and the government agencies that locational strategies for public facilities will be a major consideration in the decision-making processes. Conflicts over the rights and the management of resources will be echoed in city councils, courts, and in Congress.

ENVIRONMENTAL LAW AND JURISDICTION

It follows that if states and the federal government are concerned about protecting and preserving the environment that some legal framework will have to be designed to see that this objective is met. With the federal government showing the lead in

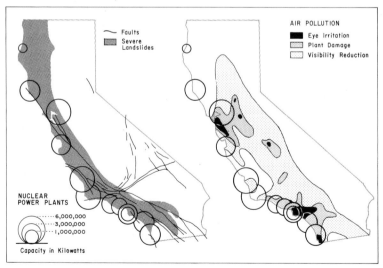

FIG. 12-5 Nuclear Power Site Locations in California. (After Peter F. Mason, "Some Geographical Considerations of Siting Nuclear Power Reactors Along the California Coast," *California Geographer*, 12 (1971), pp. 22, 24, and 26.)

noting national seriousness of the environmental problems, the National Environmental Protection Act was signed in 1970. In essence this stated that concerns of
the environment were national, not regional or restricted to only one state. It was
concerned with setting air and water quality standards as they would apply to the
nation. This was a definite step forward in the handling of pollution problems as it
demonstrated the federal government was taking the lead in recommending legislation on air and water quality and administering specific programs. Instead of
leaving problems to individual state efforts, which might be conflicting, the
national geographic basis of environmental problems was recognized. Air pollution
and water pollution are problems that cannot be confined to specific city, county,
state or even international boundary lines. If the federal government had not taken
a strong lead in this direction, a mosaic of environmental legislation probably
would have resulted between the states. The congressional legislation was instrumental in the subsequent actions taken by states as ten have passed environmental
quality acts similar to NEPA.

In addition to providing a basis for post-1969 legislation setting air and water
quality standards and enforcing them in the states, NEPA also had stipulated that
future federally financed projects must have environmental impact studies performed.[24] The effect of such impact studies is to insure that, at least on federal
lands, institutions, and projects, acceptable levels of quality are being met to deal
with the human and physical environment. To see that environmental considerations are included as a part of projects, the federal government can either challenge
a decision or NEPA provides for suits brought by individuals or environmentalist organizations.

A number of court cases have demonstrated that federally started or
conceptualized projects have had to be scrapped or alternative plans considered.
The secretary of interior refused in 1971, primarily on environmental grounds, to
authorize two proposed oil platforms in the Santa Barbara Channel. In Houston,
Texas, the Army Corps of Engineers postponed indefinitely a plan to channelize
sections of Buffalo Bayou, this for damage to the area. Federal plans for a bulk mail
handling facility in Fort Snelling, Minnesota, were dropped after it was evident it
would not be in keeping with the adjacent recreational area. Other projects that
have been stymied by citizens' groups include delayed construction of the Alaskan
pipeline, a halting of Interstate construction on the scenic Hudson River, the
suspension of the Miami jetport in the Everglades, the continued unrestricted sale
of DDT, and the protection of wildlife habitats on state and federal lands.

The regulation of uses of public lands and waters and even the management
and utilization of private holdings have seen environmental interests and legislation
become a key ingredient in contemporary society. It not only involves cooperative
efforts from the local, state, and federal governments but from various interested
groups. Agricultural, industrial, recreational, mineral, and timber interests are often
at odds with who has the jurisdiction over use of the environment and who has
priority. Frequent are the state and federal cases involving sports fishermen and
hunters vs. big dam interests supported by power companies and agriculturalists, as

along the Teton River in Idaho, or the nature groups conflicting with timber, mineral, and commercial interests for uses of federal land. With the federal government calling for impacts statements and more states beginning to pass similar legislation, the various groups desiring to use or protect the environment will be expected to clash in the courts.

Although national legislation dealing with air and water quality levels is on the books and environmental impact considerations are being requested on federal projects, there still remains much about environmental law that exhibits a geographical flavor. The Clean Air and Water Acts set national quality standards and states are to meet such programs within a specified period of time. This permits some states to be rather lax and protect their own industries should they desire. Based on the Clean Air Amendment of 1970, in April 1971 the Environmental Protection Agency established primary and secondary national ambient air quality standards for the six most widespread air pollutants—particulate matter, sulfur oxides, hydrocarbons, carbon monoxide, oxides of nitrogen, and products from petrochemicals.[25] States were given three years to develop plans to establish standards to protect public health; only fourteen states had approved plans by May 1972. Some states, cities, and air quality regions were given extensions beyond the deadline because of severe pollution mainly from automobiles. According to the 1972 legislation on water quality, the states have until mid-1977 to implement technology to reduce industrial waste discharges. Similar geographic variation in response to the federal guidelines is expected for states handling water pollution.

With the environmental legislation proposed by the states and Congress, it became necessary to provide policies that dealt with the protection and preservation of the total environment. Specific pieces of legislation were proposed and enacted that had dealt with uses and misuses of water, air, and land. What was lacking in much of this legislation was a legal framework whereby cases could be brought to the courts against industries, governments, and individuals. Such was finally incorporated in the National Environmental Policy Act that President Nixon signed on January 1, 1970. In the main this act (NEPA) was "to establish a national policy for the environment." What this act has become is the primary policy-setting federal law relating to the protection of the environment. From 1970–1972 over 200 lawsuits have been brought under NEPA. They relate mainly to federal projects involving highways and airports, water resource projects of the Corps of Engineers, public land management practices, licenses for nuclear power plants, and federally supported housing projects in cities.

Among the legal decisions rendered by the Supreme Court have been those defining the proper legal and administrative responsibility for protecting the environment (particularly where federal-state policies are not in harmony), the reinterpretation of some older little-used environmental laws, and the rights of groups and individuals to sue industries, states, and even the federal government. Since 1970 among the major environmental decisions that reached the United States Supreme Court included the underground nuclear explosions set for Amchitka Island, Alaska and the Sierra Club vs. Morton case involving a ski development on federal lands. In the latter, called the Mineral King case, the court held that the club did not have sufficient legal interest to press its claim for prohibiting constructing the development in the Sierra Nevada. However, this case was important as it did confirm the right of individual citizens and groups to outline the steps necessary for bringing environmental issues to courts of law. Other cases that were important involved the radiation regulations for nuclear-fueled generating plants. The court ruled in a case involving a power company and the state of Minnesota that such plants are subject only to regulations of the Atomic Energy Commission, not more strict ones that states may impose. In a court test involving jurisdictional limits in environmental matters, the Supreme Court ruled that the state of Illinois did not have the right to stipulate the regulations of four Wisconsin cities and two sewage commissions. This in spite of the fact that these political subdivisions caused pollution of Illinois waters. The conflicting state problems were further complicated when it was ruled that a federal district court in Wisconsin did have jurisdiction to hear Illinois' claim. In jurisdictional cases between states, the Constitution states that the Supreme Court shall hear such. In another case also involving Wisconsin the Court ruled that political subdivisions have the responsibility to abate pollution of interstate waters and of air that has an identifiable interstate watershed.[26] Thus, in these and other cases the Supreme Court is occupying an important place in the areas of environmental protection, quality, and preservation. Involved are the legal rights of the federal government, states, and local communities as well as the rights and privileges accorded industries, groups, and individuals. With greater importance attached to the environment and the quality of life, whether it involved clean air and water, public-minded land use policies, or the protection from visual blight or crowded housing, it is certain that political and geographical facets of environmental law will only increase.

With state legislatures still responsible for introducing and enforcing environmental programs, it stands to reason that some states are leaders in the protection of their environment. Others it can be said are lax in that special interests are still strong and more effective in blocking legislative actions and the effectiveness of environmental organizations. Mining interests are a case in point. With the scarring of the physical landscape and the destruction to wildlife, marine, and vegetation that is done by strip mining, still national legislation has failed to deal effectively with this problem. The result is that strip mining interests are affected by a variety of state legislation. In West Virginia, the new Surface Mining and Reclamation Act prohibits all new strip mining permits for two years in twenty-two of the fifty-five counties in the state. Also a reclamation tax is imposed and reclamation of newly mined lands must be carried out. Similar but not identical legislation over strip mining lands has been approved in Arkansas, Ohio, Illinois, Maine, Missouri, Montana, North Carolina, South Dakota, and Virginia. Examples of other industries also exist where because of their political strength in state legislatures and their contribution to the state's economy they are given favored treatment on environmental legislation. Phosphate interests in Florida and taconite mining in Minnesota are examples where tax programs and land use policies were enacted to work to their advantage. Similarly this existed for lumber interests in the South and West and Upper Great Lakes before conservation measures were introduced.

Laws and regulations have also affected the growth and development of southern Florida, California, Arizona, and neighboring states. Lax zoning laws which had little or no concern for the effect of construction on wildlife, vegetation, and coastal or inland waters led to rapid residential expansion and cheap unplanned developments in many parts of the South and Southwest. The lure of commercial interests from the Northeast or California or from Florida was that developments could be constructed easily with little state restrictions about lot size, public facilities, residential density, and destruction to the environment. It is some of these same states and areas that in the past attracted investors (major companies and individuals) to purchase and develop marshlands, swamplands, deserts, or mountains that are attempting to legislate development today. This topic is discussed at greater length below.

Geographical variations in laws affecting the environment are not restricted only to differences in the interpretation of federal standards or varying states. They also exist within political units comprising metropolitan areas. Just as some mining and industrial interests may choose to locate in a state because they can "control" legislation that may affect them, so they may choose to move from one political unit to another. In the past few years there have been actions taken by city councils and voters to protect and preserve the environment. Or they may have enacted environmental legislation affecting air, water, or noise polluters. In some cases the communities have seen companies move out and locate in other political jurisdictions. Clearly this piecemeal legislative approach is not very effective as air, water, and noise pollution are not confined to only one suburb or one socioeconomic class.

Industrial expansion in particular has followed the population shifts to the suburbs. Companies are moving from the older commercial and industrial cores in the central cities to suburban areas where land and taxes are lower, the transportation linkages to interurban and interstate movement is facilitated, and the labor force resides. According to the 1970 census almost 38 percent of all Americans now live in the suburbs compared to only 31 percent in the cities. Furthermore, in the last decade over half of the new industrial and commercial construction has taken place in the suburbs. Movements of manufacturing, retail, and wholesaling companies have been particularly acute in the largest cities. From 1965 to 1970 New York lost more than 13,000 (some by attrition but the suburbs gained 2,000); Detroit 3,500; Philadelphia nearly 3,000; Baltimore 2,500; and St. Louis 1,400.[27] The relocation of many of these concerns to suburban areas has been received with mixed feelings. Granted that the tax base will be augmented by new industrial and commercial growth but environmental headaches also result. The availability of water and sewage treatment facilities, the increased population numbers and densities, increases in traffic congestion, and the continued hassles over zoning and rezoning policies are seen as problems to individual citizens and governing bodies. The urban environmental interests enter these changing economic strategies when issues of community stability and identity, utilization of resources and revenues, and conflicting government authorities are at odds.

In an effort to handle environmental problems a number of states have banded together to deal with specific concerns about air pollution, water pollution, pest control, apportionment of water, recreation lands, water resources, and conservation. As many state leaders and legislative bodies envision the problem of handling efficiently such environmental issues, it is considered a more effective strategy to have states engage in joint efforts than to await congressional legislation. This often takes too long and in the meantime environmental conditions might worsen. As of mid-1971 there were nearly sixty agreements concerning the environment that were in effect and another twenty-five pending.[28] States may enter into Intergovernmental Environment Compacts provided they have the legislative approval of the states entering these joint compacts.

The largest number of compacts that are in effect deal with conservation and the uses of water. The Atlantic States Marine Fisheries Compact is comprised of fifteen East Coast states from Maine to Florida. On the West Coast is the Pacific Marine Fisheries Compact with five members in mid-1971. Other fishery agreements involve the Potomac River Compact (two states) and the Gulf States Marine Fisheries Compact (five states). Forest fire protection compacts exist between states in the Southwest, South Central, Middle Atlantic, and Northeast states. There are also compacts governing interstate mining and compacts to conserve oil and gas.

A number of compacts, basically on a river basin framework, handle problems relating to water in bordering states. Examples of such include the Bear River Compact (Idaho, Utah, and Wyoming); the Republican River Compact (Colorado, Kansas, Nebraska); the Klamath River Compact (California and Oregon); and the Yellowstone River Compact (Montana, North Dakota, and Wyoming). Water pollution compacts affect states in the Ohio River Valley Sanitation Compact (eight states from Illinois to Virginia and New York), the Tennessee River Basin Pollution Control Compact (three states), the New England Interstate Water Pollution Control Compact (seven states) and others in the Delaware Valley, Arkansas River, and Potomac Valley.

A number of compacts on air pollution were still awaiting the approval of one or more state legislature or Congress. Some considered were the Illinois-Indiana Air Pollution Control Compact, the Kansas-Missouri Air Quality Compact, and the Ohio-Kentucky Interstate Compact on Air Pollution (four states).

Cooperative efforts were agreed on by states in planning the land uses in rural and urban areas particularly in the northeastern quarter of the United States. The clustered and high population densities in the metropolitan areas crossing state boundaries led to these interstate compacts. Some involved industrial and others urban and even rural development efforts. Examples of compacts already existing include the New England Interstate Planning Compact (four states), the Susquehanna River Basin Compact (three states), the Delaware River and Bay Authority

Compact, the Port of New York Authority, and the Tahoe Regional Planning Compact. Interstate efforts have been noted in the establishment of recreational lands as evidenced by the Palisades Interstate Park Compact (New Jersey and New York); Pymatuning Lake Compact (Ohio and Pennsylvania); and the Cumberland Gap National Park (Kentucky, Virginia, and Tennessee).

Problems involving the environment reach beyond local and state jurisdictions to cover the concerns of nations. In the main, problems of air and water and wildlife affect all nations regardless of geographical location, economic development, or political ideology. The year 1972 marked significant progress in the field of environmental measures affecting the United States and its northern and southern neighbors. What these recognize basically is that air and water move irrespective of political boundaries and that they directly affect citizens on both sides of international borders. For example, there are at present different standards for controlling air pollution in Detroit, Michigan, and Windsor, Ontario. Detroit's deals with ambient air and Windsor's with particulate emissions. Legislation between these adjacent cities is not compatible. Most pollution in the area is derived from Detroit and thus crosses the international boundary.[29] Such problems illustrate the importance of cooperative efforts in identifying and solving mutual problems.[30]

The United States-Canadian Great Lakes Water Quality Agreement signed in April 1972 is concerned with alleviating the destruction of the Great Lakes and improving the quality of waters entering them. The lakes are important to both nations from an industrial, commercial, and until recently, recreational standpoint. The international boundary crosses through four of the five lakes and through three connecting channels; therefore, the problems affecting the lands and population clusters bordering the lakes are of concern to both the United States and Canada. Under the terms of the agreement, based in part on the Boundary Waters Treaty of 1909, an International Joint Commission was to investigate water conditions in Lake Erie, Lake Ontario, and the international section of the St. Lawrence River. Specific objectives were outlined that govern the types and levels of materials that are permitted to enter international waters. Some of the water quality standards are more stringent than the federal-state standards already established; however, the United States through intergovernmental agencies will aid the Great Lakes states and cities. The international commission is also to monitor programs of both nations. A December 31, 1975, deadline has been set for completion of certain parts of the bilateral agreement.

The problem between the United States and Mexico involves the quality of water the United States supplies its neighbor from the Colorado River. Under the terms of the Mexican Water Treaty in 1944 the United States is to supply 1.5 million acre-feet of Colorado River water annually. Although no mention was made as to the quality of such water, those waters coming into Mexico have been of such a saline nature that productive agriculture is difficult for farmers in the Mexicali Valley. Some corrective measures were taken in 1965, but the problem has remained. The joint communique issued between the presidents of the two nations in June 1972 called for the United States to take further measures to further reduce the salinity levels and present a program for such by the end of 1972. As the

Mexican government viewed the situation, it deserved quality water from the Colorado River and without some adjustments to benefit their border farmlands, the United States agricultural interests would continue to be the chief beneficiaries of these river waters. Irrigation lands in the United States dependent on such waters already have high production levels, a sharp contrast from those lands just across the border.

POLITICS OF GROWTH AND DEVELOPMENT

Changes in the population distribution of the United States especially since 1960 have basically underscored two patterns that emerged a decade earlier. First is the movement from the central city to the suburbs. The second is the movement to coastal states, that were also amenity (sun, water, varying topographies) states in the South and Southwest. The initial growth in population led to the increases in the major metropolitan centers and to new urbanization in the states of Florida, Texas, Arizona, and California. With the recent importance attached to environmental issues and quality-of-life concerns, much of the early reason to support growth and development has been called into question. Specifically, the fastest growing suburbs and states are questioning the environmental implications of continued urban growth and development. The nature of this topic has direct political implications for local and state governments as city commissions authorize construction permits and lay out zoning regulations and states administer programs regarding resources belonging to the total population. Legal forces are also involved when private property rights are questioned in line with the environmental rights of the public, whether in the planning of particular projects or in area-wide land use planning schemes. Recreational, power company, agricultural, industrial, and land development interests are all examples of controversies that are taking place over the proper utilization of the environment.

To date the actions taken by local and state governments vary from construction moratoriums to limiting population growth. Both are viewed as ways to limit growth. The opposition to previous and existing development is not simply a "no growth" philosophy but one that suggests that developing a city's resources or a state's resources needs to be carefully controlled and planned. If such is not carried out, needed services such as schools, roads, water, sewage, power and recreation might not be available in sufficient quantity in the near and distant future. Furthermore, the quality of services are important, hence the need to carefully administer and plan for effective use of the area and the numbers of people affected.

As mentioned the forms taken to deal with these environmental problems vary. The most active positions taken to date are those environmentally conscious states that are being affected by the most rapid growth and development. This list includes California and Florida but also Oregon, Colorado, some New England states, and suburban areas near Washington, D.C., and New York City.[31] It will only be a matter of time before many of the practices approved by such city commissions and state agencies are adopted by others.

Moratoriums against further building have been approved by commissions in Albuquerque, New Mexico; Fairfax County, Virginia, and Livermore and Pleasanton, California. In these and others the permits to build new developments have been withheld until new water treatment, sewage disposal, roads, and schools are made available as the existing facilities are being pressed to their maximum usage. Limiting the numbers of people has been another policy that will curtail growth and development. The San Francisco Bay Area Governments Association has adopted as a regional policy to halt the population at 5.5 million by 1980. Already there are nearly 4 million inhabitants. Density limitations have been passed by a number of Florida governments such as the counties of Palm Beach and Martin and cities of St. Petersburg-Tampa and Hollywood and Hallandale. Boca Raton as mentioned above adopted a measure restricting its dwelling units to 40,000. The concerns in these cities is partly to prevent uncontrolled growth of the city's population with little opportunity to plan for the necessary public services accompanying any residential development. Also by limiting the numbers or densities or having moratoriums it is hoped that such actions will stem the rapid migration. The Disneyworld complex near Orlando has created spillover effects of a positive and negative nature to surrounding small Florida communities. Although economic gains are desirable, the environmental damage that may result to unique areas as well as from relatively uncontrolled land developers is not necessarily desired. Similar conditions exist for recreation and tourist developments in New England, Colorado, and California.

For this reason a number of states have engaged in plans to deal with environmental problems. Oregon was one of the first to be concerned about protecting the environment, both its natural resources and its residents. During the early 1970s, the philosophy was echoed by Governor Tom McCall who said, "Come, but don't stay." This was to indicate to potential industrial developers and to potential migrants that the state was not ostensibly interested in growth per se. After much discussion by environmentalists and politicians and various citizens groups, this philosophy was echoed recently in statewide land use planning legislation. This called for carefully controlled economic growth, the protection of environmentally critical areas, and a request to raise the camping fee for out-of-state cars in state parks. Controlling the development of coastal lands 1000 feet inland was approved by California voters in a 1972 referendum. This enactment also required environmental-impact statements for most commercial developments, an innovation of increasing popularity throughout the United States. Florida has passed a series of water conservation laws and environmental legislation. Land planning was a part of the Environmental Land and Water Management Act that dealt especially with environmentally critical areas. Also a bond issue to purchase such lands was approved in 1972. Colorado voters voiced the concern for environmental vs. commercial interests with their unwillingness to finance the 1976 Olympic Games in a statewide vote in 1972. Vermont in 1970 passed a law primarily oriented to developers of second homes and ski resorts; in effect to protect lands from inappropriate or excessive development, a state permit for all commercial, industrial, and residential development above 2500 feet is required regardless of the size or acreage. Before a permit is granted, a district commissioner normally holds public hearings. In Maine the Site Location Act of 1970 is similar to Vermont's in that a permit for certain types of commercial or industrial development is required. Any development that is in excess of twenty acres or involves drilling or excavating natural resources or building structures in excess of 60,000 square feet on a single site is affected.[32] The recreational and land development interests also have been prominent in the recent controversies over the uses of the Adirondacks Park. Despite pressures for using the privately held lands for subdivisions, industries, and a jetport, the New York legislature recently approved a plan to keep the private lands permanently protected by limiting one building for each 42 acres on more than half the private land. The industrial developments will be in areas already built up and large second-house developments will be in a low density pattern.

Involved in the Adirondacks Park case and others that have come to the fore are the legal questions about property rights. In the main, the questions raised relate to the authority to regulate the uses of land, even if privately held, and the final legal authority, the state courts or the Supreme Court. In more than one legal case that has been heard the parties involve private citizens, private companies (industrial or agricultural) or environmental groups vs. a city or state government. It is basically the question of the property rights of individuals who hold lands. Individuals or groups holding land that they held for speculative purposes often find they cannot use the lands as they desire as they do not mesh with regional or state land use plans. Rather they find they have to comply with land use plans designed by governments. The Ryker Industrial Corporation in Stratford, Connecticut is an example where the company having owned land in the Great Salt Lake Meadow for more than twenty years now finds that it cannot build its new facility. The state Commissioner of Environmental Protection has denied the request as it would endanger the tidal wetlands area and endanger the shellfish. The company is asking $77 million from the state. A similar development project that was stymied by a planning agency involves a plan to build sixty second-home condominium units on the shores of Lake Tahoe, California. The developer desires to change the residential density and the Tahoe Regional Planning Authority has basically been concerned with a lower density and preservation of the unique physical environment. The company is asking for $4.5 million in compensation. Examples of compensation from developers is not limited to rural areas, as the Penn Central Railroad is asking for $8 million a year in damages because the New York City Planning Commission denied the demolition of (except for main concourse) the Grand Central Terminal. It was designated as a landmark by the city's Landmark Preservation Committee in 1967.

While some developers are seeking compensation from states and cities for property rights they feel are being violated, some citizens and groups are donating lands to the public to prevent certain types of growth and development. Especially does this hold true for individuals who have valuable natural areas or historic sites. They can donate such to public agencies or place in nonprofit land trusts and use as income tax deductions.

The question about environmental property rights promises to be of critical importance in the future. Cases involving an individual citizen suing an industrial polluter will be of one type but equally as frequent may be those individuals taking a city or state into court because of property rights being abrogated by state policies and land use plans. To date, courts in the states of California, Maine, Maryland, and Wisconsin have sustained state land use controls against individuals. The main argument taken by states is that the public interest is at stake in the particular environmental issue. For example, in 1970 a California court upheld the Bay Conservation and Development Commission's power to control the filling of San Francisco Bay. Involvement in land use controls and property rights has not been a subject handled to any great extent in recent years by the United States Supreme Court. It has preferred to leave such matters to the states. However, it is expected with the various parties involved in the environment's protection and use that questions about environmental law will reach this highest judicial body.

To handle the variety of questions and issues that arise about growth and development a number of states have implemented various land use programs and policies. As these are designed some are narrow in scope relating only to particular land uses such as recreational lands or power plant sitings while others are comprehensive in scope and operation. The most recent handbook by the Council for Environmental Quality states the concern succinctly:

> The States are concerned about possible limits on future recreation opportunities; the rapid, uncoordinated, and piecemeal industrial, commercial, and residential development going on within their boundaries; and the lack of unified criteria by which to evaluate developments proposed in environmentally critical areas.[33]

The Florida Environmental Land and Water Management Act of 1972 that is alluded to above is a comprehensive program designed to cover the major environmental concerns affecting the state and to encourage state-local cooperation. Regions of "critical state concern" are identified and recommendations for development are submitted for action. State planning agencies have been established in Virginia under a Land Use Policy Act and in Rhode Island under the Division of Statewide Planning. In Michigan the development and regulation of public and private lands and waters are coordinated by the state's Natural Resources Commission and by the Department of Natural Resources.

Some states have considered population numbers and density to be a critical part of planning for the utilization of the state's resources. Colorado and Michigan are two such states; the Environmental Commission in Colorado recommended stabilizing the population and developing a plan that considers the future ecological situation while in Michigan the Governor's Advisory Council on Environmental Quality has urged the state to adopt a zero population growth policy. Restricting or controlling expansion has been recommended in Oregon and Maine. Permits carrying environmental impact clauses are being required by several state governments; failure to comply as in California may result in a denial.

Other than economic and population considerations, a number of states have enacted legislation to govern the uses of coastal areas and wetlands. Control in these lands is desired to protect them for recreational uses as well as for being unique environmental niches. Florida, Georgia, California, Rhode Island, Oregon, New Jersey, and Virginia are states with programs to protect these areas from environmental damage. Internal rivers and waters are protected for the same reasons by laws in Florida, Massachusetts, Michigan, Oregon, and Maine. To date, eighteen states have legislation of some type to protect and preserve wildlife. Some states have wildlife they protect in addition to those 101 endangered species identified by the federal government (14 mammals, 50 birds, 7 reptiles, and 30 fish species). Problems remain in the federal-state protection of endangered species as federal authority over these now holds only on federal lands. There is a move afoot in the same states to protect all such species as well as their habitats.

Much of the recent impetus for environmental concerns as outlined in land use policies came from President Nixon's 1972 Environmental Message. The essence of this message, as in original legislation submitted to Congress, was to require states as a precondition to obtaining financial assistance, to assume the responsibility of land use matters that went beyond local jurisdictional limits. States were to protect critical environmental areas such as coastal lands and historic sites and control land use around federal installations such as interchanges and parks. Federal concern was also voiced about water treatment plants and providing low- and moderate-income housing. To insure that these be carried out the legislation called for state agencies to be established to deal with the locating and administering of land use types around airports, highways, and parks. Failure on the part of a state to develop adequate programs would result in federal funds for highway, airport, and parks being reduced starting in 1975. The result of this legislation would be to involve states in planning the growth and development of the resources.[34] Public land management, regulation, and disposal of the many federal lands in the West are also matters currently under discussion. The net effect of this federal, state, and local involvement in land use policies and planning is to hopefully result in wise utilization and protection of the nation's lands and waters. Clearly the issues involving land use have taken on more a political and legal air in the past few years as they effect subdivision zoning, wildlife protection, strip-mining reclamation, and power-plant siting.

In June 1973 the U.S. Senate approved a national land use bill that called for federal financial assistance to help states establish state-wide programs. Further, the legislation asked states to carry out land use inventories. By late 1973 the House had not voted on legislation dealing with federal and state regulations in land use matters.

FOOTNOTES

1. The most useful sources for this discussion on recent local, state, and federal developments are the 1971 and 1972 reports issued by the Council of Environmental Quality. *Second Annual Report of the Council of Environmental Quality, 1971* and *Third Annual Report of the Council of Environmental Quality, 1972*, Washington, D.C., Government Printing Office, 1971 and 1972.

2. Political geography studies in the sphere of resource management are called for in the report *The Science of Geography*, Washington, D.C., National Academy of Sciences-National Research Council, Division of Earth Sciences, Publication 1277, 1965, pp. 36–38.

3. *Second Annual Report of the Council* . . . , op. cit., p. 220.

4. The national scope of air pollution is treated by Philip A. Leighton, "Geographical Aspects of Air Pollution," *Geographical Review*, 56 (1966), 151–174; and Wilfrid Bach, *Atmospheric Pollution*, New York, McGraw-Hill, 1972.

5. The relations between air pollution levels and the degree of poverty in cities is treated in the *Second Annual Report of the Council* . . . , op. cit., pp. 189–207.

6. Gordon M. Stevenson, Jr., "Noise and the Urban Environment," in Thomas R. Detwyler and Melvin G. Marcus et al., *Urbanization and the Environment: The Physical Geography of the City*, Belmont, Calif., Duxbury Press, 1972, pp. 195–228. This book deals with the climate, geology, water, pollution, and quality of life in cities, topics that are of particular interest to understanding the urban environment.

7. The general quality of life in urban areas has been tackled by two recent geography discussions on Gainesville and Tampa, Florida. Joshua C. Dickinson et al., "The Quality of Life in Gainesville, Florida: An Application of Territorial Social Indicators," *Southeastern Geographer*, 12:2 (1972), 121–132; and David M. Smith, *The Geography of Social Well-Being in the United States*, New York, McGraw-Hill, 1973, pp. 120–134.

8. Several recent books have treated political facets of the environment such as J. Clarence Davies, III, *The Politics of Pollution*, New York, Pegasus, 1970; Frank P. Grad et al., *Environmental Control: Priorities, Policies, and the Law*, New York, Columbia University Press, 1971; James Ridgeway, *The Politics of Ecology*, New York, Dutton, 1971; Phillip O. Foss, ed., *Politics and Ecology*, Belmont, Calif., Duxbury Press, 1972; and Dennis L. Thompson, ed., *Politics, Policy, and Natural Resources*, New York, Free Press, 1972.

9. The history of federal involvement in environmental legislation is treated by Davies, op. cit., pp. 37–58; and Grad et al., op. cit., pp. 47–216.

10. The idea for another cabinet position to coordinate energy and natural resources has been discussed in the past few years. The notion was endorsed by President Nixon in June 1973.

11. *Third Annual Report of the Council* . . . , op. cit., pp. 158–162.

12. A separate discussion on the sources, problems, and solutions to urban noise is treated in the 1972 report of the Council of Environmental Quality. Ibid., pp. 206–216.

13. "Most Productive Legislative Session in History," *Congressional Quarterly Weekly Report*, November 25, 1972, pp. 3066–3067.

14. "Federal Environmental Programs," *Special Analyses of the United States Government, Fiscal Year, 1973*, Washington, D.C., Government Printing Office, 1972, pp. 296–309.

15. The growing public support for environmental issues as evidenced by the increased membership in groups is described in the *Second Annual Report of the Council* . . ., op. cit., pp. 89–95.

16. "Election Report" of the League of Conservation Voters, Washington, D.C., 1972, mimeographed statement.

17. "Environmental Vote a Factor in 50 Congress Contests," *New York Times*, November 12, 1972, p. 41.

18. Harold M. Mayer, "Politics and Land Use: The Indiana Shoreline of Lake Michigan," *Annals, Association of American Geographers*, 54 (1964), 508–523.

19. James B. Haynes, "North Slope Oil: Physical and Political Problems," *Professional Geographer*, 24 (1972), 17–22.

20. Robert Cahn, "Alaskan Oil Line Fails to Get Past Top Court," *Christian Science Monitor*, April 4, 1973, pp. 1 and 5.

21. Political problems related to resources have been examined at various scales by political geographers. Among the more valuable examples illustrating these relationships are Julian V. Minghi, "The Conflict of Salmon Fishing Policies in the North Pacific," *Pacific Viewpoint*, 2 (1961), 59–84; Robert C. Lucas, "Wilderness Perception and Use—The Example of the Boundary Waters Canoe Area," *Natural Resources Journal*, 3 (1964), 394–411; and Roger E. Kasperson, "Political Behavior and the Decision-Making Process in the Allocation of Water Resources Betweeen Residential and Municipal Use," *Natural Resources Journal* (1969), 176–211. How a population perceives the responsibility of government in dealing with natural disasters is treated in a study of New Orleans by F. Glen Abney and Larry B. Hill, "Natural Disasters as a Political Variable: The Effects of a Hurricane on an Urban Election," *American Political Science Review*, 60 (1966), 974–981.

22. A general discussion of the management of public lands and the pressures they are under from various developers is described in the *Third Annual Report of the Counsel* . . ., op. cit., pp. 133–136.

23. Peter F. Mason, "Some Geographical Considerations of Siting Nuclear Power Reactors Along the California Coast," *California Geographer*, 12 (1971), 21–29.

24. The geographer's contribution on environmental studies is amply stated by Gilbert White, "Environmental Impact Statements," *Professional Geographer*, 24 (1972), 302–309. The National Environmental Protection Act (NEPA) is described in detail in the *Third Annual Report of the Council* . . ., op. cit., pp. 221–267.

25. *Second Annual Report of the Council* . . ., op. cit., pp. 8–9.

26. General legal aspects are treated by E. Finbar Murphy, *Man and His Environment: Law*, New York, Harper & Row, 1971. Recent Supreme Court decisions involving environmental issues are discussed in the *Third Annual Report of the Council* . . ., op. cit., pp. 148–149.

27. David Holmstrom, "The Great Industrial March Into Suburbia," *Christian Science Monitor*, July 17, 1972, p. 5.

28. "Pollution Compacts: Governors vs. Environmentalists," *Congressional Quarterly Weekly Report*, July 2, 1971, pp. 1444–1447.

29. Anthony Brazel, "International Air Quality Control in the Detroit-Windsor Area," *Proceedings*, Association of American Geographers, 5 (1973), 25–30.
30. The latest agreements reached by the United States and Canada and Mexico are described in the *Third Annual Report of the Council* . . . , op. cit., pp. 82–85.
31. The problems of growth and development and their political and environmental facets are treated in a series by Robert Cahn, "Where Do We Grow From Here?" *Christian Science Monitor*, May 21, 1973, p. 9; May 23, 1973, p. 9; May 25, 1973, p. 9; May 30, 1973, p. 2; June 1, 1973, p. 11; and June 5, 1973, p. 11. The problems of rural development and subdivisions in the Southwest are illustrated in a recent geography study by Charles E. Campbell, "Some Environmental Effects of Rural Subdividing in an Arid Area: A Case Study in Arizona," *Journal of Geography*, 71 (1972), 147–154.
32. *Second Annual Report of the Council* . . . , op. cit. pp. 65–66.
33. *Third Annual Report of the Council* . . . , op. cit., p. 183.
34. Lee Guernsey, "Proposed State Land Use Policy Guidelines," *Proceedings*, Association of American Geographers, 3 (1973), 89–93.

PART III

THE FUTURE

Chapter 13

POLITICAL GEOGRAPHY OF THE FUTURE

The day will come when the only people interested
in state boundaries will be Rand McNally.

Everett Dirksen

The complexity of the present world with its associated technological achieve-
ments, sophisticated weaponry, new life-styles, color conflicts, and awareness of
human welfare necessitates that social and behavioral scientists begin to consider
seriously an investigation of such topics in future worlds.[1] Scholars faced with the
task of identifying (let alone comprehending and predicting) the significance of
salient events, processes, and patterns now and for the next several decades and
beyond realize that this is not an easy assignment. Prediction, although a goal in
science, is most difficult when political and social worlds are treated, and this is true
in the United States especially. Future events and processes that will occur in
political, psychological, social, and economic realms are too important and complicated to be restricted solely to analysis by modern-day astrologers, palm readers, and
writers of science fiction. However, many science fiction writers do seem to possess
an uncanny sense of the nature of future worlds. These worlds will be related only

in part to the present state of the world; they will be dependent on the advancement and diffusion of technological innovations, the stability of the world community, and the general development of human welfare and justice.

Geographers as well as scholars in sociology, political science, economics, psychology, planning, and history are beginning to consider in earnest the subject by discussing, forecasting, analyzing, and planning future patterns and processes.[2] Scholarly analyses treating the forecasting of geographical patterns and processes in political or social spheres do not call merely for an extrapolation of the present United States or world situation, as changes will occur that will be both unpredictable and perhaps even explosive in nature and significance. This is probably more true for political geography than other segments of the discipline. Therefore, what is needed at this juncture in geography and the other social and behavioral sciences is increased discussion of the rationale and importance of future-related research, an appreciation and respect for short- as well as long-range planning and forecasting, and the development of suitable methods and models for examining the future. Perhaps the very questions raised about the future of the United States and future worlds may be more important now than specific answers. As geographers and other social and behavioral scientists write, discuss, and analyze the future, hopefully the art of prediction will be improved and speculating about the future will become a respectable subject for scholarly inquiry and an aid for realistic spatial planning.

POLITICAL GEOGRAPHY AND THE FUTURE

This chapter discusses and analyzes a number of political patterns and processes that are likely to be illustrative of developments in the United States for the next several decades and beyond. Also a political reorganization scheme at the national level is offered. A reading of articles in politics and sociology pertaining to the future reveals that there are a number of topics of a political geography nature that merit presentation and elaboration, not only for an understanding of the future, but for the present as well. Among such future topics likely to be of importance to the political geographer interested in the United States are regional and sectional politics, voting patterns (national and particularly urban), forms of representation, political organization, political environment controversies, the power of cities, the emergence of new political pressure groups, increased political centralization, the standardization of laws and the fragility of the political institution itself. Some of these are already current concerns of political geographers dealing with the United States. However, in view of the fact that some of these political developments may take new forms and directions in the future, an understanding of these is confined strictly to political geography as the fields of political science, sociology, history, psychology, and environmental planning also contain insights useful in an examination of political space.

An analysis and understanding of the political geography of the future in part relies on completed studies dealing with political organization and behavior and with social and economic development of the United States. In particular the significance of short-term patterns and processes, and the likelihood of their continuation in the nation merits close scrutiny. Variation in thought, opinion, and analysis about politics and the future is to be expected.

THE YEAR 2000

Six major developments are suggested as potential characteristics of the political geography in the United States in the year 2000. They are (1) the erosion of boundaries, (2) the emergence of city-states, (3) the rise of new political cultures, (4) the reorientation of voting patterns, (5) centralized government planning, and (6) the politicalization of the environment. These six items are not considered mutually exclusive.

Erosion of Boundaries. In a politically developed country such as the United States, boundaries as barriers to interaction will play an increasingly insignificant role in total human planning. As the town and township boundaries have ceased to be of major significance politically in New England and the North Central states as well as in most parts of the nation for education, financial, and land use planning, so will the county boundaries and to a degree even those separating the states. Already state boundaries separating states such as Wisconsin, Illinois, Indiana, Michigan, and Ohio have lost much of their earlier economic, political, and social significance. Regional sectional boundaries reflecting inter-regional cooperation and federal planning will become more important politically and economically. The boundaries separating regions, such as the Upper Great Lakes, Appalachia, Gulf Coast, and Megalopolis, will be gradual and primarily functional in nature, not reflecting sharp economic and social and legal differences. Even the United States-Canada boundary is likely to become less and less a barrier to economic, social, and even political interaction, and the Mexican boundary even less so.

In the United States there are a multitude of administrative problems of a political geographic nature connected with the fifty states, the hundreds of metropolises, and the thousands of municipalities. This is not to mention the plethora of school, judicial, and police districts, often with greater apparent differences than similarities in organization. The role of the county unit of government is expected to continue its decline as an administration unit able to effectively handle legal, education, housing, employment, transportation, and health problems. These duties will be transferred more and more to state, regional, and federal authorities. It is considered likely that Puerto Rico, the Virgin Islands, and the Pacific Ocean island chain will eventually become officially recognized states. The redistricting and reapportionment of state and national legislative bodies will occur more often with more frequent national censuses. This will insure more equitable representation. These geographic alterations might signal the formation of some new political cultures and party alignments. By the year 2000 (and possibly earlier) attempts will probably be made to objectively reapportion the country's political-legislative space without bias or gerrymandering. Such will also be done for schools, police, fire and regional planning districts. These districts will be constructed with the aid of standardized computer-based programs. A major problem that will result will be the successful implementation of such reorganization schemes.

Emergence of City-States. As cities become more important politically they will be the major foci for redistricting, representation, and federal funding as opposed to the states. Already the current controversy over federal aid to states and major cities has been noted in Chapter 11. Combinations of metropolitan complexes, such as Chipitts (Chicago-Pittsburgh), Bowash (Boston-Washington), SanSan (San Francisco-San Diego), and many others of lesser size that will develop in the Southwest and Gulf Coast, will become the critical nodes for regional and national economic development. Already the importance of very large cities is apparent in presidential election-year politics. A plurality performance -in a few major cities such as New York, Chicago, Detroit, Philadelphia, Los Angeles, and Houston can offset the winning of many sparsely populated states. Within cities themselves the issue of representation in local, state, regional, and national political bodies will involve more than simply the proportion of representatives elected from a metropolitan area. The degree of representation from the central city, suburbs, and new towns will be critical. Political infighting may emerge at metropolitan and regional levels as planning for housing, education, health, transportation, recreation, manpower training, and environmental protection become more national and urban in scope. Local levels will likely see controversies developing over the use or misuse of urban space for transportation (routes and interchanges), industrial, residential, recreation, and institutional (churches, schools and high-rise public buildings) purposes. Zoning for specific land uses as well as intermetropolitan uses will likely acquire major political dimensions. Inadequate or politically unpopular zoning may even increase the possibility for class, color, income, or age conflicts within as well as between cities.[3] Societal and technological changes are also likely to result in different interpretations of public and private property, particularly in cities. It is also considered likely that there will be a greater consideration of the legal and environmental dimensions involving personal space in densely populated large cities.

Rise of New Political Cultures. In the United States some new political cultures and groups will emerge stemming from the population shifts to the cities' peripheries, reapportionment, occupational changes, and new values and life-styles. Some of these social changes and their effects have already been noted and popularized.[4] It is felt by some social scientists that a new political theory is needed that reflects the increasing service orientation of our economy and society instead of an agrarian or industrial philosophy.[5] The traditional two-party system as is presently known probably will continue but will undergo some dynamic internal changes.

Fractional party politics have been reflected in presidential elections in the 1960s. New political groups at local, regional, and national levels are likely to emerge that will run the ideological gamut of the political spectrum. They may form their strength primarily on the basis of differences in education, age, race, sex, religion, or even over specific issues such as racial progress, international human welfare, minority rights, the defense posture, the invasion of privacy, consumer protection, and the ecological balance. Many of these quasipolitical groups will be politically independent and small in numbers but influential and vocal in their demands. Some will choose to work outside the major political parties believing this the best way to effectuate change; others will fuse into the two major organizations. During the next several decades in all political organizations there will be greater stress placed on providing for total welfare of the individual (from child to senior citizen) in a more technologically complex and interdependent world, a need for standardized and nationalized welfare goals (health, education, retirement benefits), an emphasis on the quality and the amenities of life (leisure, open space, arts, environmental attractiveness), international justice, and disadvantaged and minority representation (such as women, blacks, Chicanos, and the handicapped). The formation of regional political attitudes whether of conservative or liberal leaning will continue to be important in national and regional politics over the next thirty years, such as are now forming in the South and Southwest.[6] Cities throughout the United States will be the foci for many of these new political groups and cultures as well as the nodes for new societal innovations. For example, San Francisco, New York City, and Boston are identified as foci for new forms of political behavior. We may observe the coalescence of urban political cultures in specific regions such as the Northeast and Southwest that will challenge specific programs, priorities, and policies of the federal government. Competition may even arise between urban areas large and small, North and South, for defense, education, welfare, housing, environmental, and transportation funds.

Reorientation of Voting Patterns. In line with the formulating and structuring of new political cultures suggested above, new voting patterns and forms of political behavior will appear. These electoral patterns will be related mainly to variations in regional philosophy, occupation types, educational attainment, not to mention contrasts in age, income, and race. The current changes occurring inside and outside the major political parties illustrate the breakdown of traditional party loyalties and the beginnings of some new forms of political action and behavior. These are reflected in recent election patterns that are rather difficult to interpret fully. For example, the voting behavior of such groups as the newly enfranchised youth, recently enfranchised blacks, veterans, the poor, labor, retired citizens, high-income whites, and residents of certain specialized communities (government employees, military personnel, university affiliates) are portents of future political developments. The growing independence of many voters and decreasing emphasis on traditional party labels lend fluidity to the existing party system and the relatively easy formation of new political groups that may garner sufficient strength individually or collectively to influence local, state, and national elections. Varying political ideologies, from left to right, that have existed and currently do, are expected to continue into the future with varying degrees of success. There may be new political or quasipolitical parties formed whose existence will have only short duration. These may influence the two major ones or more likely will challenge them on key social or economic or environmental issues in selected cities and certain regions. Stronger social and economic ties between the United States and Canada in particular are likely to see international parties and political groups appear in both countries that reflect common international interests (trade, travel, justice, urban planning, and environment).

The role of cities in national and state elections as stated above will be more important in the future than at present. Voting patterns may develop that will pit one city or metropolitan area against another. For example, there may be competition between St. Louis and Kansas City, or New York vs. Los Angeles, or Dallas vs. Houston for housing, job training, education, transportation, and environmental funds as well as government defense contracts and pilot social projects. The emerging black majority or strong minority population will be a more common phenomenon in key northern and southern cities such as St. Louis, Philadelphia, Cleveland, Detroit, Baltimore, Birmingham, and Atlanta. Some have already elected black mayors. There will doubtless be some restructuring of the present electoral system with the changes to reflect the urban and suburban electorate more than the state vote. At the congressional level the representatives will be requested to introduce and legislate more reform measures that will affect the total national (and world) economy and society rather than their own local constituency. Congressional reform may lead to representatives being elected in staggered fashion for more than two-year terms. Senators from sparsely populated rural states may lose some of their strength and representation in line with an emerging urban society, economy, and polity.[7]

On a local level, whether small city or metropolitan area, there will be more voting on societal issues such as personal privacy and rights, education bonds, health facilities, environmental improvement, housing schemes, redevelopment programs, interregional and may be international (United States and Canada) cooperation. Political candidates for many local offices are expected to run more on nonpartisan platforms than on the basis of the usual political party structure.

Centralized Government Planning. In the United States there has been increased centralization of decision making and planning at national levels for the past forty years. Many of the social and economic programs and policies instituted since then have affected the basic welfare of daily American life, not to mention the incorporation of social welfare schemes and the government bureaucracy as intrinsic to the political philosophies of both the Democrats and Republicans. This centralization at higher levels is expected to continue into the future. In future planning there will be even fewer strictly unique local problems meriting ready solutions but more problems calling for short- and long-term planning and thought at a national level. The federal government has taken the lead and many times assumed the responsibilities for programs such as education, highways, health, housing, and environmental quality, programs once considered as the domain of the state and even local administrative levels. Federal controls have led to the standardization of many existing programs such as social security, a trend likely to continue. The federal government will continue to be regarded as the chief regulator and provider of services to the society, regardless of political party representation in state, regional, and national legislative bodies. National planning with its accompanying priorities means that formulas once used to funnel monies to states for particular programs will now be used to disperse monies directly to metropolitan areas. Federal assistance to metropolitan areas already varies geographically (Chapter 11). It is likely that urban spending policies will be a crucial issue in urban, regional, and national politics in the future. The cities with their several and varied financial problems, often compounded by outmoded revenue programs and outdated political structures, are already forced to look to the national government for guidance and assistance. The need has been particularly acute for certain much-needed services, namely, housing, health, welfare, education, transportation, and environmental cleanup. In the future there is likely to be increased competition between cities but also *within* cities (central cities vs. suburbs) for government revenues. Such actions may hinder metropolitan development.

Politicalization of Environment. One major area of national concern where greater political attention will be concentrated in the short and long run involves man and his environment, both human and natural. The misuses of the natural environment for agricultural, mining, industrial, or even recreational purposes are becoming a greater concern in economic and societal development. This holds true for rural as well as urban areas throughout the nation. As these concerns are discussed and assessed there will be calls for strict legislative enforcement of policies affecting wise use of the natural environment (air, water, land, and soil) as well as controls over excess noise and odors. Accompanying such legislation will probably be federally enforced guidelines for proper care of the environment and a series of penalties for violators.

One major environmental topic where national as well as international controversy will certainly arise involves the regulation and manipulation of the weather. Once greater control over atmospheric phenomena and resulting weather patterns has been achieved, there will be legal cases in air law that may have national and maybe international significance. The effects of controlling and manipulating the atmosphere on agriculture, recreation, ecological niches, human settlement, and the military are too great not to expect some political geography problems at various scales (urban, state, national, or international).

In the decades ahead there will also be greater political ramifications on human environmental policies and programs. When societal awareness increases, life-styles change and new ones emerge, amenities are sought, and personal identity and privacy are considered desirable to preserve, political solutions may become paramount. At another level the jurisdiction of air, water, and noise pollution in interstate, interurban, and international boundaries will demand political reflection and action. The conflicting programs, policies, and roles of local, state, and national agencies and environmental groups with various planning schemes will become involved in litigation on the construction and placing of jetports, highway developments, power plants, and public recreation lands. Such cases as the Miami jetport, the Austin expressway, the Adirondacks forest lands, the Alaskan pipeline, Santa Barbara oil spills, and Lake Erie pollution have already been shown to be problems that have city or state or federal political implications.

POLITICAL REORGANIZATION

Social and economic developments affecting individual and group progress are best carried out in an organizational and administrative framework at a national level that aims to upgrade the human welfare of all residents within its jurisdictional limits. The legal and administrative structure established last century and before had as its primary goal the execution of programs reflecting economic and social changes that occurred. However, this framework presently is no longer performing efficiently or satisfactorily in many instances. Such is the case especially when the political organization of the United States is held up for close scrutiny. This situation is not considered unusual as it exists in other nations such as Canada, Great Britain, and France. It is usually considered difficult if not impossible to restructure or reorganize the existing spatial political framework at any level of the political hierarchy.

Even though a nation or society realizes this problem, namely, the anachronistic political structure and the need for political reform that accompanies societal and technological progress, any progress in thought or actual planning may at best be considered as "dreaming an impossible dream." This is not to say that social and behavioral scientists (whether political geographers, political sociologists, or political scientists), legal experts, urban planners, politicians, and administrative scientists should not attempt to seriously discuss the topic and devise new forms of political organization at all levels. It is certain that presenting alternatives to the present structure and thereby devising political reorganization schemes that are flexible and imaginative enough to effectuate societal advancement uniformly is destined to be one of the major challenges facing planners, politicians, and scholars interested in the future, not to mention the present critical need for such reform.[8]

Justification. The United States economy has changed in the past century from a rural-agricultural orientation to one where urban-industrial development and now, where more recently, services have become more important. Accompanying these economic advancements have been developments in the social sphere as well, such as expanded education and health benefits, the upgrading of minority groups, greater affluence, increased mobility, more leisure time, a search for amenities, and concern for protection of the environment from misuse. However, the political organization as it now exists is in many ways still basically reflective of the agrarian society and economy of last century. The manner in which townships and counties, not to mention states, consider political and social issues and problems affecting individuals and groups on many occasions illustrates both an unwillingness or a basic resistance to change and standardization of some basic human programs. The spatial arrangement, organization and operations of school, police, and zoning districts are still in too many cases left to local decision makers who are or may be unable to properly handle the situation for lack of talent, monies, or historical inertia. There also may be a desire to maintain local "control" or identity to preserve the antiquated political framework. Attempts to institute any reform from the "outside" are resented; furthermore, there is often even an unwillingness or reluctance to cooperate even with contiguous political units experiencing similar problems.

The current problems that large cities face in part attest to the impotency and inadequacy of the existing political structure to handle urban social problems. Mobile whites fleeing to metropolitan-detached and incorporated suburbs have taken their residences, jobs, and most importantly their talents and monies with them. This has left a residue of immobile whites and ghettoized blacks and other nonwhite minorities with a possible political victory (measured in terms of black mayors), but with insufficient monies and trained personnel and an outmoded financial structure. Urban financial crises for welfare, housing, education, transportation, and job-training are common. Having to support such services by funds from uncooperative state legislatures or a discriminatory tax base such as the property tax and one based on where residents live rather than work, presents a genuine challenge to many urban politicians, planners, and administrators. At the root of many such problems is the existing complex political structure for collecting and disbursing revenues for metropolitan areas.

One major reason for suggesting the implementation of new forms of political organization at all levels entails the ever-increasing mobility of the United States population. The economic and social characteristics of these migrants and their spatial patterns of movement have been the foci for research efforts the past several decades. Fewer have been studies treating the political ramifications associated with migration.[9] The intraurban, interurban, and cross-country migration of Americans, rich and poor, young and old, black and white, is characterized by several key political considerations. One is the scale of an individual's political identity or political territoriality. With migration (one or several times) an individual's political knowledge and "world" ceases to be with only one particular county, city, region, or state. That is, he takes his political baggage (sorted and unsorted) to his new political "world." With migration his knowledge and political concerns and political territory broaden in scope. For example, a retired Indiana businessman moving to Florida, if even only for the winter months, may alter his political perception and identity and become more national as opposed to county or state-oriented. This is because he finds that engaging in effective political action, namely, voting, in local and state elections, discriminates against the newcomer because of residency requirements. In addition he is unfamiliar with local candidates and issues. Differential state and local residency requirements, now largely erased, were often viewed as roadblocks constructed by an immobile rural society or an urban political unit not desiring "outside" influences. Such barriers to political participation do not consider the mobile urban dweller and the resident with more than local political awareness and interests. The question that arises is how much concern could the new resident (temporary or permanent) with an expanded political awareness develop when there were varying state regulations limiting or prohibiting his political participation. The migrant may have been restricted in voting but not in paying local or state taxes, both being ways in which he could identify with his new residential political space.

There is a need for eliminating gross societal inequities that are tied to the existing political organization in the states or counties or both. The increasingly mobile and more urbanized society almost dictates that local, county, city, and state variations affecting individual and group welfare and behavior be reduced substantially to provide standardization or be eliminated. Existing variations treated in previous chapters in state welfare payments, judicial standards, criminal penalties (from marijuana possession to first-degree murder), election of public officials, women's rights, education standards, health coverage, age-of-majority, marriage and divorce regulations, environmental protection, and job equality represent different interpretations of similar economic and social issues. At this juncture a question might also be raised whether states or local political jurisdictional units indeed have the "right" to administer and interpret laws with such wide variance in the mid-1970s. With a society that is acquiring more national than state or local awareness and orientation, and where centralized planning is now occurring in many areas of the economy and society, increased standardization of laws is sought. Without some reform individual rights vary markedly within the nation.

The standardization of existing social and economic variations is interpreted as meaning there will be less concern over "states' rights" or "local rights." In other words, where boundaries (county or township) represent significant variations in interpreting similar social issues, they will be eliminated or eroded. Erasing boundaries, whether they be barriers or not, with citizen approval will be no easy task in a society that has become boundary-conscious and boundary-oriented since the framework of the original colonies and territories and the settling of the West. Many of the boundaries within the United States today or within any state are not considered barriers to interaction or variations in major legal interpretations. Their existence is strictly administrative with little political and societal implication. For example, an individual driving daily to work from suburban Milwaukee to central city Chicago is likely to cross any number of boundary lines that separate and divide political space, for example, state, county, school, precinct, fire, police, sanitation, tax, water, and sanitation boundaries. Crossing these may mean nothing to him or have little impact on his social and political well-being. However, boundaries that may evoke feelings of territoriality (Chapter 3) may be those defining his private property, his exclusive housing development, his children's school district, and his suburb's police force. These segments of space, all that are identified by boundaries (*de facto* and *de jure*), he may fight to preserve and protect. Reorganizing and amalgamating such political units into large units such as metrogovernments for efficiency of tax savings may be resented.

It is often argued that political reorganization is needed in order to more efficiently handle the vast number of social, economic, and technological problems that the nation faces. In part the basis of such thought is that the current system of elected officials, whether local, state, or national, is not the best that could be devised for instituting political and social change. For example, at the national level it is felt that the present structure of electing members to the United States Senate, with two senators from each of the fifty states, is an agrarian holdover that means little in a nation that is over 70 percent urbanized, and that has its population concentrated in several major clusters. Urban areas and states such as New York, California, and New Jersey are underrepresented in this body when it is observed that the same number are elected from North Dakota, Oklahoma, and Wyoming. There are presently more people in the New York Standard Metropolitan Statistical Area than in eleven western states! Senators from the large and sparsely populated rural states often have little interest or commitment, nor do they have sufficient knowledge, to cope with many crucial urban issues that merit national legislative action. Therefore, the state as a basic unit for electing officials and a basic block in the nation's political structure is considered out-of-date. Either new states need to be formed or new political regions constituted that elect senators and electors on a more representative basis.

Members of the House of Representatives are elected from 435 districts; these districts, however, vary widely in shape and size (area and more importantly in some cases, numbers of people). This has been treated in Chapter 6. It is the manipulation of space for "political" purposes that is reflected in the calls for a more unbiased representation at local and national levels. In absence of specific legal guidelines for structuring these political units, namely, how much gerrymandering is legally possible or how much deviation is permitted in juggling the size (number of people) per district or what are the bases for drawing districts (to reflect homogeneity or heterogeneity of race, income, occupation), it is not surprising that there are groups who feel the present method of electing members demands legal clarification and reform. With political bosses or politically packed legislatures or politically influenced courts involved in constructing and approving redrawn legislative districts, it is not surprising that many cities and suburbs feel their interests are not represented by their elected representatives. Similar reactions may be felt by urban blacks, the poor, the young, the old, and even minority-party suburbs. For this reason it is felt that there is a need for greater clarity in defining the specifics of political reorganization (such as gerrymandering, compactness, district deviation) as well as standardizing the partitioning of space for elected officials at all levels. Possibly even the number of representatives necessary for effecting political legislation at a national level needs to be examined; maybe 435 is too many, especially in the light of committee assignments, the seniority system, the large number of resolutions introduced, and frequent legislative inefficiency. It may be that the entire reapportionment question needs to be considered by the United States Supreme Court. Perhaps a new computer-based and politically unbiased system that is developed and approved by a nonpolitically oriented team of planners and scholars is required, a plan not completely out of the question in the near future.

Criteria for New Regions. If it is agreed there is a need for a political reorganization of space that is more in tune with current economic and social development, it follows there must be specific criteria identified and adhered to by those urban and regional planners, politicians, or scholars charged with delimiting new regions and redrawing boundaries. A select number of operational guidelines that are designed to provide a more rational organization and administration of all political space (local to national) will hopefully avoid compounding previously made errors, some of which remain today from the political planning and dreaming of the eighteenth and nineteenth centuries.

There are at least three major underlying guidelines that can serve as the basis for devising and delimiting political space at a macrolevel in the United States. First, any new political organization scheme and any new political regions need to be primarily urban-oriented. That is, the new major political units or political regions at the national level are to be basically metropolitan, or megalopolitan in their structure. If such were the case, then states such as Chipitts, Bowash, and SanSan (maybe with new names) could be responsible for handling problems in their respective broad-scaled urban regions. Within these newly created macro-urban regions there will be a subset of political administrative regions established that will administer problems and concerns of large and small cities, semirural, and rural areas. Present existing state, county, and townships, which heretofore have served frequently as barriers to uniform economic and societal development, will be erased from maps marking political organizations. Instead boundaries within and between these city-states macrourban regions will be separating various political organizational structures that are related to broad national urban programs affecting the total welfare of all citizens. Elements in this new hierarchy of political organization will be linked from top to bottom by a series of urban threads facilitating organization and administration.

A second guideline is that these newly created urban-centered political regions be concerned with efficiency in operating and executing needed social and economic programs. The present political system within its interstate differences, hundreds of independent metropolitan centers, and thousands of municipalities is unwieldy to say the least in effectively handling administrative problems. Local, county, and state regulations in law and bureaucratic structure are often in conflict; this makes the solution to and understanding of environment, housing, education, crime, justice, and welfare problems difficult, if not impossible. Even national programs are not equally accepted or respected in all parts of political space, again due to roadblocks erected by the existing and outdated local or state political machinery. Witness the cry for states' rights. Witness also the spatial variations in flows of federal monies for welfare, model city development, education, transportation, job training, and law enforcement. These illustrate that federal policies consider to some extent the variations in existing local and state regulations prior to instituting grants-in-aid to states (Chapter 11).

A direct outgrowth of the need for greater efficiency is the third major objective, that of the development of new political regions to reflect standardization in concerns affecting the welfare of all citizens. This would literally lead to a United States, not a "nation of states." In attempting to reduce the dissimilarities that currently exist between cities, states, and regions, there should be attempts particularly to establish relatively uniform policies governing education support, welfare coverage, environmental protection, medical benefits, and the administration of justice. Attempts need to be made to reduce variations between presently existing states and regions as well as within them. It would be repeating a current political problem if in the newly developed regions there were still wide differences between the large and small cities, central city and suburbs, or the Northeast and Southwest. Some variations are expected to remain in view of the cultural and political heritage and economic and social orientation of various sections of the United States. However, with the centralization of planning at regional and national urban levels, equal coverage of programs and policies affecting all citizens would be assured within national political space. The enactment of more uniform regulations would eliminate in part the advantages or disadvantages some areas and cities currently possess. For example, the advantages of New York City to welfare recipients, Nevada for divorce, New Mexico for lax land development laws, and suburbs for better education are well known.

A NEW UNITED STATES

To date a number of social scientists have been concerned with identifying and analyzing regional political cultures and philosophy on a national as well as a regional basis. Such investigations have demonstrated that often the existing state boundaries are not necessarily the best limits used to differentiate political cultures.[10] In addition there have been attempts to classify and reclassify political units into groups with underlying similarities; these studies group entire states, not sections, into new classes.[11] The classification and regionalization schemes as well as those treating political cultures use the cultural historical threads (political "geology"), performance on various legislative programs, degree of innovativeness, spending levels and priorities, voting patterns, and a variety of social and economic indicators to ferret out areal variations. Most of the above regional treatments have been carried out by political scientists, some by sociologists and historians. Geographers, with their focus on the spatial variation and spatial organization and arrangement of phenomena, and in this case political cultures and political organization, have not contributed substantially to the regional political literature (Chapter 9). However, there have been several attempts by economists and geographers to delimit macroeconomic regions in the United States, as well as functional regions of metropolitan areas.[12] These studies on regionalization lend support to the contention that there is precedence in the geography and social science literature for suggesting alternatives to the present existing spatial structure. It appears that a combination of political and economic classifications and regionalization schemes could serve to satisfy the three criteria elucidated above as being necessary for any new political organization.

Keeping in mind the justification and rationale for a reorganization of political space, a scheme is presented that delineates a new macropolitical space for the United States. The sixteen new regions or states or city-states, as they are termed here, are delineated on the basis of similar economic orientation, social and cultural heritage, and political ideology and culture (Fig. 13-1). These states have new names. They are all oriented toward one major metropolitan area; suggested capitals for these new states are also indicated.

In constructing the new political regions, an attempt was made to identify a reasonable number of states or city-states that could justifiably handle existing and eventual societal problems. The current number, fifty, has been shown to be a rather unwieldy number when national goals and stated programs are implemented. The sixteen above are delimited on the basis of similar economic orientation, social and cultural heritage, and political ideology. Functional or economic orientation to at least one major city dictated the location of the new state capital. Current state boundaries were not considered in delimiting new political regions.

At this juncture it is deemed important to identify several criteria used to delineate certain of these new states. Regional political science and sociology literature and the regional social, political, and economic geography of the United States provide a basis for much of the actual demarcation of space. For example, the state Pacifica including Alaska and Hawaii and most of California as well as Oregon and Washington represents a cultural, economic, and political region that is different from southern California and the mountainous West. Political scientists among others have identified contrasting political cultures outside the state of Pacifica. Alaska and Hawaii were both included as their economic orientation was more tied to the northern California and Washington area than to southern California. San Francisco was selected as the capital, as this metropolitan area represents one of the major cultural and economic nodes in western United States.

The Spanish-American influence, culturally, economically, and politically, was important in delimiting the state of Angelina. In addition, the influx of young and old migrants and the impact of the space and defense industries have given this area striking homogeneity. Los Angeles, being the largest city and predominant focus for the Southwest, was selected as the capital.

Tropicana, which includes all of present-day Florida except the panhandle,

FIG. 13-1 A New United States.

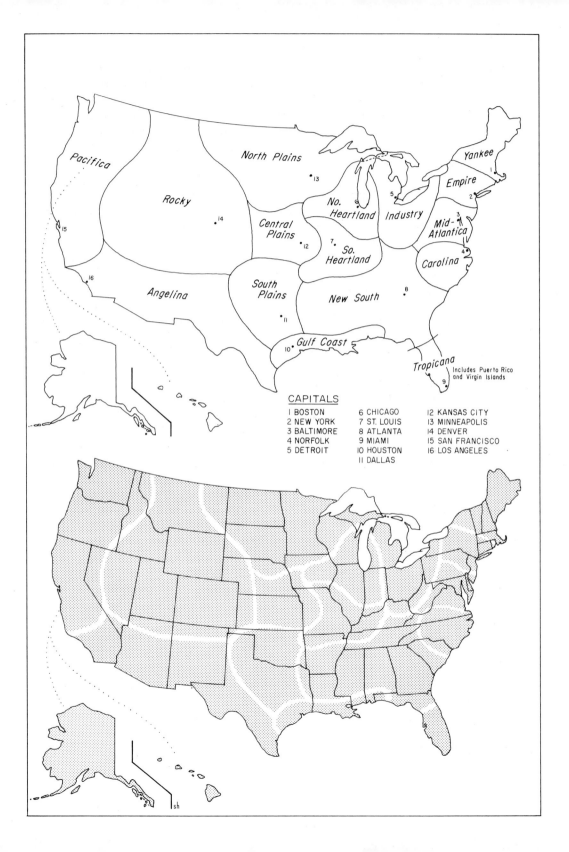

Pacifica

North Plains

Yankee

Empire

Rocky

No. Heartland

Industry

Mid-Atlantica

Central Plains

So. Heartland

Carolina

Angelina

South Plains

New South

Gulf Coast

Tropicana

Includes Puerto Rico and Virgin Islands

CAPITALS

1 BOSTON
2 NEW YORK
3 BALTIMORE
4 NORFOLK
5 DETROIT

6 CHICAGO
7 ST. LOUIS
8 ATLANTA
9 MIAMI
10 HOUSTON
11 DALLAS

12 KANSAS CITY
13 MINNEAPOLIS
14 DENVER
15 SAN FRANCISCO
16 LOS ANGELES

sh

contains an economy and culture geared particularly to the amenities of life (sun and water) and regionally to the Caribbean and Latin America. For this reason, whenever Puerto Rico and the Virgin Islands become states, they will have more in common with Florida than with other parts of the United States. As in Angelina, the attraction of migrants (especially senior citizens), the importance of space-related and defense industries and the investment in tourism and recreation activities in Florida and in nearby islands suggests this segment of space has a distinct set of similarities that separate it from north Florida and the rest of the South. Miami is the appropriate selection for the capital city.

One of the major problems in constructing new political regions involves the urbanized Northeast seaboard. A single political region comprising all of Megalopolis was out of the question. Instead three separate states were identified that, although they have many similarities, were oriented economically and politically to slightly different segments of the Northeast. The state of Yankee with Boston as capital is designed to serve as the focus for New England. New York City with its economic wealth serves as the heart of coastal Megalopolis as well as the interior of New York and surrounding states. The southern part of Megalopolis in the state of Mid-Atlantica with Baltimore as its capital was considered a transitional economic, cultural, and political area between the South and northern Megalopolis.

A final group of states treated represents the broad sparsely populated section labeled the Great Plains. Although economically this belt of states stretching from North Dakota to Texas may have striking agricultural similarities, politically and economically they are not alike. The state of North Plains is tied functionally to the upper Midwest and especially Minneapolis and St. Paul, the Central Plains to Kansas City, and the South Plains to Dallas and Ft. Worth. Politically and culturally these three states represent combinations of progressive, moderate, and conservative political philosophies where northern and central Europeans (especially in the North and Central Plains) and southerners (from the Deep and Rim South) have had historically an important imprint on the regional philosophy, an impact that remains today. In delimiting these three new states, as in others, the current state boundaries have little meaning when urban orientation and culture, society, and politics are used to delimit new political space.

The drawing of boundaries for new political regions is hampered frequently by a lack of in-depth knowledge of the social, economic, and political behavior and patterns in some urban as well as rural areas. For example, segmenting the northeast quarter of the nation is not an easy task as there are many similarities, particularly with reference to cities. Yet there are also some substantial differences. Perhaps some degree of ambiguity is behind the delimiting of all political space; there are certainly sufficient examples of such existing at the present time in the United States. For example, the number of currently existing "panhandles" suggests they were easy ways to fill voids in mapping new units (Chapter 6). Not only must the historical imprint of religious, political, ethnic, racial, and economic groups be considered in constructing new regions but also must the contemporary population movements, changing political behavior, and economic orientation of various areas. These recent dynamics are most acute in the South and Southwest.[13]

The maps should in no way be considered as masterpieces either in political planning and organization or in detailed cartography. Nor should the names of the states or the capitals be accepted without discussion and a consideration of alternatives. The maps are offered as one example of a reorganization of political space at the macrolevel that if implemented may more efficiently cope with the complex social, economic, and political problems facing the nation at the present and in the future.

REORGANIZATION SCHEMES

Problems. The implementation of the three guidelines used to delimit the sixteen new political states or administrative regions and the social, economic, and political criteria adopted will never occur without some major problems. While there will be some new concerns arising in the planning processes no matter what reorganization scheme is adopted, many problems will sound reminiscent of current conditions. The problems for the future political organization are many more than simply redrawing boundaries on a map. Therefore it is important that some of the more salient ones be identified and discussed.

It almost goes without saying that one of the major problems involved in attempting to restructure political space will be who will be assigned the task. If there can be a consensus reached by politicians, urban and regional planners, administrators, and social scientists that a basic reorganization of political space in the United States is needed (itself no easy task), then it follows that a decision must be reached regarding who will be in charge of the reorganization plans and how final judgment will be rendered. Certainly the politicians at all levels, small-town mayors, city councilmen, state representatives, governors, senators, to mention only a few, would feel they are qualified and should be involved in any such operation. On the other hand, planners and administrators at all levels of government who deal with the current political organizational complexities involved in land transactions, voter registration, welfare payments, medical benefits and business loans, would feel they should be in charge if not involved in this task. Likewise political geographers, political scientists, urban planners and legal experts would feel they could lend impartial insight into attempts to redraw existing political regions.

A reorganization task may best be solved by an arbitrary panel composed of the three broad groups mentioned above. On the other hand, maybe a new constitutional convention could be convened to discuss the reorganization of political space that reflects the contemporary and future United States. Such a convention need not be comprised solely of politicians but members of the industry, business, education, law, government, and various population segments. Another possibility would consider employing a team of independent research workers or a research corporation to feed into a computer the masses of data about numbers of people, growth, economic orientation, population structure, legislative behavior, voting patterns, spending priorities, and culture history. Then in accordance with stated objectives such as the three outlined above, cartographic representations of a new United States could be obtained that reflect maximum internal homogeneity within a specified number of new states. These could then be used as a basis for discussion and possible implementation.

Accompanying the drawing of new units of political space by computers or by panels will be a host of inherently spatial problems that merit discussion, consideration, and additional research. No matter what group or groups are charged with the task of devising new political units, there would likely always be opportunities to manipulate space. Even though it is agreed that such practices are to be avoided, care must be taken to insure that geographic bias and favoritism are not widely practiced in overt or covert fashion. It would not be difficult, for example, to have the large cities politically dominate the medium- and small-sized cities, or to have rural areas very severely underrepresented (even though they have long practiced malapportionment), or suburbs to "gang up" on central cities, or to gerrymander areas that are rich, poor, young, old, black, or Republican in order to weaken their opportunity for an effective political and social dialogue and representation. Such gerrymandering, malapportionment, and zoning plans theoretically could still be practiced especially on a microscale even though there would be more standardization of social services and attempts to legally define the areal and spatial criteria necessary for political regionalization and organization.

Boundaries, although their importance as barriers to much present-day social, economic, and political interaction will have been reduced, still will be lines on maps separating those various elements in the hierarchies and divisions of political space. With the township, county, and state boundaries of the agrarian era eliminated, the new boundaries will divide space primarily for urban-administrative purposes. These will be flexible enough to permit ready changes. With a functionally defined macrourban region that has a political organizational framework superimposed on the multitude of like-oriented urban centers, a more effective handling of social, economic, and political problems and services should be the result. Uniform codes, programs, and standards as regards to human welfare that are national in nature and scope likewise will reduce much of the current identification and importance attached to boundaries both within and between these new urban states.

Within the newly constructed regions or states there are likely to be competitive and often conflicting urban social, economic, or political interests. In much the same way that there are legislative differences between Chicago and "downstate" Illinois or New York City and "upstate" New York or southern or northern Florida, there may be substantial differences arising between coastal or inland areas, large or small cities, rich and poor sections, or rural- and urban-settled areas. In much the same light as the current regional plying for federal funds, there will be conflicting and maybe competitive interests between the newly developed urban-centered states or regions, not to mention within-state competition and conflicting interests. Regional and urban priorities may differ. Even though the boundaries separating these new states as well as the political units within them will be transitional and functional in nature, it is expected there will be competition for monies for education, housing, welfare, research and development, transportation, military-defense, environmental cleanup, and crime prevention. These will occur at the same time national planning schemes will seek greater standardization.

As stated above the task of reorganizing political space is envisaged as much more than a simple cartographic exercise devising an up-to-date map reflecting current similar social, economic, and political characteristics. It is important to remember that the restructuring and reorganization of political space basically involves people as well as area. They must be considered in macroplanning as well as in microplanning development. Although citizens of the United States are becoming more affluent, more mobile, more urban, and more politically aware, they may still find a restructuring and reorientation of their existing political world very upsetting. The attachment of a given individual to Saginaw, Michigan or Dallas, Texas, or Mill Valley, California or to the state of Utah or Alabama or Maine may be strongly reflected in his or her political identity and in the political spaces he or she knows and occupies. These feelings may hold true for one or maybe different levels of the political hierarchy (local to national). Government and urban planners and administrators, politicians, lawyers, judges, and social scientists must be cognizant of such readily nonquantifiable impressions, attachments, and feelings. During 1973, two examples of political reorganization received support in Illinois and Nebraska.[14] Western Illinois residents in sixteen counties felt neglected in state and federal services and some supported the proposed state of "Forgotonia." Similar sentiments about inadequate highway, educational, and recreational facilities in the Nebraska panhandle encouraged secession and annexation to Wyoming. Political allegiances and identity not infrequently already cross existing state lines. Even though a southern Illinois small-town resident feels alienated from Springfield or Chicago politics, he might be reticent to change his formal allegiance to a newly created political unit such as North Heartland. That change in allegiance may be more difficult than getting him to accept the forthcoming metric system. This is not to mention the problems of a low-income inner city Los Angeles black or Chicano who is told that in 1984 or 2001 he is now a member of Angelina, a political space that he may know virtually nothing about economically, socially, or politically. One example reflecting this identification problem is the Detroit suburbanite who believes his police, fire, and education systems to be the best; these he may fight to protect and retain even if told he must now identify with the state of Industry instead of Bloomfield Hills. Politics to many Americans has become identified with national goals such as housing, health, and education, however, to a sizable segment of others it is still tied to local big-city Chicago bosses, a rural Iowa county seat, or a state such as Louisiana. Ineffective and outdated as such political organization structures may be, they still represent a problem involved in the construction of a new organization and map of the United States and especially its implementation at microlevels. It is well that feelings of political identity and allegiance not be lost entirely in restructuring political space even though some reorientation of an individual's and a group's behavioral space will accompany long-waited political reforms. Many citizens have adjusted to previous political reorganization forms during their lifetimes in rural, central city, and suburban spaces.

In addition to these problems several others need to be considered. For example, how are these sixteen new states to be financed? By individual political units, a metropolitan tax, a national tax, a regional tax, or by sharing revenues from the federal treasury? If there is a broad revenue-sharing scheme akin to that instituted in 1972, what spatial criteria will be used to allocate funds? What kinds of political representation will occur within these sixteen new states as well as at the national levels? Will the new states have unicameral legislatures? Will they discuss regional or national or local problems? Will they discuss some problems at the same time? What forms of national legislative bodies will be formed? How many members are needed for regional and national legislative bodies? How will the members be elected? What will happen to the two major political parties in the light of population shifts and heightened social awareness? Will parties become less important?

A critical problem that certainly will arise is the use of computers and model-based systems in planning future political and social policies. In the same manner that they have been utilized to solve complex economic problems, so might they aid in solving social and political decisions. For example, already we know that school districts and reapportionment plans can be programmed by computers.[15]

Feasibility. The above discussion has focused on the need for political reform in the United States especially in the light of reorganizing political space from what presently exists. Much of the economic and social progress attained in the nation is dependent on how such benefits are reflected in the improvement of total human welfare. At present, many of the programs affecting individual and group welfare are related to how political space is organized and decisions executed. In short, the concern is how the political organization and administration operate spatially. It is unfortunate that the present political organization and system are in many ways ineffective and impartially handling the delivery of vital services and the administration of justice. Although most politicians, urban and regional planners, administrators, and social scientists would agree that the present system is inadequate in reaching many of the nation's citizens, little serious thought has been given to plans for more effective and efficient streamlining of the present macropolitical organization of space. One such plan for redrawing that space at a macrolevel for the United States is offered here. In this attempt several criteria reflecting economic, social, and political, similarities were utilized. It is readily admitted that other criteria and other regionalization plans can be offered.[16] It also goes without saying that there will be problems confronting the developers and political leaders who construct as well as administer new political units. Hopefully, any restructuring will be an improvement over the present organization.

Whether the thoughts, opinions, and ideas, not to mention the new political map, treated in this discussion on the future and on reorganization are accepted as valid or unrealistic is highly dependent on the individual's perception and knowledge and understanding of the current state of contemporary United States. The subject of the reorganization of political space is not exhausted here; there is ample room for more discussion and research by government planners, politicians, administrators, and social and behavioral scientists interested in the present as well as the future.[17]

FOOTNOTES

1. Commission on the Year 2000, "Toward the Year 2000: Work in Progress," *Daedalus, Journal of the American Academy of Arts and Sciences,* Summer 1967; Herman J. Kahn and Anthony J. Wiener, *The Year 2000: A Framework for Speculation on the Next Thirty-Three Years,* New York, Macmillan, 1967; Foreign Policy Association, *Toward the Year 2018,* New York, Cowles, 1968; Robert Jungk and John Galtung, eds., *Mankind 2000,* London, Allen and Unwin, 1969; and Wendell Bell and James A. Mau, eds., *The Sociology of the Future: Theory, Cases, and Annotated Bibliography,* New York, Russell Sage, 1971.
2. Among the geography references are J. Bird, "Forecasting and Geography," *Geographical Journal,* 135 (1969), 69–72; Z. Chojnicki, "Prediction in Economic Geography," *Economic Geography,* 46 (1970 Supplement), 213–222; I. P. Gerasimov, "Futurology in Soviet Geography," *Soviet Geography: Review and Translation,* 11 (1970), 521–527; Brian J. L. Berry, "The Geography of the United States in the Year 2000," *Ekistics,* 39 (1970), 339–351; M. J. Wise, "The Geographical Environment of the Future," *Advancement of Science,* 26 (1970), 429–437; B. Ryan, "Geography and Futurology," *Australian Geographer,* 11 (1971), 510–521; and Stanley D. Brunn, "Geography and Politics of the United States in the Year 2000," *Journal of Geography,* 73:4 (1973), 42–49. Two geography conferences have also been held, "First Conference on the Geography of the Future" in conjunction with the University of Western Ontario in October 1970 and "Building Regions for the Future" sponsored by the University of Montreal in February 1972.
3. Daniel Bell, "Working Session Two: The Need for Normative Statements," *Daedalus,* op. cit., p. 966.
4. One popular book is Alvin Toffler, *Future Shock,* New York, Random House, 1970.
5. Lawrence K. Frank, "The Need for a New Political Theory," *Daedalus,* op. cit., p. 812.
6. Kevin Phillips, *The Emerging Republican Majority,* New Rochelle, N.Y., Arlington House, 1969.
7. Martin Shubik, "Working Session Two: Four Futures," *Daedalus,* op. cit., p. 954.
8. Stanley D. Brunn, "Political Reorganization of the United States: A Future Perspective," Montreal, Quebec, International Conference on Building Regions for the Future, 1972, unpublished paper. Much of the ensuing discussion and map are based on this presentation.
9. Kevin Cox, "Residential Relocation and Political Behavior: Conceptual Model and Empirical Tests," *Acta Sociologica,* 13:1 (1970), 40–53; C. G. Bell, "A New

Suburban Politics," *Social Forces*, 47 (1969), 280–288; and Phillips, op. cit., passim.

10. See, for example, Herbert Jacob and Kenneth Vines, eds., *Politics in the American States*, Boston, Mass., Little and Brown, 1965; Thomas R. Dye, *Politics, Economics, and the Public: Policy Outcomes in the American States*, Chicago, Ill., Rand McNally, 1966; Frank Munger, *American State Politics*, New York, Crowell, 1966; and Charles R. Adrian, "Regional Analysis in Political Science," *Social Science Quarterly*, 49:1 (1968), 27–32.

11. Daniel J. Elazar, *American Federalism: A View from the States*, New York, Crowell, 1972; Ira M. Sharkansky, *Regionalism in American Politics*, Chicago, Ill., Rand McNally, 1968; and Norman R. Luttbeg, "Classifying American States: An Empirical Attempt to Identify Internal Variations," *Midwest Political Science Quarterly*, 15:4 (1971), 703–721.

12. Donald J. Bogue and Calvin L. Beale, *Economic Areas of the United States*, New York, Free Press of Glencoe, 1961; Brian J. L. Berry, "A Method for Delimiting Multi-Factor Regions," *Przeglad Geograficzny*, 33:2 (1961), 263–279; and Berry et al., *Metropolitan Area Definition: A Re-evaluation of Concept and Statistical Practice*, Washington, D.C., U.S. Bureau of the Census, Working Paper No. 28, 1968.

13. Stanley D. Brunn, "The New Urbanization: Emerging Patterns in the South and Southwest," Kansas City, Mo., Association of American Geographers, Annual Meeting, 1972, unpublished paper.

14. Jeffrey L. Sheler, "Petition Wants To Make Western Illinois New State," *News-Gazette* [Champaign], September 11, 1973, p. 2; and "Nebraska: Hot Panhandle," *Newsweek*, July 30, 1973, p. 23.

15. For geography examples see Michael A. Jenkins and John W. Shepherd, "Decentralizing High School Administration in Detroit: An Evaluation of Alternative Strategies of Political Control," *Economic Geography*, 48 (1972), 95–106; and Stanley Robert Lieber, "Gerrymandering and Redistricting: Computer Models with an Application for Connecticut," Pennsylvania State University, Department of Geography, M.A. thesis, 1969.

16. During late 1973 another political geographer, G. Etzel Pearcy, received national publicity for his reorganization plan that was based on thirty-eight states. This idea is described briefly and illustrated in "Boston, Plym., and Boise, Bitt.," *Time*, December 17, 1973, p. 10.

17. The author's political reorganization ideas are described in an article by David W. Hacker, "A 16-State Nation?" *National Observer*, July 28, 1973, pp. 1 and 20. It will be treated further in Stanley D. Brunn, *Towards a More Perfect Union*, New York, Oxford University Press, forthcoming 1975.

INDEX